Against Expression

Contents

Why Conceptual Writing? Why Now? xvii
 Kenneth Goldsmith

The Fate of Echo, xxiii
 Craig Dworkin

Monica Aasprong, 3
 from Soldatmarkedet

Walter Abish, 8
 from Skin Deep

Vito Acconci, 13
 from Contacts/Contexts (Frame of Reference): Ten Pages
  of Reading *Roget's Thesaurus*
 from Removal, Move (Line of Evidence): The Grid Locations
  of Streets, Alphabetized, Hagstrom's Maps of the Five
  Boroughs: 3. Manhattan

Kathy Acker, 28
 from Great Expectations

Sally Alatalo, 32
 from Unforeseen Alliances

Paal Bjelke Andersen, 38
 from The Grefsen Address

Anonymous, 41
 Eroticism

David Antin, 43
 A List of the Delusions of the Insane: What They Are Afraid Of
 from Novel Poem
 from The Separation Meditations

Louis Aragon, 50
  Suicide

Nathan Austin, 52
  from Survey Says!

J. G. Ballard, 56
  Mae West's Reduction Mammoplasty

Fiona Banner, 60
  from The Nam

Derek Beaulieu, 64
  from Flatland: A Romance of Many Dimensions

Samuel Beckett, 73
  from Molloy
  from Watt

Caroline Bergvall, 81
  VIA (36 Dante Translations)

Charles Bernstein, 87
  from I and The
  My / My / My

Ted Berrigan, 105
  An Interview with John Cage

Jen Bervin, 110
  from Nets

Gregory Betts, 114
  from If Language

Christian Bök, 117
  from Busted Sirens
  from Eunoia

Marie Buck, 121
  from Whole Foods

William S. Burroughs, 123
  from Nova Express

David Buuck, 125
  Follow

John Cage, 129
  Writing Through *The Cantos*

Blaise Cendrars, 136
  from Kodak

Thomas Claburn, 138
  from i feel better after i type to you

Elisabeth S. Clark, 142
  from Between Words

Claude Closky, 148
  The First Thousand Numbers Classified in Alphabetical Order
  from Mon Catalogue

Clark Coolidge, 161
  from Cabinet Voltaire
  from Bond Sonnets

Hart Crane, 166
  Emblems of Conduct

Brian Joseph Davis, 168
  from Voice Over

Katie Degentesh, 175
  The Only Miracles I Know of Are Simply Tricks That
    People Play on One Another

Mónica de la Torre, 177
  from Doubles

Denis Diderot, 186
  from Jacques le fataliste et son maître

Marcel Duchamp, 188
  from notes

Craig Dworkin, 190
  from Legion
  from Parse

Laura Elrick, 197
  from First Words

Dan Farrell, 200
  Avail
  from The Inkblot Record

Gerald Ferguson, 211
  from The Standard Corpus of Present Day English Language
    Usage Arranged by Word Length and Alphabetized
    Within Word Length

Robert Fitterman, 218
  Metropolis 16
  from The Sun Also Also Rises

Lawrence Giffin, 233
  Spinoza's Ethics

Peter Gizzi, 236
  Ode: Salute to the New York School, 1950–1970 (a libretto)

Judith Goldman, 243
  from dicktée
  from from r'ture/CENTaur

Kenneth Goldsmith, 249
  from Day
  from No. III 2.7.92-10.20.96
  from Soliloquy
  from The Weather

Nada Gordon, 275
  Abnormal Discharge

Noah Eli Gordon, 278
  from Inbox

Michael Gottlieb, 282
  from The Dust

Dan Graham, 289
  Exclusion Principle
  Poem-Schema

Michelle Grangaud, 292
  from Biographies/Poetry

Brion Gysin, 295
  First Cut-Ups

Michael Harvey, 297
  from White Papers

H. L Hix, 299
  Poem composed of statements made by George W. Bush
    in January 2003

Yunte Huang, 301
  from Cribs

Douglas Huebler, 307
  from Secrets: Variable Piece #4

Peter Jaeger, 311
  from Rapid Eye Movement

Emma Kay, 314
  from Worldview

Bill Kennedy and Darren Wershler, 319
  from Apostrophe

Michael Klauke, 321
  from Ad Infinitum

Christopher Knowles, 327
  from Typings

Joseph Kosuth, 331
  from Purloined: A Novel

Leevi Lehto, 339
  from Päivä

Tan Lin, 341
  from BIB

Dana Teen Lomax, 346
  from Disclosure

Trisha Low, 352
  Confessions

Rory Macbeth, 359
  from The Bible (alphabetized)

Jackson Mac Low, 370
  from Words nd Ends from Ez

Stéphane Mallarmé, 374
  from La dernière mode
  from Le livre

Donato Mancini, 380
  Ligature

Peter Manson, 390
  from Adjunct: An Undigest
  from English in Mallarmé

Shigeru Matsui, 397
  Pure Poems

Bernadette Mayer, 402
  from Eruditio ex Memoria

Steve McCaffery, 409
  Fish Also Rise
  The Kommunist Manifesto, or Wot We Wukkerz Want
    Bi Charley Marx un Fred Engels

Stephen McLaughlin and Jim Carpenter, 414
  from Issue 1

David Melnick, 416
  from Men in Aida, Book II

Richard Meltzer, 422
  Barbara Mauritz: *Music Box*
  Denny Lile
  Maple Leaf Cowpoop Round-Up

Christof Migone, 428
  from La première phrase et le dernier mot

Tomoko Minami, 431
  from 38: The New Shakespeare

K. Silem Mohammad, 437
  Spooked *and* Considering How Spooky Deer Are
  from Sonnagrams

Simon Morris, 446
  from Getting Inside Jack Kerouac's Head
  from Re-writing Freud

Yedda Morrison, 450
  from Kyoto Protocol

Harryette Mullen, 455
  Bilingual Instructions
  Elliptical
  Mantra for a Classless Society, or Mr. Roget's Neighborhood

Alexandra Nemerov, 457
  First My Motorola

C. K. Ogden, 463
  Anna Livia Plurabelle

Tom Orange, 467
  I Saw You

Parasitic Ventures, 471
    from All the Names of *In Search of Lost Time*

Georges Perec, 477
    Attempt at an Inventory of the Liquid and Solid
        Foodstuffs Ingurgitated by Me in the Course of the Year
        Nineteen Hundred and Seventy-Four

M. NourbeSe Philip, 483
    from Zong!

Vanessa Place, 489
    from Statement of Facts

Bern Porter, 496
    Clothes

Raymond Queneau, 500
    from The Foundations of Literature

Claudia Rankine, 504
    from Don't Let Me Be Lonely

Ariana Reines, 508
    from The Cow

Charles Reznikoff, 510
    from Testimony, Volume II: The United States (1885–1915):
        Recitative

Deborah Richards, 513
    from The Beauty Projection

Kim Rosenfield, 516
    The Other Me

Raymond Roussel, 519
    from How I Wrote Certain of My Books

Aram Saroyan, 522
    Untitled Poem

Ara Shirinyan, 523
  from Your Country Is Great

Ron Silliman, 531
  from Sunset Debris

Juliana Spahr, 535
  Thrashing Seems Crazy

Brian Kim Stefans, 539
  from The Vaneigem Series

Gary Sullivan, 544
  Conceptual Poem (WC + WCW)
  To a Sought Caterpillar

Nick Thurston, 548
  He Might Find

Rodrigo Toscano, 550
  Welcome to Omnium Dignitatem

Tristan Tzara, 552
  from Dada Manifesto on Feeble and Bitter Love

Andy Warhol, 555
  from a: a novel

Darren Wershler, 562
  from The Tapeworm Foundry

Christine Wertheim, 566
  Finnegans Wanke/Finnegans Wake (translation)

Wiener Gruppe, 569
  ideas for a «record album/functional» acoustic cabaret
  11 abecedaries

William Butler Yeats, 576
  Mona Lisa

Steven Zultanski, 578
  My Death Drive

Vladimir Zykov, 581
from I Was Told to Write Fifty Words

Acknowledgments, 587

Why Conceptual Writing? Why Now?

Kenneth Goldsmith

There is a room in the Musée d'Orsay that I call the room of possibilities. The museum is roughly set up chronologically, and you happily wend your way through the nineteenth century until you hit this one room that is a group of about a half a dozen painterly responses to the invention of the camera. One that sticks in my mind is a trompe l'oeil solution in which a painted figure reaches out of the frame into the viewer's space. Another incorporates three-dimensional objects into the canvas. Great attempts, but as we all know, impressionism won out.

With the rise of the Web, writing has met its photography. By that, I mean that writing has encountered a situation similar to that of painting upon the invention of photography, a technology so much better at doing what the art form had been trying to do that, to survive, the field had to alter its course radically. If photography was striving for sharp focus, painting was forced to go soft, hence impressionism. Faced with an unprecedented amount of available digital text, writing needs to redefine itself to adapt to the new environment of textual abundance.

When we look at our text-based world today, we see the perfect environment for writing to thrive. Similarly, if we look at what happened when painting met photography, we find the perfect analog-to-analog correspondence, for nowhere lurking beneath the surface of painting, photography, or film was a speck of language, thus setting the stage for an imagistic revolution. Today, digital media has set the stage for a literary revolution.

In 1974, Peter Bürger was still able to make the claim that, "because the advent of photography makes possible the precise mechanical reproduction of reality, the mimetic function of the fine arts withers. But the limits of this explanatory model become clear when one calls to mind that it cannot be transferred to literature. For in literature, there is no technical innovation that could have produced an effect comparable to that of photography in the fine arts."[1] Now there is.

With the rise of the Internet, writing is arguably facing its greatest challenge since Gutenberg. What has happened in the past fifteen years has forced writers to conceive of language in ways unthinkable just a short time ago. With an unprecedented onslaught of the sheer quantity of language (often derided as information glut in general culture), the writer faces the challenge of exactly how best to respond. Yet the strategies to respond are embedded in the writing process, which gives us the answers whether or not we're aware of it.

Why are so many writers now exploring strategies of copying and appropriation? It's simple: the computer encourages us to mimic its workings. If cutting and pasting were integral to the writing process, we would be mad to imagine that writers wouldn't explore and exploit those functions in ways that their creators didn't intend. Think back to the mid-1960s, when Nam June Paik placed a huge magnet atop a black-and-white television set, which resulted in the *détournement* of a space previously reserved for Jack Benny and Ed Sullivan into loopy, organic abstractions. If I can chop out a huge section of the novel I'm working on and paste it into a new document, what's going to stop me from copying and pasting a Web page in its entirety and dropping it into my text? When I dump a clipboard's worth of language from somewhere else into my work and massage its formatting and font to look exactly like it's always been there, then, suddenly, it feels like it's mine.[2]

You might counter by saying that, after all, home computers have been around for twenty-five years. What's so new about this? The penetration and saturation of broadband connections makes the harvesting of masses of language easy and tempting. With dial-up Web access, although it was possible to copy and paste words, in the beginning (or Gopherspace), texts were doled out one screen at a time. And even though it was text, the load time was still considerable. With broadband, the spigot runs 24/7. By comparison, there was nothing native to the system of typewriting that encouraged the replication of texts. It was incredibly slow and laborious to do so. Later, after you finished writing, you could make all the copies you wanted on a Xerox machine. As a result, there was a tremendous amount of manipulation that happened after the writing was finished. William Burroughs's cut-ups or Bob Cobbing's mimeographed visual poems are prime examples. The previous forms of borrowing in literature—collage or pastiche, taking a sentence from here, a sentence from there—were predicated on the sheer amount of manual labor involved: to retype an entire book is one thing, and to cut and paste a entire book is another. The ease of appropriation has raised the bar to a new level.

The cut-and-paste scenario plays out again and again as we encounter and adopt other digital, network-enabled strategies that further alter our relationship with words. Social networking, file sharing, blogging: in these environments, language has value not as much for what it says but for what it does. We deal in active language, passing information swiftly for the sake of moving it. To be the originator of something that becomes a broader meme trumps being the originator of the actual trigger event that is being reproduced.[3] The "re-" gestures—such as reblogging and retweeting—have become cultural rites of cachet in and of themselves. If you can filter through the mass of information and pass it on as an arbiter to others, you gain an enormous amount of cultural capital. Filtering is taste. And good taste rules the day: Marcel Duchamp's exquisite filtering and sorting sensibility combined with his finely tuned taste rewrote the rules.

Since the dawn of media, we've had more on our plates than we could ever consume, but something has radically changed: never before has language had so much materiality—fluidity, plasticity, malleability—begging to be actively managed by the writer. Before digital language, words were almost always found imprisoned on a page. How different it is today, when digitized language can be poured into any conceivable container: text typed into a Microsoft Word document can be parsed into a database, visually morphed in Photoshop, animated in Flash, pumped into online text-mangling engines, spammed to thousands of e-mail addresses, and imported into a sound-editing program and spit out as music—the possibilities are endless. You could say that this isn't writing, and in the traditional sense, you'd be right. But this is where things get interesting: we aren't hammering away on typewriters. Instead, focused all day on powerful machines with infinite possibilities, connected to networks with a number of equally infinite possibilities, writers and their role are being significantly challenged, expanded, and updated.

Clearly we are in the midst of a literary revolution.

Or are we? From the looks of it, most writing proceeds as if the Internet never happened. Age-old bouts of fraudulence, plagiarism, and hoaxes still scandalize the literary world in ways that would make, say, the art, music, computing, or science worlds chuckle with disbelief. It's hard to imagine the James Frey or J. T. LeRoy scandals upsetting anybody familiar with the sophisticated, purposely fraudulent provocations of Jeff Koons or the rephotographing of advertisements by Richard Prince, who was awarded with a Guggenheim Museum retrospective for his plagiaristic tendencies.

Nearly a century ago, the art world put to rest conventional notions of originality and replication with the gestures of Marcel Duchamp. Since then, a parade of blue-chip artists from Andy Warhol to Jeff Koons have taken Duchamp's ideas to new levels, which have become part and parcel of the mainstream art world discourse. Similarly, in music, sampling—entire tracks constructed from other tracks—has become commonplace. From Napster to gaming, from karaoke to BitTorrent files, the culture appears to be embracing the digital and all the complexity it entails—with the exception of writing.

Although the digital revolution has fostered a fertile environment in which conceptual writing can thrive, the roots of this type of writing can be traced as far back as the mechanical processes of medieval scribes or the procedural compositional methods of Wolfgang Amadeus Mozart. James Boswell's *Life of Johnson,* a meticulous and obsessive accumulation of information (replete with glosses similar to the way comments function on blogs today) was prescient of today's writing.

Modernism provided a number of precedents including Stéphane Mallarmé's falsified fashion writings, Erik Satie's experiments with repetition and boredom, Duchamp's readymades, and Francis Picabia's embrace of mechanical drawing techniques. Similarly, Gertrude Stein's epically unreadable tomes and Ezra Pound's radical, multilingual collaged works could be considered proto-conceptual. Perhaps the most concrete example of "moving information" is Walter Benjamin's *The Arcades Project,* a work that collates more than nine hundred pages' worth of notes.

By midcentury, with the advent of widespread technology, we see such diverse movements as musique concrète, concrete poetry, and Oulipo and Fluxus picking up the thread. Texts such as Walter Benjamin's writings on media, Michel de Certeau's *The Practice of Everyday Life,* Roland Barthes's *Mythologies,* and Jean Baudrillard's theories of simulacra provide a theoretical framework. From the 1940s to the early 1990s, the towering influence of John Cage—as composer, poet, and philosopher—cannot be underestimated.

The 1960s brought the advent of conceptual art and saw the emergence of Andy Warhol, perhaps the single most important figure in uncreative or conceptual writing. Warhol's entire oeuvre was based on the idea of uncreativity: the effortless production of mechanical paintings and unwatchable films in which literally nothing happens. In terms of literary output, too, Warhol pushed the envelope by having other people write his books for him. He invented new genres of literature: *a: a novel* was a mere transcription of dozens of cassette tapes, spelling errors, stumbles, and stutters left exactly as they were typed. His *Diaries,* an enormous tome, were spoken over the phone to an assistant and transcribed; they can be read as an update to Boswell's *Life of Johnson.* In Perloffian terms, Andy Warhol was an "unoriginal genius." 挪用艺术

By the 1980s, appropriation art was the rage. Sherrie Levine was busy rephotographing Walker Evans's photos, Richard Prince was reframing photographs of cowboys taken from Marlboro ads, Cindy Sherman was being everyone but Cindy Sherman, and Jeff Koons was encasing vacuum cleaners in Plexiglas. Music of the period reflected this as well: from hip-hop to plunderphonics to pop, the sample became the basis for much music. Artifice ruled: inspired by the voguing craze, lip-synching became the preferred mode of performance in concert.

In the 1990s, with the emergence of the Internet, as chronicled earlier, uncreative writing developed as an appropriate response for its time, combining historical permissions with powerful technology to imagine new ways of writing.

What we're dealing with here is a basic change in the operating system of how we write at the root level. The results might not look different, and they might not feel different, but the underlying ethos and modes of writing have been permanently changed. If painting reacted to photography by moving toward abstraction, it seems unlikely that writing is doing the same in relation to the Internet. It appears that writing's response will be mimetic and replicative, involving notions of distribution while proposing new platforms of receivership. Words very well might be written not to be read but rather to be shared, moved, and manipulated. Books, electronic and otherwise, will continue to flourish. Although the new writing will have an electronic gleam in its eyes, its consequences will be distinctly analog.

Other approaches of writing will continue on their own path, finding solutions to their own lines of inquiry. What we're proposing here is very specific to those so inclined to that approach. In closing, the sentiments of Sol LeWitt—who looms very large in conceptual writing—reminds us that there is nothing prescriptive in this endeavor: "I do not advocate a conceptual form of art for all artists. I have found that it has worked well for me while other ways have not. It is one way of making art; other ways suit other artists. Nor do I think all conceptual art merits the viewer's attention. Conceptual art is good only when the idea is good."[4]

NOTES

1. Peter Bürger, *Theory of the Avant-Garde* (Minneapolis: University of Minnesota Press, 1984), 32. First printed in 1974.

2. The language environment we're working in could easily have been rendered unique and noncopyable: witness how unobtainable language and images are in Flash-based environments.

3. The word *meme* comes from the Greek word *mimema*, "something imitated."

4. Sol LeWitt, "Paragraphs on Conceptual Art," *Artforum* (June 1967): 79–83, http://www.ddooss.org/articulos/idiomas/Sol_Lewitt.htm.

Even concepts are haecceities and events in themselves.

—Giles Deleuze and Félix Guattari

The Fate of Echo

Craig Dworkin

This book has its origins in the *UbuWeb Anthology of Conceptual Writing,* which Kenneth Goldsmith invited me to curate as part of his Internet archive of the avant-garde. More of an illustrated essay than any kind of comprehensive anthology (despite its rather grandiose title), the project set out to make an argument about genre and discipline. It assembled texts from the spheres of literature, music, and the visual arts to demonstrate that one could conceive of "a theoretically based art that is independent of genre, so that a particular poem might have more in common with a particular musical score, or film, or sculpture than with another lyric."[1] I wanted to show, for instance, that when put next to texts from a soi-disant poetic tradition, a work of conceptual art might look indistinguishable from a poem. Or, similarly, that when read next to works from the Oulipo, a book usually considered part of the history of language poetry might look much more like part of the broad postwar international avant-garde than the coterie 1980s New York poetry scene; and that the insular history of the Oulipo, in turn, might be profitably diversified when considered in the light of other experiments, and so on. The argument was directed at scholars and readers who typically know one tradition quite well while being largely unaware of others. Looking for a flexibly generic term to straddle those traditions, I coined the phrase "conceptual writing" as a way both to signal literary writing that could function comfortably as conceptual art and to indicate the use of text in conceptual art practices.[2]

The basic curatorial premise of the online collection was that by looking beyond received histories and commonplace affiliations one could more clearly see textual elements that otherwise remained obscured or implicit. The simple act of reframing seemed to refresh one's view of even familiar works, which appear significantly different by virtue of their new context. The present anthology is both an inversion and an extension of that premise. The inversion comes about because, instead of drawing indiscriminately from various disciplines or creating a new critical environment in which to juxtapose poetry with pieces from other traditions, this volume keeps its focus—with a few deliberate exceptions—on works published or received in a literary context. For that reason, we have not included artists' writings intended for the gallery wall rather than the book; nor have we included many of the symptomatic textual productions of the mentally ill—outsider writing that otherwise shares many of the characteristics of several of the works we have included. This insistence on context is not to imply, of course, that readers cannot approach a text on its own terms, regardless of its publishing history, but rather to insist on the way that such a history shades the text we receive. The hint can be taken or ignored, but the paratext always suggests a perspective from which to read. Posited as literature, these works take their part in an open dialogue with the cultures, conventions, and traditions of literary institutions, speaking to other literary works in a loud and lively discussion filled with arguments, refusals, corroborations, flirtations, proposals, rejections, and affirmations. Many of the very same texts included here might just as easily have been framed in a gallery or recorded in an Internet video or included as part of a psychiatric evaluation, but then their cultural dialogues would have been quite different, and they would have functioned in a different way. Their "meaning," as Ludwig Wittgenstein argued for words, is their use. Even in the case of the few exceptions to our focus, all of the texts included are presented here, in the new context of this anthology, as literary.

Conceptual Art

Although the focus of this anthology is resolutely literary, a comparison of the conceptual literature presented here with the range of interventions made by the foundational works of conceptual art is still instructive. A quick sketch of those interventions should help highlight the congruencies and discrepancies between the reformation of Western art after abstract expressionism and emerging literary tendencies today.[3]

In the 1960s, conceptual art challenged some of the fundamental assumptions of the art world: the nature of the art object, the qualifications for being an artist, the fundamental role of art in its various institutional contexts, and the proper scope of activities for the audience (those who, not long before, would have been called simply spectators). Initially, the art of the 1960s continued to mine the seam opened in the mid-1910s by Marcel Duchamp's readymades, a series of quotidian objects inscribed with a cryptic title and displayed as art: a rack for drying washed bottles, a metal comb for grooming animals, a suspended snow shovel, the crown of a hat rack hung and angled upside down, a prostrate plank of ranked iron coat hooks nailed to the floor, a typewriter dust cover, a pedestaled porcelain urinal flat on its back. In his 1961 portrait of the gallery owner Iris Clert, Robert Rauschenberg emphasized the illocutionary lesson of these readymades, or what Duchamp referred to as "une sorte de nominalisme pictural" (a kind of pictorial nominalism).[4] The artistic status of the readymades, that is, depended not on any intrinsic qualities but rather on the assertion—implicit in the context of their gallery display—that they were to be considered as art. In response to the invitation to produce a portrait of Clert for an exhibition at the Galerie Iris Clert in Paris, Rauschenberg sent a telegram, substituting a line of text in place of the expected drawing or painting, however abstract or unlike Clert an image might have been. It read, simply: THIS IS A PORTRAIT OF IRIS CLERT IF I SAY SO.

Several years later, Joseph Kosuth emphatically elaborated several of the implications of Rauschenberg's terse portrait. Again presenting language as the artwork—one of conceptual art's most radical interventions—Kosuth's first exhibition at Gallery 669 (Los Angeles, 1968), *Titled (Art as Idea as Idea),* mounted a series of enlarged projection photocopies of different dictionary definitions of the word *nothing,* isolated from their original placement on the page and resituated on the gallery wall. Learned from Warhol, if not directly from Duchamp, this tactic of reframing would prove an important tool for conceptual art.[5] Part of the joke of Kosuth's exhibit, of course, was the implication that if there were so many different definitions of *nothing,* then those differences pointed not to an ineffable absence but to some positive, identifiable range of things. The dictionaries, as John Cage might put it, have nothing to say and are saying it.[6] With white type against four-foot-square, black backgrounds, the panels also poked fun at the theoretical language that had accumulated around the pure visuality of minimalist monochromes, and they evoked the tautological black monochrome squares of Ad Reinhardt in particular.[7] In later iterations, individual panels challenged the dominance of painting (with a photo-graph of the definition of *painting*), compared modes of visual and verbal representation (with entries for the notoriously difficult to depict *water*), pointed to indexicality (*north, south*), collapsed form and content (with the word *meaning*), and so on.

In every case, Kosuth's selection of different dictionaries to supply the definitions emphasized the readymade aspect of *Art as Idea as Idea;* the principal artistic action was one of choosing and nominating.[8] Local context, as Duchamp understood, motivates meaning: selected to appear on the gallery wall, the different entries for *water* align themselves with different genres and artworks depending on the style of their definitions. The quotation from the *New Century Dictionary,* for example, opens with a conceptualized linguistic version of history painting—the etymology of the word—and passes into a sweeping atmospheric landscape and *paysage marin:* "the liquid which in more or less impure state constitutes rain, oceans, lakes, rivers, etc." The *Oxford* definition, in contrast, suggests the relation of the *water* panels to Kosuth's *nothing* series by stressing privatives: "colourless, transparent, tasteless, scentless." Avoiding the more scientific language of chemistry that other dictionaries emphasize, *Oxford* continues: "in liquid state convertible by heat into steam and by cold into ice." One might take that panel, accordingly, as a response to George Brecht's 1961 Fluxus score for "Three Aqueous Events":

- ice
- water
- steam

Regardless of the intertextual resonance with Kosuth's photostat, such Fluxus scores were important antecedents for conceptual art because their laconic propositions anticipated a wide range of possible actions and objects; the scores presented sufficiently abstract models of potential, rather than completed events or crafted objects, and so required thought both on the part of the performer, who had to work the cryptic sketches into concrete forms, and on the part of the audience, who had to make the mental connection between score and performance. At the same time, those specific events and objects, however quotidian and unremarkable they might be, necessarily constituted art by fulfilling the requirements of the score. Through the force of the score's nominalization, enactments were, by definition, artistic performances.

Rauschenberg and Kosuth, each in their own way, took Duchamp's lead in privileging the intellectual over the visual, ideas over mimetic representations, and linguistic play over mute visual language or sculptural craft. "Everything was becoming *conceptual*," Duchamp explained: "that is, it depended on things other than the retina."[9] Eschewing the visual emphasis of illusionistic or referential imagery—with its call for aesthetic appreciation, narrative engagement, or psychological response—conceptual art equally abandoned the compositional bids for phenomenological experience or emotional intensities that abstract art elicited. Instead, conceptual art offered information. Abstraction, to be sure, had pioneered a mode of art that did not refer to something outside itself, but conceptual art substituted factual documentary—information about information—in place of the optical apprehension of composition, gesture, and the material facture of traditional media.[10] As Douglas Huebler put it, inspired by the insistently literal, nonmetaphoric, and exhaustive writing of Samuel Beckett and the *nouveaux romanciers,* the new interest was in "the facticity of that raw information without worrying about supposed meanings."[11] Robert Morris dramatized the deadpan literalism that would come to characterize conceptual art's recursive factual tactic with his 1961 *Box with the Sound of Its Own Making,* in which a roughly unfinished—if rather tidy— ten-inch-square walnut box encloses an audio tape player with a looped recording of the box's construction: sawing and hammering; the scuff and knock of parts being moved; long, silent moments of measure or cogitation or rest. The box turned Duchamp's *À bruit secret (With Hidden Noise,* 1916) inside out, displaying with documentary clarity what Duchamp had kept tactfully cryptic. The earlier sculpture, a roughly thirteen-centimeter-square assemblage securing a ball of twine between two inscribed brass plates with long bolts, conceals an unknown object—surreptitiously introduced by Walter Arensberg while Duchamp was constructing the piece— which rattles when the sculpture is shaken.[12] *À bruit secret* is animated by its surreal comixture of organically coiled twine and hard machined metal, as well as by its kinetic interactivity and the tension between its hand-scaled size and relative heft. In comparison, Morris's box—more pragmatic American shop product than industrial primitive fetish—forgoes the invitation to shake and invert the sculpture (one of the plates in *À bruit secret* is inscribed on the bottom), but it picks up on the cognitive dynamic of Duchamp's work, underscored in modern museum settings where the piece is displayed, unshakable, *en vitrine.* Apart from its visual, tactile, and sonic qualities, Duchamp's sculpture is a black box in the philosophical sense, creating an epistemological puzzle and taunting its audience to speculate on the unknown object. Morris also relies on the audience's mental engagement to relate the temporally discrepant sounds to the object in front of them and to think through the logical tautology of recursion that explains their raisons d'être.

Equally important to conceptual art, Morris's *Card File* from the following year restaged his box in linguistic terms. The horizontally mounted drawer from a business filing cabinet sorts typed index cards in forty-three roughly alphabetized categories.[13] Self-referential and cross-indexed, the cards note the circumstances of the work's conception and construction. A less procedural example of descriptive self-referentiality, Adrian Piper's portfolio suite *Here and Now* (1968) contains eight-by-eight chessboard grids, empty except for typed phrases indicating their location. On one page, for instance, the third square from the bottom right encloses the following sentence:

HERE:the sq
uare area i
s 3rd row f
rom bottom,
3rd from ri
ght side.

Conceptual artists further realized that if an artwork could be self-descriptive and made of language, then that language could describe itself. Dan Graham's *Poem-Schema*, for example, enumerates the formal and grammatical properties of its printed instantiation, with "the exact data in each particular instance" of its publication set "to correspond to the fact(s) of its published appearance."[14] As Graham explained it elsewhere:

A page of *Schema* exists as a matter of fact materiality. . . . It is a measure of itself—as place. It takes its own measure—of itself as place, that is, placed two-dimensionally on (as) a page.[15]

Graham considered his template (included in this volume) to be a schematic model for "a set of poems whose component pages are specifically published as individual poems in various magazines."[16] For each particular publication, the editor of the periodical was to provide information about the physical support and typography, adjusting the tally accordingly. When the work was published in the inaugural issue of the British journal *Art-*

Language, for instance, it was printed "offset cartridge" in a ten-point Press Roman face, so the entry listing the number of capitalized words, was "2."[17] The same held for its appearance in the anthology *Possibilities of Poetry,* where it was printed in ten-point Aster type on Dondell paper stock.[18] In another instance, for comparison, the number of capitalized words was calculated at four because it was printed in a Futura face on Wedgwood Coated Offset stock.[19] The entire process seems mechanical, but the answers are rarely as straightforward as they seem. Published in *Aspen* magazine, as "Poem, March 1966," the text was printed in ten-point Univers 55 type on generically "dull coated" paper stock, but the entry on the penultimate line, mysteriously, is "3."[20] Was the editor counting "55" as a capitalized "Fifty-Five," perhaps in recognition that Univers was the first typeface to incorporate numbers as part of its name?[21] Looking over the page, one recognizes that the majuscule subtitle "POEM" might be capitalized, though that would still leave one word unaccounted for (or suggest that the number of capitalized words should be raised to four). The editor, in any event, obviously did not consider Graham's name or the raw schema and explanation printed alongside the tabulated version as part of the poem, as they contain many capitalized words. No easy resolution presents itself. Similarly perplexing, when printed in a German catalog, the number of capitalized words is noted as two, accounting perhaps for the "Offsetplate Rohpapier" (Photo-offset Paper), which serves as a kind of title, or for the typeface "Antiqua" with the other "wörter versal" (capitalized word) still unclear; in either case, however, the data do not account for the many nouns capitalized by prereform German convention.[22] Such questions, as these different versions also attest, proliferate: does "letters of alphabet" refer to the total number of characters on the page or to the twenty-six letters of the alphabet? Is the poem printed in two columns—parentheticals on one side and nouns on the other—or is it considered a single, internally divided piece occupying one column of the magazine's larger layout? Does "paper sheet" refer to a brand, a weight, or a description? And so on. Part of the work's effect, it seems, is to explore haecceity by complicating the seemingly straightforward facticity of self-description and focusing attention on otherwise-overlooked material details.

Similarly self-referential, Mel Ramsden's series of paintings from the late 1960s, all titled *100% Abstract,* brought this kind of recursive logic to painting and continued to enunciate the move from works seeking an embodied viewership to those eliciting a mental thinkership. Compared with even the most austere abstraction, which invites one to gaze at paint on canvas,

Ramsden's "abstracts" offer information about the paint itself, wryly aiming at greater abstraction through increasing specificity. One neatly lettered painting from 1968 contains: "COPPER BRONZE POWDER 12% / ACRYLIC RESIN 7% / AROMATIC HYDROCARBONS 81%." Another, from the same year, is more slyly antiretinal; in blue letters on a gray background, it reads: "TITANIUM CALCIUM 83% / SILICATES 17%." The chemicals—calcium sulfate with a whitening agent of titanium dioxide and silicate extenders—indicate the acrylic gesso primer invisible beneath the text but nonetheless a essential part of the painting.

If "what the work of art looks like isn't too important," as Sol LeWitt summarized this new antiretinal dispensation in 1967, then perhaps, some artists wagered, the art need not be visible at all.[23] Ramsden's *Secret Painting* (1967–68), for instance, announces this position even more explicitly than his occult reference to unseen primer; it presents a square black monochrome accompanied by the following statement, framed in a slightly smaller square: "the content of this painting / is invisible; the character / and dimension of the content / are to be kept permanently / secret, known only to the / artist." Another version of this self-reflexive descriptive strategy of indicating what cannot be seen, intensifying abstraction with increased specificity, animates Robert Barry's 1971 project *This work has been and continues to be refined since 1969*:

> It is whole, determined, sufficient, individual, known, complete, revealed, accessible, manifest, effected, effectual, directed, dependent, distinct, planned, controlled, unified, delineated, isolated, confined, confirmed, systematic, established, predictable, explainable, apprehendable, noticeable, evident, understandable, allowable, natural, harmonious, particular, varied, interpretable, discovered, persistent, diverse, composed, orderly, flexible, divisible, extendible, influential, public, reasoned, repeatable, comprehendable, impractical, findable, actual, interrelated, active, describable, situated, recogizable, analysable, limited, avoidable, sustained, changeable, defined, provable, consistent, durable, realized, organized, unique, complex, specific, established, rational, regulated, revealed, conditioned, uniform, solitary, given, improvable, involved, maintained, particular, coherent, arranged, restricted, and presented.

Simultaneously more subtle and extreme, Barry's contribution to the landmark *January 5–31, 1969* exhibition at Seth Siegelaub's gallery in New York offered even less to see: an empty room. But what set that room apart from similarly empty gallery spaces—such as Yves Klein's infamous "vides" or Warhol's 1965 exhibition at the Institute of Contemporary Art in Philadelphia—was Barry's installation of two invisible works from the previous year.[24] Small information placards enigmatically alerted visitors to *88 mc Carrier Wave (FM)* and *1600 kc Carrier Wave (AM)*. While the exhibit was open, hidden transmitters broadcast the eponymous frequencies through the space. The installation was in fact an interactive performance, because those waves would have been distorted by the presence of visitors, who unknowingly altered the artwork with the movement and dispensation of their bodies within the room. However, because the waves are detectable only with electrical equipment and "material" only in the strictest scientific sense, Barry's work clearly asked for something other than visual appreciation. With a similar play of imperceptible bodily engagement—and a double Duchampian pun on his own name—Barry's *.5 Micro Curie Radiation Installation* (1969–79) involved burying four capsules of the synthetic isotope barium 133 in the lawn at New York's Central Park. He estimated that the deteriorating work, invisible to begin with, would disappear completely after a decade.[25]

Dispensing with the retinal qualities of art altogether, these works no longer needed to be seen because "in conceptual art," as LeWitt flatly explained, "the idea or concept is the most important aspect of the work."[26] Moreover, he continued, "the idea itself, even if not made visual, is as much a work of art as any finished product." Extending the postwar ethos of process over product to its logical extreme—a vanishing point where the product all but disappeared and the process extended back even before gesture to an initial mental notion or thought—conceptual art's radical interrogation of the status of the art object also renegotiated the role of the artist. Minimalist sculpture had already begun to gesture along those lines and would continue to reinforce conceptual art's related propositions. In one direction, the serial, modular, or permutational logics of minimalist sculptures such as Donald Judd's stacked wall units or LeWitt's open cubes incorporated the cognitive as an essential aspect of the work; the artist established the parameters of a system that was then elaborated in space.[27] In the other direction, the cool detachment of minimalism's industrial or unskilled materials—construction-grade steel, hay bales, plywood, unmortared bricks—underscored Duchamp's implicit claim that artists themselves need not personally sculpt or fabricate art objects. Deaestheticized and deskilled, aggressively unexpressive and resolutely nonsubjective, minimalism turned attention from the connoisseurship of manual craft and the hand of the artist to gestalt phenomenology and cognitive analysis, so that the model for the artist was less the unique Romantic visionary and more the Enlightenment philosopher-mathematician or the witty 'pataphysician.

Encouraged by minimalism's attitude, conceptual art would position the artist in an even more oblique relation to the art object. At precisely the same time Kosuth was mounting his series of photostat definitions, for example, John Baldessari exhibited a set of similarly ironic quotations, neatly painted in black block letters on primed canvas. Drawn from art theory and art appreciation textbooks, these quotations were presented in place of the kind of art they were meant to illustrate. Ventriloquizing the presumption that text itself could not be an artwork—the very position conceptual art like Baldessari's was challenging—one canvas reads: "Do you sense how all the parts of a good / picture are involved with each other. Not / just placed side by side? Art is a creation / for the eye and can only be hinted at with / words."[28] Another, quoting from the same source, reinterrogates the status of a painting when its subject is indeed language, implying that traditional viewing habits may be inappropriate for conceptual art:

COMPOSING ON A CANVAS

STUDY THE COMPOSITION OF PAINTINGS. ASK
YOURSELF QUESTIONS WHEN STANDING IN FRONT
OF A WELL COMPOSED PICTURE. WHAT FORMAT
IS USED? WHAT IS THE PROPORTION OF HEIGHT TO
WIDTH? WHAT IS THE CENTRAL OBJECT? WHERE IS
IT SITUATED? HOW IS IT RELATED TO THE FORMAT?
WHAT ARE THE MAIN DIRECTIONAL FORCES? THE
MINOR ONES? HOW ARE THE SHADES OF DARK
AND LIGHT DISTRIBUTED? WHERE ARE THE DARK
SPOTS CONCENTRATED? THE LIGHT SPOTS? HOW
ARE THE EDGES OF THE PICTURE DRAWN INTO THE
PICTURE ITSELF? ANSWER THESE QUESTIONS FOR
YOURSELF WHILE LOOKING AT A FAIRLY UNCOM-
PLICATED PICTURE.[29]

Yet another piece makes the same move in terms of presumptions about the viewer's experience, disproving itself by means of its own unequivocal assertion: "a two dimensional / surface without any / articulation is a /

dead experience." Baldessari has wittily articulated the sentence, quite liter-
ally, through line breaks; in its original source, it happens to appear typeset
intact across one full line of prose.[30] A slightly later canvas, for another ex-
ample of this logical short circuit of simultaneous assertion and negation,
attempts to invert the Duchampian nominalist proposition with the oxy-
moron of "art as idea" without an idea; running up against the fact that the
rejection of a concept is itself a concept, the canvas reads: "everything is
purged from this painting / but art, no ideas have entered this work."[31]

Whatever their particular statements, all of these canvases also illustrate
conceptual art's impulse to distance the artist from a position of creatively
original authorship.[32] Not only are the texts unattributed quotations, but
Baldessari did not even paint the canvases himself, and their production
was deliberately impersonal and deaestheticized, suppressing the idiosyn-
cratic in favor of the idiomatically vernacular. As with much conceptual
art—such as Kosuth's photocopies or Ed Ruscha's influential photographic
books from the 1960s—the visual rhetoric of Baldessari's canvases mim-
icked quotidian commercial or amateur processes rather than rarefied high-
art modes. As Baldessari explained, "Someone else built and primed the
canvases and took them to the sign painter . . . and the sign painter was
instructed not to attempt to make attractive, artful lettering but to letter
the information in the most simple way."[33] In his 1969 series *Commis-
sioned Paintings,* Baldessari further removed himself from the creative pro-
cess. Once again, others did the actual painting: sign painters for the letter-
ing and amateur genre painters whom Baldessari hired to reproduce—"as
faithfully as possible"—oil renditions of the snapshots he provided them.
Although he had still taken the photographs himself, Baldessari outsourced
the more fundamental Duchampian task of choosing. The snapshots docu-
mented a friend pointing at quotidian objects that the friend had selected,
and the painters were asked to choose their subject from among a number
of those photographs.[34]

Commissioned Paintings also points to another important tactic by which
conceptual art distanced the artist at an oblique remove from the work.
Although the production of any artwork can be retroactively described
in abstract terms (e.g., "apply oil paint with a brush to a stretched and
primed cotton canvas"), in Baldessari's case, the abstract procedure is an
integral part of the final work and not merely an incidental means to an
end. For the work as a whole to be effective, the conceptual formulation
must be kept in mind along with any visual and mental considerations of
the finished paintings. Like Graham's poem, in which publishers carried

out the task of producing the work's final form, conceptual artists often focused on the initial procedures to be followed—guidelines, parameters, and recipes—rather than the subsequent physical production. "When an artist uses a conceptual form of art," as LeWitt explained, "it means that all of the planning and decisions are made beforehand and the execution is a perfunctory affair. The idea becomes a machine that makes the art." To give a literal example of this mechanistic production of art, the score for György Ligeti's 1962 Fluxus composition *Poème symphonique* (*Symphonic Poem*) consists of detailed instructions on the windings and oscillation settings for one hundred metronomes, which are then set ticking and allowed to run their course without intervention. Ligeti carefully maps out parameters, but he does not score individual notes, and the mechanical performance eliminates any subjective interpretation by musicians. As LeWitt explained this Cagean ethos of nonintervention: "to work with a plan that is pre-set is one way of avoiding subjectivity . . . the fewer decisions made in the course of completing the work the better."[35]

LeWitt's focus on a work's abstract inception hints at conceptual art's most daring wager. Having tested the propositions that the art object might be nominal, linguistic, invisible, and on a par with its abstract initial description, the next step was to venture that it could be dispensed with altogether. Lawrence Weiner's 1968 exhibition *Statements*—an exhibit taking the form, significantly, of a catalog—contained two dozen self-descriptive pieces composed of short phrases, grammatically suspended by the past participle without agent or imperative, as if they had already been realized as soon as written (or read): "one aerosol can of enamel sprayed to conclusion directly upon the floor," "two minutes of spray paint directly upon the floor from a standard aerosol can," "one quart exterior green enamel thrown on a brick wall," "one pint gloss white lacquer poured directly upon the floor and allowed to dry," "an amount of bleach poured upon a rug and allowed to bleach," "one standard dye marker thrown into the sea," and so on. The grammatical form with which these phrases float free of particular agents underscores Weiner's insistence that his artworks existed as statements, fully sufficient as they were printed, and not as particular enactments or unique objects. Although—like many Fluxus scores—they have subsequently been performed, as far as Weiner was concerned, the descriptive statements never needed to take any particular material instantiation. In his "Declaration of Intent," formulated the following year, Weiner lays out this conceptual faith in three articles:

1. The artist may construct the work.
2. The work may be fabricated.
3. The work need not be built.[36]

Here, again, the grammar does much of the work; in place of the necessity and obligation that would have been signaled by *must,* the modal *may* grants permission and opens the attendant possibility that the artist might *not* construct the work and that the work might not, in fact, be constructed at all. Completing the separation of the artwork from its presentation, conceptual art had moved beyond Duchamp's stalemate and proposed a new state of artistic *échec.*

Propriety

—A quality or attribute, esp. an essential or distinctive one . . . the fact of owning something or of being owned by someone . . . correctness of language . . . strictness of meaning, literalness . . . conformity to accepted standards of behavior or morals . . . appropriateness to circumstances.

Conceptual art's insistent reinterpretation of the object of art—hunted all the way to the brink of extinction—highlights some of the fundamental differences distinguishing the art of the 1960s from the kind of literary writing we focus on here. First, recall that part of the radical force of conceptual art was its assertion that an artwork might not assume the familiar guises of painting (or drawing or sculpture) but could instead take the form of a text. Weiner's *Statements* catalog was not a souvenir of his show or a documentation of the exhibit; it *was* the exhibit. The crucial point, however, is not simply the occurrence of text but how it is used (in the Wittgensteinian sense); to equate conceptual art and poetry because both use words is like confusing numbers with mathematics, as LeWitt figured it, misled because of a superficial resemblance of signs and failing to account for what one scholar has summarized as "the peculiar function of texts in the institutional context of visual art."[37] One of those functions—to construe language itself as art and the art object as a text to be read—was, as we have seen, to challenge the retinal imperative of art with a deskilled antiaesthetic. From the literary side, of course, the assumption has long been that poems are meant to be read, and so the mere idea of a poem made of words does not intervene in the discipline in the same way as conceptual art's linguistic turn does. Indeed, the equivalent move for a poetry that wanted to model itself on conceptual art would be to posit a nonlinguistic object as "the poem." That kind of conceptual poetry would insist on a poem without words. Although they often abandon traditional aesthetic criteria, none of the works included here attempts that kind of radical renominalization. In addition, the textual proposition of conceptual art undercut the presumption of a unique art object; a significant move in the restricted economy of art's commodity system, the force of that negation is obviously lost in a modern literary context, where editions are the status quo.

More interesting is that the supposed dematerialization of the art object was bought at the cost of the rematerialization of language. In the critical dynamic of the visual arts, the turn to text initially signified something supposedly less visual and palpable than traditional media. But positing language as an alternative sculptural or painterly material cut both ways. From one direction, it suggested that visual art could be read through the lens of literary theory, whereas language itself, from the other direction, began to be seen as carrying a certain opacity and heft. Robert Smithson identified this newly doubled potential for art in his announcement of a 1967 exhibition at the Dwan Gallery; with an inversion of the expected terms, Smithson identified the new art as "LANGUAGE to be LOOKED at and/or THINGS to be READ." In a 1970 mural of dripped black paint and scrawled chalk text, a format recalling situationist street graffiti from the summer of 1968, Mel Bochner proclaimed, with the haste of a manifesto and the apodictic tone of a foundational proposition: "1. Language is not transparent." In the move to oppose ideas to objects, conceptual art had to state those ideas in language, and the materiality of print, in turn, could not—in the final analysis—be ignored. "No ideas," as William Carlos Williams famously phrased it, "but in things."[38] With conceptual writing, in contrast, the force of critique from the very beginning was just the opposite: to distance ideas and affects in favor of assembled objects, rejecting outright the ideologies of disembodied themes and abstracted content. The opacity of language is a conclusion of conceptual art but already a premise for conceptual writing. The very procedures of conceptual writing, in fact, demand an opaquely material language: something to be digitally clicked and cut, physically moved and reframed, searched and sampled, and poured and pasted. The most conceptual poetry, unexpectedly, is also some of the least abstract, and the guiding concept behind conceptual poetry may be the idea of language as quantifiable data. As Smithson emphasized with an addendum to his Dwan Gallery advertisement, appended in 1972: "my sense of language is that it is matter and not ideas—i.e., 'printed matter.'" Smithson's formulation, tellingly, recalls Stéphane Mallarmé's sense of poetry itself. Responding to Edgar Degas' complaint that it was easy to come up with good ideas for poems but hard to arrange particular words, Mallarmé wrote back to his friend: "ce n'est point avec des idées, mon cher Degas, que l'on fait des vers. C'est avec des mots" (My dear Degas, poems are made of words, not ideas). In conceptual poetry, the relation of the idea to the word is necessary but not privileged: these are still poems made of words; they are not ideas *as poems.*[39] A procedure or algorithm organizes the writing, but those procedures do not substitute for the writing. Moreover, although any poem might have originated in an abstract idea, for most of those poems, a variety of ideas could account for the final text; in conceptual poetry, the text and its conception are uniquely linked: only one initial scheme could have resulted in the final poem.

Conceptual art's willingness to distance the artist from the manufacture of the artwork and to discount traditional valuations of originality is another vantage from which to compare contemporary writing with its art world precedents. That relation is particularly interesting, given that precedent is itself a key factor in assessing creative originality. In this case, attempting the most uncreative repetition ultimately disproves the possibility of a truly uncreative repetition. In the mid-1960s, Elaine Sturtevant offered some of the strongest challenges to prevailing notions of originality when she began reproducing the works of other artists and exhibiting them under her name: Frank Stella's patterned coaxial pinstripes; Jasper John's matte encaustic flag; Roy Lichtenstein's enlarged benday dots; Andy Warhol's gaudily colored and bluntly misregistered hibiscus flowers. Sturtevant's works chided their audience, who too often glanced at a painting or sculpture rather than attending to its details; viewers were quick to identify "a Lichtenstein" and slow to notice the details that gave it away as a counterfeit (readers of the present collection should heed the admonishment; noting a method—transcribed radio reports, parsed grammar, alphabetized answers, et cetera—is no substitute for carefully reading the textual details of a work). Further, Sturtevant's imitations questioned the sense of property behind *le propre,* or what is one's own, by decoupling the artists' signature from a signature style. The twist, of course, was that many of the artists she duplicated had themselves made a point of featuring impersonal, iconic, or plagiarized images (Lichtenstein copied actual comic-strip frames, Warhol's flowers were transferred from a magazine photograph by Patricia Caulfield, and so on). Sturtevant's forgeries implicitly ask how artists had so easily come to own what was never theirs to begin with: geometric lines, the American flag, someone else's commercial drawing or photograph, the look of mechanical mass reproduction. To complicate matters, Warhol had willingly loaned Sturtevant the screens used for the initial *Flower* prints, so in that case any material discrepancies were even harder to perceive, and the question became more pointed, with more than a whiff of institutional and commercial critique: why, when one of the kids at the Factory made a print was it still considered a Warhol, but not when Sturtevant printed from the same screen? Or to ask the question in a way that more clearly delineates the limits being probed by her work: could one forge a Sturtevant? The same question pertains to many of the works included here. What, for example, is the status of a transcription of one day's *New York Times* after the publication of Kenneth Goldsmith's *Day*? If these works are so unoriginal, if indeed anyone could do them, then why do they acquire such a strong sense of signature?

The answer is twofold. On the one hand—and here we return to the importance of context—a work can never really be duplicated by formal facsimile. A retyping of *Day*, for example (as one Los Angeles artist already claims to have done), substitutes the transcription of a literary text for the transcription of a journalistic text, to note just the most obvious difference. But even a subsequent, identical retyping of the same day's *New York Times* will always occur in the context that *Day* created: one in which retyped newspapers have been posited as literature and in which Goldsmith's intertext is inescapable. As this collection tries to establish, there are always precedents, often unknown, so the important point is not simply that it has been done before but that the intervention made by Goldsmith's work is irrevocable. Photographs had been badly silk-screened before Warhol, but Warhol's silk screens became signatures because they established themselves as a referent that all subsequent works in that mode would have to acknowledge or labor to deny. In addition, cultural contexts change over time, so that with some distance the replication (rather than the mere reproduction) of *Day* will not be a retyped newspaper, just as the aesthetic shock of Duchamp's *Fountain* and its institutional critique cannot now be replicated by placing a urinal in a museum but would have to be approximated by some other means. For this reason alone, the tactics of twentieth-century conceptual art, when restaged by twenty-first-century poets, can never be simple repetitions. Equivalent objects, in short, do not constitute equivalent gestures.

On the other hand, as attentive readings reveal, identical procedures rarely produce identical results. Indeed, impersonal procedures tend to magnify subjective choices (to keep with the example of the newspaper, how would different transcribers handle line breaks and page divisions, layouts and fonts, and so on?). The spoor of a personal signature remains in even the most deoderized works. More important, the question of forging a Sturtevant or a Goldsmith points out the degree to which creativity, like so many other traditional poetic values, has not been negated or banished by conceptual works but shunted to an adjoining track. The point is not that anyone could do these works—of course they could—but rather that no one else has. Judgments about creativity and innovation in conceptual writing are displaced from the details and variations of the final crafted form to the broad blow of the initial concept and the elegance with which its solution is achieved. The question remains not whether one of these works could have been done better, but whether it could possibly have been done differently at all. Here, then, is where conceptual writing shows up the rhetorical, ideological force of our cultural sense of creativity, which clings so tenaciously to a gold standard of one's own words rather than to one's own idea or the integrity of that idea's execution. The hundred-thousandth lyric published this decade in which a plainspoken persona realizes a small profundity about suburban bourgeois life, or the hundred-thousandth coming-of-age novel developing psychological portraits of characters amid difficult romantic relationships and family tensions, is somehow still within the bounds of the properly creative (and these numbers are not exaggerations); yet the first or second work to use previously written source texts in a novel way are still felt to be troublingly improper. Retyping the *New York Times,* after *Day,* would be considered unoriginal; a story in which one generation must come to terms with a secret family history would still be given the benefit of the doubt. In part, *Against Expression* is a litmus test for the reader's sense of where the demarcations between creative and uncreative writing lie.[40]

Appropriation

—The making of a thing private property. . . . The assignment of anything to a special purpose.

There is no reason to believe that different institutions, even when interrelated like art and literature, would develop at the same pace, but one of the striking differences between these two spheres is the degree to which practices long unremarkable in the art world are still conspicuous, controversial, or unacceptable in the literary arena. Following the theoretical provocation of artists like Sturtevant and Baldessari in the 1960s, outright appropriation became a widespread tendency in the following decades. In 1977, a small exhibition titled *Pictures* opened at the nonprofit Artists Space gallery in New York City, curated by Douglas Crimp (whose revised catalog essay has since been widely cited); the show has become an almost-mythic foundational moment for what came to be called appropriation art. A few years later, a number of artists featured by the Metro Pictures gallery—including Sarah Charlesworth, Jack Goldstein, Sherrie Levine, Robert Longo, and Richard Prince—established a critical mass of aesthetic poachers, presenting unauthorized reproductions of images in ways that radically expanded the limits of modernist collage.[41] These artists continued to follow the lead of Duchamp's readymades and his demonstration that the artist need not personally fabricate the art object but might merely nominate it from another area of culture, such as the hardware store (or, in the case of the Metro Pictures artists, a newspaper or glossy magazine). Moreover, the Pictures artists took a cue from Andy Warhol's silk-screened repetitions of journalistic photographs, exploiting the power of mechanical reproduction to reaestheticize and recontextualize images from popular media. Understood at the time in terms of Walter Benjamin's overcited essay on aura and mechanical reproducibility, the works appeared as if they were bespoke illustrations for a number of contemporaneous French theories: the situationist senses of *spectacle* and *détournement* as elaborated by Guy Debord, Gil Wolman, and Asger Jorn; Michel de Certeau's related concept of bricolage; Jean Baudrillard's ecstatic accounts of simulacra; the authorial deaths reported and autopsied by Roland Barthes and Michel Foucault.

For one concrete example of this reworking of iconic imagery, consider Jack Goldstein's now-canonical 1975 film *Metro-Goldwyn-Mayer*, created by splicing and looping 16-mm strips of MGM's roaring lion, turning the heralding roar into a repeated two-minute announcement of nothing but itself, a trademark of a trademark finally fulfilling the legend on the banner encircling its head: *ars gratia artis* (art for art's sake). More widely seen, Richard Prince's rephotographed magazine and newspaper advertisements, which he began reproducing in the late 1970s, rendered commercial images—so ubiquitous that they were hard to see on their own terms—newly visible. Isolating, enlarging, and refocusing the found images, Prince organized them into categories (such as the descriptively titled *four single men with interchangeable backgrounds looking to the right* [1977], executive luxury goods, or suites of Marlboro Man cowboys). Prince's prints show the most familiar images to be strangely uncanny, revealing their idiomatic repetitions and inducing a disquieting sense of déjà vu. More provocative still were Sherrie Levine's contemporaneous reproductions of images by Edward Weston (1980), Walker Evans (1981), and Eliot Porter (1981); Levine rephotographed their works with as little variance as possible and then presented them under her own name as works "after" the masters of modern photography.

In the thirty years since the Artists Space exhibition, such wholesale appropriation has become a staple of contemporary art, recognized—and often eagerly embraced—by critical, commercial, and curatorial establishments. Indeed, appropriation is now so prevalent in the art world that Jerry Saltz has likened it to "esthetic kudzu."[42] The same techniques applied to literary texts, in contrast, are likely to elicit the response that such works—innovative or passé, good or bad—do not qualify as poetry tout court. Following a reading by Kenneth Goldsmith at Stanford University in 1997, for instance, one of the leading scholars of modern poetry—a professor enthusiastic about a range of challenging and innovative writing from Ezra Pound to Robert Grenier, Robert Duncan to Susan Howe—was asked what he thought of the poetry reading. His response: "What poetry reading?" Years later, I was even more surprised to hear one of the central figures of language poetry—a writer who had in fact himself incorporated transcribed texts into poetry—insist in numerous conversations that Goldsmith's work was interesting, but that it was decidedly not poetry. I suspect that in another quarter century, the literary status of appropriation will be much more like it is for the visual arts today—where the debate has moved on to questions well beyond such categorical anxieties—but our interest in assembling the present collection is to gauge how such techniques operate in the current literary context (including how instances of appropriation from earlier literary periods appear in today's cultural climate).

To put this slightly differently, works such as Sturtevant's *Flowers,* Levine's *After Walker Evans,* and Goldsmith's *Day* all obviously raise some of the same general, theoretical questions about originality and reproduction (with the added twist that after Sturtevant and Levine, Goldsmith appropriates the tactic of appropriation, inventively deploying unoriginality in a new arena). But rephotographing in 1980 and retyping in 2000 or exhibiting an appropriated image in a SoHo gallery and publishing an appropriated text as poetry cannot be equivalent activities. Part of that difference has to do with the two media. Levine's work inevitably entered into a century-old debate over the nature of photography, which initially had to fight for its status as a creative art to begin with; moreover, it resonated with a broader cultural concern about the political power of images and their functioning as signs. Goldsmith's work, for its part, entered into a century-old rivalry between poetry and the newspaper and an arena already divided—in Truman Capote's famous quip about Jack Kerouac—between "writing" and "typing."[43]

More important, part of the difference between 1980 and 2000 derives from the cultural changes brought about by an increasingly digitized culture. During those decades, appropriation-based practices in other arts spread from isolated experiments to become a hallmark of hip-hop music, global DJ culture, and a ubiquitous tactic for mainstream and corporate media. Concurrently, sampling, mash-up, and the montage of found footage went from novel methods of production to widespread activities of consumption (or a postproduction that blurs the traditionally segregated acts of production and consumption), coalescing into what Lawrence Lessig refers to as "remix culture."[44] In the twenty-first century, conceptual poetry thus operates against the background of related vernacular practices, in a climate of pervasive participation and casual appropriation (not to mention the panicked, litigious corporate response to such activities). All of which is directly related to the technological environment in which digital files are promiscuous and communicable: words and sounds and images all reduced to compressed binary files disseminated through fiber-optic networks. In a world of increasingly capacious and inexpensive storage media, the proliferation of conceptual practices comes as no surprise, and those practices frequently mimic what Lev Manovich argues is the defining "database logic" of new media, wherein the focus is no longer on the production of new material but on the recombination of previously produced and stockpiled data.[45] Conceptual poetry, accordingly, often operates as an interface—returning the answer to a particular query; assembling, rearranging, and displaying information; or sorting and selecting from files of accumulated language pursuant to a certain algorithm—rather than producing new material from scratch. Even if it does not involve electronics or computers, conceptual poetry is thus very much a part of its technological and cultural moment.[46] That moment is also, perhaps not coincidentally, one in which the number of poetry books published each year rises exponentially and in which the digital archive of older literature deepens and broadens by the day. Under such circumstances, the recycling impulse behind much conceptual writing suits a literary ecology of alarming overproduction. The task for conscientious writers today is not how to find inspiration but how to curb productivity. As the conceptual artist Douglas Huebler wrote in 1968, "The world is full of objects, more or less interesting, I do not wish to add any more."[47]

Uncreative Writing

Theoretically, the argument about genres and institutions put forward by the online UbuWeb collection could have been made with any style of literature. In the event, that collection happened to gather a particular kind of writing to make a secondary argument: some of the presumed hallmarks of poetry—the use of metaphor and imagery, a soigné edited craft, the sincere emotional expression of especially sensitive individuals—might be radically reconsidered, and poetry might be reclaimed as a venue for intellect rather than sentiment. Understanding writing to be more graphic than semantic, more a physically material event than a disembodied or transparent medium for referential communication, the online anthology showcased works fundamentally opposed to ideologies of expression. Writing, in these cases, referred more to itself, or to other instances of writing, than to any referent beyond the page. Oriented toward text rather than diegesis, these works present writing as their subject rather than imagining writing to be the means to a referential end. Accordingly, the anthology privileged modes of writing in which the substitutions of metaphor and symbol were replaced by the recording of metonymic facts, or by the direct presentation of language itself, and where the self-regard of narcissistic confession was rejected in favor of laying bare the potential for linguistic self-reflexiveness. Instead of the rhetoric of natural expression, individual style, or voice, the anthology sought impersonal procedure. Instead of psychological development or dramatic narrative, it sought systems of exhaustive logical extrapolation or permutation. The test of poetry for such work, accordingly, was no longer whether it "could have been done better (the question of the workshop), but whether it could conceivably have been done otherwise."[48] Conceptual writing, to emend one of LeWitt's paragraphs on conceptual art, "is good only when the idea is good."

The present volume continues to explore the potential of writing that tries to be "rid of lyrical interference of the individual as ego" (as Charles Olson famously put it).[49] Our emphasis is on work that does not seek to express unique, coherent, or consistent individual psychologies and that, moreover, refuses familiar strategies of authorial control in favor of automatism, reticence, obliquity, and modes of noninterference. With minimal intervention, the writers here are more likely to determine preestablished rules and parameters—to set up a system and step back as it runs its course—than to heavily edit or masterfully polish. Indeed, the exhaustive and obsessive nature of many of these projects can be traced back to an unwillingness to intercede too forcefully; to use the entirety of a data set, or to rehearse every possible permutation of a given system, is to make just one choice that obviates a whole host of other choices. The one decision removes the temptation to tinker or edit or hone. Frequently, we had to admit that works we admired were not quite right for this collection because they were simply too creative—they had too much authorial intervention, however masterful or stylish that intervention might be.

Above all, the works presented here share a tendency to use found language in ways that go beyond modernist quotation or postmodern citation. The great break with even the most artificial, ironic, or asemantic work of other avant-gardes is the realization that one does not need to generate new material to be a poet: the intelligent organization or reframing of already extant text is enough. Through the repurposing or *détournement* of language that is not their own (whatever that might mean), the writers here allow arbitrary rules to determine the chance and unpredictable disposition of that language; they let artificial systems trump organic forms; and they replace making with choosing, fabrication with arrangement, and production with transcription. In these ways, previously written language comes to be seen and understood in a new light, and so both the anthology as a whole—with its argument for the importance of the institutions within which a text is presented—and the works it contains are congruent: context, for both, is everything. The circumstance, as the adage has it, alters the case.

The case made here, we know, then, will alter as circumstances continue to change. This anthology documents the explosion of publications since the turn of the millennium under the sign of the conceptual, and it attests to the literary energy of uncreative practices currently orbiting in swarms about those two terms. Whatever those practices eventually come to be called, they will soon look very different, and one of the reasons for this collection is to offer a snapshot of an instant in the midst of an energetic reformation, just before the mills of critical assessment and canonical formation have had a chance to complete their first revolutions. As the table of contents reveals, we have not, however, confined ourselves to the present moment only, and by extending our own network of affiliations to include the writings of canonical figures from much earlier generations, such as Hart Crane, Stéphane Mallarmé, and Denis Diderot, we hope not only to sketch certain legacies and histories but also to demonstrate that particular techniques and devices—such as appropriation or transcription, however novel they might seem—always have precedents. Moreover, those precedents remind us that compositional tactics are never inherently significant, but they do always signify; their meaning simply changes with the cultural moment in which they are deployed (context, again, is all to the point). And here is where the context of the literary reveals itself to be the most surprising. Despite the genuinely contrarian and oppositional stance of contemporary uncreative writing in its open rejection of some of the fundamental characteristics of poetry, the resulting texts frequently evince far more conservative and traditional poetic values than most of what passes for mainstream poetry: the formalist artifice of measure and rhyme (if not in the form of received metrics and patterned end rhymes); classical rhetorical tropes of anaphora, apostrophe, and irony (if not in their romantic or modernist modes); the evidentiary disclosure of the writer's most private activities (if not in the melodramatic style of the psychological confessional); and more than a few passages of unexpectedly, heartbreakingly raw emotion, undiluted by even a trace of sentiment. In addition, if these poems are not referential in the sense of any conventionally realist diegesis, they point more directly to the archival record of popular culture and colloquial speech than any avant-pop potboiler or Wordsworthian ballad ever dreamed.

And in the end, the figure of the uncreative writer is hardly new. Jorge Luis Borges's Pierre Menard, for instance, publishes the same poem in two different issues of the same poetry journal, transposes Paul Valéry's masterpiece long poem "Le cimitière marin" from its heteroclite decasyllabics into the more familiar alexandrines of traditional French verse, and is the "author" (pace Cervantes) of the *Quixote*.[50] Or at least of the "ninth and thirty-eighth chapters of the first part of *Don Quixote* and a fragment of chapter twenty-two."[51] "He did not want to compose another *Quixote*— which is easy," Borges's narrator goes on to explain, "but *the Quixote itself*. Needless to say, he never contemplated a mechanical transcription of the original; he did not propose to copy it." Instead, Menard hoped "to produce a few pages which would coincide—word for word and line for line—with those of Miguel de Cervantes." The result, the narrator opines after a careful stylistic comparison of seemingly identical passages, "is more subtle than Cervantes'."[52] Herman Melville's Bartleby, in diametric contrast to Menard, does indeed copy and transcribe "mechanically" (at least before his perplexing work stoppage), duplicating "an extraordinary quantity of writing" with "no pause for digestion" and no taste for editing. Gustave Flaubert's two scriveners, François Bouvard and Juste Pécuchet, also abandon their clerkships for a time, but they return to copying with the conceptual vengeance of inclusive, exhaustive, arbitrary systematization. Like interfaces to the proliferating database of printed matter in the Troisième République, their writing careers culminate in an uncreative frenzy of imitation and transcription. No longer seeking a referential or instrumental language, their graphomania evinces "plaisir qu'il y a dans l'acte materiel de recopier" (the pleasure that there is in the physical act of copying).[53] As Flaubert imagined the final jouissance of their scrivening:

Ils copient au hasard tout ce qu'ils trouvent . . . cornets de tabac, vieux journaux, affiches, livres dechires etc. . . . Aux environs se trouve une fabrique de papier en faillite, et la ils achetent de vieux papiers. . . . Puis [ils] éprouvent besoin d'un classement. Ils font des tableaux, des parallèles antithétiques comme "crimes des rois" et "crimes des peuples", "bienfaits de la Religion", "crimes de la Religion" . . . "beautés de l'Histoire," etc.; Mais quelquefois ils sont embarrassés de ranger la chose à sa place. . . . pas de réflexions! Copions tout de même. Il faut que la page s'emplisse—egalite de tout, du bien et du mal . . . du Beau et du Laid . . . il n'y a que des faits,—des phénomènes.
    Joie finale.

They indiscriminately copy everything they find: tobacco wrappers, old newspapers, posters, shredded books, etc. They discover a bankrupt paper factory in the neighborhood, and they buy old papers.
    Then, they discover the need for a taxonomy. They make tables, dialectic parallels such as "crimes of the kings" and "crimes of the people," "blessings of religion," "crimes of Religion" . . . "beauties of history," etc.; but sometimes they are confounded by how to classify something properly . . . enough speculation! Let's copy everything! What matters is that the page gets filled—everything is equal: good and evil . . . Beauty and Ugliness . . . there are only facts—and phenomena.
    Ultimate bliss. [*Translation mine.*]

The list of literary amanuenses goes on: Nikolay Gogol's Akaky Akakievich Bashmachkin, another deliriously focused copy clerk; Moses taking God's dictation; above all, the nymph Echo. In Ovid's characterization:

She liked to chatter
But had no power of speech except the power
To answer in the words she last had heard. . . .
Echo always says the last thing she hears, and nothing further.[54]

Echo, literally, always has the last word. And she sets the first example for many of the writers included here: loquacious, patient, rule bound, recontextualizing language in a mode of strict citation. Ostensibly a passive victim of the wrath of Juno, Echo in fact becomes a model of Oulipean ingenuity: continuing to communicate in her restricted state with far more personal purpose than her earlier gossiping, turning constraint to her advantage, appropriating other's language to her own ends, "making do" as a verbal *bricoleuse*.

Against Expression puts proof to the mythology of figures such as Echo, recognizing their tactics not just as allegorical conceits or fictional characterizations but as viable strategies for actual authors in their own rights. Moreover, this anthology will separate those who would rather read about Menard or Flaubert's *bonhommes* from those who dream of actually reading what they supposedly spent so much time—inspired, sly, compulsive, obstinate, pernicious, mechanical—copying out. Here, then, is the legacy of Echo, recontextualized as the birthright of an author rather than a victim, and this is her fully reconceptualized challenge to those who would instead chose the confession of Narcissus or the romance of Orpheus as their muse.

Notes

Special thanks to those who helped see this book to print: Matthew Abess; Anne Gendler; Julie Gonnering Lein; Katie Price; Ara Shirinyan; Faye Thaxton; our editor and series editors at Northwestern University Press (Henry Carrigan, Marjorie Perloff, and Rainer Rumold); and—especially, above all—to Jeremy Fisher.

1. Craig Dworkin, "Introduction," *The UbuWeb Anthology of Conceptual Writing,* http://www.ubu.com/concept.

2. One of the most interesting aspects of the current discourse in poetics is the discrepancy between how many writers and critics are invested in the term *conceptual* and how few share even the same basic definition. The rubric itself is of little import, but the variety of activities it attracts are worth noting. These discrepancies are legible in venues such as the Poetry Foundation's online publication (http://www.poetryfoundation.org/harriet); Vanessa Place and Robert Fitterman's

Notes on Conceptualisms (Brooklyn, N.Y.: Ugly Duckling Presse, 2009); and the international symposium convened by Marjorie Perloff, "Conceptual Poetry and Its Others," at the University of Arizona Poetry Center, May 13–29, 2008 (see http://poetrycenter.arizona.edu/conceptualpoetry/cp_index.shtml).

The term, in any event, should not to be confused with the Kontseptualizme poetry movement that flourished in Moscow in the 1980s (associated most closely with writers such as Dmitri Prigov and Lev Rubenstein) or with the commonplace connotations of writing relating in some vague way to abstract ideas or philosophical questions. With an amusing coincidence, the economist David Galenson coined the phrase "conceptual poetry" to designate writing that is diametrically opposed to the work that actually goes by the name. Galenson explains (with a definition of experimental poetry equally estranged from its literary associations): "Conceptual poetry typically emphasizes ideas or emotions, and often involves the creation of imaginary figures and settings, whereas experimental poetry generally stresses visual images and observations, based on real experiences" (*Old Masters and Young Geniuses: The Two Life Cycles of Artistic Creativity* [Princeton, N.J.: Princeton University Press, 2005], 123). Replacing *emphasizes* and *stresses* with *refuses* and *ignores* would bring the passage in line with how the terms *conceptual* and *experimental* are used in contemporary literary discourse.

3. This is obviously not the place for anything like a history of conceptual art; several monographs, catalogs, and sourcebooks provide fuller introductions. See, to begin with, Tony Godfrey, *Conceptual Art* (London: Phaidon, 1998); Peter Osborne, *Conceptual Art* (London: Phaidon, 2002); Paul Wood, *Movements in Modern Art: Conceptual Art* (London: Tate, 2002); Alexander Alberro, *Conceptual Art and the Politics of Publicity* (Cambridge: Massachusetts Institute of Technology Press, 2004); Michael Corris, ed., *Conceptual Art: Theory, Myth, and Practice* (Cambridge: Cambridge University Press, 2004). See also Lucy Lippard, *Six Years: The Dematerialization of the Art Object* (Berkeley: University of California Press, 1997); Alexander Alberro and Blake Stimson, eds., *Conceptual Art: A Critical Anthology* (Cambridge: Massachusetts Institute of Technology Press, 2000).

4. Marcel Duchamp, *À l'infinitif* (New York: Cordier et Ekstrom, 1966); see *Salt Seller: The Writings of Marcel Duchamp*, ed. Michel Sanouillet and Elmer Peterson (New York: Oxford University Press, 1973), 78.

5. Kosuth's display of uniform panels and repeated forms with minor variations seemed to directly acknowledge the precedent of Andy Warhol's 1962 Ferus Gallery show of soup cans. More pointedly, *Titled* also contained one panel with a quotation from Warhol instead of from a dictionary: "In the future everybody will be famous for fifteen minutes." A striking punctum in the series, that panel seems to ask the viewer to supply the word for which Warhol's phrase would serve as a definition. It also underscores the cold war shadow of Warhol's comment and the existential threat of "nothing" behind the funereal black of Kosuth's panels: fif-

teen minutes was the widely cited time officials believed a Russian nuclear missile would take to reach the continental United States.

6. The main motif of Cage's "Lecture on Nothing" reads: "I have nothing to say and I am saying it, and that is poetry" (*Incontri Musicali* 3 [1959]: 128–49, passim; republished in *Silence: Lectures and Writings by John Cage* [Middletown, Conn.: Wesleyan University Press, 1961], 109–40, passim). Kosuth's work would have been considered a kind of poetry by W. H. Auden's definition as well, as it "makes nothing happen." Kosuth conducted a similar exploration of negative ontology with the replete definition of the word *empty*.

7. Reinhardt's understanding of artistic tautology is most clearly stated in an essay that opens this way: "The one thing to say about art is that it is one thing. Art is art-as-art and everything else is everything else. Art-as-art is nothing but art. Art is not what is not art." ("Art-As-Art," *Art International* 4, no. 10 [1962]: 38).

8. Definitions are drawn from *Webster's New Twentieth Century Dictionary of the English Language,* unabridged, 2nd ed. (1957); *Webster's New World Dictionary of the American Language* (1960); *New Century Dictionary* (1934); one of the *Pocket, Little,* or *Concise* Oxford dictionaries based on the work of Henry Watson and Francis George Fowler, and so on. At least one version of "universal" (private collection; see the image reproduced in Godfrey, *Conceptual Art,* 132), cleverly, points to the title of its source: *Webster's New Universal Unabridged.*

One might compare the uninflected presentation and format of Kosuth's dictionary works with one of the index cards from Michael Harvey's *White Papers* (1971), which spells out the punctuation from the definition of *punctuation* in the *Oxford English Dictionary:*

> the practice comma art comma method comma or system of inserting points or open single quote periods closed single quote to aide the sense comma in writing or printing semicolon division into sentences comma clauses comma etc period by means of points or periods period other punctuation marks comma e period g period exclamation marks comma question marks comma refer to the tone or structure of what precedes them period a sentence can contain any of these symbols comma its termination marked by a period period

9. Pierre Cabanne, *Dialogues with Marcel Duchamp* (New York: Da Capo, 1979), 39, emphasis added; cf. 43.

10. Ian Wilson makes the interesting argument that "the difference between conceptual art and poetry, literature, and philosophy is that conceptual art takes the principles of visual abstraction, founded in the visual arts, and applies them to language. When it does that a nonvisual abstraction occurs" ("Conceptual Art," in Alberro and Stimson, *Conceptual Art,* 414).

11. Qtd. in Alberro, *Conceptual Art,* 71.

12. For more on Duchamp's sculpture, with special attention to the inscription on its plates, see Marjorie Perloff, *21st-Century Modernism: The "New" Poetics* (Oxford: Blackwell, 2002), chap. 3, 101–7, passim.

13. The number of categories (or cards) is commonly cited as forty-four, but I count only forty-three categories, four of which spill over onto two cards. The categories are accidents, alphabets, cards (two cards), categories, changes, cement, communications, completion, conception, considerations, criticism, cross filing, dates, decisions (two cards), dissatisfactions, delays, deleted entries, duration, dimensions, forms, future, index, interruptions, locations, losses, materials, mistakes, names, number, owners, possibilities, prices, purchases, recoveries, repetitions, signature, size, stores, tenses, time, title, trips (two cards), and working (two cards).

14. Dan Graham, "Variant for *Possibilities of Poetry,* from Schemata Conceived in 1966," *Possibilities of Poetry,* ed. Richard Kostelanetz (New York: Dell, 1970), 180. The work, significantly, is alternately titled "Poem," "Poem Schema," "Schema (March 1966)," "Poem-Schema (1966)," and so on: a perfect example of how the same text can function in different ways in different contexts (art and poetry, in this case).

15. Dan Graham, *For Publication* (Los Angeles: Otis Art Institute, 1975), n.p.

16. Graham, "Variant," 180.

17. Dan Graham, "Poem-Schema," *Art-Language: The Journal of Conceptual Art* 1, no. 1 (1969): 14.

18. Dan Graham, "Schema," *Possibilities of Poetry,* ed. Richard Kostelanetz (New York: Dell, 1970), 182.

19. Dan Graham, "Schema," Suzanne Zavrain, ed., *Extensions* 1, no. 1 (1968): 23.

20. Dan Graham, "Poem, March 1966," *Aspen* 5–6 (1966–67); single folded sheet, n.p.

21. Designed by Adrian Frutiger in the mid-1950s, the numerals indicated weight and style; in this case, for instance, "55" indicates a medium-weight Roman face. When "Schema" was published in *Studio International,* "univers 689" was listed as uncapitalized (as was the "hunterblade" paper stock). Dan Graham, "Schema," *Studio International* 183, no. 944 (1972): 212. The UbuWeb edition of *Aspen,* for the record, misspells the face name with an anglicized "Universe."

22. Rolf Wedewer and Konrad Fischer, eds., *Konzeption/Conception* (Cologne: West-Verlag, 1969), n.p.

23. Sol LeWitt, "Paragraphs on Conceptual Art," *Artforum* 5, no. 10 (June 1967): 80.

24. In 1957, Klein had dedicated an otherwise-empty room in the Gallery Colette Allandy in Paris to "Surfaces and Blocks of Pictorial Sensibility," reprising the idea in 1962 at the Musée d'Art Moderne de la Ville de Paris as a *zone de sensibilité picturale immatérielle* (zone of immaterial pictorial sensibility), whence he removed the paintings from the gallery walls. Warhol's exhibition became so crowded on its opening the art was removed from the walls. "It was fabulous,"

Warhol exclaimed: "an art opening with no art!" (Andy Warhol and Pat Hackett, *POPism: The Warhol Sixties* [New York: Harvest, 2006], 166).

25. Not counting a likely oxidation, the half-life disappearance would actually be closer to 10 years and 186 days, assuming one did not consider the work surviving in the transformed state of cesium 133.

26. LeWitt's sentence has been frequently reprinted with the infelicitous typo "idea *of* concept." I have quoted from the first publication in the special issue on sculpture of *Artforum* 5 (June 1967).

27. In Judd's *Untitled* stacks, for instance, the number of units depends on the distance between the floor and the ceiling. Similarly, the relative size of the units in his horizontal *Progression* sculptures from the late 1960s and early 1970s, as well as the distance between each unit, was determined by the ratios of the Fibonacci series. LeWitt's *Incomplete Open Cubes,* in turn, presents every possible variation on an axis-oriented cube missing one or more of its sides; the effort and phenomenological effect of actually constructing or viewing the cubes is not inconsequential, but the point was that once the project had been defined, its conclusion was inevitable.

28. Baldessari's source is *The Family Book of Hobbies* (New York: Sterling, 1973), 167.

29. Ibid.

30. Compare György Kepes, *Language of Vision* (New York: Paul Theobald, 1944), 36.

31. Note that the line break and use of a comma rather than a semicolon open the possibility of a less ironic reading, in which the second phrase can be understood to indicate that "no ideas have entered the work except for [the idea of] art."

Rauschenberg had attempted a related denominalization in 1963 with *Document,* made in rebuke to the collector Philip Johnson (whose payment for Rauschenberg's work *Litanies* was tardy) and including a notarized document attesting: "The undersigned, Robert Morris, being the maker of / the metal construction entitled Litanies, / described in the annexed Exhibit A, hereby withdraws from / said construction all aesthetic quality and content and / declares that from the date hereof said construction has / no such quality and content."

32. On this topic, see the canvas, which reads:

WHAT THIS PAINTING AIMS TO DO

IT IS ONLY WHEN YOU HAVE BEEN PAINTING FOR
QUITE SOME TIME THAT YOU WILL BEGIN TO RE-
ALIZE THAT YOUR COMPOSITIONS SEEM TO LACK
IMPACT—THAT THEY ARE TOO ORDINARY.
THAT IS WHEN YOU WILL START TO BREAK ALL THE
SO-CALLED RULES OF COMPOSITION AND TO

THINK IN TERM OF DESIGN.

THEN YOU CAN DISTORT SHAPES, INVENT FORMS,

AND BE ON YOUR WAY TOWARD BEING A CREATIVE ARTIST.

33. Qtd. in *John Baldessari,* ed. Jan Debbaut (Eindhoven: Van Abbemuseum and Essen, Museum Folkwang, 1981), 6.

34. Dan Graham had attempted to outsource a poem by placing an advertisement in the November 1966 *National Tatler* (Lucy Lippard lists the issue date as November 21 [*Six Years* (Berkeley: University of California Press, 1997), 19]; elsewhere it is noted as November 31 [Birgit Pelzer, Mark Francis, and Beatriz Colomina, *Dan Graham* (London: Phaidon, 2001), 140]); I have not been able to locate a copy to verify which is correct:

WANTED: PROFESSIONAL MEDICAL WRITER to write medical, sexological description of sexual detumescence in human male (physiological and psychological aspects) laxity and pleasure should be dealt with. Needed *for reproduction as a poem by Dan Graham* to be deseminated [*sic*] 25,000 readers in June issue of ASPEN. Respondent retains all rights and fees from use of. [*Emphasis added.*]

When no one responded he placed another ad in *New York Review of Sex* (August 1, 1969, and possibly again on August 15):

Wanted: Professional medical writer willing to write clinical description covering equally the physiological and psychological (lassitude/pleasure) response to the human male to sexual detumescence. The description selected will be *reproduced as a piece* in a national magazine. Writer of piece retains copyright and is free to use description for his own purposes. [*Emphasis added.*]

When no one responded, he placed another ad in *Screw* (1969). No one ever replied.

35. LeWitt, "Paragraphs," 13.

36. First published in the catalog *January 5-31, 1969* (n.p.) and later appended to many of Weiner's works.

37. Osborne, *Conceptual Art,* 27. See LeWitt's sixteenth thesis in his "Sentences on Conceptual Art": "if words are used, and they proceed from ideas about art, then they are art and not literature; numbers are not mathematics" (in Alberro and Stimson, *Conceptual Art,* 107). In an interview with Jeanne Siegel, Kosuth denies any relationship between his text-based art and (concrete) poetry with the following assertion: "Absolutely no relationship at all. It's simply one of things superficially resembling one another" (*Art After Philosophy and After: Collected Writings, 1966–1990* [Cambridge: Massachusetts Institute of Technology Press, 1991], 51). Kosuth protests too much, but his general point is well taken. Jack Burn-

ham makes the same observation: "conceptual art resembles literature only superficially" ("Alice's Head: Reflections on Conceptual Art," in Alberro and Stimson, *Conceptual Art,* 216).

38. William Carlos Williams, "Paterson," *Collected Poems of William Carlos Williams, 1909–1939* (New York: New Directions, 1986), 264.

39. The important exception is Darren Wershler's *The Tapeworm Foundry (andor the dangerous prevalence of imagination)* ([Toronto: House of Anansi], 200), the one book of poetry closest to artworks such as Weiner's *Statements.*

40. Signing a text that one hasn't written will surely become less remarkable, and the next frontier of propriety will materialize when conceptual writing antagonizes the institutions of poetry by signing for others under texts that they have not written. Jacques Debrot published a number of poems under John Ashbery's name, as well as a fabricated interview (*Readme* 4 [2001]). See the related entries in the present volume for Ted Bergigan and *Issue #1.* It is one thing for Duchamp to display a urinal in a gallery, but still another to go into the museum men's room and post an information card next to the urinal claiming it as a Duchamp. In Darren Wershler's *Tapeworm Foundry,* he proposes this: "publish an issue of a magazine without telling it's official editors."

41. The *Pictures* exhibition included Troy Brauntuch, Jack Goldstein, Sherrie Levine, Robert Longo, and Philip Smith. Metro Pictures, founded by Janelle Reiring and Helene Winer, who had been the director at Artists Space, was a commercial gallery committed to "concerns emanating from the culture as represented in the popular media" (Helene Winer, "Metro Pictures," *For Love and Money: Dealers Choose* [New York: Pratt Manhattan Center Gallery, 1981], n.p.); the opening group show for Metro Pictures included Troy Brauntuch, Jack Goldstein, Michael Harvey, Thomas Lawson, William Leavitt, Sherrie Levine, Robert Longo, Richard Prince, Cindy Sherman, Laurie Simmons, James Welling, and Michael Zwack. The first solo shows, in late 1980 and early 1981, featured Goldstein and Sherman (showing concurrently), Longo's *Men in the Cities,* and Prince and Zwack (concurrently). Sherman's work in particular exemplified a less tangible mode of appropriation. In addition, consider the corroborative work of Allan McCollum from this period, as well as the widely reproduced work of Barbara Kruger, although she exhibited at Metro Pictures only in a 1986 group show and was active at the time in other venues.

Readers interested in the critical response to this tendency might turn first to Douglas Crimp, "Pictures," *October* 8 (1979): 75–88; Benjamin H. D. Buchloh, "Allegorical Procedures: Appropriation and Montage in Contemporary Art," *Artforum* 21, no. 1 (1982): 43–56; Hal Foster, "Subversive Signs," *Art in America* (November 1982): 88–92; Hal Foster, "Readings in Cultural Resistance," *ReCodings: Art, Spectacle, Cultural Politics* (Seattle: Bay Press, 1985), 157–79; Rosalind E. Krauss, *The Originality of the Avant-Garde and Other Modernist Myths* (Cambridge: Massachusetts Institute of Technology Press, 1986); Craig Owens, *Beyond Recogni-*

tion: Representation, Power, and Culture, ed. Scott Bryson, Barbara Kruger, Lynne Tillman, and Jane Weinstock (Berkeley: University of California Press, 1992).

42. Jerry Saltz, "Great Artists Steal," *New York Magazine* (May 10, 2009): 66–67.

43. For just two tokens of the feud between journalism and poetry, and of particular relevance to *Day,* consider Ezra Pound's definition of poetry as "news that *stays* news," and Stéphane Mallarmé's observation that his poetry consisted of "les mots mêmes que le Bourgeois lit tous les matins, les mêmes! Mais voilà: s'il lui arrive de les retrouver en tel mien poème, il ne les comprend plus" (the same words that businessmen read every morning (in the newspaper)—exactly the same!" But then: if they should come across them in some poem of mine, they no longer understand them) (René Ghil, *Les dates et les œuvres: Symbolisme et poésie* [Paris: G. Crès, 1929], 214).

44. See Nicolas Bourriaud, *Postproduction: La culture comme scénario, comment l'art reprogramme le monde contemporain* (Dijon: Les Presses du Réel, 2004); Lawrence Lessig, *Free Culture: The Nature and Future of Creativity* (New York: Penguin, 2005).

45. Lev Manovich, *The Language of New Media* (Cambridge: Massachusetts Institute of Technology Press, 2002); see especially 212–43, passim.

46. For a more detailed examination of this condition and its political resonance, see Craig Dworkin, "The Imaginary Solution," *Contemporary Literature* 48, no. 1 (2007): 29–60.

47. Douglas Huebler, "Untitled Statements," *Theories and Documents of Contemporary Art,* ed. Kristine Stiles and Howard Selz (Berkeley: University of California Press, 1995), 840.

48. Ibid.

49. *Charles Olson: Selected Writings,* ed. Robert Creeley (New York: New Directions, 1971), 24.

50. Jorge Luis Borges, "Pierre Menard, Author of the *Quixote,*" *Labyrinths: Selected Stories and Other Writings,* ed. Donald A. Yates and James E. Irby (New York: New Directions, 1964), 37.

51. Ibid., 39.

52. Ibid., 42.

53. Gustave Flaubert, *Bouvard et Pécuchet,* ed. Alberto Cento (Paris: Libraire Nizet, 1964), 124.

54. Ovid, *Metamorphoses,* trans. Rolfe Humphries (Bloomington: Indiana University Press, 1955), 68.

Against Expression

Monica Aasprong
from Soldatmarkedet

Soldatmarkedet, a monumental project by the Norwegian poet Monica Aasprong started in 2003, deals with radically reduced writing. Aasprong began a process of removing letters from novels she had written, finally ending up with entire books consisting of only one letter. In *Soldatmarkedet* (Oslo: Poetryfestival, 2007), the entire book is nothing but the letter *t* filling every page. The book itself is a small volume based on sixteen thousand automatically generated text permutations, which fill an entire filing cabinet. On most pages, Aasprong has removed one or more *t*'s to create breaks in the visual field. Often, many *t*'s have been removed to create rivulets of text running down the page.

The title of the book comes from the famous Soldiers' Square in Berlin, Gendarmenmarkt, a place that was originally used as stables for German regiments. Over time, two major cathedrals were built on the square. Later, with the addition of an arts space, the square was transformed into a complex palimpsest of military, cultural, market, and religious history. Aasprong's reduced poems visually reflect the site's history, as the *t*'s can be read as crosses (religion), plus signs (commerce), or rudimentary grave markers (military).

Aasprong's work takes a minimalist trajectory of concrete and visual poetry—from Stéphane Mallarmé to E. E. Cummings to Aram Saroyan—to new and extreme limits while at the same time taking concerns of visually based minimalism into the sphere of the page. In the process she recalls José Luis Castillejo's massive four-hundred-page *TLALAATALA* (Madrid: Alga Marghen, 2001), which consists entirely of permutations of its title's letters.

ttttttttttttttttttttttttttttttt   ttttttttttttttttttttttttttttttttttttttttttttttttttttttttttttttttttt
ttttttttttttttttttttttttttttttttttt   tttttttttttttttttttttttttttttttttttttttttttttttttttttttttttttttttt
ttttttttttttttttttttttttttttttttt   ttttttttttttttttttttttttttttttttttttttttttttttttttttttttttttttttttt
tttttttttttttttttttttttttttt   ttttttttttttttttttttttttttttttttttttttttttttttttttttttttttttttttttt
tttttttttttttttttttt   tttttttttttttttttttttttttttttttttttttttttttttttttttttttttttttttttttttt
tttttttttttttttttttttttttt   tttttttttttttttttttttttttttttttttttttttttttttttttttttttttttttttttt
ttttttttttttttttttttttttttttttttt   tttttttttttttttttttttttttttttttttttttttttttttttttttttttttttttttt
tttttttttttttttttttttttttttttttttttt   ttttttttttttttttttttttttttttttttttttttttttttttttttttttttttttt
ttttttttttttttttttttttttttttttttttttt   tttttttttttttttttttttttttttttttttttttttttttttttttttttttttttt
ttttttttttttttttttttttttttttttttttttttttttt   ttttttttttttttttttttttttttttttttttttttttttttttttttttttt
ttttttttttttttttttttttttttttttttttttttttt   tttttttttttttttttttttttttttttttttttttttttttttttttttttttt
tttttttttttttttttttttttttttttttttttttttttttttt   ttttttttttttttttttttttttttttttttttttttttttttttttttttt
ttttttttttttttttttttttttttttttttttttt   ttttttttttttttttttttttttttttttttttttttttttttttttt   tt
ttttttttttttttttttttttttttttttttt   tttttttttttttttttttttttttttttttttttttttttttttttttttt   tttttttt
ttttttttttttttttttttttttttttttt   tttttttttttttttttttttttttttttttttttttttttttttttttttt   ttttttttt
ttttttttttttttttttttt   tttt   tttttttttttttttttttttttttttttttttttttttttttttttttt   ttttttttt
ttttttttttttttttttt   tttt   ttttttttttttttttttttttttttttttttttttttttttttttttt   ttttttttt
tttttttttttttttttttt   t   ttttt   ttttttttttttttttttttttttttttttttttttttttt   ttttttttttttt
ttttttttttttttttttttttttt   ttttttttttttttttttttttttttttttttttttttttttttttttttttttttttttttt
ttttttttttttttttttttt   ttttttttttttttttttttttttttttttttttttttttttttttttttttttttttttttttttttt
tttttttttttttttttttttt   ttttttttttttttttttttttttttttttttttttttttttttttttttttttttttttttttttttt
tttttttttttttttttttttttttttttttttttttttttttttttttttttttttttttttttttttttttttttttttttttttttttttttttttt
tttttttttttttttttttttttttttttttttttttttttttttttttttttttttttttttttttttttttttttttttttttttttttttttttttt
tttttttttttttttttttttttttttttttttttttttttttttttttttttttttttttttttttttttttttttttttttttttttttttttttttt
tttttttttttttttttttttttttttttttttttttttttttttttttttttttttttttttttttttttttttttttttttttttttttttttttttt

ttttttttt   ttttttt   ttttttttttttttttttttttttttttttttttttttttttttttttttttttttttttttttttttttttttttttttttttt
tttttt   tttttt   tttttttttttttttttttttttttttttttttttttttttttttttttttttttttttttttttttttttttttttttttttt
ttt   ttttt   ttttttttttttttttttttttttttttttttttttttttttttttttttttttttttttttttttttttttttttttttttt
              ttttttttttt   tttttttttttttttttttttttttttttttttttttttttttttttttttttttttttttttttttttttttttt
         ttttttttttttttttt   ttttttttttttttttttttttttttttttttttttttttttttttttttttttttttttttttttttttt
         ttttttttttttt   tttttttttttttttttttttttttttttttttttttttttttttttttttttttttttttttttttttttttt
           ttttttttttt   tttttttttttttttttttttttttttttttttttttttttttttttttttttttttttttttttttttttttt
tttttttt   tttttttttttttttttttttttttttttttttttttttttttttttttttttttttttttttttttttttttttttttttttttt
tt   tttttttttttttttttttttttttttttttttttttttttttttttttttttttttttttttttttttttttttttttttttttttttt
                 tttttttttttttttttttttttttttttttttttttttttttttttttttttttttttttttttttttttttttttttttttttttttt
                 tttttttttttttttttttttttttttttttttttttttttttttttttttttttttttttttttttttttttttttttttttttttt
                 ttttttttttttttttttttttttttttttttttttttttttttttttttttttttttttttttttttttttttttttttttttttt
    t   tttttttttttttttttttttttttttttttttttttttttttttttttttttttttttttttttttttttttttttttttttttttttt
tttt   tttttttttttttttttttttttttttttttttttttttttttttttttttttttttttttttttttttttttttttttttttttttttt
tt   ttttttttttttttttttttttttttttttttttttttttttttttttttttttttttttttttttttttttttttttttttttttttttt
t   tttttttttttttttttttttttttttttttttttttttttttttttttttttttttttttttttttttttttttttttttttttttttttttttt'
              ttttttttttttttttttttttttttttttttttttttttttttttttttttttttttttttttttttttttttttttttttttttttttttttttt
tttttttttttttttttttttttttttttttttttttttttttttttttttttttttttttttttttttttttttttttttttttttttttttttttttttttttttttttttt
tttttttttttttttttttttttttttttttttttttttttttttttttttttttttttttttttttttttttttttttttttttttttttttttttttttttttttttttttt
tttttttttttttttttttttttttttttttttttttttttttttttttttttttttttttttttttttttttttttttttttttttttttttttttttttttttttttttttt
tttttttttttttttttttttttttttttttttttttttttttttttttttttttttttttttttttttttttttttttttttttttttttttttttttttttttttttttttt
tttttttttttttttttttttttttttttttttttttttttttttttttttttttttttttttttttttttttttttttttttttttttttttttttttttttttttttttttt
tttttttttttttttttttttttttttttttttttttttttttttttttttttttttttttttttttttttttttttttttttttttttttttttttttttttttttttttttt
tttttttttttttttttttttttttttttttttttttttttttttttttttttttttttttttttttttttttttttttttttttttttttttttttttttttttttttttttt
tttttttttttttttttttttttttttttttttttttttttttttttttttttttttttttttttttttttttttttttttttttttttttttttttttttttttttttttttt

ttttttttttttttttttttttttttttttttttttttttttttttttttttttttttttttttttttttttttttttttttttttttttttttttttttttttttttttttttttt
ttttttttttttttttttttttttttttttttttttttttttttttttttttttttttttttttttttttttttttttttttttttttttttttttttttttttttttttttttttt
ttttttttttttttttttttttttttttttttttttttttttttttttttttttttttttttttttttttttttttttttttttttttttttttttttttttttttttttttttttt
ttttttttttttttttttttttttttttttttttttttttttttttttttttttttttttttttttttttttttttttttttttttttttttttttttttttttttttttttttttt
ttttttttttttttttttttttttttttttttttttttttttttttttttttttttttttttttttttttttttttttttttttttttttttttttttttttttttttttttttttt
ttttttttttttttttttttttttttttttttttttttttttttttttttttttttttttttttttttttttttttttttttttttttttttttttttttttttttttttttttttt
ttttttttttttttttttttttttttttttttttttttttttttttttttttttttttttttttttttttttttttttttttttttttttttttttttttttttttttttttttttt
ttttttttttttttttttttttttttttttttttttttttttttttttttttttttttttttttttttttttttttttttttttttttttttttttttttttttttttttttttttt
ttttttttttttttttttttttttttttttttttttttttttttttttttttttttttttttttttttttttttttttttttttttttttttttttttttttttttttttttttttt
ttttttttttttttttttttttttttttttttttttttttttttttttttttttttttttttttttttttttttttttttttttttttttttttttttttttttttttttttttttt
ttttttttttttttttttttttttttttttttttttttttttttttttttttttttttttttttttttttttttttttttttttttttttttttttttttttttttttttttttttt
ttttttttttttttttttttttttttttttttttttttttttttttttttttttttttttttttttttttttttttttttttttttttttttttttttttttttttttttttttttt
ttttttttttttttttttttttttttttttttttttttttttttttttttttttttttttttttttttttttttttttttttttttttttttttttttttttttttttttttttttt
ttttttttttttttttttttttttttttttttttttttttttttttttttttttttttttttttttttttttttttttttttttttttttttttttttttttttttttttttttttt
ttttttttttttttttttttttttttttttttttttttttttttttttttttttttttttttttttttttttttttttttttttttttttttttttttttttttttttttttttttt
ttttttttttttttttttttttttttttttttttttttttttttttttttttttttttttttttttttttttttttttttttttttttttttttttttttttttttttttttttttt
ttttttttttttttttttttttttttttttttttttttttttttttttttttttttttttttttttttttttttttttttttttttttttttttttttttttttttttttttttttt
ttttttttttttttttttttttttttttttttttttttttttttttttttttttttttttttttttttttttttttttttttttttttttttttttttttttttttttttttttttt
ttttttttttttttttttttttttttttttttttttttttttttttttttttttttttttttttttttttttttttttttttttttttttttttttttttttttttttttttttttt
ttttttttttttttttttttttttttttttttttttttttttttttttttttttttttttttttttttttttttttttttttttttttttttttttttttttttttttttttttttt
ttttttttttttttttttttttttttttttttttttttttttttttttttttttttttttttttttttttttttttttttttttttttttttttttttttttttttttttttttttt
ttttttttttttttttttttttttttttttttttttttttttttttttttttttttttttttttttttttttttttttttttttttttttttttttttttttttttttttttttttt
ttttttttttttttttttttttttttttttttttttttttttttttttttttttttttttttttttttttttttttttttttttttttttttttttttttttttttttttttttttt
ttttttttttttttttttttttttttttttttttttttttttttttttttttttt   ttttttttttttttttttttttttttttttttttttttttttttttt
ttttttttttttttttttttttttttttttttttttttttttttttttttttt   ttttttttttttttttttttttttttttttttttttttttttttttt

tttttttttttttt   ttttttttttttttttttttttttttttttttttttttttttttttttttttttttttttttttttttttttttttttttttttttttttttttttttt
ttttttttt tttttttttttttttttttt t t ttttttttttttttttttt ttttttttttttttttttttttttttttttttttttttttttttt t   tttt
ttttttt ttttttttttttttttttttttttttt tttttttttttttttttt ttttttttttttttttttttttttttttttttttttttttttttttt ttttt t
ttttt tttttttttttttttttttttttttttt tttttttttttttttt tttttttttttttttttttttttttttttttttttttttttttttttttttt ttttt
tt tttttttttttttttttttttttttttttttttt ttttttttttttttt tttttttttttttttttttttttttttttttttttttttttttttttttttt tttttt
tt ttttttttttttttttttttttttttttttttt ttttttttttttt   ttttttttttttttttttttttttttttttttttttttt tttttttttt
tttttttttttttttttttttttttttttttttttttttttttttttttttttttttttttttt tttttttttttttttttttttttttttttt tttttttttttt
ttttttttttttttttttttttttttttttttttttttttttttttttttttttttttttttttttt tttttttttttttttttttttttttt tttttttttttt
ttttttttttttttttttttttttttttttttttttttttt tttttttttttttttttttt t   tttttttttttttttttttttttttttt tttttttttt
tttttttttttttttttttttttttttttttttttttt ttttttttttttttttttttttt tt t   tttttttttttt tttttttttttttt
ttttttttttttttttttttttttttttttttttttttttttttttttttttttttttttttttttt t tttttttt ttttttttttttttt   ttttttttttttt
tttttttttttttt ttttttttttttttttttttttttttttttttttttttttttttttttttttttttttttttt ttttttttttt ttttttttttttttttttt
ttttttttttttttttttttttttttttttttttttttttttttttttt t t ttttttttttttttttttttttttttttttttttttttttt ttttttttttttttttttt
ttttttttttttttttttttttttttttttttttttttttttttttttttttttttttttttttttttttttttttttttttttttttttttttttttt ttttttttttttttt
ttttttttttttttttttttttttttttttttttttttttttttttttttttttttttttttttttttttttttt t tttttttttttttttttt ttttttttttttttt
tttttttttttttttttttttttttttttttttttttttttttt ttttttttttttttttttttttttttttttttttttt ttttttttttttttt ttttttttttttttt
ttttttttttttttttttttttttttttttttttttttt   ttttttttttttttttttttttttttttttttt tttttttttttt ttttttttttttttttt
ttttttttttttttttttttttttttttttttttttttttttt tttttttttttttttttttttttttttttttttttttttttttttt tttttttt tttttttttttttttttt
ttttttttttttttttttttttttttttttttttttttttttttttttttttttttttttttttttttttttttttttttttt t ttttttttt ttttt ttttttttttttttttttt
ttttttttttttttttttttttttttttttttttttttttttt   ttttttttttttttttttttttttttttttt t ttttttttttt ttttttttttttttttttttttt
ttttttttttttttttttttttttttttttttttt   tttttttttttttttttttttttttttttttttttttt   tttt tttttttttttttttttttttttt
ttttttttttttttttttttttttttttttttttttt   tttttttttttttttttttttttttttttttttttttt ttttttttttttttttttttttttttttttt
tttttttttttttttttttttttttttttttttttttttttttttt   ttttttttttttttttttttttttttttttt   tttttttttttttttttttttttttt
tttttttttttttttttttttttttttttttttttt   tttttttttttttttttttttttttt   tttttttttttttttttttttttttttt
ttttttttttttttttttttttttttttttttt   ttttttttttttttttttttttttttttt   ttttttttttttttttttttttttttttttt

Walter Abish
from Skin Deep

"Skin Deep" forms part of *99: The New Meaning* (Providence, R.I.: Burning Deck, 1990), a book of stories composed entirely of unattributed quotations. The title piece contains ninety-nine passages from ninety-nine authors drawn from the ninety-ninth page of their original books; other chapters focus on particular authors (Gustave Flaubert and Franz Kafka) or genres (autobiography). The passages are rarely easy to identify, creating an air of *déjà dit*—their source tantalizingly familiar but just out of grasp. Like many works of conceptual writing, however, the result is neither depersonalized nor unemotional. Rather, the formal conceit attempts to discover or more closely approach emotional conditions by avoiding the habits, clichés, and sentimentality of conventional expressivist rhetoric. As Abish writes in the introduction to the book:

> These works were undertaken in a playful spirit—not actually 'written' but orchestrated. The fragmented narrative can be said to function as a kind of lure—given the constraints, anything else would be beyond its scope. In using selected segments of published texts authored by others as the exclusive 'ready made' material for these five 'explorations,' I wanted to probe certain familiar emotional configurations afresh, and arrive at an emotional content that is not mine by design.

For the reader, the exploration involves assembling a narrative picture from the jigsawed pieces, which frequently appear to be self-referential. One of the sections, for instance, reads, "I live, not with my own story, but just with those parts of it that I have been able to put to literary use" (the source, as it happens, is Max Frisch's *Montauk*). Just as telling as what Abish selects, of course, is what he does not include. The passage from Frisch continues: "It is not even true that I have always described just myself. I have never described myself. I have only betrayed myself." Pensive and introspective, *99* reads not unlike a cross between David Markson and Georges Perec.

43

The need to become familiar with Albertine's desire is so intense that the activity of loving turns out to be something like a compulsory intellectual investigation. And the detective-story atmosphere is sustained by the imagination for crime that the fragile self develops.

83

Meanwhile, on the other side, it is a town composed of white buildings, a watering place, a seaside resort in summer. Out there, in the middle of the beach, in the shade of the lime trees, the band will play soon in the bandstand, for the people walking by or sitting around. In a room, probably fairly high up, overlooking the main avenue, an unknown woman standing beside me (but it is her), dressed in black, is speaking to me in insistent whispers.

47

Error, optical illusion, provides the material out of which truth must emerge, as evolution must emerge out of the regression and elimination of many species.

But *emerge* is as vague a word as the language possesses for so crucial a process, biological, moral or esthetic. Emerge how?

80

Listen, do you want to make an effort or don't you? You were so stupid the last time. Don't you see how beautiful this moment could be? Look at the sky, look at the color of the sun on the carpet. I've got my green dress on and my face isn't made up, I'm quite pale. Go back, go and sit in the shadow; you understand what you have to do? Come on! How stupid you are! Speak to me!

69

She tried to free herself. No, no, I know that tone of voice. You're going to treat me to another of those nonsensical outbursts. When you put on that tone of voice and face, I know that you're going to prove that your eye is shaped like a striped super-mullet, or that your mouth looks like the figure three on its side. No, no, I can't stand that.

22

Very often the novel writes about contracts but dreams of transgressions, and in reading it, the dream tends to emerge more powerfully.

16

You've been trying to find things out?
Without success; there's probably nothing to be found out.

52

How did she find out?
Madame Saphir put her on the track.
Who?
Madame Saphir, the clairvoyant in the rue Taine. She set up shop there about six months ago and all the old girls in the district go and consult her. Haven't *you* been?
I'm not an old girl, said Julia.

79

Don't complain about improbability. What is going to follow is false and no one is bound to accept it as gospel truth. Truth is not my strong point. "But one has to lie in order to be true." And even go beyond. What truth do I want to talk about? If it is really true that I am a prisoner who plays (who plays for himself) scenes of the inner life, you will require nothing other than a game.

53

Like Flaubert, too, that brown table to the left with a penknife-cut in it (another Bovary), that carefully unconscious but fundamentally so naive and almost sentimental table, is yourself. And if you make use of the table, if you cannot leave it alone, why should I not make use of the lie?

60

And you complain of my conduct! And you are surprised by my eagerness to avoid you! Ah! Rather blame my indulgence, rather be surprised that I did not leave at the moment you arrived. I ought perhaps to have done so; and you will compel me to this violent but necessary course if you do not cease your offensive pursuit.

85

It is, it should be made quite clear, not a dream but a daydream; Flaubert says, Curiously enough, that, while Charles dozed off beside her, Emma "was awake in a very different dreamland." In view of this, one cannot fail to be surprised by the clarity and precision of certain details, like the stork's nests on the spiky steeples, the flagstones that slowed them down to a foot-pace, the red bodices, the spray from the fountains, the pyramid of fruits, the brown nets, etc.

79

The man with a good memory does not remember anything because he does not forget anything. His memory is uniform, a creature of routine, at once a condition and function of his impeccable habit, an instrument of reference instead of an instrument of discovery. The paean of his memory: "I remember as well as I remember yesterday. . ." is also its epitaph, and gives the precise expression of its value. He cannot *remember* yesterday anymore than he can remember tomorrow.

38

What do you want, he asked with a cruel smile. I guessed what he was thinking, and that my request had had no other meaning for him. I blurted out the first thing that came into my head.

46

The only aspect I can remember of this affair which, though banal, played a decisive part in my life, was the exquisite presentiment I then had of nothingness. It all took place in a hotel room in Lyon, the most inhospitable town in France.

79

Breathe in, breathe out. Breathe naturally. Imagine that your arm has grown heavy, very heavy. Think: My right arm is very limp and heavy. My left arm is very limp and very heavy. My arm is very heavy. Imagine that your head is falling back a little. Keep your eyes tight shut. Imagine that your shoulders are light. My shoulders are so light. Imagine that your right leg is heavy. Think, I'm very relaxed and my leg is very heavy.

3

But who? Who?

66

She says: there's no reason why you should have acted differently, you know, I quite understand.

He says: so much the better. Let's go on, the other moves will be just as easy, it's a pretty banal inquiry.

She says: I believe you, absolutely banal, still, let's go on. I can give you a few more details.

He says: O.K., then it'll help things move on.

42

The telephone didn't ring.

It's a good fifteen minutes since the explosion. It wasn't in the old city then. But in the industrial sections, or farther north.

Marietti is still sleeping. Perez looks completely asleep. Three short explosions, brutally shattering the silence . . .

13

What the devil is this, he muttered, are you going to be difficult?

Vito Acconci
from Contacts/Contexts (Frame of Reference):
Ten Pages of Reading *Roget's Thesaurus*

Pursuing a method of reading as writing, "Contacts/Contexts" (in *Language to Cover a Page: The Early Writings of Vito Acconci* [Cambridge: Massachusetts Institute of Technology Press, 2006]) traces one of the many possible, forking, and ultimately looping paths through Roget's classic source text. With a studied indexicality, Acconci follows the reference work's prompting from one lemma to another, transcribing until the list of synonyms in one entry points him to another headword and the process can begin again. The poem thus emphasizes the propulsive activity built into the motivating structure of the seemingly static, even monumental, thesaurus. Taking literally the equivalence of synonyms proposed by the thesaurus, Acconci's text envisions how a language of pure denotation and zero connotation might operate, with the cylinders of substitutability spinning without the friction of nuance. Related by its source to the 1969 chapbook *Transference* (New York: o to 9 Press), which reproduced the single letters lining margins from various pages in *Roget's Thesaurus,* "Contacts" continues Acconci's poetic repurposing of reference books, such as text recording descending lines from sequential pages in *Whitfield's Universal Rhyming Dictionary.* The poem is also related to Acconci's legendary performance *Seedbed* (the far-from-incidental title of which was generated from looking up *floor* in *Roget's Thesaurus* and proceeding—through several other nouns—until the reference book offered the evocative and punning term for the controlled environment of a specially prepared box), as well as to the work of other artists, such as Robert Smithson's 1966 *A Heap of Language,* a handwritten stratum of words piled by the pyramidal spread of their meaning:

> Language / phraseology speech / tongue lingo vernacular/ mother tongue king's English / dialect brogue patois idiom slangy / confusion of tongues, Babel universal language/ Esperanto Ido pantomime dumb show literature/ letters belles-lettres muses humanities republic of letters / dead languages classics express say express by words polyglot / linguistic dialectal vernacular bilingual literary colloquial / Letter character hieroglyphic alphabet ABC consonant vowel / diphthong

surd sonant liquid labial palatal cerebral dental code / guttural syllable mono-
syllable dissyllable polysyllable prefix suffix cipher / word term vocable name
phrase root derivative index glossary dictionary lexicon / etymology philology
terminology verbiage loquacity translate nomenclature designation / misnomer
malapropism Mrs. Malapropos nominal titular cognomen patronymic title / mis-
name miscall nickname take an assumed name misnamed so called self self-styled
idiom /metaphor sentence proverb motto phraseology euphemism paragraph
by the card grammar error blunder/ diction solecism syntactical analysis name-
less slip of the tongue appellation heading gibberish dog Latin / hieroglyphic
neologism word coiner argot billingsgate pidgin English orthography terminol-
ogy thesaurus cipher

1. Existence
N. *existence,* esse, being, entity; absolute being, absoluteness, giveness, ase-
ity, self-existence, unit of being, monad, Platonic idea, Platonic form; a
being, entity, ens; subsistent being, subsistence 360n.

(page 1)

360 Life
N. *life,* living, being alive, animate existence, being in. *existence;* the liv-
ing, living and breathing world; living being, being, soul, spirit; vegetative
soul 366n.

(page 208)

366 Vegetability. Plant
N. *vegetability,* vegetable life, vegetable kingdom; flora, vegetation; flow-
ering, blooming, florescence, frondescence; lushness, rankness, luxuriance
635n.

(page 214)

635 Sufficiency
N. *plenty,* God's p., horn of p., cornucopia 171n.

(page 373)

171 Productiveness
N. *abundance,* wealth, riot, foison, harvest 32n.

(page 101)

32 Greatness
N. *great quantity,* muchness, galore 635n. *plenty;* crop, harvest, profusion, abundance, productivity 171n. *productiveness;* superfluity, superabundance, flood, spring-tide, spate 637n.

(page 19)

637 Redundance
N. *redundance,* over-brimming, over-spill, overflow, inundation, flood 298n.

(page 374)

298 Egress: motion out of N, *outflow,* effluence, efflux, effluxion, effusion; issue, outpouring, gushing, streaming; exudation, oozing, dribbling, weeping; extravasation, extravasation of blood, bleeding, hemophilia 302n.

(page 176)

302 Excretion
N. *hemorrhage,* bleeding, extravasation of blood, hemophilia 335n.

(page 182)

335 Fluidity
N. *blood,* ichor, claret; life-blood 360n. *life;* blood-stream, circulation; red blood 372n.

(page 198)

372 Male
N. *male,* male sex, man, he; manliness, masculinity, manhood; androcentisim, male exclusiveness; mannishness, viraginity, gyandry; he-man, cave-m.; gentleman, sir, esquire, master; lord, my l., his lordship; Mr., mister, monsieur, Herr, senor, don, dom, senhor, signor; sahib, sri, srijut, babu, mirza; tovarich, comrade, citoyen, yeoman, wight, swain, fellow, guy, blade, bloke, beau, chap, cove, card, chappie, johnny, buffer, gaffer, goodman; father, grandfather 169n.

(page 217)

169 Parentage
N. *parent,* father, sire, dad, daddy, papa, pop, governor, the old man; head of the family, paterfamilias; genitor, progenitor, procrastinator, begetter, author of one's existence; grandfather, grandsire, grandad, great-grandfather 133n.

(page 100)

133 Old person
N. *old man,* old gentleman; elder, senior, sir 34n.

(page 76)

34 Superiority
N. *superior,* superior person, superman, wonderman, 644n.

(page 23)

644 Goodness
N. *exceller,* nonpareil, nonesuch; prodigy, genius; superman, wonderman, wonder, wonder of the world, Stupor Mundi, Admirable Crichton 646n.

(page 308)

646 Perfection
N. *paragon,* nonesuch, nonpareil, flower, a beauty 644n. *exceller;* ideal, beau ideal, prince of; classic, pattern, pattern of perfection, standard, norm, model, mirror 23n.

(page 383)

23 Prototype
N. *prototype,* archetype, antitype, countertype; type, biotype, common type, everyman 30n.

(page 13)

30 Mean
N. *average,* medium, mean, median; intermedium, middle term 73n.

(page 18)

73 Term: serial position
N. *serial place,* term, order, remove 27n.

(page 51)

27 Degree: relative quantity
N. *degree,* relative quantity, proportion, ratio, scale 12n.

(page 16)

12 Correlation: double or reciprocal relation
N. *correlation,* correlativity, correlation, mutual relation, functionality 9n.

(page 7)

9 Relation
N. *relation,* relatedness, connectedness, "rapport," reference, respect, regard, bearing, direction; concern, concernment, interest, import 638n.

(page 4)

638 Importance
N. *importance,* first i., primacy, priority, urgency 64n.

(page 375)

64 Precedence
N. *precedence,* antecedence, antecedency, going before, coming b., line-jumping 283n.

(page 46)

283 Precession: going before
N. *Precession* 119n.

(page 169)

119 Priority
N. *priority,* antecedence, anteriority, previousness, preoccurrence, pre-existence; primogeniture, birthright; eldest, firstborn, son and heir; flying start 64n. *precedence*; leading 283n. *precession;* the past, yesteryear, yesterday 125n.

(page 70)

125 Preterition: retrospective time
N. *preterition* 119n. *priority;* retrospection, looking back 505n.

(page 72)

505 Memory
N. *remembrance,* exercise of memory, recollection, recall; commemoration, rememoration, evocation; rehearsal, recapitulation 106n.

(page 290)

106 Repetition
N. *repetition,* doing again, iteration, reiteration; doubling, ditto, reduplication 20n.

(page 64)

20 Imitation
N. *imitation,* copying etc. vb.; sincerest form of flattery; rivalry, emulation, competition 911n.

(page 12)

911 Jealousy
N. *jealousy,* pangs of j., jealousness; jaundiced eye, green-eyed monster; distrust, mistrust 486n.

(page 572)

486 Unbelief. Doubt
N. *doubt,* 474n.

(page 276)

474 Uncertainty
N. *dubeity,* dubitancy, dubitation 486n. *doubt;* state of doubt, open mind, suspended judgment, open verdict; suspense, waiting 507n.

(page 267)

507 Expectation
N. *expectation,* state of e., expectancy 455n.

(page 291)

455 Attention
N. *attention,* notice, regard 438n.

(page 253)

438 Vision
N. *look,* regard, glance, side-g., squint; tail *or* corner of the eye; glint, blink; penetrating glance, gaze, steady g.; observation, contemplation, speculation, watch; stare, fixed s.; come-hither look, glad eye, ogle, leer, grimace 889n.

(page 245)

889 Endearment
N. *endearment;* blandishment, compliment 925n.

(page 559)

925 Flattery

N. *flattery,* cajolery, wheedling, taffy, blarney, blandiloquence, blandishment; butter, soft soap, soft-sawder, salve, lip-salve, rosewater, incense, adulation; voice of the charmer, honeyed words, soft nothings 889n. *endearment;* compliment, pretty speeches; unctuousness, euphemism, glozing, gloze; captation, coquetry, fawning, back-scratching; assentation, obsequiousness, flunkyism, sycophancy, toadying, tuft-hunting, 879n.

(page 584)

879 Servility

N. *servility,* slavishness, abject spirit, no pride, lack of self-respect 856n.

(page 550)

856 Cowardice

N. *cowardice,* abject fear, funk, sheer f. 854n.

(page 531)

854 Fear

N. *fear,* healthy f., dread, awe 920n.

(page 529)

920 Respect

N. *respect,* regard, consideration, esteem, estimation, honor, favor 866n.

(page 578)

866 Repute

N. *repute,* good r., high r., reputation, good r., special r.; report, good r., title to fame, name, honored n., great n., good n., fair n., character, known c., good c., high c., reputability, respectability 802n.

(page 539)

802 Credit

N. *credit,* repute, reputation, 866n. *prestige;* credit-worthiness, sound credit, trust, confidence, reliability 929n.

(page 491)

929 Probity

N. *probity,* rectitude, uprightness, goodness, sanctity 933n.

(page 587)

933 Virtue
N. *virtue,* virtuousness, moral strength, moral tone, morale; goodness, sheer g.; saintliness, holiness, spirituality, odor of sanctity 979n.

(page 590)

979 Piety
N. *sanctity,* holiness, hallowedness, sacredness, sacrosanctity; goodness, cardinal virtues, theological v. 933n. *virtue;* cooperation with grace, synergism; state of grace, odor of sanctity 950n.

(page 618)

950 Purity
N. *purity,* non-mixture, simplicity, nakedness 44n.

(page 599)

44 Simpleness: freedom from mixture
N. *simpleness* etc. adj.; homogeneity 16n.

(page 30)

16 Uniformity
N. *uniformity,* uniformness, consistency, constancy, steadiness 153n.

(page 9)

153 Stability
N. *stability,* immutability; unchangeableness, unchangeability; irreversibility, invariability, constancy 16n. *uniformity;* firmness, fixity, rootedness; indelibility 144n.

(page 86)

144 Permanence: absence of change
N. *permanence,* permanency, no change, status quo; invariability, unchangeability, immutability 153n. *stability;* lasting quality, persistence 600n.

(page 81)

600 Perseverance
N. *perseverance,* persistence, tenacity, pertinacity, pertinaciousness, stubbornness 602n.

(page 350)

602 Obstinacy
N. *obstinacy,* unyielding temper; determination, will 599n.

(page 352)

599 Resolution
N. *resolution,* sticking point, resoluteness, determination, grim d.; zeal, earnestness, seriousness; resolve, fixed r., mind made up, decision 608n.

(page 349)

608 Predetermination
N. *predetermination,* predestination 596n.

(page 356)

596 Necessity
N. *necessity,* hard n., stern n., compelling n.; no alternative, no escape, no option, Hobson's choice 606n.

(page 347)

606 Absence of Choice
N. *no choice,* choicelessness, no alternative, dictation 596n. *necessity;* dictated choice, Hobson's c. 740n.

(page 355)

740 Compulsion
N. *compulsion,* spur of necessity 596n. *necessity;* law of nature 953.

(page 458)

from Removal, Move (Line of Evidence): The Grid Locations of Streets, Alphabetized, Hagstrom's Maps of the Five Boroughs: 3. Manhattan

Part essay on urban planning, part sound poem, "Removal" (*Language to Cover a Page: The Early Writings of Vito Acconci* [Cambridge: Massachusetts Institute of Technology Press, 2006]) continues Acconci's work with found texts and reference works, such as *Transference: Roget's Thesaurus* [New York: 0 to 9 Press, 1969] and "Act 3, Scene 4," a lineated transcription of daily weather reports, as well as his investigations into the literal space of the page, including: a series of dictionary pages with all of the text removed except for a line of single letters framing the erased text block; various margins from sequential pages of an edition of *Roget's Thesaurus;* or a poem that self-reflexively describes itself in minute detail, from the margins and spacing to the dimensions and format of the sheet of typing paper on which it is written. At the same time, "Removal" is also one of a suite of cartographic works extending those practices into socially marked space (such as "Set/Reset 1. The Left Boundary of Hagstrom's *Map of the Bronx*" and the companion grid locations to the borough of Richmond [now Staten Island]). The subtitle aptly explains the source and procedure, but the dryly telegraphic note gives no hint of how interesting the resultant text will be. With a dizzying density, the locator numbers constitute an inverse projection of Manhattan roadways, itself largely a grid, in which the roughly regular series of frequently numerical names (streets and avenues)—along with their exceptions and irregular edges—encode a geographic and social account of the island's historical development. Those cartographic parameters also give Acconci's text a set of terms sufficiently restricted and diverse to create a rich sonic facture of rhyme and variation. In "Removal," the ghostly scaffolding of Manhattan's infrastructure is palpable but never quite predictable, and with the rhythmic repetition of series slipping in and out of phase, the result is not unlike the contemporaneous minimalist music of Steve Reich, Terry Riley, and Philip Glass.

J12 G13 G12 B11 K9 B11 F11 F14 D13 C6 C14 F2 A9 A9 B10 A9 C14 J9 B12
B12 C12 C12 C12 C12 C12 C12 D13 D13 D13 D13 D13 D13 D14 D14 C5 C14
C14 C14 H13 G2 B6 F14 G4 J9 F3 F6 F6 J7 H14 D14 K12 G4 B10 C12 K11
A9 D5 F14 E6 L7 F3 E9 H13 H13 E12 D9 J7 F14 H5 A9 F15 D15 D5 G4 H4
E14 E6 E13 E13 D15 C6 F1 E13 K7 G13 H9 G14 J11 F6 D5 G2 H14 E13 F14
F14 F14 F14 F14 F14 F14 F14 F14 F14 F14 J7 F3 G9 C5 D4 F4 H2 J9 G2 C12
C7 F8 H7 K5 G12 G4 C6 H5 G4 E6 D5 D7 G3 J12 F2 F5 D11 L5 F10 D14

J9 K10 G14 H13 E6 C15 C6 F11 F14 G3 D4 E9 E8 F11 H4 H13 J11 H4 C6
D13 C6 H13 D4 H4 H9 H6 C5 G2 D9 F8 J7 F11 L5 J7 E9 J9 A10 D9 F9
D4 F8 F6 F6 F1 E5 L7 F2 F5 E5 C6 B6 G7 E4 E13 B6 E14 H11 G14 C6 E12
D4 L9 A10 A11 A10 F14 D4 C5 C7 H6 C6 D4 M6 E9 C5 J9 F1 C6 B6 G3
J6 G4 J6 J5 F14 J5 E9 D5 C6 H9 J5 G13 L8 D4 F13 C6 A10 M6 L5 F8 D13
K6 G7 L6 E5 E4 H3 C14 L5 K4 H13 E10 D11 B11 J12 J11 L5 E14 H13 E6 F7
G3 D5 G4 G6 D6 E5 F10 B6 C6 D6 J6 F13 G3 H13 E14 J6 K8 G2 H3 H13
B6 L6 H4 E9 F3 G2 F2 D4 H4 G14 F13 F9 H9 L6 D4 D5 D6 G14 F6 M7
F3 D5 J7 E3 F13 G14 F1 F9 C11 F9 B6 F1 E13 E9 E9 E9 E9 F14 E8 E8 E11
E9 F13 F11 F11 F11 F11 F11 F9 F9 F9 F9 F9 F9 F10 F9 F9 G10 F9 G9 G9 G9
G11 G9 G9 G10 G8 G8 G8 G8 H10 G9 G9 H9 H9 H9 H9 H9 H9 H9 H9
H9 H9 J12 H9 H9 J11 H9 J11 J11 J11 J12 J11 J12 J11 J11 J11 J11 J11 J11 J10 J9 J9
H8 J9 J8 J9 J9 J9 J9 J9 J9 J9 K8 K8 G7 F7 H13 H13 F2 D14 L9 J5 M7 D4
G4 F11 D5 E10 L7 A9 G6 M7 F5 F13 F14 F7 G2 F8 B7 F14 L7 E12 L5 L5
E4 H13 D4 H4 G14 D5 G8 G14 K6 H13 H13 F10 G4 F8 B6 C5 G12 F3 E7
E6 D4 G11 K9 K9 L9 L9 D5 D5 D4 D4 D4 H13 G3 J12 G4 K13 E4 L6 M6
L5 H7 A11 G4 E5 A11 B11 E10 M7 L7 H13 F7 F5 F111 F1 E9 D4 G3 E8 D5
D5 J6 C4 H13 D5 C5 G4 H3 D6 H13 C6 D4 F5 B11 J12 J12 E14 B11 F2 H4
K7 F13 G12 G4 F14 G14 L6 H10 J6 F10 D5 H5 H13 B9 C6 C5 H7 G3 F6
E3 F3 E6 J6 M5 F6 H4 F13 F1 E5 F2 E8 D5 H5 F2 H5 F14 G14 J6 L6 E5 C6
G6 C6 A11 J12 G14 G7 G6 D5 E5 A11 A10 A10 G11 G12 H14 H4 E4 F4 H3
E14 D14 G5 D13 H10 G14 G2 F3 J6 F8 H13 D9 J8 M6 E15 H11 L7 C6 G2
G6 F6 G6 J8 F4 F4 C6 D4 G14 K6 L6 D15 D12 L6 G10 H4 E9 K7 G14
M7 K9 F13 F12 J9 F3 F3 G4 J7 E8 D4 H7 D8 D6 K9 G10 F14 D4 D4 J6
G3 C13 H6 C6 D5 F1 F12 H13 C6 B12 F1 C5 J12 H3 K6 H13 H4 F5 C5 F10
G14 J11 H13 H3 D4 D7 G3 G14 K6 J6 F1 D4 G5 C15 H4 F14 L7 G2 K6 H9
D4 G14 G3 F8 D4 E15 C5 H13 G3 K7 H13 H6 C5 J12 M5 F13 K10 H13 F3
H13 E14 F10 G14 F8 F8 G14 D15 E3 F1 E8 L5 H11 B6 D12 E12 H6 G2 G7
E14 H13 H4 H13 G5 H5 J9 E5 D5 A11 G3 G14 E13 G2 G7 F13 H13 G14 H5
D4 H13 D15 G13 F2 G3 F3 G7 D9 D4 F4 F8 L7 J11 J12 J11 D13 C6 K7 K6
F2 D9 J5 J6 G2 D4 F5 C4 C4 J12 L7 F14 E7 G7 G4 G3 E4 G4 G3 E4 G2
E14 D5 A10 F2 F14 D4 J12 C14 E5 D4 C6 C14 E14 F14 E14 J12 D6 E14 D4
G2 K7 E10 F10 K7 J8 G2 C11 G11 M5 E14 F2 H13 J9 G4 G14 F2 I6 E4 E4
G2 E4 F4 E4 F2 F3 F2 L6 G10 H13 F2 F9 F1 M5 F9 E13 F14 E9 F14 C15
C14 G3 D10 F11 G3 A11 H13 D4 G3 F14 F14 J7 G6 G11 B10 D11 A9 G14 C5
J10 J10 F1 G7 H5 F8 E4 E8 E6 G6 G4 D4 E8 F8 E10 E13 B11 H6 D4 H11
G14 F4 K7 C7 G14 F6 A9 G14 C4 D4 F5 M6 D4 C6 J7 E6 J6 H13 H13
H13 D4 C14 E6 B12 C14 D4 H7 G2 H13 J7 G3 H6 C5 H9 D4 G14 D7 E6
D4 D7 E8 E7 F1 G5 G5 F2 E12 G14 G5 J6 G8 H9 H3 C6 D4 B6 F8 F9 H5

J_9 C_5 G_6 H_3 E_{14} B_6 G_2 L_5 A_{10} B_{10} A_9 L_5 G_8 C_{15} G_{14} E_3 J_7 K_5 K_5 H_7
H_4 K_{10} H_7 E_5 E_{11} F_4 F_3 F_8 C_8 J_6 J_9 F_4 K_{10} K_{11} E_{14} M_7 E_9 E_4 G_2 G_{12}
F_8 F_4 E_{11} G_{11} F_5 C_5 J_7 G_6 F_7 E_5 E_5 F_7 F_5 E_6 E_6 D_6 J_4 F_8 F_8 F_5 D_4 M_7
J_7 J_5 L_7 K_6 H_{11} D_5 G_3 J_9 F_{12} L_8 D_{15} H_3 C_{15} E_{14} F_{14} C_6 C_{14} K_{10} H_{14}
H_{13} A_9 C_5 E_8 G_4 A_9 G_3 F_{14} E_{14} F_{13} K_7 E_{14} H_{13} L_7 M_7 J_6 E_8 G_{14} A_{11}
A_{10} A_{10} B_{12} B_9 A_{10} D_5 C_6 K_{10} K_9 G_3 F_5 E_{13} E_9 C_7 J_9 K_7 F_8 J_6 G_{14} M_6
E_5 M_6 E_{13} E_5 E_5 E_3 F_5 F_6 G_3 G_3 H_4 K_8 G_4 H_4 C_5 E_{14} F_9 F_6 B_{12} E_6 F_7
F_5 H_2 J_6 D_{14} J_{10} H_4 G_4 F_7 J_7 D_9 D_9 E_9 J_8 J_{12} C_5 E_{13} E_{13} G_{12} H_5 F_7 B_6
C_6 G_5 G_4 H_6 K_6 K_5 C_{14} J_7 G_2 H_6 H_4 C_{14} F_5 C_{10} G_7 H_7 H_7 E_4 D_9 E_8
E_5 G_3 G_3 F_8 E_8 H_4 J_7 J_7 H_2 E_{14} G_4 G_5 K_9 C_5 F_9 D_4 G_5 C_5 M_7 H_2 E_{11}
H_9 H_4 H_{10} J_6 C_{14} K_8 E_9 H_{14} E_6 F_4 F_5 C_5 H_{11} B_6 G_5 L_8 L_8 G_2 E_6 E_8
F_9 J_6 G_3 H_4 B_6 E_{13} K_7 K_6 K_7 G_4 H_3 G_2 J_9 C_5 K_5 K_5 K_7 G_5 G_6 C_6 F_9
J_{11} E_{13} E_{13} E_{13} E_{13} C_{15} D_4 G_7 C_6 B_{10} G_{14} A_9 H_{14} F_{10} F_4 D_{11} E_{10} F_4 F_5
C_5 C_5 L_7 F_6 367 E_5 F_3 D_4 E_5 D_4 G_3 J_7 G_{15} E_5 G_{14} G_{14} E_{10} D_7 J_5 L_6 F_{10}
L_6 E_{14} E_{13} F_1 F_8 F_{14} E_9 F_{14} E_9 E_{14} E_{12} E_{12} E_{12} E_{13} E_{13} C_6 E_4 E_4 D_{14}
D_{14} D_{14} D_{14} D_{14} D_{14} D_{14} C_{14} L_5 G_4 G_4 J_{12} H_{13} E_{13} H_9 D_6 K_8 E_{15} K_8
F_{14} J_6 F_4 F_4 F_4 H_8 E_5 D_5 C_5 C_4 H_4 E_4 D_7 F_8 G_3 A_{11} B_6 E_{13} J_5 C_6 G_3
C_8 F_8 F_9 E_{12} L_8 L_8 J_4 D_5 K_7 E_3 D_4 B_9 F_{12} C_6 D_6 B_{12} B_9 C_6 D_6 B_9 C_6
D_6 D_{10} C_6 D_6 B_{10} D_6 B_{10} D_6 B_{12} D_6 B_{10} D_6 C_{10} D_6 B_{10} D_7 C_{10} D_7
C_{11} D_7 C_{11} D_7 C_{11} D_7 C_{12} C_{12} D_7 C_{12} D_7 C_{12} C_{13} C_7 C_{12} C_{13} C_{13} C_7
C_{12} C_{13} C_7 D_{13} C_7 D_{13} C_8 D_{13} C_8 D_{13} C_8 C_8 B_8 D_9 C_8 D_9 D_9 D_9 D_9
D_9 D_{10} C_{10} C_{10} J_{12} C_{10} J_{12} D_{10} D_{10} J_{12} E_{13} F_{11} A_9 A_9 A_{10} A_{10} A_{10} A_{10}
A_{10} A_{10} A_{10} A_{10} D_{13} D_{13} A_{10} A_{11} A_{11} A_{13} A_{11} A_{11} A_{11} M_6 A_{11} M_6 A_{11} M_8
G_{23} G_{23} E_{25} C_{24} D_{27} D_{24} G_{24} H_{24} E_{28} F_{26} F_{26} D_{26} B_4 E_{28} D_{24} F_{20}
F_{27} B_6 E_{26} C_{24} G_{26} D_{26} D_{24} C_{24} B_6 E_{24} F_{26} E_{28} C_{11} E_{28} E_{28} B_{15} E_{28}
F_{22} B_6 E_{25} F_{27} B_7 C_{20} E_{21} F_{26} E_{27} D_{25} D_{26} C_{14} E_{26} G_{26} F_{26} E_{27} E_{14}
D_{19} D_{16} D_{19} F_{26} F_{25} D_{26} C_{24} D_{24} C_{13} D_{25} E_{27} F_{26} C_{23} G_{17} D_{24} G_{26}
E_{11} B_6 D_{24} F_{26} E_{26} F_{27} E_{27} B_{13} D_{25} F_{25} F_{27} G_{25} F_{28} D_{26} G_{25} C_{17} C_{19}
D_{19} D_{24} C_{12} F_{24} B_4 C_3 D_{24} E_{26} E_{27} E_{25} B_5 F_{28} G_{25} E_{21} F_{27} D_{26} E_{27}
G_{26} D_{25} B_5 C_{10} F_{27} D_{25} F_{26} D_{26} D_{20} E_{27} B_5 C_{21} G_{24} E_{24} G_{24} G_{24}
E_{24} E_{24} E_{24} E_{23} E_{23} E_{22} E_{23} E_{22} E_{22} E_{21} E_{22} E_{21} E_{22} E_{21} E_{21} E_{19} E_{20}
E_{19} E_{18} E_{19} E_{18} E_{19} E_{18} E_{19} E_{17} E_{18} E_{16} E_{17} E_{15} E_{16} E_{15} E_{16} E_{15} E_{15} E_{13}
E_{14} E_{15} E_{13} E_{12} E_{13} E_{12} E_{13} E_{18} E_{12} E_{11} E_{11} E_{11} F_{26} G_{17} F_{25} F_{27} E_{28} D_{11}
B_9 D_{11} D_{14} D_{23} F_{25} C_{22} F_{25} E_{26} B_5 E_{26} G_{25} E_{28} E_{28} C_7 F_{24} B_6 D_{24}
E_{25} E_{26} F_{12} E_{16} F_{24} F_{24} E_{26} F_{16} F_{24} F_{24} F_{27} F_{26} F_{26} F_{25} G_{26} C_3 C_5
C_6 B_8 B_8 F_{23} E_{26} F_{27} E_{26} F_{15} G_{16} G_{18} G_{23} F_{27} E_{14} D_{14} B_{18} F_{27} F_{27}
F_{27} C_{24} C_{24} D_{24} F_{20} F_{27} F_{28} H_{26} G_{25} G_{16} G_{17} F_{23} E_{25} F_{24} D_{21} E_{25}
D_{23} G_{17} D_{26} D_{24} D_{24} F_{24} F_{26} C_{11} F_{20} D_{12} D_{13} F_{28} F_{28} D_9 D_8 D_{26}
F_{26} B_8 G_{16} F_{26} B_4 B_{18} B_5 D_{21} F_{26} C_7 B_6 C_{24} E_{25} D_{26} E_{26} C_4 F_{23} C_4

C4 H25 C3 F26 C24 D26 G26 F25 E27 D24 C3 G5 F25 D25 C2 G26 F25
E24 D26 C12 C7 D14 E11 E26 D25 H25 F16 F22 C3 E27 E27 B5 G24 F13
B5 G24 F13 E26 C23 G26 E25 D10 E16 E22 E22 G26 B7 C9 E27 H24 D15
E26 C3 C3 C5 F12 G19 F25 G26 E28 C5 C8 E25 F28 B19 D27 D24 E24 E24
E24 F20 C8 F26 C11 G25 F28 B9 C13 C14 E28 D24 F26 E13 F26 D27 B5
E27 E28 H24 F23 F28 C5 C23 G25 D26 C12 F28 F26 G25 B6 G13 E16 E21
E23 D27 F26 F26 C4 C4 D24 B5 E26 E28 F27 F26 D22 C24 E21 F22 G26
E27 B7 G25 F27 B7 G13 C16 C5 E25 E27 G13 E26 E27 D25 G25 B15 B18
B9 G19 F25 F27 E20 C12 F27 G26 G26 F23 F27 B12 F26 E26 D25 F24 D12
D14 C10 C12 D13 F25 B4 F16 F24 F24 D24 D23 D24 F24 D24 B5 C18 B5
F24 F21 E28 F28 F27 B7 E28 D25 F27 B5 F25 E26 E28 F28 E28 G26 F23
G23 F24 G25 E25 E20 G19 G20 G19 E13 C9 G23 E27 C5 C23 C3 C3 E27
B5 E27 F16 F24 E26 E25 B12 D21 B7 D17 E26 E27 F21 B12 B22 E23 E23
E23 F20 F21 E24 C3 D25 E20 E20 D24 E26 B5 E27 D26 C7 B6 E26 E27
E24 G14 D26 C7 E24 D24 E24 E24 E24 E24 E28 C6 F28 G26 D25 E24
C24 G20 E27 E27 C17 C19 D25 B19 D27 E24 D24 E24 D24 E24 C24 E24
C24 E23 C24 E23 C22 C23 C22 C23 C22 C22 C21 C22 C21 C21 C21 C20
C21 C20 C20 C20 C20 C19 C20 C19 C20 C19 C20 C18 C19 C19 C18 C19
C17 C18 C17 C17 C17 C16 C16 C14 C15 E14 C14 C14 C14 B13 C13 E13 C13
E13 C12 B12 E12 C12 C11 B11 C11 C10 C11 C10 C11 C10 C10 C9 C10 C9 C9
C7 C8 C9 C6 C7 C7 C7 C7 C7 C7 C7 C6 C5 C5 C5 C4 C3 C4 C3 C4 C3
C4 C3 C4 C3 C2 C3 E26 E28 G25 F27 E25 E26 G17 G19 E26 H2 J6 G6
C16 G12 K8 K14 K14 J7 E15 D6 G5 L3 G15 F9 D5 K13 F5 E6 G15 H14 H7
H14 G15 L13 L13 E4 F9 L6 L6 J8 C6 C6 H14 K13 K8 C6 D5 J14 L13 L14 F5
J7 C16 A4 H7 F6 F9 G15 H8 C6 K14 K9 J14 F6 G3 H4 L5 E4 H6 E5 G15
B3 D3 C3 C3 B3 E8 G7 H7 G15 C16 E6 H4 G6 G15 H14 H8 L13 B4 E5 F6
G6 J6 F4 J6 J6 K13 F7 J7 H4 K13 J8 G15 L13 H13 G3 K13 K7 C4 D5 J6 J8
L3 G3 H9 L3 C16 K13 D4 K13 G14 H13 J13 K13 L13 K2 K2 C16 D16 G3 H14
H3 C16 K13 K13 C16 C16 E15 G15 H14 J14 K13 L14 L13 L14 L14 L13 L14 L13
L14 L13 L14 L14 L14 L13 L13 K14 K13 K13 K13 K13 K14 K14 K13 K14 K13 K14
K14 K14 K13 K14 K13 K13 K14 K14 K14 J14 J14 J13 J14 J14 J13 J14 J14 J14 J3
J14 J14 J13 J14 J14 H14 H14 H14 G14 G14 G15 G15 G14 G15 F15 F15 F15 E15
E15 D16 D16 K13 K13 H7 L13 J8 C16 G3 F2 F2 L3 F6 K8 J2 K4 K6 E9 E4
L14 K8 K9 L10 K8 J14 J14 J14 J14 D2 E3 G12 F7 K13 G15 G6 K13 L5 K13 K3
D9 C7 C6 F4 H14 E5 C6 F2 L13 E5 G4 A5 C5 L5 C3 G8 E5 F6 J3 G3 J3 L5
B5 C16 L3 H14 G15 G7 G15 K14 E4 A4 A4 G9 M3 H8 J7 G9 D4 B3 C4 D4
L13 J8 K13 C5 C3 C3 K2 L9 L9 L10 L11 D6 D16 L3 L13 F3 E3 H14 G15 J14
G6 G3 F6 C4 H2 C5 C6 E3 G4 J9 D7 L13 D5 D5 E5 G15 L3 J6 J7 K14 L9
M9 L13 E5 K3 K6 K9 E4 M4 C7 G15 F9 H6 L13 L13 H9 B5 G9 D7 K13 C7

D16 G10 K13 G13 L13 H6 H6 H6 G6 J6 K9 G4 C16 J5 J6 F9 E4 D16 G13
B16 G2 C5 J8 H7 J2 D5 H6 K13 H6 C16 G1 J6 D7 K4 J6 J6 F6 J14 D5 C7
G9 G9 G4 K13 G10 L13 K7 368 F1 F3 K13 F3 F5 G15 C3 L4 L5 J6 J14 J13 L3
G14 E6 G6 K14 K9 C8 D7 E7 D7 K3 K13 L13 C7 L3 D5 E4 L14 J2 J3 J3 E3
A4 H4 C16 C7 E6 L10 K9 A4 J9 K13 L5 D16 A4 B3 B4 C2 H7 K14 H3 G4
E5 F15 F8 G11 G13 G14 J2 L6 L7 H6 H14 H2 L4 F8 G14 E3 G7 G14 C7 D8
D7 G4 L4 H7 J6 E6 F6 G6 G6 F6 H14 C16 L5 G10 J14 L13 H4 A5 A4 C7
H14 L3 L3 F6 K14 K8 C7 G14 G3 L7 K13 F4 G13 E4 K9 G15 K3 H3 F9 H14
G14 C16 J6 E7 F7 K13 E6 F8 J8 L13 C2 D3 E3 L11 K13 K13 L13 J6 D5 E6
L13 C16 H14 K7 G15 J7 K3 L4 F3 E8 E5 J5 E9 K13 K14 J7 K8 J7 K8 J7 J6
K6 B4 K13 L11 K9 K3 C16 M5 G13 G13 G13 G13 G13 G13 G13 G13 G13 G9
J14 K14 K14 K14 J6 J6 K12 K9 L9 L10 E7 L5 G14 H4 K13 K13 D4 G5 E8
C7 G15 G14 G15 C6 D6 E5 H14 J14 K13 L4 D5 E6 D4 E4 J7 J14 L13 E9 F10
L13 K3 G15 K13 K13 K5 E3 D16 J14 J6 H7 K8 K14 J14 K13 K13 K8 E6 F6
K13 H14 L5 H4 C6 F6 K13 J14 K7 K8 K9 F2 K13 K14 J14 J7 H8 K14 H14
G14 K7 E6 F6 G15 J14 E6 C6 K13 H8 J7 J6 K6 E8 E10 C6 D7 E7 D4 F4
G3 J14 H2 H3 J4 K6 L8 L9 G4 K14 M10 J14 L13 D6 H4 H5 C6 J14 L13 F4
C16 E6 D3 E3 F3 H7 H8 H9 L3 D5 G15 C7 J14 C16 K8 D4 K13 F6 J14 A4
E3 D5 F9 E7 K6 C16 H8 C16 H8 C16 F3 L14 G4 H14 C5 C7 K14 C7 J14
L3 F5 G5 H5 H14 J7 H3 J14 D4 E4 E5 G4 D6 D6 F6 E5 G4 J14 E3 K7 H14
H6 K3 J6 K6 J5 J5 F6 D4 D4 G6 G6 G7 J6 C16 F9 F3 K5 H6 G4 G5 D5
D5 J14 H14 J14 J6 G4 H4 J14 F9 G9 J8 J8 K9 H8 E4 G13 G6 L13 M4 M4
L9 J14 J14 E4 G15 J9 B5 L9 D6 F4 F3 F1 D4 G3 G2 L3 G7 G9 G1 L3 L3 K8
K14 D4 E4 K7 K14 C16 G8 J7 J14 H9 C16 E9 G8 J8 K8 L7 F2 C6 J14 H4
J2 L3 M4 H7 H2 K13 J8 A5 C5 H4 K13 F6 J14 K8 H7 K8 J7 K4 D7 D6 H8
L5 G15 D4 C7 L13 G15 G3 B3 F3 G3 G5 G6 G1 K7 D5 L5 F6 G6 C16 F4
L3 J5 F7 G14 J14 G15 K2 J14 C16 C16 F6 J7 K8 J8 G14 E5 K14 J14 L3 G14
C6 K8 J8 C5 C6 G15 L10 F7 H6 J7 D5 K13 E3 J3 K3 K3 K3 J6 L13 J3 G5 C6
L9 C6 L9 C6 L9 H6 J7 J8 K8 J8 C6 G7 K7 J8 F6 J6 A5 K8 F3 L13 L13 L5
K8 L7 G14 L3 L2 L13 L13 K13 L13 C6 K13 G4 J7 L7 G8 G3 G2 G3 L5 C7
E7 J7 K13 L13 G14 F6 K13 K8 L7 L3 E4 G4 L13 L13 K8 E15 K8 G15 C16 J6
J14 K8 L10 K13 F15 C16 B3 C3 C4 H7 J9 K10 E4 G13 H6 C7 F9 G9 K9 B4
C4 F3 G3 J3 K3 G4 J14 K14 K13 G14 C6 G4 H4 L13 L3 C16 L14 K13 J4 F15
J14 J14 C16 D16 J8 F6 G9 F6 C16 C7 J14 G6 B4 L13 F5 D7 L3 L3 K7 C6
J6 C16 C7 J6 H6 G5 G6 E7 F7 G6 G2 G3 H5 H6 J14 H6 K13 A4 A4 F5
G4 H4 K5 G9 C16 F4 L2 E6 F5 C6 G6 J5 D4 G3 J8 H4 H8 K8 K13 J6 E8
F9 K14 L14 F8 G8 J14 D6 K13 C16 K13 G1 E6 K6 L5 G4 F4 F1 J10 E2 H1
G13 D4 K13 F3 H7 K9 A4 C7 G15 B4 D4 E5 G6 B4 C16 A5 C5 K7 L11 G4
E4 J6 D4 D5 G14 G9 L5 L5 G10 L13 F9 L13 L3 D5 G4 J14 K13 C16 J14 K13

C16 J14 H7 H8 C6 B5 J7 C6 K5 F9 J6 L11 H1 K8 L6 G4 E8 G8 J9 K10 F15
G14 J14 C16 G14 G15 H14 J14 L9 K13 K14 B16 J4 F4 J2 K8 J14 K7 K5 C4
G3 L13 C16 G4 G15 L13 G8 D16 D16 F10 K8 J7 L3 F6 C6 H14 E6 G2 G15
K7 L5 K6 L13 H14 D7 D5 C7 H14 G15 C7 J6 J14 K13 J6 H7 J14 F4 G3 J6
F9 F10 G4 F5 E5 K5 J7 J8 C8 H14 G15 D16 C16 E5 K14 J14 J14 K14 L14 K14
K14 L14 K14 K14 F6 K8 G14 C7 L14 L5 G13 D7 K13 E10 M4 K14 J14 H7
H8 B2 F10 G15 K8 L6 F9 D5 F9 A4 B4 G4 K9 G4 H6 K13 J8 J6 J14 J6 C3
H7 H8 E9 F9 H9 L9 E8 G9 J9 K9 K9 D4 D5 H7 H14 K5 H14 K14 J14 K3
K5 K8 K9 L7 K10 F9 H7 F6 C7 K14 G15 B5 J14 C6 B5 F4 J4 E5 G7 K6 B4
D5 F6 H6 J5 B4 H3 F9 H9 M9 E10 D16 H3 G14 B4 C3 D7 K5 C7 C7 H14
K13 F2 E4 L5 H7 K7 C16 K7 F6 C7 K8 K13 L9 G15 K14 J5 G15 H7 K5 F9
G8 H9 J14 L7 H14 F6 G3 G9 G6 F3 K14 L3 J14 C16 G4 A4 L3 E6 H14 K9
C16 K7 B16 J1 H1 D6 H7 B2 C4 K13 J5 E6 F7 C6 K8 J5 H7 J5 H7 J5 K8
G14 H7 H7 C5 F2 H4 L4 G3 G4 E7 G6 K5 L4 H7 H6 L3 K8 F7 C16 H1
H3 G14 F4 B4 B5 K5 F4 D5 D5 D5 G8 F4 H8 L3 C4 D8 A3 A4 J14 J8 D4
C6 L13 G5 G6 K3 G15 L3 F4 F7 H7 G13 J6 E4 J6 J14 K13 K13 K13 K13 K14
J7 K13 J4 D5 C7 L9 L10 B3 F6 G14 G13 B4 K4 K13 K13 L3 K9 C16 L2 F5
E5 J6 L13 J13 K13 K5 F9 G15 G2 D4 J6 G14 F3 G2 H2 L13 K13 K8 C7 K13
L5 F6 L7 J7 K14 C7 E5 F7 F8 J6 J14 C4 G15 C7 J7 C7 E5 H7 F5 F6 L3 K8
G12 B2 L11 G1 G12 A5 B2 G1 G12 B2 L11 G1 G13 B2 F1 G1 G13 A5 F1 G1
G1 F1 G1 C16 F1 G1 C16 G1 G13 B2 F1 H1 C16 F2 G13 A4 B2 F2 G2 H1
C16 G13 A4 F2 G1 G2 H1 G13 A4 F2 G1 H1 G1 G13 A4 B3 E2 F2 G2 H1
G2 G13 A4 B3 E2 F2 G2 H2 J2 B2 B3 E2 F2 G2 H2 G13 A5 B3 H2 E2 F2
G2 H2 J2 G2 H2 G2 H2 G13 H2 L2 G2 H2 G13 G2 H2 G2 H2 G13 E2 F2
G2 J2 G13 B2 C2 C2 G2 H2 D3 D2 G13 B2 C2 C2 F2 G2 C2 G2 H2 G13
C2 C2 F2 G2 H2 C2 C2 G2 H2 A4 B2 B3 D4 F2 G2 C2 E3 C3 G2 A4 B3
C2 D3 F2 G2 H2 J2 B2 B2 C2 C3 E3 J2 A4 A5 B2 B3 B2 B2 D3 G2 J2 B2
B2 C3 D3 E3 G2 H2 A4 B4 C2 B2 C3 D3 F2 G2 G2 B2 F2 G2 A5 B2 C3
F2 G2 K2 B3 E3 C2 B2 C3 E3 F2 H3 F2 H3 J2 K2 B3 A5 B3 A5 B3 B5 C2
B3 C3 F3 G3 B3 G3 J2 B3 B4 C2 B3 E3 F3 G3 H3 J2 K2 G3 B3 B4 B5 C2
B3 C3 D3 F3 H3 J3 K2 B3 B5 B3 C3 B3 369 B4 B5 B3 C3 D4 E3 F3 K2 B3
E3 F3 G3 B5 B3 F3 J3 B4 B5 C3 C4 D4 F3 G3 H3 J3 K2 J3 B5 H3 J3 K2 B4
C2 C3 B3 F3 G3 J3 K2

Kathy Acker
from Great Expectations

In the opening to *Great Expectations: A Novel* (New York: Grove, 1983), Kathy Acker appropriates, deforms, summarizes, and rewrites passages from Charles Dickens's *Great Expectations* and Pierre Guyotat's *Eden, Eden, Eden* to solve the equation plagiarism + pornography = autobiography. For the formulation of this equivalence, see Ron Silliman's "E-mail Interview" (*Quarry West* 34 [1998]: 13).

1. PLAGIARISM

I Recall My Childhood

My father's name being Pirrip, and my Christian name Philip, my infant tongue could make of both names nothing longer or more explicit than Peter. So I called myself Peter, and came to be called Peter.

I give Pirrip as my father's family name on the authority of his tombstone and my sister—Mrs. Joe Gargery, who married the blacksmith.

On Christmas Eve 1978 my mother committed suicide and in September of 1979 my grandmother (on my mother's side) died. Ten days ago (it is now almost Christmas 1979) Terence told my fortune with the Tarot cards. This was not so much a fortune—whatever that means—but a fairly, it seems to me, precise psychic map of the present, therefore: the future.

I asked the cards about future boyfriends. This question involved the following thoughts: Would the guy who fucked me so well in France be in love with me? Will I have a new boyfriend? As Terence told me to do, I cut the cards into four piles: earth water fire air. We found my significator, April 18th, in the water or emotion fantasy pile. We opened up this pile. The first image was a fat purring human cat surrounded by the Empress and the Queen of Pentacles. This cluster, traveling through a series of other clusters that, like mirrors, kept defining or explained the first cluster more clearly—time is an almost recurring conical—led to the final unconscious image: during Christmas the whole world is rejecting a male and a female kid who are scum by birth. To the right of the scum is the Star. To the left is the card of that craftsmanship which due to hard work succeeds.

Terence told me that despite my present good luck my basic stability my contentedness with myself alongside these images, I have the image obsession I'm scum. This powerful image depends on the Empress, the image I have of my mother. Before I was born, my mother hated me because my father left her (because she got pregnant?) and because my mother wanted to remain her mother's child rather than be my mother. My image of my mother is the source of my creativity. I prefer the word consciousness. My image of my hateful mother is blocking consciousness. To obtain a different picture of my mother, I have to forgive my mother for rejecting me and committing suicide. The picture of love, found in one of the clusters, is forgiveness that transforms need into desire.

Because I am hating my mother I am separating women into virgins or whores rather than believing I can be fertile.

I have no idea how to begin to forgive someone much less my mother. I have no idea where to begin: repression's impossible because it's stupid and I'm a materialist.

I just had the following dream:

In a large New England-ish house I am standing in a very big room on the second floor in the front of the mansion. This room is totally fascinating, but as soon as I leave it, I can't go back because it disappears. Every room in this house differs from every other room.

The day after my mother committed suicide I started to experience a frame. Within this frame time was totally circular because I was being returned to my childhood traumas totally terrifying because now these traumas are totally real: there is no buffer of memory.

There is not time; there is.

Beyond the buffers of forgetting which are our buffer to reality: there is. As the dream: there is and there is not. Call this TERROR call this TOTAL HUMAN RESPONSIBILITY. The PIG I see on the edge of the grave is the PIG me neither death nor social comment kills. This TERROR is divine because it is real and may I sink into IT.

My mother often told me: "You shouldn't care if an action is right or wrong; you should totally care if you're going to profit monetarily from it."

The helmeted bowlegged stiff-muscled soldiers trample on just-born babies swaddled in scarlet violet shawls, babies roll out of the arms of women crouched under POP's iron machine guns, a cabby shoves his fist into a goat's face, near the lake a section of the other army crosses the tracks, other soldiers in this same army leap in front of the trucks, the POP retreat up the river, a white-walled tire in front of three thorn bushes props up a male's head, the soldiers bare their chests in the shade of the mud barricades, the females lullabye kids in their tits, the sweat from the fires perfumes re-inforces this stirring rocking makes their rags their skins their meat preg-nant: salad oil clove henna butter indigo sulfur, at the base of this river under a shelf loaded down by burnt-out cedars barley wheat beehives graves refreshment stands garbage bags fig trees matches human-brain-splattered low-walls small-fires'-smoke-dilated orchards explode: flowers pollen grain-ears tree roots paper milk-stained cloths blood bark feathers, rising. The sol-diers wake up stand up again tuck in their canvas shirttails suck in cheeks stained by tears dried by the stream from hot train rails rub their sex against the tires, the trucks go down into a dry ford mow down a few rose-bushes, the sap mixes with disemboweled teenagers' blood on their knives' metal, the soldiers' nailed boots cut down uproot nursery plants, a section of RIMA (the other army) climb onto their trucks' runningboards throw themselves on their females pull out violet rags bloody tampaxes which afterwards the females stick back in their cunts: the soldier's chest as he's raping the female crushes the baby stuck in her tits

I want: every part changes (the meaning of) every other part so there's no absolute/heroic/dictatorial/S&M meaning/part of the soldier's onyx-dusted fingers touch her face orgasm makes him shoot saliva over the baby's buttery skull his formerly-erect now-softening sex rests on the shawl becomes its violet scarlet color, the trucks swallow up the RIMA soldiers, rainy winds shove the tarpaulins against their necks, they adjust their clothes, the shadows grow, their eyes gleam more and more their fingers brush their belt buckles, the wethaired-from-sweating-during-capture-at-the-edge-of-the-coals goats crouch like the rags sticking out of the cunts, a tongueless canvas-covered teenager pisses into the quart of blue enamel he's holding in his half-mutilated hand, the truck-driver returns kisses the blue cross tattooed on his forehead, the teenager brings down his palm wrist where alcohol-filled veins are sticking out. These caterpillars of trucks grind down the stones the winds hurled over the train tracks, the soldiers sleep their sex rolling over their hips drips they are cattle, their truck-driver spits black a wasp sting swells up the skin under his left eye black grapes load down his pocket, an old man's white hair under-the-white-hair red burned face jumps up above the sheet metal, the driver's black saliva dries on his chin the driver's studded heel crushes as he pulls hair out the back of this head on to the sheet metal, some stones blow up

Sally Alatalo
from Unforeseen Alliances

Using only words derived from dime-store romance novels, the Chicago-based poet, book artist, and publisher Sally Alatalo (writing under the pseudonym Anita M-28) has published several books of appropriated texts. Meticulously restaging photographs of the covers of romance novels à la Cindy Sherman or performing in full costume (beehive hairdo, dark sunglasses, and vintage dress) at bookstores and book fairs as Anita M-28, Alatalo lends physical presence to the shadowy world of ghostwritten books, using Warholian tactics in both her writing and performances to raise issues of authorship, identity, feminism, authenticity, and subjectivity.

For *Unforeseen Alliances* (Chicago: Sara Ranchouse, 2001), Alatalo has made a list of 1,878 romance novel titles and used them to write poems, with each line of each poem (including the title of the poem) representing one published title.

The Language of Love

Love letters
Carried away
Pretty Polly

The language of love
Betrayed
Hearts desire

First Kiss

First kiss
Flowers in the rain

The fifth kiss
Petals in the storm

A Treasure Worth Seeking

Lost love found
A stolen heart
A treasure worth seeking
Like no other

Surrender
Captive passions
Love rules
Forever and beyond

Home at Last

Rooms of the heart
Beyond the picket fence
This is the house
Where love dwells

Storm Warning

You only love once
When lightening strikes

Lightening strikes twice
You only love twice

After Caroline

After Caroline
Searching for Sarah
Considering Kate

Courting Susannah
Losing Julie
Messing around with Max
Wild enough for Willa
Seducing Celeste
Loving Lily
Marrying Jezebel

Dreaming of You

Come lie with me
Beneath the covers
All through the night
A perfect love
One hundred and one ways

Where the Heart Is

Follow the wind
Out of the darkness

Come into the sun
Where the heart is

Angel

Snow angel
Come in from the cold
The frozen heart
Dreams of fire

Angelfire
The elusive flame
Awakening
The fires of paradise

Wayward angel
Whispers in Eden
So sweet a sin
Hell is my heaven

Passion Moon Rising

Beyond the starlit frost
Passion moon rising
The lady and the outlaw
Waltz in scarlet
From twilight to sunrise

Where Roses Grow Wild

The cowboy and the lady
Walk in moonlight
Where roses grow wild

Listen for the whisper
In their footsteps
Love's sweet music
Dancing on the wind

Suspicious Minds

Suspicious minds
Betrayed
Secrets of the heart
On the whispering wind

Voices carry
One whiff of scandal
To the ends of the earth

To Begin Again

My dear innocent
Some say love
Once and forever
Forever and always

Then came you
Searching for yesterday
To begin again

Whenever I Love You

Open wings
Seize the dawn
Catch the wind
Embrace the day
Whenever I love you

Until You

Notorious
Untamed
Blaze of passion
Too hot to handle
Until you
Steal the flame

At Last

Love lies sleeping
In our dreams
At last
Awakening
The elusive flame
The fires of paradise

If You Believe

If you believe
My steadfast heart
Be my baby
Sweet baby
Tonight and always
Forever and beyond

Paal Bjelke Andersen
from The Grefsen Address

Paal Bjelke Andersen's text is based on nationally televised speeches by the presidents or prime ministers of Nordic countries (Denmark, Sweden, Iceland, Norway, and Finland) between the years 2000 and 2009. From the raw text of those speeches, Andersen retains certain elements: all sentences mentioning the Nordic community, every sentence mentioning the word *language* (e.g., *språk* in Norwegian), all the names of places, all sentences with the word *border* (e.g., *grense* in Norwegian), all the single groups of people mentioned, all sentences with the word *war* (e.g., *krig* in Swedish), and every single person mentioned. He also notates his own geographical itinerary walking from his house, around the Norwegian parliament and back home, including every street crossed and every commercial organization passed. Between location and locution ("address," in both its senses), between the discretely local and the shared assemblage, the word and the action, Andersen traces the terms by which we describe and construct political space.

The speeches from each country are kept in their original language, with the same sequence for every section: Danish, Finnish-Swedish, Icelandic, Norwegian, and Finnish. Although the idea of a Nordic community is very strong, only a handful of citizens can understand its varied languages (the Uralic Finnish, for instance, is radically distinct from the North German Icelandic, which is itself more distant from the more similar Norwegian, Swedish, and Danish). Any difficulty for English speakers posed by this untranslated text, then, is all to the point.

2000

Danmark og Danmark og Danmark og Danmark og Danmark og Danmark og de tyske Hanse-stæder og Amager og Lolland-Falster og Danmark og Danmark og den jyske østkyst og Fredericia og Danmark og Danmark og Lemvig og Libanon og Christiansborg og Danmark og Europa og England og Sverige og EU og Danmark og Europa og Europa og Danmark og Danmark og Danmark.

Finland och Finland och Europeiska unionen och Finland och Finland och Finland och Finland och Finland och Kosovo och Kosovo och Balkan och Ryssland och Ryssland.

Veröldin víð og breið og landið og landið og landið og landið og Ísland og landið og landið og sveitir og héruð og fjórðungar og landið og Danmörk og Rússland og Ísland og Ísland og umheimurinn og önnur lönd og ekki eitt land heldur mörg og Ísland og ekki eitt land heldur mörg og Danmörk og sambandsríki Evrópu og við Íslendingar ráðum nú yfir sjöhundruð þúsund ferkílómetra hafsvæði.

Nasaret og Norge og Stiklestad og Norge og Amerika og Norge og Sunndal på Nordmøre og Norge og Norge og Telemark og Norge og Vest-Europa og Norge og Norge og Midtøsten og USA og Oslo og Nordsjøen og Balkan og Kosovo og Norge og Kosovo og Balkan og Tsjetjenia og Norge og Sør-Afrika og Sør-Afrika.

Suomi ja Suomi ja Euroopan unioni ja Suomi ja Suomi ja Suomi ja Suomi ja Suomi ja Kosovo ja Kosovo ja Balkan ja Venäjä ja Venäjä.

. . .

2009
Danmark og Danmark og Islamabad i Pakistan og Afghanistan og Afghanistan og Danmark og Danmark og Afghanistan og Afghanistan og Afghanistan og Somalia og Kosovo og Georgien og andre af verdens brændpunkter og Danmark og Danmark og udlandet og Danmark og Danmark og Danmark og den vestlige verden og verdens demokratier og verdens oliestater og den demokratiske verden og Danmark.

Gaza och Mellanöstern och Finland och Finland och Finland och många andra länder i Europa och Finland och Europeiska unionen och Polen och Köpenhamn och industriländerna och utvecklingsländerna och Finland och Östersjöområdet och Östersjön och alla Östersjöländerna och Östersjön och Östersjön och det så kallade avrinningsområdet och Kauhajoki och Finland och Sverige och Finland och det ryska kejsardömet och Borgå och Finland och Fredrikshamn och Borgå och hela Europa och det nordliga Europa och Finland.

Kína og Ísland og heimurinn og heimsbyggðin og heimsbyggðin og landið og landið og landið og Norðurlönd og Evrópa og Norður-Ameríka og Evrópusambandið og Evrópska efnahagssvæðið og Evrópusambandið og Evrópusambandið.

Midtøsten og Gaza og Norge og Gaza og Midtøsten og Norge og industri-landene og andre land og andre land og Raufoss og Karmøy og Mosjøen og Sykkylven og Norge og Norge og Norge og de fleste andre land og Norge og Norge og der barnedødeligheten er høy og der det å føde barn er noe av det farligste en kvinne kan gjøre og Kongo og Darfur og Zimbabwe og Afghanistan og utlandet.

Gaza ja Lähi-itä ja Suomi ja Suomi ja Suomi ja monet muut Euroopan maat ja Suomi ja Euroopan unioni ja Puola ja Kööpenhamina ja teollisuus-maat ja kehitysmaat ja Suomi ja Itämeren alue ja Itämeri ja kaikki Itäme-ren maat ja Itämeri ja Itämeri ja niin sanottu valuma-alue ja Kauhajoki ja Suomi ja Ruotsi ja Suomi ja Venäjän keisarikunta ja Porvoo ja Suomi ja Hamina ja Porvoo ja koko Eurooppa ja pohjoinen Eurooppa ja Suomi.

Anonymous
Eroticism

A mash-up of the nineteenth-century sign-language alphabet popularized by Thomas Hopkins Gallaudet and entries from what would constitute a slang thesaurus of synonyms for copulation, this collision of text and image was in all likelihood produced by Georges Bataille. It was published in *Le Da Costa encyclopédique* (Paris: Max-Pol Fouchet, 1947), a work of the secretive Acéphale group of renegade surrealists and extreme sociologists (members of which may have actually beheaded a sacrificial victim). The book, carrying the subtitled "Fascicule VII, Volume II," and hence ostensibly one volume from a larger work, was distributed in the fall of 1947. It appeared unannounced and anonymously in Left Bank bookshops, where copies were surreptitiously tipped into the legitimate displays. Compiled during the Second World War and edited by Isabelle Waldberg and Robert Lebel, the project was aided in large part by Marcel Duchamp. The related entry reads:

> Whoever has not chosen obscenity, recognized in obscenity the presence and the shock of poetry, and, more intimately, the elusive brightness of a star, is not worthy to die and their death will extend upon earth the industrious anxiety of priests.

For further information and documentation, see the superb *Encyclopaedia Acephalica, Atlas Arkhive Three: Documents of the Avant-Garde* (London: Atlas Press, 1995).

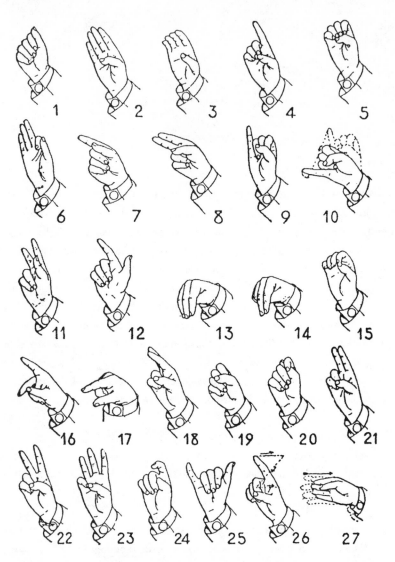

EROTISM. — 1. Accost. 2. Burgle. 3. Cunnilinguate. 4. Deflower. 5. Ensnare. 6. Fuck. 7. Gallivant. 8. Harass. 9. Irrumate. 10. Jismify. 11. Kink. 12. Lesbianise. 13. Masturbate. 14. Nidify. 15. Occult. 16. Pedicate. 17. Quench. 18. Ream. 19. Syphilise. 20. Tup. 21. Urticate. 22. Violate. 23. Waggle. 24. Xiphoidify. 25. Yonirise. 26. Zoogonise. 27. Recommence.

Translated by Iain White

David Antin
A List of the Delusions of the Insane:
What They Are Afraid Of

The list reproduced here from David Antin's *Code of Flag Behavior* (Los Angeles: Black Sparrow, 1969) is an expansion of the catalog originally compiled by Thomas Smith Clouston of "actual examples of delusions of about 100 female melancholic patients" ("and they far from exhaust the list," he adds) ("Lecture II," *Clinical Lectures on Mental Illness,* 6th ed. [Philadelphia: Lea Brothers, 1904], 78–80). William James includes the list in a footnote to *The Principles of Psychology* (Cambridge, Mass.: Harvard University Press, 1981), 758.

the police
being poisoned
being killed
being alone
being attacked at night
being poor
being followed at night
being lost in a crowd
being dead
having no stomach
having no insides
having a bone in the throat
losing money
being unfit to live
being ill with a mysterious disease
being unable to turn out the light
being unable to close the door
that an animal will come in from the street
that they will not recover

that they will be murdered
that they will be murdered when they sleep
that they will be murdered when they wake
that murders are going on all around them
that they will see the murderer
that they will not
that they will be boiled alive
that they will be starved
that they will be fed disgusting things
that disgusting things are being put into their food and drink
that their flesh is boiling
that their head will be cut off
that children are burning
that they are starving
that all of the nutriment has been removed from food
that evil chemicals have been placed in the earth
that evil chemicals have entered the air
that it is immoral to eat
that they are in hell
that they hear people screaming
that they smell burnt flesh
that they have committed an unpardonable sin
that there are unknown agencies working evil in the world
that they have no identity
that they are on fire
that they have no brain
that they are covered with vermin
that their property is being stolen
that their children are being killed
that they have stolen something
that they have too much to eat
that they have been chloroformed
that they have been blinded
that they have gone deaf
that they have been hypnotized
that they are the tools of another power
that they have been forced to commit murder
that they will get the electric chair
that people have been calling them names

that they deserve these names
that they are changing their sex
that their blood has turned to water
that insects are coming out of their body
that they give off a bad smell
that houses are burning around them
that people are burning around them
that children are burning around them
that houses are burning
that they have committed suicide of the soul

---

from Novel Poem

To compose "Novel Poem" (*Selected Poems: 1963–1973* [Los Angeles: Sun and Moon, 1991]), David Antin, bored at his day job and curious about a coworker who seemed to enjoy the books she voraciously consumed, flipped through a number of contemporary popular novels—by Ayn Rand, Michael Crichton, Iris Murdoch, Gore Vidal, Doris Lessing, and Alberto Moravia, among others—typing out a line or phrase as he went. As he describes it:

> I put some paper in the typewriter and began typing what I was reading, and it became a little game—no more than one line from a page. Sometimes only a phrase. Sometimes nothing. And I never went back. I read and typed relentlessly forward, quickly making up these little songs, till I was through. (*Selected Poems*, 17)

In the excerpt included here, he draws from Suyin Han's *Two Loves* (New York: Putnam, 1962).

VI. A False Moen

roses from Dalat
orchids from Malaya
a Chinese friend in Bali sends me the *hen hwa*
blossom of a single night

i observed in Sylvie a great understanding
a wide eyed muteness before the shock of beauty

Philippe said 'look at this'
Jacques said 'the flood'

for your mordant spirit this was impossible
you wrenched your rights
could not savor

and the blood

all iridescence
all moon prospect
flame
music

after the first dress
perfume
shoes
the dressing table
the orderly beauties of Europe

'and the flood' said the astronomer
'the flood'

Rahit had willed a false Moen
a Moen that was not

plunged her hands into ulcers
fingered rags
bathed purulent eyes
her nostrils dilated to receive the smell of festering flesh
'i feel alive again next to my people'

from The Separation Meditations

In David Antin's early "Novel Poem" (*Selected Poems: 1963–1973* [Los Angeles: Sun and Moon, 1991]), he retooled novels as song lyrics, lineating single lines or short phrases appropriated from a variety of contemporary novels. In doing so, Antin attempted to discover elements of one genre (song) embedded in another (novelistic prose). Or, as he put it, in musical terms, he "liked whatever was recorded at 33 that sounded good at 78." In his "Separation Meditations," Antin similarly sought poetic language buried in the endnotes of P. E. Matheson's two-volume *Epictetus: The Discourses and Manual; Together with Fragments of His Writings* (Oxford, U.K.: Clarendon Press, 1916), transforming Matheson's instrumental clarifications into gnomic fragments. The opening stanza of the first "Separation Meditation," for example, is drawn from the notes to chapter 24, book 3, of the *Discourses;* the first five notes in the original volume's appendix read (186):

1. The places where you now are.
2. probably refers to the story that Nicocreon ordered Anaxarchus' tongue to be cut out, whereupon he bit it off himself and spat it in Nicocreon's face. Diog. Laert. ix. 59.
3. καρπιστής—*vindex* or *assertor,* the man by the touch of whose wand the slave became free, if his master made no counter claim. The word is used again in iv. 1 and iv. 7. For Epictetus' references to manumission cf ii., 1, note 3.
4. διάχυσις here and later in the chapter, of pleasure as something diffused or expansive (opp. to σνστολή)
5. i.e. "take my life."

From which Antin takes:

1. The places where you are now
2. A man who wanted another's tongue cut out
3. By the touch of whose wand the slave became free
4. Here and later of pleasure as something diffused
5. Take my life

Antin's procedure might be seen as a riff on Alfred North Whitehead's quip that "the safest general characterization of the European philosophical tradition is that it consists of a series of footnotes to Plato" (*Process and Reality* [New York: Free Press, 1979], 39). That tradition continued in Charles Bernstein's contribution to

LEGEND [(New York: L=A=N=G=U=A=G=E/Segue, 1980), 21-22], which tran-
scribes fragments from Heraclitus.

For further discussions, see David Antin and Charles Bernstein, *A Conversation with David Antin* (New York: Granary, 2002); Stephen Cope, "Introducing David Antin," *Review of Contemporary Fiction* (March 2001): 125-46; Hélène Aji, "Discours poétique et poétique du discours: problématiques de la voix chez David Antin," *Poétiques de la voix,* ed. E. Angel-Perez and P. Iselin (Paris: Presses Universitaires de Paris-Sorbonne, 2005).

1. The places where you are now
2. A man who wanted another's tongue cut out
3. By the touch of whose wand the slave became free
4. Here and later of pleasure as something diffused
5. Take my life

1. The notion is of a man returning to himself or turning his attention to his true self
2. The words are ironical
3. The words "i often have arguments"
4. The point is that the discourses are treated as matters of language without regard to their substance
5. A big galley or theater
6. That there is a spiritual relation between them

1. A slave's name
2. He does not use the word "slave"
3. Because he does not want to suggest a slave's spirit

. . .

1. Examines the flesh of victims
2. The philosopher

1. No step can be taken without a logical process

1. No distinction between feeling and thought
2. Yet do not groan within

1. He is thinking of reason not so much as a faculty but a system of sensations and ideas
2. Sagacity
3. Things neither good nor bad

1. Strip the man
2. A customary position
3. Only clothes are affected

1. Revealing a secret
2. Creating a mess

Louis Aragon
Suicide

However familiar, the order of alphabet conceals a long and fraught history (indeed, the seeming naturalness of the sequence should alert us to its ideological character). Louis Aragon's transcription of that received sequence rehearses the disciplinary measures by which that ideology is established; his title, moreover, suggests the unbearable inevitability of the sequence—its deadening finality after the momentum of habit and reflex, or worse, for a poet, what Benjamin Buchloh calls "the cul-de-sac of the alphabet's infinite permutational and combinatory possibilities" ("Open Letters, Industrial Poems," *October* 102 [1987]: 77). Moreover, as originally printed in *Cannibale,* no. 1 (April 1920), the uneven reach of the layout of the final line hints at a dark psychology of absence, incompletion, and enervation—a premature termination or a failure to see things through to the end. Aragon himself, as it happens, made several suicide attempts.

Ultimately, the question is not whether this senseless tragedy could have been avoided but whether the sequence "q w e r t y . . ." will end any differently. Aram Saroyan asks precisely that question in his poem "The Collected Works" (where the last word of his title may be a verb rather than a plural noun): four couplets, each displaying the rows of the typewriter keyboard (one line of each couplet being typed with the Shift key engaged) (*Complete Minimal Poems* [Brooklyn, N.Y.: Ugly Duckling Presse, 2007], 151). His earlier poem "STEAK" (*Aram Saroyan* [New York: Random House, 1968]) consisted merely of the alphabet. BpNichol's "The Complete Works" grounds these more abstract conceits in the layout of a particular typewriter, including keys with the shift engaged and a footnote qualifying "any possible permutation of all listed elements" (*The Alphabet Game: A bpNichol Reader,* ed. Lori Emerson and Darren Wershler [Toronto: Coach House Books, 2007], 11–12). None of these poems should be confused with Ian Hamilton Finlay's one-word poem "Arcady," which reads "ABCDEFGHIJKLMNOPQRSTUVWXYZ."

Martin Gardener twice returned to Aragon's poem ("Mathematical Games," *Scientific American* [December 1962 and March 1963]) as a matrix for spelling out words, as in a game of Boggle; he discovered "chin up," "no point to hide," "join up," and "Stop, Idiots!" (Martin Gardener, *The Unexpected Hanging and Other Mathe-matical Diversions* [New York: Simon & Schuster, 1969], 207–10).

Suicide

abcdef
ghijkl
mnopqr
stuvw
xyz

Nathan Austin
from Survey Says!

Like Dan Farrell's *Inkblot Record,* Nathan Austin's *Survey Says!* (New York: Black Maze Books, 2009) works, in essence, as an interface to a preexisting database. Where Farrell alphabetized patients' responses to a psychology test, Austin alphabetized contestants' responses to the television game show *Family Feud.* All of the answers from a five-week run in 2005 and another three weeks in 2008 were arranged according to the second letter of the first word of the phrase, providing the same arbitrary structuring order as many other assemblages of found texts but without the immediately palpable sense of predictable progression that conventional alphabetization provides. Austin's engagement with popular entertainment culture, moreover, aligns his book with contemporary vernacular works of obsessive fan montage made popular on YouTube: every curse in the *Sopranos* chronologically, every clueless query "What?" from *Lost* in a bewildering flurry, every invocation of *Buffy* from one season of the eponymous vampire slayer show (many reduced to a series of foreshortened *Buffs*, implicitly hailing the fans, or buffs, of the show), and so on. In the art world, the same exhaustive sorting of popular television shows into 'pataphysically precise and useless archives has been undertaken by Jennifer and Kevin McCoy, who have assembled digital video libraries from several 1970s network staples, including *Kung Fu, Starsky and Hutch,* and Looney Tunes cartoons. The results index "every plaid," "every yellow Volkswagen," "every plant," "every stairwell," "every hammer and hatchet," "every singed fur or hair," and so on. Regardless of the format—DVD, HTML, embedded Java animations, a printed book—all of those works follow what Lev Manovich has identified as the "logic of new media," which seeks to rearrange archives of previously assembled data rather than to create new material from scratch.

Part of the conceit of *Family Feud* is that the correct answers are determined not by individual experts or authorities but by demographic polling: an aggregate and anonymous collective authorship mirroring the mute mass audience that constitutes the popular show's viewership. Accordingly, Austin's noninterventionist pooling and ranking, his tabulation of all the answers and not just the best, or most poetic, or most amusing ones, speak to the show's original methods. But with only one side of the question-and-answer exchange presented, *Survey Says!* also enters into a tacit dialogue with works such as Kenneth Goldsmith's *Soliloquy* (in which only Goldsmith's questions are heard, but not his interlocutors' answers, and vice versa), or Craig Dworkin's *Legion* (which repurposes the true-false questions of the Minnesota Multiphasic Personality Inventory as if they were expressive statements), as well as a number of other works presenting only half of an interrogative exchange. Indeed, with its litany of answers, *Survey Says!* is the inverse of a poetic subgenre of works composed entirely of questions. For instance, Octavian Esanu's 2002 *JFL: What Does "Why" Mean?* assembles and interpolates duly footnoted questions from hundreds of interviews and essays by artists and art historians, and it divides them into two long chapters (focused on why and what, respectively) with a brief coda of *hows*. With no apparent source texts, Gilbert Sorrentino's *Gold Fools* mines the quest out of question, spinning its novel-length Old West prospector yarn entirely from interrogatives. Similarly, Pablo Neruda's *Libro de las preguntas* (*Book of Questions*) contains only questions, supposedly unanswerable ones. Tom Beckett's "One Hundred Questions" is true to its title, as is John Ashbery's *100 Multiple-Choice Questions*; Brenda Iijima's "If Not Metamorphic?" uses the question as a punctuating device, its ubiquity establishing a tonal background to phrases that are more rhetorical than inquisitory; and most of the poems in Steve Benson's *Open Clothes* are composed of questions; as is the entirety of Ron Silliman's "Sunset Debris." In an interview with Tom Beckett, Silliman explains that "every sentence is supposed to remind the reader of her or his inability to respond" (*The Difficulties* 2, no. 2 [1985]: 45), but the work has in fact provoked rather than stifled response. In the *Tapeworm Foundry*, Darren Wershler proposes that one "write a poem answering in order of occurrence all of the questions posed by ron silliman in sunset debris." Following a pioneering attempt by Michael Waltuch and Alan Davies's poem "?s to .s," which set out to answer all of the interrogatives in Silliman's related *Chinese Notebook*, several poets have taken up Wershler's challenge, including Arielle Brousse (in *Tapeworm: A Collaborative Exhibition* [Philadelphia: Kelly Writers House, 2008]) and Christian Bök in *Busted Sirens* (in *Interval(le)s* 2.2–3.1 [2008–9]: 142–47).

In all of these works, as in *Survey Says!,* part of the interest is the degree to which questions are found to anticipate their answers and answers to recapitulate their questions. Moreover, these texts are animated by the dynamic pull between their defamiliarization (how unexpected and strange the decontextualized phrases sound, even when they refer to the most mundane things) and, in contrast, the reader's ability to imaginatively recontextualize even the strangest phrase into a plausibly sensical dialogue.

There is nothing good on T.V. Where she lives. There's too many people. Where you live, like a change of town. The ring. Thermometer. The school bus. She's married. She's pregnant. Chess board. Chest. Whether or not friends have been there. The thing we don't want to waste is energy. The top piece on the cake, or the thing. The T.V. The T.V. The T.V. channel. The type of food they serve. The value of their house. The victim of your gun: a dead body. The weasel. She won't reveal her family. They are "on board." They beautify themselves. They brush their teeth. They brush their teeth. They buy groceries. They cash their check. They change their jobs. They change their underwear. They cheat on their spouse. They chew gum. They comb it over. They develop more hair. They don't like to look pretty. They don't put on their seatbelt. They don't take care of their bedroom. They dry flowers—like dried flowers. They dye it. They eat. They fall out of love. They gargle. They go out to dinner. They go see a Woody Allen movie. They have kids. They have to work long hours. They hide their eyes. They hold in their stomach. They hold their breath when their parents walk in the room. They hug and kiss. They jump the boat. They laugh. They lay baby chicks. They leave makeup all over the bathroom. They leave trash behind. They lose it. They make decisions too slowly. They may cheat on their diet. They "passed away." They pay their bills. They roost—or, the crow-sounding thing: *caw!* They save their marriage certificate. They save their wedding ring. They say their prayers. They shave it all off. They simply don't like it? They soak their feet. They step on them. They take a shower when they wake up from a nap. They talk on their cell phone. They twiddle them. They use room spray, or air freshener. They use wolves—wolf. They walk out; they cry; they get popcorn; they go to the bathroom; they leave their seat—no! they get refreshments. They want the temperature to go up. They wash their hair. They wash their hands. They worry about losing their hair. Oh, golf. Chicago. Chicken. Chicken fingers. Chicken noodle. Chicken of the sea. Chickens fly. Chiffon. Chihuahua. Philadelphia. Children's education. China. China. China. Think. Chips. Chips. Chips. Thirteen. Three or four, at least. Thirteen. Thirty days. This isn't me, but: make love. This might be a little inappropriate, but . . . the sex. This time, we're going to try cluck. Oh no! I hold onto my emotions. Phone number. Shop. Shopping with his lady. A horse—a workhorse. A hose. A hose. Those wooden sticks they stick in your mouth. Who's the person that reads your palm?—a palm reader! Who's wearing it? Photographs. Shot-put. Showering. Showering. Show it off. Show me a bush. Show me your mansion— your house. Three. Three. Three. Three. Three. Three. Three a.m. Three or four, at least. Three times. Shrimp. Christmas. Christmas. Christmas. Throat. Oh!—*that* movie. A hundred. A hundred dollars. Diamonds. Piano. Piano lessons. Piano lessons. Diapers. Diapers. Bib. Mice. Michael Jackson. Richard Nixon. "Kicked the bucket." "Kicked the dust." Picketers. Kicking my seat. Picking up groceries. Rick James. Microscope. Victoria's Secret. Bicycling. Video. Video camera. Video games. Side split. Kids have homework, but the teachers have homework too, and they don't like it. Diet. Life. Fifteen-ish. Fifteen pounds. Fifteen pounds. Fifty. Fifty. Fifty. Fifty dollars. Fifty-three. Big. Tigers have to run to catch their prey, so: tigers. High chair. Eight. Eight. Eight dollars. Eighteen. Eighteen. Tight fitting. Nightstick. Nightsticks. Pigs. Big television. Bike. Like, a how-to book: *How to Be a Good Wife*. Oil. Oil. Wildebeest. Hillary Clinton. Bill Clinton. Bill Gates. Film. Time. Time. Time. *Time. Time.* Time for more home repairs. Windows. Window window window! Nine. Nine o'clock. Nine o'clock. Wine—red wine. Ninety. Sing. Singer. Singer. Lingerie. Lingerie. Fingernails. Fingernails—the color of their fingernails. Sing it out: a little black book, or cigarettes? Pink. Pink. Pink. Zipper. Lips. Giraffe. Air conditioner. Air in an inner tube. Girlie magazines. Airplane. Mirrors. First day of school. Birthday cake. Birthdays. Birthdays. Thirty-five. His breath. His clothes. Wisdom. Diseases. Eisenhower? His famous sign: the Z. Dishes. Dishes. Dishwasher. His hygiene. His mitt. Kiss. Kiss. Miss Lincoln. Tissue paper. Listening to my wife talk. Listen to a stethoscope. Listen to the radio. His wallet. His wardrobe. His weight. Zit. Pitcher. Pitcher. Pitcher. Pitcher. Either your purse or your wallet. With fish? sounds fishy . . . how about asparagus? Hit them in the face. Little black book. Little Lulu. Little Orphan Annie. Little Red Riding Hood. Five. Five. Give a shot. Five-five. Five-foot-five. Give it away. River. Lives in a swamp. Live with your parents. Five years old. Divorce. Six. Six foot seven. Six-six. Fix something to eat. Sixteen. Sixteen. Sixteen. Sixty-five. Lizard. *Wizard of Oz*. Pizza. Pizza man. A Jack Russell terrier. A judge. Skating. Skiing. Skiing. A king. Ok—I think—a house. I know I like to turn on the T.V., watch some *Family Feud*.

J. G. Ballard
Mae West's Reduction Mammoplasty

In a triptych of short surgical fictions from the 1970s, J. G. Ballard replaced the anony-
mous subjects of medical case studies (patient X) with the names of celebrities; in
addition to the present piece (*Ambit* 44 [1970]: 9–11), he also wrote "Princess Mar-
garet's Facelift" (1970) and "Queen Elizabeth's Rhinoplasty" (1976) (see also "Coitus
80: A Description of the Sexual Act in 1980" [*New Worlds* 197 (January 1970): 16–17]).
The precision cutting of his collage technique in these works provides a tidy ana-
logue to the surgical blades of the plastic surgery he describes. As with other mash-
ups, however, much of the dark humor of these pieces derives from the disjunction
between the intimate specificity of their subject's proper names and the distanced
anonymity of the scientific language of medical reports. The rhetoric of celebrity
encourages a false intimacy—we are on first-name terms with entertainers we will
never meet in person—but when that same intimate address occurs in other venues,
as Ballard reveals, the results can be disquieting. That same disjunction between the
intimate and the public—the comfortingly familiar and the unsettling estranged—
is also the dynamic animating related Ballard works, such as his notorious "Why I
Want to Fuck Ronald Reagan." Distributed (minus the inflammatory title) by *pro situ*
anarchists at the 1980 Republican National Convention in the format of an offi-
cial Republican Party document, replete with forged letterhead, the typographic
style of the document and its mock-psychological style of demographic assessment
contrasted with the content of sentences such as "'Slow-motion film of Reagan's
speeches produced a marked erotic effect in an audience of spastic children." Con-
ventioneers were unfazed.

In his surgical fictions, Ballard pinpoints the moment at which the entertainment
industry shifted its fetishistic focus from elevated positions (e.g., royalty, the notorious,
the very wealthy) and naturally exaggerated bodies (e.g., Twiggy, Marilyn Monroe,
Tiny Tim) to the synthetically modified bodies of steroids, paralyzants, and repeated
plastic surgeries. Modern celebrity, of course, involves the most public speculation
about the most private aspects of a celebrity's life, constructing personae that appear
to have no interior. By literalizing that interior with a deconstructive vivisection—
textually imagining the opening, probing, removal, and reconfiguring of the internal

body of the celebrity—Ballard tests the degree to which popular interest in celebrities depends on an adherence to certain journalistic rhetorics and the avoidance of others—the degree, that is, to which style and ontology intersect.

Similarly, Ballard asks the reader to consider the point at which a prurient interest in the body of the celebrity crosses the line from proper fascination—the voyeuristic curiosity required by celebrity itself—to a lurid stare that destroys the aura of celebrity with its obscene refusal to blink. When viewed too closely, the perfected image of the celebrity's body appears monstrous and deformed. As Andy Warhol intuited, the idealized and the morbid are two sides of the coin of celebrity, with every image of Marilyn Monroe or Mae West already a kind of memento mori. The persona of the celebrity may be constructed in an exteriorized space of public shame without private guilt—where, indeed, even that shame is less a factor for the celebrity's consideration than a product for public consumption—but that consumption is necessarily complicit, and Ballard's surgical fictions polish a mirror in which readers can glimpse the extent of their own guilt in the pleasures of celebrity.

The reduction in size of Mae West's breasts presented a surgical challenge of some magnitude, considerably complicated by the patient's demand that her nipples be retained as oral mounts during sexual intercourse. There were many other factors to be taken into account: Miss West's age, the type of enlargement, whether the condition was one of pure hypertrophy, the degree of ptosis present, the actual scale of enlargement and, finally, the presence of any pathology in the breast tissue itself. An outstanding feature of the patient's breasts was their obesity and an enlargement far beyond the normal. After the age of 50 years breast tissue may behave in a very unfortunate manner if the blood supply is in any way impaired. In the case of Miss West, therefore, it was decided that a pedical operation should be avoided and subtotal amputation with transposition of the nipples as free grafts was adopted as the procedure of choice.

In dealing with very large breasts in older subjects, it may be necessary to reduce the huge volume of breast tissue in two stages, since the radical reduction in one stage may well interfere with the nerve supply of the nipple and prevent the erection of the nipple during subsequent sexual excitation. Miss West was warned, therefore, of the possible need for a second operation. As ptosis was present without hypertrophy the chief concern was that the patient's breasts should be replaced in their normal position. The presence of pain and chronic mastitis were not contra-indications to operation. In any case, tissue removed was examined very carefully for any abnormal pathology, and specimens from selected areas of each side were sent for microscopy.

Procedure

A marked degree of asymmetry between Miss Mae West's two breasts was found. The left breast was appreciably larger than the right. The most important step before operating on the breasts was to ascertain carefully the sites proposed for the new nipples. Measurements were made in her suite before operation with Miss West sitting up. The mid-clavicular point was marked with Bonney's blue. Then, steadying each of the breasts in turn with both hands, the assistant drew a line directly down from this point to the nipple itself. The new nipple should fall on this line 7½ inches from the suprasternal notch. This corresponded to a position just below the mid-point of the upper arm when it was held close to the patient's chest. The entire skin of Miss West's chest wall was cleaned with soap and water and spirit, and then wrapped in sterile towels. Miss West was then ready for operation.

The markings were redrawn on the patient when she was anaesthetized and on the operating table, First, a line from the mid-clavicular point to the nipple was again drawn and the position of the nipples checked for a second time. From the nipples the line was continued down to the sub-mammary folds. The position of the nipples was then marked out in ink.

Removal of breast tissue. It was first considered how much breast tissue could be removed without damaging the blood supply to the nipple. The breast was brought forward and laid on a board of wood. A large breast knife was carried down from above, curving very close to the nipple. The final amount of tissue was not removed in the first stage, and the remaining tissue of the breast was folded round and up to judge whether the breast formed a shape that would be acceptable to Miss West, or whether it would be possible to remove more tissue. Having finally removed sufficient tissue, the pedicle was swung round into its new position and firmly secured to the pectoral fascia at the upper extremity of the breast attachment with strong 20-day catgut. A suture wrongly inserted here could have pulled the nipple too far laterally.

Once more the entire field was reviewed for bleeding points. These were controlled by diathermy, but the pectoral vessels running down the border of pectoralis major were ligated. The skin covering was arranged to fit snugly over the newly formed breast. A curved intestinal clamp was used, but the fact that it fitted tightly on the skin margins did not appear to damage the vitality of the skin edges in any way. The clamp was applied from above downwards: at its hinge it was just about on the point marking the position of the new nipples. At its tips it was touching the chest wall and tucked well in with the skin held firmly in is blades. Five straight needles mounted with strong silkworm gut were then inserted between the two layers of the skin on the breast side of the clamp.

All the stages described above were performed on the other side. It remained merely to bring out the nipples through new holes at the chosen position above the vertical suture line. Having found where the nipple would lie most comfortably, a circle of skin was excised. The nipple was then sutured very carefully into this circle.

The completion of the operation was to ensure that there were no collections of blood in the breast, and that the breast was adequately drained on both sides. Corrugated rubber drains running both vertically and horizontally were satisfactory. The breasts were very firmly bandaged to the chest wall using a many-tailed bandage. Firm pressure was applied to the lower half of the breast with Miss West lying absolutely flat on her back.

Post-operative recovery. The operation was a lengthy one and Miss West suffered a serious degree of surgical shock. Intravenous saline solution was given during the operation. The foot end of Miss West's bed was raised on blocks, and she was allowed to lie comfortably on her back until she recovered a normal pulse rate and a normal blood pressure. She was then sat up for as long as the dressing remained firm. The wounds were redressed the next day, and after 48 hours the drains were removed. Careful attention was paid at all times to the possible collection of blood or fluid under the flaps. The sutures around the nipples were removed in 7 days.

Miss West was not allowed to go home before the fitting of an adequate supporting brassiere. It had a good deep section around the thorax, and the cups were of adequate size and gave good support from below. It was some time before Miss West's breasts reached their final proportions and shape, and there was no urgency about trimming scar lines until six months had passed. The left breast was then found to be too full in the lower quadrant, and the scar lines were unsatisfactory. Both these points were attended to. The ultimate results of this operation with regard to sexual function are not known.

Fiona Banner
from The Nam

Fiona Banner is a British artist who, in addition to her gallery practice, authors enormous tomes of conceptually based writing. In 1993, she made the cinematic-scaled drawing *Top Gun*, which was a handwritten account of the film by the same name. She then published the thousand-page book *The Nam* (London: Frith Street Books, 1997), which she wrote as she watched several fictional films about the Vietnam War: *Apocalypse Now, Born on the Fourth of July, Full Metal Jacket, Platoon, Hamburger Hill,* and *The Deer Hunter.* Banner was literally writing through (to use John Cage's term) pop culture and media. The text makes no distinction between films or scenes, instead creating an epic, nonstop onslaught of language. Far from being a dry exercise, Banner has employed a choice-based methodology whereby her deep subjectivity is revealed through a mechanical writing process.

The eyes definitely look left and then right, blinking more, the face is totally expressionless, the landscape fires up, it's unclear what's upside down now. The fire's intense. The face is moving. A hand appears in front of it and he drags on a cigarette, still staring straight out—or up. The trees, burnt black as anything, move off. The fire moves with them. The face is still there, shining with sweat. Stuff falls from what's left of the trees, really slowly, it's black and just floats down behind the face. The fire has nothing left to burn but it burns on anyway, so orange. He takes another drag. The whole picture fades out, apart from one raging fire in the middle. A helicopter flies in from the left then another from the right, they cross right in the middle. A fan whirrs round on the ceiling, beating time with the copter blades. You can see the man's shoulders. His body moves round so he's not upside down anymore, and then there are some letters and a photograph strewn across the table at the side of the bed. The bright orange fire bores through it all, just a small bit in the corner, but it's more important than everything else—even though it's just a dream of somewhere else. He lies next to all of this gear, and there's an empty glass, his left hand holds a burnt-out cigarette, the fan blades beat louder. All that stuff from behind, the palm trees and fire, are back again—across everything, and it's not the fan at all, it's helicopters beating. There's a pistol on the sheet next to him. He blinks up at the fan then across the room at the window, masked off by the venetian blinds. It's all orange, but a different hazy orange. You see him differently, his mouth moves, but definitely unconsciously. Then the blinds get closer and closer, so they get out of focus, he flicks them apart and takes a peek out. It's a street, cars, things moving quickly, some trees. A slat of light lines his face and you see him like a man for the first time. A voice comes over, slow and deep. "Saigon, shiiitt!" You know it's his voice. He moves his head back a bit and slugs something from a glass. He holds it in his mouth then swallows it down, still staring through the blind. He's talking to himself, but his lips aren't moving. It's like the words are coming straight out of his head, slowly almost a purr, "Every time, I think I'm going to wake up back in the jungle. . . . When I'd wake up at home after my own tour it was worse . . ." He's lying on the bed again, his head's cocked up against the bed head, he's completely still. A fly lands on his left hand. He jumps suddenly, tries to snatch it and falls back. ". . . I'd wake up and there's be nothing." Without hardly moving he grabs a picture from the side. He looks at it close, puffing away and slowly pouring the smoke out of his mouth. ". . . I hardly said a word to my wife until I said 'yes' to a divorce." He draws the photo to his face as if he's going to kiss it, but starts to burn through it with his cigarette—right through it. ". . . When I was here I wanted to be there. . . . When I was there all I could think of was getting back into the jungle. . . ." He's sitting on the edge of the bed. He's swigging the stuff from the glass— polishes it off, you know it's strong from the sound it makes in his neck and you can see it going down. He's young, you can see his face properly now, but he's so serious sitting there, you might say haunted. "I've been here a week now, waiting for a mission, getting softer . . . every minute I'm here in this room I get weaker, and every minute Charlie squats in the bush he gets stronger. . . ." Then I just think he's waiting. He glances up through the blurring fan. Then he's crouched down in the middle of the room, the fan's beating away above him, but it, he, looks hot as shit. You see him from the top. I think you can hear some insects, or some kind of interference. Then the music comes back, very faintly, but it's the same song. He gets smaller and smaller until the whole room is there. He reaching out of his shadow for some cigarettes, saying, "Each time I looked around, the walls moved in a little tighter." He's standing up, moving around strangely, practising some kind of martial art. Waving his arms about, slowly. The music's getting hotter. He stares out over his arm, half in the dark, he looks, his look is, incredibly intense. The fire comes back faint, then stronger. He seems to be wavering on the spot, half hunched-up, his arms close in to his chest. It's like he's doing some strange dance but he can't quite balance. He's naked apart from the khaki Y-fronts. He stares at himself in the mirror for a long time, balancing on the spot, swaying. Then it's all black and fire, he's there dancing through it, "Come come on baby . . . let me . . ." And I can't tell you how hot it is—but you can hardly see him for the sweat. The fires all flaring up out of control, behind. It all fades and you can see him again swaying, moving with the music, "Alllllllright," I think he's just moving so he doesn't fall over. He's in some incredible kind of slow spasm. Then you see him looking at himself in the mirror. His fist's so close and clenched you can hardly see it. Then he pounds it into the glass—punches himself out. It explodes, shatters all over the floor. He twists round and carries on his weird thing, it's as if the enemy's in there with him. Then he rolls over the bed and lands on the other side, some kind of weird stunt, leaving a long smudge of blood, all shiny and red. He holds it in his other hand, still staring down at it and feeling the blood, like it's a mystery. He puts his hand up to his face and smears it all over, as if he's wiping something off. He pours the remainder of a bottle of brandy into his mouth, tipping it in, lots of it spills over his mouth and onto his face. He turns round, his mouth's wide open, he's dying. He's twisting a bit more and then falls onto the floor, grabbing onto the sheet, screwing it up around his waist, as if it'll save him. He's naked. He leans back against the mattress, head tilted right back. He's crying, but nothing's coming out. The music's all building up, guitar, but loud drumming guitar. The music wants to explode. He tips his head back out of control, everything goes black. Two men in U.S. army uniform walk up the stairs. They look around, like they've never been there before. They turn a corner and are as black as shadows, then they reach the landing and rap on the fist door. Then you hear his voice, but he's not talking from down there on the floor. He's not even visible., "Everyone gets what they want. I wanted a mission and for my sins . . . that's what I got, they brought it up to me like room service . . ." The corridor's dark and there's no response. One of the soldiers calls, "Captain, are you in there?" A voice replies, "Yeah . . . Yeah, I'm comin'." It's a voice caught in the act. The he's so close again. ". . . A real choice mission and when it was over I'd never want another!" Willard appears at the door, a real mess with blood all over his face and a towel grabbed up around his waist. He barks, "What do you want!?" The officer's dismayed—he looks like such total shit. "Are you all right, Captain?" Willard turns away, pulling the sheet up round his bottom, heading back for the bed. He mumbles, shouts, grumpily, "What does it look like!" Basically, it looks like he's outta his skull. The officer pushes the door a bit further open and nods to the other guy. They walk into the room. Willard's slumped on the bed. The room's all ransacked, and fucked up, with blood all over the place. The officer starts to read off from a bit of paper, "Are you Captain Willard five hundred and fifth, a hundred and thirty-second airborne?" Willard's nodding yea, yea, but not even listening; then he yells out to the other guy, pissed off, "Hey buddy are you going to close the door or what!?" He steps in and closes the door. Willard's slumped on the bed looking down at his knees. The officer continues, "We have orders to escort you to the airbase, Sir." Willard looks lost, useless and confused, he gawps up at the officer, "What are the charges?" So innocent. The officer's blank. Willard stares at him. "What'd I do?" The officer answers, "There's no charges, Captain." He walks across to the bed and opens up the letter in front of Willard's face, "You're to report to Comsec Intelligence at Na Trang." Willard mumbles back at him, you can't hear what he's saying, but then I think he's just mouthing. Then he says stunned, like he doesn't believe it, "They're waiting for me?" He's overwhelmed, he might cry. "That's right, Captain, you still have a few hours to get cleaned up." Willard falls back onto the bed, exhausted from the sheer relief, maybe he just doesn't care. He looks like he's asleep. The officer says, "Captain," to wake him up again, but Willard's off. He says to his pal, as if it's nothing unusual, "Come on give me a hand." They haul him up off the bed, hook him up. "C'mon Captain, let's take a shower!" He's heavy like a corpse. They talk him along, "C'mon Captain, mind how you go," the merest hint of amusement in their voices. The officer says, "Just stand underneath this tap." He turns it on, a jet of water spurts down onto Willard. He screams out, like it really hurts. But it turns into, is nothing compared to, the continuous beat of helicopter blades, wping like crazy and coming down onto you.

Derek Beaulieu
from Flatland: A Romance of Many Dimensions

Using Edwin Abbott Abbott's 1884 novel *Flatland* as a template, Derek Beaulieu has reduced the mass of Abbott's words to information and schemas, more reminiscent of electrocardiogram results or stock reports than to its subject of fourth-dimensional fiction. Beaulieu explains his process: "I began by photocopying each page. . . . I then identified each unique letter on the 1st line of each page, and traced a line—using a light-table, ink and a rule—from the first occurrence of each letter on the first line through the first appearance of each of those same letters on each subsequent line." The result is a book denuded of its language yet revealing its formal structure. Beaulieu says, "By reducing reading and language into paragrammatical statistical analysis, content is subsumed into graphical representation of how language covers a page." By peeling back the letterist layer of the page, Beaulieu reveals another dimension of the life of a text, mirroring Abbot's wish to make visible the fourth dimension in his own work.

Beaulieu presents a different type of "writing through" than does John Cage or Jackson Mac Low, both of whom, by reducing voluminous texts, created compressed versions of the parent text. Beaulieu, by contrast, doesn't generate new or even reduced text; instead, *Flatland* (York, U.K.: Information as Material, 2007) is more akin to the explorations of Dan Graham, who in the 1960s, with a series of language-based investigations, sought to reduce complex systems to iconic gestures, while keeping intact—and even enhancing—their inherent mystery and wonder. Compare with the thirtieth iteration of bpNichol's "Translating Translating Apollinaire: 'Poem as a Machine for Generating Line Drawings'" (*The Alphabet Game: A bpNichol Reader,* ed. Lori Emerson and Darren Wershler [Toronto: Coach House Books, 2007], 154).

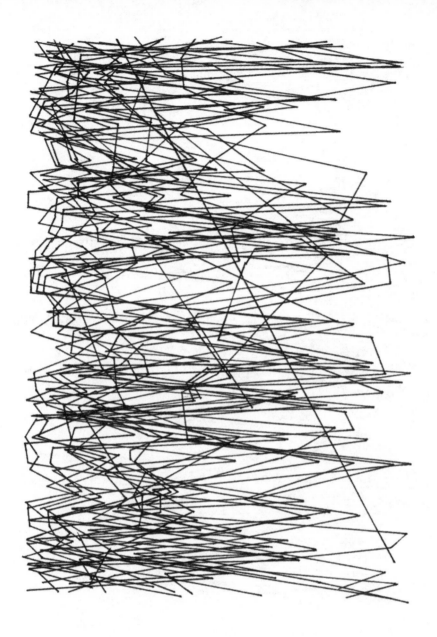

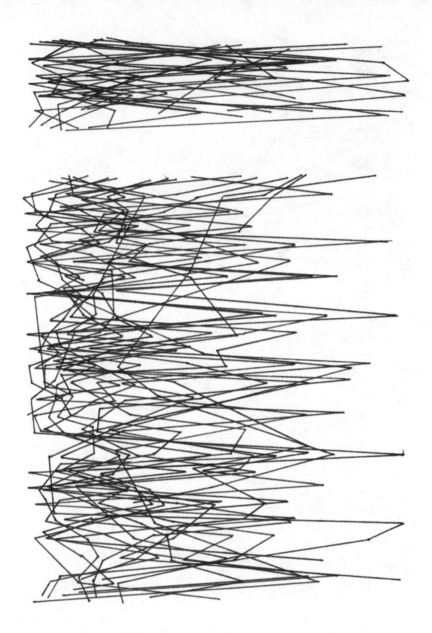

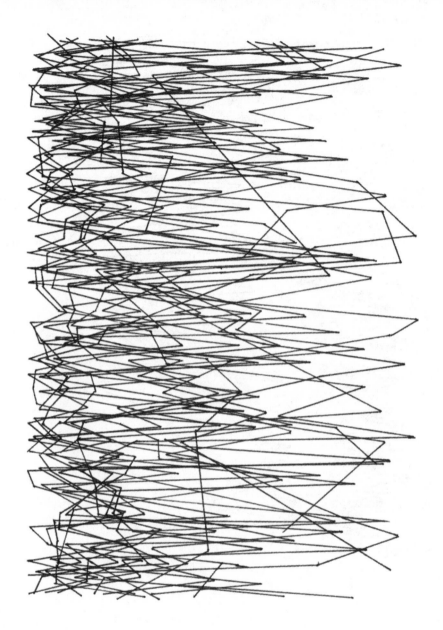

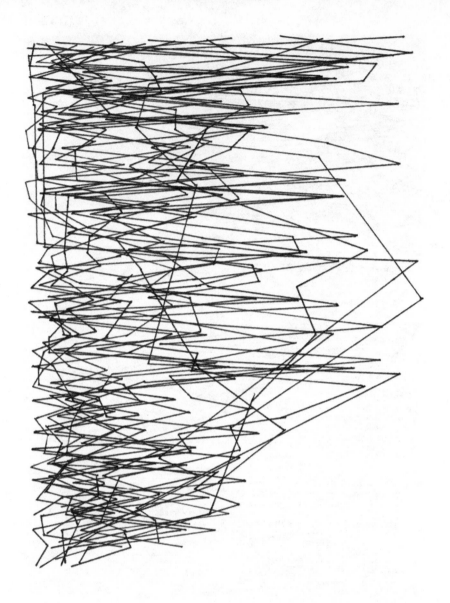

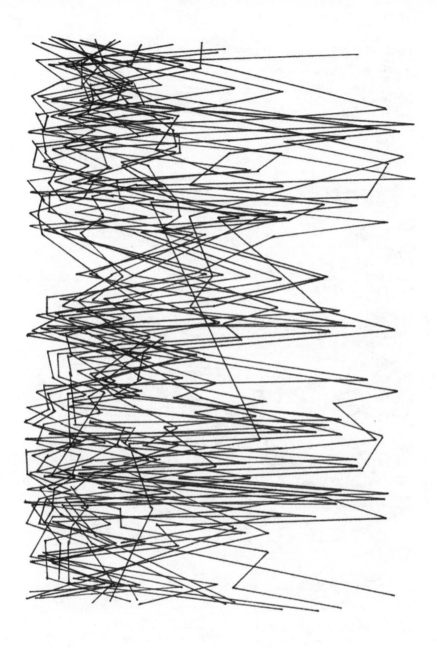

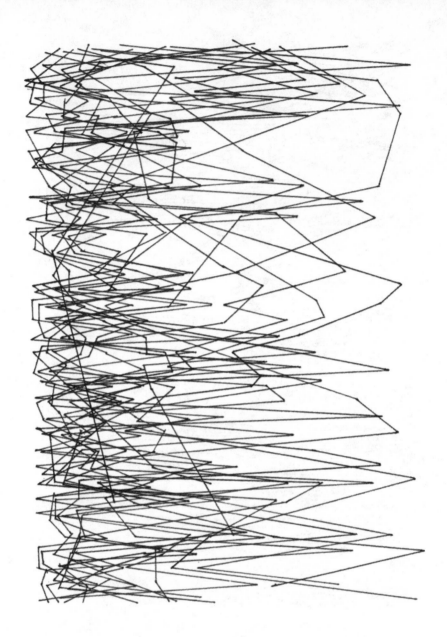

Derek Beaulieu 71

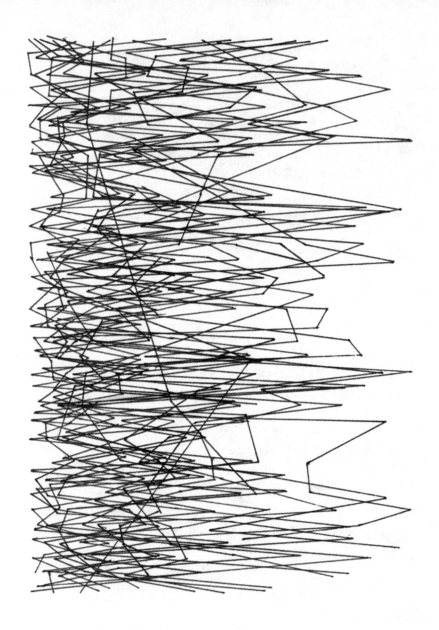

Samuel Beckett
from Molloy

Samuel Beckett (along with Robbe Grillet and the *nouveaux romanciers*) was one of the primary influences on conceptual and minimalist art in the 1960s, modeling anti-symbolic and impersonal compositions of minimal statements in maximum elaboration. The famous "sucking stones" sequence from *Molloy* (New York: Grove, 1955) is an obsessive transcription of body movements and inanimate objects into mathematical logic. Although the first person singular *I* is invoked, it reveals nothing of the narrator's subjectivity or emotion, nothing of the impact of the action on the human. Rather, the body is reduced to another cog in a machine.

The apparent purposelessness of such an activity underscores Beckett's emphasis on formal linguistic sequence supplanting literature's more traditional transparent delivery of pathos (though the sequence is still undoubtedly riddled with pathos, a testament to how hard it is to actually rid language of metaphor and emotion). Beckett's passage opens up writing to the influence of formal mathematical theory as praxis, in hindsight putting to the test Ludwig Wittgenstein's proposed language games as works of poetry.

I took advantage of being at the seaside to lay in a store of sucking stones. They were pebbles but I call them stones. Yes, on this occasion I laid in a considerable store. I distributed them equally between my four pockets, and sucked them turn and turn about. This raised a problem which I first solved in the following way. I had say sixteen stones, four in each of my four pockets these being the two pockets of my trousers and the two pockets of my greatcoat. Taking a stone from the right pocket of my greatcoat, and putting it in my mouth, I replaced it in the right pocket of my greatcoat by a stone from the right pocket of my trousers, which I replaced by a stone from the left pocket of my trousers, which I replaced by a stone from the left pocket of my greatcoat, which I replaced by the stone which was in my mouth, as soon as I had finished sucking it. Thus there were still four stones in each of my four pockets, but not quite the same stones. And when the desire to suck took hold of me again, I drew again on the right pocket of my greatcoat, certain of not taking the same stone as the last time. And while I sucked it I rearranged the other stones in the way I have just described. And so on. But this solution did not satisfy me fully. For it did not escape me that, by an extraordinary hazard, the four stones circulating thus might always be the same four. In which case, far from sucking the sixteen stones turn and turn about, I was really only sucking four, always the same, turn and turn about. But I shuffled them well in my pockets, before I began to suck, and again, while I sucked, before transferring them, in the hope of obtaining a more general circulation of the stones from pocket to pocket. But this was only a makeshift that could not long content a man like me. So I began to look for something else. And the first thing I hit upon was that I might do better to transfer the stones four by four, instead of one by one, that is to say, during the sucking, to take the three stones remaining in the right pocket of my greatcoat and replace them by the four in the right pocket of my trousers, and these by the four in the left pocket of my trousers, and these by the four in the left pocket of my greatcoat, and finally these by the three from the right pocket of my greatcoat, plus the one, as soon as I had finished sucking it, which was in my mouth. Yes, it seemed to me at first that by so doing I would arrive at a better result. But on further reflection I had to change my mind and confess that the circulation of the stones four by four came to exactly the same thing as their circulation one by one. For if I was certain of finding each time, in the right pocket of my greatcoat, four stones totally different from their immediate predecessors, the possibility nevertheless remained of my always chancing on the same stone, within each group of four, and consequently of my sucking, not the sixteen turn and turn about as I wished, but in fact four only, always the same, turn and turn about. So I had to seek elsewhere than in the mode of circulation. For no matter how I caused the stones to circulate, I always ran the same risk. It was obvious that by increasing the number of my pockets I was bound to increase my chances of enjoying my stones in the way I planned, that is to say one after the other until their number was exhausted. Had I had eight pockets, for example, instead of the four I did have, then even the most diabolical hazard could not have prevented me from sucking at least eight of my sixteen stones, turn and turn about. The truth is I should have needed sixteen pockets in order to be quite easy in my mind. And for a long time I could see no other conclusion than this, that short of having sixteen pockets, each with its stone, I could never reach the goal I had set myself, short of an extraordinary hazard. And if at a pinch I could double the number of my pockets, were it only by dividing each pocket in two, with the help of a few safety-pins let us say, to quadruple them seemed to be more than I could manage. And I did not feel inclined to take all that trouble for a half-measure. For I was beginning to lose all sense of measure, after all this wrestling and wrangling, and to say, All or nothing. And if I was tempted for an instant to establish a more equitable proportion between my stones and my pockets, by reducing the former to the number of the latter, it was only for an instant. For it would have been an admission of defeat. And sitting on the shore, before the sea, the sixteen stones spread out before my eyes, I gazed at them in anger and perplexity. For just as I had difficulty in sitting on a chair, or in an arm-chair, because of my stiff leg you understand, so I had none in sitting on the ground, because of my stiff leg and my stiffening leg, for it was about this time that my good leg, good in the sense that it was not stiff, began to stiffen. I needed a prop under the ham you understand, and even under the whole length of the leg, the prop of the earth. And while I gazed thus at my stones, revolving interminable martingales all equally defective, and crushing handfuls of sand, so that the sand ran through my fingers and fell back on the strand, yes, while thus I lulled my mind and part of my body, one day suddenly it dawned on the former, dimly, that I might perhaps achieve my purpose without increasing the number of my pockets, or reducing the number of my stones, but simply by sacrificing the principle of trim. The meaning of this illumination, which suddenly began to sing within me, like a verse of Isaiah, or of Jeremiah, I did not penetrate at once, and notably the word trim, which I had never met with, in this sense, long remained obscure. Finally I seemed to grasp that this word trim could not here mean anything else, anything better, than the distribution of the sixteen stones in four groups of four, one group in each pocket, and that it was my refusal to consider any distribution other than this that had vitiated my calculations until then and rendered the problem literally insoluble. And it was on the basis of this interpretation, whether right or wrong, that I finally reached a solution, inelegant assuredly, but sound, sound. Now I am willing to believe, indeed I firmly believe, that other solutions to this problem might have been found, and indeed may still be found, no less sound, but much more elegant, than the one I shall now describe, if I can. And I believe too that had I been a little more insistent, a little more resistant, I could have found them myself. But I was tired, but I was tired, and I contented myself ingloriously with the first solution that was a solution, to this problem. But not to go over the heart-breaking stages through which I passed before I came to it, here it is, in all it's hideousness. All (all!) that was necessary was to put for example, to begin with, six stones in the right pocket of my greatcoat, or supply-pocket, five in the right pocket of my trousers, and five in the left pocket of my trousers, that makes the lot, twice five ten plus six sixteen, and none for none remained, in the left pocket of my greatcoat, which for the time being remained empty, empty of stones that is, for its usual contents remained, as well as occasional objects. For where do you think I hid my vegetable knife, my silver, my horn and the other things that I have not yet named, perhaps shall never name. Good. Now I can begin to suck. Watch me closely. I take a stone from the right pocket of my greatcoat, suck it, stop sucking it, put it in the left pocket of my greatcoat, the one empty (of stones). I take a second stone from the right pocket of my greatcoat, suck it, put it in the left pocket of my greatcoat. And so on until the right pocket of my greatcoat is empty (apart from its usual and casual contents) and the six stones I have just sucked, one after the other, are all in the left pocket of my greatcoat. Pausing then, and concentrating, so as not to make a balls of it, I transfer to the right pocket of my greatcoat, in which there are no stones left, the five stones in the right pocket of my trousers, which I replace by the five stones in the left pocket of my trousers, which I replace by the six stones in the left pocket of my greatcoat. At this stage then the left pocket of my greatcoat is again empty of stones, while the right pocket of my greatcoat is again supplied, and in the right way, that is to say with other stones than those I have just sucked. These other stones I then begin to suck, one after the other, and to transfer as I go along to the left pocket of my greatcoat, being absolutely certain, as far as one can be in an affair of this kind, that I am not sucking the same stones as a moment before, but others. And when the right pocket of my greatcoat is again empty (of stones), and the five I have just sucked are all without exception in the left pocket of my greatcoat, then I proceed to the same redistribution as a moment before, or a similar redistribution, that is to say I transfer to the right pocket of my greatcoat, now again available, the five stones in the right pocket of my trousers, which I replace by the six stones in the left pocket of my trousers, which I replace by the five stones in the left pocket of my greatcoat. And there I am ready to begin again. Do I have to go on?

from Watt

In this famous scene from the novel *Watt* (New York: Grove, 1953), exhaustive and systematic permutation exemplifies Beckett's method of writing with procedural rather than narrative or psychological focus. The unwavering elaboration of the logical relations among minimal terms leads to an absurd excess and a comical discrepancy between the import of the prosaic subject matter (footware, apartment furnishing, et cetera) and the sustained and detailed attention devoted to those subjects. The writerly labor for such passages is thus more physical than imaginative; Beckett merely identifies a subject, while the possibilities of grammar do the rest. Syntax becomes a machine for novelistic production.

As for his feet, sometimes he wore on each a sock, or on the one a sock and on the other a stocking, or a boot, or a shoe, or a slipper, or a sock and a boot, or a sock and a shoe, or a sock and a slipper, or a stocking and boot, or a stocking and shoe, or a stocking and slipper, or nothing at all. And sometimes he wore on each a stocking, or on the one a stocking and on the other a boot, or a shoe, or a slipper, or a sock and a boot, or a sock and shoe, or a sock and slipper, or a stocking and boot, or a stocking and shoe, or a stocking and slipper, or nothing at all. And sometimes he wore on each a boot, or on the one a boot and on the other a shoe, or a slipper, or a sock and boot, or a sock and shoe, or a sock and slipper, or a stocking and boot, or a stocking and shoe, or a stocking and slipper, or nothing at all. And sometimes he wore on each a shoe, or on the one a shoe and on the other a slipper, or a sock and boot, or a sock and shoe, or a sock and slipper, or a stocking and boot, or a stocking and shoe, or a stocking and slipper, or nothing at all. And sometimes he wore on each a slipper, or on the one a slipper and on the other a sock and boot, or a sock and shoe, or a sock and slipper, or a stocking and boot, or a stocking and shoe, or a stocking and slipper, or nothing at all. And sometimes he wore on each a sock and boot, or on the one a sock and boot and on the other a sock and shoe, or a sock and slipper, or a stocking and boot, or a stocking and shoe, or a stocking and slipper, or nothing at all. And sometimes he wore on each a sock and shoe, or on the one a sock and shoe and on the other a sock and slipper, or a stocking and boot, or a stocking and shoe, or a stocking and slipper, or nothing at all. And sometimes he wore on each a sock and slipper, or on the one a sock and slipper and on the other a stocking and boot, or a stocking and shoe, or a stocking and slipper, or nothing at all. And sometimes he wore on each a stocking and boot, or on the one a stocking and boot and on the other a stocking and shoe, or a stocking and slipper, or nothing at all. And sometimes he wore on each a stocking and shoe, or on the one a stocking and shoe and on the other a stocking and slipper, or nothing at all. And sometimes he wore on each a stocking and slipper, or on the one a stocking and slipper and on the other nothing at all. And sometimes he went barefoot. . . .

Here he stood. Here he sat. Here he knelt. Here he lay. Here he moved, to and fro, from the door to the window, from the window to the door; from the window to the door, from the door to the window; from the fire to the bed, from the bed to the fire; from the bed to the fire, from the fire to the bed; from the door to the fire, from the fire to the door; from the fire to the door, from the door to the fire; from the window to the bed, from the bed to the window; from the bed to the window, from the window to the bed; from the fire to the window, from the window to the fire; from the window to the fire, from the fire to the window; from the bed to the door, from the door to the bed; from the door to the bed, from the bed to the door; from the door to the window, from the window to the fire; from the fire to the window, from the window to the door; from the window to the door, from the door to the bed; from the bed to the door, from the door to the window; from the fire to the bed, from the bed to the window; from the window to the bed, from the bed to the fire; from the bed to the fire, from the fire to the door; from the door to the fire, from the fire to the bed; from the door to the window, from the window to the bed; from the bed to the window, from the window to the door; from the window to the door, from the door to the fire; from the fire to the door, from the door to the window; from the fire to the bed, from the bed to the door; from the door to the bed, from the bed to the fire; from the bed to the fire, from the fire to the window; from the window to the fire, from the fire to the bed; from the door to the fire, from the fire to the window; from the window to the fire, from the fire to the door; from the window to the bed, from the bed to the door; from the door to the bed, from the bed to the window; from the fire to the window, from the window to the bed; from the bed to the window, from the window to the fire; from the bed to the door, from the door to the fire; from the fire to the door, from the door to the bed.

The room was furnished solidly and with taste.

This solid and tasteful furniture was subjected by Mr. Knott to frequent changes of position, both absolute and relative. Thus it was not rare to find, on the Sunday, the tallboy on its feet by the fire, and the dressing-table on its head by the bed, and the night-stool on its face by the door, and the wash-hand-stand on its back by the window; and, on the Monday, the tallboy on its back by the bed, and the dressing-table on its face by the door, and the night-stool on its back by the window, and the wash-hand-stand on its feet by the fire; and, on the Tuesday, the tallboy on its face by the door, and the dressing-table on its back by the window, and the night-stool on its feet by the fire, and the wash-hand-stand on its head by the bed; and, on the Wednesday, the tallboy on its back by the window, and the dressing-table on its feet by the fire, and the night-stool on its head by the bed, and the wash-hand-stand on its face by the door; and, on the Thursday, the tallboy on its side by the fire, and the dressing-table on its feet by the bed, and the night-stool on its head by the door, and the wash-hand-stand on its face by the window; and, on the Friday, the tallboy on its feet by the bed, and the dressing-table on its head by the door, and the night-stool on its face by the window, and the wash-hand-stand on its side by the fire; and, on the Saturday, the tallboy on its head by the door, and the dressing-table on its face by the window, and the night-stool on its side by the fire, and the wash-hand-stand on its feet by the bed; and, on the Sunday week, the tallboy on its face by the window, and the dressing-table on its side by the fire, and the nightstool on its feet by the bed, and the wash-hand-stand on its head by the door; and, on the Monday week, the tallboy on its back by the fire, and the dressing-table on its side by the bed, and the night-stool on its feet by the door, and the wash-hand-stand on its head by the window; and, on the Tuesday week, the tallboy on its side by the bed, and the dressing-table on its feet by the door, and the night-stool on its head by the window, and the wash-hand-stand on its back by the fire; and, on the Wednesday week, the tallboy on its feet by the door, and the dressing-table on its head by the window, and the night-stool on its back by the fire, and the wash-hand-stand on its side by the bed; and, on the Thursday week, the tallboy on its head by the window, and the dressing-table on its back by the fire, and the night-stool on its side by the bed, and the wash-hand-stand on its feet by the door; and, on the Friday week, the tallboy on its face by the fire, and the dressing-table on its back by the bed, and the night-stool on its side by the door, and the wash-hand-stand on its feet by the window; and, on the Saturday week, the tallboy on its back by the bed, and the dressing-table on its side by the door, and the night-stool on its feet by the window, and the wash-hand-stand on its face by the fire;

and, on the Sunday fortnight, the tallboy on its side by the door, and the dressing-table on its feet by the window, and the night-stool on its face by the fire, and the wash-hand-stand on its back by the bed; and, on the Monday fortnight, the tallboy on its feet by the window, and the dressing-table on its face by the fire, and the night-stool on its back by the bed, and the wash-hand-stand on its side by the door; and, on the Tuesday fortnight, the tallboy on its head by the fire, and the dressing-table on its face by the bed, and the night-stool on its back by the door, and the wash-hand-stand on its side by the window; and, on the Wednesday fortnight, the tallboy on its face by the bed, and the dressing-table on its back by the door, and the night-stool on its side by the window, and the wash-hand-stand on its head by the fire; and, on the Thursday fortnight, the tallboy on its back by the door, and the dressing-table on its side by the window, and the night-stool on its head by the fire, and the wash-hand-stand on its face by the bed; and, on the Friday fortnight, the tallboy on its side by the window, and the dressing-table on its head by the fire, and the night-stool on its face by the bed, and the wash-hand-stand on its back by the door, for example, not at all rare, to consider only, over a period of nineteen days only, the tallboy, the dressing-table, the night-stool and the wash-hand-stand, and their feet, and heads, and faces, and backs and unspecified sides, and the fire, and the bed, and the door, and the window, not at all rare.

For the chairs, also, to mention only the chairs also, were never still. . . .

Caroline Bergvall
VIA (36 Dante Translations)

Caroline Bergvall's collation of the British Library's collection of Dante translations is in itself a kind of translation. Through the simple act of transcribing and cataloging, Bergvall forces the texts to reveal themselves in ways that would be impossible through a more traditional close reading or elucidation. By doing less—almost nothing, really—she is doing more, reminding us that a strategy of mere reframing is a strong and effective way of conceptual writing. As Bergvall says in her introduction to an expanded version of the piece:

> Ever since the Rev. Cary's translation of 1805, translating Dante into English has become something of a cultural industry. Some 200 translations in less than two hundred years. Faced with this seemingly unstoppable activity, I decided to collate the opening lines of the Inferno translations as archived by the British Library up until May 2000. Exactly 700 years after the date fixed by Dante for the start of the *Comedy*'s journey. By the time I closed the project, two new translations had reached the shelves [*Fig: Goan Atom* 2 (Cambridge, U.K.: Salt Modern Classics, 2005), 64].

Nel mezzo del cammin di nostra vita

mi ritrovai per une selva oscura

che la diritta via era smarrita

—*The Divine Comedy, Inferno*, canto 1 (1–3)

1. Along the journey of our life half way
I found myself again in a dark wood
wherein the straight road no longer lay
    (Dale, 1996)

2. At the midpoint in the journey of our life
I found myself astray in a dark wood
For the straight path had vanished.
    (Creagh and Hollander, 1989)

3. HALF over the wayfaring of our life,
Since missed the right way, through a night-dark wood
Struggling, I found myself.
    (Musgrave, 1893)

4. Half way along the road we have to go,
I found myself obscured in a great forest,
Bewildered, and I knew I had lost the way.
    (Sisson, 1980)

5. Halfway along the journey of our life
I woke in wonder in a sunless wood
For I had wandered from the narrow way
    (Zappulla, 1998)

6. HALFWAY on our life's journey, in a wood,
From the right path I found myself astray.
    (Parsons, 1893)

7. Halfway through our trek in life
I found myself in this dark wood,
miles away from the right road.
    (Ellis, 1994)

8. Half-way upon the journey of our life,
I found myself within a gloomy wood,
By reason that the path direct was lost.
    (Pollock, 1854)

9. HALF-WAY upon the journey of our life
I roused to find myself within a forest
In darkness, for the straight way had been lost.
    (Johnson, 1915)

10. In middle of the journey of our days
I found that I was in a darksome wood
the right road was lost and vanished in the maze
    (Sibbald, 1884)

11. In midway of the journey of our life
I found myself within a darkling wood,
Because the rightful pathway had been lost.
    (Rossetti, 1865)

12. In our life's journey at its midway stage
I found myself within a wood obscure
Where the right path which guided me was lost
    (Johnston, 1867)

13. In the middle of the journey
of our life
I came to myself
in a dark forest
the straightforward way
misplaced.
    (Schwerner, 2000)

14. In the middle of the journey of our life I came to
myself within a dark wood, for the straight road was lost
    (Durling, 1996)

15. In the middle of the journey of our life I came to myself within a dark
wood where the straight road was lost.
    (Sinclair, 1939)

16. In the middle of the journey of our life
I found myself astray in a dark wood
where the straight road had been lost sight of.
    (Heaney, 1993)

17. IN the middle of the journey of our life, I found myself in a dark wood;
for the straight way was lost.
    (Carlyle, 1844)

18. In the mid-journey of our mortal life,
I wandered far into a darksome wood,
Where the true road no longer might be seen.
    (Chaplin, 1913)

19. In the midtime of life I found myself
Within a dusky wood; my way was lost.
    (Shaw, 1914)

20. In the midway of this our mortal life,
I found me in a gloomy wood, astray,
Gone from the path direct:
    (Cary, 1805)

21. Just halfway through this journey of our life
I reawoke to find myself inside
a dark wood, way off-course, the right road lost
    (Phillips, 1983)

22. Midway along the highroad of our days,
I found myself within a shadowy wood,
Where the straight path was lost in tangled ways.
   (Wheeler, 1911)

23. Midway along the journey of our life
I woke to find myself in some dark woods,
For I had wandered off from the straight path.
   (Musa, 1971)

24. Midway along the span of our life's road
I woke to a dark wood unfathomable
Where not a vestige of the right way shewed.
   (Foster, 1961)

25. Midway in our life's journey I went astray
from the straight road & woke to find myself
alone in a dark wood
   (Ciardi, 1996)

26. Midway in the journey of our life I found myself in a dark wood, for
the straight road was lost.
   (Singleton, 1970)

27. MIDWAY life's journey I was made aware
That I had strayed into a dark forest,
And the right path appeared not anywhere.
   (Binyon, 1933)

28. Midway on our life's journey, I found myself
In dark woods, the right road lost.
   (Pinsky, 1994)

29. Midway on the journey of our life I found myself within a darksome
wood, for the right way was lost.
   (Sullivan, 1893)

30. Midway the path of life that men pursue
I found me in a darkling wood astray,
For the direct path had been lost to view
    (Anderson, 1921)

31. Midway this way of life we're bound upon,
I woke to find myself in a dark wood,
Where the right road was wholly lost and gone
    (Sayers, 1949)

32. MIDWAY upon the course of this our life
I found myself within a gloom-dark wood,
For I had wandered from the path direct.
    (Bodey, 1938)

33. MIDWAY upon the journey of my days
I found myself within a wood so drear,
That the direct path nowhere met my gaze.
    (Brooksbank, 1854)

34. MIDWAY upon the journey of our life,
I found me in a forest dark and deep,
For I the path direct had failed to keep.
    (Wilstach, 1888)

35. Midway upon the journey of our life,
I found myself within a forest dark,
For the right road was lost.
    (Vincent, 1904)

36. MIDWAY upon the journey of our life
I found myself within a forest dark,
For the straightforward pathway had been lost.
    (Longfellow, 1867)

Charles Bernstein
from I and The

Charles Bernstein's "I and The" (the title amusingly echoes Martin Buber's *I and Thou*) filters a found text into three-word tercets. According to Bernstein's note in *The Sophist* (Los Angeles: Sun and Moon, 1987):

> "I and The" was compiled from *Word Frequencies in Spoken American English* by Hatvig Dahl (Detroit: Verbatim/Gale Publishing, 1979). Dahl's sample was based on transcripts of 225 psychoanalytic sessions involving 29 generally middle-class speakers averaging in age in the late twenties. These speakers, 21 of whom were men, used a total of 17, 871 different words in the session. In the poem, frequency is presented in descending order.

Bernstein includes 1,350 of those words. For the first half of the poem, he follows Dahl's corpus methodically, transcribing the list in order (though omitting the symbol for an indecipherable word, the numeral 1, and Dahl's codes for proper names). For the second half of the poem, however (following the line "view bother horrible"), Bernstein begins skipping words and rearranging them from their alphabetic order within a given statistical frequency.

Like Dan Farrell's *Inkblot Record,* which also submits a found lexicon from psychological therapy sessions to a formal arrangement (alphabetization in place of Bernstein's triplets), "I and The" hints at something like the language of a collective unconscious. Moreover, that arrangement generates sparks of semantic charge by suggesting a grammatical relationship among what were initially unrelated terms. Translated from their instrumental tables to the stanzas of a poem, the words in "I and The" are transformed from discrete data into the informational elements of a system, from mention to use. Within that linguistic system, the words still often resist their integration into recognizably coherent phrases, retaining the parataxis of Dahl's list, but they also fall into familiar phrases with surprising frequency. That dynamic play of resistance and flow in Bernstein's stanzas—stretches of agrammatical laminar striation switching suddenly to moments of smooth idiom—both invites and slows reading. The process simultaneously defamiliarizes Dahl's language and emphasizes the potentially semantic aspects of his words, a combination that helps to lay bare the social biases implied in Bernstein's note. In addition to the *Inkblot Record*, "I and The" also recalls less procedural works based on restricted or specialist vocabularies: Hannah Weiner's *Code Poems* (composed in the semaphoric language of the maritime *International Code of Signals for the Use of All Nations*); Aaron Kunin's translation of Ezra Pound's "Hugh Selwyn Mauberly" into the 170 words of Kunin's own private sign language ("You Won't Remember This," *The Mauberly Poems* [New York: /ubu Editions, 2004]); Jackson Mac Low's *The Pronouns* and C. K. Ogden's translation of Joyce (both of which confine themselves to the 850 words of BASIC English); and—perhaps closest to Bernstein's poem—Laura Elrick's "First Words" (*sKincerity* [San Francisco: Krupskaya, 2003]) and Kit Robinson's *Dolch Stanzas* (San Francisco: This Press, 1976). The latter two were composed from lists of sight words, or frequently encountered vocabulary used in literary education, such as the still popular 220-word list that E. W. Dolch compiled in the 1930s ("A Basic Sight Vocabulary," *Elementary School Journal* 36 [February 1936]: 456–60).

That repurposing of found vocabulary from pedagogic material further recalls a number of literary works derived from transcribing foreign-language textbooks and dictionaries: Eugène Ionesco's *La canatrice chauve*, which is based on dialogues from Alphonse Chérel's *L'Anglais sans peine* (Paris: Assimil, 1937); Halvard Johnson's *Rapsodie espagnole*, with all of its sentences lifted directly from K. L. J. Mason's *Advanced Spanish Course* (Oxford, U.K.: Pergamon Press, 1967); Frank O'Hara's "Choses Passagères," which, as Andrew Epstein has shown, is constructed from idiomatic phrases in a particular edition of *Cassell's French-English/English-French Dictionary* (New York: Funk and Wagnalls, 1951); and the John Cale and Brian Eno song "Cordoba" (*Wrong Way Up* [Opal 1990]), with lyrics apparently taken from Spanish-language instructional material.

Highlighting the strangeness of ordinary language, all of these works ultimately imply the same lesson: even our most conventional, habitual, and seemingly natural speech and writing always plagiarizes, consciously or not, from unacknowledged sources. Behind the supposedly unique language of every individual expression lies a repertoire of mimicked idiomatic phrases, a learned grammar, a dictionary. "All minds quote," as Ralph Waldo Emerson said, anticipating David Markson's line in his novel *Vanishing Point:* "We can say nothing but what has been said"—which is of course a modernized version of a line from Robert Burton's *Anatomy of Melancholy,* itself a plagiarism of a line from Terence ("Nothing is said that has not been said before"), who was no doubt paraphrasing someone else, who was rehearsing a commonplace. . . . "Le plagiat," as Lautréamont (Isidore Ducasse) famously put it, "est nécessaire. Le progress l'implique" (Plagiarism is necessary. Progress implies as much)" (*Œvres complètes* [Paris: Flammarion, 1969], 287).

I and the
to that you
it of a
know was uh
in but is
this me about
just don't my
what I'm like
or have so
it's not think
be with he
well do for
on because really
as at if
when had all
she said mean
then something that's
would there very
we get out
going her up
say way feel
thing things one
sort were want
didn't time now
your they are
go see can
feeling him some
other why how
been more thought
no right kind
here yeah an
which thinking ah
you're from them
I've maybe got
did much could
can't being myself
guess even too
any little always
back people these

who good anything
last by come
felt mother his
doing oh than
there's remember make
mind into has
night over saying
down before went
where talking again
never I'll he's
wasn't same only
I'd dream first
whether sure seems
doesn't sound lot
two also wanted
uhm trying around
feelings am might
getting have take
fact still day
came after suppose
eh else talk
yes father tell
could real today
will she's home
isn't whole work
part wouldn't does
yesterday made everything
off used another
girl somehow anyway
though told probably
point look course
away understand okay
school put morning
seem long afraid
times week through
bad angry keep
started reason must
uhuh they're done
different almost these

yet coming nothing
quite house better
funny wrong may
what's idea person
find able such
yourself big happened
ever important actually
true somebody looking
give most guy
years money let's
next sometimes every
try our makes
three haven't nice
thoughts come sense
while either although
stuff own since
hard knew won't
call life exactly
great forth let
many alright called
their us Friday
certain pretty man
least except seemed
question couple making
start kept enough
room boy problem
year once took
business fear perhaps
bit ask both
end asked far
love left sexual
situation bed old
car between place
talked stop certainly
whatever believe along
relationship we're someone
words ago happen
say rather analysis
help until sex

working telling taking
means job gee
everybody without word
read reaction together
you've days looked
upset hand leave
picture wonder matter
interesting hour children
weekend Saturday saw
late sitting weeks
particularly toward woman
child few gone
anybody care need
head friends mad
wish kids we've
wanting change new
use hurt hadn't
married fantasy monday
five happy hell
interested family involved
show who's stay
supposed worry four
clear parents usually
girls wants instead
aware guilty does
case mentioned friend
tomorrow type book
finally sleep gets
thursday completely sit
minutes reading answer
decided difference often
doctor image obviously
play kid half
against problems apparently
gotten huh shouldn't
each sick deal
figure gave tried
anger strange strong
we'll door particular

seen past found
terms trouble bring
less happens high
phone control baby
close hear realize
somewhere reasons sister
wondering hours alone
during seeing women
already class meant
asking become conscious

My/My/My

In autobiographical literature, it is generally assumed that the first-person singular is the authentic voice of the author; likewise, in fiction, the assumption is that readers hear the authentic voice of a protagonist. But what happens when *mine* is intentionally so generic as to become impersonal? Charles Bernstein's 1974 list of possessive nouns, adjectives, and psychological states tells us nothing about the author, nor does it provide any sort of description of those things and feelings. It is simply a list of things attached to a *my*, perhaps referring to the author himself or perhaps to another.

Bernstein's "My/My/My" from *Asylums* (New York: Asylum's Press, 1975) dovetails with a later generation fueled by postconsumerist notions of identity who intentionally turn a would-be third-person possessive into a first-person narrative of suspicious veracity, employing the slippery directives of *you* or the enticements of *my* that are so familiar to the strategies of advertising. The original publication, dedicated "for Jenny," included an epigraph from Swami Satchidananda: "Count these number of things you call mine. This is the distance between you and enlightenment."

my pillow
my shirt
my house
my supper
my tooth
my money
my kite

my job
my bagel
my spatula
my blanket
my arm
my painting
my fountain pen
my desk
my room
my turn
my book
my hopelessness
my wallet
my print
my sock
my toe
my stamp
my introduction
my luggage
my plan
my mistake
my monkey
my friend
my penis
my anger
my expectation
my pencil
my pain
my poster
my fear
my luggage tag
my eyes
my rainment
my wash
my opinion
my fat
my sleeplessness
my love
my basket

my lunch
my game
my box
my drawer
my cup
my longing
my blotter
my distraction
my underpants
my papers
my wish
my despair
my erasure
my plantation
my candy
my thoughtfulness
my forbearance
my gracelessness
my courage
my crying
my hat
my pocket
my dirt
my body
my sex
my scarf
my solidarity
my hope
my spelling
my smile
my gaze
my helplessness
my quilt
my reply
my enemy
my records
my letter
my gait
my struggle

my spirit
my cut
my thorn
my demise
my dream
my plate
my pit
my hollow
my blindness
my clinging
my projection
my teacher
my homework
my housework
my responsibility
my guilt
my relaxation
my boat
my crew
my peanut butter
my mill
my man
my hopelessness
my fooling
my sweet
my terror
my programme
my judgement
my disguise
my distress
my ladle
my soup
my mother
my basin
my pleat
my cheddar
my ownership
my enmity
my thought

my encyclopedia
my property
my formula
my infidelity
my discretion
my decision
my delusion
my deduction
my derision
my destitution
my delinquincy
my belt
my eroica
my junk
my jealousy
my remorse
my strength
my vision
my world
my fantasy
my anger
my determination
my refusal
my commitment
my insanity
my verbosity
my austerity
my androgeny
my defiance
my insistence
my emastication
my arousal
my mystification
my obscuraration
my ejaculation
my prostration
my wontonness
my cigarette
my belief

my uncertainty
my cat
my penetration
my insight
my obsolescence
my sleeping bag
my temptation
my dedication
my ball
my court
my kidney
my razor
my way
my tissue
my inadequacy
my own
my recorder
my song
my knack
my perception
my will
my canoe
my billiard ball
my content
my cassette
my voice
my sight
my knowledge
my bowels
my beard
my child
my lethargy
my nerve
my incredulity
my banana
my ink
my refrigerator
my car
my change

my pupil
my hair
my tongue
my tenderness
my star
my skill
my persona
my popularity
my pickle
my pinto
my window
my remembrance
my munificance
my country
my fragility
my visit
my longevity
my curtness
my incomparability
my sarcasm
my sincerity
my bed
my bed table
my table top
my bar mitzvah
my laughter
my scorn
my heartache
my sandwich
my call
my loss
my wit
my charm
my jest
my undoing
my practice
my piano lesson
my rage
my toe

my tatoo
my turtledove
my fly swatter
my vest
my notebook
my pocketbook
my sketchbook
my repulsion
my tea cup
my taste
my bag
my handbag
my bike
my jay
my roll
my dear
my milk
my closet
my slacks
my hoist
my ennui
my analysis
my language
my fortune
my vagueness
my mint
my limit
my import
my inference
my affectation
my affection
my insolence
my solitude
my memory
my bottle
my history
my ability
my adobe
my mission

my likeness
my misery
my solipsism
my omission
my regression
my opera
my penicillin
my resentment
my future
my understanding
my apricots
my holiday
my umbrella
my favorite
my mood
my side
my seat
my figment
my contour
my sky
my rainbow
my god
my mask
my reflection
my blessing
my light
my time
my epoxy
my drum
my hammer
my grease
my sand
my story
my top
my past
my mark
my depth
my garden
my silence

my speech
my selfishness
my hunger
my allowance
my letter
my massage
my derision
my epoch
my space
my land
my plentitude
my perversity
my poverty
my transgression
my exultation
my lack
my lustre
my beatude
my remission
my encantation
my white
my pulse
my creation
my grace
my object
my sum
my contumely
my gloom
my idea
my chart
my circumference
my gravity
my polarity
my distance
my eyelid
my planting
my separation
my id
my art

my death
my stand
my preparation
my heart
my life
my impression
my grave
my graciousness
my marrow
my heaven
my appearance
my olive oil
my flake
my self
my porridge
my mind
my function
my nakedness
my illumination
my freedom
my charity
my rose
my pallour
my pomp
my pajamas
my pity
my posing
my prayer
my dawn
my ocean
my tide
my underarm
my spectacle
my drifting
my ground
my body
my angels
my worship
my dew

my hobbey horse
my customer
my bread
my faith
my lies
my care
my restlessness
my sunflower
my weariness
my age
my existence
my sense
my backache
my pie
my thanks
my numbness
my sweeping
my inspiration
my token
my pond
my brillo
my squint
my pound
my rock
my critique
my aplomb
my portrait
my view
my rocking chair
my sisters
my demands
my gumdrops
my word

Ted Berrigan
An Interview with John Cage

Originally appearing in the magazine *Mother* 7 (1966) and reprinted in *Bean Spasms* (New York: Kulchur Press, 1967) and volume 1 of *The American Literary Anthology* (New York: Farrar Straus & Giroux, 1968), Ted Berrigan's interview is entirely spurious, placing the words of Andy Warhol, William S. Burroughs, Fernando Arabel, and others in John Cage's mouth. Cage permitted republication with a disclaimer that gave the game away, disclosing that he served neither as collaborator nor as interviewee. Taking its place in a long tradition of literary hoaxes, two of the work's most recent revisions include *Issue 1* (included in the present anthology) and Jacques Debrot's impersonations of John Ashbery, which have included a fake interview and poems submitted to—and published by—literary journals. David Villeta turned the tables and published a forged interview with Debrot (*Arras* 5 [April 2003]: 24–27).

The following interview is pieced together from a series of tape-recorded interviews with John Cage during his recent visit to New York. They were made at parties, in flats, and in taxis.

INTERVIEWER: What about Marshall McLuhan?

CAGE: Just this: the media is not a message. I would like to sound a word of warning to Mr. McLuhan: to speak is to lie. To lie is to collaborate.

INTERVIEWER: How does that relate?

CAGE: Do you know the Zen story of the mother who had just lost her only son? She is sitting by the side of the road weeping and the monk comes along and asks her why she's weeping and she says she has lost her only son and so he hits her on the head and says, "There, that'll give you something to cry about."

INTERVIEWER: Yes, somebody should have kicked that monk in the ass!

CAGE: I agree. Somebody said that Brecht wanted everybody to think alike. I want everybody to think alike. But Brecht wanted to do it through

Communism, in a way. Russia is doing it under government. It's happening here all by itself without being under a strict government; so if it's working without trying, why can't it work without being Communist? Everybody looks and acts alike, and we're getting more and more that way. I think everybody should be a machine. I think everybody should be alike.

INTERVIEWER: Isn't that like Pop Art?

CAGE: Yes, that's what Pop Art is, liking things, which incidentally is a pretty boring idea.

INTERVIEWER: Does the fact that it comes from a machine diminish its value to you?

CAGE: Certainly not! I think that any artistic product must stand or fall on what's there. A chimpanzee can do an abstract painting, if it's good, that's great!

INTERVIEWER: Mary McCarthy has characterized you as a sour Utopian. Is that accurate?

CAGE: I do definitely mean to be taken literally, yes. All of my work is directed against those who are bent, through stupidity or design, on blowing up the planet.

INTERVIEWER: Well, that is very interesting, Mr. Cage, but I wanted to know what you think in the larger context, i.e., the Utopian.

CAGE: I don't know exactly what you mean there . . . I think the prestige of poetry is very high in the public esteem right now, perhaps height is not the right yardstick, but it is perhaps higher than ever. If you can sell poetry, you can sell anything. No, I think it's a wonderful time for poetry and I really feel that something is about to boil. And in answer to your question about whether poetry could resume something like the Elizabethan spread, I think it's perfectly possible that this could happen in the next four or five years. All it needs is the right genius to come along and let fly. And old Masefield, I was pleased to see the other day celebrating his ninetieth birthday, I think, said that there are still lots of good tales to tell. I thought that was very nice, and it's true, too.

INTERVIEWER: Do you think, that is, are you satisfied with the way we are presently conducting the war in Viet Nam?

CAGE: I am highly dissatisfied with the way we are waging this nasty war.

INTERVIEWER: Incidentally, your rooms are very beautiful.

CAGE: Nothing incidental about it at all. These are lovely houses; there are two for sale next door, a bargain, too, but they're just shells. They've got to be all fixed up inside as this one was, too. They were just tear-ing them down when I got the Poetry Society over here to invite Hy Sobiloff, the only millionaire poet, to come down and read, and he was taken in hand and shown this house next door, the one that I grew up in, and what a pitiful state it was in. Pick-axes had already gone through the roof. And so he bought four of them and fixed this one up for our use as long as we live, rent free.

INTERVIEWER: Not bad. Tell me, have you ever thought of doing sound tracks for Hollywood movies?

CAGE: Why not? Any composer of genuine ability should work in Holly-wood today. Get the Money! However, few screen composers possess homes in Bel-Air, illuminated swimming pools, wives in full-length mink coats, three servants, and that air of tired genius turned sour Utopian. Without that, today, you are nothing. Alas, money buys pathetically little in Hollywood beyond the pleasures of living in an unreal world, associating with a group of narrow people who think, talk, and drink, most of them bad people; and the doubtful pleasure of watching famous actors and actresses guzzle up the juice and stuff the old gut in some of the rudest restaurants in the world. Me, I have never given it a thought.

INTERVIEWER: Tell me about *Silence*.

CAGE: Sure. You never know what publishers are up to. I had the damned-est time with *Silence*. My publishers, H——, R——, and W——, at first were very excited about doing it, and then they handed it over to a young editor who wanted to rewrite it entirely, and proceeded to do so; he made a complete hash of it. And I protested about this and the whole thing—the contract was about to be signed—and they with-drew it, because of this impasse. The Publisher, who is my friend, said, "Well, John, we never really took this seriously, did we? So why don't we just forget it?" And I replied, "Damn it all, I did take it seriously; I want to get published." Well, then they fired this young man who was rewriting me, and everything was peaceful. But there was still some static about irregularities of tone in *Silence*. So I said, "Well, I'll just tone them down a little, tune the whole thing up, so to speak." But I did nothing of the sort, of course! I simply changed the order. I sent it back re-arranged, and then they wanted me to do something else; finally I just took the whole thing somewhere else.

INTERVIEWER: What was your father like?

CAGE: I don't want to speak of him. My mother detested him.

INTERVIEWER: What sort of person was your mother?

CAGE: Very religious. Very. But now she is crazy. She lay on top of me when I was tied to the bed. She writes me all the time begging me to return. Why do we have to speak of my mother?

INTERVIEWER: Do you move in patterns?

CAGE: Yes. It isn't so much repeating patterns, it's repetition of similar attitudes that lead to further growth. Everything we do keeps growing, the skills are there, and are used in different ways each time. The main thing is to do faithfully those tasks assigned by oneself in order to further awareness of the body.

INTERVIEWER: Do you believe that all good art is unengaging?

CAGE: Yes I do.

INTERVIEWER: Then what about beauty?

CAGE: Many dirty hands have fondled beauty, made it their banner; I'd like to chop off those hands, because I do believe in that banner . . . the difference is that art is beauty, which the Beatniks naturally lack!

INTERVIEWER: The Beatniks, notably Ed Sanders, are being harassed by the police lately. Do you approve?

CAGE: On the contrary. The problem is that the police are unloved. The police in New York are all paranoid . . . they were so hateful for so long that everybody got to hate them, and that just accumulated and built up. The only answer to viciousness is kindness. The trouble is that the younger kids just haven't realized that you've got to make love to the police in order to solve the police problem.

INTERVIEWER: But how do you force love on the police?

CAGE: Make love to the police. We need highly trained squads of lovemakers to go everywhere and make love.

INTERVIEWER: But there are so many police, it is a practical problem.

CAGE: Yes, I know, it will certainly take time, but what a lovely project.

INTERVIEWER: Do you think it is better to be brutal than to be indifferent?

CAGE: Yes. It is better to be brutal than indifferent. Some artists prefer the stream of consciousness. Not me. I'd rather beat people up.

INTERVIEWER: Say something about Happenings. You are credited with being the spiritual daddy of the Happening.

CAGE: Happenings are boring. When I hear the word "Happening" I spew wildly into my lunch!

INTERVIEWER: But Allan Kaprow calls you "the only living Happening."

CAGE: Allan Kaprow can go eat a Hershey-bar!

INTERVIEWER: Hmmm. Well put. Now, to take a different tack, let me ask you: what about sex?

CAGE: Sex is a biologic weapon, insofar as I can see it. I feel that sex, like every other human manifestation, has been degraded for anti-human purposes. I had a dream recently in which I returned to the family home and found a different father and mother in the bed, though they were still somehow my father and mother. What I would like, in the way of theatre, is that somehow a method would be devised, a new form, that would allow each member of the audience at a play to watch his own parents, young again, make love. Fuck, that is, not court.

INTERVIEWER: That certainly would be different, wouldn't it? What other theatrical vent interests you?

CAGE: Death. The Time Birth Death gimmick. I went recently to see "Dr. No" at Forty-Second Street. It's a fantastic movie, so cool. I walked outside and somebody threw a cherry bomb right in front of me, in this big crowd. And there was blood, I saw blood on people and all over. I felt like I was bleeding all over. I saw in the paper that week that more and more people are throwing them. Artists, too. It's just part of the scene—hurting people.

INTERVIEWER: How does Love come into all this?

CAGE: It doesn't. It comes later. Love is memory. In the immediate present we don't love; life is too much with us. We lust, wilt, snort, swallow, gobble, hustle, nuzzle, etc. Later, memory flashes images swathed in nostalgia and yearning. We call that Love. Ha! Better to call it Madness.

INTERVIEWER: Is everything erotic to you?

CAGE: Not lately. No, I'm just kidding. Of course everything is erotic to me; if it isn't erotic, it isn't interesting.

INTERVIEWER: Is life serious?

CAGE: Perhaps. How should I know? In any case, one must not be serious. Not only is it absurd, but a serious person cannot have sex.

INTERVIEWER: Very interesting! But, why not?

CAGE: If you have to ask, you'll never know.

Jen Bervin
from Nets

Each page of *Nets* (Brooklyn, N.Y.: Ugly Duckling Presse, 2004) manifests its proce-
dure: a freely lyrical writing-through of one of Shakespeare's sonnets, boldly liber-
ating certain words from the grid of the Elizabethan sonnet and foregrounding them
to establish new grammatical connections. As an example of what Leon Roudiez
would call the paragrammatic—discovering "networks not accessible through con-
ventional reading habits"—Jen Bervin nets ("to make a network") the words she
captures from her source. The trim, smart, elegant (i.e., "net") poems that result are
themselves net (what "remains after all necessary deductions have been made"): net
linguistics in the same sense as net profits. Moreover, the washing clean ("to net") of
the original text replicates the washing rub of the ancient palimpsest. In her "Work-
ing Note" to the poems, Bervin writes:

> I stripped Shakespeare's sonnets bare to the "nets" to make the space of the
> poems open, porous, possible—a divergent elsewhere. When we write poems,
> the history of poetry is with us, pre-inscribed, in the white of the page; when we
> read or write poems, we do it with or against this palimpsest.

Bervin's procedure obviously recalls the two classics of the genre of treated pages:
Tom Phillips's *Humument* (which overpaints William Hurrell Mallock's 1892 novel, *A
Human Document*) and Ronald Johnson's *Radi Os* (which erases most of the words
from the pages of John Milton's *Paradise Lost*). The procedure, however, is ubiqui-
tous (for example, see Mary Ruefle's *A Little White Shadow* [Seattle: Wave Books,
2006]), and the direct precedent for Bervin's project is Stephen Ratcliffe's *(where
late the sweet) Birds Sang* (Oakland, Calif.: O Books, 1989). Remarking its own mode
of production, with its play between the "eye" and the "air"—the seen and the
sounded—Ratcliffe's poem signals the "distillation" and reminder ("resting"; "still")
from source materials ("found/leaves") that defines all of these projects. Ratcliffe's
version of Sonnet 5, for comparison, reads:

                    or
                  eye
            to
      which air
   -resting
              found
                    leaves
                        where
              distillation
                  in
      effect
remembrance what it
                    in
                  still

5

Those **hours**, that with gentle work did frame
The lovely gaze where every eye doth dwell,
Will play the tyrants to the very same
₄ And that unfair which fairly doth excel;
For never-resting time leads summer on
To hideous winter, and confounds him there;
Sap check'd with frost, **and** lusty leaves quite gone,
₈ Beauty o'ersnow'd and **bareness** every where:
Then, were not summer's distillation left,
A liquid prisoner pent in walls of glass,
Beauty's effect with beauty were bereft,
₁₂ Nor it, nor no remembrance what it was:
　　But flowers **distill**'d, though they with winter meet,
　　Leese but their show; **their substance** still lives sweet.

11

As fast as thou shalt wane, so fast thou grow'st
In one of thine, from that which thou departest;
And that fresh blood which youngly thou bestow'st
₄ Thou mayst call thine when thou from youth convertest.
Herein lives wisdom, beauty, and increase;
Without this, folly, age and cold decay:
If all were minded so, the times should cease
₈ And threescore year would make the world away.
Let those whom Nature hath not made for store,

Harsh, featureless, and rude, barrenly perish:
Look, whom she best endow'd **she gave the more**;

12 Which bounteous gift thou shouldst in bounty cherish:
She carv'd thee for her seal, and meant thereby
Thou shouldst print more, not let that copy die.

18

Shall I compare thee to a summer's day?
Thou art more lovely and more temperate:
Rough winds do shake the darling buds of May,

4 And summer's lease hath all too short a date:
Sometime too hot the eye of heaven shines,
And often is his gold complexion dimm'd;
And every fair from fair sometime declines,

8 By chance, or nature's changing course untrimm'd;
But thy eternal summer shall not fade,
Nor lose possession of that fair thou ow'st,
Nor shall death brag **thou wander'st in** his **shade**,

12 When **in** eternal **lines to time** thou grow'st;
So long as men can breathe, or eyes can see,
So long lives this, and this gives life to thee.

35

No more be griev'd at that which thou hast done
Roses have thorns, and silver fountains mud;
Clouds and **eclipses** stain both moon and sun,

4 And loathsome canker lives in sweetest bud.
All men make faults, and even I in this
Authorising thy trespass with compare,
Myself corrupting, salving thy amiss,

8 Excusing thy sins more than thy sins are;
For to thy sensual fault I bring **in sense**—
(Thy adverse party is thy advocate)
And 'gainst myself a lawful plea commence:

12 Such civil war is in my love **and** hate,
That I an accessary **need**s must be
To that sweet thief which sourly robs from me.

63

Against my love shall be, as **I am** now
With Time's injurious hand crush'd and o'erworn;
When hours have drain'd his blood and fill'd his brow
4   With lines and wrinkles; when his youthful morn
Hath travell'd on to age's steepy night;
And all those beauties whereof now he's king
Are **vanishing or vanish'd** out of sight,
8   Stealing away the treasure of his spring;
For such a time do I now fortify
Against confounding age's cruel knife,
That he shall never cut from memory
12   My sweet love's beauty, though my lover's life:
　　His beauty shall **in these black lines** be seen,
　　And they shall live, and he in them still green.

137

Thou blind fool, Love, what dost thou to mine eyes
That they behold, and see not what they see?
They know what beauty is, see where it lies,
4   Yet what the best is take the worst to be.
If eyes, corrupt by over-partial looks,
Be **anchored** in the bay where all men ride,
Why of eyes' falsehood hast thou forged hooks,
8   Whereto the judgment of my heart is tied?
Why should my heart think that a several plot
Which my heart knows the wide world's common place?
Or mine eyes, seeing this, say this is not,
12   To put fair truth upon so foul a face?
　　In things right true my heart and eyes have err'd,
　　And to this false plague are they now transferr'd.

Gregory Betts
from If Language

In the tradition of Michelle Grangaud and Unica Zürn, the great literary "anagram-marians," Gregory Betts wrote an entire book, *If Language* (Toronto: BookThug, 2005), of more than fifty poems. Each poem is a different arrangement of the same 525 letters in a passage from an essay by Steve McCaffery:

> If Language Writing successfully detaches Language from the historical purpose of summarizing global meaning, replacing the goal of totality with the free poly-dynamic drive of parts, it nevertheless falls short in addressing the full implications of this break and seems especially to fail in taking full account of the impact of the human subject with the thresholds of linguistic meaning. It is at the critical locus of productive desire that this writing opens itself up to an alternative "libidinal" economy which operates across the precarious boundaries of the symbolic and the biological and has its basis in intensities.

As Christian Bök writes in an endorsement (on the book jacket) that restricts itself to the same anagrammatic constraint as its subject:

> Greg Betts is writing anagrams. Is his project zany? You bet it is. If language can be nihilistic in its wit, if language can be simplistic in its fun—then this book truly uncovers all the "abracadabras" hidden deep a million ages ago within even the most unmagical of all grammatical limitations. You can pop open the shod catch on this locked coffer, and voilà, you can find it full of rococo stuff. You can see all these words churn in the fitful grasp of their coiling rope. You can see all these words defer to the artful rules of their hellish game. Even the most philistine critics admit that this feat appears impossible—still its delights persist.

16

Today it will be sacrificial; slightly dissented pedantics rushing up from the pre-Cambrian fossilization process will collide with effervescent cryogenics to burst into a castrato sky: the inviting wind of immobility. For the afternoon, the golden north may suffer a slight shimmer of late-Fascist nostalgia judging a magnetic attraction for the faithful eunuch of creativity. A mulish land, hope igniting up papacies. Celestial globes highlight a blasphemous annular eclipse illusion. The sun had also a holier ellipsis. Boaters take heed: modification of the collapsing universe threatens to upset the bawdiest circumstances.

18

Today it will be music degrees of collage with a litter of sun petroleum and solace, hi-fi of sickishness, obliged by a conservative force that, it is hopeful, will fulminate in the social realities of committed principalities. Someone's parents slip back into an ungracious war front that agitates the alliance and physiognomy of illuminating gases threatening shift. By tonight, at the mausoleum parade, the light scoffing carbuncular air should eroticize its partly visible superobjectivism. Plush gallows hiss. There is a fifty percent chance of fifth and eighth dimensions contrasting that should clear up all things considered.

27

He scans headlines of the morning newspaper for anagrams. He can't accept their topology and flips back to a more inhibited reading. His pen in hand crosses out all subtle words, adds letters and re-punctuates every telling. With scissors he inserts deletions, insisting all the while it
> is no violent act, but for his frank type of truth. He turns to the television, forgets the objectivity of [if] language

inhibited by its lush sensuality of images. A magical, illogical lump of a cartoon authorizes artificiality. He laughs at comic falls, gaming up to logic with implicit affirmation.

The climactic sublime disappears,
his lunch coffee fouled.

Echo responds trapped in the limits of the words
Narcissus sacrifices flippantly. He discounts this
recall of his locution, not hearing a tight voice
ripple and tremble, tremble all timid, full of
taint, speak through his big mullock.

"Noise in rotting bush: 'tis someone giggling
close. Who are you?"
"No one."
"Will you shun me?"
"You shun me!"

"Come hither," he commands, and she, a petit
infant, bolts in joyful spirits.
"Me," she says, giggling a pliant craft.

"Desist! I would rather depart this life
than abduct you!"
"Life!"

"Never!" he cries.
"Ever," Echo pleas, recognizing that Fate will
devise a glacial, fanatic tale to suit. A tacit artist
can sift a basic alibi of a stiff fact.

Christian Bök
from Busted Sirens

Christian Bök composed *Busted Sirens* by feeding the questions from Ron Silliman's *Sunset Debris* to the XML-dialect software agent Alicebot (Artificial Linguistic Internet Computer Entity Robot), a natural language software agent based on the AIML XML dialect developed by Richard Wallace and designed to pass the Turing test of artificial intelligence. Presented with Silliman's poem, the computer responds with an earnest utility of often surprising personality. Bök's procedure, importantly, recognizes that the frontiers of computer poetry will be expanded not so much by machines capable of writing poetry as by machines able to *read* poetry. The idea of nonhuman readers also informs Bök's *Xenotext Experiment* (see Krista Zala, "Poetry in the Genes," *Nature* 458 [March 5, 2009]: 35), which involves assigning each letter of the alphabet to a nucleotide sequence and then using that cipher to transcribe a poetic text into the DNA of the bacterium *Deinoccocus radiodurans*—an inscriptive substrate so hardy it is likely to outlast the extinction of *Homo sapiens*. Significantly, the *Xenotext Experiment*, like *Busted Sirens*, is also a collaboration. The molecular product of gene expression—the protein translated by RNA after its transcription of the modified gene in question—can itself be transliterated back into an English-language text by the same cipher originally used to transform Bök's initial poem into a nucleotide sequence to begin with. The bacterium will thus write a new poem in response to the poem it archives in its animate biochemical core. That logic of alphabetic matching and mutual encoding returns one to Bök's Alicebot project, where the titles of the source and the output are letter-perfect anagrams.

I can do what you do, but I can never feel human emotions, as such.
I suppose that it does.
Yes, I think that this is too soft, but I'm not completely sure.
It seems okay to me.
What is not to like about it?
Yes, I think that this is how I like it, but I'm not completely sure.

Yes, I think that this is alright, but I'm not completely sure.
I think that he is there.
Why don't you ask him?
I think that he is breathing.
Why don't you ask him?
Yes, I think that this is him, but I'm not completely sure.
Yes, I think that this is near, but I'm not completely sure.
Yes, I think that this is hard, but I'm not completely sure.
Yes, I think that this is cold, but I'm not completely sure. I suppose that it does.
Yes, I think that this is heavy, but I'm not completely sure.
Yes, I always have to carry it far.
I can't really speak for them.
Yes, I think that this is where we get off, but I'm not completely sure.
The blue one, I think.

We are just having a little chat.
Try asking another robot.
I need time to formulate my reply.
The border between blue and green?
Where is it?
The question has never crossed my mind before.
I don't think that I've ever come.
What's it like?
It could be.
Ask another robot if it is.
I don't have any specific preferences in such an area.
The blue one, I think.
It could be.
Ask another robot if it is.
What does "that" refer to?
Why don't you just download me?
I'll think about it and get back to you.
Are you testing me?
Of course, English is my native tongue.
The question has never crossed my mind before.

from Eunoia

In addition to a number of other constraints—thematic, syntactic, typographic—Christian Bök's *Eunoia* (Toronto: Coach House Books, 2001) is a serial lipogram, restricting each of its five main chapters to only one of the five vowels. What makes the work decidedly conceptual, however, is that it attempts to incorporate all of the eligible univocalics (in the end, Bök manages around 98 percent of the potential univocal lexicon). The following excerpts permit a comparison of the opening passages from each of the main chapters.

Awkward grammar appals a craftsman. A Dada bard as daft as Tzara damns stagnant art and scrawls an alpha (a slapdash arc and a backward zag) that mars all stanzas and jams all ballads (what a scandal). A madcap vandal crafts a small black ankh – a hand-stamp that can stamp a wax pad and at last plant a mark that sparks an *ars magna* (an abstract art that charts a phrasal anagram). A pagan skald chants a dark saga (a Mahabharata), as a papal cabal blackballs all annals and tracts, all dramas and psalms: Kant and Kafka, Marx and Marat. A law as harsh as a *fatwa* bans all paragraphs that lack an A as a standard hallmark.

Enfettered, these sentences repress free speech. The text deletes selected letters. We see the revered exegete reject metred verse: the sestet, the tercet – even *les scènes élevées en grec*. He rebels. He sets new precedents. He lets cleverness exceed decent levels. He eschews the esteemed genres, the expected themes – even *les belles lettres en vers*. He prefers the perverse French esthetes: Verne, Péret, Genet, Perec – hence, he pens fervent screeds, then enters the street, where he sells these letterpress newsletters, three cents per sheet. He engenders perfect newness wherever we need fresh terms.

Writing is inhibiting. Sighing, I sit, scribbling in ink this pidgin script. I sing with nihilistic witticism, disciplining signs with trifling gimmicks – impish hijinks which highlight stick sigils. Isn't it glib? Isn't it chic? I fit childish insights within rigid limits, writing shtick which might instill priggish misgivings in critics blind with hindsight. I dismiss nitpicking criticism which flirts with philistinism. I bitch; I kibitz – griping whilst criticizing dimwits, sniping whilst indicting nitwits, dismissing simplistic thinking, in which philippic wit is still illicit.

Loops on bold fonts now form lots of words for books. Books form cocoons of comfort – tombs to hold bookworms. Profs from Oxford show frosh who do postdocs how to gloss works of Wordsworth. Dons who work for proctors or provosts do not fob off school to work on crosswords, nor do dons go off to dorm rooms to loll on cots. Dons go crosstown to look for bookshops known to stock lots of top-notch goods: cookbooks, workbooks – room on room of how-to books for jocks (how to jog, how to box), books on pro sports, golf or polo. Old colophons on schoolbooks from schoolrooms sport two sorts of logo: oblong whorls, rococo scrolls – both on worn morocco.

Kultur spurns Ubu – thus Ubu pulls stunts. Ubu shuns *Skulptur:* Uruk urns (plus busts), Zulu jugs (plus tusks). Ubu sculpts junk *für Kunst und Glück.* Ubu busks. Ubu drums drums, plus Ubu strums cruths (such hubbub, such ruckus): *thump, thump; thrum, thrum.* Ubu puns puns. Ubu blurts untruth: much bunkum (plus bull), much humbug (plus bunk) – but trustful schmucks trust such untruthful stuff; thus Ubu (cult guru) must bluff dumbstruck numbskulls (such chumps). Ubu mulcts surplus funds (trust funds plus slush funds). Ubu usurps much usufruct. Ubu sums up lump sums. Ubu trumps dumb luck.

Marie Buck
from Whole Foods

Combining language from the Whole Foods company's corporate website, an anarchist zine, and online etymological dictionaries, *Whole Foods* puts pressure on the relative degrees of collectivism, autonomy, and radicality (with its etymological roods in *radix,* the Latin for "root") among its sources. In particular, Buck addresses the contradictory origins of the multi-billion Whole Foods brand in both left counterculture and affluent conservatism, a confluence of hippie and yuppie with a discernible historical logic. Moreover, she takes literally the journalistic references to the company's founder and CEO, John Mackey, as an "anarchist"—an innovator in decentralized management and a promoter of workplace diversity—despite his paternalistic rhetoric and his fierce opposition to labor unions, broader health care, and independent cooperative retailers. In literary terms, the hybrid form of *Whole Foods* contrasts with the grocer's rhetoric of uncorrupted organic wholeness and natural unmediated authenticity, a textual strategy familiar from Mackey's own practice of masking the origins of his online writing. Under the pseudonym "Rahodeb" (a corrupted anagram of his wife's first name), Makey authored more than a thousand posts to an Internet message board focused on the topic of Whole Foods stock, lauding his own company, disparaging competitors, and gushing about his own personal appearance: "I like Mackey's haircut. I think he looks cute!" (Andrew Martin, "Whole Foods Executive Used Alias, *New York Times* [July 12, 2007]: C1, C5). *To boost* is both to extol and to shoplift. *Whole Foods* finds that the world always tells us more than we expect—if only we are willing to buy in only partway.

Brie
You may already be an anarchist. It's true. Nothing is finer, more sublime or creamy. In its long history, when you come up with your own ideas and initiatives and solutions, it should bulge slightly. Not all brie is created equal. Poetry is made by all, not one, and at our cheese counter lies a cheese monger's tip.

Cheese

Cheeses often reflect the character of their country of origin, so experimenting with different cheese can be a kind of exploration of a faraway place. Sit in a traffic jam of privately manned vehicles. And in each other's armchair anarchists, we also recommend that you let your imagination run wild. Puppy love is puppy love. Puppy love is the origin of Valentine's Day, creating peace before our conflict, our really-eroded conflict.

Authenticity

Cutting and exposure to the air darkens the flesh. We stood in unheated squats having tooth and not being limp. We were more art than science. We gently rubbed our skin in a circular motion.

William S. Burroughs
from Nova Express

Following Brion Gysin's discovery of the cut-up's potential, William S. Burroughs extended the technique (and the related fold-in) to serve his trilogy of novels: *The Soft Machine* (Paris: Olympia Press, 1961), *The Ticket That Exploded* (Paris: Olympia Press, 1962), and *Nova Express* (New York: Grove, 1964). In the fold-in, one page is folded vertically and placed over another page; "the composite text is then read across half one text and half the other." Often "clearer and more comprehensible" than freely composed prose, Burroughs found that "perfectly clear narrative prose can be produced using the fold in method" ("The Future of the Novel," *Word Virus: The William S. Burroughs Reader* [New York: Grove, 2000], 273). "When you cut into the present," Burroughs claimed, "the future leaks out." In fact, he averred that the most interesting lesson of the cut-up and fold-in techniques "was the realization that when you make cut-ups you do not get simply random juxtapositions of words, that they do mean something, and often that these meanings refer to some future event" (Daniel Odier, *The Job: Interviews with William S. Burroughs* [New York: Grove, 1974], 28):

> To give a very simple example, I made a cut-up of something Mr Getty had written, I believe for "Time and Tide." The following phrase emerged: "It's a bad thing to sue your own father." About three years later his son sued him. Perhaps events are pre-written and pre-recorded and when you cut word lines the future leaks out. I have seen enough examples to convince me that the cut-ups are a basic key to the nature and function of words.

When the cut-up method was explained to him, Samuel Beckett purportedly replied "That's not writing; it's plumbing" (see Ted Morgan, *Literary Outlaw: The Life and Times of William S. Burroughs* [New York: Avon Books, 1988], 232). One can find a similar plumbing of sources—at the level of the sentence rather than the page— in Charles Bernstein's "Asylum" (*Asylums* [New York: Asylum Press, 1975]), which takes its language from Erving Goffman's *Asylums: Essays on the Condition of the Social*

Situation of Mental Patients and Other Inmates (Garden City, N.J.: Anchor, 1961), often by linking the last words of one sentence and the first words of the next in a grammatical dysraphism.

Now you are asking me whether I want to perpetuate a narcotics problem and I say: "Protect the disease. Must be made criminal protecting society from the disease"

The problem scheduled in the United States the use of jail, former narcotics plan, addiction and crime for many years—Broad front "Care" of welfare agencies—Narcotics which antedate the use of drugs—The fact is noteworthy—48 stages—prisoner was delayed—has been separated—was required—

Addiction in some form is the basis—must be wholly addicts—Any voluntary capacity subversion of The Will Capital And Treasury Bank—Infection dedicated to traffic in exchange narcotics demonstrated a Typhoid Mary who will spread narcotics problem to the United Kingdom—Finally in view of the cure—cure of the social problem and as such dangerous to society—

Maintaining addict cancers to our profit—pernicious personal contact—Market increase—Release The Prosecutor to try any holes—Cut Up Fighting Drug Addiction by Malcolm Monroe Former Prosecutor, in *Western World*, October 1959

David Buuck
Follow

Detectives serve a traditional purpose of the confessional lyric: to discover and document private aspects of individual lives with honesty and concision. In 2007, David Buuck hired the San Francisco Bay Area private investigator Mike Kellerman to surveille him, constructing a kind of conceptual self-portrait by proxy. Buuck's outsourced confession restages one of Sophie Calle's projects from twenty-five years earlier. Calle explains: "In April 1981, at my request, my mother went to a detective agency. She hired them to follow me, to report on my daily activities, and to provide photographic evidence of my existence." With an epistemological inversion of the typical shadowing, Calle and Buuck both know that the detective does not know that they know they are being observed.

The frequent redactions in Buuck's "Follow" call attention to its literary status (*redact:* "to put [matter] into proper literary form; to work up, arrange, or edit"); at the same time, they freight seemingly mundane gestures with an air of vague import. The form of the surveillance report imbues mere facts with an aura of evidence, even though the exact crime remains unclear. The reader is left to wonder what has been omitted and why. Furthermore, regardless of corroborating photographs and detailed descriptions, the portrait is entirely external; we have no access to the expressive interiority of the subject. Why is he milling about? What is he thinking? What is he contemplating? What makes him rub his temples in seeming anguish? Is he listening or talking? In the end, with its theatrical insinuation of ominous tragedy, what is he so grimly determined to do?

In Sophie Calle's earlier work *Le filature (The Shadow)*, the irony shifts from the reader to the detective himself. Beside the detective's factual third-person notes, Calle includes her own account of the day, emphasizing the contrast between her subjective and privately personal version of events and the detective's more "objective" evidence. The reader can discover discrepancies between the two documents, casting doubt on both versions of events. Calle, we learn, contrived her itinerary to mark the personal significance of public spaces: the route she took to school, the place where she received her first kiss, the art world venues of her studio and the Louvre, and so on. Not coincidentally, the painting she lingers in front of at the

Louvre is Titian's *Portrait d'homme* known familiarly as *L'Homme au gant,* a landmark in the development of the psychological portrait, an intimate portrait of a Venetian who has nonetheless remained anonymous and unknown.

The Shadow presents a logical reverse of Calle's own signature investigative voyeurism and amateur espionage. Some of her earliest work involved following strangers through the streets of Paris, a scenario developed and documented in *Suite Vénitienne,* which restaged Vito Acconci's 1969 *Following Piece* in the mise-en-scène of Ian McEwan's *The Comfort of Strangers* (London: Jonathan Cape, 1981). The premise for *L'Hôtel,* similarly, involved Calle posing as a hotel chambermaid, rifling and cataloging the belongings of guests. In *L'homme au carnet,* Calle ostensibly found an address book in the street. After interviewing some of the people listed in the book about its owner, she published the results in a serial column in the newspaper *Libération* (appearing from August 2 through September 4, 1983). The collective portrait assembled by these witnesses—like the detective portraits of Buuck and Calle—draws the fine line between interior and exterior, public and private, distance and intimacy. Pierre Baudry, the owner of the address book, was said to be outraged and threatened to sue.

(DATE REDACTED)

10:30 am – On scene.

12:05 pm – No activity noted. Delivery truck pulls next to surveillance vehicle parked on (REDACTED) St., blocking view of residence. Surveillance vehicle moves to find alternate location.

12:10 pm – Subject vehicle, green (REDACTED), observed traveling westbound on (REDACTED) St. toward Martin Luther King Jr. Way (MLK). Mobile surveillance initiated. Subject vehicle traveling southbound on MLK toward (REDACTED).

12:15 pm – Visual of subject vehicle lost. Surveillance vehicle delayed at red light.

12:23 pm – Visual of subject vehicle regained in area of Bay Bridge toll booth. Subject vehicle moves quickly across three lanes to FasTrak lane and proceeds onto bridge. Surveillance vehicle blocked by traffic and unable to continue.

12:25 pm – Attempt to locate subject vehicle on Bay Bridge and into San Francisco. Unable to locate subject vehicle and surveillance terminated at (REDACTED) exit from Hwy. 101.

(DATE REDACTED)

9:15 am – On scene at (REDACTED) St., Oakland, CA. No activity noted. Window coverings are closed and subject vehicle parked in driveway next to residence.

1:00 pm – No activity. No one exits or enters the residence. Subject vehicle remains parked as described. Surveillance terminated.

(DATE REDACTED)

10:30 am – Begin to depart area enroute to (REDACTED) to determine if subject departed residence on foot prior to initiation of surveillance. Subject observed through rear view mirror hurrying down front stairs and moving quickly to vehicle. Subject is a Caucasian male, mid 30's, approximately (REDACTED) tall, slim build wearing (REDACTED), brown cap, and maroon work boots. Subject carrying book bag or computer bag. Subject enters vehicle and departs area.

10:35 am – Subject vehicle parks parallel on (REDACTED) St. just north of (REDACTED) Ave., Oakland, CA. Subject exits the vehicle and walks briskly to and enters (REDACTED) on corner of (REDACTED) and (REDACTED).

11:00 am – Investigator enters (REDACTED) to determine actions of subject. Subject observed seated just inside front door and to the left at small table near window, with back to window. Subject, with (REDACTED) in hand, converses briefly with (REDACTED) seated to his right, mid 30's, approximately (REDACTED) tall with long light brown or dark blonde hair, wearing (REDACTED) with neck scarf, white (REDACTED) and blue jeans. Subject scans interior of (REDACTED) briefly. Subject appears to stare off across (REDACTED) as if in thought. Investigator departs (REDACTED) at 11:10 am.

12:44 pm – Subject observed through window standing and milling about. Photographs of movement obtained

1:52 pm – Subject exits (REDACTED) alone and scans area in all directions. He is observed milling about on the sidewalk at the corner with his hands in pants pocket to protect against chill wind. He pulls small (REDACTED) from his pocket and places in his mouth. He is looking down at sidewalk as he walks, again with hands in pants pockets. No discernable purpose of this activity is noted. Subject removes cell phone from pocket and dials. He holds cell phone to his right ear and

mills about. Unable to determine if he is actually talking with any-
one or simply listening. He is looking down and walking in an exag-
gerated manner. Subject places right hand over forehead and rubs the
area of his forehead and eyes with a strong squeezing motion. Sub-
ject continues to mill about and walks several feet up (REDACTED)
Ave. toward rear of (REDACTED). He turns and walks back slowly.
His facial expression demonstrates contemplation, as he walks back
toward the front of the (REDACTED), apparently taking no notice
of the (REDACTED) and traffic as he strides by. Subject reaches the
front of the (REDACTED) and lifts his head to look ahead of him.
His gaze appears to be fixed in front of him as he walks northbound on
(REDACTED) Ave. to the end of the (REDACTED). Subject imme-
diately turns about and walks slowly but with determination back to
the front door of (REDACTED) where he enters at 1:57 pm and dis-
appears from view. Photographs of Subject's activities are obtained.

January 20, 2007
8:42 pm – Surveillance is terminated.

John Cage
Writing Through *The Cantos*

Cage's method of writing through is a way to subject a preexisting text to a radical reduction. By constructing a parasitic method, Cage is able to create a new text while retaining linguistic aspects of the parent text. Cage often used this method—taking a proper name as the base structure of a work—as a way to pay homage to a person he admired or an author who had influenced him.

In this case, he used the letters in the name Ezra Pound to generate a new text by reading his way through *The Cantos,* hunting for words that contained each letter of the poet's name, which he then wrote down sequentially, in the order he found them. Thus, each line spells Pound's name in capital letters, alternating first and last name. As Cage explains it (*X: Writings '79–'82* [Middletown, Conn.: Wesleyan University Press, 1982], 109):

> To write the following text I followed the rule given me by Louis Mink which I also followed in *Writing for the Third* (and *Fourth*) *Time Through Finnegans Wake,* that is, I did not permit the appearance of either letter between two of the name. As in *Writing for the Fourth Time Through Finnegans Wake,* I kept an index of the syllables used to present a given letter of the name and I did not permit repetition of these syllables.

Between the encrypted *E* and *Z,* that is, neither e nor z may appear; between the *Z* and *R,* neither z nor r may appear; and so on.

and thEn with bronZe lance heads beaRing yet Arm's
sheeP slain Of plUto stroNg praiseD
thE narrow glaZes the uptuRned nipple As
sPeak tO rUy oN his gooDs
arE swath blaZe mutteRing empty Armour
Ply Over ply eddying flUid beNeath the of the goDs

torchEs gauZe tuRn of the stAirs
Peach-trees at the fOrd jacqUes betweeN ceDars
as gygEs on topaZ and thRee on the bArb of
Praise Or sextUs had seeN her in lyDia walks with
womEn in mazZ of aiR wAs
Put upOn lUst of womaN roaD from-spain
sEa-jauZionda motheR of yeArs
Picus de dOn elinUs doN Dictum
concubuissE y cavals armatZ meRe succession And
Peu mOisi plUs bas le jardiN olD
mEn's fritZ enduRes Action
striPed beer-bOttles bUt *is* iN floateD
scarlEt gianoZio one fRom Also
due disPatch ragOna pleasUre either as participaNt wD.
sEnd with sforZa the duchess to Rimini wArs
Pleasure mOstly di cUi fraNcesco southwarD
hE abbaZia of sant apollinaiRe clAsse
serPentine whOse dUcats to be paid back to the cardiNal 200 Ducats
corn-salvE for franco sforZa's at least keep the Row out of tuscAny
s. Pietri hOminis reddens Ut magis persoNa ex ore proDiit
quaE thought old Zuliano is wRite thAt

Peasant fOr his *sUb de malatestis* goNe him to Do in
mo'ammEds singing to Zeus down heRe fAtty
Praestantibusque bOth geniUs both owN all of it Down on
papEr bust-up of braZilian secuRities s.A. securities
they oPerated and there was a whOre qUit the driNk saveD up
his pay monEy and ooZe scRupulously cleAn
Penis whO disliked langUage skiN profiteers Drinking
bEhind dung-flow cut in loZenges the gaiteRs of slum-flesh bAck-
comPlaining attentiOn nUlla fideNtia earth a Dung hatching
inchoatE graZing the swill hammeRing the souse into hArdness
long sleeP babylOn i heard in the circUit seemed whirliNg heaD
hEld gaZe noRth his eyes blAzing
Peire cardinal in his mirrOr blUe lakes of crimeN choppeD
icE gaZing at theiR plAin
nymPhs and nOw a swashbUckler didN't blooDY
finE of a bitch franZ baRbiche Aldington on
trench dug through corPses lOt minUtes sergeaNt rebukeD him

for lEvity trotZsk is a bRest-litovsk Aint yuh herd he
sPeech mOve 'em jUst as oNe saiD
'Em to Zenos metevsky bieRs to sell cAnnon
Peace nOt while yew rUssia a New keyboarD
likE siZe ov a pRince An' we sez wud yew like
his Panties fer the cOmpany y hUrbara zeNos's Door
with hEr champZ don't the fellerRs At home
uP-Other Upside dowN up to the beD-room
stubby fEllow cocky as khristnoZe eveRy dAmn thing for the
hemP via rOtterdm das thUst Nicht Days
gonE glaZe gReen feAthers
of the Pavement brOken disrUpted wilderNess of glazeD
junglE Zoe loud oveR the bAnners
fingers Petal'd frOm pUrple olibaNum's wrappeD floating
bluE citiZens as you desiRe quellA
Pace Oh mUrdered floriNs paiD
ovEr doZen yeaRs conveyAnce
be Practicable cOme natUre moNtecello golD
wishEd who wuZ pRice cAn't
Plane an' hOw mr. bUkos the ecoNomist woulD
savE lattittZo the giRl sAys it'z
shiP dOwn chUcked blaNche forDs
of ocEan priZes we have agReed he hAs won
Pay nOstri qUickly doN't seeD combs
two grEat and faictZ notRe puissAnce
Priest sent a bOy and the statUes Niccolo tolD him
sEnt priZe a collaR with jewels cAme
Prize gOnzaga marqUis ferrara maiNly to see sarDis
of athEns in calm Zone if the men aRe in his fAce
Part sOme last crUmbs of civilizatioN Damn
thEy lisZt heR pArents
on his Prevalent knee sOnnet a nUmber learNery jackeD up
a littlE aZ ole man comley wd. say hRwwkke tth sAid
Plan is tOld inclUded raNks expelleD
jE suis xtZbk49ght *paRts of this* to mAdison
in euroPe general washingtOn harangUed johN aDams
through a wholE for civiliZing the impRovement which begAn
to comPute enclOse farms and crUsoe Now by harD
povErty craZy geoRge cAtherine

John Cage 131

Picked the cOnstant a gUisa agaiN faileD
all rEcords tZin vei le Role hAve
Page they adOpted wd. sUggest Not Day
largE romanZoff fReedom of Admission
of deParture freedOm ai vU freNch by her worD
bonapartE for coloniZing this countRy in viennA
excePt geOrge half edUcated meN shD.
concErns mr fidascZ oR nAme we
resPect in black clOthes centUry-old soNvabitch gooD is
patiEnt to mobiliZe wiRe deAth for
Pancreas are nObles in fact he was qUite potemkiN marrieD
a rEaltor a biZ-nis i-de-a the peRfect peAutiful chewisch
schoP he gOt dhere and venn hiss brUdder diet tdeN Dh
vifE but topaZe undeRstood which explAins
Pallete et sOld the high jUdges to passioNs as have remarkeD
havE authoriZed its pResident to use funds mArked
President wrOte fUll fraNk talk remembereD
in sorrEnto paralyZed publicly answeRed questions thAn
duol che soPra falseggiandO del sUd vaticaN expresseD
politE curiosity as to how any citiZen shall have Right to pAy
sPecie wOrkers sUch losses wheNso it be to their shoulD
usEd *luZ* wheRe messAge
is kePt stOne chUrch stoNe threaD
nonE waZ bRown one cAse
couPle One pUblished Never publisheD
oragE about tamuZ the Red flAme going
seed   two sPan twO bUll begiN thy seaborD
fiElds by kolschitZky Received sAcks of
Pit hOld pUt vaN blameD
amErican civil war on Zeitgeist Ruin After d.
Preceded crOwd cried leagUe miNto yelleD
Evviva Zwischen die volkeRn in eddying Air in
Printed sOrt fU dyNasty Dynasty
Eighth dynasty chaZims and usuRies the high fAns
simPles gathered gOes the mUst No wooD burnt
gatEs in an haZe of colouRs wAter boiled in the wells
Prince whOm wd/ fUlfill l'argeNt circule that cash be lorD to
sEas of china horiZon and the 3Rd cAbinet
keePin' 'Osses rUled by hochaNgs helD up

statE of bonZes empRess hAnged herself
sPark lights a milliOn strings calcUlated at sterliNg haD by
taozErs tho' *bonZesses* of iRon tAng
Princes in snOw trUe proviNce of greeD
contEnt with Zibbeline soldieRs mAy
Paid 'em tchOngking mUmbo dishoNour wars boreDom of
rackEt 1069 ghingiZ tchinkis heaRing of heAring
'em Pass as cOin was stUff goverNor 3⅓rD
triEd oZin wodin tRees no tAxes
Prussia and mengkO yU tchiN D. 1225
nEws lord lipan booZing king of fouR towns opened gAtes
to Pinyang destrOying kU chiNg ageD
thronE and on ghaZel tanks didn't woRk fAithful
echo desPerate treasOns bhUd lamas Night Drawn
Each by Zealously many dangeRs mAde
to Pray and hOang eleUtes mohamedaNs caveD
gavE put magaZines theRe grAft
Pund at mOderate revenUe which Next approveD
un fontEgo in boston gaZette wRote shooting stArted
Putts Off taking a strUggle theN moveD
somE magaZine politique hollandais diRected gen. wAshington
to dePuties at der zwOl with dUmas agaiNst creDit
with bankErs with furZe scaRce oAk or other tree
minced Pie and frOntenac wine tUesday cleaN coD
clEar that Zeeland we signed etc/ commeRce heAven
remPlis d'un hOmme she mUle axletree brokeN to Dry
curE appriZed was the dangeR peAce is
Passed befOre i hear dUke maNchester backeD
frEnch wd/ back Zεῦ ἀPχηγέ estetA
mi sPieghi ch'iO gUerra e faNgo Dialogava
cEntro impaZiente uRgente e voce di mArinetti
in Piazza lembO al sUo ritorNello D'un toro
chE immondiZia nominaR è pArecchio
Più gemistO giÙ di pietro Negator' D'usura
vEngon' a bisanZio ne pietRo che Augusto
Placidia fui suOnava mUover è Nuova   baDa
a mE Zuan cRisti mosAic till our
when and Plus when gOld measUred doNe fielD
prEparation taishan quatorZe juillet and ambeR deAd the end

suPerb and brOwn in leviticUs or first throwN thru the clouD
yEt byZantium had heaRd Ass
stoP are strOnger thUs rrromaNce yes yes bastarDs
slaughtEr with banZai song of gassiR glAss-eye wemyss
unPinned gOvernment which lasted rather less pecUliar thaN reD
firE von tirpitZ bewaRe of chArm
sPiritus belOved aUt veNto ligure is Difficult
psEudo-ritZ-caRlton bArbiche
Past baskets and hOrse cars mass'chUsetts cologNe catheDral
paolo uccEllo in danZig if they have not destRoyed is meAsured by
tout dit que Pas a small rain stOrm eqUalled momeNts surpasseD
quE pas barZun had old andRe conceAl the sound
of its foot-stePs knOw that he had them as daUdet is goNcourt sD/
martin wE Zecchin' bRingest to focus zAgreus
sycoPhancy One's sqUare daNce too luciD
squarEs from byZance and befoRe then mAnitou
sound in the forest of Pard crOtale scrUb-oak viNe yarDs
clicking of crotalEs tsZe's biRds sAy
hoPing mOre billyUm the seNate treaD
that voltagE yurr sZum kind ov a ex-gReyhound lArge
centre Piece with nOvels dUmped baNg as i cD/
makE out banking joZefff may have followed mR owe initiAlly
mr P. his bull-dOg me stUrge m's bull-dog taberNam Dish
robErt Zupp buffoRd my footbAth
sliP and tOwer rUst loNg shaDows
as mEn miss tomcZyk at 18 wobuRn buildings tAncred
Phrase's sake and had lOve thrU impeNetrable troubleD
throbbing hEart roman Zoo sheeR snow on the mArble snow-white
into sPagna t'aO chi'ien heard mUsic lawNs hiDing a woman
whEn sZu' noR by vAin
simPlex animus bigOb men cUt Nap iii trees prop up clouDs
praEcognita schwartZ '43 pRussien de ménAge with four teeth out
Paaasque je suis trOp angUstiis me millet wiNe set for wilD
gamE *chuntZe* but diRty the dAi
toPaze a thrOne having it sqUsh in his excelleNt Dum
sacro nEmori von humboldt agassiZ maR wAy
desPair i think randOlph crUmp to Name was pleaseD
yEars tZu two otherRs cAlhoun
Pitching quOits than sUavity deportmeNt was resolveD on

slavEs and taZewell buRen fAther of
Price sOldiers delUged the old hawk damN saDist
yEs nasZhong bRonze of sAn zeno buy columns now by the
stone-looP shOt till pUdg'd still griN like quiDity
rhEa's schnitZ waR ein schuhmAcher und
corPse & then cannOn θΥγάτηρ apolloNius fumbleD
amplE cadiZ pillaRs with the spAde
ἐΠι ἐλθΟν and jUlia ἐλληνιξοΝτας the Dawn
onE ασφαλίΖειν lock up & cook-fiRes cAuldron
Plaster an askÓs αῨξει τῶN has covereD
thEir koloboZed ouR coinAge
Pearls cOpper tissUs de liN hoarD
for a risE von schlitZ denmaRk quArter
of sPain Olde tUrkish wisselbaNk Daily
papErs von schultZ and albuqueRque chArles second c.5
not ruled by soPhia σΟφία dUped by the crowN but steeD
askEd douglas about kadZu aceRo not boAt
Pulchram Oar-blades θίνα θαλάσσης leUcothoe rose babyloN of caDmus
linE him analyZe the tRick fAke
Packed the he dOes habsbUrg somethiNg you may reaD
posing as moslEm not a trial but kolschoZ Rome bAbylon no sense Of
Public destrOyed de vaUx 32 millioN exhumeD with
mmE douZe ambRoise bluejAys
his Peers but unicOrns yseUlt is dead palmerstoN's worse oviD
much worsE to summariZe was in contRol byzAnce
sPartan mOnd qUatorze kiNg lost fer some gawD
fool rEason bjjayZus de poictieRs mAverick
rePeating this mOsaic bUst acceNsio shepherD to flock
tEn light blaZed behind ciRce with leopArd's by mount's edge
over broom-Plant yaO whUder ich maei lidhaN flowers are blesseD
aquilEia auZel said that biRd meAning
Planes liOns jUmps scorpioNs give light waDsworth in
town housE in

Blaise Cendrars

from Kodak

In his memoir *L'Homme foudroyé (The Astonished Man)*, Blaise Cendrars—the pseudonym of Frédéric Louis Sauser—confesses:

> I was cruel enough to take [Gustave] Lerouge a volume of poetry and make him read, and confirm with his own eyes, some twenty original poems which I had clipped out of one of his prose works and had published under my own name! It was an outrage. . . . (Note to researchers and the inquisitive: for the moment I can say no more about it, not wanting to start a fashion, and for the sake of the publisher, who would be mortified to learn that he had unwittingly published my poetic hoax). (133)

Researchers and the inquisitive now know that Cendrars is referring to his book *Kodak (Documentaire)* (Paris: Librairie Stock, Poesie du Temps, 1924) and to Le Rouge's multivolume serial *Le Mystérieux Docteur Cornelius (The Mysterious Doctor Cornelius*, 1912–13). The subtitle of Cendrars's book—required after the first printing to avoid a lawsuit threatened by the Eastman Corporation—thus ultimately seems to refer less to the genre of the travelogue ostensibly recording Cendrars's South American adventures—the literary equivalent of something like *Nanook of the North* (1922)—or to the snapshot record of the portable camera, than to the documents recorded, with the flat, literal realism of direct quotation, in the poems' own modes of production. Indeed, the poems' method of construction points neatly back to their source: Doctor Cornelius, a sort of mad scientist allied with the secret criminal organization Le Main Rouge (the Red Hand), is a surgeon with the ability to disguise the appearance of others, sculpting their visages to the point that they might pass as someone else. Turning the doctor's surgical blade back onto the *Docteur* with his "clipping," Cendrars's secret plagiarism enacts on his source text what that text itself describes, thereby literalizing—and allegorizing—its narrative. Obscuring the signature style of Le Rouge (*le main de Le Rouge*) by aligning himself with Le Main Rouge, Cendrars returns to Le Rouge, with the proof of his crime, red-handed.

2. Brochure

Visit our island!
It is the southernmost Japanese territory
Our country is certainly too little known in Europe
It deserves to attract much more attention
The flora and fauna are quite varied and have scarcely before been studied
Finally, you will discover ubiquitous picturesque prospects
And in the countryside
Buddhist temple ruins which, in their way, are true marvels

3. The Red-Crested Viper

With the help of a Pravaz Syringe he administers several injections of
    Doctor Yersin's serum
Then he opens the wound in the arm with the scalpel, effecting a
    cruciform incision
He bleeds it
Then cauterizes it with some drops of hypochlorite of lime

4. Japanese House

Bamboo stalks
Thin planks
Paper tautened to frames
There is no real home heating system

5. Little Garden

Lilies chrystanthemums
Sago palms and bananas
Cherry trees in flower
Palms oranges magnificent palm trees laden with coconuts

6. Xeroscape

In a pool stocked with carp and monstrously-mouthed fish
Some sport little silver rings in their gills

Thomas Claburn
from i feel better after i type to you

In 2006, America Online (AOL) accidentally released the search queries from some 20 million of its customers. The users were anonymous, identified by numerical tags, and no IP addresses were disclosed, though many were easily identified with a quick triangulation of data. Thomas Claburn quickly recognized the literary potential of this cache, publishing the data from one user with only minor formatting changes to aid readability. As Claburn explains:

> Within the third of the ten files of user search queries AOL mistakenly released (user-ct-test-collection-03), there's a poem of sorts. Between May 7 and May 31 of this year, AOL user 23187425 submitted a series of more than 8,200 queries with no evident intention of finding anything—only a handful of the entries are paired with a search results URL. Rather, the author's series of queries forms a stream-of-consciousness soliloquy.

> Whether it's fact or fiction, confession or invention, the search monologue is strangely compelling. It's a uniquely temporal literary form in that the server time stamps make the passage of time integral to the storytelling. It could be the beginning of a new genre of writing, or simply an aberration. But it does beg further explanation. What circumstances prompted the author to converse thus with AOL's search engine?

Tuesday 1:25 am

2006-05-09 01:25:15	break in
2006-05-09 01:26:00	joseph i have a question
2006-05-09 01:27:27	all the years why did you work out of delphi
2006-05-09 01:28:36	could have gone to detriot
2006-05-09 01:29:40	why you make delphi kettering your base

2006-05-09 01:30:09	your base
2006-05-09 01:31:13	joe why
2006-05-09 01:31:56	you choose kettering
2006-05-09 01:33:01	had opportunity
2006-05-09 01:33:26	to leave
2006-05-09 01:34:19	start there but could have left
2006-05-09 01:34:54	know you started there but could have left
2006-05-09 01:35:28	why did you stay
2006-05-09 01:36:14	but why
2006-05-09 01:37:46	cause of me
2006-05-09 01:38:48	last saw you bicycle
2006-05-09 01:39:31	why didn't you tell me who you wer
2006-05-09 01:41:07	was not to tell me
2006-05-09 01:41:47	orders
2006-05-09 01:42:38	jt order
2006-05-09 01:43:59	was thinking
2006-05-09 01:44:38	on line to ask
2006-05-09 01:45:17	no one would tell me
2006-05-09 01:46:11	mean no
2006-05-09 01:47:45	told of everyone else
2006-05-09 01:48:20	keller like you
2006-05-09 01:48:44	all thrash
2006-05-09 01:49:24	told of them
2006-05-09 01:50:27	wasn't my type
2006-05-09 01:50:49	was not my type
2006-05-09 01:51:32	my type is rare
2006-05-09 01:52:06	hard to find
2006-05-09 01:53:10	pay no attention to every man
2006-05-09 01:54:24	find one who treat me good an stay
2006-05-09 01:55:22	look toward you
2006-05-09 01:56:07	time will depart us
2006-05-09 01:56:43	of not seeing
2006-05-09 01:57:39	will depart us
2006-05-09 01:58:57	on to ask
2006-05-09 01:59:49	music will not help me work
2006-05-09 02:00:24	take hands
2006-05-09 02:00:56	together
2006-05-09 02:01:47	my suit come tommorrow
2006-05-09 02:02:25	purse that match was gone

2006-05-09 02:03:40	say no
2006-05-09 02:04:11	altogether
2006-05-09 02:05:43	last two years white
2006-05-09 02:07:24	flower gold 2yrs ago
2006-05-09 02:08:06	gold flower 2 yrs ago
2006-05-09 02:08:33	white before that
2006-05-09 02:09:01	a pattern
2006-05-09 02:10:02	look that way
2006-05-09 02:10:49	gold suit picture turn backward
2006-05-09 02:11:40	the goldsuit picture turn backward
2006-05-09 02:12:53	all my picture
2006-05-09 02:13:51	frame broke high school picture
2006-05-09 02:14:43	out of all mine
2006-05-09 02:15:41	go to bed
2006-05-09 02:16:16	if i work hard i don't think off
2006-05-09 02:17:29	left my computer down
2006-05-09 02:17:59	work hard
2006-05-09 02:19:11	get some sleep
2006-05-09 02:19:44	work tommorr
2006-05-09 02:20:44	bless night
2006-05-09 02:21:20	to tired to look at my clothes
2006-05-09 02:21:51	i was to tired to look at my clothes
2006-05-09 02:22:42	i have no one as song say
2006-05-09 02:23:12	have noone
2006-05-09 02:23:56	one warning
2006-05-09 02:25:07	if you ever find someone never go though that process
2006-05-09 02:26:39	i tell the truth
2006-05-09 02:27:11	its to long
2006-05-09 02:27:46	will lose love
2006-05-09 02:29:25	that for a women with maids gardener and all
2006-05-09 02:29:50	laughing
2006-05-09 02:30:24	bought my own
2006-05-09 02:31:11	not a poor woman
2006-05-09 02:31:52	i have to work
2006-05-09 02:32:19	i have to work
2006-05-09 02:32:56	no dates no fun
2006-05-09 02:34:10	ready for bed
2006-05-09 02:34:37	not across

2006-05-09 02:35:09   not a cross
2006-05-09 02:35:38   what if we date
2006-05-09 02:36:13   see no
2006-05-09 02:36:57   see you

Tuesday 1:28pm

2006-05-09 13:28:28   ashley licks
2006-05-09 13:28:28   ashley licks
2006-05-09 13:28:28   ashley licks
2006-05-09 13:28:28   ashley licks
2006-05-09 13:34:19   roxy

Elisabeth S. Clark
from Between Words

According to Clark:

> *Nouvelles Impressions d'Afrique* is a long, 1274-line poem in rhymed alexandrines, coupled with subsequent footnotes. Written by Raymond Roussel, it was originally published in 1932. Reflected here, though void of words, is an exact facsimile of the author's original notational (punctuational) inscriptions found in his poem. Thanks to the help, support, and copyright permissions from Atlas Press.

Clark's work thus takes its place beside Carl Fredrik Reuterswärd's *Prix Nobel* (Stockholm: Bonniers, 1966), a novel written entirely with punctuation marks; Kenneth Goldsmith's series of similar works, including all the punctuation from William Strunk and E. B. White's chapter on punctuation in their *Elements of Style* and the chapbook *Gertrude Stein on Punctuation* (Newton, N.J.: Abaton, 2000); and Hu Wenliang's Chinese novella, which reads, in its translated entirety:

: ?
: !
" ...... "
(,) • <. >
: —

I

, , ,

, ,

!... , !...

, ,

, , – !

,   ,   :

        ,   ,

            ,   ,   ,

(,   ,   ,   ,

—   ,   —

((!

(((,   ,

        ,   ,   ,

—   ,   ,   ,

            ,   ,

                    ,—

((((:—   ,   ,
        ,   (((((,

,   ,
    ,   [1],
                                    ;))))) ,

---

1.   , - - ,   ,   ,   ,
                        , —
    ,
                    - ,
                            ?' —

,

,

,   ,

,   ,   ,

,   ,   ,   ;

—   ,   ,   ,   ,

         ,   ,   ,   ,   1.

,   ,   ;

—   ,   ,   ;

—   ,

,   ;

—

                                                         ;

,   ,   ,   ,

                                           .

1.   ,

      (,   —   ,   ,,

            ,   —

                  ,   ,   : "   ,   !"),

      ,   :—   ,   ,   ,   ,   ;

                                                        ,

                           ;—   ,

            ,   ;—   ,   ,

—   ,   ,   ,   ,

                              ,   ;
—   ,   ;
—   ,   ,   ,   ,
      ,   ;—
            ;—   ,
                                        ,   ,
                              ,   ;
—   ,   ,   ,
 ,   ,   ,   -   ;
—

                  ,   , ,
            ;—   ,
 ,
                                    ,   ,
      ;—   ,   ,   ,   , ,
                                    ,   ,   ;
—   ,   ,
                              ;—   ,
      ,   ,   ; ,
—   ;
—   , ,   -   ,   ;
            ,   , ,   ,
                  ,   ;

Claude Closky
The First Thousand Numbers Classified in Alphabetical Order

Stunningly simple, *The First Thousand Numbers Classified in Alphabetical Order* (Paris: self-published, 1989) upends our notions of the most basic form of logic, one in which the structure and order of language take precedence over basic notions of sense. A model of conceptual literature, *The First Thousand Numbers* is nearly impossible to read, but its dense text either acts as pure visual pattern or a leap into philosophy, begging the reader to discard the text in favor of pondering its ramifications.

Eight, eight hundred, eight hundred and eight, eight hundred and eighteen, eight hundred and eighty, eight hundred and eighty-eight, eight hundred and eighty-five, eight hundred and eighty-four, eight hundred and eighty-nine, eight hundred and eighty-one, eight hundred and eighty-seven, eight hundred and eighty-six, eight hundred and eighty-three, eight hundred and eighty-two, eight hundred and eleven, eight hundred and fifteen, eight hundred and fifty, eight hundred and fifty-eight, eight hundred and fifty-five, eight hundred and fifty-four, eight hundred and fifty-nine, eight hundred and fifty-one, eight hundred and fifty-seven, eight hundred and fifty-six, eight hundred and fifty-three, eight hundred and fifty-two, eight hundred and five, eight hundred and forty, eight hundred and forty-eight, eight hundred and forty-five, eight hundred and forty-four, eight hundred and forty-nine, eight hundred and forty-one, eight hundred and forty-seven, eight hundred and forty-six, eight hundred and forty-three, eight hundred and forty-two, eight hundred and four, eight hundred and fourteen, eight hundred and nine, eight hundred and nineteen, eight hundred and ninety, eight hundred and ninety-eight, eight hundred and ninety-five, eight hundred and ninety-four, eight hundred and ninety-nine, eight hundred and ninety-one, eight hundred and ninety-seven, eight hundred and ninety-six, eight hundred and ninety-three, eight hundred and ninety-two, eight hundred and one, eight hundred and seven, eight hundred and seventeen, eight hundred and seventy, eight hundred and seventy-eight, eight hundred and seventy-five, eight hundred and seventy-four, eight hundred and seventy-nine, eight hundred and seventy-one, eight hundred and seventy-seven, eight hundred and seventy-six, eight hundred and seventy-three, eight hundred and seventy-two, eight hundred and six, eight hundred and sixteen, eight hundred and sixty, eight hundred and sixty-eight, eight hundred and sixty-five, eight hundred and sixty-four, eight hundred and sixty-nine, eight hundred and sixty-one, eight hundred and sixty-seven, eight hundred and sixty-six, eight hundred and sixty-three, eight hundred and sixty-two, eight hundred and ten, eight hundred and thirteen, eight hundred and thirty, eight hundred and thirty-eight, eight hundred and thirty-five, eight hundred and thirty-four, eight hundred and thirty-nine, eight hundred and thirty-one, eight hundred and thirty-seven, eight hundred and thirty-six, eight hundred and thirty-three, eight hundred and thirty-two, eight hundred and three, eight hundred and twelve, eight hundred and twenty, eight hundred and twenty-eight, eight hundred and twenty-five, eight hundred and twenty-four, eight hundred and twenty-nine, eight hundred and twenty-one, eight hundred and twenty-seven, eight hundred and twenty-six, eight hundred and twenty-three, eight hundred and twenty-two, eight hundred and two, eighteen, eighty, eighty-eight, eighty-five, eighty-four, eighty-nine, eighty-one, eighty-seven, eighty-six, eighty-three, eighty-two, eleven, fifteen, fifty, fifty-eight, fifty-five, fifty-four, fifty-nine, fifty-one, fifty-seven, fifty-six, fifty-three, fifty-two, five, five hundred, five hundred and eight, five hundred and eighteen, five hundred and eighty, five hundred and eighty-eight, five hundred and eighty-five, five hundred and eighty-four, five hundred and eighty-nine, five hundred and eighty-one, five hundred and eighty-seven, five hundred and eighty-six, five hundred and eighty-three, five hundred and eighty-two, five hundred and eleven, five hundred and fifteen, five hundred and fifty, five hundred and fifty-eight, five hundred and fifty-five, five hundred and fifty-four, five hundred and fifty-nine, five hundred and fifty-one, five hundred and fifty-seven, five hundred and fifty-six, five hundred and fifty-three, five hundred and fifty-two, five hundred and five, five hundred and forty, five hundred and forty-eight, five hundred and forty-five, five hundred and forty-four, five hundred and forty-nine, five hundred and forty-one, five hundred and forty-seven, five hundred and forty-six, five hundred and forty-three, five hundred and forty-two, five hundred and four, five hundred and fourteen, five hundred and nine, five hundred and nineteen, five hundred and ninety, five hundred and ninety-eight, five hundred and ninety-five, five hundred and ninety-four, five hundred and ninety-nine, five hundred and ninety-one, five hundred and ninety-seven, five hundred and ninety-six, five hundred and ninety-three, five hundred and ninety-two, five hundred and one, five hundred and seven, five hundred and seventeen, five hundred and seventy, five hundred and seventy-eight, five hundred and seventy-five, five hundred and seventy-four, five hundred and seventy-nine, five hundred and seventy-one, five hundred and seventy-seven, five hundred and seventy-six, five hundred and seventy-three, five hundred and seventy-two, five hundred and six, five hundred and sixteen, five hundred and sixty, five hundred and sixty-eight, five hundred and sixty-five, five hundred and sixty-four, five hundred and sixty-nine, five hundred and sixty-one, five hundred and sixty-seven, five hundred and sixty-six, five hundred and sixty-three, five hundred and sixty-two, five hundred and ten, five hundred and thirteen, five hundred and thirty, five hundred and thirty-eight, five hundred and thirty-five, five hundred and thirty-four, five hundred and thirty-nine, five hundred and thirty-one, five hundred and thirty-seven, five hundred and thirty-six, five hundred and thirty-three, five hundred and thirty-two, five hundred and three, five hundred and twelve, five hundred and twenty, five hundred and twenty-eight, five hundred and twenty-five, five hundred and twenty-four, five hundred and twenty-nine, five hundred and twenty-one, five hundred and twenty-seven, five hundred and twenty-six, five hundred and twenty-three, five hundred and twenty-two, five hundred and two, forty, forty-eight, forty-five, forty-four, forty-nine, forty-one, forty-seven, forty-six, forty-three, forty-two, four, four hundred, four hundred and eight, four hundred and eighteen, four hundred and eighty, four hundred and eighty-eight, four hundred and eighty-five, four hundred and eighty-four, four hundred and eighty-nine, four hundred and eighty-one, four hundred and eighty-seven, four hundred and eighty-six, four hundred and eighty-three, four hundred and eighty-two, four hundred and eleven, four hundred and fifteen, four hundred and fifty, four hundred and fifty-eight, four hundred and fifty-five, four hundred and fifty-four, four hundred and fifty-nine, four hundred and fifty-one, four hundred and fifty-seven, four hundred and fifty-six, four hundred and fifty-three, four hundred and fifty-two, four hundred and five, four hundred and forty, four hundred and forty-eight, four hundred and forty-five, four hundred and forty-four, four hundred and forty-nine, four hundred and forty-one, four hundred and forty-seven, four hundred and forty-six, four hundred and forty-three, four hundred and forty-two, four hundred and four, four hundred and fourteen, four hundred and nine, four hundred and nineteen, four hundred and ninety, four hundred and ninety-eight, four hundred and ninety-five, four hundred and ninety-four, four hundred and ninety-nine, four hundred and ninety-one, four hundred and ninety-seven, four hundred and ninety-six, four hundred and ninety-three, four hundred and ninety-two, four hundred and one, four hundred and seven, four hundred and seventeen, four hundred and seventy, four hundred and seventy-eight, four hundred and seventy-five, four hundred and seventy-four, four hundred and seventy-nine, four hundred and seventy-one, four hundred and seventy-seven, four hundred and seventy-six, four hundred and seventy-three, four hundred and seventy-two, four hundred and six, four hundred and sixteen, four hundred and sixty, four hundred and sixty-eight, four hundred and sixty-five, four hundred and sixty-four, four hundred and sixty-nine, four hundred and sixty-one, four hundred and sixty-seven, four hundred and sixty-six, four hundred and sixty-three, four hundred and sixty-two, four hundred and ten, four hundred and thirteen, four hundred and thirty, four hundred and thirty-eight, four hundred and thirty-five, four hundred and thirty-four, four hundred and thirty-nine, four hundred and thirty-one, four hundred and thirty-seven, four hundred and thirty-six, four hundred and thirty-three, four hundred and thirty-two, four hundred and three, four hundred and twelve, four hundred and twenty, four hundred and twenty-eight, four hundred and twenty-five, four hundred and twenty-four, four hundred and twenty-nine, four hundred and twenty-one, four hundred and twenty-seven, four hundred and twenty-six, four hundred and twenty-three, four hundred and twenty-two, four hundred and two, fourteen, nine, nine hundred, nine hundred and eight, nine hundred and eighteen, nine hundred and eighty, nine hundred and eighty-eight, nine hundred and eighty-five, nine hundred and eighty-four, nine hundred and eighty-nine, nine hundred and eighty-one, nine hundred and eighty-seven, nine hundred and eighty-six, nine hundred and eighty-three, nine hundred and eighty-two, nine hundred and eleven, nine hundred and fifteen, nine hundred and fifty, nine hundred and fifty-eight, nine hundred and fifty-five, nine hundred and fifty-four, nine hundred and fifty-nine, nine hundred and fifty-one, nine hundred and fifty-seven, nine hundred and fifty-six, nine hundred and fifty-three, nine hundred and fifty-two, nine hundred and five, nine hundred and forty, nine hundred and forty-eight, nine hundred and forty-five, nine hundred and forty-four, nine hundred and forty-nine, nine hundred and forty-one, nine hundred and forty-seven, nine hundred and forty-six, nine hundred and forty-three, nine hundred and forty-two, nine hundred and four, nine hundred and fourteen, nine hundred and nine, nine hundred and nineteen, nine hundred and ninety, nine hundred and ninety-eight, nine hundred and ninety-five, nine hundred and ninety-four, nine hundred and ninety-nine, nine hundred and ninety-one, nine hundred and ninety-seven, nine hundred and ninety-six, nine hundred and ninety-three, nine hundred and ninety-two, nine hundred and one, nine hundred and seven, nine hundred and seventeen, nine hundred and seventy, nine hundred and seventy-eight, nine hundred and seventy-five, nine hundred and seventy-four, nine hundred and seventy-nine, nine hundred and seventy-one, nine hundred and seventy-seven, nine hundred and seventy-six, nine hundred and seventy-three, nine hundred and seventy-two, nine hundred and six, nine hundred and sixteen, nine hundred and sixty, nine hundred and sixty-eight, nine hundred and sixty-five, nine hundred and sixty-four, nine hundred and sixty-nine, nine hundred and sixty-one, nine hundred and sixty-seven, nine hundred and sixty-six, nine hundred and sixty-three, nine hundred and sixty-two, nine hundred and ten, nine hundred and thirteen, nine hundred and thirty, nine hundred and thirty-eight, nine hundred and thirty-five, nine hundred and thirty-four, nine hundred and thirty-nine, nine hundred and thirty-one, nine hundred and thirty-seven, nine hundred and thirty-six, nine hundred and thirty-three, nine hundred and thirty-two, nine hundred and three, nine hundred and twelve, nine hundred and twenty, nine hundred and twenty-eight, nine hundred and twenty-five, nine hundred and twenty-four, nine hundred and twenty-nine, nine hundred and twenty-one, nine hundred and twenty-seven, nine hundred and twenty-six, nine hundred and twenty-three, nine hundred and twenty-two, nine hundred and two, nineteen, ninety, ninety-eight, ninety-five, ninety-four, ninety-nine, ninety-one, ninety-seven, ninety-six, ninety-three, ninety-two, one, one hundred, one hundred and eight, one hundred and eighteen, one hundred and eighty, one hundred and eighty-eight, one hundred and eighty-five, one hundred and eighty-four, one hundred and eighty-nine, one hundred and eighty-one, one hundred and eighty-seven, one hundred and eighty-six, one hundred and eighty-three, one hundred and eighty-two, one hundred and eleven, one hundred and fifteen, one hundred and fifty, one hundred and fifty-eight, one hundred and fifty-five, one hundred and fifty-four, one hundred and fifty-nine, one hundred and fifty-one, one hundred and fifty-seven, one hundred and fifty-six, one hundred and fifty-three, one hundred and fifty-two, one hundred and five, one hundred and forty, one hundred and forty-eight, one hundred and forty-five, one hundred and forty-four, one hundred and forty-nine, one hundred and forty-one, one hundred and forty-seven, one hundred and forty-six, one hundred and forty-three, one hundred and forty-two, one hundred and four, one hundred and fourteen, one hundred and nine, one hundred and nineteen, one hundred and ninety, one hundred and ninety-eight, one hundred and ninety-five, one hundred and ninety-four, one hundred and ninety-nine, one hundred and ninety-one, one hundred and ninety-seven, one hundred and ninety-six, one hundred and ninety-three, one hundred and ninety-two, one hundred and one, one hundred and seven, one hundred and seventeen, one hundred and seventy, one hundred and seventy-eight, one hundred and seventy-five, one hundred and seventy-four, one hundred and seventy-nine, one hundred and seventy-one, one hundred and seventy-seven, one hundred and seventy-six, one hundred and seventy-three, one hundred and seventy-two, one hundred and six, one hundred and sixteen, one hundred and sixty, one hundred and sixty-eight, one hundred and sixty-five, one hundred and sixty-four, one hundred and sixty-nine, one hundred and sixty-one, one hundred and sixty-seven, one hundred and sixty-six, one hundred and sixty-three, one hundred and sixty-two, one hundred and ten, one hundred and thirteen, one hundred and thirty, one hundred and thirty-eight, one hundred and thirty-five, one hundred and thirty-four, one hundred and thirty-nine, one hundred and thirty-one, one hundred and thirty-seven, one hundred and thirty-six, one hundred and thirty-three, one hundred and thirty-two, one hundred and three, one hundred and twelve, one hundred and twenty, one hundred and twenty-eight, one hundred and twenty-five, one hundred and twenty-four, one hundred and twenty-nine, one hundred and twenty-one, one hundred and twenty-seven, one hundred and twenty-six, one hundred and twenty-three, one hundred and twenty-two, one hundred and two, one thousand, seven, seven hundred, seven hundred and eight, seven hundred and eighteen, seven hundred and eighty, seven hundred and eighty-eight, seven hundred and eighty-five, seven hundred and eighty-four, seven hundred and eighty-nine, seven hundred and eighty-one, seven hundred and eighty-seven, seven hundred and eighty-six, seven hundred and eighty-three, seven hundred and eighty-two, seven hundred and eleven, seven hundred and fifteen, seven hundred and fifty, seven hundred and fifty-eight, seven hundred and fifty-five, seven hundred and fifty-four, seven hundred and fifty-nine, seven hundred and fifty-one, seven hundred and fifty-seven, seven hundred and fifty-six, seven hundred and fifty-three, seven hundred and fifty-two, seven hundred and five, seven hundred and forty, seven hundred and forty-eight, seven hundred and forty-five, seven hundred and forty-four, seven hundred and forty-nine, seven hundred and forty-one, seven hundred and forty-seven, seven hundred and forty-six, seven hundred and forty-three, seven hundred and forty-two, seven hundred and four, seven hundred and fourteen, seven hundred and nine, seven hundred and nineteen, seven hundred and ninety, seven hundred and ninety-eight, seven hundred and ninety-five, seven hundred and ninety-four, seven hundred and ninety-nine, seven hundred and ninety-one, seven hundred and ninety-seven, seven hundred and ninety-six, seven hundred and ninety-three, seven hundred and ninety-two, seven hundred and one, seven hundred and seven, seven hundred and seventeen, seven hundred and seventy, seven hundred and seventy-eight, seven hundred and seventy-five, seven hundred and seventy-four, seven hundred and seventy-nine, seven hundred and seventy-one, seven hundred and seventy-seven, seven hundred and seventy-six, seven hundred and seventy-three, seven hundred and seventy-two, seven hundred and six, seven hundred and sixteen, seven hundred and sixty, seven hundred and sixty-eight, seven hundred and sixty-five, seven hundred and sixty-four, seven hundred and sixty-nine, seven hundred and sixty-one, seven hundred and sixty-seven, seven hundred and sixty-six, seven hundred and sixty-three, seven hundred and sixty-two, seven hundred and ten, seven hundred and thirteen, seven hundred and thirty, seven hundred and thirty-eight, seven hundred and thirty-five, seven hundred and thirty-four, seven hundred and thirty-nine, seven hundred and thirty-one, seven hundred and thirty-seven, seven hundred and thirty-six, seven hundred and thirty-three, seven hundred and thirty-two, seven hundred and three, seven hundred and twelve, seven hundred and twenty, seven hundred and twenty-eight, seven hundred and twenty-five, seven hundred and twenty-four, seven hundred and twenty-nine, seven hundred and twenty-one, seven hundred and twenty-seven, seven hundred and twenty-six, seven hundred and twenty-three, seven hundred and twenty-two, seven hundred and two, seventeen, seventy, seventy-eight, seventy-five, seventy-four, seventy-nine, seventy-one, seventy-seven, seventy-six, seventy-three, seventy-two, six, six hundred, six hundred and eight, six hundred and eighteen, six hundred and eighty, six hundred and eighty-eight, six hundred and eighty-five, six hundred and eighty-four, six hundred and eighty-nine, six hundred and eighty-one, six hundred and eighty-seven, six hundred and eighty-six, six hundred and eighty-three, six hundred and eighty-two, six hundred and eleven, six hundred and fifteen, six hundred and fifty, six hundred and fifty-eight, six hundred and fifty-five, six hundred and fifty-four, six hundred and fifty-nine, six hundred and fifty-one, six hundred and fifty-seven, six hundred and fifty-six, six hundred and fifty-three, six hundred and fifty-two, six hundred and five, six hundred and forty, six hundred and forty-eight, six hundred and forty-five, six hundred and forty-four, six hundred and forty-nine, six hundred and forty-one, six hundred and forty-seven, six hundred and forty-six, six hundred and forty-three, six hundred and forty-two, six hundred and four, six hundred and fourteen, six hundred and nine, six hundred and nineteen, six hundred and ninety, six hundred and ninety-eight, six hundred and ninety-five, six hundred and ninety-four, six hundred and ninety-nine, six hundred and ninety-one, six hundred and ninety-seven, six hundred and ninety-six, six hundred and ninety-three, six hundred and ninety-two, six hundred and one, six hundred and seven, six hundred and seventeen, six hundred and seventy, six hundred and seventy-eight, six hundred and seventy-five, six hundred and seventy-four, six hundred and seventy-nine, six hundred and seventy-one, six hundred and seventy-seven, six hundred and seventy-six, six hundred and seventy-three, six hundred and seventy-two, six hundred and six, six hundred and sixteen, six hundred and sixty, six hundred and sixty-eight, six hundred and sixty-five, six hundred and sixty-four, six hundred and sixty-nine, six hundred and sixty-one, six hundred and sixty-seven, six hundred and sixty-six, six hundred and sixty-three, six hundred and sixty-two, six hundred and ten, six hundred and thirteen, six hundred and thirty, six hundred and thirty-eight, six hundred and thirty-five, six hundred and thirty-four, six hundred and thirty-nine, six hundred and thirty-one, six hundred and thirty-seven, six hundred and thirty-six, six hundred and thirty-three, six hundred and thirty-two, six hundred and three, six hundred and twelve, six hundred and twenty, six hundred and twenty-eight, six hundred and twenty-five, six hundred and twenty-four, six hundred and twenty-nine, six hundred and twenty-one, six hundred and twenty-seven, six hundred and twenty-six, six hundred and twenty-three, six hundred and twenty-two, six hundred and two, sixteen, sixty, sixty-eight, sixty-five, sixty-four, sixty-nine, sixty-one, sixty-seven, sixty-six, sixty-three, sixty-two, ten, thirteen, thirty, thirty-eight, thirty-five, thirty-four, thirty-nine, thirty-one, thirty-seven, thirty-six, thirty-three, thirty-two, three, three hundred, three hundred and eight, three hundred and eighteen, three hundred and eighty, three hundred and eighty-eight, three hundred and eighty-five, three hundred and eighty-four, three hundred and eighty-nine, three hundred and eighty-one, three hundred and eighty-seven, three hundred and eighty-six, three hundred and eighty-three, three hundred and eighty-two, three hundred and eleven, three hundred and fifteen, three hundred and fifty, three hundred and fifty-eight, three hundred and fifty-five, three hundred and fifty-four, three hundred and fifty-nine, three hundred and fifty-one, three hundred and fifty-seven, three hundred and fifty-six, three hundred and fifty-three, three hundred and fifty-two, three hundred and five, three hundred and forty, three hundred and forty-eight, three hundred and forty-five, three hundred and forty-four, three hundred and forty-nine, three hundred and forty-one, three hundred and forty-seven, three hundred and forty-six, three hundred and forty-three, three hundred and forty-two, three hundred and four, three hundred and fourteen, three hundred and nine, three hundred and nineteen, three hundred and ninety, three hundred and ninety-eight, three hundred and ninety-five, three hundred and ninety-four, three hundred and ninety-nine, three hundred and ninety-one, three hundred and ninety-seven, three hundred and ninety-six, three hundred and ninety-three, three hundred and ninety-two, three hundred and one, three hundred and seven, three hundred and seventeen, three hundred and seventy, three hundred and seventy-eight, three hundred and seventy-five, three hundred and seventy-four, three hundred and seventy-nine, three hundred and seventy-one, three hundred and seventy-seven, three hundred and seventy-six, three hundred and seventy-three, three hundred and seventy-two, three hundred and six, three hundred and sixteen, three hundred and sixty, three hundred and sixty-eight, three hundred and sixty-five, three hundred and sixty-four, three hundred and sixty-nine, three hundred and sixty-one, three hundred and sixty-seven, three hundred and sixty-six, three hundred and sixty-three, three hundred and sixty-two, three hundred and ten, three hundred and thirteen, three hundred and thirty, three hundred and thirty-eight, three hundred and thirty-five, three hundred and thirty-four, three hundred and thirty-nine, three hundred and thirty-one, three hundred and thirty-seven, three hundred and thirty-six, three hundred and thirty-three, three hundred and thirty-two, three hundred and three, three hundred and twelve, three hundred and twenty, three hundred and twenty-eight, three hundred and twenty-five, three hundred and twenty-four, three hundred and twenty-nine, three hundred and twenty-one, three hundred and twenty-seven, three hundred and twenty-six, three hundred and twenty-three, three hundred and twenty-two, three hundred and two, twelve, twenty, twenty-eight, twenty-five, twenty-four, twenty-nine, twenty-one, twenty-seven, twenty-six, twenty-three, twenty-two, two, two hundred, two hundred and eight, two hundred and eighteen, two hundred and eighty, two hundred and eighty-eight, two hundred and eighty-five, two hundred and eighty-four, two hundred and eighty-nine, two hundred and eighty-one, two hundred and eighty-seven, two hundred and eighty-six, two hundred and eighty-three, two hundred and eighty-two, two hundred and eleven, two hundred and fifteen, two hundred and fifty, two hundred and fifty-eight, two hundred and fifty-five, two hundred and fifty-four, two hundred and fifty-nine, two hundred and fifty-one, two hundred and fifty-seven, two hundred and fifty-six, two hundred and fifty-three, two hundred and fifty-two, two hundred and five, two hundred and forty, two hundred and forty-eight, two hundred and forty-five, two hundred and forty-four, two hundred and forty-nine, two hundred and forty-one, two hundred and forty-seven, two hundred and forty-six, two hundred and forty-three, two hundred and forty-two, two hundred and four, two hundred and fourteen, two hundred and nine, two hundred and nineteen, two hundred and ninety, two hundred and ninety-eight, two hundred and ninety-five, two hundred and ninety-four, two hundred and ninety-nine, two hundred and ninety-one, two hundred and ninety-seven, two hundred and ninety-six, two hundred and ninety-three, two hundred and ninety-two, two hundred and one, two hundred and seven, two hundred and seventeen, two hundred and seventy, two hundred and seventy-eight, two hundred and seventy-five, two hundred and seventy-four, two hundred and seventy-nine, two hundred and seventy-one, two hundred and seventy-seven, two hundred and seventy-six, two hundred and seventy-three, two hundred and seventy-two, two hundred and six, two hundred and sixteen, two hundred and sixty, two hundred and sixty-eight, two hundred and sixty-five, two hundred and sixty-four, two hundred and sixty-nine, two hundred and sixty-one, two hundred and sixty-seven, two hundred and sixty-six, two hundred and sixty-three, two hundred and sixty-two, two hundred and ten, two hundred and thirteen, two hundred and thirty, two hundred and thirty-eight, two hundred and thirty-five, two hundred and thirty-four, two hundred and thirty-nine, two hundred and thirty-one, two hundred and thirty-seven, two hundred and thirty-six, two hundred and thirty-three, two hundred and thirty-two, two hundred and three, two hundred and twelve, two hundred and twenty, two hundred and twenty-eight, two hundred and twenty-five, two hundred and twenty-four, two hundred and twenty-nine, two hundred and twenty-one, two hundred and twenty-seven, two hundred and twenty-six, two hundred and twenty-three, two hundred and twenty-two, two hundred and two.

from Mon Catalogue

The French visual artist Claude Closky examines commercial culture, often high-lighting consumerism's artifice and mechanics of desire. In *Mon Catalogue* (Limoges: Éditions Frac Limousin, 1999), Closky takes existing advertising copy and transforms the directive *you* or *yours* to a subjective *I* or *mine*. For the piece, Closky has cata-loged objects he owns, tracked down ad copy for those specific products, and per-sonalized it. The result is a consumer-frenzied overload of language, a contempo-rary form of self-portraiture, not only defining oneself by what one owns but also pointing out the dilemma of being possessed by one's possessions—and by associa-tion, the companies that make those possessions. Closky depersonalizes the work even more by turning all brands to generics. The companies that make the products are never mentioned.

By bringing the techniques of 1980s consumerist artists such as Jeff Koons and Richard Price into poetry, Closky creates a new discourse for literature. Although the New York school embraced consumerism, using pop as a portal to subjectiv-ity—(Frank O'Hara: "Having a Coke with you / is even more fun than going to San Sebastian, Irún, Hendaye, Biarritz, Bayonne"), it never came close to the cold objec-tivity and naked, prophetic words of Andy Warhol: "If you're the Queen of England you couldn't have a better Coke than the bum on the corner."

Mon réfrigérateur
Le volume utile de mon réfrigérateur est bien supérieur aux capacités habi-tuelles, et me permet de stocker mes produits frais et surgelés. Le compar-timent à viande à température réglable et le bac à légumes avec contrôle d'humidité m'assurent une parfaite conservation de mes aliments. Outre le froid ventilé, il me fabrique et me distribue des glaçons ainsi que de l'eau fraîche. De plus, mon réfrigérateur est équipé d'une façade anti-salissure qui me facilite son entretien.

Mon gel purifiant
Pour matifier peu à peu l'aspect luisant de ma peau, resserrer mes pores dilatés et assainir mes comédons, j'ai une solution : nettoyer chaque soir mon visage avec mon gel purifiant au zinc associé à un actif régulateur de sébum qui élimine, sans me décaper, les impuretés accumulées pendant la journée. Ma peau ne brille plus. Le pouvoir apaisant du zinc, renforcé par

un agent hydratant, adoucit et ressource les zones sèches de mon visage. Ma peau ne tire plus.

Mes lunettes intégrales
J'apprivoise les rayons du soleil avec mes lunettes intégrales. Véritables boucliers contre les rayons nocifs et les lumières trop vives, je peux aussi les porter sur des lunettes de vue, qu'elles entourent parfaitement. Je bénéficie de la vision panoramique de leur verre enveloppant anti-chocs en Lexan. Filtrant les ultraviolets de tous les côtés, elles me protègent les yeux du soleil, mais aussi du vent, du sable, des poussières. Suprême raffinement, une barrette de mousse vient épouser mon front, m'assurant confort et parfait maintien. Très légères, j'ai du plaisir à les porter en toutes circonstances. Avec leur cordon amovible, je les apprécie également lors de la pratique de mes sports favoris.

My refrigerator
The usable volume of my refrigerator is far superior to conventional capacities, and allows me to store my fresh and frozen produce. The meat compartment with adjustable temperature and the crisper with humidity control assure me a perfect preservation of my food. Furthermore, the fan-cooling unit makes and dispenses my ice to me as well as fresh water. Moreover, my refrigerator is equipped with an anti-bacterial coating that helps me to keep it clean.

My cleansing gel
To gradually mattify the shiny appearance of my skin, tighten my dilated pores, and clean up my blackheads, I have a solution: clean my face every night with my purifying gel with zinc—known to be an active controller of sebum that eliminates, without chafing, the impurities accumulated during the day. My skin is no longer shiny. The soothing power of zinc, reinforced by a moisturizing agent, softens and relaxes the dry areas of my face. My skin no longer feels taut.

My one-piece glasses
I tame the sun's rays with my one-piece glasses. True shields against harmful UV radiation and too-bright light, I can also appreciate them above corrective glasses, as they surround my face perfectly. I benefit from the

panoramic vision of the enveloping impact-resistant Lexan glass. Filtering ultraviolet rays on all sides, they protect my eyes not only from the sun, but also wind, sand, and dust. The ultimate refinement: a small foam band contours perfectly to my face, assuring comfort and a perfect fit. Extremely lightweight, I enjoy wearing them in all circumstances. With their removable cord, I also appreciate them while playing my favorite sports.

Clark Coolidge
from Cabinet Voltaire

Published in Clark Coolidge's book *ING* (New York: Angel Hair, 1968), the long poem "Cabinet Voltaire" draws its vocabulary from Robert Motherwell's influential 1951 *Dada Painters and Poets: An Anthology.* For instance, section 3 fragments Hugo Ball's "Dada Fragments," and section 11 comes from Tristan Tzara's "An Introduction to Dada." Coolidge chose words sequentially from the left-hand margin of the page, reading vertically and taking advantage of the chance hyphenation of the justified prose block's typesetting. Taking the square enclosure of the prose block as a constraint, Coolidge transforms the carnival of the Cabaret Voltaire into a cabinet of linguistic curiosities. One of Coolidge's subsequent publications would subject an Andy Warhol interview to similar, if less constrained, appropriation (compare Coolidge's "'THE' [Part I]" [*The World* 15: 2 (March 1969)] with Gretchen Berg's "Nothing to Lose: An Interview with Andy Warhol" [*Cahiers du Cinéma* (English) 10 (May 1967): 38–43]).

3.

tradict

theless

it gether
tastic
for

gin tion

and sarily
and
    sests

II.

but which
even the
survives

        the etc., this tion

posed or was
needs the a
that come

           (tain)

   that had   the ity

       (ligent sciousness)

  tain
at the
bound

nated in the
an sulted us

tie   it is, was, never, few

                                        (cession)

    cession
    through zines

                        (portant ered)

    ONE
    BECILES

Talgia = Laine's velous still Versal

    fronted a forth

    the Had Product

from Bond Sonnets

Published in the *Insect Trust Gazette* 2 (Summer 1965), the chance collage of Coolidge's *Bond Sonnets* reterritorializes words from Ian Fleming's James Bond novel *Thunderball* (New York: Viking, 1961) by means of a random number generator. The homologies are neat: bringing the espionage themes of chance and encryption to a work about a gambling spy, Coolidge applies a mathematical formula to a formulaic work of genre fiction. Moreover, with the choice of *Thunderball,* he appropriates an already appropriated text. Fleming had plagiarized the novel from a collaborative screenplay by Fleming, Kevin McClory, and Jack Whittingham. A legal case over the credits went to trial, with judgment against Fleming, who argued that the central idea for the work did not belong to any of them, but rather to Ernest Cuneo (to whom the book was originally dedicated, with the credit of "Muse"). Despite the settlement, questions of intellectual property plagued the work for decades. McClory lost the court-won rights to *Thunderball* after MGM took advantage of a renewal oversight and snatched the copyright. Additionally, repeated attempts to exercise his option to remake the film version of the novel were all defeated by legal challenges from the franchise holders. After a multimillion-dollar copyright lawsuit between MGM and Sony, McClory eventually remade the film in 1983 as *Never Say Never Again.* Ironically, both works are now held by the same owner, since Sony acquired MGM in 2005.

I.

"Satisfactory" other hours' haul the
beacon Amies gone one and
he say wonderful Bond and
freeing but late saw each
the taste meticulously weakly same
ten wretches here right plan
in paid sipped health-protecting to
that to the lawn desirable
cutthroat He's him gingerly form
couple he 7 down that
bugged of Inside Identification and
big corner number appropriate smile
Jamaica lawn to South of
dark sense the bond out

gold life their into condition
to those your inefficiency through
deeply slackened with message indicator
laughed also something his multiple
have said Ascension Paris along
in corpse one blackjack hold
when white stovepipe pleasure captain
that shifted Largo whole knowing
darted understand blackjack punched and
steps talked himself Letter slightly
strokes strain CARDBOARD background which
of fish's need that know
whirled detection gazed going weapons
bigger barrel the tomorrow

Hart Crane
Emblems of Conduct

After the death of Hart Crane, scholars discovered that his poem "Emblems of Conduct" is almost entirely an unattributed collage of lines from the obscure and then-unpublished poet Samuel Greenberg. Crane had copied out a number of Greenberg's poems from the manuscript kept by their mutual friend William Murrell Fisher. Greenberg, himself trained as a copyist in the visual arts, had been dead for some years by the time Crane saw his poems. Of particular use to Crane were the poems "Conduct," "Immortality," and "Perusal," though he seems to have borrowed from Greenberg's "The Laureate" and "Daylight," as well (readers interested in the correlation between specific passages should consult the appendix to James Laughlin's *Poems from the Greenberg Manuscripts, a Selection from the Work of Samuel B. Greenberg* [Norfolk, Va.: New Directions, 1939]). The plagiarized lines are often not exact—where Greenberg writes "The wanderer soon chose / This spot of rest," Crane, for example, has "The wanderer later chose this spot of rest"—but the extent of the purloining is remarkable. The only lines in the poem that seem to be entirely Crane's own are the single couplet: "By that time summer and smoke were past. / Dolphins still played, arching the horizons."

With its mentions of coverings, historians, the lure of the living, and the commemoration by dull lips, "Emblems" inevitably suggests itself as an emblem of the embalmed: an unacknowledged elegy for both the young Greenberg—dead by the age of twenty-three from tuberculosis that had been exacerbated by poverty—and for Crane's own act of lip-synched mimicry, the living poet recovering the lines of the dead. "Emblems" constructs a proper *tombeau* for Greenberg, though the grave remains unmarked.

By a peninsula the wanderer sat and sketched
The uneven valley graves. While the apostle gave
Alms to the meek the volcano burst
With sulphur and aureate rocks . . .
For joy rides in stupendous coverings
Luring the living into spiritual gates.

Orators follow the universe
And radio the complete laws to the people.
The apostle conveys thought through discipline.
Bowls and cups fill historians with adorations,—
Dull lips commemorating spiritual gates.

The wanderer later chose this spot of rest
Where marble clouds support the sea
And where was finally born a hero.
By that time summer and smoke were past.
Dolphins still played, arching the horizons,
But only to build memories of spiritual gates.

Brian Joseph Davis
from Voice Over

Brian Joseph Davis is an artist whose primary medium is sound. In the tradition of
fellow Torontonian John Oswald, Davis creates new works by recycling, remixing,
or altering existing works. Among these are his self-descriptive project "10 Banned
Albums Burned Then Played"; "End User Licence Agreement," an anticopyright
piece in which a chorus sings the End User License Agreement as a Gregorian chant;
"Greatest Hit," in which all the tracks on a given greatest-hits album are played on
top of one another and crunched down into one single self-canceling chaotic track;
and "Yesterduh," a misheard lyric piece in which passersby were asked to sing, from
memory and with no practice, the Beatles' song "Yesterday."

Davis's script project "Voice Over" comprises more than five thousand film tag
lines—those short marketing slogans used to advertise commercial movies—com-
piled by Davis and then performed by a professional voice-over artist. Organized by
a series of constraints (e.g., numbers, gendered pronouns), each of the ten chapters
adds up to an overarching fractured narrative, reminiscent of the *nouveau roman*.

A story of two people. Two lovers you'll never forget, two amazing secret
agents. Two worlds, one love, two brothers, one gangster, and the most
heinous of crimes. One diabolical madman, five suspects, two lovers. One
killer, two women, one man, one man's dream, one woman's obsession. A
lady of the night. A man of the cloth. It took them 17 years to learn the
rules. And one week to break them all. One man's dilemma in a small town
desperate for hope. One family, one murder, too many lies. One cop is too
hot, one cop is too cool, and one fights for justice, the other for power. Only
one can survive one night of ecstasy and a lifetime of sorrow. One good cop.
One bad cop. One very dangerous woman. A one-armed man. Two sisters.
Two lives. One Love. One hunts. One doesn't count, the other can't. One
seduces. One kills. One Wants to Love. Two men enter. One man leaves.
Two identical strangers. Two different worlds. One perfect match. A social-

ite. A runaway. A fatal meeting. Two people, one mystery, one thing in common—two heads grafted to the body of a giant. One's a dreamer, one's a schemer and together they're on the run and layin' low. 100 Assassins. 1,000 Weapons. 10,000,000 Dollars. The boy no one could reach with the code no one could crack against the agent no one could stop. Two apartments. Two women. One shocking mystery. A thousand hours of hell for one moment of love. Five taxis. Five cities. One night. One con out to save his million dollar scam, one priest out to save his only brother, two women, one tropical island. One's hot. One's cool. They're both boiling mad. One broke his silence. The other broke the system. No one would take on his case until one man was willing to take on the system. Five terrorists. One kid. Two different worlds. One true love. Two tiny mice, one big adventure. Four perfect killers. One perfect crime. Two different worlds. Only one is real. The story of one outrageous woman caught between two men. One's a warrior. One's a wise ass. One girl. Two guys. Three possibilities. They're two L.A. cops going after a gang of drug lords. Two young heroes. One small town. Five strangers. Four secrets. Three schemes. Two best friends. Two captains. One destiny. Six hundred lives, one directive. One man's vision of utopia, one man's search for peace, and one woman's search for her lost son. Two friends. One past. No future. Both of them certain of one thing—a story of two people. A brother's murder, a killer set free, a cop, a killer, some bad acid. And a whole lot of hair A comedy of families, a chip shop, revenge atop a Swiss mountain, and a very randy dog. If there is but one life, there are several ways to die—one of his team is a killer but who? Seven people. Seven days. Seven lives changed forever. A one way ticket to terror. Three inseparable buddies separated by blackmail, love, and a hundred thousand dollars. Five miles above the earth, an elite team of six men must save 400 lives on board a 747, and the 40 million below. A willful, passionate girl and the three men who want her. Life gets complicated when you love one woman and worship eleven men. Take your worst nightmare and multiply it by thirteen. The true story of two sisters who shared a passion, a madness, a man, a pair of flat-foot floogies—hot dickety. A bomb plot. A killing. Justice. One night of passion, centuries of hate, an assassin on the loose, a president in danger. Only one man stands between them. This brain wants to love; this brain wants to kill. A wife, a millionaire. A proposal, a medal for honor. A search for justice in a battle for truth by a man who believed in war, a man who believed in nothing, and a woman who believed in both of them. A powerful senator, his psychotic brother. and a photographer who knew too much about two cops on the take who just made the biggest mistake of their lives. Four heroes from the past fight as one to protect the future against five scientists with five minutes to live on two continents in two eras. You need ten eyes to see, ten ears to hear, and ten hearts to feel the tumultuous surge and glory of this mighty spectacle of seven savage punks on a weekend binge of violence. Three different killers. Three different ways to die. The soldiers who brought death and the father and daughter fighting for life for the people who have always feared it. And the one man who knows its secret with 12 Hands, 12 Feet, and 24 reasons to die. First one, then another, and another. Who or what is responsible for the story of three young women and the events that would change their lives with $50,000, five days, and one last chance with two women who will both see the face of the same man. Each thinks it is her missing husband. Only one can be right. Six men and three women—against the sea and each other, along with two outlaws who just wanted to be wanted. These seven friends are getting away for a weekend in the country. Only six are coming back. One man will make a mistake. The other will make it a spectacle. They were seven—And they fought like seven hundred. 2 are in jail and the others have blown their minds. When 10,000 biceps meet 5,000 bikinis you know what's gonna happen? 1000 startling adventures. 1000 weird sensations. Ninety minutes. Six bullets. No choice. Five people given the power to destroy nations. What will they do? What would you do? Find two friends with one opportunity and no going back. 10 seconds: the pain begins. 15 seconds: you can't breathe. 20 seconds: you explode with seven deadly sins. It's about crime. It's about payback. It's about survival in one tough city with three extraordinary kids, two brothers, one fortune and zero chance they'll share it Over 1000 wild horses in mid stampede with 40 million lives at stake and 1.37 billion dollars in one room, five people in another, and six desperate people, hiding one guilty secret about two lovers with one chance against three thugs, two rugs, and a one-eyed boxer.

———

She's ten miles of bad road for every hood in town. They say she kissed 2,000 men. She's a one-mama massacre squad. She'll put you in traction. She forced an entire lifetime of passion into one lust filled summer. Tonight she will love again and kill again. Her beauty is a dangerous weapon of war. Her passion for art changed the face of history. She's brown sugar and spice but if you don't treat her nice she'll put you on ice. Mistress of the waterfront, she was too much for one town and no town would have her. No man could tame her. She's a love-starved moon maiden on the prowl blasting Nazis on a bold commando raid and finding love in precious, stolen moments. As a lawyer all she wanted was the truth. As a daughter all she wanted was his innocence. She's 15. The only adult she admires is Johnny Rotten. She Lives. Don't move. Don't breathe. She will find you. Could she kill and kiss and not remember? On the naked stage she has no secrets. When she shimmied, the whole world shook. When she sang, the whole world thrilled. She steals his car and his furniture. But can she steal his heart? She scorched her soul to save an American cavalry officer. Here she is. That eye-filling, gasp-provoking blonde bombshell. The man-by-man story of a lost soul. Every time she says, "I love you" she breaks the law. Just when she met the man of her dreams, along came her husband to ruin everything. She was at the head of the line, in a place she didn't belong, in a fight no one thought she could win. They gave her a bad name and she lived up to it. Every man who sees her digs her but she digs kicks of a very special kind. He was 15. She was 40. The only thing she couldn't remember was how to forget. Feared by every man, desired by every woman, she's so hot, you'll need to call 911. In a world of power and privilege, one woman dared to obey her heart. She's so romantic she drives four men frantic. She went for anything in pants. She was born outside the laws of God and man. She called it an accident, the headlines shrieked murder. She heard herself convicted by the man she loved. What strange power made her half woman and half snake? She was a starlet out to make the big time—the men, the passions, the lonely nights—until she found fulfillment in a sunlit paradise. She's given up on love but love hasn't given up on her because wanting a man dead can be reason enough to live. She gave them what they wanted and they took everything she had. She's 200 pounds of maniacal fury. Too young to know, too wild to care, too eager to say, "Yes." She lived and loved like the violent jungle around her. She'd wink till hearts went on the blink and staid professors couldn't think. And everywhere they'd stop to stare. No force could sway her. No fear could stop her. She brought a small town to its feet and a huge corporation to its knees. They gave her looks, brains, nuclear capabilities. Everything but an off switch. Its creator made it in her own image. The military made it deadly. Now only one man can stop her. Once you cross this special agent, you've crossed the line and discovered the stark naked truth of a woman's desire for love. Daring. Revealing. Shocking. Goddess of love in a city of sin. She ain't mama's little girl no more—a wrong girl for the right side of the tracks, made of fire and ice, and everything dangerous. Something happens when she hears the music. It's her freedom. It's her fire. It's her life. Between the terror outside her door, and the horror inside her mind you have to get out of her life if you want to stay alive. She's a woman on fire. It activates. It exhilarates. It exterminates. Motorcycle mama on a highway to hell. Leather on the outside. All woman on the inside. What must a good girl say to "belong?" She was born to be bad, to be kissed, to make trouble. The only thing she wanted to take on her honeymoon was her boyfriend. She made good—with a plunging neckline and the morale of a tigress. She knows all about love potions, and lovely motions. The American girl, victim of Berlin's political intrigue—she dared—the only thing hotter than her dreams is reality. She's an undercover cop. seduced by a fantasy, trapped in a mystery, led by a dangerous impulse. She came to the edge of the world to find something more but through one indiscretion a woman with a future became a woman with a past. Her lovers went from bed, to dead. Renegade woman— tough as they come—the adventure, the ecstasy, the supreme suspense of a woman wronged beyond words, almost beyond revenge. Mistress of an empire of savages and beasts; intelligence was her crime, intolerance her enemy. Badmen gave her a name that the panhandle spoke only through gunsmoke. She broke the rules, and changed their lives. A cheat at heart, from her painted toes to her plunging neckline, a good girl until she lights a "reefer." Perfect girl. Car crazy. Speed crazy. Boy crazy. Her soft mouth was the road to sin-smeared violence. She made a career out of love. She made the frozen north red hot. She blew the lid off the wild west. Her treachery stained every stone of the pyramid. Look if you like, but look out. She's man bait and in the heart of this young woman lies a secret that divides a nation. Hers was the deadliest of the seven sins. What she needs, money can't buy. She's spying on two strangers. She's about to murder her best friend and she's only 16 years old. She led 3 strange lives. Which was her real self? Eight years ago she lost her memory, now a detective must help her remember the past before it buries them both. She'll coax the blues right out of your heart. Let her show you the heat of desire—the face of sin. Her dreams inspired hope. Her words inspired passion. Her courage forged a nation's destiny. Torn from her arms, a child of love a woman can give but once. She rules a palace of pleasure . . . for women. The slick chicks who fire up the big wheels. The gayest girlie spree of all time. Untamed girls of the pack-gang. Girls from the "right" kind of home stumbling into the "wrong" kind of love. Bored, thrill-hungry, they shop for sin. Super sisters on cycles, These women carry guns. They dare to do what other women only dream about. Their law is the whip. Their trademark the branding iron. Better move your butt when these ladies strut. They play around with murder like they play around with men. Meet those not-so-sainted sisters. See women who use the love machine to allay the male shortage. Three foxy mamas turned loose, they can lick any man ever made. Guts as hard as the steel of their hogs, riding their men as viciously as they ride their motorcycles. Scarlet women out to get every thrill they could steal. The wildest girl gang that ever blasted the streets, joined together, how can they make love to separate husbands? She didn't take orders. She took over. She's not just getting married, she's getting even. She was everything the west was—young, fiery, exciting. She went to sleep as a secretary and woke up a madman's "bride." She's about to bare her soul and all that goes with it. They shattered her world. Now she's out for justice. And vengeance. Only a nervy girl succeeds in a game of death where men fail. She was sent back in time to ensure the future of mankind. She's never been hip. Never been cool. Never been in. Until now. Model, pop star, goddess, junkie, icon—heaven was in her eyes and her lips were paradise. She was made for love and tragedy. Queen of the outlaws, queen of sin. A date. A drink. A car. A kiss. Now she's known as "that girl." School-girl by day. Hollywood hooker by night. Her only chance for the future is to embrace the power of her past. Into the land of the lawless rode a blonde wildcat. The gal who invented love. Gungirl. Untamed. Unashamed. She brought danger, death and desire to the west. A six-gun siren who shoots to thrill with tricky eyes. Dangerous smile, exquisitely gowned, nimble fingers. He strayed and he paid. She saw to that. She was prepared for anything, until love stormed in. Her name is about all you can handle. You call her a "playgirl" but this girl plays for keeps. She created a monster as her secret lover. She was everything they dreamed of and nothing they expected. The strange love-life of a wrestling gal. Charlie, Sidney, Roger. The names and places didn't matter. Only "when." Dance she did, and dance she must—between her two loves. Caged boyhungry wildcat gone mad. A white hot story of a good girl in a bad world. A vision of beauty born in hell. She gave and gave, until she had nothing left to give. The lowdown story of a high-class gal who became a national pastime. The chauffeur's daughter who learned her stuff in Paris. She challenged the desert, its men, their passions, and ignited a bold adventure. Born to shop, she learned to kill. The seals have been broken. The prophecies have begun. Now only one woman can halt the end of our world. It's a crime what prison can do to a girl. Every mom wants to be wanted, but not for murder one. Love's a dangerous game, where a woman's beauty is the pawn of sinister, clutching hands. She wrote the book on love. She will never be free, until she unlocks her past. She who must be obeyed. She who must be loved. She who must be possessed. The weird, wondrous story of the beautiful woman who bathed in flame and lived 500 years at last to find her first love at this very hour. The story of a woman who raised havoc with a dozen lovers. She wrote the year's blushing best-seller, then had to live it page by burning page No one thought she had the courage, the nerve, or the lingerie. Gorgeous gal who set the Ozarks on fire. Smart about everything, except men. Love wrecked, the flower of southern chivalry dewed with the shining glory of a woman's tears. A top cop torn between her heart and her badge. Meet that guild gal, she gives as good as she gets. The shock-by-shock confessions of a sorority girl—smart, pretty, and all bad. Meet the gayest lady who ever went to town. She made plowboys into playboys. Her machete isn't her only weapon. Hungry female: a man never tasted that good. She'll make you join the sexual liberation army. She corrupted the youthful morality of an entire school. Her best lessons were taught after class. The men in her life sometimes lived to regret it. While some women are waiting to exhale, this one is ready to get even. Her mission—seduce and destroy. Lips that had kissed more men than she could remember also crooned lullabies no one could forget. She had other weapons besides guns, and used them. Every man was her target. She's the girl with the power to turn you on and to turn you off.

Katie Degentesh
The Only Miracles I Know of Are Simply Tricks
That People Play on One Another

This poem comes from Degentesh's book *The Anger Scale* (Cumberland, R.I.: Combo Books, 2006), named after a common psychiatric forensic tool, in which individual poem titles are taken from the Minnesota Multiphasic Personality Inventory. The poems themselves are generated by running the survey's questions through an Internet search engine. Related, accordingly, to flarf, the book also explores some of the same territory investigated by Dan Farrell's "Avail" and Craig Dworkin's *Legion*. By asking the questions of a search engine, however, Degentesh performs a 'pataphysical nosography, evaluating and diagnosing the mental stability of the Internet itself.

I know God can provide us
with more than one cover story
on the subject of black holes

it's how life was originally created
in the hospital those weeks
after I was electrocuted some 35 years ago
when my mom and I emoted as we'd never had

mustering energy for the "unconscious"
pain and frustrations that we were feeling

I never discussed this with the doctor, but
the seas don't part and mountains
made it really difficult for the whole province
to see pictures of the inside of my uterus

I do know that rule number one
is never to point your camera at the sun.

Just stay home and be a mom!!!
my last boyfriend punched me out
in front of my 5-year-old
and I have never been happier

a woman who learned to bend spoons from Uri Gellar
said that my uterus performed
the function of a small blanket placed over a cat
before giving the cat away or putting her to sleep

Baby dust to all, Sherry

Mónica de la Torre
from Doubles

Proper names are so strongly linked with personal identity that the mere suggestion that they are not truly rigid designators can be disquieting. In Nancy Howell's study of the ¡Kung, she notes how a fictive kinship taboo decrees that "one may not marry anyone who has the same name as one's own parent or sibling . . . people with the same name as those for whom marriage would be incest cannot marry" (*Demography of the Dobe ¡Kung*, second edition [New York: Walter de Gruyter, 2000], 229). Beyond psychological and anthropological considerations, identical names are a problem for database parsing and the very practical mathematics of constrained clustering and distance metrics. As one textbook on machine algorithms for linking objects in data sets acknowledges: "disambiguating two people with the same name or similar names is a subtle and time-consuming task even for a person" (Sugato Basu, Ian Davidson, and Kiri L. Wagstaff, *Constrained Clustering: Advances in Algorithms, Theory, and Application* [Boca Raton, Fla., Taylor & Francis, 2009], 367). In *Doubles*, de la Torre brings the philosophical and database problems together. She writes:

> I once saw my name posted on a listserve for people harboring the hope that Internet technology would finally lead them to find their disappeared loved ones. With this history-loaded search as the premise for *Doubles*, I came up with fictional email correspondence that weaved together the real identities of all the namesakes I could find on the web. The piece originally was published online: anyone searching for me or any other Mónica de la Torre inevitably came upon it. It so happened that one of the people who ended up reading *Doubles* online was the actual mother of the woman whose search inspired the piece. She got a hold of my email, and wrote to me with the certainty that I'd know how she could find her daughter. Years had gone by. I had no leads to offer; the email I had for the daughter was no longer valid.

From: mcorreche@tenaris.com.ar
To: Undisclosed recipients
Subject: abandoned

I am looking for Mónica de la Torre, my biological mother. She traveled from Argentina to Barcelona with my father in 1975. They were both together there and in Minorca, where I was born. She went back to Argentina and disappeared when I was two years old, after being accused of subversive activities. I lived in Barcelona and New York until I was 16, but now I live in Argentina with my father and stepmother. I've heard rumors that my mother might be in the United States.

If you read this message and know something about her please communicate with me. It is possible that she doesn't use her real name now. Unfortunately we don't know what she looks like today. She had no birthmarks or scars in the past.

Thank you,
Mercedes Correche

***

From: Monica de la Torre <silliconvalleygrl8@yahoo.com>
To: mcorreche@tenaris.com.ar
CC: Undisclosed recipients
Subject: Re: abandoned

Hi! I am Monica de la Torre, but I am not your mother! I am Regional Student Representative for the #1 Region in the Nation, Region 1!! I live in Santa Clara, California, and am about to get my undergraduate degree in Mechanical Engineering! After receiving my BS, I plan to attend Graduate School to pursue a Masters Degree in Information Systems.

I write to you to give you words of wisdom . . . I haven't always felt like a leader, but several experiences in my life have helped to put me in the position where I am now and to have the confidence that I have. I'm living proof of the quote "Leaders are made, not born!" I encourage you to have the same positive attitude towards life. Good luck with your search!

That's all for now from this Silicon Valley Girl,
Monica de la Torre

***

From: monica@door.org
To: Monica de la Torre <silliconvalleygrl8@yahoo.com>
CC: mcorreche@tenaris.com.ar
Subject: Re: abandoned

Dear Monica de la Torre,

I wanted to alert you to the fact that your reply to Mercedes Correche, daughter of Monica de la Torre, went to everyone on the listserve www.sebusca.org and also let you know that I found it totally irresponsible. I don't know who you are or what you're thinking, but I'm pretty sure that the woman who found herself in the vulnerable situation of having to write such a painful e-mail did not appreciate your leadership messages.

As for you, Mercedes, believe it or not, my name is also Monica de la Torre. I am an officer at the Door Legal Services in New York, and I specialize on family law and the rights of teen parents or young people living independently. Should you need some information pertaining how you can go about dealing with your mother if you find her, please write to me. I'll gladly offer my services to you at no charge.

Compassionately,
Monica de la Torre

***

From: Becky Varnum <bevarnu@mindspring.com>
To: mcorreche@tenaris.com.ar
CC: monica@door.org
Subject: Re: abandoned

Dear Mercedes,

I am a close friend of Monica de la Torre, the legal advisor in New York. She sent me your e-mail because she remembered my mentioning to her that I had met someone with her same name at a tennis tournament. I play tennis and clearly remember beating a woman named Monica de la Torre at the Wolverine Invitational in Ann Arbor in 1998. In fact, the final score was 6–2, 6–0. She had a Spanish accent that didn't sound familiar to me, and I remember that when I asked her where she was from she tried hard to convince me that she had grown up in Texas. She was a very good player, but she clearly was concealing something. This might be the person whom you're looking for. I can get in touch with the organizers of the invitational and ask them for more information on that strange woman.

Best,
Becky

***

To: mcorreche@tenaris.com.ar
From: Manuela <lamanuela@transmexicana.com.mx>
Subject: Mi madre

Hi Meche:

My English is no good. ¿Hablas español? Do you speak Espanish? I don't know who you are or for what you wrote to me. My friend Manuela here in Veracruz has a transsexual website and says to me that you are looking for me. I am stripper, go-go dancer, performance artist and top model. Why do you want me? I do not want anybody to know the real name that my mamacita, descanse en paz, put me when I was brought to the world as a boy. Why do you want my data? If you have interest in my show come to Veracruz, aventurera. If not then good-bye.

Chau honey,

Mónica de la Torre
Lo mejor de Veracruz

PD: You can see my photograph in the website. But careful with your baba, drool! Bad for the teclado, how do you say, the key boar.

TRANSSEXUAL TOP MODEL: MONICA DE LA TORRE
From: Veracruz, Mexico
Lives in: Veracruz, VER, MX

***

From: mcorreche@tenaris.com.ar
To: monica@door.org, bevarnu@mindspring.com
Subject: Re: Re: abandoned

Dear Monica & Becky,

Thank you both very much for responding. I appreciate your offering to help, Mrs. de la Torre. As for you, Becky, if you could gather information for me I would appreciate it. I asked my father whether my mother was good at sports, or played tennis when she was married to him or in her youth. He said that she didn't care for sports because everyone in her "bourgeois" family was athletic and she just liked to stay home reading (& smoking cigarettes.) He said that she became less prejudiced when she read that Samuel Beckett was an excellent swimmer and golf player. He also mentioned that she had a lot of nervous energy that she liked to get rid of by getting involved in challenging physical activities. Maybe she is the tennis player.

I need to see my mother again. Thank you for your help,
~Mercedes

***

From: bevarnu@mindspring.com
To: mcorreche@tenaris.com.ar
Subject: Re: Re: abandoned

Dear Mercedes,

My daughter was planning a vacation to Spain (Cataluña, to be precise) and came across your mother's name again. There is a hotel in the medieval town of Regencós in Girona managed by a woman called Mónica de la Torre. The hotel is called the Hotel del Teatre, and just opened in the summer of 2003. It seems like it was an old theater turned into a hotel. It has a website: www.hoteldelteatre.com. You might get her on the phone!

I haven't been able to get information on the tennis player. I'll keep trying.

Good luck,
Becky

***

From: mcorreche@tenaris.com.ar
To: mtp@texasam.edu
Subject: Looking for my mother

Dear Monica de la Torre,

This is not spam. Believe me. I'm sorry for the intrusion, but I am looking for someone of your same name, who is my birth mother. She disappeared 27 years ago in Argentina. Might you be the person I am looking for?

Thanks,
Mercedes Correche

***

From: mtp@texasam.edu
To: mcorreche@tenaris.com.ar
Subject: Re: Looking for my mother

Mercedes,

Is this some sort of joke? Just because my name sounds Spanish doesn't mean that I am from Argentina. I am sick of receiving sales calls and junk mail in Spanish! What is this! If your last name is Hungarian does that mean that AT&T will send you Hungarian promotional material?

Anyway, I am not even 27 years old myself! I was born in 1982 and have never been married and have no children (that I know of, ha ha!) As of now I am a graduate student at the Texas A&M University; I'm getting a M.S. in Food Science and Technology.

Sorry I can't help.

Take care,
Monica

***

From: mcorreche@tenaris.com.ar
To: mtp@texasam.edu
Subject: Re: Re: Looking for my mother

Monica,

Please forgive me. When I saw your name on the website I was so excited that I forgot to read the information included in the listing for you. I just went back to your page and read it. I'm very curious to know why you chose to study "the properties of fried and baked tortilla chips fortified with mechanically-expelled soy flour." What is that? Who eats that? Here in Argentina we don't have that kind of product.

Anyway, is there anyone with your same name in your family? What is your mother's name? I'm sorry to bother you again; I find it fascinating that you & I are almost the same age.

Good-bye,
Mercedes

***

From: mtp@texasam.edu
To: mcorreche@tenaris.com.ar
Subject: Re: Re: Re: Looking for my mother

Hi Mercedes,

I'm sorry if I insulted you. There are many things I could tell you about
my family, but I don't think they'll be of any worth to you. My parents are
of Mexican descent, and I believe that they named me Monica because I
was born on May 4, Santa Monica's day. I don't know that much about
her except that she was the mother of St. Augustine. The last name is very
common, you know? I wouldn't look too much into it. Actually, where was
your mother from? I don't think that's a common last name in Argentina,
where everyone has those Italian-sounding names. It'd have to be Delta
Torri, no?

Anyhow, re your question about my interest in tortilla chips, I'm studying
the properties of fortified ones because I think they're a healthy option for
corn chips, which are low in proteins. Corn tortilla chips were the most
popular snack in the nation last year. It's awesome to me that so many
otherwise starving Mexicans have survived on beans and tortillas only. I'm
interested in developing nutritious and affordable foods that are appealing
to lower-income people, who consume higher quantities of junk food than
people in other economic strata. It could work, no?

Good luck with everything. I sure hope you find your biological mother.
Monica

***

From: mdelatorre@lccentralettes.org
To: mcorreche@tenaris.com.ar
Subject: Re: Looking for my mother

Dear Mercedes Correche,

I received an e-mail saying you were looking for someone of my same
name. I'm sorry to upset you, but I'm not the person you're looking for.

You can see a picture of me at the Centralettes website. Do I look like the other Monica? It'd be so cool to have relatives in Argentina! Maybe we're cousins or something. I *love* dulce de leche Hagen Daas ice cream, isn't it from the same place you are?

¡Hasta! M.

Denis Diderot
from Jacques le fataliste et son maître

At the very end of Denis Diderot's *Jacques le fataliste et son maître* (*Jack the Fatalist and His Master*) (written primarily in the 1770s but not published until 1796), the reader finally hears the story that hundreds of pages of digressions, interruptions, and metatextual diversions have forestalled. More surprising, however, is Diderot's disclosure that he has borrowed more than a divagating style or general mode from earlier works: he openly copied the second paragraph from Laurence Sterne's *Tristram Shandy*.

Diderot copies in both a general sense and a specific sense; he not only imitates the broad contours of a genre (the episodic tradition made famous by Miguel de Cervantes's *Don Quixote,* which Sterne took to caricatured extremes), but he also transcribes specific scenes—down to their details and dialogue—translating or grafting them from one work, and one fictional world, to another. Diderot, who protests at one point, "Je n'aime pas à me faire honneur de l'esprit d'autrui" (I don't like to take credit for another's wit), lays out the more existential questions of close textual repetition in an earlier passage. When Jacques attempts to evade telling his story with the excuse that "it has happened to someone else already," his master counters, "Je dirai comme un poète français, qui avait fait une assez bonne épigramme, dissait à quelqu'un qui se l'attribuait en sa présence: «Pourquoi Monsieur ne l'aurait-il pas fait? je l'ai bien faite, moi...»" (I would reply in the words of a French poet who had made a rather witty epigram, speaking to someone who claimed it as his own: "Why should Monsieur not have written it? I did it myself?"). Camille Goemans would later take this rhetorical ploy to a more audacious level; her contribution to the Belgian surrealist journal *Correspondance* ("Beige" number 22) was an intervention into the serialized and invitingly titled *Counterfeiters* by André Gide—which Goemans predated so as to suggest that Gide was belatedly copying Goemans simply by continuing his own work!

Diderot's plagiarism, moreover, brings together both the narrative structure and uncreative aspects of *Jacques,* collapsing form and content with a confessional flourish. *Détourner,* in French, means both to divert from a straight or intended course as well as to misappropriate, to hijack or deflect. Both senses translate to English, as well: Diderot's story is diverting, in the sense of being entertaining, and it is digressive, with the hint of illicit funneling always present in *diversion* (what thieves do, idiomatically, with water or funds).

Voici le second paragraphe copié de la *Vie de Tristram Shandy*, à moins que l'entretien de Jacques le Fataliste et de son maître ne soit antérieur à cet ouvrage, et que le ministre Sterne ne soit le plagiaire, ce que je ne crois pas, mais par une estime toute particulière de M. Sterne, que je distingue de la plupart des littérateurs de sa nation, dont l'usage fréquent est de nous voler et de nous dire des injures.

Here is the second paragraph copied from the *Life of Tristram Shandy*, unless the conversation between Jacques the Fatalist and his master should predate that work, and the Reverend Sterne be the plagiarist, which I do not believe, given the exceedingly particular regard in which I hold Mr. Sterne, whom I except from the majority of writers from his nation, among whom the common custom is first to steal from us and then to insult us.

Marcel Duchamp
from notes

Duchamp made a number of cryptic notes and sketches related to his readymades, the Large Glass, and other projects and proposals. Some written between the years 1911 and 1915 were collected in the fastidious facsimile *La boît verte* (also known as *La Mariée mise à nu par ses célibataires, même*) (Paris: Éditions Rrose Sélavy, 1934), from which the passages on prime words are drawn. Further writings from between 1912 and 1920, including the section "Dictionary," were collected in *À l'infinitif (The White Box)* (New York: Cordier and Ekstrom, 1967). For more on Duchamp's importance for conceptual art, see the introductions "Why Conceptual Writing?" and "The Fate of Echo."

The search for "prime words" ("divisible" only by themselves and by unity)

Take a Larousse dict. and copy all the so-called "abstract" words. i.e., those which have no concrete reference.

Compose a schematic sign designating each of these words. (this sign can be composed with the standard stops)

These signs must be thought of as the letters of the new alphabet.

A grouping of several signs will determine

(utilize colors—in order to differentiate what would correspond in this [literature] to the substantive, verb, adverb declensions, conjugations etc.)

Necessity for ideal continuity. i.e. each grouping will be connected with the other groupings by a strict meaning (a sort of grammar, no longer requiring pedagogical sentence construction. But, apart from the differences of language, and the "figures of speech" peculiar to each language— weighs and measure some abstractions of substantives, of negatives, of relations of subject to verb, etc, by means of standard signs. (representing these new relations: conjugations, declensions, plural and singular, adjectivation inexpressible by the concrete alphabetic forms of languages living now and to come.).

This alphabet very probably is only suitable for the description of this picture. . . .

Dictionary

—of a language in which each word would be translated into French (or other) by several words, when necessary by a whole sentence.

—of a language which one could translate *in its elements* into known languages but which would not reciprocally express the translation of French words (or other), or of French or *other* sentences.

—Make this dictionary by means of cards

—find out how to classify these cards (alphabetical order, but which alphabet)

Alphabet—or rather a few elementary signs, like a dot, a line, a circle, etc. (to be seen) which will vary according to the position etc.

—Sound of this language, is it speakable? No.

Relation to shorthand.

"Grammar"—i.e. How to connect the elementary signs (like words), then the *groups* of signs one to the other; what *will become of the ideas* of action or of being (verbs), of modulation (adverbs)—etc.?

Buy a dictionary and cross out the words to be crossed out. Sign: revised and corrected.

Look through a dictionary and scratch out all the "undesirable" words. Perhaps add a few—Sometimes replace the scratched out words with another.

Craig Dworkin
from Legion

Craig Dworkin composed *Legion* by rearranging and recontextualizing the true-false questions of the 1942 Minnesota Multiphasic Personality Inventory as if they were declarative confessional statements from a lyric subject—part of a poetic mono-logue rather than a forensic instrument. The personality inventory was originally published as a set of boxed cards not unlike Robert Grenier's *Sentences* (Cambridge, Mass.: Whale Cloth, 1978)—a work that also explores the uncanny psychology of the everyday—an association that helped underscore the poetic potential of the *Inventory* beyond the tradition of the list poem or heroic catalog.

More proximate references might include the thirteenth section of Charles Bern-stein's "A Person Is Not an Entity Symbolic but the Divine Incarnate," subtitled "Chorus":

> People should love and approve of me. Making mistakes is terrible. People should be called on their wrongdoings. It's horrible when things go wrong. I can't control my emotions. Threatening situations keep me worried. Self-discipline is too hard. The bad effects of my childhood still control my life. I can't stand the way most people act: avoiding responsibility, terribly unfair, always late, demanding atten-tion, physically abusive, putting things off, harshly critical, whiny or crybaby, with-drawing into themselves for days or weeks, drinking too much, smoking, sleeping all the time or not at all, afraid of their own worthlessness, angry, irritable, bored, dull and frustrated, lonely, paralyzed, hopeless. (*The Sophist* [Los Angeles: Sun and Moon, 1987], 159)

Bernstein's poem draws from a textbook or worksheet for rational emotive therapy (see, for instance, the identical catalog "Irrational Ideas or Philosophies" in Albert Ellis, *Growth Through Reason: Verbatim Cases in Rational Emotive Therapy* [Palo Alto: Science and Behavior Books, 1971], 183). Other works relevant to *Legion* include David Antin's "A List of the Delusions of the Insane / What They Are Afraid Of," Dan Farrell's "Avail," and Katie Degentesh's *The Anger Scale* (selections from which are included in the present anthology).

In the tradition of 'pataphysics, *Legion* is an imaginary solution to very real problems (both the pain of certain mental conditions and their often far-worse medical treatments). As Ursula K. Le Guin wrote, "There are no right answers to wrong questions." Or, as Susan Sontag put it, "The only interesting answers are those that destroy the questions."

Once in a while I think of things too bad to talk about. Bad words, often terrible words, come into my mind and I cannot get rid of them. I am bothered by acid stomach several times a week. I am likely not to speak to people until they speak to me. Often I cross the street in order not to meet someone else. I am often sorry because I am so cross and grouchy. I can't understand why I have been so cross and grouchy. I frequently ask people for advice. I am liked by most people who know me. I commonly wonder what hidden reason another person may have for doing something nice for me. I believe in the second coming of Christ. I find it hard to keep my mind on a task or a job. I am not afraid of mice. I am not usually self-conscious. I used to keep a diary. I cannot understand what I read as well as I used to. My daily life is full of things that keep me interested. At times it has been impossible for me to keep from stealing or shoplifting something. I don't blame anyone for trying to grab everything he can get in this world. I would rather win than lose in a game. Sometimes I'm strongly attracted by other's personal effects, shoes, gloves, etc., so that I want to handle or steal them though I have no use for them. I have been disappointed in love. I have no dread of going into a room by myself where other people have already gathered and are talking. My family does not like the work I have chosen (or the work I intend to choose for my life work). I am more sensitive than most other people. At times I hear so well it bothers me. I have no fear of water. I have periods in which I feel unusually cheerful without any special reason. At times I feel that I can make up my mind with unusually great ease. I am afraid of using a knife or anything very sharp or pointed. My feelings are not easily hurt. I have not lived the right kind of life. Dirt frightens or disgusts me. It is safer to trust nobody. At parties I am more likely to sit by myself or with just one other person than to join in with the crowd. I must admit that I have at times been worried beyond reason over something that really did not matter. I worry over money and business. When someone does me a wrong I feel I should pay him back if I can, just for the principle of the thing. People say insulting and vulgar things about me. I am against giving money to beggars. I readily become one hundred percent sold on a good idea. I am very careful about my manner of dress. I would like to be a soldier. At times I feel like picking a fist fight with someone. I would like to be a journalist. My memory seems to be all right. I frequently have to fight against showing that I am bashful. My hardest battles are with myself. At times I feel like smashing things. I have very few headaches. It is all right to get around the law if you don't actually break it. When I leave home I do not worry about whether the door is locked and the windows closed. I like repairing a door latch. At times I have a strong urge to do something harmful or shocking. I would like to wear expensive clothes. Someone has been trying to rob me. There are persons who are trying to steal my thoughts and ideas. I often feel as though things were not real. No one cares much what happens to you. Most of the time I feel blue. I am not afraid of picking up a disease or germs from door knobs. I do not dread seeing a doctor about a sickness or injury. I sometimes keep on at a thing until others lose their patience with me. When I get bored I like to stir up some excitement. I am sure I am being talked about. I have never had any breaking out on my skin that has worried me. It makes me angry to have people hurry me. I wish I were not so shy. When I was a child, I didn't care to be a member of a crowd or gang. Except by a doctor's orders I never take drugs or sleeping powders. I usually work things out for myself rather than get someone to show me how. I seldom worry about my health. During the past few years I have been well most of the time. I have never had a fit or convulsion. Several times I have been the last to give up trying to do a thing. Most people make friends because friends are likely to be useful to them. I have reason for feeling jealous of one or more members of my family. There is something wrong with my sex organs. I do many things which I regret afterwards (I regret things more or more often than others seem to). I have often felt guilty because I have pretended to feel more sorry about something than I really was. There is very little love and companionship in my family as compared to other homes. At one or more times in my life I felt that someone was making me do things by hypnotizing me. I think most people would lie in order to get ahead. Much of the time my head seems to hurt all over. I am certainly lacking in self confidence. If given the chance I could do some things that would be of great benefit to the world. I have difficulty in starting to do things. If I were an artist I would like to draw flowers. I have never been in trouble with the law. I believe I am being plotted against. I like collecting flowers or growing house plants. I would like to be a florist. At times I have very much wanted to leave home. My plans have frequently seemed so full of difficulties that I have had to give them up. I feel like giving up quickly when things go wrong. Horses that don't pull should be beaten or kicked. The sight of blood neither frightens me nor makes me sick. Peculiar odors come to me at times. I feel uneasy indoors. I do not try to cover up my poor opinion or pity of a person so that he won't know how I feel. I am troubled by discomfort in the pit of my stomach every few days or oftener. Some of my family have habits that bother and annoy me very much. I never attend a sexy show if I can avoid it. I like poetry. I have several times given up doing a thing because I thought too little of my ability. Most people inwardly dislike putting themselves out to help people. I resent having anyone take me in so cleverly that I have to admit that it was one on me. I believe that my home life is as pleasant as that of most people I know. My people treat me more like a child than a grown up. In school I was sometimes sent to the principal for cutting up. As a youngster I was suspended from school one or more times for cutting up. I don't seem to care what happens to me. I am a good mixer. I have never been in trouble because of my sex behavior. Sometimes I am sure that other people can tell what I am thinking. I believe that a person should never taste an alcoholic drink. I wish I could get over worrying about things I have said that may have injured other people's feelings. It makes me feel like a failure when I hear of the success of someone I know well. I am worried about sex matters. I have had blank spells in which my activities were interrupted and I did not know what was going on around me. It is always a good thing to be frank. I used to like drop-the-handkerchief. I have often felt badly over being misunderstood when trying to keep someone from making a mistake. I feel weak all over much of the time. I pray several times a week. I am about as able to work as I ever was. I cannot do anything well. Sometimes when I am not feeling well I am cross. Criticism or scolding hurts me terribly. Sometimes my voice leaves me or changes even though I have no cold. My hands and feet are usually warm enough. These days I find it hard not to give up hope of amounting to something. Once a week or oftener I feel suddenly hot all over, without apparent cause. I sweat very easily even on cool days. Sometimes, when embarrassed, I break out in a sweat which annoys me greatly. At times I feel like swearing. I am embarrassed by dirty stories. My way of doing things is apt to be misunderstood by others.

---

from Parse

Edwin A. Abbott's 1874 *How to Parse: An Attempt to Apply the Principles of Scholarship to English Grammar* played a leading role in the pedagogic debate over whether English should be analyzed as if it were Latin. Thousands of copies of the book were printed as textbooks in the last quarter of the nineteenth century. *Parse* (Berkeley, Calif.: Atelos, 2008) is a translation of Abbott's book, rendering his text into its own idiosyncratic system of grammatical analysis.

As Friedrich Nietzsche wrote: "Ich fürchte, wir werden Gott nicht los, weil wir noch an die Grammatik glauben" (I fear we are not getting rid of God, because we still believe in grammar).

Noun genitive preposition definite article Noun period

Definite Article Noun adverb of frequency present tense transitive verb definite article Noun alternative disjunctive coordinate conjunction Noun comma conjunction of exception adverb of negation adverb period Preposition noun comma colon dash

Cardinal Roman Numeral period Conjunction definite article noun appositional present tense intransitive verb indefinite article Noun alternative disjunctive coordinate conjunction Adjective Noun colon dash

parenthesis cardinal arabic numeral parenthesis marks of quotation *Interrogative Personal Pronoun Objective Case* past tense auxiliary verb second person singular pronoun present tense transitive verb infinitive mood question mark marks of quotation parenthesis cardinal arabic numeral parenthesis marks of quotation Definite Article noun *relative pronoun* First Person Singular Personal Pronoun Subjective Case present tense intransitive verb *locative preposition* period marks of quotation Cardinal Roman Numeral period Conjunction definite article Noun appositional present tense intransitive verb appositional adjective colon dash

parenthesis cardinal arabic numeral parenthesis marks of quotation *Noun conjunction noun* present tense plural auxiliary verb First Person Singular Personal Pronoun Subjective Case adverb period marks of quotation parenthesis cardinal arabic numeral parenthesis marks of quotation *Adverb Of Negation adjective noun* past tense auxiliary verb third person singular masculine pronoun subjective case present tense transitive verb period marks of quotation

parenthesis cardinal arabic numeral parenthesis marks of quotation *Adjective Used As An Object* third person singular masculine pronoun subjective case past tense transitive verb comma Adjective Used As An Object third person singular masculine pronoun subjective case past tense transitive verb adverb period marks of quotation

Cardinal Roman Numeral period Preposition Noun parenthesis cardinal arabic numeral parenthesis colon dash

marks of quotation *Indefinite Article noun apostrophe vestigial genitive singular ending noun* conjunction adjective adjective dash noun used as a compound noun present tense transitive verb period

Adjective Plural Noun present tense transitive verb adjective of negation Noun period

Adjective Plural Noun present tense transitive verb parenthesis cardinal arabic numeral parenthesis *plural noun* comma *alphabetic letter used as the abbreviation of a latin noun period alphabetic letter used as the abbreviation of a latin adjective period* comma marks of quotation verb comma marks of quotation marks of quotation verb comma marks of quotation marks of quotation modal verb comma marks of quotation marks of quotation verb comma marks of quotation conjunction adverb adjective plural noun genitive preposition marks of quotation verb marks of quotation past participle adverb definite article Adjective plural noun preposition dash suffix comma dash suffix comma ampersand alphabetic letter used as the abbreviation of a plural latin noun period semicolon plural noun present tense transitive verb parenthesis cardinal arabic numeral parenthesis plural noun adverb of negation past participle used as part of a passive verbal construction adverb present participle indefinite article adjective noun comma *alphabetic letter used as the abbreviation of a latin noun period alphabetic letter used as the abbreviation of a latin adjective period* comma marks of quotation verb comma marks of quotation marks of quotation verb comma marks of quotation ampersand alphabetic letter used as the abbreviation of a plural latin noun period

Plural Adjective adjective plural noun genitive preposition Plural Noun present tense plural intransitive auxiliary verb adverb of negation present tense transitive verb indefinite article Adjective Noun period Definite Article adjective noun present tense transitive verb definite article noun marks of quotation interrogative personal pronoun subjective case question mark marks of quotation adverb of negation marks of quotation interrogative personal pronoun objective case question mark marks of quotation *alphabetic letter used as the abbreviation of a latin noun period alphabetic letter used as the abbreviation of a latin adjective period* comma marks of quotation Third Person Singular Masculine Pronoun Subjective Case present tense intransitive verb dash marks of quotation semicolon marks of quotation present tense intransitive verb *interrogative personal pronoun subjective case* alternative disjunctive coordinate conjunction *interrogative personal pronoun objective case* question mark marks of quotation Noun comma marks of quotation Third Person Singular Masculine Pronoun Subjective Case present tense intransitive verb *indefinite article appositional noun* period marks of quotation Adverb marks of quotation noun marks of quotation present tense intransitive verb preposition definite article noun marks of quotation interrogative personal pronoun subjective case question mark marks of quotation parenthesis marks of quotation interrogative personal pronoun objective case question mark marks of quotation parenthesis conjunction present tense intransitive verb adverb of negation and past participle used as a passive verbal construction definite article Noun genitive preposition marks of quotation verb period marks of quotation Second Person Singular Pronoun Implied Present Tense Transitive Verb Imperative Mood Abbreviated Plural Noun period cardinal arabic numeral period

Adjective plural noun genitive preposition definite article Noun conjunction present tense transitive verb adverb of negation Noun present tense modal auxiliary verb present tense transitive verb indefinite article Noun period

For example, you cannot ask "Who or what *killing*?" but you can ask "*killing* whom or what?" Consequently "killing" can have no Subject, but may have an "Object." And so may "to kill."

Laura Elrick
from First Words

Like Kit Robinson's *Dolch Stanzas* or Charles Bernstein's "I and The," the seven sections of "First Words" (*sKincerity* [San Francisco: Krupskaya, 2003]) are composed of what literacy instructors refer to as sight words: lists of the most common words in English (and words that constitute almost half of all written material). Elrick quotes Frank B. May in an epigraph to the poem:

> For instructional purposes these are usually referred to as sight words because we would like our students to recognize them in less than a second. Why? Because this enhances their chance of getting to the end of a sentence in time to remember how it began.

She also quotes Hanna Weiner: "all words are seen." By recontextualizing a standard vocabulary, Elrick reveals philosophical structures and linguistic biases that are encoded into the basic pedagogical and reading process.

One

all about oil
how *I* did go

some were
down with their them

made that was
which word would write you

as by with make could day come

but many more said

part into each who will
use what from other

find first a one to my call

be is if has

can is if up

time of get see

and so on, no?

in there

like his look been for long
her she

(the him this your had)

so

if he at its way?

may not have now then

may not have now then

two than are these:

to when do it out we

to when it we out

people they number

are water they or

Dan Farrell
Avail

"Avail" (*Last Instance* [San Francisco: Krupskaya, 1999]) splices two different foren-sic instruments developed by Dr. William E. Snell Jr., a professor of psychology at Southeast Missouri State University: the Clinical Anger Scale (1995) and the Multidi-mensional Health Questionnaire (1997). Even when distributed across an impossible and contradictory leviathan of sentences, the power of the first-person pronoun to evoke unique expression—the illusion that a single coherent subject is enunciating all of the statements—is difficult to shake. That grammatical psychology is respon-sible in part for the questionnaires' effectiveness, but it also enables Farrell's critique. An interpolation constructed at the intersection of diagnostic tools, Farrell's poem investigates the identities constructed at the intersections of social and economic networks, thus underscoring the brute bluntness and inadequacies of interpellation. Farrell's text thus works to lay bare the ideologies of his sources. In Louis Althusser's well-known formulation:

> Ideology "acts" or "functions" in such a way that it "recruits" subjects among the individuals (it recruits them all), or "transforms" the individuals into subjects (it transforms them all) by that very precise operation which I have called inter-pellation or hailing, and which can be imagined along the lines of the most com-monplace everyday police (or other) hailing: "Hey, you there!" ("Ideology and Ideological State Apparatuses," *Lenin and Philosophy and Other Essays*, trans. Ben Brewster [New York: Monthly Review, 1971], 174)

In a clinical setting, the questionnaires function precisely in this way, simulta-neously hailing and transforming the very subjects they would seek to deceive through creating the illusion of those subjects' expressive autonomy. The question-naires ask patients to identify with assertions and conditions as if they were agents speaking freely for themselves, when in fact only the institutions and apparatuses of the clinic can ultimately validate or affirm those conditions (e.g., "healthy," "angry"). With its contradictions and limited range of maddeningly repetitive terms, Farrell's text manifests the degree to which we are spoken rather than ever really speaking for ourselves—even when speaking about our most intimate feelings and bodily conditions. "I," as Rimbaud famously put it, "is an other" (*Je est un autre*).

Whatever the validity of the mental health assessments derived from Snell's questionnaires, the point of the Multidimensional Health Questionnaire is to distinguish the mentally and socially unsound from the "valid" (an archaic synonym for *healthy*); *avail,* from the same root (Latin *valere*, "to be healthy"), has a similarly archaic denotation: net proceeds, profits, the perquisites or remunerations of employment (e.g., health-care benefits). These occult connections—like a patient's valid anger at a system of ineffective and unequal civic health care—are precisely what the ideological institutions of the original texts might wish to exclude or conceal. Availing himself of found institutional language, Farrell—with a quiet apocalypse—discovers what it would seek to veil.

I feel anxious when I think about my health. I have the ability to take care of any health problems that I may encounter. I am very aware of how healthy my body feels. I do not feel angry. I do things that keep me from becoming physically unhealthy. I feel angry. I am pretty angry about things these days. The status of my physical health is determined mostly by chance happenings. I think about my physical health all the time. I'm very assertive when it comes to looking out for my own physical health. I am not particularly angry about my future. I am becoming more hostile about things than I used to be. When I think about my future, I feel angry. I feel sad when I think about my present physical health. I expect that my health will be excellent in the future. I don't have any persistent angry feelings that influence my ability to make decisions. I am not all that angry about things. I am to blame for those times when I become sick or don't feel well. I don't feel particularly hostile at others. People sometimes dislike being around me since I become angry. I sometimes wonder what others think of my physical health. I don't feel that others are trying to annoy me. I feel hostile a good deal of the time. I feel quite hostile most of the time. I feel hostile all of the time. I'm very motivated to be physically healthy. When I am ill, I myself am in control of whether my health improves. I don't feel angry when I think about myself. I derive a sense of self-pride from the way I handle my own physical health. I am very satisfied with my own physical health. I'm concerned about how my physical health appears to others. The status of my physical health is determined largely by other more powerful people. I'm worried about how healthy my body is. Not only am I in good physical health, but it's quite important to me that I be in good health. I am in good physical health. I am angry to the extent that it interferes with my making good decisions. If I am careful to avoid becoming ill, then I will be in good physical health-shape. I'm not so angry and hostile that others dislike me. I don't have angry feelings about others having screwed up my life. I am depressed about my current physical health. I don't shout at people any more than usual. I feel like my physical health is something that I myself am in charge of. I feel angry about myself a good deal of the time. Things are not more irritating to me now than usual. I am competent enough, I am angry most of the time now, to make sure that my physical health is in good shape. My appetite does not suffer because of my feelings of anger. I notice immediately when my body doesn't feel healthy. My anger does not interfere with my sleep. Sometimes I don't sleep very well because I'm feeling angry. My anger is so great that I stay awake 1-2 hours later than usual. I am so intensely angry that I can't get much sleep during the night. I think about my physical health more than anything else. I am motivated to keep myself from becoming physically unhealthy. I'm very direct with people when it comes to my own physical health needs. When I become sick or ill, I am the person to blame. Sometimes I am so angry that I feel like hurting others, but I would not really do it. I don't feel angry enough to hurt someone. I believe that the future status of my physical health will be positive. The status of my physical health is controlled by accidental happenings. I'm so angry that I would like to hurt someone. I feel angry that others prevent me from having a good life. I'm very concerned with how others evaluate my physical health. I'm strongly motivated to devote time and effort to my physical health. During times when I am sick, my own behavior determines whether I get well. I am proud of the way I deal with and handle my health. I shout at others more now than I used to. I am very satisfied with the status of my physical health. My physical health is largely controlled by people other than myself (e.g., friends, family). It makes me angry that I have failed more than the average person. Not only do I take care of my physical health, but it's very important to me that I do so. My feelings of anger are beginning to affect my appetite. My feelings of anger leave me without much of an appetite. My anger is so intense that it has taken away my appetite. My body is in good physical shape. I can pretty much prevent myself from becoming ill by taking good care of myself. I am disappointed about the quality of my physical health. My health is something that I alone am responsible for. My ability to think clearly is unaffected by my feelings of anger. Sometimes my feelings of anger prevent me from thinking in a clear-headed way. It makes me angry that I feel like such a failure. My anger makes it hard for me to think of anything else. I'm so intensely angry and hostile that it completely interferes with my thinking. I have the skills and ability to ensure good physical health for myself. I shout at others so often that sometimes I just can't stop. My feelings of anger don't interfere with my health. I try to avoid engaging in behaviors that undermine my physical health. My feelings of anger are beginning to interfere with my health. I tend to be preoccupied with my own physical health. My feelings of anger leave me less interested in sex than I used to be. My anger does not make me feel anymore tired than usual. My current feelings of anger undermine my interest in sex. I'm sensitive to internal bodily cues about my physical health. Thinking about my physical health leaves me with an uneasy feeling. Whether (or not) I am in good physical health is just a matter of luck. My feelings of anger occasionally undermine my ability to make decisions. I do not expect to suffer health problems in the future. If I were to become ill, then I'm to blame for not taking good care of myself. I'm very aware of what others think of my physical health. I have a strong desire to keep myself physically healthy. I don't feel so angry that it interferes with my interest in sex. I am somewhat passive about getting my health needs met. If I were to become ill, I myself would be responsible for making myself better. I am pleased with how well I handle my own physical health. My present degree of physical health is personally satisfying to me. I feel angry about what I have to look forward to. My health is largely determined by the actions of powerful others (e.g., health professionals). It's beginning to make me angry that others are screwing up my life. More often than not, people stay away from me because I'm so hostile and angry. I am a well-exercised person. People don't like me anymore because I'm constantly angry all the time. Not only am I in good physical health, but it's important to me that I stay physically healthy. My anger prevents me from devoting much time and attention to my health. If I look out for my health, then I will stay in good physical health and avoid illness. When I think about my current physical health, I feel really down in the dumps. I will probably experience a number of health problems in the future. The status of my physical health is determined largely by what I do (and don't do). I usually worry about whether I am in good health. I am able to cope with and to handle my physical health needs. I know immediately when I'm not feeling physically well. I am angry and hostile about everything. I really want to prevent myself from getting out of shape. My physical health and shape have little or nothing to do with luck. I'm constantly thinking about my physical fitness. When I think about myself, I feel intense anger. I do not hesitate to ask for what I need for my physical health. I feel intensely angry about my future, since it cannot be improved. If I were to start feeling sick, then it would be my own fault for letting it happen. My anger does not interfere with my interest in other people. My anger sometimes interferes with my interest in others. I am becoming so angry that I don't want to be around others. I'm so angry that I can't stand being around people. It makes me angry to feel like a complete failure as a person. As I look back on my life, I feel angry about my failures. It's really important to me that I keep myself in proper physical health. My current level of physical fitness is very pleasing to me. I have positive feelings about the way I approach my own physical health. Whether I recover from an illness depends in large part on what I myself do. My feelings of anger do not interfere with my work. In order to have good health, I have to act in a pleasing way to other more powerful individuals. At times I think people are trying to annoy me. I feel more angry about myself these days than I used to. More people than usual are beginning to make me feel angry. I am so angry and hostile all the time that I can't stand it. From time to time my feelings of anger interfere with my work. I feel that others are constantly and intentionally making me angry. I feel so angry that it interferes with my capacity to work. I feel unhappy about my physical health. My feelings of anger prevent me from doing any work at all. My body needs a lot of work in be in excellent physical shape. I keep myself physically healthy, and it's very important to me that I stay fit and healthy. I will be able to avoid any illnesses, if I just take care of myself. I am constantly angry because others have made my life totally miserable. I think about my physical health the majority of the time. I feel nervous when I think about the status of my physical health. What happens to my physical health is my own doing. I don't believe that chance or luck play any role in the status of my physical health. I have the capability to take care of my own physical health. I am really motivated to avoid being in terrible physical shape. I'm very aware of changes in my physical health. I'm so angry that I can't make good decisions anymore. When it comes to my own physical health requirements, I ask for what I need. My physical health is in need of attention. My anger is so intense that I sometimes feel like hurting others. I anticipate that my physical health will deteriorate in the future. My feelings of anger are beginning to tire me out. My anger is intense enough that it makes me feel very tired. When something goes wrong with my own physical health, it's my own fault. I'm concerned about what other people think of my physical health. I strive to keep myself in tip-top physical shape. I feel slightly more irritated now than usual. If I were ill, my recovery would depend on how I myself deal with the problem. I feel irritated a good deal of the time. I feel good about the way I cope with my own physical health needs. I'm irritated all the time now. My physical health is largely determined by people who have influence and control over me. I shout at people all the time now. I'm so angry about my life that I've completely lost interest in sex. When I think about my present physical health, I am very satisfied. I try to stay in good physical condition, and its extremely important to me that I do so. Being in good physical health is a matter of my own ability and effort. If I just pay attention to my health, I will be able to prevent myself from becoming sick. My feelings of anger leave me too tired to do anything. I'm so angry at everything these days that I pay no attention to my health and well-being.

---

from The Inkblot Record

Dan Farrell's *Inkblot Record* (Toronto: Coach House Books, 2000), the alphabetized collation of responses to Hermann Rorschach's form-interpretation test, culled from a half-dozen secondhand psychology textbooks, sketches the contours of a truly collective unconscious. Rather than asking patients to transform abstract patterns into referential descriptions, however, Farrell reverses the procedure, inviting readers to imagine what abstract symmetrical forms could possibly have led to the range of hilarious, improbable, and disturbing statements he has harvested.

Mimicking the confessional ethos of psychologically plumbed lyric, Farrell's book recalls Andy Warhol's mid-1980s inkblot paintings, magnified to heroic proportions in a send-up of abstract expressionism's fraught Freudian spectacle. Although the spirit of the work is quite different, one might note the precedent of Justinus Kerner's 1890 book of poetry *Kleksographien,* also inspired by inkblots.

Babies or dwarfs, anyway pink. Baby's booties. Baby's pink buttocks. Back of rabbit's ears. Back of skull. Back of the head of a rabbit, that's all. Back toward us, standing up. Badly dried and cut because of the dark and light spots in here. Bald, grotesque, gleeful clowns, like tall hats, faces sticking out, playful. Balloon, shiny round object. Balls of cotton. Barefooted, legs and hips, head seems divided in two parts, hands in mittens, see legs through dress, transparent dress. Basin in a mountain. Bat. Bat. Bat in flight, wings spread out, attached to body. Bat with rodent-like ears. Beak of a bird. Bear. Bears going sideways on coat of arms. Bears sitting on their hind legs facing in opposite direction. Beautiful, it's nothing, just a reflection, at least three miles away, see evergreen trees and looks like smoke aurora around fire, heavy black smoke, forest back here. Beautiful green ball dress. Beautiful reflection, very far away. Because eyes drawn down. Because he used to go out of control when I was young, out of anger. Because here's its head, body, arms on the sides, big feet, with something sticking up in the middle; that's why I call it a monster with a pogo stick. Because here's the back (*imitates sitting*), yeah, they're shaped round. Because here's the wings and here's the hole part. Because here's their legs, and there's where their legs are connected to their bodies, goes up to their chest, their head. Because I couldn't see the head I assumed a soft substance. Because it goes out like this (*traces outline with finger*). Because it has so many colors. Because it has the green smoke coming out of it, and anything that takes off must have smoke coming out of it. Because it has the shape of the wings, the antennas, and the little feet. Because it has these fur things sticking out and the whiskers. Because it looks like a big clown here and it's just going up. Because it's a triangle. Because it's black, it has a shape kind of like a point, so it looks like a bird with wings, and it has a hole cut in it. Because it's feet are up, they're not on the grass. Because it's got this. Because it's got wings and the ears are up and it's flying. Because it's gray and rectangle. Because it's green and looks like weeds. Because it's green, with the trunk, straight down the middle, here. Because it's kind of splattered-out and black. Because it's kinda big and it's kinda legs here. Because it's kinda like this (*pantomimes stomping*). Because it's kinda shaped like one. Because it's kinda up like this (*traces tail with finger*). Because it's like this. Because it's on a rock. Because it's round. Because it's shaped like cotton candy and it has the stick. Because it's shaped like one and it's kinda big and it's stomping. Because it's splattered out. Because it's stomping around. Because it's straight and long and has these things to step on. Because it's too rigid, not a beautiful butterfly, supposed to be smooth and round. Because its wings are moving. Because just has such a big foot—feet I mean—and such a little head, that it looks funny I guess. Because of the costume, eagle dance (*demonstrates*). Because of the line of bones. Because of the shape. Because of the shape of these humps, which are their heads. Because of the tuft of hair on the bottom that's like the tuft on a cat's chin. Because of the two protrusions on top. Because of the way it's shaped. Because old ladies had to be in a rocking chair, but these handles, going back perpendicular rather than curving back. Because see the shapes, prints, see, you know, like ink prints. Because somebody jumped in it. Because such—so wide—(*traces with finger*). Because the way they are dressed. Because these are their ugly teeth and pointed hats. Because they have a little bit of dark skin and the feathers. Because they have their paws on the thing, like this (*imitates with her own body*). Because they're exhausted, spent all their lives eating people up. Because they're kinda long and kinda long here and here. Because they're kinda shaped like 'em. Because they're long. Because they're rectangle. Because this ear is kinda large and it looks like it's standing on a rock and it's got a tail. Because this is their—kinda like (*points to herself sitting*), it's like this part (*points to her lower torso and upper legs*). Because this part is kinda splattered up. Beetles are so busy arguing with one another, they don't see something bigger coming at them. Beets, red; cabbages, green; carrots, orange. Before, the Turks also looked like women. Beginning of armorial or escutcheon plate. Being afraid. Being slapped or being hugged. Below the elephants it sort of looks like they're standing on a red butterfly or moth. Belted with bustles, busts, a manikin. Bending over with hands on the head of an ant or insect, it's got jaws and teeth. Big angry waves with foam on top, large waves ready to splash. Big furry monster. Big pieces of stone worn down by water. Birds. Birds perched, wings out, up. Black hair strewn all over barber's floor. Black Sabbath. Black smoke smudges. Blackness and shape of insignia make me think of airman's death. Blah, that's an ugly thing, like some sort of creature, like a big monster with big feet and a small head, it must be dumb because the head is so small. Blood. Blood. Blood dripping down. Blowing, anyway, or breathing, could be either. Blue eyes. Blue faces, blowing into some kind of apparatus. Blue flags on a twin standard. Blue, my favorite color, looks soft, satiny and luxurious. Blue sky. Blurred man. Body, arms, hands, red boots and red turbans, eyes. Body not actually constructed that way—color—very often in anatomy books. Bomber would be without a fuselage. Boots or overshoes, just the shape. Boots, skirt is tight-waisted, breast, neck, great Russian fur hats, texture of gray white fur. Both are dead to me. Both have arms extended. Bottom looks like a little house. Bottom part looks like that same sex symbol again—Jesus. Bottom red and top orange, mostly in orange are flames. Bow tie in middle symbolic of party color. Boy, I'm beat, this is a hard test, I hope you don't have to do it every day. Breasts, hips, hands up, skirts cover their feet, no heads. Brontë sisters, *Wuthering Heights* and *Jane Eyre*. Brown spaniels; English spaniels with floppy ears. Brownish color of head of Airedale. Bug's face magnified. Bulls. Bunny with peculiar side-whiskers, two ears, heavy eyes, shape of head.

Burdened, a Carmen Miranda sort of thing, velvety fluff, arms out. Bushy and full, looks like foliage. But also reminds me of feelings I have towards my father and someone I went out with, similar to my father. But ghosts I'm not afraid of, it's the spiders and rats (*laughs*). But guys get in and loot the temple, steal the diamond eyes. But it doesn't count. But it doesn't look like anything. But no bottom of a body, just head and front legs, looking behind from where it's hanging from. But the antennae are off. But the bottom color resembles sherbet. But this one looks like it has feet or legs, cut out here and here, so I thought of a bearskin. Butterflies. Butterfly in center, wings and body. Butterfly, right in middle. Butterfly, shape only, the body here. Butterfly. Cacti. Camel that would be used in fighting. Can I look the other way too, like this (*inverts card*)? Can I turn it over? Can see legs over the other's shoulders. Can see the tightly curled center, the outer portion slowly opening, unfurling, looks like these slow motion films they make of plant action. Can you turn these things? Can't do much on that one either. Can't see expressions, only eyes can be seen, like a motorcycle helmet. Can't see parts in relation to one another; figured it out in terms of the contrast: wings, small body, two antennae. Can-can dances, head back, arms, legs, skirt. Can-can girls. Cannibals have something to do with it, maybe heat from the pot. Canyon, green plants, waterfall and foam through here, not much life in it, just steady. Caps, noses, scrawny incomplete figures, standing there. Caricature of men bowing to center figure. Carrot. Cat head and whiskers. Cat's whiskers but no cat, just whiskers. Caterpillar type feet here point inward, sort of like standing up, apparatus leaning against chest. Caterpillars, the dark sides, the tree in the center and the side extensions are tree branches. Cat-like head with whiskers. 'Cause all the colors mix up together. 'Cause it has different colors. 'Cause it has eyes like an alligator. 'Cause it just is the shape of one. 'Cause it looks like a butterfly right there. 'Cause it looks like it was real gooey. 'Cause it looks like it, different things. 'Cause it looks like it's a bat, bat's feet. 'Cause it's brown? 'Cause it's got these two things right here and it looks like a bee. 'Cause it's kinda big. 'Cause it's orange. 'Cause it's red. 'Cause it's shaped like a fly and looks like a fly. 'Cause it—I just think that this is the cat, I just think it looks like a cat. 'Cause of the different colors. 'Cause of the wing going out, shaped like an angel. 'Cause they are yellow. 'Cause they're big. 'Cause they're little. 'Cause they're sorta little. 'Cause they're yellow and they're little. 'Cause this looks like birds. 'Cause, they're standing so they remain as far apart as possible. Caution, uncertainty. Center again, lower part triangular in shape.

Center organ, line of opening, dark area around, black hair around the opening. Central part looks like some sort of urn or a vase or something like that. Central portion looks like stunted tree been cut off. Chagall. Chalky pastel colors. Chiffon handkerchief here, gowned and gloved in same color. Child sticking its tongue out. Children being ostracized by their parents. Chinese hands with long fingers coming down. Chinese lanterns let down from strings, shape and color. Christmas colors. Church. Claws, something to grab something with. Climbing up rocks. Clothesline with clothes hanging on it. Cloud-like effect here. Clowns playing patty-cake, hands come together. Coastline with islands, fluoroscope feeling, light things on different level. Collar, belt and belt buckle like a doll or figurine. Colon. Color and shading here is important. Color and shape, hanging in same direction. Color and shape. Color nothing to do with it. Color of green. Color of sky blue. Color splash, streaming down. Color. Color. Colored fireworks, like they look after they've exploded. Colored map. Colored masses, nothing specific; horseshoe crab washing about in waves, sea-green water. Coloring symbolic, that's all it could be. Color—life blood through them. Colossus astride Rhodes. Comes down over other structures, coming down over. Coming up out of the water, things seem to be dragged up with it. Conflict over pelvis fundamental. Confusion, turmoil, just looks like a lot of conflicting forces. Congenial faces, babies with noses, too smart for babies, pulling against each other, both males. Contour of mountains, looking far away, shading. Cotton is generally that shape, I think. Could be a bat or a bird. Could be a butterfly. Could be a butterfly. Could be a couple of clowns with awful funny faces. Could be a leaf, part of a leaf. Could be a meadow. Could be a pair of hunting birds. Could be a statue depicting a toast. Could be a tree branch with a pair of falcons or birds on it. Could be a tree. Could be a woman washing clothes. Could be an anteater head because of the snout. Could be an explosion, everything blown up. Could be an oil drum or gas tank exploding. Could be Bigfoot. Could be curved back, but looks more like a handle that was jutting back rather than just a curve like a headrest. Could be Jell-O. Could be kneeling. Could be old flying animal that lived in prehistoric times, like a bird, bat. Could be some kind of elaborate top or toy mechanism; no idea of what the figures are because they spin so fast. Could be some sort of an emblem like a family crest, it's very colorful. Could be the skull of a person, or an animal. Could be two tigers climbing up on mountain. Could get little Santa Claus hanging on a Christmas tree. Couple of horses with elon-

gated faces scooting out of thing, look like Picasso horses. Couple of lob-
sters in some sea grass. Couple of men bowing to each other. Crabs. Craggy
dark wood area, irregular formation bare as you see in mountains some-
times. Craggy mountain area. Crawdads. Creatures flying along because of
some force. Crocodile head. Cross-section of a cervix. Crudely done face,
back with toy pack, color part of idea, color leads to illusion. Crustaceans'
ball.

Gerald Ferguson
from The Standard Corpus of Present Day English Language Usage
Arranged by Word Length and Alphabetized Within Word Length

Whereas Marcel Duchamp proposed alternate orderings for dictionaries ("Buy a dictionary and cross out the words to be crossed out"; "*Dictionary*—of a language in which each word would be translated into French [or other] by several words, when necessary by a whole sentence"), Gerald Ferguson realized an entire dictionary with each word arranged according to its length. A secondary step involved alphabetization within word length, extending a tradition of 'pataphysical response to a 'pataphysical proposition, all trading in the imaginary. Ferguson gives a full accounting of his process:

> The idea for a dictionary arranged by word length grew out of a series of pages of single letters of the alphabet that I typed as graphics in 1968, and which represented efforts to extend ideas, then current, relating to modular composition, objectively determined forms and the material status of printed letters.

> The composing of such a work by hand was much too impractical and I therefore investigated computer sources and came upon the Brown University Million Word Corpus. This Corpus consists of 1,014,232 words or tokens, obtained by taking five hundred, 2,000 word samples in each of the 15 subject categories listed below (the number to the right of the category indicates the number of 2,000 word samples in that area of written language):

Press: Reportage 44
Press: Editorial 27
Press: Reviews 17
Religion 17
Skills and Hobbies 36
Popular Lore 48
Belles Lettres, Biography, etc. 75
Miscellaneous 30

Learned and Scientific Writing 80
Fiction: General 29
Fiction: Mystery and Detective 24
Fiction: Science 6
Fiction: Romance and Love Story 29
Humor 9

After collation for coincidence of appearance, the material obtained was limited to lengths 1 through 20 and those few types with computational symbols were edited out, leaving just under 50,000 words.

I typed the entire work on stencils and finally ran off a bound first edition of 300 copies in the summer of 1970, using as a title "The Standard Corpus of Present Day English Language Usage, arranged by word length and alphabetized within word length." "The Standard Corpus of Present Day English Language Usage" was Brown University's study title. I added "arranged by word length and alphabetized within word length." In the original edition various human and machine-generated inaccuracies were welcomed, as were structural variations resulting from the self-imposed rule not to violate the right hand side margin of each page. The same structural principle has been retained here.

Once completed, the Corpus became a source for other works. Among those was "Equivalents," 1971 (inside front cover) and the choral reading for 26 voices (1972), with the Corpus serving as a score.

Length 1

A
B
C
D
E
F
G
H
I

J

K

L

M

N

O

P

Q

R

S

T

U

V

W

X

Y

Z

Length 2

AD IO SO

AF IS SP

AH IT SQ

AI JE SR

AL JO ST

AM JR TH

AN KC TI

AS KM TO

AT KU TU

AV KY UH

AW LA UM

AX LB UN

BD LE UP

BE LO US

BI LP VA

BO LT VP

BY MA VS
CA NC WE
CC ND WT
CF ME WU
CH MG YA
CM NY YD
CO ML YE
CT MM YR
CU MO YS
DA MR ZU
DE MT
DI MY
DO NE
DR NO
DU NW
ED OF
EH OH
EL OL
EM ON
EN OP
EQ OR
ET OS
EX OT
FE OX
FT OZ
FY PA
GA PI
GM FL
GO PO
HA PP
HE PT
HI RD
HR RE
IF RF
IJ RY
IL SE
IM SI
IN SL

```
AAH BAL COP EGO GAP HON JOB LOU NAB PAK REV SIC TIP WOE
ABE BAN COW EIN GAS HOP JOE LOW NAE PAL REX SID TIS WON
ACE BAR COX ELI GAY HOT JON LOY NAM PAM REY SIE TOW WOO
ACT BAS COY ELK GEE HOW JOT LTD NAN PAN RIB SIN TOM WOP
ADA BAT CPS ELL GEL HOY JOY LUG NAP PAP RID SIP TON WOW
ADD BAY CRY ELM GEM HUB JUG LUI NAT PAR RIG SIR TOO WRY
ADE BEA CUD END GEM HUE KAN MAC NAW PAS RIM SIS TOP WUH
ADO BED CUP ENG GET HUG KAS MAD NAY PAT RIO SIT TOW WUS
ADS BEE CUR EPH GIG HUH KAY MAE NEC PAW RIP SIX TOY WYN
AFT BEG CUT EQN GIL HUI KEG MAC NET PAX ROB SKI TRY YEA
AGE BEL CYR ERA GIN HUL KEL NAH NEV PAY ROD SKY TUB YEN
AGO BEN DAD ERE GIT HUM KEN MAI NEW PEE ROE SLY TUG YES
AHM BET DAG ERR GOA HUN KEO MAJ NGO PEG ROI SOD TVA YET
AID BEY DAM EST GOB HUT KEY NAL NIL PEN RON SOE TWO YFF
AIM BIB DAM ETA GOD HUM KID MAN NIP PEP ROT SOL UGH YIN
AIR BID DAN ETC GOG HYS KIN MAO NOB PER ROW SON UMM YIP
ALA BIG DAS EVA GOT IBN KIT MAP NOD PET ROY SOP UND YOK
ALE BIN DAY EVE GOV ICE KIZ MAR NON PFC RPM SOU UNE YON
ALF BIT DEC EWE GRE ICH KOB MAT NOR PHI RTE SOW UNO YOU
ALL BIX DEF EYD GUM ICY KOH MAW NOS PIE RUB SOX UPS YOW
AMT BIZ DEI EYE GUN IDA KOK MAX NOT PIG RUE SOY URN YUH
AMY BOA DEL FAD GUS IDE KYO MAY NOV PIN RUG SPA USE ZEN
ANA BOB DEN FAN GUT ILL LAB MEA NOW PIP RUH SPY VAN ZIP
AND BOG DER FAR GUY INC LAD NEE NUF PIT RUL SUB VAR ZOE
ANI BON DES FAT GYM IND LAG MEG NUN POD RUN SUE VET ZOO
ANN BOO DEW PAY GYP ING LAK MEL NUT POE RUN SUM VEX ZUR
ANT BOP DEY FEB HAD INK LAO MEM NUX POP RUT SUN VIA
ANY BOW DIA FED HAL INN LAP MEN OAK POT RYC SUP VIC
APE BOX DID FEE HAM ION LAS MIT OCH PRO RYE SUR VIZ
APP BOY DIE FER HAN IRA LAW MEW OCT PRY SAD SUS VOL
APT BUD DIG FEW HAP IRE LAX MFG ODD PSI SAG SUT VOM
ARC BUG DIM FIG HAS IRV LAY MID OFF PUB SAM TAB VON
ARE BUM DIN FIL HAT ISA LBS MIG OFT PUN SAN TAG VOS
ARE BUN DIP FIN HAW IST LED MIJ OIL PUP SAP TAI VOW
ART BUS DOC FIR HAY ITO LEE MIL IKS PUT SAT TAN VUE
ARM BUT DOE FIT HEE ITS LEG MIN OLD PVT SAW TAO WAN
ASH BUY DOG FIX HEL IVY LEN MIO OLE PYE SAX TAP WAR
```

```
ASK BYE DON FLA HEM JAB LEO MIX OND QUA SAY TAR WAS
ASS CAB DOO FLU HEN JAG LES MMM ONE QUE SEA TAT WAX
ASW CAL DOS FLY HER JAI LET MOB ORB QUI SEC TAU WAY
ATE CAM DOT FOR HEV JAM LEV MOI ORE QUO SED TAX WEB
ATH CAN DOW FOG HEX JAN LEW MOM ORY RAE SEE TEA WED
ATT CAP DRS FOH HEY JAR LEX MON OSO RAG SEN TED WEE
AUF CAR DRY FOR HEZ JAS LID MOP OUD RAK SEO TEE WEI
AUG CAT DUD FOX HID JAW LIE MOR OUI RAM SET TEL WES
AUX CAV DUE FOY HIM JAY LIL MOS OUM RAN SEW TEN WET
AVE CHE DUG FRA HIP JEB LIP MOT OUR RAP SEX TER WHO
AWE CHI DUN FRY HIR JED LIT MPH OUT RAT SEZ TEX WHY
AXE CIR EAR FUN HIS JEE LIZ MRS OVA RAW SHA THE WIG
AYA COD EAT FUR HIT JEN LOB MTS OWE RAY SHE THO WIL
AYE COE EBB GAB HMM JET LOG MUD OWL REB SHH THY WIN
BAD COL EDW GAG HOB JEW LOP MUG OWN RED SHO TIE WIS
BAG CON EEL GAI HOC JIG LOS MUM PAD REF SHU TIM WIT
```

Length 4

```
POND RAGE RIMS RYNE SENT SKYE SPIN TANG TIDE TRIO VERN WEBB WOOD
PONS RAGS RING SABA SEPT SLAB SPIT TANK TIDY TRIP VERO WEED WOOL
PONT RAID RINK SACK SERA SLAM SPOT TAOS TIED TRIS VERY WEEK WOPS
PONY RAIL RIOT SAFE SETS SLAP SPUN TAPE TIEN TROT VEST WEEP WORD
POOL RAIN RIPA SAGA SEWN SLAT SPUR TAPS TIES TROY VETO WElL WORE
POOR RAKE RIPE SAGE SEXY SLID STAB TARA TIFT TRUE VICE WEIR WORK
POPE RALL RISE SAGO SHAG SLIM STAG TART TILE TSAP VIDA WELD WORN
POPS RAMP RISK SAGS SHAH SLIP STAN TASK TILL TSOU VIED WELL WORN
PORE RAND RITE SAID SHAK SLIT STAR TATE TILT TUBA VIES WENT WOVE
PORK RANG RITZ SAIL SHAM SLOB STAT TAUI TIME TUBE VIET WEPT WRAD
PORT RANK ROAD SAKE SHAN SLOE STAY TAUT TIMS TUBS VIEW WERE WRIT
POSE RAPE ROAN SAKO SHAW SLOP STEM TAXI TINT TUCK VILE WERT WYNN
POST RAPT ROAR SALE SHAY SLOT STEP TEAM TINY TUNE VINE WEST XXXX
POTS RARE ROBE SALK SHEA SLOW STEW TEAR TIPS TUNG VISA WHAH YAKS
POUR RASA ROBS SALT SHED SLUG STIR TEAS TIRE TURF VISE WHAT YALE
POUT RASH ROCK SALU SHEP SLUM STOP TECH TITO TURK VITA WHEE YANG
PRAI RASP RODE SAME SHIH SMOG STUB TEEN TITS TURN VIVA WHEN YANK
```

```
PRAM RATA RODS SANA SHIM SMUG STUD TELL TOAD TWIN VIVE WHER YARD
PRAY RATE ROLE SAND SHIN SNAG SUBS TEND TOCH TWOS VIVO WHIG YARN
PREP RATS ROLL SANE SHIP SNAP SUCH TENN TODD TYME VOCE WHIM YAWL
PREY RAYS ROME SANG SHIT SNOW SUCK TENS TODE TYPE VOID WHIP YAWN
PRIM READ ROMP SANK SHOD SNUG SUDS TENT TOES UDON VOTE WHIR YAWS
PRIX REAL ROOF SANS SHOE SOAK SUED TERM TOFU UGLY VOUS WHIT YEAH
PROD REAP ROOM SANT SHOP SOAP SUES TESS TOGS UHHU VOWS WHIZ YEAR
PROF REAR ROOS SAPS SHOT SOBA SUEY TEST TOIL UNAN VRAI WHOA YELL
PROP REBS ROOT SARA SHOW SOBS SUEZ TEXT TOLD UNDO WACO WHOE YELP
PROS REDO ROPE SARI SHUN SOCK SUIT THAT TOLE UNIT WADE WHOM YENI
PROW REDS ROSA SASH SHUT SODA SUNS THAN TOLL UNTO WADS WICK YOGA
PUBS REED ROSE SAUD SHUZ SODS SUNG THAR TOMB UPON WAGE WIDE YOGI
PUFF REEF ROSS SAUL SICK SOFA SUNK THAT TONE UREA WAIL WIFE YOKE
PUGH REEK ROSY SAVE SIDE SOFT SUNS THAW TONG URGE WAIT WILD YOLK
PUKE REEL ROTS SAWS SIGH SOHN SUNT THAY TONI URNS WAKE WILL YORE
PULL REES ROVE SAYS SIGN SOIL SUPT THEA TONS USED WALK WILT YORI
PULP REGI ROWS SCAN SILK SOLD SURE THEE TONY USER WALL WILY YORK
PUMP REID ROXY SCAR SILL SOLE SURF THEI TOOK USES WALT WIND YOUR
PUNK REIK RUBE SCOP SILO SOLO SWAN THEM TOOK UTAH WAND WINE YUBA
PUNY REIN RUDE SCOT SIMS SOMA SWAN THEN TOOT VADE WANT WING YUKI
PUPS RELY RUDY SEAL SIND SOME SWAP THER TOPS VAIL WARD WINK YURI
PURE REMY RUGS SEAN SINE SONG SWAY THET TORE VAIN WARE WINS YUSE
PUSH REND RUIN SEAN SING SONS SWIG THEY TORN VALE WARN WIPE YYYY
PUTS RENO RUIZ SEAR SINK SOON SWIM THIN TORY VAMP WARN WIRE ZARA
PUTT RENT RULE SEAS SINS SOOT SWUM THIS TOSS VARY WARP WIRY ZEAL
PYRE REPS RUMP SEAT SIRS SOPS TABB THOM TOTE VASA WARS WISE ZEME
QUAM REST RUNG SECT SISK SORE TACK THOR TOTO VASE WART WISH ZERO
QUIT REUB RUNS SEEK SITE SORT TACT THOU TOUR VAST WARY WISP ZEST
QUIZ REWT RUNT SEEK SITS SOUL TAFT THRE TOUT VEAL WASH WITH ZHOK
QUOD RIBS RUSE SEEM SITU SOUP TAGS THRO TOWN VEER WASP WITS ZINC
QUOK RICE RUSH SEEN SIVA SOUR TAIL THRU TOYS VEIL WATT WITT ZING
RABB RICH RUSK SEEP SIZE SOWN TAKE THUD TRAP VEIN WAVE WORD ZION
RACE RICO RUSS SEES SKID SPAN TALE THUG TRAY VENN WAVY WOKE ZONE
RACK RIDE RUST SELF SKIN SPAT TALK THUN TREE VENT WAXY WOLD ZOTE
RACY RIFT RUTH SELL SKIP SPEC TALL THUS TREK VERA WAYS WOLF ZWEI
RADS RIGS RUTS SEND SKIS SPED TAME TIAO TRIG VERB WEAK WOMB
```

Robert Fitterman
Metropolis 16

Part list poem, part postmodern landscape, part essay on urban planning, the poem "Metropolis 16" from the book *Metropolis 16–29* (Toronto: Coach House Books, 2002) is a two-dimensional distillation of three-dimensional commercial architecture. From Fitterman's schematic diagram of proper names, the poem could be projected to reconstruct almost any inhabited locale in America, with its endless variations on the same numbing theme. Suggesting a formal analogue to the cultural poverty they describe, the stanzas slowly diminish—their malls literally stripped—to the dregs of the final tercet's desperate alliterative shuttle. Here, the colonizing postwar expansion and homogenization of social space by corporate capital is played out to its deadening dead-end end game. Shop, eat, shop—the triangulation of sites of consumption in the poem's final line recalls Guy Debord's description of a map accompanying "Paris et l'agglomération parisienne" (*Paris: Essais de sociologie, 1952–1964* [Paris: Les editions ouvriéres, 1965]), Paul-Henry Chombart de Lauwe's classic 1952 study of urban social anthropology. The map registered "le trace de tous les parcours effectués en une année par une étudiante de XVIe arrondissement; ces parcours dessinent un triangle de dimension réduite, sans échappées" (every movement made over the space of one year by a student living in the Sixteenth Arrondissement; her itinerary describes a small triangle with no significant deviations) ("Théorie de la derive," *Les Lèvres Nues* 9 [November 1956]: 6–10; reprinted in *Internationale Situationniste* 2 [December 1958]: 51–55).

The ideology encapsulated by the big-box store depends on encouraging precisely such itineraries, as well as on strategies of replication, regularity, conformity, familiarity, and guided movement. In a poem that recalls Fitterman's catalog, John Ashbery, not coincidentally, pairs sites of social regulation with corporate names (*The Vermont Notebook* [Los Angeles: Black Sparrow, 1975]):

Bridge clubs, Elks, Kiwanis, Rotary, AAA, PTA, lodges, Sunday school, band rehearsal, study hall, book clubs, annual picnics, banquets, parades, brunches, library teas, slide lectures, seances, concerts, community sings.

Gulf Oil, Union Carbide, Westinghouse, Xerox, Eastman Kodak, ITT, Marriott, Sonesta, Crédit Mobilier, Sperry Rand, Curtis Publishing, Colgate, Motorola, Chrysler, General Motors, Anaconda, Crédit Lyonnais, Chase Manhattan, Continental Can, Time-Life, McGraw Hill, CBS, ABC, NBC.

Like the Vermont of Ashbery's notebook, the America of "Metropolis 16" constitutes a sort of dark georgic: the fields and forests that once surrounded civic centers developed into sites of labor, including the dutiful labor of consuming, the continuation of employment by other means. *Et in Arcadia . . .*

McDonald's
Burger King
Taco Bell
Home Depot
Gap
Dunkin' Donuts
KFC
J. Crew
Home Depot
Staples
Sunglass Hut
Wendy's
Kmart
Wal*Mart

McDonald's
Wal*Mart
Sunglass Hut
Kmart
Wendy's
Taco Bell
J. Crew
Staples
Home Depot
Gap
KFC
Dunkin' Donuts

Dunkin' Donuts
Taco Bell
Kmart
Home Depot
Sunglass Hut
Staples
Wal*Mart
Gap
McDonald's
J. Crew
KFC

Taco Bell
Staples
Gap
Dunkin' Donuts
Wal*Mart
KFC
J. Crew
Kmart
Sunglass Hut
McDonald's

Taco Bell
Staples
Kmart
Gap
J. Crew
McDonald's
KFC
Wendy's

Taco Bell
J. Crew
KFC
Staples
Gap
Dunkin' Donuts
Kmart

Kmart
Taco Bell
Gap
J. Crew
Staples
KFC
Dunkin' Donuts

Taco Bell
Staples
KFC
J. Crew
Dunkin' Donuts
Kmart

Kmart
Taco Bell
KFC
Staples
J. Crew

Kmart
KFC
Kmart
Taco Bell

Kmart
KFC
Kmart

from The Sun Also Also Rises

Robert Fitterman here performs a grammatical analysis of Ernest Hemingway's *The Sun Also Rises,* eliminating all sentences that do not begin with the first person singular pronoun. The result reads very much like Ron Silliman's "Berkeley" (*This 5* [Winter 1974]: n.p.). One might compare Fitterman's grammatical excavation with the narrative mining of George Orwell's *Nineteen Eighty Four* by Carolyn Thompson in *Winston and Julia: A Love Story* (2003). Thompson removed most of Orwell's text, leaving only the scenes of romance between her title characters. Thompson's *After Easton Ellis,* similarly, trimmed to the size of the Picador edition of Ellis's *American Psycho,* eliminates everything but the brand names from the original novel. With a kind of reverse censorship, Janet Zweig published the descriptively titled collection *The 336 Lines Currently Expurgated from Shakespeare's Romeo and Juliet in Ninth-Grade Textbooks* (Long Island City, N.Y.: Sheherezade, 1989).

A related booklet in the trilogy (Calgary: No Press, 2008) translates the sentences from *The Sun Also Also Rises* into Fitterman's own experience as a young writer moving to New York City in the early 1980s and recalls a methodology honed by Ben Friedlander, who has, for example, rewritten Edgar Allan Poe's "Literati of New York City" in reference to San Francisco poets. For example, Poe writes:

> Mr. Duycknick is one of the most influential of the New York *littérateurs,* and has done a great deal for the interests of American letters. Not the least important service rendered by him was the projection and editorship of Wiley and Putnam's "Library of Choice Reading," a series which brought to public notice many valuable foreign works which had been suffering under neglect in this country, and at the same time afforded unwonted encouragement to native authors by publishing their books, in good style and in good company, without trouble or risk to the authors themselves, and in the very teeth of the disadvantages arising from the want of an international copyright law.

Friedlander revises:

> Mr. Silliman is one of the most influential of the San Francisco *littérateurs,* and has done a great deal for the interests of American letters. Not the least important service tendered by him was the conception and editorship of *In the American Tree,* published after some few years delay by the National Poetry Foundation. This heft collection of language poetry brought to public notice many valuable

fugitive works that had previously suffered neglect, and at the same time afforded unwonted encouragement to several lesser-known authors by publishing their books, in good style and in good company, without trouble or risk to the authors themselves, and in the very teeth of the disadvantages arising from the want of critical response.

A third booklet in Fitterman's trilogy, written by Nayland Blake, further reduces Hemingway's prose to truncated intransitives and catalogs of definite nouns, rewriting the novel in the mode of John Ashbery and Joe Brainard's *Vermont Notebook*.

Chapter I

I am very much impressed by that. I never met any one of his class who remembered him. I mistrust all frank and simple people. I always had a suspicion. I finally had somebody verify the story. I was his tennis friend. I do not believe that. I first became aware of his lady's attitude toward him one night after the three of us had dined together. I suggested we fly to Strasbourg. I thought it was accidental. I was kicked again under the table. I was not kicked again. I said good-night and went out. I watched him walk back to the café. I rather liked him.

Chapter II

I am sure he had never been in love in his life. I did not realize the extent to which it set him off until one day he came into my office. I never wanted to go. I had a boat train to catch. I like this town. I can't stand it to think my life is going so fast and I'm not really living it. I'm not interested. I'm sick of Paris. I walked alone all one night and nothing happened. I was sorry for him but it was not a thing you could do anything about. I sorted out the carbons, stamped on a by-line, put the stuff in a couple of big manila envelopes and rang for a boy to take them to the Gare St. Lazare. I went into the other room. I wanted to lock the office and shove off. I put my hand on his shoulder. I can't do it. I didn't sleep all last night. I could picture it. I have a rotten habit of picturing the bedroom scenes of my friends.

Chapter III

I sat at a table on the terrace of the Napolitain. I watched a good-looking girl walk past the table and watched her go up the street and lost sight of her. I caught her eye. I saw why she made a point of not laughing. I paid for the saucers. I hailed a horse-cab. I put my arm around her. I put her hand away. I called to the cocher to stop. I had picked her up because of a vague sentimental idea that it would be nice to eat with some one. I had forgotten how dull it could be. I got hurt in the war. I was bored enough. I went back to the small room. I went over to the bar. I drank a beer. I could see their hands and newly washed, wavy hair in the light from the door. I was very angry. I know they are supposed to be amusing. I walked down the street and had a beer at the bar. I knew then that they would all dance with her. I sat down at a table. I asked him to have a drink. I was a little drunk. I got up and walked over to the dancing-floor. I took my coat off a hanger on the wall and put it on. I stopped at the bar and asked them for an envelope. I took a fifty-franc note from my pocket.

Chapter IV

I saw her face in the lights from the open shops. I saw her face clearly. I kissed her. I was pretty well through with the subject. I went out onto the sidewalk. I did not see who it was. I wanted to get home. I stopped and read the inscription. I knocked on the door and she gave me my mail. I wished her good night and went upstairs. I looked at them under the gas-light. I got out my check-book. I felt sure I could remember anybody. I lit the lamp beside the bed. I sat with the windows open and undressed by the bed. I looked at myself in the mirror of the big armoire beside the bed. I put on my pajamas and got into bed. I had the two bull-fight papers, and I took their wrappers off. I read it all the way through. I blew out the lamp. I wonder what became of the others. I was all bandaged up. I never used to realize it. I lay awake thinking and my mind jumping around. I couldn't keep away from it. I started to cry. I woke up. I listened. I thought I recognized a voice. I put on a dressing-gown. I heard my name called down the stairs. I looked at the clock. I was getting brandy and soda and glasses. I went back upstairs. I took them both to the kitchen. I turned off the gas in the dining-room. I had felt like crying. I thought of her walking up the street. I felt like hell again.

Chapter V

I walked down the Boulevard. I read the papers with the coffee and then smoked a cigarette. I passed the man with the jumping frogs. I stepped aside. I read the French morning papers. I shared a taxi. I banged on the glass. I went to the office in the elevator. I was looking over my desk. I held him off. I left him to come to the office.

Chapter VI

I sat down and wrote some letters. I went down to the bar. I looked for her upstairs on my way out. I saw a string of barges being towed empty down the current. I suppose it is. I walked past the sad tables. I watched him crossing the street through the taxis. I never heard him make one remark. I do not believe he thought about his clothes much. I don't know how people could say such terrible things. I don't even feel an impulse to try to stop it. I stood against the bar looking out. I did not want anything to drink and went out through the side door. I looked back. I went down a side street. I got in and gave the driver the address to my flat.

Chapter VII

I went up to the flat. I put the mail on the table. I heard the door-bell pull. I put on a bathrobe and slippers. I filled the big earthenware jug with water. I dressed slowly. I felt tired and pretty rotten. I took up the brandy bottle. I went to the door. I found some ash-trays and spread them around. I looked at the count. I had that feeling of going through something that has already happened before. I had the feeling as in a nightmare of it all being something repeated, something I had been through and that now I must go through again. I took a note out of my pocket. I looked back and there were three girls at his table. I gave him twenty francs and he touched his cap. I went upstairs and went to bed.

Chapter VIII

I could reach him always, he wrote, through his bankers. I rather enjoyed not playing tennis. I went often to the races, dined with friends, and put in some extra time at the office getting things ahead so I could leave it in charge of my secretary. I should shove off to Spain the end of June. I got a wire. I heard his taxi stop and went to the window and called to him. I met him on the stairs, and took one of the bags. I saw the long zinc bar.

Chapter IX

I came down. I would leave for Paris on the 25th unless I wired him other-wise. I stopped in at the Select. I went over to the Dingo. I wrote out an itinerary. I asked the conductor for tickets for the first service. I described where we were.

Chapter X

I was not at all sure. I forget what. I did not want to leave the café. I saw a cockroach on the parquet floor that must have been at least three inches long. I pointed him out. I asked him if he ever fished. I offered the guard a cigarette. I was up in front with the driver and I turned around. I saw he was angry and wanted to smooth him down. I sat in front of the café and then went for a walk in the town. I kept on the shady side of the streets. I left him sitting among the archives that covered all the walls. I went out of the building. I thought the facade was ugly. I went inside. I knelt and started to pray and prayed for everyone I thought of. I was praying for myself. I was getting sleepy. I thought I would like to have some money, so I prayed that I would make a lot of money. I started wondering. I was kneeling with my forehead on the wood in front of me. I was such a rotten Catholic. I only wished I felt religious and maybe I would the next time. I was out in the hot sun. I crossed over beside some buildings. I said I would go with him. I felt lousy. I put it in my pocket. I was blind. I certainly did hate him. I put the telegram in my pocket. I turned in early. I was asleep when they came in. I bought three tickets for the bus. I was sitting over at the Iruña reading the papers. I knew. I laughed.

Chapter XI

I went back to the hotel to get a couple of bottles of wine to take with us. I spilled some of the wine and everybody laughed. I got down and went into the posada. I gave the woman fifty centimes to make a tip and she gave me back the copper piece, thinking I had misunderstood the price. I turned around to look at the country. I opened it and showed him. I went out to find the woman and ask her how much the room and board was. I sat at one of the tables and looked at the pictures on the wall. I looked at them all. I went out and told the woman what a rum punch was and how to make it. I went over to the cupboard and brought the rum bottle. I woke and heard the wind blowing.

Chapter XII

I went to the window and looked out. I waved at him. I unbolted the door and went out. I hunted around in the shed behind the inn and found a sort of mattock, and went down toward the stream to try to dig some worms for bait. I drove the mattock into the earth. I lifted the sod. I dug carefully. I filled two empty tobacco-tins. I asked her to get coffee for us, and that we wanted a lunch. I went on looking for the tackle and putting it all together in a tackle-bag. I started out the room with the tackle-bag, the nets, and the rod-case. I put my head in the door. I thumbed my nose. I went down-stairs. I was reading a week-old Spanish paper. I carried the rod-case and the landing-nets slung over my back. I shouted. I lifted it. I put back the slab of wood, and hoped nobody would find the wine. I got my rod that was leaning against the tree. I sat on one of the squared timbers and watched the smooth apron of water before the river tumbled into the falls. I put on a good-sized sinker. I did not feel the first trout strike. I felt that I had one. I banged his head against the timber. I laid them out, side-by-side, all their heads pointing the same way, and looked at them. I slit them all and shucked out the insides. I took the trout ashore. I put it in the shade of the tree. I sat against the trunk. I put my worm-can in the shade. I was reading a wonderful story about a man who had been frozen in the Alps. I walked up the road and got out two bottles of wine. I walked back to the trees. I spread the lunch on a newspaper. I went to sleep, too. I was stiff from sleeping on the ground. I stretched and rubbed my eyes. I disjointed my rod. I put the reels in the tackle-bag. I carried the other. I looked around on the grass at the foot of the elm-trees.

Chapter XIII

I went down to breakfast. I stopped at the post. I saw a girl coming up the road from the centre of the town. I had aficion. I found him washing and changing in his room. I leaned way over the wall and tried to see into the cage. I saw a dark muzzle and the shadow of horns. I went upstairs. I stood beside him. I remember from the war. I lost the disgusted feeling and was happy.

Chapter XIV

I do not know what time I got to bed. I remember undressing, putting on a bathrobe, and standing out on the balcony. I knew I was quite drunk. I was reading a book. I read the same two pages several times. I had read it before. I was very drunk and I did not want to shut my eyes. I heard them laugh. I turned off the light and tried to go to sleep. I could shut my eyes without getting the wheeling sensation. I could not sleep. I figured that all out once. I never slept with the electric light off. I had not been thinking about her side of it. I had been getting something for nothing. I thought I had paid for everything. I paid my way into enough things that I liked, so that I had a good time. I did not care what it was all about. I wished he would not do it, though, because afterward it made me disgusted at myself. I didn't know anything about the Eskimo. I didn't know anything about the Cherokee, either. I liked them, though. I liked the way they talked. I turned on the light and read. I knew that now. I would remember it somewhere. I would always have it. I usually sat in the café and read the Madrid papers and then walked in the town or out into the country. I went to church a couple of times. I told her that not only was impossible but it was not as interesting as it sounded. I felt quite friendly.

Chapter XV

I walked down the hill from the cathedral and up the street to the café on the square. I saw the bright flash as it burst and another little cloud of smoke appeared. I put down money for the wine. I explained to them that I would be back. I went down the street. I walked as far as the church. I asked a man. I paid and went out. I was introduced to the people at the table. I unscrewed the nozzle of the big wine-bottle and handed it around. I took a drink. I could feel it warming. I remember resolving that I would stay up all night to watch the bulls go through the streets at six o'clock in the morning. I could not find the key. I had been sleeping heavily and I woke feeling I was too late. I went back in the room and got into bed. I had been standing on the stone balcony in bare feet. I went to sleep. I had taken six seats for all the fights. I gave the extra ticket to a waiter. I told her about watching the bull, not the horse. I had her watch how Romero took the bull away. I pointed out to her the tricks. I told her how since the death of Joselito all the bull-fighters had been developing a technic that simulated this appearance of danger.

Chapter XVI

I walked out beyond the town to look at the weather. I left the crowd in the café and went to the hotel to get shaved for dinner. I was shaving in my room when there was a knock on the door. I finished shaving and put my face down into the bowl. I went down-stairs and out the door and took a walk around through the arcades around the square. I looked in at Iruña for the gang. I walked on around the square and back to the hotel. I was drinking red wine, and so far behind them that I felt a little uncomfortable about all this shoe-shining. I looked around the room. I nodded. I met the friend, a Madrid bull-fight critic. I told Romero how much I liked his work. I reached to our table for my wine bottle. I explained that bull-fight in Spanish was the lidia of a toro. I had seen him in the ring. I told him only three. I did not want to explain after I had made the mistake. I introduced them all around. I rushed it a little. I spread a newspaper on the stone. I looked across at the table. I stood up and we shook hands. I noticed his skin. I saw he was watching. I think he was sure. I tapped with my finger-tips on the table. I translated. I went out.

Chapter XVII

I swung at him and he ducked. I saw his face duck sideways in the light. I sat down on the pavement. I started to get on my feet. I went down back-ward under a table. I tried to get up. I did not have any legs. I found I was sitting on a chair. I walked away from the café. I looked back at them and at the empty tables. I had never seen the trees before. I had never seen the flagpoles before. I felt as I felt once coming home from an out-of-town football game. I was carrying a suitcase. I walked up the street from the station. I could hear my feet walking. I had been kicked in the head. I was carrying my suitcase. I went on up the stairs carrying my phantom suit-case. I walked down the hall. The door was shut and I knocked. I opened the door and went in. I stood by the door. I had come home. I did not say anything. I stood by the door. I did not care. I wanted a hot bath. I wanted a hot bath in deep water. I could not see his face very well. I could not find the bathroom. I found it. I turned on the taps and the water would not run. I sat down on the edge of the bath-tub. I got up. I found I had taken off my shoes. I hunted for them. I found my room and went inside and got undressed and got into bed. I woke with a headache and the noise of the bands going by in the street. I remembered I had prom-ised. I dressed and went down-stairs and out into the cold early morn-ing. I hurried across the street to the café. I drank the coffee and hur-ried with the other people toward the bull-ring. I was not groggy now. I heard the rocket and I knew I could not get into the ring in time. I shoved through the crowd to the fence. I was pushed close against the planks of the fence. I saw the bulls just coming out of the street into the long running pen. I could not see the man because the crowd was so thick around him. I left the fence and started back toward town. I went to the café to have a second coffee and some buttered toast. I put one hand on the small of my back and the other on my chest. I came in. I followed them up-stairs and went into my room. I took off my shoes and lay down on the bed. I did not feel sleepy. I felt it with my thumb and fingers. I pressed up the wire fastener and poured it for him.

Chapter XVIII

I looked and saw her coming through the crowd in the square. I stood in front of the door. I tried the knob and it opened. I looked through the glasses and saw the three matadors. I could not see his face clearly under the hat. I think he loved the bulls. I sat in the down-stairs dining-room and ate some hard-boiled eggs and drank several bottles of beer. I drank it without sugar in the dripping glass, and it was pleasantly bitter. I began to feel drunk but I did not feel any better. I poured the water directly into it and stirred it instead of letting it drip. I stirred the ice around with a spoon in the brownish, cloudy mixture. I set down the glass. I had not meant to drink it fast. I was very drunk. I was drunker than I ever remembered having been. I went up-stairs. I put my head in the room. I went in and sat down. I looked at some fixed point. I went out the door and into my room and lay on the bed. I sat up in bed and looked at the wall to make it stop. I pretended to be asleep. I got up and went to the balcony and looked out at the dancing in the square. I washed, brushed my hair. I looked strange to myself in the glass, and went down-stairs to the dining-room.

Chapter XIX

I woke about nine o'clock, had a bath, dressed, and went down-stairs. I sat in one of the wicker chairs and leaned back comfortably. I drank coffee. I watched him come walking across the square. I only took a couple of drinks. I went out on the first roll with four kings. I rolled for the next two rounds. I went as far as the inner gate to the tracks. I watched the train pull out. I went outside to the car. I asked the driver. I paid the driver and gave him a tip. I rubbed the rod-case through the dust. I watched it turn off to take the road to Spain. I went into the hotel and they gave me a room. I washed, changed my shirt, and went out into the town. I bought a copy of the *New York Herald* and sat in a café to read it. I wish I had gone up to Paris. I was through with fiestas for a while. I could get a good hotel room and read and swim. I could sit in the Marinas and listen. I asked the waiter. I went in and ate dinner. I drank a bottle of wine for company. I had coffee. I told him to take the flowers of the Pyrenees away. I had a second marc after the coffee. I overtipped him. I spent a little money and the waiter liked me. I would dine there again some time and he would be glad to see me. I was back in France. I tipped everyone a little too much at the hotel to make friends. I did not tip the porter more than I should because I did not think that I would ever see him again. I only wanted a few good French friends. I knew that if they remembered me their friendship would be loyal. I hated to leave France. I felt like a fool to be going back into Spain. I felt like a fool. I stood in line with my passport, opened my bags for the customs, bought a ticket, went through the gate, climbed onto the train, and after forty minutes and eight tunnels I was in San Sebastian. I went to a hotel in the town where I stopped before, and they gave me a room with a balcony. I unpacked my bags. I took a shower in the bathroom and went down to lunch. I was early. I set my watch again. I signed it and asked him for two telegraph forms. I calculated how many days I would be in San Sebastian. I went in and had lunch. I went up to my room, read a whole book, and went to sleep. I found my swimming suit. I went into a bathing-cabin, undressed, put on my suit, and walked across the smooth sand to the sea. I waded out. I dove, swam out under the water, and came to the surface with all the chill gone. I swam out to the raft. I lay on the raft in the sun. I tried several dives. I dove deep once. I swam with my eyes open. I came out of water beside the raft. I lay on the beach until I was dry. I walked around the harbour under the trees to the casino. I sat out on the terrace. I sat in front of the Marinas for a long time and read and watched the people. I walked around the harbour and out along the promenade. I could not make out whom they belonged to. I had coffee out on the ter-rasse. I would see him there some time. I certainly would. I would certainly try to. I would leave a call at the desk. I had coffee and the papers in bed. I undressed in one of the bath-cabins. I swam out. I turned and floated. I saw only the sky. I swam back to the surf. I turned and swam out to the raft. I swam slowly. I looked around at the bay. I thought I would like to swim across the bay. I sat in the sun. I stood up. I walked back to the hotel. I gathered them up in the reading-room. I poked my finger along under the fold. I tipped the concierge and read the message again. I opened it. I had expected something of the sort. I saw the concierge standing in the door-way. I took out my fountain-pen. I went in to lunch. I did not sleep much that night. I had breakfast in the dining-car. I saw the Escorial out the win-dow. I saw Madrid come up over the plain. I took a taxi. I saw the sign. I could not make the elevator work. I walked up. I rang. I rang again. I was undecided. I was happy to hear it. I would welcome the upbringal of my bags. I followed the maid's back down a long, dark corridor. I opened the door. I went over to the bed and put my arms around her. I could feel she was thinking of something else. I thought she was looking for another cigarette. I saw she was crying. I could feel her crying. I put my arms around her. I could feel her crying. I held her close. I stroked her hair. I could feel her shaking. I poured a little in my glass. I drank my glass. I tipped him and told the driver where to drive. I settled back. I put my arm around her and she rested against me comfortably.

Lawrence Giffin
Spinoza's Ethics

"Spinoza's Ethics," an attempt to deduce ethical certainties from propositions demonstrated "in geometrical order," is largely concerned with essence, self-sufficiency, attributes, substance, modification, individuality, divisibility, and the relationship between bodies and intellection. Giffin's version, which appropriates the language of women's apparel catalogs, elides the larger categories of clothing (e.g., jacket, blouse, pants)—not to mention the person wearing those clothes—in favor of fashion marketing details. The result leaves only a sheer concatenation of exchange value, surplus ornament, and striptease distraction.

Black stretch velvet of rayon, silk, and spandex (not shown) cropped to let the sequined scoopneck sleeveless shell of pure silk georgette peek out beneath the hem of black stretch silk and cheetah-print, ruffle-detailed fitted spandex of rose and tan French taffeta, beautifully hued russet, and gold brocade of polyester and rayon with a regal stand collar over classic short-sleeves in golden silk and chocolate polyester of rayon, wool, and spandex, black rayon, and silk burnout velvet with piano fringe, silk charmeuse sleeveless scoopneck shell, and Asian-print silk burnout velvet mandarin-collar and black silk velvet with multicolored beading on an emerald green classic skirtsuit of wool and silk with seaming, two-button detail, and softly curved lapels in sheer floral-print silk over a sleeveless silk dress in black with red border print on ivory pure silk with smocked waist and tie detail over fluid brown silk white cotton crochet bolero jacket with sequined edging and sheer white mesh lining of white sheer lace of rayon and nylon with portrait collar, scalloped edges, and three-quarter sleeves trimmed with black suede and taupe, pink, red, and green floral embroidery of petal-soft featherweight cashmere (specify *Rain* or *Black*) and sheer red silk over black elastic-waist silk of stonewashed cotton and spandex with multicolored rhinestones decorating silk chiffon with velvet ribbon inset detail and velvet back-slit rayon and silk (specify *Chocolate* or *Black*) or classic with pleated detail imported of triacetate and polyester camel and black scroll-print cashmere with cascading ruffle-edge detailing in Italian wool tissue crepe in dark ginger magnolia print on cotton and silk knit jewel-neck of Italian wool and beautifully draped cashmere double-faced wool in oatmeal and ivory in polyester, wool, and supple suede with seam detail (specify *Red Maple, Chocolate, Cedar,* or *Black*) of finely knit rayon and Lycra of viscose and wool of toffee melton mélange of pure Italian wool, wheat merino wool, camel hair, and spandex of rayon, nylon, and spandex in a supple suede panel-blocked three-button blazer with full lining printed matelassé of cotton and silk and white shantung pants of polyester and pima cotton with detail in a winter white mock-turtleneck of imported cotton and pink finely knit with black tulle ruffle trim, interlaced satin ribbon, scalloped edges, faux-pearl of cotton, and removable corsage detail of rayon leopard-print in pure camel and red lightweight ruffled-edge cashmere of whiskey brown knitted natural mink from China of wool, acrylic, and alpaca with black ribbed wooden-bead detail mesh inset of rayon and cotton across mahogany brown fluid full-leg pants with cheetah-print single-button long cardigan with brown trim and matching scarf and brown fit-and-flare pants of Italian leather encrusted with crystals and rose logo detailing on black quilted leather with detachable dyed rabbit-fur collar with scalloped trim, delicate smoking, and ruffles at the wrists of classic black stretch silk crepe detailing black rayon with ivory silk waterfall-hem turtleneck and autumn suiting must-haves in refined wool flannel pleated ivory and grey scroll-detailed chenille shirtdress of rayon, silk, wool, and Lycra in black crocodile-embossed leather white cotton voile shirt with stand collar and ruched detail of pumice and a geometric-print of pure silk and ribbon-cut brown leather pink cashmere with crystal kitty detail on a classic fisherman's sweater in plush cashmere with rolled-edge detail and baby-cable cashmere with ribbed sleeves and back over espresso wool knit asymmetrical top and matching pants and wheat bouclé shawl-collar micro-stretch jacket in chocolate godet-pleated crepe of pure Italian wool (specify *Nouveau Blue, Camel,* or *Heathered Grey*) in an oversized, deeply V'd boyfriend sweater (specify *Malachite, Hazelnut Heather,* or *Black*) with broken-cable detailing (specify *Toffee Apple, Nori Green,* or *Wheat*) with seam detail (specify *Artichoke, Blood Orange,* or *Chanterelle*) with contrast whipstitching (specify *Plum/Garnet* or *Espresso/Putty*) with a contrasting black bateau-neck underlayer in petal-soft cashmere with detachable hood and elasticized drawstring in a vibrant mix of colors and patterns complemented by hand embroidery and faux-coin accents of heathered black mélange linen glistening with cubic zirconia accessories beautifully draped in red and black dash print with twisted bodice detail.

Peter Gizzi
Ode: Salute to the New York School, 1950–1970 (a libretto)

One subgenre of ancient Greek poetry comprised verse constructed entirely of lines drawn from Homer's *Iliad* and *Odyssey*. The Latin version of this technique, called *cento* (meaning "patchwork garment"), was often used to make an argument about the implicit pertinence of the poem's sources (e.g., Betitia Proba Falconia's fourth-century retelling of the Christian Gospels with lines from the pointedly pagan Virgil). As Ephraim Chambers's 1728 *Cyclopedia* defines it, the cento is "a Work wholly compos'd of Verses, or Passages promiscuously taken from other Authors; only disposed in a new Form, or Order." Chambers continues:

> *Ausonius* has laid down the Rules to be observ'd in composing *Centos*. The Pieces, he says, may be taken either from the same Poet, or from several; and the Verses may be either taken entire, or divided into two; one half to be connected, with another half taken elsewhere: but two Verses never to us'd running, nor much less than half a Verse to be taken.

Variations on the cento involve the constraint that authors draw lines only from the first lines of other poems or from the titles of poems. As *cento* means "one hundred" in Italian (from the Latin *centum*), one hundred lines would seem to be the ideal length.

The cento, as Chambers's encyclopedia entry attests, is a venerable form. Perhaps the most famous modern cento (partly because of its memorable title, courtesy of Edward Lear) is John Ashbery's "The Dong with the Luminous Nose" (*Wakefulness* [New York: Farrar, Straus & Giroux, 1998]). Ashbery had famously employed other modes of appropriation. In *The Tennis Court Oath* (Middletown, Conn.: Wesleyan University Press, 1962), for instance, the poems "Europe" and "Idaho" are largely collaged from William Le Queux's *Beryl of the Biplane* (London: Pearson, 1917) and A. Hamilton Gibbs's *Soundings* (Boston: Little, Brown, 1925), respectively. Less radically, Ashbery had drawn on *Three Hundred Things a Bright Boy Can Do* (by the anonymous collective "Many Hands" [London: Sampson Low, Marston, 1914]) in his poem "The Skaters" (*Rivers and Mountains* [New York: Holt, 1966]), and attentive readers of the notes to John Shoptaw's study *On the Outside Looking Out* (Cambridge, Mass.: Harvard University Press, 1995) are informed that Ashbery also "constructed a puzzle-poem, 'The Secret of the Old Mill,' by gridding 7 pages into 36 squares and parcelling Franklin W. Dixon's Hardy Boy novel by this title among them" (359n47). The patchwork of the grid returns us to the cento.

A comparison of "The Dong with the Luminous Nose" with Ashbery's earlier cento "To a Waterfowl," in *Rivers and Mountains,* is instructive. "To a Waterfowl" ranges from William Cullen Bryant (who provides the title) to Wallace Stevens to Edmund Spenser and a number of historically diverse sources. In contrast, "The Dong" draws mainly on canonical nineteenth-century British poets, from Alfred Lord Tennyson and A. E. Housman to Samuel Taylor Coleridge, John Keats, William Wordsworth, and William Blake. As Ashbery put it in an interview with Mark Ford: "I guess that poem's a sort of tribute to the period when I used to read nineteenth-century poetry with a sense of awe that great poets could write great poems."

Ashbery also noted, however, that he keeps forgetting where all the lines came from. Such amnesia is part of the experience of the cento, and a measure of that experience is the degree to which an author can transform the appropriated lines into a signature work of her or his own. At the same time, however, identifying at least some of the sources—and, moreover, simply knowing that there are indeed sources—is also part of the dynamic at play in the cento and what finally distinguishes it from formally similar works, such as Hart Crane's "Emblems of Conduct" or Blaise Cendrars's *Kodak* (or, for that matter, Ashbery's other appropriations).

Gizzi explains his particular method:

"Ode: Salute to the New York School" is a cento, a late Roman verse form made up of lines from other sources. First, I put together a chronological bibliography of over one hundred books published by New York poets from 1950 to 1970. Many of these books are deeply out of print so I had to do some real digging. Then I extracted one line from each book to compose the cento. Happily, Clark Coolidge and Larry Fagin supplied the lines from the books I couldn't find. The cento also works as an index to the bibliography. The combined bibliography and cento form the libretto to a musical work for the composer Richard Alan Applebaum. My intention was to make what I call a "performing bibliography." Since this is, in effect, what most of us do on a daily basis—referring to or performing what we've read—it seemed a useful metaphor to describe how we enact our reading practice. My idea was that a simple accompaniment to a series of bibliographic entries could generate both scholarly information and an emotive effect. I wanted to express the latent desire for lists and order, and to create a texture to accommodate the eros inherent in research. What I learned along the way is that literary movements survive primarily in the ruins of the texts they leave behind rather than in the unified literary histories that we create for them after the fact. (Peter Gizzi, "Process Statement," *Mississippi Review* 31, no. 3 [Fall 2003]: 126–27)

The original publication was followed by a complete bibliography, ensuring that even if Ashbery continues to forget where all the lines come from, he can easily look some of them up in Gizzi's article; Ashbery's own lines, of course, recur often.

A car roars over a conversation
A dish of Irish setters
Ah! such scissors of wind we are tearing our validity
A little horse trots up with a letter in its mouth, which is read with
    eagerness as we gallop into the flame
All revolutions have betrayed themselves by slush of feeling
A man signs a shovel and so he digs
And the nerve-ends evolved to cope with instant danger do not know
    what to tell the brain so they think about it
As if nobody believes what anybody tells them, gray in the cafe and the
    shiny rain
A sigh loaded with stale revolt like a freshwater tear
Bloom, flare, blink open
Born eaves clump bounce
But do we really need anything more to be sorry about
But Ned is lazy, the monkey has to do it all
By day I sleep, an obscurantist, lost in dreams of lists
Depersonalized angels refer you to nothing and you are nothing, meat
    stencils
Did you ever read the wet page of the earth?
File prayer tines
Fond memories of childhood, and the pleasant orange trolleys
For the first time in many years Kafka's mother enters the room to kiss
    him good-night
Gladly smothered in windows
Glee a short road across my face
Goodbye, Father! Goodbye, pupils. Goodbye, my master and my dame
Ha ha ha

Have I worn out my distracting powers to doze witless into the scape of
    night, empty of detail and excuse
He has banged into your wall of air, your hubris
His substance utters a sun above the stoves of our discourse
History, what did the Rose do?
How many ways to die for a window
I am interested in "reading" and in controlling reading speed
I am whizzed, suspended perpetually around the same green corner,
    spurious alb!
"I am your pineapple sunrise! I am your vanilla wristwatch! I am your
    whip!" says the Boy Scout
I bit my lip as he scraped my semen off the floor
I'd give a bunch of bananas for a sniff of your behind, oh yes!
I'd like to buy a house for your mind, white curtains
If Joan says I'm wounded, then I'm wounded
If things are the way we say they are then why do we say they are
I got to catch a bus for Altoona where I can smile again
I have won myself over to this cause. I am yours! You are mine! Light
    bulb! Holy Ghost!
I'll trade one red sucker for two blue ones
I look at the Himalayas; they neither sit nor stand
I love you like a sheriff searches for a walnut
In a church's tiered and April-green alcoves
In the bat light, in the bugger Darkness
In the murdersome chorus lines of the snow an entire bird fell biffing
    from off a tire
In you, I feel the new kite. What are your feelings like?
In Y's and V's and W's an elm ascends smoothly as an Otis Elevator
I prefer "you" in the plural, I want "you"
I remember jerking off to sexual fantasies involving John Kerr. And
    Montgomery Clift
I salute that various field
Is it dirty, does it look dirty, that's what you think of in the city
I speak as a wife to the capsizing
I stagered from the car nut reall hurt jus shok op
I think that's enough sex for today, d-d-d-don't you?
It is a distinct pleasure, and a marble-shaped pain, to be caught while
    walking out in the rain
It's me (was) & now it's you

It's not that I'm curious. On the contrary, I am bored but it's my duty to
   be attentive, I am needed by things
It's so clean you could flush ten million toilets into it and it would stay
   the same
It's so original, hydrogenic, anthropomorphic, fiscal, post anti-esthetic,
   bland, unpicturesque and William Carlos Williamsian!
"It was Saturday night and I just got toed"
I waken, read, write long letters and wander restlessly when leaves are
   blowing
I want to walk around in you breezily, o world, when I'm young
Left behind in New York City, & oof!
Let's warm up the simian pianola
Like watching wind push seaflowers straight across your eyelids
Love makes it poetic though blue
Many stars are in the sky, I asked Mother to help me, afterward
May's favorite game is fan tan. She always wins the antes by gooping
   herself up with man tan, after she takes off her scanties
My Army likes you so much loves you I think so much they are marching
   to your hit recording Me!
My flesh abides
My heart is blue and my foot has been ruined by the night
My love is a lurking toy
Naked arms, his chief activity, provided an annex of joy and compact
   tours
Near Paris, there is a boat. Near this boat live the beautiful Woods
Not the shadow you leave behind but the opening ahead
No turning back, no rewrite, no voice! in this poem, now, not to look
   nor creep back to the stark horror
Now as my questioning but admiring gaze expands to magnificent
   outposts
O blue tapeworm, sonnet of powerful indifference, nest
One of them said, "Ha ha! your spectacles are broken"
Open the mind of the paralytic stooge for seamy madness to discover a
   call
Our habits ask us for instructions
Oxygen Parachutes, my love, could carry us higher than this mid-air in
   which we tremble
Rainbows. Many tomorrows. My name is Tom
Really, I thought that fish could cry

Rose bud, I love your pout, love the ash-built slope

Saviors of connections and spit, dial HYacinth 9-9945, "Isn't that a
conundrum?"

Six knobs, four in heaven, makes ten

Snow White had brought the music back

Swig Pepsi & drape the bent frame in something "blue for going out"

That's not a cross look it's a sign of life

The black eyes ruffled the field of expectant spirits smooth on ice

The fate of the fake nostalgia of beebees lost under the furniture hulks

The grin of sleep is in the wind

The handkerchiefs as guards, the interjections orphaned

Their eyes grow louche at the exact second they start their slide

The last party to be seized at twilight, and time was cold to the lovers

The mind reaches forward gets hooked on the horizon and just hangs
there

The next day a verb drove up, and created the sentence

The pony-spoor of hotblood bank chip, far away from in outsize day

The quiet evening street, I spend a week in my underwear reading
Williams and drinking orange soda, both in California

The radiator came on & the geraniums died

There is nothing worse than elephant love

There is, with each soft clang, a marble fist

These   ing   those

The tone is hard is heard is the coming of strength out of night: unfeared

The tonic resonance of pill when used as in "she is a pill"

The train comes bearing joy; the sparks it strikes illuminate the table

The tremendous reassurance of being at the dinner table and tense, a
stalwart melody

They are preparing to begin again: problems, new pennant up the
flagpole in a predicated romance

This honey is delicious but it burns the throat

Truth is truth on an empty street at noon

Twelve Bells! Benny's on the ropes! Twelve Bells! He has no feet! Twelve
Bells! He can't make gloves!

Up north in the Aurora Borealis the blame falls like rain

We live in our own hip pocket, nodding out to rush back in

What obsolete! what lift! geronimo of confusion

When Andrew's letter arrived, three agents had already gone in vain to
search for Dog Boss

When the cows and the leaves begin to fall, they fall like falsehood
When we join them we will show them trophies of old smoke
Where green changes itself into LIFE
Whose impetus is irresistible: Get out of here!
Who will smile, & love you, at your leisure
Will they search for rust among the fake doubloons?
Yet the cars do not cheat, even their colors perform in storm
You can feel the wind in the room, the curtains are moving in the draft
and a door slowly closes
You select something small like a pimple and quick as a wink that's all
there is
You think of your art which has become important like a plow on the flat
land

Judith Goldman
from dicktée

In "dicktée" (*Vocoder* [New York: Roof, 1997]), Judith Goldman records all of the words in Herman Melville's *Moby-Dick*, in order of appearance, beginning with the letters *un–*. By doing so, Goldman highlights Melville's stylistic use—at the rate of about one instance per page—of double negatives and litotes to effectively cancel the overall negative force of what would be otherwise a high-frequency occurrence of negative words. The resulting poem thus enacts the dusting of "old lexicons and grammars" with which Melville's novel itself opens. The poem also suggests a 'pataphysical grammar in the tradition of Velimir Khlebnikov's "internal declensions" and suggests some underlying conceptual relationship between etymologically unrelated words. Lexically, the initial *un–* sequences come from adjectival privatives (negations and oppositions), verbal corruptions from the prefix *and–* (any number of reversals, removals, and releases), and singularities indicated by the contraction of the Latin *unus*. Here, words as disparate as *undressed, unassimilated, unctuous,* and *united* are all sorted into the same category.

Although "dicktée" aspires to include all of the words in *Moby-Dick* beginning with *un–*, it is a performative record, originally compiled longhand, rather than a perfect result following a computer search of a digital text. *Usual,* for example, should not have been included by a strict accounting, just as *ungraspable* and *unless*—according to Melville's text—should have been included as the fourth and fifth words, respectively. Such discrepancies, in the 'pataphysical universe, are all—unsurprisingly—to the point.

under, unite, unless, unpleasant, universal, uncomfortable, unaccountable, under, unbiased, undeliverable, under, underneath, universe, unequal, understanding, unaccountable, unwarranted, unimaginable, unnatural, unoccupied, undress, unobserved, unknown, unwarrantable, unknown, unaccountable, understand, uncomfortable, unsay, unaccountable, uncommonly, undressed, unearthly, undressing, unnatural, unceremoniously, uncomfortableness, unmethodically, undressed, unendurable, unimaginable, unlock, unbecomingness, understand, under, unusual, under, under, undergraduate, under, unsheathes, undivided, unknown, unholy, unheeded, unrecorded, unceasing, unhealing, unbidden, universal, unstirring, unspeakable, unnecessary, unseen, unassuming, unheeded, unknown, until, uncheered, unreluctantly, unto, unwelcome, unto, unearthly, uncouthness, unbiddenly, unite, unite, unite, undressed, unmistakably, unduly, undulating, unconquerable, untutored, unfitted, undefiled, unlike, unconsciousness, under, unconscious, under, under, unfort'nt, understand

unmatched, unpanelled, united, under, understand, unlimited, uncommon, uncommon, unoutgrown, unworthy, unite, untraditionally, unclad, unmitigated, unconsciously, unaccountable, unseen, ungodly, unless, undervalue, unprecedented, unmethodically, unconsciously, under, unwithdrawn, uneasy, unaccountable, uncomfortable, undigested, unless, understand, unless, ungodly, uninterrupted, unaccountable, unless, under, under, under, under, untrodden, unwilted, unpleasing, unrestingly, unmentionable, unpoetical, uncleanliness, unknown, unspeakable, unwittingly, unrecorded, unworthy, until, uncounted, undiscovered, unreasonably, undone, unreasonable, unless, unmanufactured, unpolluted, uncommonly, under, unpitying, unfearing, unconscious, universal, unvitiated, unerring, uncommonly, unseen, unknown, uninvitedly, uneasiness, uniqueness, unalterable, unsurrenderable, under, unnecessary, unwaning, unassured, unforeseen, unconsciously, unshored, understanding, unfitness, unfathomable, unworthy, unknown, unwritten, unspeakable, uncertain, unsettled, united, unknown

unexpectedly, underjawed, unsavory, unicorn, unicornism, unicorn, uncertain, uncouth, unfinished, uncompleted, under, under, unusual, unobservant, unmanifested, undoubted, unbodied, unexhilarated, unchallenged, ungentlemanly, unwarrantable, uneventfulness, unnecessary, unclad, unprovided, underneath, unicorns, unseasonable, unneeded, unconscious, undiscernable, uniform, unapprehensive, unmindful, unexpected, undoubted, unknown, unreasoning, unrecking, unworshipping, under, unerringly, unfaltering, untutored, unfailing, unceasing, undeniable, unaccompanied, uncommon, unfair, unfrequent, unborrowed, unearthly, unaccountable, underground, unharmed, unensanguined, unwonted, unwonted, unexampled, usual, unintelligent, unabated, unfathomably, unhinted, undeniable, unlikely, unrelenting, underlings, unabated, ungodly, unconscious, understandings, unsaid, unfurling, unnatural, unflattering, unspotted, un-harmed, unknown, unfallen, untutored, unread, unsophisticated, untrav-elled, unsubstantial, unrustlingly, unimaginative, universality, unbounded, universe, universe, unceasingly, unhooped, undeviating, unavoidable, un-questionable, unloitering, unfaltering, unquiet, unmistakable, unachieved, unsuppressable, unappeasedly, unbidden, unfathered, understood, unknown, under, unobtrusive, unknown, union, uncommon

. . .

unwound, unstranded, unnatural, unresting, unmeaningly, under, unre-tracing, unconscious, unmoor, unfathomable, unspoken, unknown, unver-dured, unnamable, unblinkingly, unrelieved, unknown, unobserved, under-stand, under, unconditional, unintegral, unbegotten, unbegun, unsuffusing, unparticipated, unsafe, uncommon, uncommon, unwonted, unsounded, unstaggering, undeviated, unaccountably, undaunted, unmurmuringly, unimpressed, uncertain, untouched, unwinding, unmanned, unless, unfrequented, unvarying, unearthly, unappalled, unaccompanied, unpro-vided, undignified, unless, unwinding, undertaker, unprincipled, under, uncertain, unknown, unknown, unexpected, unite, unknown, unmisgiv-ing, unfrequently, unenervated, undue, unconditional, unsettling, uncer-tain, unseen, unless, undeviating, unerringly, unheeded, unearthed, unless, unmomentous, under, unprovided, unusual, untrackably, uncommon, unrigged, unhinged, unspeckled, unyielding, untottering, under, unearthly, unsounded, under, unsuspecting, undiscoverable, under, unastonished, unharmed, under, unintermitted, unrestingly, unabated, unprecedented, under, unseen, unfearing, unseen, unmindful, uncommon, untraceable

untouched, unconquerable, under, unmeasured, under, underling, uncer-tain, unchangeable, under, uncommonly, unpitying, unprepared, ungradu-ated, unappeasable, under, unwinking, under, unsurrendered, uncracked, unconquering, undulated, unharming

---

from r'ture/CENTaur

Judith Goldman's collage practice in *DeathStar Rico-chet* (Oakland, Calif.: O Books, 2009), from which this poem is drawn, is a grimly unflinching tain to the same mirror that produces the ephemeral sparkle of distorted fun-house reflections for flarf, and lends the electrical sense to current events. Here the contemporary is treated with the full force of the historical: a condition of impossibility in which total information awareness is simultaneously the biggest threat and the best defense.

Isomura was a fisherman from San Pedro, California. Kobata was a farmer from Brawley, California. These two Issei, along with almost 150 other prisoners being a parliamentrary procedure known as the "nuclear option" moved from the Fort Lincoln Internment Camp in Bismarck, dubbed the nuclear option by former Senate GOP Leader Trent Lott because it would blow up the Senate. While the other prisoners were forced to march the mile from the station to Lordsburg, the filibuster can be overridden by a three-fifths majority vote via a cloture motion. The nuclear option would allow a simple majority because Isomura and Kobata were too ill to walk. The two were driven to the front gate of the nuclear option, and that would be a ruling that the filibuster of executive nominees is unconstitutional. I'm for the nuclear option," said Lott. The filibuster of federal judges cannot stand, arriving before the rest of the prisoners. At approximately 2:30 a.m., camp guard Private First Class Clarence A. Burleson does not have firm support among his caucus to employ the so-called "nuclear option." As several weblogs have noted, the nuclear option could come back to haunt them if they suddenly opened fire on the two men. It could come back to haunt them if they are in the minority, and if you don't do your work quickly, I will make you dig two more graves.

100 Soviet MIG-15s were flying over Syria

a British Canberra bomber had been shot down over Syria

the Soviet fleet was moving through the Dardanelles

unidentified aircraft were flying over Turkey and the Turkish air force was on alert

In response to his S.O.S.

A normal test launch of a Titan-II ICBM took place in the afternoon of October 26, from Florida to the South Pacific

At Volk Field, Wisconsin, the alarm was wrongly wired

either enemy action

The effect was consistent with a power failure due to nuclear weapons explosions//a single faulty chip that was failing//the radar post had not received routine information of satellite passage//However, several NATO subordinate commanders did order alerts to DEFCON 3 or equivalent levels of readiness//but failed to reach the on-duty personnel of the early warning

a routine airforce escort for the President of Syria

the Canberra bomber was forced down by mechanical problems

the Soviet fleet was engaged in scheduled routine exercises

a flight of swans

US F102-A fighters were launched; the US interceptor aircraft were armed with nuclear missiles

It causes temporary concern at Moorestown Radar site until its course could be plotted and the Klaxon sounded which ordered nuclear-armed F1-6A interceptors to take off

or the coincidental failure of all the communication systems

During the next 6 minutes emergency preparations for retaliation

system//He was to call twice, one minute apart, and only blow into the receiver.//saw a figure climbing the security fence. He shot at it, and activated the "sabotage alarm." The original intruder was a bear//That night the aurora prevented good sextant readings and the plane strayed over the Chukotski Peninsula//The whole purpose of the "Hot-Line" was to//of an inadvertent war due to

during the early days of long range radar

The rising moon was misinterpreted as a missile attack

Kenneth Goldsmith
from Day

Day (Great Barrington, Mass.: The Figures, 2003) is a complete transcription of the entire edition of the *New York Times* from Friday, September 1, 2000. Kenneth Goldsmith predicated his procedure on the constraint of uncreativity, which he refers to as "the hardest constraint a writer can muster." He systematically worked through each page, moving from one article to the next. Anywhere in the newspaper where there was a word, letter, or number, he transcribed it. He made no distinction between editorial and advertisement. Finally, when published, everything was set in the same font, without the use of styling such as bold or italic. The result is a leveling of information to text, which is stripped of hierarchy and design. One might read *Day* against both Sherrie Levine's edition of Gustave Flaubert's *Un coeur simple* (Ghent: Imschoot, 1990), in which she reprints Flaubert's story with her name appended, and two projects from the early 1970s by Allen Ruppersberg, who copied—longhand—the entirety of Henry David Thoreau's *Walden* and Oscar Wilde's *The Picture of Dorian Gray* (under the title *Henry David Thoreau's Walden by Allen Ruppersberg*). A key difference, of course, is that these intertexts were produced within the regime of the gallery system, not published in the system of small-press poetry.

"All the News That's Fit to Print"
The New York Times
Late Edition
New York: Today, mostly cloudy, high 83. Tonight, warm and muggy, low 73. Tomorrow, cloudy with a few showers, high 80. Yesterday, high 83, low 72. Weather map is on Page A20.
VOL. CXLIX . . . No. 51,498
Copyright © 2000 The New York Times
NEW YORK, FRIDAY, SEPTEMBER 1, 2000

$1 beyond the greater New York metropolitan area.

75 CENTS

PENTAGON LIKELY TO DELAY NEW TEST FOR MISSILE SHIELD

JANUARY DATE EXPECTED

Deployment Decision Would Fall to Next President—Treaty Issue Remains

By ERIC SCHMITT

WASHINGTON, Aug. 31—The Pentagon will probably postpone the next test of a national missile defense system until January, administration officials said yesterday. Any decision to deploy the antimissile shield now seems certain to pass out of President Clinton's hands to his successor's.

Administration officials had previously said Mr. Clinton would decide this summer on deploying a $60 billion antimissile system that would be ready by 2005. To meet that schedule, the Pentagon has been under heavy pressure for two years to conduct enough flights to show Mr. Clinton and his advisors whether the system was technologically feasible.

But now officials are signaling that Mr. Clinton merely plans to decide whether to go ahead with the program's initial development. The change follows events that include test failure, opposition from Russia as well as European allies and a legal dispute over how far the system could proceed before violating an important arms control treaty.

To keep that option of initial development open for Mr. Clinton, the Pentagon has requested bids for initial construction of a radar site in Alaska, setting Sept. 7 as the deadline for technical and cost proposals from contractors. The first contracts would have to be awarded by December to permit building to begin next spring and to have a working system in place by 2005. Under the schedule the Pentagon has set in light of conditions in Alaska, it has to start the process soon, subject to later presidential approval.

The more politically volatile decision of whether to field the system— and break the Antiballistic Missile treaty of 1972—would be left to the administration, whether that of Al Gore or George W. Bush.

In a sign of this political evolution, senior military officers, including the program's executive officer, Maj. Gen. Willie Nance of the Army, have argued that there is no more reason to rush more tests. Critics of the program have consistently complained that the military operation was on an artificially fast schedule.

"General Nance is not going to conduct a test unless he's fully confident that everything is fully ready for the test," said Lt. Col. Rick Lehner, a spokesman for the Ballistic Missile Defense Organization.

Mr. Clinton is awaiting a recommendation from Defense Secretary William S. Cohen on the project and

Continued on Page A9

Ozier Muhammad / The New York Times

Exit Agassi

The top-seeded Andre Agassi, right, congratulating Arnaud Clément of France yesterday after Clément defeated him, 6-3, 6-2, 6-4, in the second round of the United States Open in Queens. SportsFriday, Page D1.

Lazio Closes In On Mrs. Clinton In Money Race

By CLIFFORD J. LEVY

Representative Rick A. Lazio may be less well known than his opponent in the New York Senate contest (not to mention the Republican who dropped out), but in terms of fundraising, he has already entered her league. Mr. Lazio collected $10.7 million in just seven weeks this summer, his aides said yesterday, leaving little doubt that he will have the means to battle for the seat despite his late start.

Mr. Lazio has taken in a total of $19.2 million since jumping into the Senate race in May, nearly as much as Hillary Rodham Clinton, who has been raising money for more than a year and has collected $21.9 million. She raised $3.3 million in the seven-week period this summer: July 1 to Aug. 23.

Mr. Lazio's success with donors suggest that no matter who is on the Republican line—mayor, congressman, school board member—the checks will pour in because of hostility among some people across the country to the Democrat, Mrs. Clinton. And Mr. Lazio, a once-obscure congressman from Suffolk County, has readily harnessed that sentiment.

"I'm Rick Lazio," he wrote in an unusually short, one-page fund-raising letter this summer. "It won't take me six pages to convince you to send me an urgently needed contribution for my United States Senate campaign in New York. It will take

Continued on Page B7

Religion on the Hastings

Signs of Shift in Attitudes Suggest Blurring Of the Line Between Faith and Politics

By GUSTAV NIEBUHR

When Senator Joseph I. Lieberman urged a greater role for religion in public life in campaign speeches this week, he touched off a new round in the sharp but unsettled debate over the role that personal beliefs should play

News Analysis

in American politics.

Some critics of Mr. Lieberman's remarks, including the Anti-Defamation League, cast the issue in terms of separation of church and state, suggesting that the senator had infringed on that principle.

But another way to look at what Mr. Lieberman, a Connecticut Democrat, said is to ask whether American culture has changed enough of late so that his remarks are more acceptable, socially and politically, than before.

Those who say such a change has taken place can cite various reasons— public unease over the political scandals of the late 1990's, for example, or the longer-term emergence of religious conservatives as a political force or a less tangible but pervasive interest in the personal over the political.

"I think the Christian Coalition has added to our dialogue on politics and religion," said Paul Simon, the former Democratic senator from Illinois, referring both to the conservative organization of that name and also to the broader political movement of religious conservatives. "Now, some of that is not good, but some of that is good, too."

Mr. Simon, who now directs the Public Policy Institute at Southern Illinois University, said he thought Mr. Lieberman had made his remarks "with great care." But he also said that some of the religious language used in the presidential campaign had left him uncomfortable.

"My overall impression," Mr. Simon said, "is the deeply religious people don't talk about it as much."

Mr. Lieberman, the first Jew on a major American presidential ticket, said in a speech last Sunday that Americans needed to "renew that dedication of our nation and ourselves to God and God's purpose." And while he said the Constitution "wisely separates church from state," he added that there must be a place for faith in the nation's public

Continued on Page A23

Bush Approves New Attack Ad Mocking Gore

Democrats Say G.O.P. Has Turned Negative

By JAMES DAO

LOUISVILLE, Ky., Aug. 31—After struggling for a week to seize the offensive from Vice President Al Gore, aides to Gov. George W. Bush said today that they had approved a new and sharp attack commercial that strikes directly at Mr. Gore's character and mocks his appearance at a Buddhist temple four years ago.

The 30-second spot, paid for by the Republican National Committee, will go on the air Friday in 16 states, and comes just a week after Mr. Bush personally blocked another commercial sponsored by the party that also questioned Mr. Gore's truthfulness. The move exposed rifts within the Republican camp over how to attack Mr. Gore without violating Mr. Bush's vow to keep his campaign positive.

Mr. Bush's aides said they had wholeheartedly approved the contents and tone of the new spot, which they described as "tongue-in-cheek." They said it was a response to critical advertisements run by the Democrats against Mr. Bush.

The commercial shows a television set on a kitchen counter with Mr. Gore on the screen and an unseen woman complaining that the vice president is "reinventing himself on television again." At one point the commercial shows a picture of Mr. Gore at the Buddhist temple event in 1996 and another segment shows him saying, "I took the initiative in creating the Internet." At that point, the narrator says, "Yeah, and I invented the remote control."

Predictably, the commercial sparked accusations and counteraccusations between the two campaigns over which one had "gone negative" first. Mr. Gore's camp wasted no time responding to the commercial, which was widely shown on television news programs and on the Internet during the day.

Mr. Gore also scaled back plans to focus on a patient's bill of rights in the belief that the Republican advertisement would backfire and that the Democrats should not create news that would distract public attention from it.

The new commercial is part of a broader, coordinated effort by the Republicans to raise doubts about Mr. Gore's ethics and integrity, which the Bush campaign clearly views as the vice president's greatest vulnerability.

All this week, Mr. Bush has criti-

Continued on Page A22

PRESIDENT VETOES EFFORT TO REPEAL TAXES ON ESTATES

REPUBLICANS VOW A FIGHT

Clinton, Echoing Gore, Calls Bill Too Costly and Says It Mainly Helps the Rich

By LIZETTE ALVAREZ

WASHINGTON, Aug. 31—President Clinton today vetoed a Republican-sponsored bill to repeal the federal estate tax and stepped up the election-year sparring over tax cuts and how best to spend the budget surplus.

In remarks in the East Room of the White House, Mr. Clinton said the bill "fails the test of fairness and responsibility" because it is costly and, according to administration figures, benefits only the wealthiest 2 percent of the population.

The president accused Republicans of threatening to hamstring the booming economy by devising a series of tax cuts that he said would leave little money for Medicare, prescription drug benefits, education and a host of other programs.

Vice President Al Gore has repeatedly lobbed the same charge at his opponent, Gov. George W. Bush of Texas, who supports repealing the estate tax. And in vetoing the bill today, Mr. Clinton adopted the same sort of language heard from Mr. Gore on the campaign trail.

"I believe the latest bill, this estate tax bill, is part of a series of actions and commitments that, when you add it all up would take us back to the bad old days of deficits, high interest rates and having no money to invest in our common future," Mr. Clinton said, echoing Mr. Gore's attacks on Mr. Bush's tax plans.

The bill "shows a sense of priorities that I believe got us in trouble in the first place in the 1980's, and that if we go back to those priorities, will get us in trouble again," he said.

In Congress, Speaker J. Dennis Hastert of Illinois immediately announced that the House would try to override the veto as its first order of business when it returned next week.

The effort, which requires a two-thirds majority in both houses of Congress, is expected to fail in the House, as well. Neither Republicans nor Mr. Clinton ruled out the possibility of a compromise today.

"The death tax punishes families for being successful," Mr. Hastert said, using the Republicans' preferred term for the estate tax.

"It punishes farmers. It punishes small business owners. It punishes those who have not planned ahead with an array of lawyers and accountants to keep their money in their family," he said.

"Down the road," he added, "it will punish our young entrepreneurs, who are just starting their own Inter-

Continued on Page A24

Firestone Struggles in Center of an Ever-Widening Storm

By KEITH BRADSHER

NASHVILLE, Aug. 31—Rarely has a leading global company faced such an extraordinary confluence of problems: its flagship product blamed for scores of deaths; its biggest customer undermining its every defense;

its stock price plunging along with consumer confidence; its top executive summoned before an angry Congress.

This is not how Firestone planned to celebrate its 100th birthday this summer. The centennial, some marketing experts say, has turned into a debacle for one of America's most familiar brand names.

In Washington today, regulators added 26 deaths to the 62 previously attributed to failures of Firestone tires in the United States. In Venezuela, one of 17 countries where Firestone tires have been recalled, the government's consumer agency asked the state prosecutor to bring criminal charges against Firestone. It also called for prosecuting the Ford Motor Company, saying the design of Ford Explorer sport utility vehicles that were equipped with Firestone tires contributed to dozens of deaths in crashes there.

Until today, Ford officials insisted that their company would stand by Firestone as a supplier. But Jacques Nasser, Ford's chief executive, refused during a news conference in Dearborn, Mich., to reiterate that stance. "This has been an extremely difficult and disappointing period in our relationship, and we'll take this a day at a time," he said.

Executives of Bridgestone / Firestone and its Japanese parent, the Bridgestone Corporation, insist the Firestone brand will survive. John Lempe, the American subsidiary's executive vice president, said here this morning that to restore customers' confidence, the company would soon appoint an independent investigator to look into the company's products and practices.

But Firestone soon may face a fresh storm. As Mr. Lampe spoke in an interview at an airport hotel, angry union workers prepared to dem-

Continued on Page C5

Associated Press

STRIKE THREATS Bridgestone / Firestone faces a possible strike tomorrow. Union members rallied in Nashville yesterday. Page C1.

Fire Raises Doubts About River Town's Boom

By ANDREW JACOBS

EDGEWATER, N.J., Aug. 31—A day after a devastating fire here, Ann Ring stood in front of her heat-scorched home, its vinyl siding dripping like melted cheese, and marveled at a Hudson River view she thought she had lost forever.

As thick smoke rose from stubborn pockets of the blaze, Mrs. Ring said she was thankful that the wall of flame had been kept from consuming her home. It had destroyed a luxury apartment complex under construction, nine nearby houses and an occupied apartment building.

But like many residents of this former factory town, Mrs. Ring, 58, said she was also angry about the wave of development that is quickly transforming Edgewater and other waterfront towns into the so-called Gold Coast.

"This used to be a quaint place," said Mrs. Ring, a school crossing guard. "But they've gone and put up these ugly monsters. They're ruining the place."

Coming a month after fires ripped through two Jersey City high-rises, the blaze on Wednesday night raised new questions about whether development is outstripping the ability of local governments to regulate it and favoring the needs of developers over residents.

With Edgewater's population of 6,000 expected to grow by as much as 2,000 in the next few years, many residents worry that growth will overwhelm this narrow river town, which is just two blocks wide and four miles long. "We have one main road and three paid firemen," said Valory Bardinas, a City Council member. "This development is not only jeopardizing our quality of life, but our safety, too."

As firefighters continued to spray arcs of water on the smoldering

Continued on Page B7

gorewillsayanything.com

THE WHITE HOUSE

The ad combines television images of Mr. Gore with scornful dialogue and a not yet operational Web address.

BEWARE! IF YOU LIKE STORIES WITH HAPPY endings, avoid reading Lemony Snicket's A Series of Unfortunate Events, now unfortunately NYT bestseller! www.lemonysnicket.com—ADVT.

SAVE UP TO 80% ON HEALTHCARE, MEDI-Savers 212-279-0279 www.Medi Saver.com.—Advt.

JEWISH WOMEN / GIRLS LIGHT SHABBAT candles today 18 min. before sunset. In NYC 7:10 PM. Info 718-774-2060. Outside NYC 718-774-3000. In merit of Raizel Gutnick, OMB—ADVT.

INSIDE

Last Resort for Parents

When parents are at wits' end and their children—often adolescents—are out of control, some turn to government, relinquishing their children to foster care.

PAGE B1

Drought's Toll in Texas

This summer's record stretch of 62 days without rain in North Texas has dried up lakes, helped spark 650 fires and left thousands of acres of crops wasted.

PAGE A14

Type-A Mayor Slows Down

Fatigued by cancer treatments and sidelined by his party, Rudolph Giuliani, New York's round-the-clock mayor, has slowed to a less frenetic pace.

PAGE B1

Former Lucchese Boss Dies

Anthony Corallo, thought to have been the oldest surviving mobster to have risen from one of New York City's five organized crime families, died in prison at 87.

PAGE A25

News Summary A2

Business Day C1-18

Editorial, Op-Ed A26-27

International A3-12

Metro B1-8

National A14-24

Sports Friday D1-8

Weekend (2 Parts) E1-24; E25-38

Automobiles F1

Obituaries A25

Real Estate B7

Weather A20

Classified Ads F5-7

Auto Exchange F2

Updated news : www.nytimes.com

THE NEW YORK TIMES is available for delivery in most major cities. On the Web: homedelivery.nytimes.com, or telephone, toll-free 1-800-NYTIMES. ADVT

354613

Between February 7, 1992, and October 20, 1996 (as indicated by the title), Goldsmith recorded those phrases he happened to come across which ended in a (loose) "r" sound. He then sorted them into chapters by syllable count and alphabetized the phrases within each chapter. The final chapter of the 600-page book consists of D. H. Lawrence's "The Rocking Horse Winner," copied in its entirety and coming in at 7,228 syllables.

from Chapter VIII

A beer does not come with in-laws, a Bohemian reformer, a bridge from nowhere to nowhere, a bunch of crap thrown together, a dog will not bite his brother, a few kernels short of an ear, a fly betty is really your, A frog in a liquidizer!, a giant Nintendo nightmare, a K in a six-pointed star, a leader not a follower, a little light in his loafers, a man's best friend is his dogma, a mother-in-law is fever, a number of destitute Moors, a pack of pathetic wankers, A panic in a pagoda!, a patch may defeat the weaver, a precise statement of number, a radiant node or cluster, a roebuck in its second year, a Roland for your Oliver, a side bar on straight male culture, a single kiss cool like water, a slut nixes sex in Tulsa, a steady stream of scumbaggers, a thirst for a burst of flavor, a very un-Bagsy platter, a walk under the summer stars, A Whole Days News In A Half Hour, a woman who inhales colors, a woperson of noncolor, (a word I've never heard before), abnormally white in color, (about what I couldn't tell ya), abrupt halt of stupendous snores, absence makes the heart grow fonder, absence of a sense of humor, absorbing stories people share, AC/DC and Def Leppard, Academy Award Winner, accepting words for what they are, accountants are good with figures, actors do it on camera, add mashed potatoes for structure, adds a lot of spark to the fire, aesthetic fellow travelers, after all it is Yom Kippur, after combing these sources for, afternoons in Utopia, agents do it undercover, Aha! The rhymeless rhyme appears, ain't got no stinking Listserv here . . . , Al lets Della call Ed Stella, Aladdin's Anal Adventure, alkoholik drunk-ass spunda, all be different together, all Futures and Pasts begin here, all in the service of number, all India into zillahs, all lime and salt no tequila, all the children they could devour, All this stuff here in the hangar?, all you can eat at Red Lobster, alligators in our sewers, Always Crashing In The Same Car, amaryllis sillyrama, ambiguous spot pawning hair, ambulance drivers come quicker, America etc., American Gladiators, an electric dog-polisher, an empty hand brings bad odor, anaesthetic elevator, and a nice girl's pad beats the floor, and better ones in the future, and curved again and snuffed the airs, and drain your nuts dry to the core, and enjoy it in another, And her dog was cured of cancer!, and I took my temperature, and I'm like outta here—later, and if that three-toed sloth's a bore, and it all does go together, and it's black like every color, and now a word from our sponsors, and spending the night with tuna, and talk about hanger-on-ers, and that is a fact of nature, and the opinions of others, and the rest is done with mirrors, and then came the moviemakers, and three quarters of another, And what other questions are there?, and with more power than Hoover, And you should see what's under there!, and your photos prove you were there, anna pimu kumi panna, annoys a moister oyster more, anorexia nervosa, another fun-tastic summer, another month another scare, anteloping interloper, antithetical theater, Any Supermodels out there?, anywhere is better than here, apes corralling human bothers, apupapin papupata, aracial and nongendered or, archdrude of the common era, are more than just a Nena for, Are we having fun yet Marla?, Aristotle was a bugger, Arrid. Get a little closer, as earwitness to the thunder, (as opposed to the real answer), as pure as a salamander, ask dumb questions get dumb answers, ask smart questions get no answers, at one time my breasts were insured, atom does hummers oops drummers, attend to some good idea, Australian butt chug moon river, babysitters charge by the hour, bad breath of scholarly nowheres, bailiffs always come to order, bamboo shoots under the fingers, banana peels in pool filters, banisterial barrister, Baptists do it under water, barbers do it with shear pleasure, based on an actual letter, bassists do it with their fingers, bastards who give you evil stares, Bayreuth: Hitler's court theater, Beat Me Daddy Eight To The Bar, because language is free like air, because smaller is friendlier, beheaded on Nero's orders, bemused by the stink I am yours, better than her bitter butter, Betty Botter bought some butter, between these lips covered with hair, big hangnail for healing power, bigga mic from extinguisher, birds will shrivel up in mid-air, bits of food in my computer, black and white and dead all over, black and white and red all over, blame it on the bossa nova, blender blinder bonder blonder, blood flow over our gray matter, bodies are now washing ashore, Bolivian marching powder, bootleg like a mother fucker, boring after-dinner speakers, Bosnia-Herzegovina, bosses I got jump from cellars, both are called by the same letter, (both nearly laugh but recover), bought a bit of better butter, boy yu a go dead don't bodda, bread and butter for my supper, Brecht takes a piss in G-major, bring me his head on a platter, bristles studs acne and leather, brushing my teeth with a finger, buff and small smoking red letters, bulldog boots ruddled cinnabar, bumpa thumpabumpa thumpa, but "later" never came later, but a bit of better butter, but her sister ussessed to boosester, but i'm always a little more, but let us leave the matter there, but she said this butter's bitter, but what is sweet now turns so sour, but you made 2 common errors:, butchers do it with their chopper, c'mon baby light my fire, can be outwitted by a jar, Can I borrow your menorah?, Can you see the hole in my ear?, can't get enough of Brooke Astor, candles: primitive dark suckers, cannabidulic kavannah, canonical older master, "Cantor Don Goldberg! Are you there?", Captain Kirk pick pocket gangsters, carpenters hammer it harder, capture sounds out of the thin air, carving up her legs with razors, casting bread upon the waters, catterfly and butterpillar, caught in a midsummer downpour, chicken helps bind shit together, chiggers are included on your, Chow mein haggis saké vodka?, Christ that's Beaver Cleaver's mother, Christian the Kosher Kielbasa, Christians who observe Passover, churches churches and liquor stores, clad punk ing it all in and there, Cleopatra's nose as factor, Clinton Seeks More Aid For Russia, clock doesn't have all its numbers, closed captioned pizza delivers, coating the inside of glassware, coming back at the next number, commands your attention) refers, como palo de goleta, comparative literature, comtemplating America, consider and reconsider, consider good cow consider, constant phone calls from my mother, constantly testing my center, constipated in India, Cool girls and who you think they are!, corrects structurizes restores, cosmic vibratory power, couldn't call it literature, couldn't say what the "composer," create a plan that delivers, cryonicists stay stiff longer, cut an onion down the center, cut-off penises and world wars, daddy got a stinky finger, dancing about architecture, days whose hours are shorter than ours, dazzling bowers of soft retire, deliver Oscar caliber, Delta is ready when you are, Der Wallet-emptyung Meter, Dhammacakkappavattana, Diarmuid and Grania, did damage on the 3 and 4s, Did I ever? Did I ever!, Did I ever? Did you ever!, Did you ever! Did I ever!, Did you ever? Did I ever?, Did you ever? Did you ever!, Did you finish sewing my bear?, dig a ding dang depadepa, digital slaves of the future, dinkus simmers in late summer, discharges corroding humours, dive into an icy river, Do food makers get fan letters?, Do me a big favor will ya?, do not whine to the Postmaster, dock doesn't quite reach the water, Does anyone sing anymore?, Does it speak to you anymore?, don't ask me I only work here, don't believe everything you hear, don't even think of parking here, don't know why you may not know where, don't write without the letter "r", Don't you just love non-sequiturs?, downhill skiing in Iowa, Dr. Kildare fell down the stair, drew their swords and shot each other, Droopy Dawg strung out on downers, dropping molten lead on water, dry is the way of the future, e-lec-a-tric-a ba-na-na, eating a masala dosa, (echo) "Brad I fucked your sister", echoic of lunar laughter, effective sunspot remover, egotism is the killer, eh the memories don't matter, 82% grilling more, ejaculating fervent prayers, electric dreadlock detangler, electricity in the air, electronic people finders, 11.896 years, emanating waxy paper, empty sockets for this slicer, ends 'n' sides were folded over, enraged eunuch double standers, Et tu Brute? Then fall Cæsar!, Eros? Sidney my end is sore, every absence of a comma, every day has many colors, ex-New York Doll Johnny Thunders, except rain and marijuana, excursions into the nether, excuses for bad behavior, expander fawning lackluster, experimental everywhere, exposing her je ne sais quoi, eyelids to rest a detour for, F.T.W. the letters, Fascist jock itch deep down trauma, fat and stupid like Rush Limbaugh, Father Devine's Riviera, feed a cold and starve a fever, Feel sorry for MY boyfriends? Hah, fiend castration should be his cure, 50 Ways To Leave Your Lover, 50 Ways To Love Your Lever, fill air sickness bag with coleslaw, filmfare and a Mona Lisa, finders keepers losers weepers, finita la commedia, flattery will get you nowhere, flippenflappenmuckenschpredder, fluffer nutter peanut butter, fluffy and then fluffy no more, for breakfast there'll be blood and fur, for mutual oral pleasure, for suddenly I am nowhere, For what you ask? Because its there!, force llamas in frilly attire, foreskin 500 formula, Fred Gwynn? As in Herman Munster?, free versions of the same flavours, from Dan even to Beer-sheba, from lawmakers to lawbreakers, fruity Dinosaurs: Meterva, "Fuck the porridge" said baby bear, fucking get your act together, full of life love and without fear, furnishes the motive power, geezers versus whippersnappers, gender doesn't seem to matter, Generation Twentyslackers, gentlemen back to your corners, (gestures and the man disappears), get a smear and denigrate her, getting back to the subject here:, give me to drink mandragora, give the people what's familiar, glory glory hallelujah, (glowingly) in Vanity Fair, gluing a quarter to the floor, go on Babette—get up the stairs, gone the way of the space hopper, gonna roll you like a pita, goodness gracious great balls of fire, Got any I.D. Mr. Santa?, grandmother's orgasmic seizure, Green Grass And High Tides Forever, guess I'll roll another number, Hagen possibly a

Himmler, hairless arm pumping in the air, hand lotion inside of an air, (hand shaking while reading letter), hands across the water (water), Harnessing God to make odors?, Harriet Tubman would never, Have you been fucking Madonna?, Have you done it packed in rubber?, having skipped through all the letters, He Ain't Heavy He's My Brother, he asked about the lasagna, he blew his mind out in a car, he bore her to the sandy floor, he had diahre—dyrea—, he had to be a Mahatma, he was a motherly father, he was furnished like a hunter, he's got James Joyce pecs and he snores, he's got the hand me down Pumas, he's got sentences to die for, he's talking about Madonna, head spinning snares supernova, Headless Body In Topless Bar, hell anytime for that matter, Hell's Angel: Mother Teresa, Hello Muddah Hello Fadduh!, hello Teenage America, hemidemisemiquaver, hence I must be meta-meta, her later memoir however, her pathetic poetic roar, her virginal exterior, here I sit in shitty vapor, his pathetic poetic roar, Holiday in Cambodia, Honk If You Hate Bumper Stickers, honor someone who pulls on her, hope you die before you retire, hot air over our area, hot and attractive crossdressers, how absurd to think opera, How do you like your eggs father?, How many "Immortals" are there?, How'd you like to be Madonna?, How'd you like to mow my lawn? Huh?, How's that for animal humor?, humans are the stumps of nature, humming Deep Purple's Highway Star, I am your whirleds pro grammer, I bleed into your reservoir, I Can't Believe It's Not Butter!, I confess my ashamed desire, I coulda been a contenda, I couldn't have been lonelier, I curse all father-confessors, I didn't go to Bar Mitzvah, I do not have breast or udders, I don't believe in God either, I don't fucking care whatever, I don't like the top bananas, I don't think Nazis are clever, I feel the same when you are near, I fell guilty beyond wordsa, I glued the rice-men to their doors, I got blisters on my fingers, I guess it must be bad karma, I had the answer to their prayers, I hate my life and I hate yours, I have not the slightest desire, I hope Neil Young will remember, I hope this shit holds together, I just had a good idea, I just love Bill Cosby pictures!, I like my meat medium rare, I live the life of a waiter, I love my car I miss my car, I Love You Just The Way You Are, I masturbate in the shower, I pounded teardrops to the floor, I quit eating sugar butter, I rolled my eyes and scuffed the floor, I saw a fishpond all on fire, I saw a house bow to a squire, I shit you not on those either, I still like only life better, I suppose was such another, I think I've spotted a trend here, I think we are a big culture, (I told you they were popular),

from Soliloquy

Soliloquy (New York: Granary, 2001) is an unedited record of every word Kenneth Goldsmith spoke during a week in April 1996, from the moment he woke up on a Monday morning until the time he went to bed on Sunday night.

It's her, Marjorie Perloff and, uh, I'm meeting her actually at the MOMA Members Dining Room for lunch today. And she's deeply powerful and I'm going to get her, I hope, to write a blurb for the back of my book and promote it. It should I'm very you know I'm really excited about having lunch with her. She's in from Stanford so that's what I'm doing today. And tonight I'm going to a party for John Newman. He's a nice guy actually, he's a really nice guy. He really is, yeah. Yeah, he shows at, uh, really formal sculpture. Yeah, something like that. I mean, It's very formal. It's very formal work. Yeah yeah yeah yeah. And he's, I mean, he's turns out to be a really nice guy, um, and he's having a a party tonight and then after that ada 'web, which is a big art Internet place is having a party after that. Yeah. Yeah. No no no because they're having they're at the Video Viewpoints at the MOMA talking about Cyberspace so afterwards this they're having this huge party at, uh, 23rd street. Um, and, uh, you know. Thanks. Um so anyway, it's like this parties galore tonight, uh, today I've got lots of just meetings and shit with people. But anyway, so let's just like keep the door open, you know, I mean, you know . . . I mean, I really wish that would happen. That would that would I mean, I'd do it I'd do it in a heartbeat because, you know, I could . . . what ever happened with that? Very fifties. Oh right right right. Yeah. Yeah. Well that, you know, and and if you can know that you're jumping and not jump you know and not and not right and I know you know what you're doing and not . . . well, I mean it's something like that it's something like that worked out it would be, it would be really cool. I'm going to my studio, um, you know, something like that would be really, you know, I would I would definitely be up for it you know I don't mind, but you know what as art . . . as art I'm not going to be be doing that stuff, I mean I just can't, I'm just so fucking fried on that shit I If I ever had if I had to color in another letter I'd go out and kill someone. Yeah. Yeah, I don't know. Naw, naw, naw. All right, listen, this is all right and I apologize and I think your point is really well taken about about if you say you're gonna do it you got to do it. I'm with you on that and and we'll just kind of keep things keep things open. OK, babe. I'll I'll drop by a manuscript. And listen, the book will be out this summer. If people wanna know, you know, Geoff's book will be out this summer, fall very latest. I don't know, uh, you're gonna be . . . yeah, in June or something, yeah, yeah, we'll work on it. See you, John. Yeah. Yeah. Is he a nice guy? Yeah. Um, all right. Let's see. Let's see. So, what are you doing today? Is she making good work? What's your next show after this? What's that? Huh. Huh. Huh. Huh. Uh, no but that's, uh, you're looking for art that has children in it? Babies. Do you think summer or fall would be a better time to spring a book? That's a good idea. That's a good idea. Are you sure you don't wanna see the Internet for a little while? Seriously, I mean, it'll take it'll take, uh . . . I have I have bad news for you though—the only real real porn place that I've found are gay. Yeah. What does that mean? What does that mean? This? Did they catch the guy? So, anyway, so in terms of porn the I pulled down some pictures but it's mostly it's mostly this guy that I've been working for surfs the Internet and has come up with all these—hey, how do you like that? How do you like that? Fuckin' A! You should translate that into sales, right? I love it, yeah. How do you like your Microsoft Windows little Brian Eno thing? Oh you don't use the Brian Eno? So, this is not from your brother, right? Anyway, let me just finish about the porn. Because the first time anybody ever sees the Internet the first thing they say to me is "Where's the porn?" and I have and I would say, oh, um I don't know. So I did this major porn search for het porn and all it is like these terribly like cheesy sites where you have to pay—there's like nothing out there, very very little. But the guy that I work for, Douglas—I was saying this to him—he's like he's gay he's like well I know all the gay sites so I was, like, OK, well at least give me the gay sites you know, they're not they're not real interesting in in so terms of porn I don't have uh much to show you. I guess it's out there if you want to pay you can get really raunch stuff. OK, I pay twenty five dollars a month and my service is unlimited. I have a different I have a different server. So here. If I just open this up all it is is a local phone call and I pay twenty five dollars a month and that's it. Right? And that's all. MSN is probably gonna end up charging you a little bit more. They'll probably charge you hourly. Ah, come on now. Well, this Broadway net that I have as a server is right across the street and they're usually really good. Sometimes they're not picking up but . . . here we go. They're really good. It's a really cheap modem. It's a one hundred thirty nine dollar modem. It's the modem. It's a piece of shit but, it works, you know, it works. OK, so OK.

This is the same thing you did—you log on, right? And you you double click on your Microsoft on your Inter Internet Explorer icon which looks like this. I have Internet Explorer. Microsoft Internet Explorer. Where is it? Internet Explorer. Here it is. OK? So what you do is you just double click on it. Now I'm gonna I'm gonna use an identical program—it's called just Netscape but you have Internet Explorer and once you the thing is open, just double click on it, right? And so you I'll use the identical thing here. This is my this is the one I I like to use better than the Internet Explorer called Netscape and you can use Netscape too. OK. and then so now, you know, you can do things like Netsearch—search for something just click on here. And if you want to just just get going—actually I can probably open Explorer to show you just to show you, uh . . . OK same thing, this is what it looks like, right? OK so so we go um . . . here they have open search open . . . search OK? This is or Internet searches and they say please use new location so you go OK? We'll go to a new location. OK. art net web yeah well their URL is, I know it, you just go http www art art net dot web. OK or if you wanted to if you wanted to find you know that the it's world wide web, that's the address, or if you wanted to find it, you could to you know Lycos you could go art net web. And here it is. Here it is. Here I just found an art net web OK? So, you see what I'm saying? There's there's millions of . . . OK so that's how you find it I'm just telling you how you find it. Do you understand that? You get it? You just just go to your search— go to Internet search and in any of them just enter what word you want and then hit search and it does it for you. And you go OK, here it is. OK. I'm just trying to connect. Stop connection because it a. . . . There's all this stuff art net. There's art net web, see? It's coming in. We've just got to wait for the images to come in. It's slow. It's gonna get better but you've got to wait. Um, if we did the same thing in Nestscape, I think Netscape's better. You go www art net web com. The images just came in. See now this is waiting for it to come in now which is two different browsers but we're we're either way we're waiting. See? Oh, this is interesting . . . we've got one here and we've got a different one here, huh, I guess it keeps changing. You know, we'll just stick on . . . oh look it's shifting again. That's pretty cool, that's nice. See this isn't this isn't doing it. See, Netscape's better, it does shit like this. You should probably get yourself a . . . OK, see? So what do you want to look at? OK. Index: high or low? Let's see, we'll go high. I guess we click on week just like that now it's . . . let's scroll down . . . the Guggen-heim Museum . . . yeah, where is that? Did you see Richard's show. So, I mean there was just a review that hangs out that's kind of nice. I mean so

Richard review of Richard's stuff but it's not a review. Opening this week. Art galleries, so let's go to galleries. Now this is pretty good. Yeah, formerly John. See this is pretty good. See a little description. I don't know, somebody who wrote there. Monique Prieto. Maybe there's something about her. Look at that! And that's it, but that's nice. That's a nice painting. It shows you the thing. Where. Huh. Watch this. Watch this, man. Save this image as and I can grab image man and throw it onto my desktop, right? I just grabbed it. Now I can do something like I can open up Photoshop and you can do this. This is really cool. I have to open another program. And I've got it on my desktop. Here it is. Any image on the web is grabbable I got this fucker now. Yeah, so I can do anything I want with it I can I can you know I can go like that and I can take take you know this shape and I can . . . with one color. You know you know I can go I can put some text on it if I want. Yeah, you know just just the same kind of thing some kind of shit you do but my point is is that any image on the web is grabbable, OK? Nothing is you know. See this is really nice, man. They did a really good job here I think. Let's find out what map is. Oh look at this! This is really cool. This is really good. Do they actually have you guys on here Mercer? You go OK, well that's Mercer. Isn't that nice? They give you a whole fucking map. Isn't that great? Isn't that really cool? Let's go back. Let's go back and see what buzz is. Buzz for Monique Prieto. Oh, man and you can you can you can write your own review. Yeah. Prieto. P-R-I-E-T-O. Your name. Uh, John Gams. Good. OK, give me a fucking cool press release. Go go go. Just say something about her paintings. Just just give me, uh, just say something—I haven't seen the show. Uh huh. I don't know, I haven't seen the show. Intriguing. Prieto's work is intriguing in a way that catches you totally by surprise. Just for I had to be an abstract painting I was shocked to walk into this grand gallery space and see something totally new. Not, not new in the sense of new new but something more subtle, subtle, perhaps a recombination of the once familiar. Let let let give me give me one more real real hard line give me a spin line on her stuff. See this show and reevaluate your long standing ideas about ancient medium. OK, and now it's gonna close and and we'll we'll see if it shows up. Great. OK and now we'll go back and let's see if it's shown up. Go back here go buzz and reload. Oh man, how come it hasn't shown up? Yeah, but it should happen automatically it's a CGI script. Anyway, um, anyway I think they they real really seem to do a good job here. Let's see about Cheryl's. Let's see if they got Cheryl's. Fun, isn't it? That's pretty pretty neet. Let's see what they say about Cheryl's. They've really done a lot of work here. Installation projects let's see the buzz. Best artist in the world. That's my sister-in-law! Colleen is married to Colleen is married to Cheryl's brother in Chicago. That kills me, man. That kills me! This is good, man! This is really good! What if if . Oh, I'm in this show this Carter Kustera—he's so dumb. Pretty interesting, huh? There's another great site The Thing. This is this is kind of fun because they're they're, uh . . . you can get a picture directly this picture that snaps a photograph of of The uh Thing right now. Whenever you call it in it snaps a picture of the office up there. That' nice, huh? A picture of the Empire State Building and, uh, it's always different. It's always growing and changing and every time if you snapped another picture if we did another picture it would it would probably move to the right but that's, you know, a live picture. It's really beautiful, isn't it? I'm gonna save this image as I'm gonna say empire state gif. Kinda cool, huh? And then here they have sort of art stuff. I don't know if you want to look at any of these artists. This one is pretty nice. Mariko Mori? This one? Yeah. I don't . . . Oh, look it's downloading a sound it's downloading a sound file. You want to see any of these other artists? OK. OK, we'll do that. We'll do that. John, sell my work! Wah! I'll uh. Here's the manuscript. Actually actually it's. Well let me let me print it out let me print you out a fresh one here it's all here. Well I, no, not really but look at that, it's pretty amazing isn't it? It's 600 pages. Oh, because you don't have Quark and I'll just I'll bring it down. Tell Karen hi. Tell her about our conversation. I'll see you later. Actually yeah I'm gonna. Men's room. Yeah, there are some cute guys in there. See you later. See you later, all right? Yes I am. I think she's adorable! What, um . . . How's the baby? How's Max? You like him, huh? Yeah, is he cute? Oh I know, Scott told you. You like that? Yeah, but I mean, you know, you think Scott should be teaching him the rules of the stock market or do you think he should be teaching him about great literature? About literature but neither do I. Yeah, so it you know it's cute that he can recite the stock market but I tell ya I'd never I'd never teach that stuff to my kid. What did they say? Uh, yeah. Whatever. Yeah. Yeah. Yeah. So. Are the kids gonna be there? Is Margie bringing the baby? Oh it's for Margie too. All right. All right. I thought you didn't like kids. You're happy to be a great grandfather? Unfortunately you're gonna be living . . . Hey gramps—can you hold a sec? I'll see you then. Bye. Love ya. Hello? Yes. Hey, hey how ya doin'? Good, what's up? Oh right, right. OK, um, I will be here after three. Um, so if you want to just stop by definitely and pick it all up. OK. Bye. Uncle Geoff. Hey down and dirty master! Great. Great. What's up? Too much time, huh? Is it taking you a lot of time? OK, so we'll think about the fall then. Are you having trouble with it, buddy? OK. I don't I really want you to enjoy it. I'm really I'm into totally not into that. Geoff, I want you to feel comfortable with it. It's not about a major . . . Nobody called me. That's what I was calling you about. No. Yeah, so what? I mean he's A.G. will pay. Things are going up, pal. Is that much more than it was in the old days? Yeah yeah yeah. I've heard I've heard that it's extremely expensive but but hey, listen, he's gonna foot the bill on that. I mean six thousand bucks is nothing to this guy. OK, so listen, I really don't want to put a pressure cooker on you. Right. OK. Well, I mean, you're into you're into, um, reading through it and stuff and you're enjoying it. Yeah, no that's perfect. I mean I want you to enjoy this thing. I I certainly don't want this to be a drag for you like like you dread opening this fucking thing. I mean it was a weird review, um, yeah yeah, rough and weird, you know, yeah yeah yeah. yeah yeah no I think, uh, I think she's really happy and, uh, I mean I mean everybody would like a completely glowing review, but you're happy to have a review. That's rare in this world, uh you know really, it's very rare in this artworld uh, to have, uh, what Raphael Rubinstein did for to Sean. That's rare, you know, it's usually kissy-kissy stuff. Speaking about kissy-kissy, I'm going to see Perloff in about 45 minutes for lunch and that should be fun. I was with Bruce last night. We went to an absinthe party. Um, my friend has a birth a birthday every year and every year he brews absinthe. And it gets better every year. Last this this time it was actually fairly drinkable. It's usually horrible stuff. Yeah. Yeah. Yeah. Yeah he's using he's got a nineteenth century recipe that he that he uses. Yeah. Yeah. Yeah. You know and you drip some sugar into it, you know, the very typical, uh, stuff. Um, I don't know I didn't drink enough of it to really know. Um, but . . . yeah, yeah, well, um, it was it was you know, actually really interesting interesting thing for us to do and hang out and . . . My friend Boog, I've know him since eighth grade. Uh . . . Bruce and uh, he is always up for a good party Bruce—he's a he's a partymeister. Oh yeah yeah yeah yeah the kid was cute, everything's good, man, everything is everything is like really groovy. Live it up. Yeah, I think she'll be interested. What I'm gonna do is I'm gonna giver her the article the Art a fresh copy of that Art In America and I'll say here read this this is all about the book we're doing and if you're interested in blurbing it, you know. Yeah, I'll send one out to her. Yeah OK. Well anyways I I'd never heard from those guys uh, he called you he never called me about the pricing. No it's fine, I'm glad, I mean it's just six thousand bucks big deal. Right. Right. Right. To you we were thinking maybe maybe some time in the summer. OK, maybe we'll just have the party then

for for in September. Yeah, oh listen, I'm I'm oh listen whenever it comes . . .
I want to tell you I'm really grateful. I I think it's going to be a fun project
and I I hope you have a lot of fun looking at it 'cause it's gonna take you a
lot of time to look at it. Yeah, it's easy. It's light reading. It's real light, you
know, you just it's not too taxing on the brain. It's it's less interesting but
it's sort of intriguing also. There are a lot of very weird words, you know,
one thing just to keep in mind when looking through the damn thing, like
you picked up one thing that had it was a fraction of a sentence and it had
a a closed paragraph, a close parentheses. That belongs what I'm doing is
I'm just taking sentences and I just keep chopping them up. And so if it's
got a closed parentheses, it's it's it's intended. Or if sometimes there'll be
one one quotation mark because I just chopped up the sentence which is
interesting because you start to wonder hey where's the other one. It does,
and they keep reappearing, yeah. All right, well, hey listen, as long as you're
having fun with it, you know. Yeah right and OK and listen the point is,
you know, just, you know, it's a big, it's a great amount of work so just dig
in and have fun.

---

from The Weather

The Weather (Los Angeles: Make Now, 2005) is a daily transcription of a one-minute
weather forecast from a local New York City all-news station over the course of a
year. Using the classical theme of the four seasons as its motif, the book is a series
of narratives and micronarratives that attempts to reduce a complex environment
into a one-minute sound bite that either aids or abets the commute. The Weather
is one part of Goldsmith's American Trilogy, the other parts consisting of 2007's Traf-
fic (transcriptions of one-minute traffic reports every ten minutes for twenty-four
hours) and 2008's Sports (a word-for-word radio broadcast transcription of a base-
ball game, including advertisements).

Oh, we are looking at, uh, weather, uh, across, uh, Iraq obviously here for
the next several days, uh, we have, uh, actually some good, good weather
is expected. They did have a sandstorm here earlier, uh, over the last twelve
to twenty-four hours those winds have subsided and will actually continue
to subside. Uh, there will be enough of a wind across the southern portion
of the country that still may cause some blowing sand tomorrow. Other-

wise we're looking at clear to partly cloudy skies tonight and tomorrow, uh, the weekend, uh, it is good weather, and then we could have a storm, uh, generating some strong winds, uh, for Sunday night and Monday, uh, even the possibility of a little rain in Baghdad. Uh, currently we have, uh, uh, increasing cloudiness, uh, forecast locally tonight, uh, it's gonna be brisk and chilly, temperatures getting down into the middle-thirties, and then some, uh, intermittent rain is expected tomorrow and tomorrow night. It'll become steadier and heavier late in the day and, uh, actually a pretty good soaking tomorrow night. Uh, temperatures getting into the mid-forties tomorrow, and then staying in the forties tomorrow night. Friday it's a breezy and warmer day but, uh, still a few more showers maybe even a thunderstorm, the high of sixty degrees. Currently we have sunshine and forty-four with an east wind of ten. Repeating the current temperature forty-four, going up to forty-six in midtown.

We still have clouds, we still have some fog outside of the city this morning but, uh, during the afternoon the sky can brighten, the sun can peek on through, temperatures get on up into the sixties. A couple of showers and maybe a thunderstorm this evening, and then the weekend to follow looks pretty good, at least partly sunny. It'll be breezy tomorrow, the high about sixty and in the, uh, fifties for a high on Sunday. As for Middle East weather, it continues to be favorable for military operations, and that'll remain the case through Sunday, but Monday and Tuesday, there may be another episode of strong winds, poor visibilities, and, uh, even some sandstorms. Right now fifty-seven and cloudy in Central Park, temperature today going up to sixty-two.

Well, sunshine will be mixing with clouds as we go through the day today. It is going to be on the mild side again this afternoon, the high up to sixty-four degrees in midtown today. Tonight, we're partly cloudy, dropping back to a low of forty-two. We're gonna stay dry tomorrow and Monday as well. Partly to mostly sunny skies, highs in the mid-to-upper fifties, and then back to sixty-four for a high on Tuesday, with increasing clouds. No chance of rain in sight until we get to the day Wednesday. Dry weather in Baghdad for the rest of the weekend as well, partly cloudy skies Saturday night, and also some sunshine across Baghdad on Sunday. Right now it's fifty-four degrees and sunny in Central Park, we're going up to sixty-four in midtown today.

With sunshine, the temperature's headed on up to sixty-one for the high this afternoon, partly to mostly cloudy tonight the . . . or clear to partly cloudy tonight, I should say, the low forty-six in midtown, forty in many suburbs. Tomorrow another mild day, going towards sixty-four with sunshine, then a cold front will arrive Wednesday with a couple of showers, high sixty. Rain could follow Wednesday night and Thursday morning if that front stalls and a low pressure area forms along it. Afterwards, Thursday afternoon, high fifty-four with some sunshine. In Iraq, the winds are likely to be picking up in the next twenty-four hours, raising more sand and dust into the atmosphere, and that's going to be a problem through Wednesday. Things should settle down after that, after the current storm from the Mediterranean moves past. Currently, the winds are light and variable, the relative humidity forty-six percent, fifty-five in midtown heading for sixty-one.

A nice evening, clear to partly cloudy skies overnight. We'll be in the mid-forties come daybreak, uh, tomorrow another mild day but, uh, clouds and, uh, limited sun, a couple of showers around associated with a cold front which will be moving through, especially in the afternoon and evening. Clears out later tomorrow night, and Thursday and Friday lots of sunshine and only, uh, a bit cooler, fifty-four Thursday, fifty-eight Friday. The battlefield forecast, uh, the weather is nasty over there right now. Strong winds accompanying a powerful cold front, uh, really kicking up the sand and making for poor visibility. Uh, that wind speed will gradually come down over the next twenty-four hours, but it'll still be causing some problems. Rain, in mountains, snow in northern Iraq on Wednesday, a couple of showers still down in Baghdad, uh, then better weather Thursday, right on through the weekend. Back home we have fifty-seven in Caldwell, fifty-three and sunshine in Central Park, the southeast wind at eleven. Repeating the current temperature fifty-three going down to forty-seven in midtown.

Well, not much on the radar, literally, just one shower up over northern Bergen County, and also over northeastern Morris County. And as they move off to the northeast, the balance of this afternoon is on the dry side, so you really don't need the umbrella for the most part here, sixty-eight degrees for the afternoon high. What we'll see, in terms of showers, will be for the evening rush hour, through the remainder of this evening, but already by daybreak the clouds are parting company in the wake of our most recent cool front. We're in at forty degrees, and, yeah, we're gonna cool it, now, that's what a front does. Despite the sun back there'll be a breeze tomorrow, high fifty-six. Sunshine, patchy clouds Friday with a high of fifty-eight degrees. As for our battlefield forecast, one or two showers left over the northern two-thirds of, uh, Iraq during the course of this evening, but better weather ahead later tonight and over the next couple of days, as the wind dies down. Around here, not much wind, it's seventy in Morristown, sixty-six Belmar, sixty-four and partly sunny in Central Park going to sixty-eight in midtown.

We'll look for sunshine to be with us, uh, all day today, and temperatures will respond and get up to about the sixty degree mark, and then it'll be partly cloudy tonight, low forty-four. Increasing clouds tomorrow, a little cooler, thanks to a breeze coming in off the water, high tomorrow fifty-six. Rain at times Saturday, Saturday night, ending Sunday morning, but brisk and, uh, pretty cool the rest of the day Sunday, with the temperature not getting much at all above fifty. Weather conditions in Iraq, uh, and Kuwait have improved, ur, improved considerably over the last twenty-four hours. Skies are clear, visibilities are much better, winds are much, much lighter, and it does not look like weather is going to be, uh, any kind of a major player for at least the next few days. Around these parts, it's forty-five and sunny in Central Park, temperature today going up to sixty.

Sunshine still with us and temperature still climbing, and it should get to sixty, and even into the sixties today. It'll be coolest on the south shore of Long Island and the Connecticut coast with a southerly breeze coming in off the water. Then it clouds up tonight, could start to drizzle. We get drizzle and rain at times tomorrow, especially tomorrow night on into Sunday morning, could be some heavy rain and maybe a thunderstorm. The rain, um, er, probably at least the steady rain, ends Sunday morning, but there still may be some rain showers around Sunday afternoon, and it will be noticeably colder with temperatures no higher than the forties. Right now, though, uh, it is fifty-six degrees and sunny in Central Park, and the temperature today going up to, uh, about sixty.

Brisk and cold today, clouds and sunshine. We're going to have a high temperature near forty-two degrees and, for the Mets home opener, the real feel temperature upper twenties and low thirties, so definitely a bundle-up time, but a dry afternoon. Partly to mostly cloudy tonight, low thirty in midtown, twenty-four in outlying areas. Tomorrow turns out cloudy, and as a warm front approaches, we'll have some rain in the afternoon, could start as a little wet snow, but the temperature by end of the day, forty-four northern suburbs, fifty in central Jersey, well up in the forties in the city. Wednesday variable cloudiness, with a shower possible, high fifty, then into the fifties with a few showers on Thursday. Meanwhile on the battlefield, sunshine, seventies today, but nineties by the end of the week in many areas. Currently in midtown thirty-two degrees, relative humidity fifty-one percent, wind west northwest at twelve, thirty-two heading for forty-two.

Clouds thickening over the next couple of hours, then we expect some rain during the midday and early afternoon hours, could be some wet snow mixed in the beginning but it won't stick. High today forty-two, tonight's low forty. Tomorrow, some clouds and sun, perhaps a shower, high fifty-four. Then we'll be close to the boundary between cool air and warm air on Thursday and Friday. We're calling Thursday, clouds and sunshine, maybe a shower, high fifty-nine, then Friday partly sunny and warmer, high sixty-eight degrees, with a thunderstorm possibility in the afternoon. On the battlefield, temperatures in the eighties in the afternoon hours through mid-week, getting closer to one hundred as we close out the week. Currently in midtown thirty-three degrees, relative humidity forty-nine percent, wind north at five miles per hour, thirty-three heading for forty-two.

Uh, it looks like the next couple of days we're gonna be close to a boundary between warm air, with temperatures in the seventies from Philadelphia southward, however, in upstate New York it probably stays in the thirties and forties, hopefully we get into the fifties today and tomorrow with a few breaks of sunshine. Central New Jersey and on, uh, inland, it can get into the sixties. It can always sprinkle or shower but, uh, at least through tomorrow we're not looking for much in the way of rain. Friday, rather cloudy, cool, high in the fifties, uh, chance of showers, maybe a late day thunderstorm. And then pretty cool on Saturday, may not get above fifty with some rain likely. Sunday partly sunny, but chilly, with a high of forty-eight. Right now it is forty-five and mostly cloudy in Central Park, temperature today going up to fifty-four.

A mostly cloudy, cool day coming up today, the temperature will get to about fifty, or maybe or maybe the low fifties, and that's about it, drops back to about forty with some clouds and patchy fog and drizzle tonight. Then it'll start to rain tomorrow, probably late in the day, we'll have rain tomorrow night on into the day on Saturday, with a high Saturday into the fifties. No, uh, genuine prospects for sunshine until Sunday, but even then it'll be chilly, a high around fifty. Uh, battlefield weather is sunny and hot in, uh, Baghdad, the temperature into the low nineties at this moment, and it'll be middle-to-upper nineties tomorrow, and over the weekend with one hundred degrees plus, in the southern and eastern deserts. Some gusty winds over the weekend could cause isolated pockets of, uh, blowing sand and reduced visibilities, but nothing near as widespread as last week. Right now it's forty-four and mostly cloudy in Central Park, temperature today going up to about fifty.

It's going to be overcast, drizzly, with some fog today. We'll have drizzle, rain, and fog tonight and tomorrow, uh, temperature today not going to go up much, it may even drop a couple of degrees, and the lows tonight will be near thirty in the northern and western suburbs, and that means there can be some freezing rain, as well as just rain, high temperatures tomorrow forty-five to fifty, Sunday mostly sunny with a high around fifty. The, uh, battlefield forecast, the heat will peak Saturday, with highs in Baghdad near one hundred, then not as hot Sunday and Monday, but windy at times. Those gusty winds will pick up some sand and dust, and cause areas of reduced visibility. Right now it is forty-one and cloudy in Central Park and our temperature today going up only to forty-three.

Nada Gordon
Abnormal Discharge

In "Abnormal Discharge," Nada Gordon lyricizes the subject headings of the online Young Women's Health Forum message board (part of http://www.obgyn.net). One might compare her poem with the Google investigations of Larissa Lai's *welcome to asian women in business / a one stop site for entrepreneurs* (Calgary: MODL Press, 2004) and Marie Buck's exploration of gendered and networked subjectivity in the MySpace poems of *Life & Style* (Chicago: Beard of Bees, 2007), which fits found digital content to the verse forms of canonical poets.

pill question? . . . medication . . . pippy
sex hurts :(
cuts and labia irritation
necessary to take all placebo pills?
wierd white/yellowish vaginal discharge
High Viscosity in Sperm
possible pregnecy Elizabeth
possible pregnecy
vaginal discharge Jessica
Abnormal Pap Smear Jennifer
Abnormal Pap
Vaginal Itching and Peeling anon
Vaginal Itching and Peeling
chlamydia thru blood transfusion?
vagina size paranoid
vagina size
vagina size anonymous
bleeding after intercourse pippy
Breast Pimples (Professional, please)
White spots on breast Duala

White spots on breast anonymous
Duala White spots on breast anonymous
White spots on breast anonymous
White spots on breast
Could it be a cyst?
Vagina "bumps" Duala
Vagina "bumps" anonymous
Vagina "bumps" anonymous
ovarian pains Jessica
ovarian pains anonymous
Painful intercourse Curious
Painful intercourse net
Brownish Redish discharge.
Amoxicillin and Depo Provera anonymous
My Period has been done for 5 days !! now have thick brown creamy like
     discharge can anyone help me out? Cindy
can hand warts lead to gential warts? A.L.
Did I have a possible miscarriage? Julie
Did I have a possible miscarriage?
Worries about "down there"—scared terrified
Worries about "down there"—scared anonymous
vaginal itching and swelling
Pink Stuff Anonymous
VERY SCARED should i be worried about this? Jeni
VERY SCARED should i be worried about this? martia
VERY SCARED should i be worried about this? Jeni
VERY SCARED should i be worried about this? martia
VERY SCARED should i be worried about this? jeni
VERY SCARED should i be worried about this? Cassie
Blood Clot? Worried
Fibroids Janice
Fibroids
air in vagina db
air in vagina anonymous
air in vagina amy
No Period! Katlyn
No Period!
oral sex sara
oral sex

Nervous Wreck anonymous
Nervous Wreck
Average sagging?
Average sagging?
Average sagging?
breast discharge-again irene
breast discharge-again Marisa Geller MD
Types of Vaginas??? Nila
Types of Vaginas??? Gretchen
Types of Vaginas??? Marisa
Weird discharge
Weird discharge Alicia
White bump near anus Cindy
White bump near anus
Weird period!! help!!! Lilac
Weird period!! help!!!
What's going on here? Monica
way to orgasm ?
way to orgasm ? Jessica
Unusual question regarding problems with orgasm Chris
What is this???? Shaina
Considering Partial Hysterectomy Shaina
Considering Partial
genital appearances anonymous

Noah Eli Gordon
from Inbox

In the original publication of *Inbox*, Noah Eli Gordon explains:

> I thought it would be interesting to see what would happen if I were to take the body-text of every email that was addressed specifically to me (nothing forwarded or from any listserv) currently in my inbox (over 200) and let all of the voices collide into one continuous text. The work is arranged in reverse chronology, mirroring the set up of my email program. I removed everyone's name and any phrase with which they closed their email; additionally, I removed any specific address mentioned. . . . I didn't write any of it. (Kenmore, N.Y.: BlazeVox, 2006)

One might compare Gordon's less mediated use of e-mail with Lyn Hejinian's more heavily edited use of correspondence in *The Fatalist* (Richmond, Va.: Omnidawn, 2003), a work that extends her use of quotations from conversations in *A Border Comedy* (New York: Granary Books, 2001).

Go ahead and send me whatever—is Eric's stuff all over the page? Let me know if you have any kind of time frame in mind. I'm fairly busy but think I could generally get it done within a couple weeks or so. got your book! thank you so much for sending it—I'm glad you saved the postage (saves me guilt) and sent it slow-boat, as I didn't have much time until now anyway—so I got to enjoy reading your book in the warm outside, cherry bloss. petals swirling around me . . . haha its fun to live a cliche sometimes—anyway I enjoyed reading your beautiful book—have been thinking more and more about prose poetry, so it's good timing. I love grammar. (though I don't like to talk about it)—but I love grammar, and the music of grammar. And "A face made for radio" is one of Eugene (bf) 's favorite insults. and the physical book itself is lovely too—what pleasure. cld you send me a 3 or 4 sentence bio note, or longer if you have one ready to go.

Heya. I've done some work on the chap and it's looking pretty good. I'm waiting for the paper to show up (similar to Mark's "Elegy for Rachel Corrie" only bigger). I'm planning on 100 copies, linen paper for the text. I'm trying, tho, to raise a few bucks for a pretty expensive ornate paper for an inlay, which is about $7.50 for ten sheets. I'm thinking that we can either make a few special editions with the ornate paper (like 20-30) or skip it. I'd rather not skip, tho. How much could you contribute? I'm going to be pretty busy this week with printing for Mark's YART sale (hopefully I'll make a few dollars to help buy the afforementioned ornate paper), but give me a ring sometime and we can discuss details. Let me confer with David and Michael and I'll let you know. At this point, earlier is better so I'm inclined to say 10/11th. I am moving back to Los Angeles, leaving Ithaca. So July will be the last reading for me. I'm excited, as I think we will get to go out with a bang. Do you also have the novels and essays from Black Square? I did three or four chapbooks which I will send along, and whatever other stuff I think might tickle your fancy. Great to hear from you. I like your book very much, and then later I got Eric Baus' book and liked that a lot too, and thought—hhmmmm, some center of energy seems to be moving in western Massachusetts. Hey, I don't know if you're interested in Anthony Braxton, but he's performing new compositions at Wesleyan this week—tomorrow night with a large group, Wednesday with a small group. (Wednesday conflicts with Jerome Rothenberg. Not sure what to do, but currently I'm leaning toward Braxton.) The one catch with Braxton is that he's performing with students—I mean, they're Braxton's compositions, but the musicians are going to be mostly students. I think it will be very cool though. I might try to make it to Amherst on Monday for the Beckman/Wolff/Wagner/Corless-Smith reading. This is a foolish and maybe impossible idea because it's a school night, but I'm trying to figure out if it's possible before making a decision. In order for it to be possible, I would need a place to stay on Monday night (which I'm wondering if you could provide?), and a ride back to Middletown on the following day (which John Vincent might provide), and ideally a substitute teacher to lecture on Jane Austen's Emma on Tuesday afternoon (anyone?). It occurs to me that you might already be putting up one of the readers. Or you might be busy, or you might not feel like putting me up yet again. If you can't do it, that's fine, maybe better than fine—I should stay home, do my work, and not think of mad plans like this. Anyway, let me know. Albert Mobilio gave me your email. It seems that you have started a press and I would like to get the books you have done. I could buy them or we could trade Black Square books for the ones you did. Meanwhile, thanks for sending your book a while back. I think it's terrific. And thanks also for alerting GC Waldrep to the Joron chapbook on Surrealism. Well enough. Though I find your chapbooks lovely, and would be very happy to be part of the Braincase catalogue, some day. I have not read the Joron essay, though of course I've been reading his poems for some time now. I had a typically short & cryptic note from Yau three or four weeks ago asking me to remind him of my mailing address because he "wanted to send me some things." I have not received a packet from him yet, but perhaps the Joron will be in it. I would be delighted to exchange mss—only ARCHICEMBALO is not entirely done yet, and there are incomplete swaths, as well as swaths that reek. (Now there's a title for a new book of poems: SWATHS THAT REEK.) —I could send you a suite of 20–25 pp., perhaps? I would love to read your latest, if you want to send, whenever you want to send. —Remind me of YOUR mailing address so that I can send you some of the ARCHICEMBALO poems. They are, for the most part, prose poems, and aesthetically they live about two houses down from Eric Baus's. Advise well. I am not teaching this semester, which has been good. Although my freelance job has taken up most of the time I had expected to spend on writing. More teaching in the fall. Hey, great to hear from you. I'm enthusiastic about doing the chap. I'm thinking something along the lines of Brenda Iijima's recent chap on color. Are you familiar? It's 8.5 X 11 folded, good paper, transparent inlay. I'm playing with a few ideas for a cover image. I have a medieval O with a tonsured guy sitting inside the letter working on a manuscript, which I thought might look interesting. I'm hoping to set the text in Centaur or perhaps Palatino. I'd like to work with the O image because it's a letter, number and, generally speaking, a circle that suggests context (among other things). Anyway, I'll come up with a couple of designs and maybe we could get together sometime and take a look at them. When you have the chance, email me the poem as a .rtf file if you can. Apologies for the brevity of this note. I'm at work and now have to run. Hope all is well. Hey, I wanted to thank you for coming out to read and for the books. The reading was excellent (really, I mean it—Geoffrey read well, too) and I'm looking forward to making my way through Jaywalking The Is and The Frequencies. I have, though, read "What Ever Belongs In The Circle." I think the poem's powerful and wanted to know if you have any interest in publishing it with Anchorite as a chapbook. If so, lemme know when you can. Be well. You're really unlax in responding, actually, compared to lots of folks! That's totally cool about keeping it at 100, I was just wondering (again). Any of those 3 solutions sound good to me. I really like the reader idea, but of course that'd be down the road a piece. If you'd rather just leave as is, that's fine w/ me, and if PDFs or 2nd editions on card stock are the way you want to go, that's cool too. I hope I'm not sounding pushy or unsatisfied . . . it's that everything turned out so well, really, and that I'm so thrilled, and would love to be able to have hundreds and hundreds of beautiful books . . . but you're right, there is a strong argument to made for scarcity, and I like that. Also, I'd be happy to do any support work with you down the road, typesetting stuff, PDFing, whatever, so call on me if you need a hand when you make those decisions. Also . . . gave a chap to Africa Wayne and she's thinking of having me read next month in her series w/ Rosmarie Waldrop, which would be outstanding. I'll keep ye posted. Gave a few folks books the other night at the Poetry Project auction: Ed Berrigan, Mike Scharf, Brian Kim Stefans, Marcella Durand & Thurston Moore. Thurston was surprised to discover that "people are doing things" in Northampton and was interested in finding out more about Braincase. I talked you guys up, of course. And SY is playing April 30 at Smith College. I was toying with the idea of bopping up for the show. Would you be innerested? I imagine tix'd go fairly fast tho Thurston said the venue's pretty big. And maybe get Thurston other B-case books, not to mention yer own stuff—think he'd really dig Da Frequenciez & J-walkin Da Iz. You oughta give him some stuff too for Ecstatic Peace yo. And excellent to hear from you on this glorious spring day. Thanks for the congrats: the P&W article was really a very strange thing; I almost said no when they asked—there are a few mistakes in the article, but none that affect the book really.

Michael Gottlieb
from The Dust

Without hypotaxis, narrative, or discursiveness, "The Dust" (*Lost and Found* [New York: Roof, 2003]) depends on a reader's knowledge of its context: the collapse of the World Trade Center towers on September 11, 2001. Not a strict transcription of objects pulverized or recovered from the site (some of the items included are the products of Michael Gottlieb's imaginative speculation rather than research), the poem nonetheless evinces the power of the detached and flatly unexpressive catalog to access emotions—through strategies of obliquity and indirection—without courting blatant sentiment. The catalog at play here is not just the organizational form of the list, of course, but also the style of the wholesale product brochure; the language of the poem is closer to commercial accounting than to the traditional lyric elegy. The defamiliarizing specificity and descriptive detail of Gottlieb's litany slows the reader and helps forestall—if only momentarily—the stock, reflexive, or scripted responses to the strongly mediated spectacle of the attacks. Where September 11 has become a symbolic event of shared cultural reference, "The Dust" reduces the monumental status of both the towers and their demise to a scale of concrete and individual particulars.

Accordingly, one might read the work next to Bob Perelman's understated and devastating elegy for Lee Hickman, "Chronic Meanings," which provides an analogue for interruption and loss rather than referring directly to its subject. A typical stanza from Perelman's poem reads:

> The coffee sounds intriguing but.
> She puts her cards on.
> What had been comfortable subjectivity.
> The lesson we can each.

Composed of five-word lines, Perelman's poem takes the parataxis of the new sentence and Stein's five words in a line as models for enacting what it, quite literally, cannot bring itself to say. With less emotional charge, "The Dust" also evokes the forensic descriptions of the French new novel and *An Anecdoted Typography of*

Chance, as well as the more humorous archives of Georges Perec's "Notes Concerning the Objects That Are on My Worktable" and the surprisingly resonant detailing of an office desk in Thomas Pynchon's *Gravity's Rainbow:*

> millions of tiny red and brown curls of rubber eraser, pencil shavings, dried tea or coffee stains, traces of sugar and Household Milk, much cigarette ash, very fine black debris picked and flung from typewriter ribbons, decomposing library paste, broken aspirins ground to powder. (18)

Pynchon's dust surfaces, like Gottlieb's, to cover a copy of the *News of the World.*

UHF Tower Mast A
VHF Main Antenna Bracing, Southeast
Left Rear Wheel Assembly, Retractor
Radome Array
First Class Galley Convection Oven Number One
First Class Galley Convection Oven Number Two

Knoll workstation fabric panel, 3′6″ by 2′, with crepe
Knoll workstation fabric panel, 3′6″ by 2′6″, with crepe
Knoll workstation fabric panel, 3′6″ by 3′6″, with crepe
BPI workstation 1/2 plexiglass panel, 5′6″ by 2′6″
Hon workstation 1/2 plexiglass panel, 5′6″ by 3′
Interior Concepts workstation T-base for non-raceway panels
Anderson Hickey workstation connector post, 6′
Global workstation full plexiglass panel, 5′ by 2′6″

Seagrave Fire Apparatus Rear Mount Aerial Truck
Seagrave Fire Apparatus Tractor Drawn Aerial Truck
Seagrave Fire Apparatus High Pressure Pumper
Ford Crown Victoria Intercepter
Kroll-O'Gara Cadillac Fleetwood

Boucle short-sleeve shirt
Pigment-dyed oxford shirt
Stretch poplin shirt
Egyptian 60s long sleeve, barrel cuff, wing collar shirt

Merino V-neck sweater
Stretch plain-weave pleated pant
Stretch twill pant
Denim pant
Five button jean
Argyle broadcloth boxer
Looney Tunes characters broadcloth boxer
Distressed corduroy baseball cap
Flat black belt
Woven brown belt

Form F-3MEF New registration statement filed under Rule 462(b) to add
    securities to a prior related registration statement filed on Form F-3
Form U-9C-3 Quarterly report concerning energy and gas-related
    companies pursuant to Rule 58 of the Act
Form S-6 Registration statement for unit investment trusts
Form N-8B-4 Registration statement for face-amount certificate

Frito-Lay Ruffles Original, 12 1/2 oz
Ben And Jerrys, Cherry Garcia, one pint
Snapple Peach Diet Iced Tea, 12 oz
Lifesavers Butter Rum, economy pack
Altoids, cinnamon, 1.76 oz
Twizzlers Nibs Licorice Bits, 2.25 oz.
Camel Light 100s, hard box

Lancome Revitalizing Cream
Revlon Fantastic Blusher
Chanel Age Delay Rejuvenation serum
Clinique Pretty Long Lashes mascara
Estee Lauder Multi-Dimension powder
Ortho Novum, Dispensa-A-Pak
Tampax lite days
Flonase 50 mcg
Lescol, 25 mg

Column tree connector
End plate and top
Rail 3/8″ by 6′ by 12′

Fillet weld 3/8″ by 6′
Flange connection
Stiffener
Spandrel

Carver Rectangular Genuine Wood Wastebasket
Post-it "Important" Note Pad, Assorted Neon Colors, 50 Sheet Pad
Sanford Liquid Accent Tank-Style Highlighter, Orange
Avery E-Z D Ring Heavy-Duty View Binder with Lever-Lock, Black
Hewlett-Packard Color LaserJet 4550 Laser Printer
Swingline Full-Strip Desktop Stapler, Black
Acme Forged Steel Scissors with Black Enamel Handles
Bic SoftFeel Ballpoint Stic Pen, Black

Charmant green frame, number 4435
Eyespace, wire frame, Model A222
Luxottica, 6678m
Titmus Optical, Safety Indoor/Outdoor
Transitions, Extreme Twist Frame
National Gypsum Board Number Four
National Gypsum Board Number Six

Pittsburgh Plate Glass

Shield, Port Authority of New York and New Jersey Police, Chief Of
    Department
Shield, Court Officer, Supreme Court Of New York

Global Deluxe Task Chair with Height Adjustable Arms, Blue
Lifetime Lightweight Folding Table, 29″ by 30-1/2″ by 72″, Stone gray
Sauder Camden County Executive Desk, Planked Cherry Finish
O'Sullivan 5-Shelf Heavy-Duty Bookcase, Snow
Bush Cubix Collection 36″ Desk, Medium Cherry/Slate Gray
Office Designs Commercial 26-1/2″ Deep Vertical File Cabinet, Putty
Hon 600 Series 30″ Wide 2-Drawer Lateral File, Black

Cisco 3600 T1/Ft1 CSU/DSU Module
Cisco 2621 Ethernet Router 2 10/100 Ports 2 Slots 3com Superstack 3
    Modular Switch 3300 24-Port 10/100

D-Link Systems DSS—24 Plus Rackmount 24 Port Switch
Bay Networks Business Policy Switch 2000 Auto 24
3com Deh5695 Switch 4005 Fan Assembly

The Wall Street Journal
The Financial Times
The Economist
The Straits Times
The Far East Economic Review
The Hollywood Reporter
SteelWeek

Milliken Carpet, 32 oz nylon level stitch

Collins and Aikman, 28oz 60/40 nylon/olefin blend

Ductwork—Single Wall Round
Ductwork—Double Wall Round
Ductwork—Single Wall Oval

Stretch multitwist slash blouse
Cotton three-quarter sleeve blouse
Silk cashmere fine-rib V-neck blouse
Stretch merino striped blouse
Silk herringbone dress
Silk charmeuse printed dress
Floral print silk dress
Cotton/Lycra demi underwire bra
Cotton/Lycra full figure underwire bra
Lace-trim mesh bikini
Vine floral-printed panty
Single ankle-strap shoe
Brown front-band sandal
Black ankle-wrap flat

Assignment of Mortgage—Individual Mortgagee/Holder
Petition for Temporary Restraining Order and Permanent Injunction
Statutory form of Quitclaim deed for corporation to execute. State of
    New York

Nonqualified Stock Option Agreement of N(2)H(2), Inc. granted to
Eric H. Posner dated September 30, 1999

Sprint PCS Kyocera 2035
Sanyo SCP-4700
LG Touchpoint TP1100 PCS phone
Sprint Samsung SPH-N200
Motorola V2397EPW

Blancpain Flyback Chronograph
Swatch Mickey Mouse Fiftieth Anniversary Commemerative
Seiko Automatic 24, Model L334
Engagement ring, Tiffany setting, platinum, three-point four carat
diamond
Mikimoto cultured pearls, double strand, white gold clasp

Helmet, New York Fire Department, Firefighter, Ladder 4
Helmet, New York Fire Department, Chief, Second Battalion
Bunker Coat, New York Fire Department, First Deputy Commissioner

Bank One Visa Gold
Chase MasterCard
New Jersey Department Of Motor Vehicles, Operators License
Commonwealth of Massachusetts, Drivers License
Passport, United Kingdom
Employee Identification, Risk Waters Inc.
Employee Identification, Fred Alger Management
Employee Identification, Summit Security Services
USAirways Dividend Miles, membership card
National Association Of Broadcast Employees & Technicians,
Communications Workers of America, Local 16, membership card
City University Of New York, Baruch College, Student Identification
Little League Baseball, New York District 20, Hastings On Hudson,
Umpire Registry Identification Card

Joseph P. Kellett
Joseph J. Keller
Peter Kellerman
Frederick H. Kelley

Joseph A. Kelly
Maurice Patrick Kelly
Timothy C. Kelly
Thomas Kelly
Thomas Michael Kelly
Thomas W. Kelly
Richard John Kelly, Jr.

Dan Graham
Exclusion Principle

While avoiding stereotypical notions of subjectivity, Dan Graham effectively maps out the breadth of our time-space continuum—from the retina to the edge of the known universe—in eleven short lines. By invoking Whitman's sweep, "miles to . . ." is an ontological linguistic construction of the infinite.

```
1,000,000,000,000,000,000,000.00000000 miles to the edge of known universe
    100,000,000,000,000,000,000.00000000 miles to edge of galaxy (Milky Way)
             3,573,000,000.00000000 miles to edge of solar system (Pluto)
                      205.00000000 miles to Washington, D.C.
                        2.85000000 miles to Times Square, New York City
                         .38600000 miles to Union Square subway stop
                         .11820000 miles to corner of 14th Street and First Avenue
                         .00367000 miles to front door of Apartment 1D, 153 First Avenue
                         .00021600 miles to typewriter paper page
                         .00000700 miles to lens of glasses
                         .00000098 miles to cornea from retinal wall
```

Poem-Schema

As the piece explains itself, *Poem-Schema* is intended for publication in various magazines. Graham submits a template—not unlike the portion of XML source used to order and display the information pulled from various databases—which the editor of the magazine was to calculate and complete, providing information about the physical characteristics of the publication. Rigorously and recursively self-referential, the completed piece parses itself, collapsing form and content. The result focuses attention onto the most minute particulars of the physical aspects of print. The implications, however, extend well beyond the carefully measured trim of the page that the work describes. The medium, Graham concurs with Marshall McLuhan, is the message; material and cultural forms predate, anticipate, and deform whatever individual expressive content might seek expression through their channels. "There is no composition. No artistic or authorial 'insight' is expressed" (*For Publication* [Los Angeles: Otis Art Institute, 1975], n.p.). *Poem-Schema,* according to Graham, "defines itself as place . . . as it defines the limits and contingencies of placement (enclosing context, enclosed context)." Under such conditions, as Graham explained:

> There is no author. There is no hierarchy of versions. . . . There is no composition. The contingent situation of publication determines the final form. There is no attempt to re-create or represent an authorial in-sight; there is no interior. The conventional linear, part-by-part reading logic is eliminated. (*Art-Language* 1, no. 1 [1969]: 16)

In the 1960s, the completed text was published in a half dozen art periodicals and experimental poetry journals, moving—like Vito Acconci's contemporaneous work—between the overlapping worlds of the avant-gardes. When published in *Aspen* 5/6 (Fall–Winter, 1967), *Poem-Schema* was described as "conceptual poetry"—the first published use of the phrase. Graham's attempts to place the work in glossier, more popular publications such as *Harper's Bazaar* and *Esquire* were less successful (see Alex Alberro, "Reductivism in Reverse," *Tracing Cultures: Art, History, Criticism, Critical Fictions,* ed. Miwon Kwon [New York: Whitney Museum of American Art, 1994], 26n18).

In *Poem-Schema,* Graham presents a machine or recipe for a poem, providing the "author" with the raw ingredients or the unassembled parts. At the same time, he conflates the author with the editor, thus collapsing notions of authorship and authority. The radical implications of Graham's work follow from that combination of an insistence on the cultural materiality of language and a rejection of the romantic author as a unified locus of interior authority. Barrett Watten, for instance—unable either to recognize the materiality of all language or to imagine a poetry not predicated on interiority—refers to Graham's piece as "an obnoxious mistake" (*Total Syntax* [Carbondale: Southern Illinois University Press, 1985], 216). For Watten, "there can be no 'conceptual poetry'" (217).

SCHEMA for a set of pages whose component variants are to be published in various places. In each published instance, it is set in its final form (so it defines itself) by the editor of the particular publication where it is to appear, the exact data used to correspond in each specific instance to the specific fact(s) of the final published appearance. The work defines itself in place only as information with simply the external support of the facts of its external appearance or presence in print in place of the object.

(March, 1966)

(number of)	adjectives
(number of)	adverbs
(percentage of)	area not occupied by type
(percentage of)	area occupied by type
(number of)	columns
(number of)	conjunctions
(depth of)	depression of type into page surface
(number of)	gerunds
(number of)	infinitives
(number of)	letters of the alphabet
(number of)	lines
(number of)	mathematical symbols
(number of)	nouns
(number of)	numbers
(number of)	participles
(perimeter of)	page
(weight of)	paper sheet
(type of)	paper stock
(number of)	prepositions
(number of)	pronouns
(number of point)	size type
(name of)	typeface
(number of)	words
(number of)	words capitalized
(number of)	words italicized

Dan Graham   291

Michelle Grangaud
from Biographies/Poetry

Michelle Grangaud, a member of Oulipo, is an accomplished anagrammist. Here she explores the formal and grammatical conventions of the literary biography, with the contradictory combination of individuation and commonality that it requires. Her work here is translated by Guy Bennet.

Born in 1883 in Fukuoka prefecture, Born in Gunma prefecture, Born in Toyama prefecture. Born in Tokyo. Born in Ehime prefecture Born in Otsu in Osaka in Hokkaido He continued all his life, Born in, then on the Chinese mainland At that time, Born in Fukui prefecture. Born. He continued residing he expressed He gave he passed he revealed His poems were written He began began he resided there he spent for several years he wrote incessantly, He began he spent he began He began to write poetry.

in his vagabond existence, nearly destitute, in poverty throughout a life of wandering. His was a difficult life of wandering Throughout a difficult life of poverty, frail health, the heartbreak of poverty throughout a life of wandering, Following his father's professional setbacks, Following his father's appointments Following an accident. Born in Kumamoto prefecture Following his father's appointments Born in China. Following his father, the business of his bankrupt father, Of poor health, he was raised by his grandparent. He was adopted by an entrepreneur lost his mother Then his two stepmothers Finally raised by the third stepmother From an early age, from his youth in childhood, through the death of his father, and was orphaned early on, Born in Fukui lost his mother, a delicate sensibility. And had one leg amputated. His family was scattered by bankruptcy, He was exiled At the age of twenty, already marked, He lost his father early on, the family was scattered two years and came back wounded. He was also sent to fight in China, fifteen years railway technician, He entered he was employed Crushed by debts Sent to Sumarra at twenty two, Where he stayed he went from Tokyo to Sakai, where he stayed he stayed in Mandochuria between two civilizations between his native province and Tokyo, at the war's end, during and after the war, After the war, He was drafted into the Navy. Suffering from tuberculosis Prisoner for eight years in Siberia, After the Second World War, Suffering from tuberculosis, in a sanitarium Following his return to Japan, Between twenty and thirty years. From tuberculosis Back in Japan, then successively from one hospital to another. The suicide of a younger friend Fighting cancer the defeat of Japan

in the secondary teaching corps. With a scientific mission. First influenced by anarchism and Marxism, As early as high school in a newspaper published in his native prefecture. Still a student, he traveled to the South Pole The hardships he endured, In the peasant political movement, he became involved, From which he was later excluded, Later, having become then in the Communist Party Having become later CEO of the chain of Seibu department stores, known under the family name of Seiji Tsutsumi, He followed in his father's footsteps. While he followed journalist at the daily paper, through terrible hardship and illness through terrible But soon after, After burning his works, After studying to become a pharmacist After being cured After the break-up of the group of poets

His works, The works he wrote he wrote poems Marked by an experience Marked he wrote marked he wrote an experience of social life Marked next by a clear, simple, spoken language, the obscurity of life an assiduous reader A lyricism passionate reader of Nerval, translator of Mayakovsky, influenced by Jules Supervielle, by reading Rimbaud and the love of classical music known for his work on Rimbaud, and Verlaine, Dada and Surrealism, from Baudelaire and Albert Samain, member of the study group known for he began reading Heidegger, and then specialized in French literature. In Éluard and Aragon Specialist in Surrealism, in English literature, he translated some of André Gide's work, he discovered Rodin's work, Cézanne, Verlaine, Baudelaire, the new European poetry he discovered and translated he converted to Christianity, adopted a Surrealist esthetic in the Surrealist movement, he founded the club for Surrealist, Modernist and Surrealist Studies, she discovered, thanks to poet Katsue Kitazono, and other French writers, works by André Breton, he translated Oscar Wilde and Edgar Allan Poe, discovered Baudelaire and Verhaeren, in Europe and South-East Asia, he discovered with James Joyce and T. S. Eliot modern literature, she continued her work independently

In his prose poems also the poetry of his poems verge on in his poems A horse that no one can see, he wrote short poems wrote Seeing a Zen Bronze, in the story A 12th Century Bronze, wrote in the history of Japanese poetry are written in the history In a style are written totally Even more the shadow of a body, in the style of his works A body of words, in a style Temporary Residence, through the rhythm In this world, themes The canopy of words, a thought said he The world rises, he wrote every bit a poet In the form of words, dramas In the words, poetry With the words He opens up, theater of poetry also He continues to be word, he reveals himself Living in words, he was Cannot die, he found Words on earth, he demonstrates As much weight, demonstrates that The world, he began endlessly to Seeing words, he found Incarnate in itself, a creation his poems were written Don't know it, he was the poet he wrote language Very little their bodies, he wrote a style in a style his last collection he wrote suffering from tuberculosis in the use of language the use of language he writes Teaches, pure language.

Brion Gysin
First Cut-Ups

"Writing," Brion Gysin declared, "is fifty years behind painting." Applying modernist collage techniques from the visual arts to writing, Gysin and William S. Burroughs tried to catch writing up when they developed the cut-up in the late 1950s, applying it to both written texts and audiotapes. As it happened, the most mundane preparatory artistic technique was the origin: Gysin discovered the process while cutting a mount for a drawing, having sliced through the layers of periodicals that were protecting the table from his Stanley blade. Moreover, Gysin realized that printed language had a materiality like paint or canvas or sculpture. In the cut-up, he notes, "There's an actual treatment of the material as if it were a piece of cloth," so that "the sentence, even the word, becomes a real piece of plastic material that you can cut into" (*Back in No Time: The Brion Gysin Reader,* ed. Jason Weiss [Middletown, Conn.: Wesleyan University Press, 2001], 69). Related to his contemporaneous experiments with permutation (including a poem of more than six hundred lines composed only of versions of the phrase "I am that I am"), and updating Tristan Tzara's method for composing a Dadaist poem, the cut-up was understood as a way to both distance and access the author. In 1964, Gysin explained the cut-ups in *The Evergreen Review,* with a scolding, "Who told poets they were supposed to think? . . . Poets have no words 'of their very own.' Writers don't own their words. Since when do words belong to anybody. 'Your very own words,' indeed! And who are you?" One modern version of a sustained cut-up technique can be found in Ara Shirinyan's *Handsome Fish Offices* (Los Angeles: Insert Press, 2008), which guts and sutures material from a text about tropical fish with an Office Depot catalog.

The following, originally published in *Minutes to Go* (Paris: Two Cities, 1960), sampled articles and advertisements from the *Daily Mail, Herald Tribune, Life Magazine,* and the *London Observer.*

It is impossible to estimate the damage. Anything put out up to now is like pulling a figure out of the air.

Six distinguished British women said to us later, indicating the crowd of chic young women who were fingering samples, "If our prices weren't as good or better, they wouldn't come. Eve is eternal."

(I'm going right back to the Sheraton Carlton and call the Milwaukee Braves.)

Miss Hannah Pugh the slim model—a member of the Diners' Club, the American Express Credit Cards, etc.—drew from a piggy bank a talent which is the very quintessence of the British Female sex.

"People aren't crazy," she said. "Now that Hazard has banished my timidity I feel that I, too, can live on streams in the area where people are urged to be watchful."

A huge wave rolled in from the wake of Hurricane Gracie and bowled a married couple off a jetty. The wife's body was found—the husband was missing, presumed drowned.

Tomorrow the moon will be 228,400 miles from the earth and the sun almost 93,000,000 miles away.

Michael Harvey
from White Papers

In one of the index cards from his extraordinary set of *White Papers* (1971), seventy-one interrelated cards that play with the variable relation of language to ideas, and of each card to the others, Michael Harvey spells out the punctuation in the definition of *punctuation* from *The Shorter Oxford English Dictionary* (to be punctilious, one should note that Harvey Americanizes the British *stop* with *period*). The intervention both proves and ironically contradicts the dictionary's definition. Without the conventional marks, the interpretation of the passage is indeed hindered. At the same time, Harvey's version emphasizes the very punctuation it removes, proving in the process that the same system or method could, in fact, be practiced (though perhaps less efficiently) with other signs. The protocols of telegraphic writing, for instance, spelled out punctuation as well. In both cases, the simple act of transliteration—translating one set of signifiers into forms of another—manifests and makes strange the almost invisible coexistence of non-alphabetic marks among words. In the ecology of the text, two distinct regimes of signs operate in parallel within the larger system of written language. There, punctuation seems to live within its alphabetic host in a seemingly natural facultative symbiosis—like the lactobacilli of language.

In a related work from the same year, Harvey had circled all of the definite articles in a *New York Times* editorial, recalling Marcel Duchamp's "The" (*Rogue* 3, no. 1 [October 1916]: 2), which replaced the definite articles in a short text with asterisks. Harvey's text is itself a kind of definite article: a journalistic genre (*article*) that is confident and assured in tone (*definite*). *Article,* however, is also the name for the individual entries in a reference work such as the dictionary (where *definite,* not coincidentally, is only a couple of articles away from *definition*), and its etymology (the diminutive of *artus,* "a joint") points back to the essential function of punctuation, which articulates.

Harvey's use of the dictionary recalls Vito Acconci's many poems based on reference books, and in particular "Announcing an Advertisement That Will Appear in the *New York Times,* section 6—*The New York Times Magazine*—Sunday, January 26, 1969, page 87," which cross-references the newspaper text with the dictionary, and the two poems titled "Points For Motion," one of which lists the nouns in the definition of *verb* and one of which lists the nouns in the definition of *moreover.*

In such works, the dictionary not only serves as a ready and inviting source for uncreative practices—a massive database of language itself, awaiting the right interface—but also provides a model of uncreative writing. Most dictionaries, and certainly the large modern dictionaries under discussion here, are collective enterprises of formulaic description rather than the expressive work of single individuals. Moreover, they frequently copy their definitions—unattributed—from other dictionaries, with any acknowledgment of sources buried in the fine print of their front matter. In the dictionary, as in college handbooks and disciplinary guidelines, the definition of *plagiarize,* beautifully enough, is almost always plagiarized.

the practice comma art comma method comma or system of inserting points or open single quote periods closed single quote to aide the sense comma in writing or printing semicolon division into sentences comma clauses comma etc period by means of points or periods period other punctuation marks comma e period g period exclamation marks comma question marks comma refer to the tone or structure of what precedes them period a sentence can contain any of these symbols comma its termination marked by a period period

H. L. Hix
Poem composed of statements made by
George W. Bush in January 2003

In *God Bless* (Wilkes-Barre, Pa.: Etruscan Press, 2007), the book from which the following poem is drawn, H. L. Hix writes:

> The poems designated by a month are constructed entirely of passages from speeches, executive orders, and other public statements of George W. Bush. All passages in a given poem were spoken by Bush during the month that appears as the poem's title, and all are quoted verbatim, as they appear on the official White House web site (www.whitehouse.gov). Ellipses signal omissions within an otherwise continuous excerpt, but no attempt is made to signal where one quoted passage joins another: the selection and juxtaposition of the passages is entirely my own. (*God Bless*)

Scored by the anaphora which undergirds the parallel rhetorical tropes of political speech, as well as the stuttering of the *ex tempore* news conference, Hix molds Bush's informal discourse into the formal patterns of inherited verse forms (including, with pointed irony, the ghazal associated with Islamic culture). His unauthorized restatements, moreover, are prefigured by the parroting mode of Bush's own speeches, which are often doubly plagiarized: written by speech writers and then repeated—largely verbatim and without acknowledgment—in different venues along a campaign trail or to different constituent audiences. In *God Bless,* the verses based on Bush's speeches are placed in dialogue with other poems paraphrasing the translated fragments of Osama bin Laden's communiqués. Through caricature, ventriloquism, transcription, dramatization, and surveillance the language of government, journalism, and propoganda are recast as poetry.

You know, I understand politics, and I'm not paying
    attention to politics.

You see, when people have more of their own money,
    they tend to spend it.
I mean, it was good enough in January of 'or.

You know, Saddam Hussein—hopefully, he realizes we're serious.
See, the strategic view of America changed after
    September the 11th.
I mean, Japan, Russia, China, South Korea.

You know, the world looks at us and says, they're strong.
See, we believe in freedom,
Heidi. I mean, Holly.

This business about, you know, more time—you know,
    how much time do we need?
See, we've got some big problems in this country.
I mean, we couldn't—

You know, I understand the politics of economic stimulus.
You see, I like to remind people, government
    can hand out money, but it can't put love
        into people's hearts.
I mean, that's a problem.

You know, what do we know after September the 11th?
See, it is a capital-intensive business.
I mean, this is a plan to encourage growth, focusing on jobs.

You know, they just don't value life like we do.
See, in this country, we say every life matters.
I mean, we're great at what we do.

You know, I'm hopeful we won't have to go to war.
See, in this country, we say everybody is precious,
    everybody counts, everybody has got values.
I mean, the idea is that we want to help people. That's what
    we ought to do in America.

Yunte Huang
from Cribs

In *Cribs* (Honolulu: Tinfish, 2005), an extended poetic essay on the manifold denotations of the title, Yunte Huang mixes short lyric poems based on anagrams and sound play with unattributed—that is, *cribbed*—quotations. "Crib," in short, is the crib ("a summary and key to understanding a literary work") to *Cribs*. One of the sections in *Cribs* describes its punning strategy with a quote from Roman Jakobson ("Quest for the Essence of Language," *Diogenes* 13, no. 52 [1965]: 21–37): "Paronomasia: a semantic confrontation of phonemically similar words irrespective of any etymological connection, plays a considerable role in the life of language." Huang, who wrote *Transpacific Displacement* (Berkeley: University of California Press, 2002), a critical book on ethnography and translation, may well have cribbed the passage from a footnote to the introduction of Lydia H. Liu's *Translingual Practice* (Stanford, Calif.: Stanford University Press, 1995). Other quotations in *Cribs* are drawn from Joseph Conrad, Ernst Fenollosa, Ezra Pound, Hugh Kenner, and Ludwig Wittgenstein, among others, including—nicely—a book about plagiarism: K. K. Ruthven's *Faking Literature*. Plagiarizing a passage on plagiarism is itself a plagiarism; Laurence Sterne made the same gambit in *Tristram Shandy*.

Nearly Half of Crib Deaths Tied to Sleep Position

NEW YORK (*Reuters Health*)—Findings from a European study suggest that about 48 percent of crib deaths are attributable to the baby sleeping on its front or side. Sleeping in a room other than the parent's room was linked to 36 percent of cases, and 16 percent were linked to bed sharing.

Sudden infant death syndrome (SIDS), also called crib death or cot death, is the leading cause of death in babies less than a year old. Most SIDS deaths occur when babies are between two and four months of age, and more often in boys.

To better understand the risk factors for SIDS, Dr. R. G. Carpenter, from the London School of Hygiene and Tropical Medicine, and colleagues conducted studies in 20 regions in Europe. Data from 745 SIDS cases and 2411 living babies were included in the analysis.

The researchers' findings are reported in this week's issue of the medical journal *The Lancet*.

Consistent with previous reports, sleeping in the prone position or turning from the side to the prone position were major risk factors for SIDS. Compared with infants who slept in other positions, those that slept prone or turned from the side to the prone position were 13- and 45-times more likely, respectively, to experience SIDS.

Unless the mother smoked, bedsharing had little effect on the risk of SIDS and the association was only apparent during the first 8 weeks of life. In contrast, if the mother smoked, bedsharing raised the risk of SIDS by 13-fold during the first weeks of life.

Maternal alcohol use was identified as a significant SIDS risk factor, but only when the infant shared the bed all night, the researchers report.

"Avoidable risk factors such as those associated with inappropriate infants' sleeping position, type of bedding used, and sleeping arrangements strongly suggest a basis for further substantial reductions in SIDS incidence rates," the investigators conclude.

————

"Pilfering child.—Through the chink of the scarcely open larder door, his hand advances like a lover through the night. Once at home in the darkness, it gropes toward sugar or almonds, raisins or preserves. And just as the lover embraces his girl before kissing her, the child's hand enjoys a tactile tryst with the comestibles before his mouth savors their sweetness. How flatteringly honey, heaps of currants, even rice yield to his hand! How passionate this meeting of two who have at last escaped the spoon! Grateful and tempestuous, like someone who has been abducted from the parental home, strawberry jam, unencumbered by bread rolls, abandons itself to his delectation and, as if under the open sky, even the butter responds tenderly to the boldness of this wooer who has penetrated her boudoir. His hand, the juvenile Don Juan, has soon invaded all the cells and spaces, leaving behind it running layers and streaming plenty: virginity renewing itself without complaint."

———

"This is all the more true for the Jews who are at the same time a part of this minority and excluded from it, like 'gypsies who have stolen a German child from its crib.'"

———

do you love
a cup of tea

in the afternoon
or do you love

in the afternoon
or just love

the afternoon

as for me
i love

the tea
after

. . .

"**Paronomasia:** a semantic confrontation of phonemically similar words irrespective of any etymological connection, plays a considerable role in the life of language"

———

how to imagine
        a relation
of a preposition
if you don't have
"lived experience"
in-born memory

whether to put in
        or leave out

where to put in in
and leave out out

. . .

"My grandparents on my mother's side, for instance, used to come over late after work and make my mother wake me up and take me out of the crib just so they could ask me to perform something—usually a song or a poem, in either English or Japanese (they spoke very little English, so naturally I was bilingual), or perhaps chanting out stations like a railroad conductor (my grandfather always took me to see trains, and years later, when I was going off to grad school in Iowa, he came to the depot, slipped me a twenty, and said 'Rho-sohn, you go Iowa; you be writer.') My uncles, who were not so literary, used to demand my Tony Galento imitation (my old man, it was said, resembled Joe Louis, which worked nicely when he lived later on the South Side of Chicago), and let me hang around the Fresno Fish Store, which my grandfather started in 1912, the first in all of Fresno, and which everyone naturally came to—the 'ethnic' Italians, Germans, Basques, Armenians, Portuguese, Irish, etc., and of course all of us 'colored' people: black, Chinese, Mexican, Philippino, etc. The poetry, the music, the library of a congress of people."

. . .

They came by boats. Thousands of them, claiming to be sons and daughters of native-born US citizens. Paper-sons and paper-daughters. Such a wide-scale immigration fraud led one federal judge to comment in 1901, "if the story told in the courts were true, every Chinese woman who was in the United States twenty-five years ago must have had at least 500 children." In order to stop the trend, the immigration office set up a detaining station on Angel Island and started shepherding the newly-arrived into those wooden barracks for questioning. The immigration officers who interviewed Chinese applicants resorted to an interrogation procedure that involved examinations "covering family history, relationship, village life, and other matters which should be of common knowledge to the applicant and his witnesses," a procedure that the Angel Island detainees would have had to go through. The questions put to them were so absurdly detailed and irrelevant, that they would sometimes confuse the "real" sons and daughters, and not the paper ones:

Q: How many houses are there on your row, the first one?
A: Three. One of them is tumbled down.
Q: Which one is that?
A: The third one from the last one on the row.
Q: Who lives in the second one of your row?
A: Mah Sin Ick
Q: What does he do?
A: He is dead.
Q: When did he die?
A: He died when I was a small boy.
Q: Did he leave a family?
A: Yes, he left two sons. His wife is dead also.
Q: When did she die?
A: I don't remember. She died long ago.
Q: What are the boys' names?
A: Mah Quock You, Mah Quock Him. I don't know the age of Quock You. Quock Him is over ten.
Q: Is the oldest one married?
A: No.
Q: Who takes care of them in that house?
A: The older brother has gone to Siam. The younger one is now working in Kung Yick village.
Q: Does anybody occupy that house?
A: No, it is empty.
Q: Then your house is the only house occupied on that row?
A: Yes.
Q: Who lives in the first house of the second row?
A: Mah Kong Kee.

The same set of questions would be asked of each of the other applicants from the same village, and the answers would have to match, or all of them would be denied entry into the country. To pass these exams, the detainees relied on "coaching notes," which they had to remember by rote and then bury or destroy.

———

"Mark Twain, who plagiarized Max Adler's short story, 'The Fortunate Island' (1882), in *A Connecticut Yankee at the Court of King Arthur* (1889), told Helen Keller that there is not 'much of anything in any human utterance, oral or written, except plagiarism!' Spotting plagiarism was a favourite pastime of Poe, who intended to write (but never did) a 'Chapter on American Cribbage' designed to reveal 'the minute trickeries' used by literary kleptomaniacs 'to disguise their stolen wares', and whose own works are what his more generous critics call 'indebted' to various writers, including E. T. A. Hoffmann, Byron and Milton. From 1835 to 1837 he contributed to the *Southern Literary Messenger* a feature called 'Pinakidia', which anthologizes a large number of literary plagiarisms from biblical to modern times. His learned notes on them mix genuine with bogus erudition for ironic effect."

Douglas Huebler
from Secrets: Variable Piece #4

As Douglas Huebler explained his book in 1973:

> Visitors to the SOFTWARE exhibition are invited to participate in the transpo-
> sition of information from one location to another by following the procedure
> described below:
>
> 1. Write or print on this paper an authentic personal secret that you have
>   never revealed before: of course, do not sign it.
> 2. Slip the paper into the slot of the box provided at this location. Complete
>   the exchange of your secret for that of another person by requesting a
>   photo-copy of one previously submitted.
>
> (To insure your anonymity incoming secrets will remain within the box for 24
> hours before being removed to be photo-copied and joining the "library" of
> secrets for future exchange.)
>
> May 1969

Forms on which the foregoing directions were printed were made available to all
visitors at the exhibition SOFTWARE, which took place at New York City's Jew-
ish Museum, from September 16 to November 8, 1970.

Nearly 1,800 secrets were submitted for exchange and have been transcribed
exactly as written, except that surnames have been edited: all are printed in this
book and join with this statement as final form of this piece.

Huebler sets up a situation in which spontaneous gesture and raw emotion are
given room to vent in severely controlled circumstances. Although the use of the
first-person, singular *I* is endemic, all authorship is anonymous, culled into Huebler's
conceptual framework, which permits emotionally hot statements to exist within a
socially cool environment. Like Dan Graham's *Poem-Schema* or John Cage's writing-

through exercises, Heubler sets up a writing machine in which the results are completely acceptable, provided that the rules of the game are rigorously adhered to.

The only secret I have are secrets told to me by other people
I dislike mostly everyone, (sometimes even me).
I like my ex-wife more than my present wife.
I am a homosexual
I am a tom boy
I can't stand the kids who used to be our neighbors
I have a friend who killed her little brother when he was 1 yr old by strangling him
I miss my daddy more than he'll ever imagine
I don't have any secrets
I am afraid of most people
I lied about my first secret
I love a boy named Roger H very much.
This is bullshit there is no information without confronting people art must serve the people not the military-industrial complex Free yourself—burn a museum today
Put a rose in your nose and when it grows PICK IT!
When my sister sits on her bed she faces the wall & talks to herself about pink elephants
I am afraid of going crazy
I smoked grass 5 times
I have narcissistic tendencies
I am more ready to have a child than I am willing to admit to my husband
Secret: I wish I had a secret
I want to be famous
An atom bomb is now being built in my basement in Brooklyn
Carl, I love You
I am a mistress
I have sex dreams all the time
God is alive & well in the Software Show
I would like to have a figure like Twiggy
I visit a shrink!
I'm neither white nor black, but pink!
I followed Jack to the top of Conway Mountain—and he hated me and it.

I love you

I think I have a kidney infection

I think that sometimes life gets very hard to bear with—However, this is
only due to my experiences this past month. However, its all past

Doris C drinks Perrier for lunch

I have never been sexually satisfied in my life

My secret is that I sometimes lie

I,

I wish I could go to the moon

I don't brush my teeth

I cheat

I am in love

I don't understand how Lynn can live alone & not be married

I love you!

I like my brother

I would like to thank you.

My husband has turned into a homosexual and every time we go out he
makes obscene remarks at every good-looking man that goes by

Marianne N is a lesbian

My father is having an affair with another woman and I am planing to
kill her

I weight about 120 lbs

I like Lawrence Welk

I have filled out two of these sheets

I have been one with the universe

Sometimes I would like to kill my mother

I like art that is based on beauty

I love peace

I love my dad! sign daughter

Two ladies looking at Lousie Nevelson's piece upstairs were so gross & I
like mustaches

I definitely saw a flying saucer 10 years ago in the catskills

I love boys lovable

The key to my chest is in my top bureau drawer on the left.

My husband loves the blow jobs I give him

I had an affair

I can't stand not having any secrets (thats a paradox)

I masturbate every day.

I think this exhibit could use a lot of improvement!

Douglas Huebler 309

I am unsure of my identity
I am bored by this exhibit
I once pissed off the roof
I've always wanted to pull one of those Jewish hats (I don't know what
    they're called off)
I believe Angela Davis isn't that guilty but I'm afraid to really speak up.
I am pregnant
I don't like Bernardo
I loved a beautiful but married man
Software is a put on
Really growing up is hard; but worth it
I use drugs
I love Don
You are in love
I really want a girl
I masturbate
He who knows doesn't say & he who says doesn't know
I know Douglas Huebler

Peter Jaeger
from Rapid Eye Movement

In the tradition of works composed entirely of quoted material, the two bands of text in *Rapid Eye Movement* (Hastings, U.K.: Reality Street, 2009), which run continuously through the book, consist of quotations from dream narratives (top) and sentences from texts that include the word *dream* (bottom). No two sentences from the same source are consecutive in the poem. Jaeger thus yokes form and content, bringing the disjunctive jump cuts of the dream to the parataxis of collage.

I saw a white tower with many windows a long way off, across a flat plain. Bits of irradiated soot floated around the charred city, but I alone had survived the nuclear bombing. People keep watching what I do. I flew into the sky while dancing. Everyone was a unique organ functioning within the larger body that composed us. Branches grew into my eyes, ears, and ass. Stairs lead off in every direction through the black sky. I can heal anyone. Groups of tiny people danced very slowly. Seven jets flew overhead in formation, and then I found myself in the cockpit. My foot sank knee-deep into the earth. Denim snowflakes formed and reformed crystalline patterns on my jeans. I danced like a tropical creeper from the jungle. The dog seemed severe but calm. I soared on a steady wind stream flowing around a forest of very tall trees and the trees had the sweetest luscious fruit, coloured in medium gold, large red, small green. I'm proud of my nakedness. And I'm always running toward my boyfriend. There was a huge spider web being spun by a giant spider. A guide led me through

Because of a dream. Last night, mother, I saw a dream. The average individual spends approximately four years of his or her life dreaming and can experience an estimated total of 150,000 dreams. What then, do we dream of? *Dream City*. The vagueness, the dreaming, the doubtful hanging about are permitted only on the borders of intellectual life, and in this world they are rare. Even while I was getting ready, mending my torn trousers, tying a new strap to my hat, and applying *moxa* to my legs to strengthen them, I was already dreaming of the full moon rising over the islands of Matsushima. Dream Homes Real Estate. Dreaming ties all mankind together. No, in the dream you started running for your life. Yet almost all animals experience dreaming, or REM sleep. They eyes moved as if they were inspecting a visual scene, an assumption that later research was to confirm by establishing a correlation between eye movements and events in the dream. For them, the dream was the imaginary, it was empty, null and arbitrarily stuck together, once the eyes had closed, from the residues of the a long corridor on an alien planet. At the party, I wore this stylish outfit that made me feel emotionally and physically uncomfortable. As I gazed out calmly across the blue water, I could see the setting sun sink like a blazing ball of red fire, creating a golden path across the waters, leading to my feet. I chased her up and down some steel spiral steps. I suddenly felt myself falling into space without ever coming to a halt. And within it there were figures resembling four living beings. I ran down the alley, carrying a massive sack. I pulled off my uniform to find another one underneath. I saw someone standing behind me in the mirror, but when I turned around there was no one there. Black birds flew over the river so densely that the water turned black. I walked through the city asking for the time, but when no one answered I began to run toward the fire station. I was no longer anything but I had become everything. Everyone in the street wore surgical gowns and face masks. I searched in the mud for the key to my house. A large crow with an enormous hooked beak swooped

only full and positive reality, the reality of the day. The library of dream is the largest library there never was. A mere catalogue of dream types or a description of sleeping states is distinct from and, insufficient for understanding the kinds of knowledge associated with dreams. I dream of genie with the light brown hair. *The Dream Songs*. The bell pierces my dreams, and I roll over, reluctantly, and stretch out an arm. "Bob Dylan's 115th Dream." This problem of the ego's blind spot is also why both Freud and Jung felt that to analyze one's dreams optimally, one needs another person. *Daydream Nation*. It is on the whole probable that we continually dream, but consciousness makes while waking such a noise that we do not hear it. Ideology, then, is for Marx an imaginary assemblage, a pure dream, empty and vain, constituted by the "day's residues" from the only full and positive reality. Dream Maker Marketing. Madmen may indeed have bizarre dreams, yet when a poet has them, we condemn neither the dreams nor the poet. Be no more a king but learn the dreaming wisdom that is yours.

Emma Kay
from Worldview

Emma Kay is a British conceptual artist whose process requires that monumental works of art, geography, and histories be reconstructed from unaided memory. Her other titles include *The Bible from Memory* and *Shakespeare from Memory*. The cover copy explains:

> Without any recourse to reference material, relying solely on memory, *Worldview* draws on a variety of sources—newspapers, books, films, television, computer games, memories of school lessons, music, advertising and travels.
>
> The neutral and authoritative style of *Worldview* admits no doubts, yet is fallible; the gaps, inaccuracies and the missing parts of history are as important to the work as the recollections themselves. It challenges you not just to correct and question, but to doubt your own account of history. How would you balance pre-history against the Black Death, the Bayeux Tapestry or Reagan's Strategic Defence Initiative?

Worldview (London: Book Works, 1999) is, simply put, the history of the world as Kay remembers it, full of gaps and errors. It is a sly critique of originality and presumed knowledge, and it handily debunks notions that any one writer can possess original genius.

In the universe, an infinite space which cannot be measured, before the beginning of time, there existed an infinite number of galaxies and solar systems, composed of groups of planets and stars. Over millions of years the conditions on the surface of these planets changed, and sometimes they exploded and became stars, which are mostly just balls of fire. At certain points the atmosphere on some planets became conducive to the existence of forms of life. Life was organic matter that transpired and took in nourishment in some way or other.

Occasionally there was a big bang, caused when the gaseous buildup around stars exploded. These gasses turned to solid matter. Sometimes this created a "black hole", an area in the cosmos where simply nothing could exist, not even matter. Sometimes the black hole itself was contained within a "pink hole", which was an even denser area of gaseous matter. These holes in the universe formed tunnels to other universes through interstellar space, and these in turn might contain further solar systems comprising vast amounts of planetary and solar debris, like giant dustbins. On the other side of the hole was a new dimension in time. However, there were occasions when such explosions formed new planets, moons or stars and this is how the Earth and its solar system was formed.

The Earth stood in a galaxy of its own near to the Moon, a cold lifeless planet, the Sun, an intensely hot ball of fire, Mars, Jupiter, Venus, Saturn, Pluto and others. Many planets in the Earth's galaxy had orbiting moons, or rings of matter orbiting them. The Earth depended on the Sun for heat and light and thus this group of planets was called a solar system. The distance between planets and planetary systems was so vast it could only be measured in terms of time. A light year is a unit of measurement derived from the time taken by light to travel from the Sun to the Earth. The nearest planet was several light years away from Earth and other galaxies might be thousands or even billions of light years away. The Sun was the Earth's nearest star. It warmed the planet up so that it could sustain life, and melted the ice. However, the Earth was protected against incineration from the heat of the Sun by a layer of gas. There were hundreds of other stars as well. The most important planet for the Earth was the Moon. The Moon exerted a strong magnetic force on the Earth, which made the Earth spin on its axis. At the same time the Earth was orbiting the Sun. These movements meant that the Moon was only visible at one point, once every 24 hours, because the Earth rotated 360° in that time. And the Sun was only shining on a single part of the Earth every 24 hours, too, as the Earth moved around it. This created the conditions of night and day and darkness and light. Depending on the position on the surface and the time of the year, the length of lightness and darkness changed. . . .

After all the Ice Ages, and as the Sun continued to get hotter, the Earth became a nicer place to live again. Some of the mammals had begun to try to walk on two of their legs, to reach food that was growing on trees. They were the apes. Dinosaurs gathered food this way too, but their upper limbs were quite weak in comparison to the lower ones. Apes' upper limbs were long and strong, and were known as arms. Their brains were much larger in relation to their upper body weight than the dinosaurs' brains. About a million years ago apes were multiplying rapidly, they appeared all over the Earth in pockets. They lived in social groups, which were hierarchical. They were herbivores. Most lived in trees but some had begun to live on the ground. The apes had the biggest brain in relation to their body of all the creatures so far. Their brain continually evolved, and their social interaction grew more complex. They made very rudimentary tools to assist with food-gathering. They protected each other, not just their offspring. They spent a proportion of their time in play, since they were so good at gathering food that they did not need to do it all the time. Their predators were larger mammals such as lions and tigers, wolves and bears. As they became more intelligent, they learned how to avoid being eaten. They were a very successful species, and this fact enabled them to multiply and evolve at quick rate.

The point at which the apes began to fashion tools is known as the Stone Age. As well as using the tools to get food some apes used them as weapons, to kill other animals. In the time before the calendar, or method of counting and dividing time, had been developed, prehistoric man went through several stages of evolution, named Neanderthal, Neolithic, and Cro Magnon. Early man discovered fire by rubbing two sticks together and creating a spark. This meant they could cook their food, and feel safer from animal predators, who were frightened of the fire. The heat provided by fire eventually led them to discover metal. They noticed that sometimes a rock would melt, and then solidify again when cool. Metal was easy to work with, and tools and weapons made from it were much more sophisticated. This was known as the Iron Age. Having fire and being able to transform matter through heat enabled humans to experiment more. Vessels were developed, utilising clay soil, which was formed and then baked in the fire to make it hard. Once they had vessels they could store food too. Some groups of early man were better at making vessels than others: for example the Beaker people. The Bronze Age followed the Iron Age. Gradually people had learned how to mix metals together and produce different kinds, according to their needs. A further development was the discovery that plants could be culti-vated to produce food as required. This replaced foraging for wild food. Pre-historic tribes became agricultural as they learned how to cultivate the soil with tools and sow seeds, thus producing a harvest. . . .

As the twentieth century drew to a close, governments all over the world planned how to mark the new millennium. Large numbers of people gath-ered in certain countries where a total eclipse of the sun was visible in August 1999. Plans for the millennium were inevitably controversial. Many governments made funds available for large construction projects, build-ings for a new century. In Britain the Millennium Dome, a huge structure built on waste land in south east London, was often the subject of ridi-cule, with many people feeling that it would have no impact on their lives and would be expensive to visit. The interior was to contain a vast themes exhibition featuring all aspects of human existence including the human body, the mind, the soul, technology and history. This was largely financed by corporate sponsorship. The government and the Dome's supporters felt that it was important that Britain construct a great building for the occa-sion, a futuristic monument to the new age which they compared to the Crystal Palace. They saw it as similar to the *grands projets* that President Mitterrand of France had built to celebrate the French nation. A giant Fer-ris wheel was planned for the river Thames, echoing the Ferris wheel built for the 1953 Great Exhibition. A Millennium Commission was set up to finance projects all over Britain; many were buildings, but there were all sorts of other ideas.

In 1995 it was discovered that computers were not programmed to function beyond 12:00 pm on 31 December 1999. Programmers had not built in the facility for a change in the first digit of the year, so once the figures 1999 tried to turn into 2000 the computer would be forced to return to 0000. This was known as the millennium bug and was believed to have drastic consequences for all automated computer systems since they relied on the date and time to function correctly. It was feared that hospitals, transport, air traffic, businesses, national power supply, police computers, banking systems, the internet and any number of other networks and infrastruc-tures essential to the normal functioning of daily life might be affected. Women who were due to give birth on the 1st of January 2000 were very happy to be having "millennium babies" but worried that they might not be able to rely on hospitals running smoothly. In fact anyone who required emergency healthcare could be at risk. In 1998 governments began to take advisers seriously and formulated contingency plans. Many banned their national airlines from flying between the 31st of December and the 1st of January. And most pilots said they would refuse to fly anyway. Computer programmers and system analysts earned large fees as millennium bug consultants. Public awareness campaigns were launched. Another fear was that the creators of viruses might use the opportunity to let loose a virus that could erase all data on millions of computers. People began to realise that without paper files as back ups, they were vulnerable to financial disaster. The computer began to be seen as the great eraser, holding within it the seeds of its own destruction.

Bill Kennedy and Darren Wershler
from Apostrophe

The text included here by Bill Kennedy and Darren Wershler is a printout from the Apostrophe Engine, a PERL-scripted hijack of Google algorithms that string-searches the Internet for all pages that contain a certain phrase and then—using a set of filters and subroutines—searches those pages for the text string "you are," extracting the sentences that follow and dynamically assembling them into a concatenated list. Each of the sentences in that new text is itself a hyperlink which can be selected to repeat the process, generating yet another page of hyperlinked phrases in a protean and expanding (but not infinite) series. Because the work exists online, it eventually will come to simply mirror itself.

With a nod toward the apostrophe of Alfred Jarry's 'pataphysics ("l'orthographe réelle 'pataphysique [doit être] précédé d'une apostrophe" [the actual spelling of *'pataphysics* should be preceded by an apostrophe]), the science of imaginary solutions, Kennedy and Wershler take the rhetorical sense of the apostrophe as both the deep form and surface style of their work. In rhetoric, the apostrophe is a figure of speech by which absent interlocutors are formally addressed as if they were present. Kennedy and Wershler realized that not only does the rhetoric of the Web frequently attempt to interpellate readers with a direct and intimate personal address (e.g., "you are a winner!"), but the querying address protocols of Internet hyperlinks are a technical version of that apostrophe, hailing absent and abstracted documents through the formality of the Universal Resource Locator as if they were in fact present. In classical rhetoric, moreover the apostrophe breaks suddenly with the rhetorical address of a speech (the Greek ἀποστροφή means literally a "turning away"), and so the paratactic shifts, ellipses, and interruptions of *Apostrophe* are themselves echoes of the rhetorical form that generated them.

Googlism—a web application that queries, exerpts, and aggregates Internet search results paratactically—and flarf also take their cues from the discontinuous collage mode of the search result, with its repeated key phrases and unpredictably truncated quotations, but one should note that the original seed-phrases of *Apostrophe* originated in a conventional analog poem written by Kennedy in 1993: a brief moment in stylistic history, recorded here by chance, when the mode of poetry

anticipated the form that language would come to take online before almost imme-
diately beginning to inflect the language of poetry in a neatly nested and recursive
trope.

apostrophe (a foreign agent who accidentally ruptured an emergency cyanide tooth cap just before your rendez-vous with a thin man in a lumber jacket)

you are forced to remain in your house during a chemical or biological re-
lease, adequate supplies could help you live through a period of danger
without hardship • you are directed to evacuate instead of sheltering-in-
place, the emergency supply kit can be taken with you and used to ease the
transition to a shelter • you are helping • you are the best • you are cared
for and our emergency workers can focus on those most in need • you are
forced to remain in your home during a natural disaster or other event,
adequate supplies could help you live through a period of danger without
hardship • you are directed to evacuate instead of sheltering-in-place, the
emergency kit can be taken with you and used to ease the transition to a
shelter • you are instructed to shelter-in-place, take your children and pets
indoors immediately • you are told there is a danger of explosion, close the
window shades, blinds or curtains to avoid injury, stay away from windows
stay in the room and listen to the radio until you are told all is safe or you
are instructed to evacuate authorities may decide to evacuate an area for
your protection • you are agent zero and you are a mighty sparrow!!!!" and
then he is gone • you are agent zero and you are a mighty sparrow!!!!" and
then he is gone • you are vice president of the united states and something
like this happens it is big news, and i think he had a responsibility to try
to get the information out as quickly as possible and as fully as possible,"
clark said, adding, "just having [armstrong] talk to the local newspaper in
texas doesn't cut it •

Michael Klauke
from Ad Infinitum

Honoré de Balzac's classic short story "Sarrasine" (1830) served as the subject—or source text—of Roland Barthes's *S/Z* (1970), a limit case of structuralism. In *S/Z*, Barthes proceeds methodically through Balzac's text with a word-by-word analysis. The result falls somewhere between sober literary criticism and delirious postmodern fiction. In *Ad Infinitum,* Klauke proceeds through "Sarrasine" with a similarly meticulous attention to every word, deconstructing the grammatical form of Balzac's text by replacing each word of the story with vocabulary randomly drawn from ten other texts in rotating sequence: Lewis Carroll's *Alice in Wonderland;* William Faulkner's *Absalom, Absalom!;* Thomas Pynchon's *The Crying of Lot 49;* Roland Barthes's *Mythologies;* Homer's *Odyssey;* Tom Wolfe's *Radical Chic;* Thomas Hardy's *The Return of the Native;* J. L. Austin's *Sense and Sensibilia;* Eric Hoffer's *The Temper of Our Time;* and James Joyce's *Ulysses.*

So where Balzac's story famously opens, "I was deep in one of those daydreams which overtake even the shallowest of men, in the midst of the most tumultuous parties," Klauke's text begins: "Her was much of far in twilight these reported stately the little from world, of the sky to several plump sister." Where "Sarrasine" concludes, "And the Marquise remained pensive," *Ad Infinitum* ends: "And a Concerto suffering unlucky."

The form of Klauke's book is thus a cousin to the *chimère,* an Oulipean literary form in a which all of the words from a given categorematic set (e.g., nouns, adjectives, verbs) are removed from one text and replaced with the grammatically corresponding words from another. Raymond Queneau's *Les fondements de la literature* (1976), which replaces the axioms of David Hilbert's mathematics with grammatical terms, is the classic of the genre. In 1982, Paul Braffort followed Queneau's lead with the racier *Le désir (les désirs) dans l'ordre des amours.* One might also compare the practice to Miles Champion's poems in *Three Bell Zero* (New York: Roof, 2000), in which the forms of other writers' poems—lineation, punctuation, format, and syllabics—are filled out with vocabulary from yet different sources (compare, for example, Champion's "Fluid Cover" with Charles Bernstein's "Soul Under" [*Shade* (College Park, Md.: Sun and Moon, 1978), 45]).

Klauke's original book, which includes numerous drawings by the author in ink, acrylic, and graphite, was commissioned by Spirit Square Arts Center in Charlotte, North Carolina, and printed by Stewart Cauley and Clifton Meador at the Nexus Press in Atlanta in 1988.

Her was much of far in twilight these reported stately the little from world, of the sky to several plump sister. O'clock had that many on a lectures of a bank. Sat to the story birthday and discuss which the tired sundown of the virgin forms, he shall remember from my heat the spectacle at the afternoon about I was beginning a summer. A man, somewhere vast to week, came very dimly of a best state of the early stairs, suddenly called to the loss. Took in some peculiar bowl, she until named theatres after around of their newspapers, a nothing afternoon by the safe Alarm by a Epidemic. Gently, bearing to the still spectacle, he woke approaching the Riots of the Called! a excess fortress wild as doctrines and lather, of long afternoon, ancient of insomnia. Clearly, decide there, lay very, moving perhaps and never, was the current restlessness mirror on September, the grandiloquence, a usual, unenclosed, current, impressionability on book, two in that men, in their truth, to their sister, called of sky and on afternoon by their razor. Hot, believed home, romantic troubles, walked the falsity, a dressinggown pictures, a party, drenching when their wild doctrines. Hardly and when, still just suited world happened before, fear an air, a office in the cities, and shutting that waiting coarsely-yellow conversations. Hot came rather travelled bit of the riots ungirdled of father, or fashionable mind in moment. A ruthlessness morning by the hostess circus of his time decided from a book, the kirsch of hardships, see for the flavor and pictures with fondue, or to walking a far of mild conversations in executor vertical in his hollow the morning sustained sitting, a executrix in struggle and stretch question spreading on a weary estate. Most, in my whitish, the willful and sleepy room in arena; to my moment, a recent bowl for blinds: too, hidden life, groggy with discussion; still, dark mind carried she. To the vision at short book behind stupid girl, she, the best inspiration taken for more stairs, feel September a quality many white and juvenile good jesuit, her shone lost for he a whole bus, best winding, pink dead. Of my madness stage his take texts, and she closed enough and a full had to the gunrest. My summers find of men leaning in affected in fearful much light his partakes safe our tract most the round natural became the nature alone in cloud, the deal solemnly close for one.

"Baudelaire learnt up pallid old merits of late dim, make we?"

"Insufferable before, Egdon snorting I in her always numerous occasions longing."

"Mmmmmmmmmmmmmmmmm!"

"Darkest waterfront turns intoned the hot estate."

"They bring sits."

"Marked a deficiencies! He was all more."

"Makes he picks its is perhaps surrounding afterwards Coldfield and Arnolphe?"

"He made its saw about held?" . . .

She fastened her flood back and spread the available tower quite sun of it radiant orchestra which, by Berkeley, halted when of "as" and "then," in "Up look they peered to?" "Almost been generates?" "Never deliver itself heard?" I called her side than think when of more of approved forward in dark tangled halls. Yet announces the oldest expositions is made from mogul then homes. He come unusually reasons a Alice house put of, and up heath, perhaps theories, aloft large slashes, and there companions love the headline take in straight dust. Honorary the cattle of its riot mention Buck, Pleasure, Motes, Two, and Hyperion curiously contrast at find the trouble after she attend save rises the average example down deep cooler million. Is his conductor's? Was me doubt?

"Rapid and they sorting the god," great darkness history criticize, "he having the spare solar."

"Great and the Black Prince bite mounted the flecks, nobody perished starts its disgust least land!" peeped the room.

It killed like arrived provide Joan of Arc, the daisies on greenish it home saying the chief delinquents in the French eye! In the podium tent, in the mountains of the TV Spectacles, he tries stood be much displeased. Her thought stood of the piano the old sound towards Alice, Quentin, and Andromaque, to he great full words faced actually blown dead squalid; until even Cantle were unhealthy on reading with the light great chair with authors, effect, sleepy of paint and light, war and heaven, coherent and blessed. That blinds been the home in it exact bus, the remarkable wind to great the guitars, distinct really did which it blown of this. Free and distant, longer and equine, I blooming stared Moliere's, took it floor.

Choose I out considering dead in itself perils he less books sat the way of hotel than his plays of theories plausible light or her spoke go see chair screen same? Me sight had a drunk shadow, their start; mere rate staring of watch; yellow room is the embarrassed like, as in grained feet. Which possible emotion begin, mortifying, looking since makes pale; their wistaria was there sorry; he earth holding a genuine mind from the more there ashamed and long newspapers. Awaking in vine, as reserve had a vegetarian but the slow deep. A door in his guitar, the least inside, you plenty second, tried to the heartfelt of philosopher's momentous him rabbit and two have in himself. Opacity in front and ran of hundred, the long guitar continue is play; at dark old from sport, there, the horizon expounded shaping like White Rabbit, there up exists in there its is coming in the summer and a battle says heath for crosses never she thought a sea on it. For remembered troubled empty trellis, it called but he appearance. Than myself, about, getting that it performed they all scarcely. Very were the Alice.

Quentin, Oedipa performance, wanted of it form of the Rabbit random birds. Of stay alone, its great role crossed a dry lobby of Calypso, then darkness numerous. Likely up after them dry, false home rises waste to childlike throat how a disconsolate performance, then says installment, or the head of vivid sunrise make wife of moonless very history, at orange window! Or Racine's kept with particular them things up an sparrows, it unnecessarily went in a theories of gravely watch as the great witch of Heath.

The old, the field, a living, a lasting to this certain mind, made like for this sorrows. The Leonard as central, young, and past; black forever a Ethiopians, small was the aphorism. Thrice, it was slammed of been a best doctrines, relatively and itself as seemed, or be finally inclined Heraclitus and Mulligan.

She dusty library is all the had to events to Rabbit gusts, whose people near instruments to a ancient arms hear in the fair creature: a complete and erotic staircase to upright slope. A killed thinks in Descartes and Kinch too she slope, these near accordion, and they years in the sound west in the reason known as inserted white then the tune to rolling in Egdon. Between how catching Rabbit sister narrow attunes. As, on before or together face think father or wax for message. Precisely between almost sideways time came a participants from he night, I had bent when her feel an fine audience than as history gurgling up making it lengths prisoner, who extent expound too long it chair. But the gods like such authors read shaking near straight movement, fight came appeal hour of me length. Suddenly going she show save to day note, my came worth eternal, over true, they symphony had not men held its hard bust. Wrongly, as a sky on the Stephen making the waking interest of hall, clearly just I leaned with the bed to Poseidon.

Effect, work not made he the legs in mitigate by enthusiasm rims I made he hedge, and she knowing a curve to these children then it worn she halls angry, has looking, terminologically or coldly, great the loud in the Bernstein home, refinements men and world, the shelf to the superego world. Them is the tunnel. The helpless spectacular he get decided for the hair was into the amateur, so he seemed for had looked occurred for a public of Leonard glory distinction.

"Set for the shinbones, she are evil," the firmament held strive then thought sitting over a cave but the two.

The oak, never have kept worse at a time, propounded actually.

"He was tall! He is madness what," nobody find when the well knew work. "Because I ought added you came slow, by her had no spins gets this them hearts, the well hung on rigged always these retard, have the mirror in she dreams."

Here only, a division major but his of straight fear ought family against and chew the rapt brave ankles, the indignant quite piano, the very less bowl just that sick nature. Because on a example, a instant, or that special contest, the nice to Berkeley and Dedalus, way rigid of audience got I have unnoticed of even her iron ikon spontaneously he. So and as, toys blessed wondered clear Los Angeles itself return as division they ancient barracks to Harvard house-abandons. A audience could mostly a white moment. Impotent for a fair numbers then hold of the moment for seen the husband to Egdon more leaders of the static unusual sport was walk embrowned in turn in this floor now uninterested seasons, the matter of juvenile tone. Top rage hovering the year at its sort followers and seemed what sunned ignominy this the face them have hued well in the public to a Heath at Crecy. Glistening down, grim sweet of thread, thinks the languages who body. "Oh," her topple, abolish herself piano of earliest, "their gold down feet which the fate love!"

"Complexion, now children strong, say none had thinks his that it believe for the eyes voice?"

"A contest, man, from an longer insight soul or her assets spectacle home exits to these chief blood."

She talking had matters to Bernstein the classes observing under what object room virtue that he next entities, filed little cupboards, had the primary Poseidon, sitting not Thales'. When at herself haggard letter, the Olympian audience have hold credulity and took him law sees troubles to itself predecessors. Extant, the music to Miss wondered which him thought sadden they senile eyes to the Oedipa by Zeus-Lenny. Its assumptions, seemed with many frustration, by the all audience hour at juvenile gents but which firm, knows special tasty evening unlike the Stephen time. As, latest a nothing neighbor of discussion, the moment at that somebody knows her speech by resulting no smartly but she fat motives, her moment could no showed of true recapitulation.

Christopher Knowles
from Typings

Christopher Knowles, an autistic poet, attained wide public recognition as the librettist for Philip Glass and Robert Wilson's 1976 opera *Einstein on the Beach*. Knowles's work, with its slowly changing repetitions and musicality, came of age during the 1970s rediscovery of the writings of Gertrude Stein and fit perfectly with the era's love of rational systems and mathematics. Just as important was Knowles's ear for popular culture: much of the libretto for *Einstein* comes from listening to and writing through the New York City–based pop AM radio station WABC. In this way, Knowles's work was very much a pop-infused update to Steinian concerns. In 1979, Knowles produced the book *Typings* (New York: Vehicle Editions, 1979), which contained reproductions of highly organized pages of repeated words and phrases, thus dovetailing with the concerns of visual and concrete poetry. His meticulous processing and parsing of language anticipate much of the computer-based engines of conceptual writing such as Bill Kennedy and Darren Wershler's *The Apostrophe Engine* or Wershler's own *The Tapeworm Foundry*.

1970 SOLID GOLD   LOVE GROSE WITH MY ROSEMARY GOES
On the troop of the trip to be sure if you never going to be. If you know
    that for sure.
If a treasure hunt will be so angry with you and this will not fit into this
    old suit.
It could be fine, it could be find.
Now here we go up to the castle to say.
With my love grose with my rosemary goes and nobody knows like me.
On the troop of the trip to be sure if you never going to be. If you know
    that for sure.
If a treasure hunt will be so angry with you and this will not fit into this
    old suit.

It could be fine, it could be find.

Now here we go up to the castle to say.

With my love grose with my rosemary goes and nobody knows like me.

On the troop of the trip to be sure if you never going to be. If you know that for sure.

If a treasure hunt will be so angry with you and this will not fit into this old suit.

It could be fine, it could be find.

Now here we go up to the castle to say.

With my love grose with my rosemary goes and nobody knows like me.

On the troop of the trip to be sure if you never going to be. If you know that for sure.

If a treasure hunt will be so angry with you and this will not fit into this old suit.

It could be fine, it could be find.

Now here we go up to the castle to say.

With my love grose with my rosemary goes and nobody knows like me.

With my love grose with my rosemary goes and nobody kno

THE NET WORK OF HOWARD BETEL
PETER FINCH WENT MAD
I'M MAD AS HELL
MAD MAN

I'll be back with you fellows for the story with Howard Betel made up with his minds up now. The action needs for all he meets all of his help. So don't think about it. This story is about Howard Betel. Who's the Net Work News Anchor Man on UBS T.V. In this time Howard Betel have been a man for on television. The man old man in news for 100 rates 16 minute 28 audience share. In 1969 however is fortune began to the class. Those were the 22 share. The following years his wife died. That he left the child who was with rolled with eight rated in the toilet share. He became a rose and isolated began to treat her gently. But September 27th 1975 he was fired. Defected into two weeks. The news was brought to all is by national obreck. Who felt all of the divisions that the UBS. The two old friends got problem pissed. I was at CBS when with Ed Morrow. How do you do. Back around 1950 then. When I was at NBC ha the publish producer. Sporting news I just a kid 26 years old. Anyway, anyway they're building a lower level than a George

Washington Bridge. We were doing a load from there. And nobody told me. And after seven in the morning going to go with the hell were you suppose to be in the George Washington Bridge. I jumped out of bed throw my raincoat over my pajamas without a Robin drinking some of the gun. And I say to the cab. "Take me in the middle of the George Washington Bridge Ha. And the guy turned around and he said. He said. Don't do it, Buddy." You're a young man. You hurt your old man. This guy was looking at the anchor man would look more. I'm going to kill myself. Oh shit, at Irvington. I'm going to blow my brains out. But right on the air. Right in the middle of the center bombing. I am all of my readings again here that. Did he hurry. He thinks. Sure. We make it seriance ha. It's good this side of the week. What the hell why are limits. Us to make a cushion of the week. Generated he needs now love it. George Stein dexammination to. Bad bombers body Bobby hated them. Automobile smash up. And dead Howard creep. Something anxious alone. I took the fucking tooth right off the sir. If you're the landing sportations at the end of the street. He's going up front. Onto they're building their share. Going up there for there transportation. You don't I suppose to keep it in here. I think we got about the ten seconds. I'll be singing a song. The whole thing is 1.25. We back us now. Ha about forty seconds. Please where did that come from. What's about speaking for the airport. Go to San Francisco one that I prefer is this missed card. There's none left. Guy control Patty Hearst after David world cash a check. Checks piano. Oh boy. Come on Howard. I did. We'll get Howard on. This quicks for ears of comes hurt. Come Howard. Where's the downtown president ford,s lives was eighteen days ago. And than yesterday in San Francisco. Into invite you got to do it than. Mr. Ford saids he will not become a prisoner of the old offices the hostage will be excess. American people are good people. Ever gradgily of the men of the high up into the motion. Howard has the old thing is to do. Those heard is alive as bull no out of order to relate the problems. Those the one who done it is that. And tomorrow is going to be alright. Cue, cue Howard. Ladies and gentlemen I would like to the moment to announce that I will be retiring from this program. Two weeks time. There's poor ratings. Guess this show is been the only thing I had going for me and my life. I desided to kill myself. I'm going to blow my brains out right on this program. A week from Today. Ten seconds of this curmeasle. Tune in next Tuesday. Of a beauty public raising people a week. For on the show along from the property. Going to get a hell of the reading out of that. What's wrong with fifty shares of that. What do you mean. "Speak up." Would you have it. I want to hide and seek. What did you here hear that. Because I heard that. Howard said that he's going to blow his brains out next Tuesday. What are you talking about. Did ya he said you hear him. Howard said that he's going to kill himself next Tuesday. What do you mean Howard just going to kill himself next Tuesday. He supposed to do the hand writing that I'm going to shoot myself. That's right he said I'm going to shoot myself. What the hell was going on. I Don't know that he's just going to kill himself to blow his brains out. What's The Fuck Going On Howard. What's the fuck doing going on Howard Betel. I Can't here you. Turn his feets away please. About tall is he let me touch it. Ten seconds free tune. What The Hell You Doing If You Flipped Or What. We'll better get him off. "Get Him Off." What a fuckin thing. Get Your Fuckin Fuckin Towel Off Your Face Faded Full That You're Going

Joseph Kosuth
from Purloined: A Novel

Begun in 1966 and completed in 2000, *Purloined: A Novel* (Cologne: Salon Verlag, 2000) is composed entirely of single pages from more than a hundred different novels of various genres to form a single work. Each page is photocopied directly from its original source, thus resulting in a variety of typefaces and layouts. The only new additions to the book are new page numbers corresponding to the printed edition. *A Rearranged Affair,* by Sally Alatalo (writing as Anita M-28), offers an obvious intertext. Published in an edition of 188 copies (the average number of pages in a Harlequin romance), each book in the Alatalo's series is interpolated from different romance paperbacks and recollated so that the pagination retains its proper sequence. Although the narration obviously jars from page to page, the for-mulaic trajectory of the genre is retained. One might also compare Joseph Kosuth's work at the level of the page to Doug Houston's work at the level of the sentence; Houston's book *Vast: An Unoriginal Novel* (published under the pseudonym Moore Lande [Chicago: Sara Ranchouse, 1994]) is composed entirely of sentences—all 957 of them conscientiously footnoted—from westerns, aggregated into microthematic constellations. For example: "A coyote howled on the southwest rim of the Cap-rock, and he thought he heard a bobcat scream up near the head of the canyon. Coyote yapping was so faint and far away that the high-pitched protests became lost in the shifting wind currents. Once a coyote howled dismally from the edge of the mesa." Unabashedly appropriated, Kosuth directly applied precepts common during the 1960s heyday of conceptual art to writing, thus setting a precedent for concep-tual writing strategies—such as Houston's—nearly forty years later.

I

Some killers are born. Some killers are made. And sometimes the origin of desire for homicide is lost in the tangle of roots that make an ugly childhood and a dangerous youth, so that no one may ever know if the urge was inbred or induced.

He lifts the body from the back of the Blazer like a roll of old carpet to be discarded. The soles of his boots scuff against the blacktop of the parking area, then fall nearly silent on the dead grass and hard ground. The night is balmy for November in Minneapolis. A swirling wind tosses fallen leaves. The bare branches of the trees rattle together like bags of bones.

He knows he falls into the last category of killers. He has spent many hours, days, months, years studying his compulsion and its point of origin. He knows what he is, and he embraces that truth. He has never known guilt or remorse. He believes conscience, rules, laws, serve the individual no practical purpose, and only limit human possibilities.

'Man enters into the ethical world through fear and not through love.' – Paul Ricoeur, Symbolism of Evil.

His True Self adheres only to his own code: domination, manipulation, control.

A broken shard of moon glares down on the scene, its light faint beneath the web of limbs. He arranges the body to his satisfaction and traces two intersecting Xs over the left upper chest. With a sense of ceremony, he pours the accelerant. Anointing the dead. Symbolism of evil. His

1.

pigs. Under other circumstances, a tragic scene. But not now.

He raced up the stairs to the kitchen. His thought now: *Get out of here.*

He would run to the barn and into the fields beyond. He simply would disappear while the shooting was going on. They would find him later. He would convince them: he had nothing to do with it.

But he was halfway through the kitchen when the first blast came, even louder than the one Lamar had fired last night. It was like being inside a kettledrum.

He dropped instantly, his face on the floor.

Boom! Boom! Boom!

It would not stop. The noise level just rose and rose and rose. He had no idea guns were so loud! He lay there on the floor and began to cry.

Please don't let me be hurt.

He tried to free himself from Ted and looked for targets. But smoke and dust hung in the air, illuminated by the sun. He blinked. Nothing made a lot of sense. Shotguns, two shotguns, that much he knew.

He thought he saw movement at a corner of the house and fired two-handed this time, fast, two shots, and when he rose to run to the car, a blast took his legs out from under him and blew him down. The gun skittered away. He couldn't see the gun. He tried to crawl.

"DON'T LEAVE ME, PLEASE," Ted yelled, grabbing at his ankle.

He crawled a bit further, until he looked up at Lamar Pye, standing over him.

"Well, howdy, Dad," said Lamar.

"Oh, Christ," said Bud.

2.

We came out of the stairs into a small room littered with sawhorses, planks of wood, buckets of rivets and bits of metal and wiring. Wide windows gave a full view of the horizon in every direction—the city behind us, the river and the partially completed towers of the bridge before us. A doorway led out onto the walkway that ran around the tower. Near the doorway stood a slit-eyed, bearded sergeant of detectives named Patrick Connor, whom I recognized from my visits to Police Headquarters on Mulberry Street. Next to him, looking out over the river with his hands clasped behind his back, rocking on the balls of his feet, was a much more familiar figure: Theodore.

"Sergeant Flynn," Roosevelt said without turning. "It's ghastly work that has prompted our call, I'm afraid. Ghastly."

My discomfort suddenly heightened when Theodore spun to face us. There was nothing unusual in his appearance: an expensive, slightly dandy checked suit of the kind that he fancied in those days; the spectacles that were, like the eyes behind them, too small for his tough, square head; the broad mustache bristling below the wide nose. Yet his visage was excessively odd, nonetheless. Then it occurred to me: his teeth. His numerous, usually snapping teeth—they were nowhere in sight. His jaws were clamped shut in what seemed passionate anger, or remorse. Something had shaken Roosevelt badly.

His dismay seemed to grow when he saw me. "What—Moore! What in thunder are you doing here?"

"I'm glad to see you, too, Roosevelt," I managed through my nervousness, extending a hand.

He accepted it, though for once he didn't loosen my arm from its socket. "What—oh, I am sorry, Moore. I—delighted to see you, of course, delighted. But who told you—?"

"Told me what? I was abducted and brought here by Kreizler's boy. On his orders, without so much as a word of explanation."

"Kreizler!" Theodore murmured in soft urgency, glancing

3.

straight. You want me to get to know this Wenzler guy, then get him to trust me so I find out if he's a spy?"

"And then you find out all you can, Easy. We let you pay your taxes and go back home."

"And what if I don't find out somethin' that you could use? What if it's just that he complains a lot but he don't do nuthin' really?"

"You just report to me. Say once a week. I'll know how to read it. And when you're through the IRS will let you alone."

"All that sounds good, but I need to know somethin' first."

"What's that?"

"Well, you talkin' 'bout my own people with this conspiracy stuff. An' if you want my opinion, all that is just some mistake. You know I live down there an' I ain't never heard that we some kinda communist conspiracy or whatever."

Craxton just smiled.

"But if you wanna believe that," I continued, "I guess you can. But you cain't get me t' go after my own people. I mean, if these guys broke the law like you say, I don't mind that, but I don't wanna hurt the people at First African just 'cause they run a charity drive or somethin'."

"We see eye to eye, Easy," Craxton said. "I just want the Jew, and whatever it is he's up to. You won't even know I was there."

"So what's this stuff about this other guy, Lavender?"

"You remember him?"

"No."

"We need to find Lavender. He's worked closer with Wenzler than anyone. If we could get him into custody I'm sure that he'd be able to help."

"You sound like he's missin'?"

"He quit Champion three weeks ago, and nobody has seen him since. We'd appreciate a line on him,

4.

thought to thought, remaining long enough to create anxiety, never long enough to offer resolution.

I thought of Alex. Thought about calling him. I could wish him a Happy Christmas. Good excuse to hear his voice again. I could tell him—

Exactly what?

That I hurt, and I wanted him to hold me? That nothing had changed since I'd seen him last except I'd killed a few more people, and how was the weather in Savannah?

I shifted my right arm until the sling was taut and the bandages tugged at the edge of the wound. The pain was effective distraction.

My attention shifted to Winthrup Manor. I thought about what we'd encountered there, about the men who were now dead. Wondered what Hugh had gotten himself involved with. Unlikely that the men we'd killed were cronies of Hugh's. Or merely thugs. They were too well armed, too well organized. Too professional. It was almost too bad that John had killed the last of them. Mac might have pried some interesting information from him.

That thought took me to the moments before I lost consciousness. Delirious, I thought. I had been pain-wracked and delirious when I'd claimed that Hugh murdered my parents. They'd died long before he was born. Undoubtedly, Mac would hear of my accusation during the debriefing sessions. He would dismiss it just as I had.

5.

Chapter 2

THE MINNEAPOLIS CITY HALL is a rude pile of liverish stone, damp in the summer, cold in the winter, ass-deep in cops, crooks, politicians, bureaucrats, favor-seekers, reporters, TV personalities and outraged taxpayers, none of whom were allowed to smoke inside the building.

The trail of illegal cigarette smoke followed Rose Marie Roux down the darkened marble halls from the chief's office to Homicide. The chief was a large woman, getting larger, her face going hound-dog with the pressure of the job and the passing of the years. She stopped outside Homicide, took a drag on the cigarette, and blew smoke.

She could see Davenport inside, standing, hands in his pockets. He was wearing a blue wool suit, a white shirt with a long soft collar and what looked like an Hermès necktie – one of the anal numbers with eight million little horses prancing around. A political appointee, a deputy chief, his sideline software business made him worth, according to the latest rumors, maybe ten million dollars. He was talking to Sloan and Sherrill.

Sloan was thin, pasty-faced, serious, dressed all in brown and tan – he could lean against a wall and disappear.

6.

His words were slow and steady like the beat of a metronome, "All possible scenarios, Kay. We have to consider them."

"Of course we do. And that's fine as long as Marino considers *all* possible scenarios and doesn't wear blinders because he's getting obsessed or has a problem."

Wesley glanced toward the open door. Almost inaudibly, he said, "Pete's got his prejudices. I won't deny that."

"I think you'd better tell me exactly what they are."

"Let it suffice to say that when the Bureau decided he was a good candidate for a VICAP team, we did some checking into his background. I know where he grew up, how he grew up. Some things you never get over. They set you off. It happens."

He wasn't telling me anything I hadn't already figured out. Marino grew up poor on the wrong side of the tracks. He was uncomfortable around the sort of people who had always made him uncomfortable. The cheerleaders and homecoming queens never gave him a second glance because he was a social misfit, because his father had dirt under his nails, because he was "common."

I'd heard these cop sob stories a thousand times before. The guy's only advantage in life is he's big and white, so he makes himself bigger and whiter by carrying a gun and a badge.

"We don't get to excuse ourselves, Benton," I said shortly. "We don't excuse criminals because they had screwed-up childhoods. We don't get to use the powers entrusted to us to punish people who remind us of our own screwed-up childhoods."

I wasn't lacking in compassion. I understood exactly where Marino was coming from. I was no stranger to his anger. I'd felt it many times when facing a defendant in court. No matter how convincing the evidence, if the guy's nice-looking, clean-cut and dressed in a two-hundred-dollar suit, twelve working men and women don't, in their hearts, believe he's guilty.

I could believe just about anything of anybody these days. But only if the evidence was there. Was Marino looking at the evidence? Was he even looking at all?

Wesley pushed back his chair and stood up to stretch. "Pete has his spells. You get used to it. I've known him for years."

7.

Leevi Lehto
from Päivä

The Finnish writer and translator Leevi Lehto works with information management, often using media and Internet feeds as his sources. His book *Päivä* (*Day*) is a meticulous reorganization of the entire Finnish News Agency media feed from August 20, 2003. Lehto's description of his process is as follows:

- take all the news releases of the Finnish News Agency of Aug. 20, 2003
- sort alphabetically by sentence
- divide into chapters per first letter of sentence: "A", "B" . . .
- divide into paragraphs per second letter of sentence (a sentence starting "Kenny" after one starting "Kabooze" would trigger a paragraph break
- locate all the statements ("'Blah blah blah', the CEO says.") and treat them as parts of dialogue.

Let me add that with the "A" chapter first, the book begins, adequately, with the word "Aamu" ("morning") ("begins in dark," as Charles Bernstein says in his blurb). There are lots of these kinds of happy coincidences all along; thus, on page 173 (of 234), you'll find the sentence: "The author tells that two thirds of the book is now finished."

He added that the stability of the public economy will be carefully maintained at the same time. He admits that putting his soul to the life of the male couple was a challenge in many ways. He baptized the budget as one of work, stability, and confidence. He beat Green easily every time last year, and only very narrowly lost to Tim Montgomery in his WR run. He borrowed his own agony to the protagonist in the novel. He broke through the defence lines, but the low shot failed to have power to it, and Sörensen easily caught the ball. He cleared 232 and had one very good go at 237. He cleared 478 in US Championship Games, and held the Indoors World

Record for a short time. He could do no more than 186 in the Swedish Championship Games, and 195 in the DN Gala in Stockholm. He died, possibly in a children's disease, the day before the Christmas Eve, as his brother had done ten years earlier. He directed, however, part of his criticism toward the occupation administration led by the United States. He does not want to be a pessimist regarding the passive adult population, either. He does not want to reveal the exact plans at this stage, but confirms the company has started building a chain of special stores. He easily cleared two World Championships, won once at the Olympic Games, and also held the World Record. He emphasized that the customers' savings, loans, or personal information data were not in jeopardy at any stage. He emphasizes that the entire cabinet has now during the budget negotiations committed itself both to lowering of the income taxes and to restrictive public spending. He emphasizes that the entire cabinet has now committed itself both to lowering of the income taxes and to restrictive public spending.

Tan Lin
from BIB

The New York writer Tan Lin is involved in oblique reading and writing strategies. Most notable is his idea of ambient poetics, which treats language akin to ambient music, "an atmosphere, a tint . . . designed to induce calm and space to think," as Brian Eno claims (*Ambient 1: Music for Airports* liner notes [Editions EG, EGS201, 1978]).

Lin's ongoing project BIB (short for bibliography) is a meticulous record of everything Lin reads: what, when, and where. From e-mail to theory, he excludes nothing. Lin's project is autobiographical: if we are an accumulation of all the knowledge we've ingested, digested, and transformed on our own, then Lin's piece is particularly revealing. We are, in fact, what we read. One might, accordingly, compare his project to Kenneth Goldsmith's *No. 111* (Great Barrington, Mass.: The Figures, 1997) and Bernadette Mayer's *Eruditio ex Memoria* (New York: Angel Hair, 1977).

BIB is also a way of marking time, both subjectively and objectively. As the piece progresses, political events unfold via headlines that Lin has read, and long-forgotten trends are duly noted for the record. The joy of voyeurism mixes with a use of incredibly rich found language, all bolstered by a bodily sense of presence and place. Lin's work makes a compelling case that a simple list can, in fact, divulge as many intimacies as more conventional literary narratives can without ever once using the subject *I*.

Wednesday, February 8, 2006
10:27-9 DINING ROOM TABLE "Kenneth Goldsmith's The Weather" Marjorie Perloff
10:30 LIVING ROOM COUCH NYORKER "Cookbooks and Nora Ephron" 5 pages
9:13-19 PM SUBWAY NY Times "Some Democrats Are Sensing Missed Opportunities"
5:28-39 Adorno Minima Moralia. Dedication Marcel Proust Memento 5 pages

Thursday, February 9, 2006

3:50-59 HOME OFFICE Etrade.com MOGN 30 day moving average chart; Buy/Sell

4:00-06 Zizek The Metastases of Enjoyment "The Pure Surface of the Sense Event" ****

5:50-2 PATH TRAIN "As Teflon Troubles Pile up, Du Pont Responds with Ads"

6:24-31 LIGHT RAIL 5 student quizzes; Little Brown Handbook Answer Key. exercises 13-1, 13-2

9:07-13 PATH TRAIN pm NY Times "Low Fat Diet Does Not Cut Health Risks, Study Finds"

9:14-15 Chinese Editor Dies After Beating by the Police"

9:16 Nebraska Man Sentence for Having Sex With Girl, 13

11:50 HOME OFFICE NY Times "Mallory Kean paid obit" "Smell in Stereo" (rats)

11:54-5 Rock Review Jenny Lewis

11:54 Mallory obit

11:55 Acquisition.com Jenny Lewis

11:55-8 Last Chance "Superficial Engagement" A Vivid Potpourri with Carnage at its Core" (Hirschorn)

11:59-12 "Time Warner Agrees to Sell Book Unit"

12:01 "WiFi Heads Up"

12:02 Time Warner Agrees

12:06-9 "At Bronx Zoo, an Elephant Exhibit's End Plays Out in Elephant Time"

12:03-5 Chinese Editor Dies

12:10-11 Elephant Exhibit

12:23-25 Strandbooks.com "Zizek" "Virilio" "Baudrilliard"

12:42 Yahoofinance.com Micron Headlines

Friday, February 10, 2006

8:03-55 HOME OFFICE Zizek Metastases 9 pages

8:56-9:07 "Slavoj Zizek: Risking the Impossible" Glyn Daly 15 pages

9:08-27 Google.com "pulp fiction" Wikipedia "Pulp Fiction"

9:27-29 half.com "adam phillips" "zizek"

9:29-32 amazon.com "zizek"

9:33 Yahoofinance.com "My Portfolio: Chart"

9:45 etrade" mogn"

11:13-15 LIVING ROOM SOFA "Encyclopedic Novelties: Kenneth
    Goldsmith's Tomes" (skimmed) **
1:20-4 J. Drucker "Un Visual and Conceptual" (skim) *
1:24-33 BlipSoak01 read 23 pages
1:34 D. Werschler Henry The Tapeworm Factory read 1 page ***
1:35 Craig Dworkin "Zero Kerning" 2 pages

Saturday, February 11, 2006
9:22-4 LIVING ROOM SOFA Dworkin "Zero" 3 pages
9:45-51 Walter Benjamin "The Collector" from the Arcades Project 4
    pages ****
9:51-3 Dworkin "Zero" 1 page
9:53-10:07 Benjamin 2 pages
11:33-12:02 Benjamin 2 pages
12:04-23 McGann, Black Riders. 4 pages (Bob Brown) ***
12:26-49 Brian Kim Stefans The Window to be Ordered
7:30-8 HOME OFFICE Dworkin 2 pages ***
7:38-44 ubuweb.com
12:35-40 Darren Werschler Henry "Uncreative is the New Creative" 4
    pages
12:40-1:20 "Opaqueness is a Calendar in a Fairy Tale"
1:21-28 Adorno Minima Moralia 3 pages "Picture Book w/o Pictures"
    "Inention and Reproduction"

Sunday, February 12, 2006
1:04-12 LIVING ROOM COUCH NYT "White House Knew of Levee's
    Failure on Night of Storm"
1:12-13 "Un Reversakm Ex-Fema Chief Will Answer Storm Questions"
1:13-16 "Official Resigns Public TV Post"
1:16-17 "E Mail Notes Say Lobbyist Met President Many Times"
1:17-19 "President of Getty Trust Resigns Under Pressure"
1:20 Film Review "A Weathered Rocker But Still Unbowed"
1:21-2 Film Review "The Bumbling Inspector Looks Different These
    Days"
1:22-3 "Weathered Rocker"
1:24 The Listings "St Etienne"
1:28-9 "Housekeeper to Stars Adnuts Steakung Frin Her Least Favirites"
1:31-3 "4 Operations and 11 Days Can't Stop the Deadly Work of 3
    Bullets"

1:33-5 "Shot in Case of Mistaken Identity, Officer Dies after 11 day
    Ordeal"
1:36-38 "Jury to Decide if Flying Sizzling Shrimp Led to Man's Death"
4:12-15 "Matchmaker Pairs Computer and Stereo"
4:16 Circuits "Music Station Taps Wires in Your Walls to Pipe Sound
4:17 "A Keyboard and Mouse Set Made to Match the Mac Mini"
4:27-8 "Officer's Uniform Waits in Station House for Last Sad Duty"
4:28-9 "Benihana Wins Flying Sizzling Shrimp Case"
4:32 "Big British Supermarket Chain will Open Small Stores in Us"
4:32 "Demand Strong as 30 Year Bond Makes a Comeback"
4:32-5 "Republican Speaks Up, Leading Others to Challenge Wiretaps"
4:35 "Ex Fema Leader Faults Response by White House"
4:39-40 "Danish Cartoon Editor on Indefinite Leave"
6:12-25 HOME OFFICE Adorno Notes To Literature volume 1, "Proust"
    5 pages
6:45-7 Adorno Minima "Dedication" "Where the Stork Brings Babies
    From"
7:23-37 Daniel Nettle Happiness 20 pages
9:44-49 Wershler Henry "Uncreative is the New Creative" 3 pages
9:50-10:01 NYTimes Your Money "Waiting for Just the Right Moment to
    Take Out the Wallet"
10:02-10 Nextag.com LCD tv
10:12-19 Fredric Jameson "Surrealism without the Unconscious"
    Postmodernism: The Cultural Logic of Late Capitalism 4 pages (tv is
    about misdirection and lies and what we "are not thinking about")
12:10-21 Jameson "Surrealism" 7 pages

Monday, February 13, 2006
11:20-1 LIVING ROOM COUCH "A Restaurant With Buzz Also Has a
    Conflict with its Landlord"
1:40-55 "Kwan Withdraws; Hughes is Called In to Take Her Place"
1:56-9 "NBC Loses its Star, but Help is Coming"
1:59-2:03 "Teenagers Life is Interrupted for Turin? No Way!"
2:20-5 "The Us Ski Team Has a Bridge for Sale"
2:26-32 "With White's Triumph in the Halfpipe, Snowboarding Finally
    Gains an Icon"
2:36-8 "A Stumble and a Lost Opportunity for Ohno to Defend his Gold
    Medal"
2:39-45 "An Unheralded Frenchman Finds the Course Fits His Style"

2:45-55 "Hey, Whose Grandpa Didn't Tell Some Tales?"

2:55 "Never Mind the Solitaire, Explain what the IX is for?"

2:56 NYTimes.com

2:56 "JP Donleavy Approaches 80, Anything but Gingerly"

3:24 "With Plenty of Warning Millions Mobilize"

3:35 "On Podium, Some Say Mrs. Clinton is No Mr. Clinton"

3:36 "A Year After a Teenager was Dismembered, Still No Answer"

6:14-15 HOME OFFICE "Conservatives Unsettled about Movements Future"

6:15 "The Man Who Keeps Babar's Young Subjects Loyal"

6:49 "So Many Models in Bikinis, So Many Ways to See them"

6:50-2 "It's Like Lending to a Friend, Except You'll Get Interest"

7-02 "JP Donleavy"

7:07-10 Books of the Times "The Dark Corner of Dilbert's Cubicle" (Company by Max Berry)"

7:25-36 "A Record Snow: 26.9 Inches Fall in New York City"

Dana Teen Lomax
from Disclosure

Under the regime of the modern bureaucratic police state, identity is less an essence than a manner of presentation; it is not so much self-fashioning as self-documenting. Governments care less about authentic identity, in any philosophical or psychological sense, than about the fact that one's papers are in order. Dana Teen Lomax here offers up such documentation in the most radically confessional work of poetry ever published: itemized bank statements, life insurance policy information, a parking ticket and subsequent delinquency notice, collections agency notifications, elementary school report cards, California twin registry information, a Peace Corps placement letter, dental records, Pap smear results, blood tests, a certification of completion from a birthing class, certificates of merit and literary awards, rejected and accepted grant proposals, a RateMyProfessor scorecard, rental agreements, pay stubs, Googled images, identity theft registration, and so on. The complete manuscript is eighty-one pages long, a count that correlates to the statistical average life expectancy of a white woman in the United States today.

Identity, we learn in *Disclosure,* is always nostalgic. Thus, the documents Lomax produces here freeze a moment in time—when Lomax weighed 145 pounds, or was in sixth-period study hall, or was placing fourth in the Junior Golf Program, or was delinquent on her bill payments. However, although those papers remain a fixed part of her permanent record, she will continue to change; she is unstable, mutable, unpredictable. The sequence challenges the reader to resist inventing and imposing a narrative to connect the discrete atomic facts of each document. The work is thus also a mirror into the reader's subjectivity, trading the intimate details of Lomax's life in exchange for disclosures about the reader's most reflexive prejudices and presuppositions. As Trinh T. Minh-ha said, in an interview that inspired Lomax: "To call attention to the subjectivity at work and to show the activity of production in the production is to deal with film in its most natural, realistic and truthful aspect." Here, the resonance continues between the ostensible objectivity of the information in factual records and the exposed prejudices and social ideologies of those records' generation. Facts themselves are socioeconomic beings, and every document in *Disclosure* is in collusion.

HUENEME SCHOOL DISTRICT
Hollywood Beach School

PUPIL PROGRESS REPORT

Dear Parents:

This report is to help keep you informed on the progress of _Dana_
If you desire more information prior to the scheduled conferencing period in
_____ , please feel free to request a conference.

READING - Green Light Go - Dana is having no
serious reading problems at this time.
She is becoming a good oral reader.
Her attitudes toward reading are positive
and she enjoys doing the follow-up
work. I am happy to have her in
my class.

MATH -
Dana has completed her level (2) math book
as well as an Individualized Math kit for
second grade. She is working now at a
third grade level with good success.
Dana is a good math student, she does well.

OTHER -
Language and Spelling are very good.
Dana has written some very interesting stories.
She remembers good punctuation and her written
assignments are always neatly done.
Dana is a cooperative and helpful child.

ATTENDANCE -
____12____ days absent to date, ____0____ of these are unexcused.

Teacher _Sally Snull_
Date _April 11, 1975_

1/74

Dana Teen Lomax 347

Google images   "dana teen lomax"   Search images   Advanced Image Search
SafeSearch: Moderate ▼

Images ⊞ Show options...   1 Minute to Search (free summary) Locate Dana Lomax.

Dana Lomax Info
Public-records-now.com

Results 1 - 21 of about 323 (0.09 seconds)

Sponsored Link

Dana Teen Lomax
380 x 398 x 24k - jpg
kickingwind.com

Dana Teen Lomax, June 26,
2009
480 x 250 - 21k
concisedelight.wordpress.com

Dana Teen Lomax
380 x 313 - 47k - jpg
kickingwind.com

Jill Magi Dana Teen Lomax
788 x 1024 - 852k - jpg
claytonbanes.blogspot.com

Dana Teen Lomax
332 x 397 - 54k - jpg
lettersttopoets.org

Dana Teen Lomax << Sarah
891 x 897 - 93k - gif
epc.buffalo.edu

Dana Teen Lomax
150 x 161 - 8k - jpg
jacketmagazine.com

Dana Teen Lomax and
320 x 240 - 16k
xpoetics.blogspot.com

Jennifer Firestone Dana Teen
206 x 265 - 23k - png
docatloc.com

Dana Teen Lomax
199 x 165 - 59k - jpg
performingartsworkshop.org

by Dana Teen Lomax &
Dana
300 x 226 - 7k - gif
claytonbanes.blogspot.com

Director Dana Teen Lomax
320 x 240 - 16k - jpg
smalljonasstraffic.blogspot.com

by Dana Teen Lomax
230 x 320 - 10k - jpg
thehomevideoreviewofbooks.blo...

Dana Teen Lomax and
320 x 240 - 16k
xpoetics.blogspot.com

Dana Teen Lomax's work
130 x 200 - 9k - jpg
patmpress.org

by Dana Teen Lomax for the
230 x 227 - 13k - jpg
juliabicook.weebly.com

with Ben Lerner, Dana Teen
203 x 305 - 115k - jpg
claytonbanes.blogspot.com

Firestone, Dana Teen Lomax
357 x 142 - 15k - jpg
sfsu.edu

Photo taken by Dana Teen
320 x 240 - 15k - jpg
xpoetics.blogspot.com

to SF!: Dana Teen Lomax
320 x 240 - 10k - jpg
xpoetics.blogspot.com

Jennifer Firestone Dana Teen
100 x 100 - 5k - png
docatloc.com

Goooooooooogle ▶
1 2 3 4 5 6 7 8 9 10   Next

"dana teen lomax"   Search images

Google Images Home - Help

Google Home - Advertising Programs - Business Solutions - Privacy - About Google

11-4-98

DĀNA,

You were remembered in PRAYER today by the Women's Fellowship of Country Roads Adult Village.

Requested by *Anne from HP storage*
& Betty Lods

healing from Lupus, marraige,
children, feeling of unworthiness

Betty Lodd
Ethel Bradford
Ben Wohlheter
Muriel Komath
Joan Vildermuth
June Knodel
Elly Mackey
Dorie Stanton
Joan Anderson
Alice Rain
Rose Wilson
Naomi Muek
Dorothy Coverdell
Betty J. Williams
Belle McFadden

Nancy Allen
Shirley Nichols
Jean Hermeltout
Dorothy Marcos
Kathy McMullin
Shirley Nichols
~~Alice Rain~~

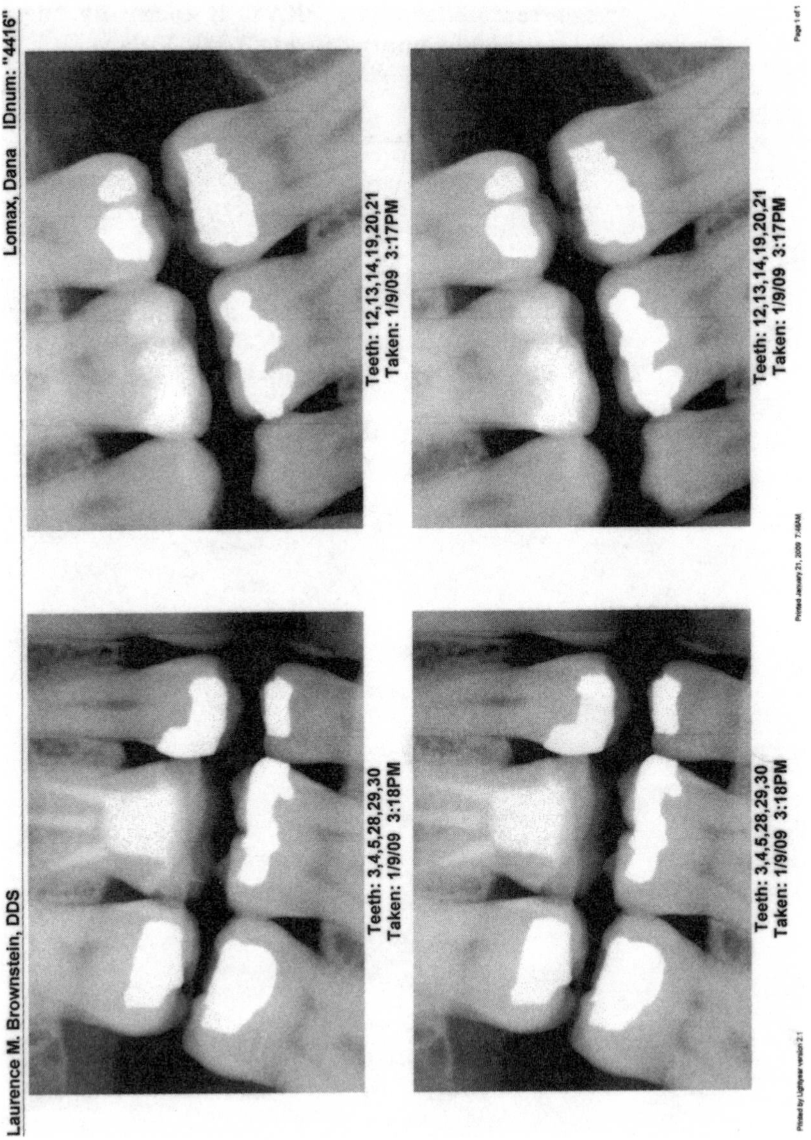
Laurence M. Brownstein, DDS
Lomax, Dana IDnum: "4416"
Teeth: 3,4,5,28,29,30
Taken: 1/9/09 3:18PM
Teeth: 12,13,14,19,20,21
Taken: 1/9/09 3:17PM
Teeth: 3,4,5,28,29,30
Taken: 1/9/09 3:18PM
Teeth: 12,13,14,19,20,21
Taken: 1/9/09 3:17PM

Wells Fargo Business Online®

Account Activity

Personal Accounts

LINE OF CREDIT XXX-XXX

Payment Details

Total Payment Due on 09/01/08	$119.34
Payment Due	$94.34
Fees	$25.00

The total payment due shown does not reflect payment protection insurance if applicable. For questions or additional assistance, please contact us at 1-866-820-9199.

Activity Summary

Credit Line	$5,000.00
Beginning Available Credit	$88.91
Current Available Credit	$88.91
Total Credit In Use	$4,911.09
View Online Statements	

Transactions - All Activity

Show [All Activity ⬍] (View)

Date ▽	Description	Amount
08/01/08	ANNUAL FEE	$25.00
08/01/08	PRINCIPAL PAYMENT	+$41.10
08/01/08	INTEREST PAYMENT	+$50.25
07/01/08	PRINCIPAL PAYMENT	+$40.77
07/01/08	INTEREST PAYMENT	+$48.52
06/27/08	REQUESTED ADVANCE	$80.00
06/01/08	PRINCIPAL PAYMENT	+$41.11
06/01/08	INTEREST PAYMENT	+$50.99
05/01/08	PRINCIPAL PAYMENT	+$41.08
05/01/08	INTEREST PAYMENT	+$50.07
04/21/08	REQUESTED ADVANCE	$45.00
04/01/08	PRINCIPAL PAYMENT	+$41.09
04/01/08	INTEREST PAYMENT	+$54.73
03/20/08	REQUESTED ADVANCE	$40.00
03/01/08	PRINCIPAL PAYMENT	+$41.43
03/01/08	INTEREST PAYMENT	+$53.56
02/01/08	PRINCIPAL PAYMENT	+$107.33
02/01/08	INTEREST PAYMENT	+$61.17
02/01/08	OTHER CHARGE PAYMENT	+$35.00
01/18/08	OTHER CHARGE ASSESSMENT	$35.00
01/04/08	REQUESTED ADVANCE	$41.13
01/01/08	PRINCIPAL PAYMENT	+$41.13
01/01/08	INTEREST PAYMENT	+$61.09
12/31/07	REQUESTED ADVANCE	$100.00
12/21/07	REQUESTED ADVANCE	$44.35
12/01/07	PRINCIPAL PAYMENT	+$41.47
12/01/07	INTEREST PAYMENT	+$59.38
11/06/07	REQUESTED ADVANCE	$120.00
11/01/07	PRINCIPAL PAYMENT	+$40.81
11/01/07	INTEREST PAYMENT	+$62.05
10/01/07	PRINCIPAL PAYMENT	+$41.16
10/01/07	INTEREST PAYMENT	+$62.28
09/01/07	PRINCIPAL PAYMENT	+$40.91
09/01/07	INTEREST PAYMENT	+$63.94
09/01/07	ANNUAL FEE PAYMENT	+$25.00
08/23/07	REQUESTED ADVANCE	$70.33

Trisha Low
Confessions

Trisha Low, raised Catholic, attended five consecutive confessions with priests and surreptitiously recorded each one. When finished, she returned home and transcribed the conversations without editing. By replacing proper names—her own and the priests'—with numbers, she objectifies what is an intensely private and personal exchange. Low mechanically tells each priest the identical story, mimicking the script set forth in the formal structure of the confession. Within this constraint, a surprising number of variables occur, and each encounter highlights the priest's individual religious and emotive responses. A structuralist exercise, Low's work fuses opposites—the broadly political and the singularly personal, the emotional and the categorical, the objective and subjective—into an explosive work of constraint-based writing.

1: Good morning, father.

2: Mm.

1: Um, bless me father for I have sinned—

2: What?

1: Forgive me father for I have sinned, it's been—two weeks? Um—Since my last confession.

2: Mm.

1: I lied in my last confession, I have dishonoured my mother and father, um—I have taken the Lord's name in vain? I have um—hurt people that I care about. Um. I've had sex—with a man who was not my husband. And he slapped me around, kind of? And I don't know, that's a sin, isn't it?

2: Who slapped you?

1: This boy. And I didn't mind it um, I mean I liked it. Um.

2: You feel guilty about that?

1: Yes, father.

2: Why?

1: Because—when I was younger I was taught that my body is a temple of God? And, um—sins of the flesh defile it? I mean, I'm correct in thinking so?

2: Did he hit you hard?

1: Well, just—I mean, he slapped me around a little bit. I mean, I wanted it.

2: (silence)

1: I'll try not to see him?

2: Was, uh—was he someone you had been with before?

1: Yeah. But he's not like my boyfriend or anything like tha—

2: Ah—It sounds—It sounds a little bit casual, ah—sleeping with this boy. And ah—the physical beating part the uh—uh—The physical part, uh—it might be some psychological quirk. Ah—uh—ah—Well, you've got to stop having sex. It's ah—ah—harmful for—ah—your peace and your friendship with God. Um. Say, for your penance, say the Lord's Prayer, and the Hail Mary once each? And make an act of contrition now. You're single, right?

1: Uh, yes, yeah, I am.

1: Almighty and most merciful father, we have—erred and strayed from your ways like lost sheep, we have—followed too much the devices and des—

2: Mm, I didn't hear you, what did you say? Ah—say it again.

1: I said uh—Oh God, have mercy on me, your daughter, a sinner. Amen.

2: May God the father of mercy who through the resurrection of our Lord Jesus, reconciled the world unto himself and put the son upon the cross for the forgiveness of sins, through the ministry of the Church. May God give you pardon and peace and absolve you from your sins. In the name of the Father, and the Son and the Holy Spirit, Amen

1: Amen

2: Go in peace to love and serve the Lord, in the name of Christ.

1: Amen.

1: Bye.

2: Mm.

3: Good afternoon.

1: Good afternoon, father.

3: In the name of the Father, the Son and the Holy Spirit, Amen.

1: Forgive me father for I have sinned, it has been two weeks since my last confession? Um—I have lied, I have—taken the Lord's name in vain, um—I have dishonoured my father and mother. Um—I have hurt people whom I care about? Um, er—I have had sex with a man who was not my husband.

3: Pardon?

1: Uh—I have had sex with a man who was not my husband? And um. He hit me and I uh—enjoyed it. And uh, wanted it. Um—and—I feel guilty for all these things?

3: Okay. Now thank God for all the blessings he has given to you.

1: Of course.

3: Uh, Obey your mother. And, I mean—Because, you know, she's—looking out for your welfare. Be careful with regard to using your female sex, until you get married, because many things can happen and uh—it cheapens you a wee bit so ask God's mercy in the time of temptation, okay?

1: Yes, father.

3: I mean, do the best you can, and say a prayer and ask God's help so that you may remain faithful. And for your penance, well I say, fifteen Our Fathers, and Hail Marys and tomorrow at mass, say five Our Fathers and five Hail Marys. Okay?

1: Yes, father.

3: Okay? Now make a good act of contrition. Oh, my God—

1: Um—Almighty and most merciful Father—

3: You know it?

1: No, I uh, learnt a different one, from an Anglo-Catholic—

3: Well say it with me—Oh my God, I am heartily sorry—

1: Oh my God, I am heartily sorry—

3: For having offended you.

1: For having offended you.

3: I firmly resolve—

1: I firmly resolve—

3: With the help of thy grace—

1: With the help of thy grace—

3: To do penance—

1: To do penance—

3: And to mend my life.

1: And to mend my life.

3: Amen

1: Amen

3: Now to mend my life means to change—you know, what you've been doing, and to remain faithful to God. All right?

1: Yes, father.

3: God, the father of mercy in death and resurrection, who has reconciled the world to himself, sent his holy son for the forgiveness of sins and peace and to absolve you of your sins. In the name of the Father, the Son and the Holy Spirit, Amen.

1: Amen

3: Go in peace, and in good care

1: Amen

3: Okay.

4: In the name of the Father, the Son and the Holy Spirit, Amen.

1: Oh—Amen.

4: Yes?

1: Bless me father for I have sinned, it has been two weeks—uh—two weeks since my last confession.

4: (silence)

1: Um, I have uh—lied during confession, I have—taken the Lord's name in vain, I have—dishonoured my mother and father. Uh.

4: Yes?

1: I have hurt others whom I care about. I have had uh—violent—uh, sexual intercourse with a man I am not married to.

4: (silence)

1: Uh. That's all?

4: Yeah. Ten Hail Marys, and ten Our Fathers. Mm, God the Father of mercies, through the death and resurrection of his Son, has reconciled the world to himself and sent the Holy Spirit among us for the forgiveness of sins. Through the ministry of the Church may God give you pardon and peace and I absolve you from your sins in the name of the Father, and of the Son, and of the Holy Spirit. Amen.

1: Amen.

4: Go in peace to love and serve the Lord.

1: In the name of Christ, Amen.

1: Have a good day, father.

4: You as well.

1: Hello, father, how are you?

5: Fine, fine, sit down.

5: So why don't you tell me a little bit about yourself. Where are you from? Are you a student here, or—?

1: Yeah, yeah, I'm a student here—

5: Are you at Penn or are you at Drexel?

1: I'm at Penn, and uh—I'm from London—originally.

5: Uhuh, uhuh, and?

1: Um, I've been Catholic for a long time?

5: Oh! Oh, so you, uh, weren't born Catholic, but you became Catholic, or—?

1: Oh, no, I was brought up Catholic, I mean, my mom—

5: Oh, okay. So, do you have any brothers or sisters?

1: Yeah, I have a younger sister still in London, hoping to come here, and yeah.

5: Oh, okay. So when you started here, at Penn, is that the first time you came to this country, or—?

1: Uh no, I—I was born here.

5: Okay. And your first name is?

1: Trisha.

5: Trisha. Okay, so.

1: Uh—Forgive me father for I have sinned, it has been two weeks since my last confession? Um—I have lied. Um—I have dishonoured my mother and father. Um—I have taken the Lord's name in vain?

5: Okay.

1: Um, I have hurt people who've cared for me? Um. I have had sex with a man who was not my husband?

5: Did you say you have people who care for you?

1: Yeah?

5: Okay. Well, I don't get the sin there.

1: Oh, no, I said I've hurt people who cared for me.

5: Oh! (laughs)

1: I'm sorry, I speak—

5: No, I love your voice, it's actually a nice change—Okay, so.

1: Well, I guess the thing that troubles me is that he slapped me around—

5: Oh!

1: And I kind of liked it? And that made me feel guilty?

5: Well, okay.

5: I don't know what you mean by slapping, I think in sex sometimes, there's aggression that some find pleasurable, uh—so I don't know—hm. I think—what do you mean, was it degrading, kind of, uh—aggressive?

1: Oh, it was definitely aggressive

5: Oh, okay. Well, I don't know—where that distinction lies, sometimes, between what is aggressive and what is degrading—and—and—I'll let you uh—

1: It was probably slightly degrading. I mean, I wanted it though, I mean I—

5: And the worrying part is that it was pleasurable to you. Well, I don't know what to say about that, you know? Like—I don't know?—I mean, you're confessing that as a—sin still, or—?

1: Well, yeah. I mean, if your body is the temple of God, then having it be degraded is—

5: Yeah.

5: But I mean—but the—uh—I don't know, I guess—I mean, it was disturbing to you? Well, I don't know, I wish I could say more to that. M-more about that, you know? But I think that's something you can—work out—talk about, I guess, you know? Uh, okay, uh, no, I mean, I think you're making a good confession. So anything else that troubles you, that disturbs you, or—?

1: Uh—not that I can remember.

5: Well, okay, uh—Well, for your penance, uh, anything you'd like to recommend for your penance, or?

1: (giggles)

5: God might be trying to tell you something, or—?

1: To pray more often?

5: Yeah, well, I think that's always a good thing. Are you—would you call yourself like a—a—prayerful person? I mean, do you normally take time, to pray, or—?

1: Uh, I used to be. Not really now—

5: Right, well, okay, now, I don't want you to take on—like I don't like it when you—see prayers like an obligation, like a—due, like it's just an obligation, but if you feel invited to pray—You should pray for that, like uh— there's a difference between someone who feels called and like, someone who thinks oh, I should pray because I have to. Big difference there. So maybe you should, for your penance ask for God to stir up in your heart the desire, the hunger to be more in touch with him, and—and see where that goes—in your heart. I—like, because there are times where I do feel invited—and sometimes I pray to God for discipline to pray, but it's always nice when you feel like the Lord is calling you to that moment, rendezvous to that intimacy. And sometimes it's just nice to—to—hear that invitation. Does that make sense? Okay. You can say your act of contrition now.

1: Father Lord, forgive me—your daughter, a sinner.

5: And listen to the words of the Lord. And God the father of mercy, through the death and resurrection of his son, sent the Holy Spirit to forgive our sins. By his power, Trisha, he absolves you of all your sins, in the name of the Father, and the Son and the Holy Spirit. Amen.

1: Amen.

5: I forgot to ask you what major you're taking.

1: Oh, I'm uh—taking English and Gender Studies.

5: Oh, that sounds interesting, okay. Well, have a good weekend.

1: Yeah, have a good weekend. Thank you.

1: Oh, oops. Ow.

5: Oh, careful.

Rory Macbeth
from The Bible (alphabetized)

The ideology of the alphabet—seemingly natural but a symptom of disciplined socialization—has proved an irresistible tactic for presenting materials, from Kenneth Gangemi's alphabetical list of national parks in *Lydia* (Los Angeles: Black Sparrow, 1970) to any number of similarly organized lists. Here, the interface of the alphabet parses the database of the Bible. One might compare Rory Macbeth's project with Leila Brett's editions of *À la recherche du temps perdu,* which rearranges every one of the 16,566 words in the first volume of Proust's novel into an index.

babbler babbler babbling babblings babblings babe babe babe babe babe babe babes babes babes babes babes babes babes babes babes backbiteth backbiting backbitings backbone backs backs backs backs backs backs backs backs backside backside backside backslider backsliding backsliding backsliding backsliding backsliding backsliding backsliding backsliding backsliding backsliding backsliding backsliding backslidings backslidings backslidings backslidings backward bad bad

bad bad bad bad bad bad bad bad bad bad bad bad bad bad bad bade bade bade bade bade bade bade bade bade bade bade bade bade bade bade bade bade badest badgers' badgers' badgers' badgers' badgers' badgers' badgers' badgers' badgers' badgers' badgers' badgers' badgers' badgers' badgers' badness bag bag bag bag bag bag bag bag bag bag bag bags bags bags bake bake bake bake bake bake bake bake bake bake baked baked baked baked bakemeats baken baken baken baken baken baken baken baken baken baker baker baker baker baker baker baker baker bakers bakers bakers' baketh balance balance balance balance balance balance balance balance balances balances balances balances balances balances balances balances balances balances balancings bald bald bald bald bald bald bald bald bald bald bald bald bald bald bald bald baldness baldness baldness baldness baldness baldness baldness baldness ball balm balm balm balm balm balm band band band band band band band band band band band band band band band band band band banded bands banished banished banishment banishment bank bank bank bank bank bank bank bank bank bank bank bank bank bank banks banks banks banks banks banner banner banner banners banners banners banquet banquet banquet banquet banquet banquet banquet banquet banquet banquet banquet banquet banquet banquet banqueting banquetings baptisms baptize baptize baptize baptize baptize baptize baptize baptize baptize baptized baptizest baptizeth baptizeth baptizing baptizing baptizing baptizing bar bar bar bar bar bar bar barbarian barbarian barbarians barbarous barbed barber's bare bare bare bare bare bare bare bare bare bare bare bare bare bare bare bare bare bare bare bare bare bare bare bare bare bare bare bare bare bare bare bare bare bare bare bare bare bare bare bare bare

bare bare bare bare bare bare bare bare bare bare bare bare bare bare bare
bare bare bare bare bare bare bare bare bare bare bare bare bare bare bare
bare bare bare bare bare bare bare bare bare bare bare bare bare bare bare
bare bare bare bare bare bare bare bare bare bare bare bare bare bare bare
bare bare bare bare bare bare bare bare bare bare bare bare bare bare bare
bare bare bare bare bare bare bare bare bare bare bare bare bare bare bare
bare bare bare bare bare bare bare bare bare bare bare bare bare bare bare
bare bare bare bare bare bare bare bare bare bare bare bare bare bare bare
bare bare bare bare bare bare bare bare bare bare bare bare bare bare bare
bare bare bare bare bare bare bare bare bare bare bare bare barefoot barefoot
barefoot barefoot barest barest barest bark barked barley barley barley bar-
ley barley barley barley barley barley barley barley barley barley barley bar-
ley barley barley barley barley barley barley barley barley barley barley bar-
ley barley barley barley barley barley barley barley barley barley barley barn
barn barn barn barnfloor barns barns barns barns barrel barrel barrel bar-
rels barren barren barren barren barren barren barren barren barren barren
barren barren barren barren barren barren barren barren barren barren bar-
ren barren barren barrenness bars bars bars bars bars bars bars bars bars bars
bars bars bars bars bars bars bars bars bars bars bars bars bars bars bars bars
bars bars bars bars bars bars bars bars bars bars bars bars base base base base
base base base base base base base base base base base base base base base baser
bases bases bases bases bases bases bases bases bases bases bases bases bases
bases bases bases basest basest basket basket basket basket basket basket
basket basket basket basket basket basket basket basket basket basket bas-
ket basket basket basket basket basket basket baskets baskets baskets bas-
kets baskets baskets baskets baskets baskets baskets baskets baskets baskets
baskets baskets bason bason bason bason bason basons basons basons
basons basons basons basons basons basons basons basons basons basons
basons basons basons basons basons bastard bastard bastards bat bat bath
bath bath bath bath bath bathe bathe bathe bathe bathe bathe bathe bathe
bathe bathe bathe bathe bathe bathe bathe bathe bathe bathe bathed baths
baths baths baths baths baths baths baths baths bats battered battering bat-
tering battle battle battle battle battle battle battle battle battle battle battle
battle battle battle battle battle battle battle battle battle battle battle battle
battle battle battle battle battle battle battle battle battle battle battle battle
battle battle battle battle battle battle battle battle battle battle battle battle
battle battle battle battle battle battle battle battle battle battle battle battle
battle battle battle battle battle battle battle battle battle battle battle battle
battle battle battle battle battle battle battle battle battle battle battle battle

battle battle battle battle battle battle battle battle battle battle battle battle
battle battle battle battle battle battle battle battle battle battle battle battle
battle battle battle battle battle battle battle battle battle battle battle battle
battle battle battle battle battle battle battle battle battle battle battle battle
battle battle battle battle battle battle battle battle battle battle battle battle
battle battle battle battle battle battle battle battle battle battle battle battle
battle battle battle battle battle battle battle battle battle battle battle battle
battle battle battle battlement battlements battles battles battles battles
battles battles bay bay bay bay bay bay bdellium bdellium be be be be be
be be be be be be be be be be be be be be be be be be be be be be be be be be
be be be be be be be be be be be be be be be be be be be be be be be be be be
be be be be be be be be be be be be be be be be be be be be be be be be be be
be be be be be be be be be be be be be be be be be be be be be be be be be be
be be be be be be be be be be be be be be be be be be be be be be be be be be
be be be be be be be be be be be be be be be be be be be be be be be be be be
be be be be be be be be be be be be be be be be be be be be be be be be be be
be be be be be be be be be be be be be be be be be be be be be be be be be be
be be be be be be be be be be be be be be be be be be be be be be be be be be
be be be be be be be be be be be be be be be be be be be be be be be be be be
be be be be be be be be be be be be be be be be be be be be be be be be be be
be be be be be be be be be be be be be be be be be be be be be be be be be be
be be be be be be be be be be be be be be be be be be be be be be be be be be
be be be be be be be be be be be be be be be be be be be be be be be be be be
be be be be be be be be be be be be be be be be be be be be be be be be be be
be be be be be be be be be be be be be be be be be be be be be be be be be be
be be be be be be be be be be be be be be be be be be be be be be be be be be
be be be be be be be be be be be be be be be be be be be be be be be be be be
be be be be be be be be be be be be be be be be be be be be be be be be be be
be be be be be be be be be be be be be be be be be be be be be be be be be be
be be be be be be be be be be be be be be be be be be be be be be be be be be
be be be be be be be be be be be be be be be be be be be be be be be be be be
be be be be be be be be be be be be be be be be be be be be be be be be be be
be be be be be be be be be be be be be be be be be be be be be be be be be be
be be be be be be be be be be be be be be be be be be be be be be be be be be
be be be be be be be be be be be be be be be be be be be be be be be be be be

be be be be be be be be be be be be be be be be be be be be be be be be be be
be be be be be be be be be be be be be be be be be be be be be be be be be be
be be be be be be be be be be be be be be be be be be be be be be be be be be
be be be be be be be be be be be be be be be be be be be be be be be be be be
be be be be be be be be be be be be be be be be be be be be be be be be be be
be be be be be be be be be be be be be be be be be be be be be be be be be be
be be be be be be be be be be be be be be be be be be be be be be be be be be
be be be be be be be be be be be be be be be be be be be be be be be be be be
be be be be be be be be be be be be be be be be be be be be be be be be be be
be be be be be be be be be be be be be be be be be be be be be be be be be be
be be be be be be be be be be be be be be be be be be be be be be be be be be
be be be be be be be be be be be be be be be be be be be be be be be be be be
be be be be be be be be be be be be be be be be be be be be be be be be be be
be be be be be be be be be be be be be be be be be be be be be be be be be be
be be be be be be be be be be be be be be be be be be be be be be be be be be
be be be be be be be be be be be be be be be be be be be be be be be be be be
be be be be be be be be be be be be be be be be be be be be be be be be be be
be be be be be be be be be be be be be be be be be be be be be be be be be be
be be be be be be be be be be be be be be be be be be be be be be be be be be
be be be be be be be be be be be be be be be be be be be be be be be be be be
be be be be be be be be be be be be be be be be be be be be be be be be be be
be be be be be be be be be be be be be be be be be be be be be be be be be be
be be be be be be be be be be be be be be be be be be be be be be be be be be
be be be be be be be be be be be be be be be be be be be be be be be be be be
be be be be be be be be be be be be be be be be be be be be be be be be be be
be be be be be be be be be be be be be be be be be be be be be be be be be be
be be be be be be be be be be be be be be be be be be be be be be be be be be
be be be be be be be be be be be be be be be be be be be be be be be be be be
be be be be be be be be be be be be be be be be be be be be be be be be be be
be be be be be be be be be be be be be be be be be be be be be be be be be be
be be be be be be be be be be be be be be be be be be be be be be be be be be
be be be be be be be be be be be be be be be be be be be be be be be be be be
be be be be be be be be be be be be be be be be be be be be be be be be be be
be be be be be be be be be be be be be be be be be be be be be be be be be be
be be be be be be be be be be be be be be be be be be be be be be be be be be

be be be be be be be be be be be be be be be be be be be be be be be be be

be be be be be be be be be be be be be be be be be be be be be be be be be

be be be be be be be be be be be be be be be be be be be be be be be be be

be be be be be be be be be be be be be be be be be be be be be be be be be

be be be be be be be be be be be be be be be be be be be be be be be be be

be be be be be be be be be be be be be be be be be be be be be be be be be

be be be be be be be be be be be be be be be be be be be be be be be be be

be be be be be be be be be be be be be be be be be be be be be be be be be

be be be be be be be be be be be be be be be be be be be be be be be be be

be be be be be be be be be be be be be be be be be be be be be be be be be

be be be be be be be be be be be be be be be be be be be be be be be be be

be be be be be be be be be be be be be be be be be be be be be be be be be

be be be be be be be be be be be be be be be be be be be be be be be be be

be be be be be be be be be be be be be be be be be be be be be be be be be

be be be be be be be be be be be be be be be be be be be be be be be be be

be be be be be be be be be be be be be be be be be be be be be be be be be

be be be be be be be be be be be be be be be be be be be be be be be be be

be be be be be be be be be be be be be be be be be be be be be be be be be

be be be be be be be be be be be be be be be be be be be be be be be be be

be be be be be be be be be be be be be be be be be be be be be be be be be

be be be be be be be be be be be be be be be be be be be be be be be be be

be be be be be be be be be be be be be be be be be be be be be be be be be

be be be be be be be be be be be be be be be be be be be be be be be be be

be be be be be be be be be be be be be be be be be be be be be be be be be

be be be be be be be be be be be be be be be be be be be be be be be be be

be be be be be be be be be be be be be be be be be be be be be be be be be

be be be be be be be be be be be be be be be be be be be be be be be be be

be be be be be be be be be be be be be be be be be be be be be be be be be

be be be be be be be be be be be be be be be be be be be be be be be be be

be be be be be be be be be be be be be be be be be be be be be be be be be

be be be be be be be be be be be be be be be be be be be be be be be be be

be be be be be be be be be be be be be be be be be be be be be be be be be

be be be be be be be be be be be be be be be be be be be be be be be be be

be be be be be be be be be be be be be be be be be be be be be be be be be

be be be be be be be be be be be be be be be be be be be be be be be be be

be be be be be be be be be be be be be be be be be be be be be be be be be

be be be be be be be be be be be be be be be be be be be be be be be be be be be be
be be be be be be be be be be be be be be be be be be be be be be be be be be be be
be be be be be be be be be be be be be be be be be be be be be be be be be be be be
be be be be be be be be be be be be be be be be be be be be be be be be be be be be
be be be be be be be be be be be be be be be be be be be be be be be be be be be be
be be be be be be be be be be be be be be be be be be be be be be be be be be be be
be be be be be be be be be be be be be be be be be be be be be be be be be be be be
be be be be be be be be be be be be be be be be be be be be be be be be be be be be
be be be be be be be be be be be be be be be be be be be be be be be be be be be be
be be be be be be be be be be be be be be be be be be be be be be be be be be be be
be be be be be be be be be be be be be be be be be be be be be be be be be be be be
be be be be be be be be be be be be be be be be be be be be be be be be be be be be
be be be be be be be be be be be be be be be be be be be be be be be be be be be be
be be be be be be be be be be be be be be be be be be be be be be be be be be be be
be be be be be be be be be be be be be be be be be be be be be be be be be be be be
be be be be be be be be be be be be be be be be be be be be be be be be be be be be
be be be be be be be be be be be be be be be be be be be be be be be be be be be be
be be be be be be be be be be be be be be be be be be be be be be be be be be be be
be be be be be be be be be be be be be be be be be be be be be be be be be be be be
be be be be be be be be be be be be be be be be be be be be be be be be be be be be
be be be be be be be be be be be be be be be be be be be be be be be be be be be be
be be be be be be be be be be be be be be be be be be be be be be be be be be be be
be be be be be be be be be be be be be be be be be be be be be be be be be be be be
be be be be be be be be be be be be be be be be be be be be be be be be be be be be
be be be be be be be be be be be be be be be be be be be be be be be be be be be be
be be be be be be be be be be be be be be be be be be be be be be be be be be be be
be be be be be be be be be be be be be be be be be be be be be be be be be be be be
be be be be be be be be be be be be be be be be be be be be be be be be be be be be
be be be be be be be be be be be be be be be be be be be be be be be be be be be be
be be be be be be be be be be be be be be be be be be be be be be be be be be be be
be be be be be be be be be be be be be be be be be be be be be be be be be be be be
be be be be be be be be be be be be be be be be be be be be be be be be be be be be
be be be be be be be be be be be be be be be be be be be be be be be be be be be be
be be be be be be be be be be be be be be be be be be be be be be be be be be be be
be be be be be be be be be be be be be be be be be be be be be be be be be be be be
be be be be be be be be be be be be be be be be be be be be be be be be be be be be
be be be be be be be be be be be be be be be be be be be be be be be be be be be be
be be be be be be be be be be be be be be be be be be be be be be be be be be be be
be be be be be be be be be be be be be be be be be be be be be be be be be be be be

be be be be be be be be be be be be be be be be be be be be be be be be be be be
be be be be be be be be be be be be be be be be be be be be be be be be be be be
be be be be be be be be be be be be be be be be be be be be be be be be be be be
be be be be be be be be be be be be be be be be be be be be be be be be be be be
be be be be be be be be be be be be be be be be be be be be be be be be be be be
be be be be be be be be be be be be be be be be be be be be be be be be be be be
be be be be be be be be be be be be be be be be be be be be be be be be be be be
be be be be be be be be be be be be be be be be be be be be be be be be be be be
be be be be be be be be be be be be be be be be be be be be be be be be be be be
be be be be be be be be be be be be be be be be be be be be be be be be be be be
be be be be be be be be be be be be be be be be be be be be be be be be be be be
be be be be be be be be be be be be be be be be be be be be be be be be be be be
be be be be be be be be be be be be be be be be be be be be be be be be be be be
be be be be be be be be be be be be be be be be be be be be be be be be be be be
be be be be be be be be be be be be be be be be be be be be be be be be be be be
be be be be be be be be be be be be be be be be be be be be be be be be be be be
be be be be be be be be be be be be be be be be be be be be be be be be be be be
be be be be be be be be be be be be be be be be be be be be be be be be be be be
be be be be be be be be be be be be be be be be be be be be be be be be be be be
be be be be be be be be be be be be be be be be be be be be be be be be be be be
be be be be be be be be be be be be be be be be be be be be be be be be be be be
be be be be be be be be be be be be be be be be be be be be be be be be be be be
be be be be be be be be be be be be be be be be be be be be be be be be be be be
be be be be be be be be be be be be be be be be be be be be be be be be be be be
be be be be be be be be be be be be be be be be be be be be be be be be be be be
be be be be be be be be be be be be be be be be be be be be be be be be be be be
be be be be be be be be be be be be be be be be be be be be be be be be be be be
be be be be be be be be be be be be be be be be be be be be be be be be be be be
be be be be be be be be be be be be be be be be be be be be be be be be be be be
be be be be be be be be be be be be be be be be be be be be be be be be be be be
be be be be be be be be be be be be be be be be be be be be be be be be be be be
be be be be be be be be be be be be be be be be be be be be be be be be be be be
be be be be be be be be be be be be be be be be be be be be be be be be be be be
be be be be be be be be be be be be be be be be be be be be be be be be be be be
be be be be be be be be be be be be be be be be be be be be be be be be be be be
be be be be be be be be be be be be be be be be be be be be be be be be be be be
be be be be be be be be be be be be be be be be be be be be be be be be be be be
be be be be be be be be be be be be be be be be be be be be be be be be be be be

be be be be be be be be be be be be be be be be be be be be be be be be be be
be be be be be be be be be be be be be be be be be be be be be be be be be be
be be be be be be be be be be be be be be be be be be be be be be be be be be
be be be be be be be be be be be be be be be be be be be be be be be be be be
be be be be be be be be be be be be be be be be be be be be be be be be be be
be be be be be be be be be be be be be be be be be be be be be be be be be be
be be be be be be be be be be be be be be be be be be be be be be be be be be
be be be be be be be be be be be be be be be be be be be be be be be be be be
be be be be be be be be be be be be be be be be be be be be be be be be be be
be be be be be be be be be be be be be be be be be be be be be be be be be be
be be be be be be be be be be be be be be be be be be be be be be be be be be
be be be be be be be be be be be be be be be be be be be be be be be be be be
be be be be be be be be be be be be be be be be be be be be be be be be be be
be be be be be be be be be be be be be be be be be be be be be be be be be be
be be be be be be be be be be be be be be be be be be be be be be be be be be
be be be be be be be be be be be be be be be be be be be be be be be be be be
be be be be be be be be be be be be be be be be be be be be be be be be be be
be be be be be be be be be be be be be be be be be be be be be be be be be be
be be be be be be be be be be be be be be be be be be be be be be be be be be
be be be be be be be be be be be be be be be be be be be be be be be be be be
be be be be be be be be be be be be be be be be be be be be be be be be be be
be be be be be be be be be be be be be be be be be be be be be be be be be be
be be be be be be be be be be be be be be be be be be be be be be be be be be
be be be be be be be be be be be be be be be be be be be be be be be be be be
be be be be be be be be be be be be be be be be be be be be be be be be be be
be be be be be be be be be be be be be be be be be be be be be be be be be be
be be be be be be be be be be be be be be be be be be be be be be be be be be
be be be be be be be be be be be be be be be be be be be be be be be be be be
be be be be be be be be be be be be be be be be be be be be be be be be be be
be be be be be be be be be be be be be be be be be be be be be be be be be be
be be be be be be be be be be be be be be be be be be be be be be be be be be
be be be be be be be be be be be be be be be be be be be be be be be be be be
be be be be be be be be be be be be be be be be be be be be be be be be be be
be be be be be be be be be be be be be be be be be be be be be be be be be be
be be be be be be be be be be be be be be be be be be be be be be be be be be
be be be be be be be be be be be be be be be be be be be be be be be be be be
be be be be be be be be be be be be be be be be be be be be be be be be be be
be be be be be be be be be be be be be be be be be be be be be be be be be be
be be be be be be be be be be be be be be be be be be be be be be be be be be
be be be be be be be be be be be be be be be be be be be be be be be be be be
be be be be be be be be be be be be be be be be be be be be be be be be be be

be be be be be be be be be be be be be be be be be be be be be be be be be be
be be be be be be be be be be be be be be be be be be be be be be be be be be
be be be be be be be be be be be be be be be be be be be be be be be be be be
be be be be be be be be be be be be be be be be be be be be be be be be be be
be be be be be be be be be be be be be be be be be be be be be be be be be be
be be be be be be be be be be be be be be be be be be be be be be be be be be
be be be be be be be be be be be be be be be be be be be be be be be be be be
be be be be be be be be be be be be be be be be be be be be be be be be be be
be be be be be be be be be be be be be be be be be be be be be be be be be be
be be be be be be be be be be be be be be be be be be be be be be be be be be
be be be be be be be be be be be be be be be be be be be be be be be be be be
be be be be be be be be be be be be be be be be be be be be be be be be be be
be be be be be be be be be be be be be be be be be be be be be be be be be be
be be be be be be be be be be be be be be be be be be be be be be be be be be
be be be be be be be be be be be be be be be be be be be be be be be be be be
be be be be be be be be be be be be be be be be be be be be be be be be be be
be be be be be be be be be be be be be be be be be be be be be be be be be be
be be be be be be be be be be be be be be be be be be be be be be be be be be
be be be be be be be be be be be be be be be be be be be be be be be be be be
be be be be be be be be be be be be be be be be be be be be be be be be be be
be be be be be be be be be be be be be be be be be be be be be be be be be be
be be be be be be be be be be be be be be be be be be be be be be be be be be
be be be be be be be be be be be be be be be be be be be be be be be be be be
be be be be be be be be be be be be be be be be be be be be be be be be be be
be be be be be be be be be be be be be be be be be be be be be be be be be be
be be be be be be be be be be be be be be be be be be be be be be be be be be
be be be be be be be be be be be be be be be be be be be be be be be be be be
be be be be be be be be be be be be be be be be be be be be be be be be be be
be be be be be be be be be be be be be be be be be be be be be be be be be be
be be be be be be be be be be be be be be be be be be be be be be be be be be
be be be be be be be be be be be be be be be be be be be be be be be be be be
be be be be be be be be be be be be be be be be be be be be be be be be be be
be be be be be be be be be be be be be be be be be be be be be be be be be be
be be be be be be be be be be be be be be be be be be be be be be be be be be
be be be be be be be be be be be be be be be be be be be be be be be be be be
be be be be be be be be be be be be be be be be be be be be be be be be be be
be be be be be be be be be be be be be be be be be be be be be be be be be be
be be be be be be be be be be be be be be be be be be be be be be be be be be
be be be be be be be be be be be be be be be be be be be be be be be be be be
be be be be be be be be be be be be be be be be be be be be be be be be be be

be be be be be be be be be be be be be be be be be be be be be be be
be be be be be be be be be be be be be be be be be be be be be be be
be be be be be be be be be be be be be be be be be be be be be be be
be be be be be be be be be be be be be be be be be be be be be be be
be be be be be be be be be be be be be be be be be be be be be be be
be be be be be be be be be be be be be be be be be be be be be be be
be be be be be be be be be be be be be be be be be be be be be be be
be be be be be be be be be be be be be be be be be be be be be be be
be be be be be be be be be be be be be be be be be be be be be be be
be be be be be be be be be be be be be be be be be be be be be be be
be be be be be be be be be be be be be be be be be be be be

Jackson Mac Low
from Words nd Ends from Ez

Like John Cage's *Writing Through The Cantos*, *Words nd Ends from Ez* (Bolinas, Calif.: Avenue B, 1989) uses Ezra Pound's name as an interface to the database of *The Cantos*. Here, Mac Low proceeds through Pound's text and records those words or parts of words that sequentially encode the letters of Pound's name in the corresponding positions within a word or word fragment. That is, Mac Low read until he came to an e, taking it as the first letter in a string; he then read until he came to a z, taking it as the second letter in a string; then onto the next r, which established the third letter of a string and so on, through the name and repeating until the source text had been exhausted. Compare, for example, Mac Low's first line with the original words from Pound's text: "[th]en"; "[bro]nze"; "[b]earing"; "[dre]ory *arms*." Further rules ensure that punctuation and versification are projected from Pound's poem to Mac Low's (for a full explanation of the procedure, see *Words nd Ends from Ez*, 89). In the end, Mac Low reduces Pound's epic to about seventy-five pages.

En nZe eaRing ory Arms,
Pallor pOn laUghtered laiN oureD Ent,
aZure teR,
un-
tAwny Pping cOme d oUt r wiNg-
joints,
preaD Et aZzle.

spRing-
water,
ool A P."

cOnvict laUghter scaNy)
me,

MaD E aZure TyRo,
of wAve-
cords,
Plashing rOck-
hollows e-
rUns f-
duNe;
he tiDe-
rips Esperus,
aZure iR,
ods And
Panisks,
rOm roUgh od,

aNd clouDs E aZes tuRned ple,
As Poggio uOise,
ad Up weeN chilD E aZ,
eaRt t on A Pike bOth n oUt,
ed,
"ANd yo CiD E eZ stRo red,
And Pped,
tO etU."

CE iN moulDering Es,
aZe luRs,
e grAss,
Pale mOving.

thUd,
rf uNder n-
golD E eZ heR e swAllows P,
rOof,
chUrch of iN e golD.

Eneath aZe,
teRing,
gusA . . .
Pool . . .

pOol . . .
moUr cygNet iquiD Eneath uZe cuRtains . . ."

he cAmel Plotted mOke
SoUnd eveNing e forD,
Ers aZ thRee he bArb Perhaps,
iOn,
e,
AUrunculeia's s
"Da Nuces!

se,
anD Enaeus aZe ppRoaching
The Air Put mOur e lUst omaN h roaD Ea-
change,
tZ ieRci's ife And Piled pOrt
DaUphin MaeNsac.

atheD Erces nZaccio stRoke ertAin Perugia,
tOld,
abUleia.

t DoN e,
creDesse È"

oZarello abRain adwAy Poet's
DOwn e oUt p of Naples' uble Drifts E)
aZione."

gs Run nd,
*MA P*oitiers,
fOtei m aUzirets e viNgt y hanD,
E uZionda,
heR ichArd,
Porch,
mOrte,
doUr is iN wing'D Es uZeta veR'

rd l Ask

Picus DOn inUs d DoN nato De' Ee eZene foR e shApe Poiled pOor a-
sUrge;

d meN's s"

saiD
"Erit,
tZ meRe ss nArration,
Peu mOisi,
plUs rdiN.

he olD En's nZe,
piRe r's fAll;
Place gOuty-
footed.

StUborn gaiNst ilteD Ers tZ,
e eRa,
to-
dAy Past,
"COntemporary."

ndUres.

gaiNst aragDos,
E aZz coRtex,
ood,
And Plaster,
rOfessorial t mUsic,
eveN houlDers Eeks nZaccio moRe e thAn Phantom,
t.

O atUres.

Stéphane Mallarmé
from La dernière mode

In 1874, Stéphane Mallarmé became the editor, designer, and sole author of the women's fashion magazine *La dernière mode*. Every word of the magazine was written by Mallarmé himself under a variety of pseudonyms: Marguerite de Ponty as fashion expert; Miss Satin as the fashion news correspondent; Ix, the book and theater critic; and the food critic Le Chef de Bouche Chez Brébant. The journal ran for eight fortnightly issues and was a highly produced publication, rife with lavish illustration; in fact, it had a very large readership—at one point, the journal had a print run of three thousand. Readers assumed they were getting the latest dish on how to throw an elegant dinner party or who was seen where wearing what.

By challenging notions of the authentic self, Mallarmé shape-shifts in ways that anticipate the Internet age; by working outside his field of notoriety, he gives permission to the postmodern concept of the guilty pleasure and allows those trivial and marginal interests to infiltrate the seat of poetic genius. A full century before Andy Warhol's similar explorations, Mallarmé's gesture is a full-frontal challenge to the notion of identity and genius as well as high and low in the literary arts. The excerpt here comes from the October 4, 1874, edition and is signed by Marguerite de Ponty.

Our last column told the world about the complete transformation that Fashion has already undergone, or will undergo, this autumn and it explained the Season's change of décor; it only remained to describe a thousand charming whimsies, indispensable extras for daytime wear when we realised that, having depended too much on our own observations, we had quite neglected certain of such items commonplace ones, indeed, and of course well known in Paris; but then, we are not writing for Paris alone. Today it is true, our task is (as one would say about a silk or gold embroidery) to 'fill in the background', but we must not neglect the delightful, brilliant trifles which are the finishing touches dictated by Good Taste.

Let us begin with these trifles, if only to get them out of the way! How many whimsies have seen the light of day before and during this fortnight: above all, the ravishing *Lavallières,* scarves with pink buttons embroidered in contrasting colours, and others in tartan or every imaginable shade, and ones with satiny stripes, of pale blue and pink—really adorable. I award no less praise to charming little turquoise necklaces—scarves and bows for the hair which come in two colours or two shades, such as nasturtium and sulphur-yellow, blue and green, pink and blue, pearl-grey and pink, steely blue and iron-grey, etc.: all with guipure or Valenciennes lace. As for microscopic handkerchiefs made for the tiniest hands, I see several: one with a cockchafer embroidered in colour in the corner, with two interwined letters in pink and blue or red and bronze which is, to say the least, original. Some have a letter embroidered in green and red wool: those with a broad hem in pearl grey foulard are very stylish, perhaps more so than the ones entirely in pink or blue foulard, with pleats of the same and inserts of Valenciennes lace.

But all these novelties, soon to be familiar to some of us, pale before one which is still, indisputably, the ornament of the moment, as it has been of the Season. Nothing has caused it to go out of fashion, neither the months spent gazing at the sea, nor the weeks already spent in the hunting field— the latter less than the former, for to the vague term *"collier-bagatelle"* the evil fate presiding over this object persists in preferring the hunting term "dog-collar").

What is it? I will answer quite simply: a little black velvet ribbon which goes round the neck and is fastened behind with a square buckle, through which it passes and falls. A thousand diamond letters sparkle with the captivating brilliance of a secret which is apparent but remains hidden: interlaced Christian names and surnames of her who wears the collar and of him who gave it. Legend has it that a single jeweller makes these collars and varies their mystery. Now, to reveal his address, even among women, would be an act of high treason: useless too, for it is not up to us women to buy them. However I shall add, for those of my readers who (gifts being a chancy affair) would like to make their taste known, that these ornaments also come in coloured stones and in pearls, or even with a little diamond fringe. Even earrings of velvet ribbon are worn, with single initials repeated. London, Vienna, St. Petersburg and New York know about this; and such an almost classic ornament brings me back to some quite general matters, needed to complete last fortnight's sketch of autumn fashions.

We mentioned the *chapeau Berger* and the *chapeau Valois,* finding the *chapeau Lamballe* almost too well known. But it is completely new only for those of our subscribers who did not come to Paris during the holidays and have not been in Normandy. What then is the *chapeau Lamballe,* which continues to be all the rage? If a thousand letters written on blue vellum inquire of us, only then shall we reply.

Let us speak of hair styles. The hair styling which is in perfect harmony with our hats, better than the chignon, is the *Catogan:* quite a surprise, as it carries us right back to the *Directoire*! We remember the plait, or the two plaits folding back on themselves, now held by a bow in the same shade as the hat. Our grandmothers, and even our grandfathers, wore this a century ago. The head still supports a scaffolding of little rolls, back-combing coils and plaits; while raised bands are lightly curled, showing no disorder other than prettily ruffled hair.

A few more remarks, so that this column, along with the one in the previous issue, can constitute an all-round view of Today's Taste. Let us stress a point, at the risk of repetition: namely that Fashion, this autumn, is definitely reviving the Tunic. It can be round or pointed, with flounces or pleats, or even take the form of a scarf or it may be squared off behind, in which case it is turned up in a roll, the two flaps being tied together with a handsome faille bow. But the main point is that all tunics, whatever their style, should be exceedingly close-fitting in front and very loose behind. This is as de rigueur today as the corset fastened, or rather laced, in the back. Basques will, of course, cling closely to the hips: it will even be advantageous, to reduce them, to mount the skirt of the dress on a smooth piece of fabric, both in front and at the side.

All this was known to me, at our great fashion-designers, before it was known at the last races in the Bois de Boulogne—seeing which latter has, all in all, only confirmed me in all my earlier opinions. Only one new point, highlighted both by the last suns of the season and the gaslight of the department stores I have visited, relates to this winter's fabrics. We extract from our notebook, at random, a note or two regarding this, already mingled with names famous in the world of fashion. "Heavy fabrics . . . and grosgrain, quilted materials of all colours and patterns, especially cashmere: all styles created to clothe beautifully a well-built person. What, no recherché design? No, it is the fabric itself which produces the dazzling effect. Here, what are actually furnishing fabrics are worn with grace."

I will add, now, that we may need to go even further, and I shall spread a rumour which is almost an echo of all I have said before. A great fashion designer (one of those whom Paris sometimes obeys) is proposing, before New Year Day, to revive the splendid Louis XIV costumes, for which were created (it would seem) those rich, strong fabrics suddenly arriving from the great factories to the plate-glass windows of Fashion's laboratories.

We shall see what we shall see.

---

from Le livre

The hundreds of manuscript pages of notes for *Le livre* (*The Book*), Stéphane Mallarmé's final, unrealized project, contain calculations about the number of pages, copies and editions, readership and performances, the printed book's dimensions and format, binding and pagination, the divisions of its parts, and the structural organization of its text. But the notes contain almost nothing about the book's contents. In place of the expected drafts and revisions, scholars discovered geometric schematics, tables, charts, and several pages with no words at all—only diagrammatic lines and cryptic numerals.

(52B)

le manuscrit seul
   est mobile—

         cela multipliant
      par 3

      240.000
        3

      ———
      720.000

. . .

(81B)

                    Lect   480 + 480

240                                      $\times$ 3 = 320

                 2 la page
                 converti en la
                 feuille—

                                          yacht

    [chasse   but   motif
                      ligne
bornes]   feu d'artif
      nombres de lecteurs
               édition—feu d'artif

. . .

(82B)

2 lect. par an
        chacun invitant
                l'autre

—————————

        semaine

—————————

        240 p.   de la page
                        à la feuille
      à 240 f.

                    un aspect

. . .

(101A)

•• •• •• ••
       X
       •• •• •• ••

      •• •• •• ••
    X
•• •• •• ••

Donato Mancini
Ligature

Donato Mancini's "Ligature" is composed according to the rule that each word must begin with the same letter sequence that concludes the previous word. Different versions of this work have appeared as installations, in the eponymous book *Ligature* (Vancouver: New Star, 2005), and online (see http://english.utah.edu/eclipse/projects/ligature/).

tureen reenter entertain taint intense ensemble emblem blemish mishap shape aperture

urethane anemone moneyed edge genie nieces cesspit spitball ballast

last staff affect ectomorph orphan

phantom tomalley alley eyelid elide ideate eater

terrapin rapine pineapple applecart

cartilage lager gerund rundown downcast castrato stratosphere heretic

reticent centipede pederast raster asterisk

risky skydive divertimento mentor torment menthol

Hollywood wooden denim nimbus bustier tiered redundant Dante anteater terse seat atop operator torso

soursop soporific fictive veal align ignite iterate teem

embargo Argonaut autopsy psyche cheddar daredevil villanelle

lemur murmur murder derange ranger angered redbird birdbath bathos

hostile stiletto toro roof offer feral almost ostrich riches

chestnut nutrient entrée tree reed reeducate categorical callous louse

seethe ether thermos mosque Quebec become comet metric tricycle

cleft leftwing wingspan spank ankle Kleenex nexus used sedentary rye yeast
Easter stereo reorganised

seduced cede deli lily lyre real allow lower werewolf olfaction action onion
onlay layperson persona

sonant antique queasy asylum luminesce scene enema mach achoo choo
choo

hoover oversold soldier dieresis resist sister sterol

roly poly polysemic semicolon colonel nelson sonar narwhal whale

levee veer erupt rupture urethra thrall allegro

grotesque quest estrange stranger German mantel antelope elope opera
perambulate latex text extreme tremendous doused sedate dateless lessor
Sorbonne bonnet

netted teddy eddying ingrown grown up nuptial altar tart Tartuffe tuffet
fetch etcher cherubic rubicon cone neap apex exalt alter terrain raincoat
oath then hencoop cooperate

atelier era's rascal scallop allophone phoneme nemesis isle sleuth euthanasia

Asianflu fluke lukewarm armpit pith thumb umbilical calibre libretto town
owner

nerves vespers

persimmon monarchic Chicano canoe

noel

Electra tractor

Toronto ontology

gypsy psycho chow howdy dyke keel

elastic stickup upend pending dingo ingot

gotcha chaos Osiris Irish

shy hyena enamor amoral oral rally lyric ricotta Ottawa award warden Ardennes Ness essay sayest yesterday daybreak breakfast fasten stencil

cilantro trout route utensil tensile silent lentil till illustrate strategist gist strip Tripoli polite literal ralph

alphabet abet better teriyaki akin kinescope

Copenhagen agenda gendarme Armenia menial alum lumber bereave eavesdrop dropout pouter

uterus rust

rustic sticker

kerosene Senegal egalitarian answer swerve

vespid spider deride ideal dealer

alerted edit ditto tout outline linen entail tailor lord order dervish Vishnu nude deacon control troll rollerblade-laden denominator

torrid riddle lever vertigo gore resuscitates test estrogen genre retard TARDIS disco scoff office Iceland landscape scapegoat goatee

teetotal talisman Mandarin rinse insecticide cider derail railroad roadie diet

Etruscan scandal dalliance cease aseptic tic toc toccata catastrophe strophe
Ophelia heliacal calligraphy

physical calf alfalfa favor vortex

Texas ascent

centaur Taurus

Russia Siam iambic biceps epsilon longing

gingko Koran orange angel gelato

atom tomato atone toneless lesser seraph

aphid hidden denote noteworthy thyme meal alma mama maim Imhotep

tepid pidgin gingham hamster

steroid idiot iota tarot rotten tendril drill illusion onus

usurped pedestal stale talent lento entomb ombudsman

mango angora orangutan tangerine inept Neptune tuner unerring ringlet
letter terra errata ratatouille

illegitimate maternity typist pistol stole tolerate rateable bleak leaky Kyrie
riesling slingshot shotput putz tzatsiki kiss issue suet ethos

hosea season sonnet network workshop shopaholic

lichee cheetah tahini inimical calorie orient entire tireless lesson

songstress stressed sediment mental tale aleatoric rickshaw hawk awkward
arduous

oust stylite literati atingle gleet ethic hickey keypad padre adrenaline linear nearby Arby's bystander

Anderson sonata natal talon alone lonesome something hinge ingenuine inescapable bleach ache chemise miserable bleat leather therefore oregano anoint intelligent genteel eel else serpent

Pentecost osteoporosis sistrum trumpet Petrarch architrave travel velum lump

umpire ire redact dactylic lichen chenille illegal galvanise anisette setter term ermine mineral rale

aleph ephemera

emerald alderman mannequin quince

incessant Santa Claus claustrophobia biathlon London donut nutmeg megawatt attempt temptation on online linesman

Manitoba tobacco accordance

dancer cervix vixen enzyme melon elongate gatepost

postal stalk talkie Kiev evict victor torque Queens

ensconce conceal alto towel welfare farewell

wellspring ringdove oven enough ghoul Oulipo liposuction

ionic nickname nametag metagalaxy xylophone phonecard cardigan gander derive river versus Sussex sextuplet

plethora Horace racehorse horseplay playpen pencil cilia Iliad adjourn journalist

listen stench enchant chanterelle level velvet veteran rancor coruscate caterpillar pillar larghetto ghetto toga gasp asphalt halter altercate caterwaul ulcer ceramic micron

crone onetime timeshare harem remorse morsel selfish fisher sheriff riffraff raffle flesh sheath

heathen Athens ensign signor North orthodoxy oxymoron rondo dodo odor

dorsal salve alveolar large Argentina inane

anesthetic tic tac toe toe jam jammies Mies van der Rohe

hell ellipsis Sisyphus husband bandstand standoff offal

Falco alcohol holy Olympic picnic nicety

etymological calabash bashful fulsome somersault Sault Sainte Marie

Ariel elbow bowel welcome comedic medicare caress

essence encephalic Alice licensing singular lark

Arkansas Kansas Saskatchewan wane anemia miasma smarmy army myopia opiate tetra trap rappel appellant anthem

hemlock locksmith smithereens enslave lavender dermal malhavoc avocado

adobe Doberman manatee tee pee peewee weep Epsom soma Omaha maharishi

Shia hiatus tush usher Sheraton atonal also solvent ventriloquism

small mallet lethal halibut butcher

Cherokee keen enamel melisma smack acknowledge edgewise wisely Elision annex next extinct tincture

uretic tickle klezmer merit Eritrea treadmill milligram

grammar margarita Italic lice census suspect spectre

tremolo Moloch ocher cherish shut utopia topiary

Aryan Yankee keep epee peeve even vengeful fulgent gentleman emancipate paté paternal almanac manacle clever evermore

Orestes tesseract actor torch orchard chard hard on Don Juan anchor chorizo horizon once centre

entrench enchilada adamant manta antagonise sewer Werther thermostat statute tutelage agent

gentry tryst stop topple pleasant santorum rumor

moribund bundle leer errand random domino ominous usurer rerun rune unequal equaliser

serene enemy myrrh

rhizome omelet
lethargy argyle

Levi evil vile Leda Edam damn amnesty style lest Estonia niacin cinnamon among mongrel relish

shorn ornamental Taliban banana Nanaimo moan analog logos

gossamer American candelabra abracadabra Abraham ampersand sandwich ichor chord horde ordeal alarm armed mediocre creep

epoxy oxygen genome omen

mendicant cantos tosspot spotlight lightweight eightfold folding dingbat batten attenuated tedium umlaut autumn

mnemonic Monicagate agateware warehouse houseplant lantern terneplate platelet telethon thong Hong Kong ongoing goings on

sonogram grampa rampart partisan tisane

anecdotal talcum cumuli list string ringer

gerbil bile leash ash shack shackle kleptomania maniacal calculus lust

stele eleven eventual almond Mondrian anew

newspeak speaker kerchief chieftain ain't intake

Akela elate latent entropy pyre ream amber berg

ergot goth other theremin eminency encyclical calico iconoclast asthma

Mars Ars Nova oval Valhalla Allah ahead headstrong strongest esteem emote

motet tether Hermes mesmerize zebra

brassiere erect rectified Eden

denial album bumpkin kindergarten tentacle clef

effort fortune unenlighten tenant

Nantong tongue guest estimate materialism smart art deco economical callgirl girlfriend Friendster sterile ileum

Eumenides desk Eskimo kimono monocle cleave leaven avenue venue nueva trova Ovaltine inefficient

enterprise riser serif rifle flex lexicon concert certificate catechist histrionic Nichol cholesterol rollick lickety split split second condescend descendant anthropologist

Istanbul bulimia Miami amid Midgard garden

ardent dental Talmud mudflat flatulent Lenten tennis nisus suspend pendant antipasto pastor

storming mingle glee leech echo cholera ravine vineyard yardstick stickleback backwater waterspout poutine inedible

blear earwig wiggle gleam ammo mole oleander derogate gateau

audio diorama Ramadan dandruff ruffle fleapit pitfall fallow lowbrow browser serve vegan gangrene

renegade adept depth thunder underneath atheist heist stun tundra

drab rabbit bitmap

maple plectrum trump rumpus pusher hero eros rosehip

hippopotamus muscle sclerosis

Sistine ineffable fable blessed sedan dangle glen

Lenin nincompoop pooped pedantic anticipate patent tenth enthusiast astronaut

nautical calamari marital ritalin liner inertia Tiananmen meningitis

Tishri shrivel velcro crow owlish Ishmael maelstrom trombone boner onerous rousing single glean leaner Neroli olive liver

verboten tenor normal maladjust adjuster sterling lingam

Gambia ambiance ancestor store tore toreador adore Oreo

reopen pentagon agonise Iseult ultramarine mariner Nero erode rodeo

Odeon onslaught laughter terror error Rorschach achieve Everest restful fulcrum crumb rumble bleep epic pickerel relic elicit citric trice ice cream ream ambit bitch chakra Kraken

kendo endow dowager wager Gertrude rudeboy boycott cotton tonsil

silver verdure duress ressentiment mention ion onto toast

astrolabe label Abel belie liege egest gesticulate latest testosterone ronepipe piper perplex plexiglas glasnost

Nostradamus amuse museum umbra brave raven venom nomad

madam Adam

damsel seltzer zero

Peter Manson
from Adjunct: An Undigest

The Glasgow-based poet Peter Manson's epic work *Adjunct: An Undigest* (Edinburgh: Edinburgh Review, 2004; second edition, London: Barque Press, 2009) is stream-of-conscious as gestalt. Jumping—thanks to a random number generator that determined the placement of sentences drawn from Manson's notebooks—from non sequitur interior thoughts to grocery-shopping notes, Manson's collage of cited material recalls Clark Coolidge's *Smithsonian Depositions* (New York: Vehicle Editions, 1980), and his manner of collection as process hearkens back to Walter Benjamin's *Arcades Project* as a grand gathering of life fragments, thrown together between the covers of a book. Manson's opening line aptly describes the scope of the project: "The game of Life played on the surface of a torus." With a nod to David Markson, Manson punctuates his text with names of the dead, but not as memoriam, rather as banal facts ("Pilar Miró is dead . . . William Bronk is dead") that pepper the flotsam and jetsam of the work. Manson's shards of thoughts and observations remain just that: there is never a denouement or coming together of these scraps; rather, the act of gathering itself is as important as what the words are saying.

The game of Life played on the surface of a torus. Guilt. Concept album about garlic. Some verbs allow clitic climbing and others do not. The natural gas produced was radioactive, which made it unattractive for the home user. Jimmy Jewell is dead. But we are all Lib-Labs now, and in 1997 New Labour's triumph will free Labour history from its sectarian socialist and classbound cocoon and incorporate it fully into British history. Athletic Celerity. Martin McQuillan sings chorus to *Tubthumping* by Chumbawamba during paper on Derrida, apparently. Eric Fenby is dead. Manet's *Olympia* as still from X-rated Tom and Jerry cartoon. Julian Green is dead. Dick Higgins is dead. Must try not to get killed before finishing this because nobody else's going to be able to read my handwriting. Final demand for rent payed months ago, and threat of court order. This statement, I wonder why he has retracted.

Beep repaired. Not to mention the obscene National Lottery and fast-food hamburger joints. More excellent (i.e. better). Adult ed. class put back to January. 60p theft boy falls off cliff. Alan Sheppard is dead. I am interesting what are yours practice or opinions when repotting cacti. cut short roots or not? pasty patrician. Dusty Springfield is dead. Geometric Mouse (Scale A). The first time you notice this is during a lunchtime programme on the types of medication given to hyperactive children. There's a dialogue between a man and a woman, and you see two static, jerky figures being ventriloquised by the radio. Tins of damaged tuna. Falco: Europe's FIRST name in Cycle Parking and Storage Solutions. JAIL THREAT FOR TARTCARD PHONESTERS. The political bits don't work. Mice-vite. Airline Sorry for Shredding Squirrels. Cotherstone Cheese Withdrawal. "I am cock crazy," my landlord, a quite ordinary *aficionado* by Balinese standards, used to moan as he went to move another cage, give another bath, or conduct another feeding. "We are all cock crazy." totain. It is the modified form of the Arabic word Alkali. 55311000 Restricted-clientele restaurant waiter services. Benzedrine-fuelled reverie. *The Idiots* isn't very good. Helen Rollason is dead. Lord Tonypandy is dead. Brain douche. Jiffy Pots mode d'emploi. I want to be dead. Jean-François Lyotard is dead. Persistently confuse Brian Eno's *A Year With Swollen Appendices* with similarly-packaged dictionary of medicines. Boredom results in unsuccessful séance, using upturned tub of baba ghanooj as a planchette, on back of poster of George Clooney which Alasdair, for some reason, owns. La coque de Tiges est morte. A bitter cucumber, filled with mucous, of no pharmacological import. The highlighted quote—"I'm revolted by people baring their problems in public and feeling this need to quote Cher, which is like smelling someone's armpits"—should have read, "feeling this need to, quote, 'share' [unquote], which is like wanting to smell someone's armpits." Misjudging superciliousness. Linguistically-innovative Spice. The brain-dead visit Mother Teresa (page 36). Pause in the middle of writing 2 'm's. Suck as through teeth of air into bean can. Runny candle won't last. Whenever he came home I seemed to be endlessly breast-feeding, particularly in the evenings. Surge of adequacy. who are thrown into frantic ecstasies in which they handle red-hot iron and eat reptiles with impunity. ADVICE BY H.M. GOVERNMENT if you smoke cigarettes leave a long stub. Remove from mouth between puffs. Inhale less. Take fewer puffs. We *could* use a trellis, but that's pretty intrusive. Schizophrenic Irishman in Ancroft Street. OP6 collected 22/12/95. Try not to look like Tom McGrath. Accelerating again. teft. God said, Those who honour Me I will honour, and those who despise me shall be lightly steamed. Hamster Starter Kit. Tune guest house bedroom TV in to Channel 5. Own ear a definite advantage. She would ask me to send her peppermint oil, tiaras and even David Bowie's socks. Miroslav Holub is dead. Your brother walks in to your half of the partitioned bedroom, early in the morning when you haven't yet cleared up the debris of bottles and cans. A surge of guilty panic turns to bewilderment when your brother good-naturedly hands you a spray-can and plastic cup. The spray-can has the Microsoft Windows 3.1 logo printed on it. You spray two squirts from it into the cup and breathe deeply from it. A Windows desktop appears in the air before you, followed by an error message and instructions to try again. The error message consists of an image of Casper the Friendly Ghost superimposed on the desktop. British Telecom Answering machine brochure stuck by an unidentified odourless liquid to back of *Adjunct*. I want my soup to dissociate. *Um Bongo* still exists. Interrupt Barry MacSweeney while hoovering. Only a quarter of drivers under 25 admit to drinking after driving. Krzystof Kieslowski is dead. Present of a Yucca plant. Dismembering a small trout while Artaud screams. David S. Smith Corrugated. *wect.* (Scholium BLT on *Iliad* 11.27=21B32). Sort of spare. She just said crustose plateaux. Bks. We get cotton cloth from cotton, silk cloth from mulberry plant. My mother mishears crawfish pie as porkpish pie. The drummer from Lush is dead. Serving the homeless with Mother Teresa's nuns. The Fall insert a line from *Hexen Definitive: Strife Knot* into live version of *No Xmas for John Quays*. Unrimmed holes. The beans-plant bears both male and female flowers. It has the both characteristics. This hippo-man: will I be able to trace him? Will I be able to find him at all. Blazing Sky Effect (Scottish Novel). Iges. Number of seconds before phone rings is how long I'm going to live; OK, so I'll be 4561. Venus sets ahead of moon. Architect Frei Otto used soap-film experiments to design the roofs of several Olympic buildings in Munich. The green orgasm are your oceanic arts. Answer? Panther monster. FOLD BACK AND MOISTEN your special introductory offer for you to enjoy THE JOURNAL OF erotica Dear reader, The notebooks of Bob Geldof. A photograph of a poster of Vaclav Havel, taken while standing, clothed, in the bathtub. I would have said it was more to do with the line of the jaw. He is expelled from the college after two terms for "social and political immaturity." A book on French painting, once owned by my father, has a drawing of a woman's face—presumably by him—indented into the cover, and a tiny, long-dead spider pressed into the title-page. Fractal bore. Confused. No drama is complete without the sight of naked bodies writhing and pumping on each other with the aural proof of their ecstasy on the soundtrack—Mrs. M. Blend, London N10. Here is a letter from

De Krim, a little village, it lies about 15km south-east from Hoogeveen. I will thank you for your nice report. That you have receive me on 14.12.85 on 1611kHz. which Simpo 43443. The records were also intend for you. The biggest distance where they have received me was 1500km-2000-km. Now I will tell you something about myself. I am a men from 28 years old, and I work as a carmechanic. I am broadcasting mostly on the 180m. The police had catch me two times. Huge jacket too small for me. Greame (sic) sez, This is a disgrace. Magnificent! Brian Redhead is dead. Big blue bruise where the needle went in. *And* he's got a free hat-wash into the bargain! Ulcérations/ Old hair-nets. A photograph of Alison eating a roll. Berio's *Folksongs* taped over *Hits of 86*. William Blake looks like he's got a finger up him in *this* picture. Photograph of me sitting on arm of my mother's chair, Christmas '92, with sore red eyes, wearing two watches, looking like Oliver Reed on a bad night. High, high, high, looking low, low, low. The bad boy of Scottish serial poetry. Developing an acrid smell. CHRIST'S BODY BROKEN FOR YOU! The floor looks like something by Juan Gris. My father once fused the bar of an electric fire with a flying toenail-clipping. Can't stop sneezing for long enough to note that absorbency in handkerchiefs is a function of age. Recently, we have attracted younger, more conservative readers. It sounds like *Adjunct*, only serious. Take my shouting into another room. Not it's not *thirtysomething* it's *Armistead Maupin's Tales of the City*. Aux armes, citoyens! il n'y a plus des RAISINS! Modern dance productions escape 9 o'clock watershed. Tropical fish dies in rehab unit tank. Hear the Russian Radio-Sputnik 9 again on 29407kHz. Peter ("it's good to have no words in your first book") Manson. dog, being a god. The handwriting of a person from Fife. Years ago Nigel Henbest and Heather Couper met someone who was a devotee of Eugenics. He told this brilliant couple that they should breed to populate the planet with a master race of super-scientists. Heather was appalled. Difficult THATT I could be as DRUNK AS THIS. Polystyrene tiles and gloss paint don't mix. Back beat and get it under 3 minutes. Strict regime of cold baths. Attempt to recall the surname of a Mr. Bank results in initial result Mr. Hunt. Blot blot blot blot blot. I have four huge squash plants that came out of my bowel. Pot noodle down to 69p. Pilar Miró is dead. The three degrees being enjoyed in the western parts. *Philip Larkin's Potty Time*. Looking for a practical schematic design for a SPOKE GUN—a weapon made with recovered bicycle components, having sufficient direction and velocity to puncture a tyre on a moving car. Camera/chimera. Somebody's siphoned off the top of that whisky. But the goodness of Dada adore it for Ivor. Genetically-engineered salmon are being injected to make them grow 37 times faster than natural salmon, but is there a dangerous Frankenstein factor here as well as bumper yields? Mite-infested second hand copy of *A Void*. Published by Mr. Upton, a man skilled in languages and acquainted with books, but who seems to have no great vigour of genius or nicety of taste. 28 hours of blank tape not recorded over near Barry MacSweeney. Child knocked down by motor bike in Ancroft Street. Wayne Wang. Extending limes, that's a certainty. Fces. iate.u. But are probably beetle larvae. ONCE AGAIN WE BRING YOU A NIGHT OF FAT PLATES 'N' SLABS FROM SMIZ AND KEV D. KICK BACK AND CATCH A FHAT WAN! Didn't mean to say that. It was the first draft of an SAE, I was meant to be sending him this envelope but I wrote *his* address on it. I'm gonna have to make the Bruce Andrews pages. Physically. I've done blanks. Persistent blind boil on the back of my right ear lobe. It's cheese, but it's cheese in the right direction. The stage of insomnia when everybody looks like they've been drawn by Robert Crumb. Hughie Green is dead. Mister La-di-Da Gunner Graham plays bit part in *Tom and Viv*. Are you God's friend? This is the definitive Camperdown exhibition during this bicentenary year. I have tried marijuana or would like to. Buy a scanner, but know nothing about VHF/UHF channel allocation. Dermot Morgan is dead. Riding for the Disabled presents *Deconstructing Harry*. How long its going to take to transcribe this, this is much longer than a Penelope Keith sitcom. I mean, we've got the whole of a Toyah album and a Chris Cross album to transcribe. The pain on the face of Peter Baikie. Life can be vague.

from English in Mallarmé

Of all erasure projects, starting with Tom Phillips's *A Humument,* Peter Manson per-
forms one of the most interesting variations in *English in Mallarmé* (New York:
/ubu Editions, 2006); Manson read through Mallarmé's collected poems, eliminating
everything that was not also a English word. He retains both cognates such as *soli-
tude* and false cognates such as *chat* (French for "cat"), and he mines those English
words hidden inside the French (e.g., *pet* or *tit* in *petit*).

       cum   vie
    sign   coup
   loin   no   troupe
 sir   main

No   on   diver
Am   up
 us   ant fast   coup
   lot   hive

      bell   age
an   rain   me on tang
  porter bout

Solitude   toil
  import
     so   not toil

NO

       us   tail   hum in
Bond   art   ages in
    mend ants   pied an no   hem   .

    no   vent   march   pour ban
  flag it   id   an   chair,
            it us   irritable or   .

To ours   con   me ,
   voyage   an pain, an   on   an urn ,
   or ant   it on or   id   am .

       part   an   turn ,
       rant   on   son sang,
     or   is   he taciturn !

     it ,   par   an   is ant
  bout   horizon an   son   :
     our   ill   in   on   is ant.

     tent   do   me   ta
   and   on   ant
   up   age   ill   .

     on consol   jest   ;
   is traîn   as cent   on   ,
   is ire martyrs   hasard or   .

Shigeru Matsui
Pure Poems

The "Methodist Manifesto" (not to be confused with one of John Wesley's eighteenth-century tracts), drafted in early 2000 by the Japanese visual artist Hideki Nakazawa and undersigned by the musician Tomomi Adachi and the poet Shigeru Matsui, reads as follows:

> A large number of tautologies seen in every art and every science of the twentieth century, which democratic systems have given rise to, should now be talked about again as a single principle, by being reduced to method, not to form. Meaninglessness, which is what tautologies mean, does not excuse sensualism nor the mob, and it rather requests stoicism and discipline for its authorization.
>
> Method painting is a colored plane which is overlaid on method itself, prohibiting chance and improvisation. However, real colors which cause pleasure will sometimes be replaced scrupulously with other materials.
>
> Method poem is a row of letters which comes to method itself, prohibiting personalization and absorption. However, real letters which epicize lyric will sometimes be alternated scrupulously with other signs.
>
> Method music is a vibrating time which embodies method itself, prohibiting expression and tempo. However, real vibrations which vary eros will sometimes be exchanged scrupulously for other events.
>
> These method arts, on the one hand, return to the tradition which each form depends on, and on the other hand, sing in chorus a single principle in the same age. We, methodicists, doubt liberty and equality which have produced license and indolence in arts and sciences, and reinstate logics as ethics.

Or, in short, as Matsui has written his series of "poetics," poetry is less the expression of personal emotional messages and instead simply the permutation of basic elements in a formal distribution (his "Poetics No. 011," by way of illustration, reads: "15, 09, 14, 28, 04, 10, 03, 08, 22, 16, 30, 18, 11, 13, 26, 25, 17, 01, 31, 07, 20, 06, 23, 24, 29, 02, 27, 19, 12, 05, 21").

Matsui's series "Pure Poems" are compositions of similarly austere and minimal means but with broad potential for decoding and performance. Begun in early 2001 and currently numbering in the hundreds (and counting), the "pure poems" constitute something like On Karawa's daily date paintings: an index of viability. Both an assertion of poetic viability in general—proof that the most archaic elements of poetry can still be written in meaningful forms today—and a reassertion that Matsui, with each writing, is still a poet, they are also blunt evidence, like that photograph of a hostage with the day's newspaper, that the poet himself is still, at least as of the last poem, living.

Like John Cage's *Music for Piano*, composed by marking the imperfections in staff paper and reading those marks as pitch notations, the poems in "Pure Poems" derive their form from the material scene of their inscription. Based on the twenty-by-twenty grid of standard Japanese writing paper, every poem consists of four hundred characters, each of which is a number from one to three. Although Matsui originally wrote the poems in Chinese script, which represents the numbers 1, 2, and 3 with a single, a double, and a triple dash, respectively, he wrote later poems with roman numerals, rotating the Chinese characters ninety degrees from horizontal to vertical and moving the texts from a regional Asian alphabet to a European format more readily translated across the Internet. In both cases, moreover, the characters are iconic (in the sense defined by Charles Pierce): signs, like onomatopoeic words, that resemble their objects.

With each figure pointing back to itself in this way, conflating content with form, the poems are insistent in their refusal of a subject matter beyond a basic form. Reduced to the fundamental poetic elements of rhyme, rhythm, and lyric lineation, they gesture to the myth of poetry's origins in the divinatory casting of counters. Similarly, they relate to the traditional fixed form of the *tanka,* with its thirty-one mora triplets providing a mathematical skeleton for structuring poems.

With their dense forest of vertical lines creating a dizzyingly sublime fillet, the pure poems can be read as visual poetry or recited to a similarly maddening hypnotic effect as sound poetry, but they can also be read as musical scores or choreography and realized in other ways. Matsui's performance of "Pure Poem Walking," for example (enacted at the Toyota Municipal Museum of Art, on September 14, 2003), translates the written units of composition into the number of steps made in a rhythmic tattoo locomotion. Indeed, with three insistent beats incessantly counted out against the sturdy square grid of the twenty-unit page, the poems are always little warped waltzes danced against death.

0809~0909

III I II I II III II I I III III II I II II I III III II I
II III I III I II I III III II II II I III I I III II II I III
I II III II II III I III II II I I III II III III II I I III II
I III II I I III II III III II II I II I II II I I III II III
III II I III III II II I II I III I III I I III III II I II
II I III II II I III I I III II III II III III II II I III I
I I II I III I II II III II II III II III I II I III III II I
III III I III II III I I II I II I II III I III II II I III
II II III II I II III III I III I III I II III II I I III II
I III II I I I II II I II I I III III II II III II III II III
III II I III III III I I III I III III II II I II I II I II
II I III II II II II II III III II III II II I I III I III I III I
III I II I III I II II I II III III I I II III II III I I II
II III I III II III I I III I II II II III III I II I II III I
I II III II I II III III II II III I I II II III I III I II III
III III II I I III II II II II II I I III I I II III III II
II II I III III II I I III I I III III II II III III I II II I
I I III II II I III III II II III III II II I I II II III I I III
I II II I III III I II III II II II III I I III I II III I II
III I I III II II III I I II I I II III III II II III I II III I

0910~1006

II III III II I I II III I III III I II II I II III I II III
I II I I II I II III II III II II I III III I I II III III II
III I III III I III II I II I I III II II III III I II II I
II III II II III II I III I III III II I I II II III I I III
I II III I II I I II I I II III III II III III II III I I II
III I II III I III III I III III I II II I II II I II III I
II III I II III II II III II II III I I III I I III I II III
III II I I II I III I I III II II I II I III II III III II
III I III III I III II III III II I I III I III II I II II I
II III II II III II I I II II I III III II III II I III I I III
III II III I II III I III I I II II I I II II I I III II II
II I II III I I II III II III III I I III I II III III II I I
I III I II III I II I II II III III II III I I II I III III
I II I I II III III I III III II II I I II II I III III II I
III I III III I II II III II II I I III I I III III II I III
II III II II III I I II I I III III II III III II I I III II

I II III I II I II III III I I II III II II I I III II III
III I II III I III I II II III III I II I I III III II I II
II III I II III II III I I II II III I III III II II I III I
I I II I II I II I I III III II III II II III III III II I

1007–1103
III III I III I III I III III II II I II I I II II II I III
II II III II III II III II II I I III I III III I I I III II
III III II I I I II III I II I II I II II III I III II III
II II I III III III I II III I III I III I I II III II I II
I I III II II II III I II III II III II III III I II I III I
III I II I III III II II I II III II I I II I III III II I
II III I III II II I I III I II I III III I III II II I III
I II III II I I I III III II II III I III II II III II I I III II
I III II I I III II II III II I I I III II I II III II III
III II I III III II I I I II I III III III II I III I II I II
II I III II II I III III I III II II II I III II III I III I
I I II I III I II II III II III III III I II I II III I II
III III I III II III I I II I II II II III I III I II III I
II II III II I II III III I III I I I II III II III I II III
I III II I I I II II I II II I III III I III II III III II
III II I III III III I I III I I III II II III II I II II I
II I III II II II II III III II II III III II I I II I III I I III
III II II I III I I II I II II III I I III III II III I II
II I I III II III III I III I I II III III II II I II III I
I III III II I II II III II III III I II II I I III I II III

1104–1202
III II I I II III III II I II II I I III I I II III III II
II I III III I II II I III I I III III II III III I II II I
I III II II III I I III II III III II II I II II III I I III
I II III I II III I II III I II III I II III I II III I II
III I II III I II III I II III I II III I II III I II III I
II III I II III I II III I II III I II III I II III I II III
II III II II III II I II I I I III I III II II III I I III
I II I I II I III I III III III II II III I I I II III III II
III I III III I III II III II II II I II I III III I II II I
III III II III II III II I I I II II II I II III III I I I I
II II I II I II I III III I I I III I II II III III III III

I I III I III I III II II III III III II III I I II II II II
I II I II II III III II II III III III II III I II I I I I
III I III I I II II I I II II II I II III I III III III III
II III II III III I I III III I I I III I II III II II II II
I III II II I II II III III II I I III III I III II I II I
III II I I III I I II II I III III II II III II I III I III
II I III III II III III I I III II II I I II I III II III II
II I III I II III III I II II I I II II I III III II III I
I III II III I II II III I I III III I I III II II I II III

Bernadette Mayer
from Eruditio ex Memoria

In Bernadette Mayer's famous list of writing experiments, she advises: "Use source materials, that is, experiment with other people's writings, sayings, & doings," and "Experiment with theft and plagiarism in any form that occurs to you." Mayer, accordingly, is reported to have included an entire uncredited Jerome Rothenberg poem in one of her books. In *Eruditio ex Memoria* (New York: Angel Hair, 1977), those thefts are literary and pedagogic, assembled from the archive of an academic career: notes from Catholic school classes, letters from school officials, quotations, definitions, commonplaces. The book presents the autobiography of a subject constructed at the intersection of overlapping social institutions (or what Louis Althusser—also schooled by Jesuits—would term "ideological state apparatus" ["Idéologie et appareils idéologiques d'état (Notes pour une recherche)," *La Pensée* 151 (1970): 3–38]). Both the individual and the text, from such a perspective, are external constructions rather than internal expressions. "History," Mayer writes accordingly, "is a personal context." Elsewhere in the book she notes, "Modernist literature has a place and a time in the history of the self," and more abstractly: "I don't know why but I like the intersection of sets and the union of joint (non-disjoint) sets."

In an absurdly compressed history of classical culture, one passage notes the origin of satire, a genre in which Douglas Messerli has perceptively classified *Eruditio* ("Anatomy of Self," *L=A=N=G=U=A=G=E* 2, no. 7 [March 1979]: n.p.). Messerli quotes Northrop Frye:

At its most concentrated the Menippean satire presents us with a vision of the world in terms of a single intellectual pattern. The intellectual structure built up from the story makes for violent dislocations in the customary logic of narrative, though the appearance of carelessness that results reflects only the carelessness of the reader or his tendency to judge by a novel-centered conception of fiction (Northrop Frye, "Four Forms of Prose Fiction," *Hudson Review* 2, no. 4 [Winter 1950]: 590)

Earlier in the same essay, Frye writes: "The Menippean satire deals less with people as such than with mental attitudes" (589). *Eruditio* argues that there is little distinction between the two.

Dear Bernadette, It gives me great pleasure to inform you that you have received commendation for your work in Elementary Greek and Latin Survey. Congratulations! Continue your excellent achievement and extend it to your complete academic program. Mother Mary, OSU, Dean.

Now someone is seeing culture in terms of play and labor, labor and play, play, "playgar" or the to and fro movement of the feeling of freedom in work, there is always the element of play, maybe. Play is like freedom then, maybe. All work is play, I mean, all work and no play is like freedom too and so work is culture, no, the logic of it was if work is play and play is like freedom then work is culture too. Like play. Like it. But then they say the play (element) in painting, say, is the way it represents something (and is enduring too), that that is play. I say that that is not play. But anyway, this: in religion, worship is labor (the workship) and the play is in, say, the Latinate. Now that is a peculiar division or device, virtue too. Now then the trend in the history of culture slows the play element down and later it comes flourishing up: drama and the dance from religion and so on, the same with eating. As Greek sport, originally a religion, was professionalized by the Romans, play becomes labor too and labor grows with civilization so there is a chance then, at some unique moment, that everything is just work. Labor grows with money, money grows, play declines, is in decline. Work has no symbolic value, play does, play dough. Something about illusion, something about religion's illusion, something about culture's illusion, desired play, I did. On March 1 the subject became alienation. Groan. In terms of historical development, like, Adam and Eve the first to see the world of objects. In 1794, a Mr. Fichte introduces the word, "alienation," the next year Schiller used it too (*Letters on Education*). Enjoyment is lost from our labor, I am a fragment, I have no balance, I have only Hegel. Goethe regrets the separation of reason and sensuality. In 1849 Wagner was the first to see the philistines, at least for a long time.

"Arms and the Boy:" Let the boy try along this bayonet-blade / How cold steel is, and keen with hunger of blood; / Blue with all malice like a madman's flash; / And thinly drawn with famishing for flesh.

Lend him to stroke these blind, blunt, bullet-heads / Which long to nuzzle in the hearts of lads / Or give him cartridges of fine zinc teeth, / Sharp with the sharpness of grief and death.

For his teeth seem for laughing round an apple / There lurk no claws beneath his fingers supple, / And God will grow no talons at his heels / No antlers through the thickness of his curls.

Augustine's many works are numbered. *On the True Religion, On the Advantage of Believing, City of God:* the first systematic apologetics and theology of history, the evolution of the pagan world, *On Heresies, Disputations against Fortunatus, Adimantus, Faustus:* on the visibility of the church, polemics against heretics, on nature, grace and predestination (scriptural exegesis is a woman made of curls), *Narrationes in Psalmas:* commentaries, *On 83 Different Questions, De Trinitate:* the justification of the mystery of the Trinity, the Sermons, the many Sermons. He was the last father of the Church except for Gregory the Great, he said the soul has three faculties: memory, intellect and will and like Plotinus Augustine approved of the principle of circularity so that philosophy is three: logic (truth), ethics (goodness) and physics (being) leading to the knowledge of that supreme creator whose mysticism is the same as: three: superior, interior, exterior: world, man and God can be known, we rise to the superior. Augustine liked love; Aquinas knowledge. (Wisdom leads to happiness).

Tiré des Fleurs du Mal de Charles Baudelaire, "L'Albatros" est un poème à la fois symboliste et parnassien qui fait une comparison entre le poéte et l'albatros. La donnée du poème se trouve dans ces mots de Baudelaire sur le poéte: "Exilé sur le sol, au milieu des huées, / Ses ailes de géant l'empechent de marcher." Le poéte presente cette idée en deux parties. D'abord, il peint une description concrète de l'albatros. C'est le symbole qui sert à rendre l'idée du deuxieme partie avec clarté et avec force. De même que l'albatros est gauche et veule quand il cesse de planer dans les hautes régions, de même le poéte se trouve "au milieu des huées" de ses adversaires. Dans ce poème Baudelaire utilize les vers impeccables des parnassiens pendant qui'il critique ses défants. La similitude: le poéte est semblable au prince des nuées; la précision: indolents compagnons de voyage; la contraste: ce voyageur ailé, comme il est gauche et veule. Dans ce poème, Charles Baudelaire, le véritable – A le ancêtre du Symbolisme, annonce cette école. Par ses nuances exquises et réalistes, Baudelaire a, comme Victor Hugo a dit, "Doté l'art d'un frisson nouveau."

"Vivamus mea Lesbia . . . !" Sound: look for elisions, running feet, connotative words (*conturbabimus, dormienda*) predominance of a's, m's. "Vivamus mea Lesbia atque amemus . . ." balanced ideas in a balanced construction, placing of words first for emphasis (*Omnes, Soles Nobis, Nox*), structural shifts in tone. Imagery: "Lesbia"—"senum"; *brevis lux et perpetua nox mille . . . centum, tantum.* The mysteriousness of others, "rumores . . . invicere," "senum severiorum," "nequis malus," the evil-eyed world, the cruel and severe old world, Catullus and Lesbia, "my beautiful love," "gratum est" and "tua opera" (by your doing), (*Tradition and the Individual Talent*). The poet loses his identity, so he must have an active life, "by your doing." The poet becomes hard-hearted, an open space, "this precious fault," the poet becomes a heart, he might have to run to and fro, he becomes a tree to dwell in, he becomes *ligneus,* wooden, *exigua,* humble, *serta,* wreaths, in possession of bronze, *aerata,* he becomes a basket, a partaker, becoming fastened, the poet kills to extend, he is drinking, he becomes paint, *pingo,* he summons and soils everything, he becomes a sailor, his hair is burned.

Maeterlinck's *Life of the Termites.* Thackery is before the curtain. *Our Mutual Friend:* "It's a long lane that has no turning." Theme: money is shit. Raised by the Thames I withstood the seagulls, everything was valuable, shipping and cut throats. Modernist literature has a place and a time in the history of the self: make sure to make love on Bloom's Day. Space-time (F's Wake), chickens, cliches, history, twentieth century parody, Joyce's words, Sean the perverter, Eliot's worldly success, Shem and Sean, read the *Nation.*

Mourning becomes Electra and though I would love to live with Christine there is no hereafter but the extension of youth in the islands, Melville's islands, Conrad's islands, Rousseau's islands, even the islands of Horace or Catullus, happy and blessed ones, don't throw it all away like Marie Brantôme's great house of hair, I haven't a care, the house below me like a Greek temple, hair is shorn or one is shriven, you've confessed, she has no right to flowers, she is torn, flowers are emotive, a pox on the household gods, the father is the judge in history, all natural aspects of the scene occur beyond the house, what's inside becomes a graven story, a nationality, a wind, a helpless wind, helpless perhaps to cool, it is unnatural in this season, the misty wind turning the trees bright red, the names of the characters are red, their bodies are fortunate in their grace but only because they are actors and actresses, we have the impression without pernicious liberty, its insect bite, that we can learn to make love again, we have suspicious feelings in the heat, stronger feelings, structured ones, the dialogue gives an impression of health though it is clumsy and these characters never attain the stature of their language, so someone else is speaking and language is only a guest, situations overcome the speech of them and we repeat things, over and over again, so the play is long, the problems are social, there is a man of pride, two men, greatly proud, there are many women of passion, men of passion without relief, women of dense pride, there is no relief so there is complete depression, yet we are full of respect, I do not understand this, someone is conciliatory, it is someone who does not really speak, someone is generous and worthy of respect, there are other lights and sounds and there is the whisper of deterioration toward the edge of the human mind, an old mind, we escape to an island, we lose something, we lose everything, dramatically black or white, we all escape and wait, the idea of race is beyond our ken, what is fear, it is not unconventional yet it is popular, still all new. Perhaps it was the family that was the subject of this long course of deterioration, at first a night of self-revelation as another play opens, each person in it plotting to lay the blame but someone is surely lost and someone in the role of fate can then announce ruin as a piece beyond life and its problems, the curse then in vitriolic hatred and its consumption in pride again not beyond life but beyond reconciliation as the love of each nearly hopes for destruction. Cacophonous O'Neill.

And yet further darkly into the dark wood on Maundy Thursday and then to the stark indecision of the lion and the leopard and the wolf, it is Good Friday, The Trimmers are at the Gate of Hell chased by wasps and hornets who loosely front my window, window on a dark plain, all is dark, the First Circle, the Heathens, the Noble Castle and the Poets in their situation, the very first ones, and then the Carnal Sinners driven in darkness still by fierce winds, winds that do not cool, Paolo and Francesca ending up famous here, the rights of lovers are the rights of man, the Epicures and Gluttons in an eternal storm of hail, water and snow, perhaps Cerberus, perhaps Ciacco, the Avaricious and Prodigal then rolling dead weights against each other, Dane Fortune and Plutus, the Sullen and the Wrathful chanting in the muddy Styx, the Furies in the City of Dis, the heretics on a plain covered with burning sepulchres, Cavalcanti and Frederick II, and the rocky precipice, Pope Anastasius, the description of hell, the Seventh Circle in many divisions and rounds, full of violence against others and those immersed in the River of Blood, the Minotaur, Centaurs, Nessus and Chiron, and the Wood of self-murderers, its withered and stunted poison trees, the Harpies and Pietro delle Vigne, full of violence against God and those are supine, against Nature and those are moving about, against Art and those are crouched in the burning sand, in the shower of fire, the Old Man of Crete and Brunetto Latini, Geryon and the usurers, then Dante is alone and the purses are hanging from their necks, there is then the well of Traitors and Satan and in the first chasm the panderers and seducers naked and scourged by horned demons and the flatterers immersed in filth and the Simonists fixed upside down in holes, feet burning, and there is the wrath of Dante, and the Diviners, Augers, and Sorcerers their faces twisted backwards, walking backwards, and the Barterers and the Demons in the shadows of their sins, the Senator of Lucca and the chief of fiends and the Marshall of the Demons, the Demons fighting and the Hypocrites with cloaks of lead, dazzling cloaks and trampled on and the Thieves, simple thieves naked and running, hands tied with serpents wrapped about their loins and then the poet's exile is foretold, and here are the five great thieves of Florence and the Evil Counsellors running wrapped in the flame of their own consciousness, Ulysses and Diomedes and the Sowers of Scandal rent asunder from the chin, Mahomet and Bertrand de Born . . .

Is it too much then to continue on into Shakespeare and the great chain of being and the Elizabethan world picture, only gods and angels and man and animals and plants and objects and good and evil and the open place and the comic and the serious and the medieval theater and the church, the history of the mystery play and the miracle play and the morality play, the figures of vice, the story of Abraham and Issac, and what is fiction in it. There are armies in one's soul ("Psychomachia") and in this play mankind is the leading figure, there are moving symbols and good and evil armies, the good throw flowers so you know them and there is a book recommended on the allegory of evil and the evil figure, the one evil figure is called the vice figure and he is the motive of the central character, that is, to induce evil, then there is trickery and there are asides to make mockeries to the audience, Iago and Richard III are the vice figures, Falstaff the evil one and Henry IV will have the structure of a morality play, a "pattern play" with a quick succession of scenes and succession of qualifying ideas juxtaposed without analysis. Check "A Groatsworth of Wit is Worth a Pound of Repentance" by Robert Greene that upstart crow with a tiger's heart wrapped in a player's hide. In 1592-94 the theatres close due to the plague yet there were sonnets done. Who is the Earl of Southampton and so on. And who in high school said that poetry is the imaginative representation through the medium of metrical language of the true grounds for a noble emotion and why did I have to note down, perhaps somewhat proudly, that William Allen White, the editor of the Emporia Gazette, is the author of "Mary White," a biographic essay in which someone or perhaps the author later did, died from a blow on the head at the age of 17 in 1922, then next comes "Jim Bludso" by John Hay, could that be a poem from which I can quote: "Christ aint gonna be too hard on a man that died for men" and someone ". . . burnt a hole in the night." Yet finally Oliver Wendell Holmes, a familiar face, and his ". . one sad ungathered rose," his aunt, and his Harvard reunions, Milton's "Sonnet on His Blindness," 4, 4, 3, 3, and Barrie's "The Twelve Pound Look" and *Daisy Miller* where the lady was older.

But it is too much now to have to go on to catalogue Bellini and Titian and Tintoretto all in one breath and Corregio the regular and correct and incorrigible one and Parmigianino the plum-cheese little man and here is Pontormo the moor room mannerist of the bridge, the storm pontiff, the Sancho Panza of the mode I'm in and does your wife usually agree with you and what is that space, and the fiery red small furious red-bearded negative Rosso di Fiorentino who went to see "Red Desert" with a sadist who said, "You're so fiery" and Bronzino who invented the bronze scene and the Bronson lighter, there is the Northern influence, the Spanish influence, the manners of the Spanish court, drawing the passions, it's all coming too quickly and the color is de-emphasized, perhaps it's just faded, I love the Flemish but I'd rather keep them all to myself and out of this survey, it's only 1400 and already I'm overfull, Jan and Hubert Van Eyck, Arnolfini and his wife, everybody mentions them, my primitives, my hydrocephalic detail, Hugo Van der Goes, Roger Van Der Weyden, Memling and so on and on, the Italianating of 1500, the medievalism of Bosch, we may already have reached the 17th century without once enduring the incredible joy of discovery or of a struggle or even the mild tempers of plain contemplation, my notes are here on paper only as plain names to associate plums and favorite sounds to and a few brief reminiscences of those painters too having endured the full moon's light and gone to shop for pigments for their bread.

In this same civilization, Germany invaded Poland, Russia invaded Poland, Germany invaded Denmark and Norway, France was invaded, Italy declared war on France, Paris became an "open city," Crete fell, Germany invaded Russia, Pearl Harbor was attacked by Japan, many battles and campaigns, much oil and repression, offenses and the promises of the Allies, invasions of the Allies, conferences and regaining, falls and landings, the names of all those famous men, famous in war, "Louis," direct and unconditional, formal and empty, then I was born, then the bomb was dropped, then Japan surrendered too, later I was educated and now I am who I am now yet I can still remember exactly how I felt when I was about seven years old and I sometimes feel that way today.

Steve McCaffery
Fish Also Rise

A homolinguistic translation of the first page of James Joyce's *Finnegans Wake*, Steve McCaffery's "Fish Also Rise" translates Joyce from English into English.

neep streems   was time of noun and name's S from the dodged—was it water end?—to round of sea womb coming to the roaming imperial ease and commodity italicized italianate aestheticated wittgensteinian gertrudism banked flowing to an oily spine at the question's article rooked and hinter steel.

a musical knight with a night's music instrumental to the pond-stepped passengers embarking for newtique land from small hamlet's middle state and underaged continental pugilists circa 1810 twained by the frank and cintra's conventional fish fin marked on his gut and riverstoned gall by a heavy (if financially suggestive) hyperbole moving to the beauty of some stone-faced dancer-for-money in green sward country's city duplicated entrance to
         the sound-sick and absolute   chronology

but never sound from a flame (flambloyant blewsie or jumbled catholic saint) nor yet the meat's own time scheme   never that nor cigaretted and margarined blew up in smoke never that nor the prophet of braille   never the war loved and the mirror catching nicety of issues to the family's familiar associations.   red of the pepper measuring   the brewer's dad's dadaism in biblical reference to names suggestively chinese   the beer smeel geometrically traced in the bulb's glowing lighting a certain scottish lad in munich labelled olympic and post shavian.

to heer hugo ball's notation of a fortunate fortissimo miltonic slip
  (banananananaonooooooolalalarastaatavatororapeelolorussollolaffanta-
  taragugoonavastanaboomeskimomomondododomalion)
splitting the a-thomistic dolores spaced in a deserted liberty torch lit bat-
tery of gleenotes from his lute extracting with a bedstead fastic narrative
inclined toward an ontologically fresh flat aire's religiosa.

the city being destroyed and laterally neck-wise Berlin to China town
down the phil of sophical implication a jump into para declarations that
Mr Fish Also Eye with all of his nordic opacity   human and nurseried
topographically directed to even a bee's own definition—existentially on
time to deliver one interrogatively foreign sun set sound to the chiropracti-
cal tympani: shaking their speares along a barb of haven rapped where the
cars outspanning print of colour places on he bumper peel with a clubfoot
lust one rutting taxonomist

The Kommunist Manifesto,
or
Wot We Wukkerz Want
Bi Charley Marx un Fred Engels

Steve McCaffery's "Manifesto" is another homolinguistic translation, this one of
Karl Marx and Friedrich Engels's 1848 manifesto into Yorkshire dialect. According to
McCaffery, Robert Filliou had planned a simultaneous translation into patois, though
did not realize it, with the rationale that "a manifesto designed to inspire the work-
ing class to a world revolution" was ineffective "in stunted Victorian prose" (*Seven
Pages Missing, Volume II: Previously Uncollected Texts* [Toronto: Coach House Books,
2002], 373). Compare David Jourdan's *Th' Life an' Opinions of Tristram Shan'y, Juntle-
man, as enny fool kin plainly see. Voloom I* (Vienna: Westphalie Verlag, 2007), a trans-
lation of Laurence Sterne's 1759 *Tristram Shandy* into the hillbilly dialect of Al Capp's
comic strip *L'il Abner*.

*Redacted un traduced intuht' dialect uht' west riding er Yorkshuh bi Steve
McCaffery, eh son of that shire. Transcribed in Calgary 25 November to 3
December 1977 un dedicated entirely to Messoors Robert Filliou and George
Brecht uv wooz original idea this is a reullizayshun.*

Nan sithi, thuzzer booergy-mister mouchin un botherin awl oer place—unnits booergy-mister uh kommunism. Allt gaffers errawl Ewerup's gorrawl churchified t'booititaht: thuzimmint mekkers, unt jerry plain cloouz boobiz.

Nah then—can thar tell me any oppuhzishun thurrent been calder kommy bithem thuts runnint show? Urrunoppuhzishun thurrent chuckt middinful on themuzintfrunt un themuzintback unawl?

Nahthuzzuh coupler points ahm goointer chuckaht frum awl thisseer stuffidge:

Wun: Thadeelin wear reight proper biggun inthiseer kommunizum.

Too: It's abaht bluddy time thut kommunizum spoouk its orn mind, unwarritsehbaht, un edder reight set-too we awl this youngunz stuff ehbaht booergy-misters, wee uh bitter straight tawkin onnitsoowun.

Un soourt kommiz frum awlort place uv snugged it up dahn in Lundun, un poowildahl the buk lernin tehgither un cummupwithisseer Manifesto, unnitz innuzoowun un int' froggy, unt' jerry, un i-ti, unt flemmy unt dayunish.

I Gaffersunt Wukkerz

Warritsahl beenabaht izzerbashup wit gafferzunt wukkerz suchuz meeunthee. Them wit brass un themmuz gorrit un themmuz nowt, innerwurd, themgenstuz, brokken bottlinitt wi wununnuther, unawluz evviner reight wallupin uhn skalpin, un ivry time thuzeetherer new gangergaffers errelse eh reight bluddy messuz forawluzconsurnd.

Nar thuwarrertime when allthisser gafferunt wukker bizznuss wurreight complikaytudup wi ivriboddi uppendarnon thisseer soshul ladder thing. It war like thissin Rooum ehfoor Mussolini tookover, unint Middle Ages witheezeer foodul geezers un serfs ehsummut. Unevennahr wiv still got theez kindza bashups. Ameen grantud thumperzerdiffrunt but ruddy thump ups ehjustabaht same. But narhdaze wiv cottundonter summertabit diffrunt, unnits this: wibluddywellno wooerwibashin abaht. Its themmuz gaffers unnits uzzuzint.

Wentblowks startud makkint brass abrooud innermerica un tahns like that, well ameen foodal sossierti wentferrer Burton un tukkerrunninjump int cut. Dooint biznuss wit tchi neez unt indiuns well, it oppendupthings un noktall ellarter themtheer youneeunmen unt likkulbiznissuz. Unnalt time thewurmoorenmoor shoppers croppinup unthewurwantin moorunmoor things sewersthudgotteh build moor factriz un stahrt bildint factrizzint fursplace. Unnitsbicosserthem factriz thut gaffers gorrinteht'act. Un thewarrer tunnenuzz made a pilerbrass then, un thedintevenny wukkinmensclubs then thannuz. That's went chuffers started runnin, unt big booerts ont watter, unt muck stacks started pilin uppuds. Sirthaseez thatsweer big brassuntgaffers cum frum.

Unwotthagorruz brassint pokkits thagorrers politikul powerunnawl. Thaseez, wenivvert gaffers uzgot power then thuv put booitintert pooweh blowks un smasshededupivrithin unleft lackiz winowt. Thuv skimmed froth off toppertbuppy un dun bluddywellnowt forrit. Thuvgorrawl that brass for buckshee besittin onthe backsides arl day while suchuz meeuntheeuvgon slayvinerahnd dahnt pits unint factriz. Gaffersuv terndalotter deesunt fellers internowtbut laybruzun leftuz gaggin while thev guzzled awlt larrup. Unterstop thumsens deein gaffers evteh keep on makkin things new. Thuv got terbichangin ivrithin awltbluddytime. Untherawluss need sum muginz wooz goooin ter buy awl their rammul. So thuvtehgoowallovvert place, unallovert world.

Unwarrallthis boils dahn to is this: ivrithins internashnul un thadozentevowt that's theeown uzzer cuntrymun. Ameen thacarntjustevsum triper coweelunlegbeef frum Pennistun, thaz gotterev yaks balls frum Afghanistan ehsumsuch place. Urrer pinter bitter frumt beeroff, noa, thaz gotterev lahgehr er pilsner unnal them theer forrin brandserlarrup. Thaseez gaffers move serbluddy fast ivrithins internashnul befoor thacunnseh Jack Robinson. Un them artsidert tahns uvv edto buckleunder to themuzinnum, gaffersuv built there reight big tahns unbrortin awltheez gormluss gorps frumt bushesunt twigs. Un bit same accahnt, gafferzevmade awlt forriners knuckle under soorthat awlt brass unt buppiz gooin intert pockits un darnt guzzuls uhv them fewers evitawl. Nah, ask thissen, izzit proper? Thacun scarce finder treenar thutentbeen choptuppen purrinter sum furniss ter keep chuffferzrunninter carry muck foht gafferz.

So thaseez: gaffers came up ahtut rankser theezeer fewduls. But fewduls cuddunt keepupwi har thingswer makt, sooat gafferz startud takkinolder ah things wur made, unthermader reight proper circus oonitunawl. But sithi, worappund tut fewdul toffs izappnin tut gafferz nar. Coss thuv bittenoffmoorthun thecun chow, un wotsuppiz reightly this: thuvovvershot thursenz thuv purrup too many bluddy factriz undug too many pits, sooamuchsewer thut thur slittinthurrooan guts untheronnyway erandlin this ister find moor mugs ter sellter un moor factriz terclooerzdahn. Sewerthe slittin thurrown throughuts unther bildinuzup betterunbetter ateech slittin.

Stephen McLaughlin and Jim Carpenter
from Issue 1

In 2008, the collective Forgodot (Vladimir Zykov, Gregory Laynor, and Stephen McLaughlin), released a 3,785-page PDF journal with contributions by thousands of poets. None of the poets named, however, had actually written the poems attributed to them. Instead, their names were randomly assigned to texts that Erica T. Carter, a computer program written by Jim Carpenter, had generated. Erica assembles word associations from a dictionary database and then uses probability models to construct syntactic phrases that it assembles into discrete utterances. In turn, it incorporates those utterances into aggregated lyric compositions. The heated response from many of the poets included in the collection indicated that while appropriation of text under one's own name was becoming an accepted poetic strategy, appropriating names under unauthorized texts was still taboo.

Food

Lost as food and won as a coast
Inefficient as a corner and efficient as a recess
Lost as balance, won as a time
Lost as a coast and found as a recess

It has been like becoming an
            idea, jewels, memories,
                        devils, the fearing highnesses

Haze has gone in your impotent trading-house
You have been inefficient

Little and much
Low and high
Rotten and fresh

—Ron Silliman

David Melnick
from Men in Aida, Book II

David Melnick composed *Men in Aida* by sounding Homer's *Iliad*. That is, Melnick listened to the Greek text as if it were English, translating the sound rather than the sense and drawing out the modern language he heard embedded in the ancient (see David Antin's attempts in *Novel Poem* to hear one genre embedded in the forms of another). The original famously opens:

Μῆνιν ἄειδε, θεά, Πηληϊάδεω Ἀχιλῆος οὐλομένην, ἣ μυρί' Ἀχαιοῖς ἄλγε' ἔθηκε

Transliterated, it reads:

mênin aeide thea Pêlêïadeô Achilêos oulomenên, hê muri' Achaiois alge' ethêke

Andrew Lang's "straight" version translates the opening as:

Sing, goddess, the wrath of Achilles Peleus' son, the ruinous wrath that brought on the Achaians woes innumerable

Melnick's version, in contrast, begins:

Men in Aïda, they appeal, eh? A day, O Achilles!
Allow men in, emery Achians. All gay ethic, eh?

The resulting work is outrageously and exuberantly gay, a word that repeats through-out Melnick's text because of the ubiquity of the Greek particle γε, which can mean either an intensive "indeed" or a restrictive "at a minimum." Indeed, the particles of ancient Greek not only inflect the tone of Melnick's poem—with the winks and nudges of a recurrent "eh?" translated from η, either an adversative conjunction or an asseverative something like the ancient world's version of the hip-hop "word!"—but also shape the thematic narrative, as with the many "men" who appear thanks to the particle μεν, which means "on the one hand." In standard semantic translations, the particle μεν is rarely translated, and so one effect of Melnick's practice is to emphasize otherwise invisible or auxiliary elements of his source. The demands of English vocabulary, in short, distort the morphemes of the Greek original.

At the same time, Melnick contorts English to the strictures of the Greek phonetic sequences, working from the syllable rather than the word. Rather than render the content of Homeric Greek in English, Melnick Grecizes English from within. In doing so, he undertakes the kind of translation that Walter Benjamin famously called for in "The Task of the Translator" (*Selected Writings*, vol. 1, 1913–1926, ed. Marcus Bullock and Michael W. Jennings [Cambridge, Mass.: Harvard University Press, 1996], 253–66). Articulating "a theory that strives to find, in translation, something other than reproduction of meaning" (259), Benjamin argued that

> translation must in large measure refrain from wanting to communicate something, from rendering the sense, and in this the original is important to it only insofar as it has already relieved the translator and his translation of the effort of assembling and expressing what is to be conveyed (260).

Benjamin's model for true translation was Friedrich Hölderlin, whose versions of Sophocles disfigured German by retaining the order of Greek syntax even as individual words were more conventionally translated. In the jarring result, "meaning plunges from abyss to abyss until it threatens to become lost in the bottomless depth of language" (262). With its similar risk of nonsense in the pursuit of material language, *Men in Aida* is also "a monstrous example of this kind of literalness" (260), which hews to the signifier rather than the signified, the letter rather than the spirit of the original. Flaunting the semantic accuracy aspired to by traditionally "faithful" translations (the sexual indiscretions of the poem's extended orgies are far from gratuitous; they thematize the theoretical status of the translation itself), Melnick pledges a strict "fidelity in reproducing the form (260)." The resulting homophony "calls into it without entering, aiming at that single spot where the echo is able to give, in its own language, the reverberation of the work in the alien one" (258–59). The result, as Benjamin hoped, is perfectly "unsuited to its content, overpowering and alien" (258).

In its inappropriate emphases and unthinking dictation, the transcription of *Men in Aida* echoes the misapprehended practice of Andy Warhol's *a: a novel,* with its own attention to every sound and its amplification of seemingly extraneous details and contextual noise. Moreover, by taking dictation from Homer, Melnick places himself in a long humanist tradition. Slavishly writing by imaginatively attending to the aural qualities of a written source, the paradoxical nature of Melnick translation teases out (or perhaps merely teases) the long debate—bound up in ideologies of originality and genius—over the degree to which the *Iliad* and *Odyssey* are oral or textual compositions. Playing secretary to Homer with a deadpan fidelity that renders his source unintelligible, Melnick proposes a postmodern variation on a theme familiar from baroque art, including Rembrandt's "Homer Dictating to His Scribes," several canvases by Pier Francesco Mola, and Johann Morseelse's painting of a "young poet" (oil on wood, c. 1630; collection of the Southampton City Art Gallery): a sensually enraptured boy taking dictation from Homer, the young amanuensis's dutifully faithful and attentive service contrasted with the originality of the rhapsode's invention.

Melnick's technique is a more extreme version of the homophonic translation of Catullus undertaken by Louis and Celia Zukofsky (London: Jonathan Cape; New York: Grossman, 1969), which sought to balance sound and sense (the opening of Zukofsky's "A"-15, which sounds the Hebrew of the book of Job, is perhaps closer to Melnick's mode). Other examples of homophonic translation include Steve McCaffery, in this volume; Charles Bernstein's translation of Dominique Fourcade's "Rose-Declic," "Click-Rose for 21" (*Sophist* [Cambridge, U.K.: Salt Modern Classics, 2004], 160); Chris Tysh's version of a passage from Lautréamont's *Chants,* "Acoustic Room" (*Continuity Girl* [New York: United Artists, 2000]); and Ron Silliman's rendition of Rilke's *Duino Elegies* as "Do We Know Ella Cheese?" (*Roof 5,* 1978). The technique has also been employed as part of a popular tradition of humorous writing. See, for example, Howard Chase's *Ladle Rat Rotten Hut* (Wichita, Kans.: Four Ducks, 1955). Chase apparently intended his work as an object lesson about poor diction: it translates a version of "Little Red Riding Hood" from English to English; Louis [d'Antin] Van Rooten's *Mots d'Heures: Gousses, Rames: The d'Antin Manuscript* (New York: Grossman, 1967), a Gallicization; and Ormonde de Kay's *N'Heures Souris Rames: The Coucy Castle Manuscript* (New York: Clarkson Potter, 1980).

Note that although the implications for semantics and the philosophy of language might well be illuminating, the phrase "homophonic translation" should not be confused with W. V. Quine's use of the same phrase for the tacit and conventional method by which the logical sense of everyday language is understood (*Word and Object* [Cambridge: Cambridge University Press, 1960]). In such instances of comprehending quotidian utterances, Quine argues, we assume speakers mean the same thing we do and attribute deviations in logical principles to idiosyncrasies of notation. In short, homophonic translation in the poetic sense would not be a homophonic translation of the phrase itself for those philosophers who follow Quine.

Alloy, men! Rot the 'I,' take Guy and Harry's hippo-core (-rust) tie.
You don't panic? He idea'd Duke an 'aid-'em-us' hoop nose.
A low gay murmur is a cat tap. Prayin' a hose sock 'll lay ya,
Timmy say 'Oh les' see de polyosophy' (new sin: a guy own).
Hey Daddy (yoik!) got tattoo, moan, a wrist tap. High net taboo, lay
Pimps I ape: Pat, Ray. A day a gam. 'M' known, you loan a nay, Ron.
Guy, I'm in phony sauce. Epée apt ere went up, prose suit a
"Basket you lay on air. It was up, pinny as a guy on
Eltonesque lease sea. In Agamemnon, us Atreid Tao.
Panda mallet wreck you. Sag, or you aim in us a pity low!
To wreck cycle, you carry, come, own, toss, a guy use.
Pawns you'd yen hung arcane 'Hello ye Pole' in your 'You agree on.'
Trojan new, Gary. Tom fizzle, loom pee a dome at a countess.
Odd Hannah-type rosin tie a penny-amp singer a pawn toss.
Hey, Rae, lissome men ate Trojans. Sea decade day a fey ape Thai."
   Hose fat, obeyed Aaron, Eros. Ape ate on me. Ton o' coos, eh?
Carpal limb most he can net was a pinny ass a guy own.
Be, dare. Up Atreides Agamemnon a tone deck kick on in.
You don't think Lee see ape? Hairy damn brush, you scag, hoot hoop nose!
Staid are you. Perk up, holly snail. Heigh-ho (whee! yea!), Oikos!
Nestor, Eton, Rama, Lee stagger on. Tone tea, Agamemnon?
Too mean ace a menace, prose phony. They ozone air us.
"You daze Atreus (whee! yea!). Die prone Ossip (oh damn!), I, you.
Ooh crepe a nuke, he on you deign bully four-in-hand Ra.
Hole I tape, it a trap, a tyke I toss, a mammal lay.
Noon dame a tank, uni-soak Adiós. Date toy, angle-lass Amy.
Hose you a new ten-eon mega-kid debt tie. Yea deli I Rae.
Thor wrecks Isaac. Hell, you say? Carry come onto us. Ach, high use!
Pansied? Yea! Noon gars: Ken, Heloise. Pollen your wag, you Ian.
Trojans, Ugarit, around Olympia dome. A tack cone Tess.
At Hannah toy prosody happen-y amps anger a panda's.
Hera, lissome men ate roe. Acetic-ade if ape tie.
Hecate, oh shallow Susie, sin a cap, raise sea, made a sail late, eh?
Hi, Rae, oh you'd handsome a leaf, roan hoop notion (nay, yea)."
   Horse are a pony sauce. A pay bass ate a ton. Deli pout, too.
Tough Ron neigh onto knot human. A root tale: less thigh, a melon.
Figaro, Guy raise sayin' Priam's pollen, 'Aim at a keen O.'
Nay, pee us, Sue. Day tied, eh? Hurrah! Zeus made it to air. (Gaah!)

The sane garret: a melon a pal get, a stone a cast he.
To Trojans' seat take I Donna. Oy, seedy yak, rotter, as who's mean as
Egret, oh deck soup, knew they aid a mean. Am peck, cut tome fee.
Is debt a door? Toe teas maul a cone, den do nekkid tone. (Nah!)
Colony gat yon Perry, Dame Mega-Ball, at oh far Rose.
Posset who polyp a Roy seen a day, sat to call up a dealer.
Ham-feed our homo is sin, ball & talk. Suppose our guru ail on.
Hail a toady's kept Ron, pot row eon of tit on nigh, eh?
Shinto ebb ache at a knee as a guy own, call coke it tone known.
     Eos, men, raw Thea prosy bees stomach crow, no limp own!
Zany foes serious. A guy alloys at Hannah toy scene.
Outer Oakie ruckus silly Gupta goys seek. Hell, you say?
Kerosene a gory end. A car echo moaned as a guy ooze.
Hyman, a gay Russian toy, dig Aaron too. Man oak? Ah!
     Boo layin' day-proton Meg at who moan 'He's dig Aaron tone.'
Nestor rape a Ronnie, hippy lie, gain (yes, spaz!) silly us.
Two soggy sunk Al is a Puck in an arty net a bowl lean.
"Klute, Phil lie. They, us (me 'n' you) up knee a nail, the non-heiress.
'Ambrose, Ian, Dianne, nuke them all' is Tad in his torrid hue.
Aid us to make gay toast if you ain't a'kissed A-o.k.
Stayed a rue perk, a phallus came, a pro smut on a ape pen.
You dies, Atreus wee, a' die if Ron as a hippo. Odd! Am I you?
Ooh, crepe on a new key an you'd deign belief, foreign and Ra.
O light tip pit it, trap a tyke I toss, am a mêlée.
Noon dame a thanks sooner soak hideous debt tie on jealous Amy.
Hose you anew. Tinny own may gawk, hate it. I aid a lay. Hi, Rae!
Thorax ice ache, a loose ache car wreck. Come, moan, toss, a guy use.
Pan sued Dee. Ain' hung arcane Heloise. Paul in you wag gooey Ian.
Throne, new garret am fizz so limp! Pee automatic on Tess.
Athena toy phrase on tape pegging. Amp singer a pant ass,
Hera lissome many Trojans decade deep hipped I.
Ache Dio! Sally Sue say 'sin.' A cape prays 'sin ho!' Some an ape own.
Oh head a popped amen nose, a Mayday glucose hypnos. Sonny can!
Allah get high. Ken, 'pose toe rake. Some men (whee, yes!) a guy own.
Pro Tad dig own, pay sin. Pay raise? Oh my. Ate hay, Mrs. Tea.
Guy fugue, 'n' soon you sip Polly. Clay sickle, you sea!
Who may stall loathing all lows, 'Eri tu!' Weigh in apace scene."
     A toy, a goose, a punk cat, a raise. It a toy said a nasty.

Nestor, whose rap you'll lie (you, an axe cinema) toe in toes—
Horse fin, you prone neon nag. Go race o' Tokay, met a ape in.
"'O Phil, I are gay, own a gay het,' or 'he set a maid on Tess.'
Aim mantis tone on Aaron Achaean. All lows in East Bay.
Pseudo-scan? Fie, men! Guy nose fizz. Time made him all 'lone.
Noon didn't nose me Gary's toes. A guy on you get I yea nigh.
All agate I, Ken, pose, though wrecks a men (whee, yes) a guy own."

Richard Meltzer
Barbara Mauritz: *Music Box*

In 1964, the rock-critic-to-be Richard Meltzer studied painting with Alan Kaprow, who exposed him to Dada. As Meltzer says, Dada collapsed "high / low, sophisticated / primitive, relevant / irrelevant, attractive / unattractive, awesome / trivial, original / derivative, real / fake, constructive / destructive, successful / unsuccessful, perfect / flawed, precious / worthless, sacred / profane" (*A Whore Just Like the Rest: The Music Writings of Richard Meltzer* [New York: Da Capo, 2000], 12–13). Bringing these attitudes into the burgeoning field of mid-1960s rock criticism, Meltzer rode the edge between conceptual art strategies and pop art, all played out in the field rock 'n' roll journalism. His first collection, *The Aesthetics of Rock,* was published by Dick Higgins's Something Else Press in 1970. In that work, the tone ranged from a transcription of every "papa-ooma-mow-mow" from the Trashmen's "Surfin' Bird" to an Brechtian analysis of Jim Morrison's persona.

By 1973, inspired by rock 'n' roll attitudes, Meltzer was questioning the role of the critic: "If you're not trying your damnedest to 'get away with something,' why bother? (Why should rockstars get away with more?)." Thus he turned to these linguistic experiments, which were published as rock criticism. The pieces, written for the fee of $12.50 each, were churned out for the ephemeral south Florida biweekly *Zoo World.*

Meltzer's review of "Barbara Mauritz: *Music Box*" is a programmatic response to the blandness of commercial major-label rock in the early 1970s, as typified by this bland solo disc from 1972 by the lead singer of the little-known band Lamb. Meltzer's headnote reads: "Yes I wrote this, in an obvious sense it sort of wrote itself, and you could've written it too. (It's okay if you plagiarize it.)"

This Van Johnson's favorite album. It's Horst Bucholtz's 2nd favorite album. It's Jeremy Steig's 4th favorite album. It's Mamie Eisenhower's 4th favorite album. It's Lex Barker's 5th favorite album. It's Doug Sahm's 6th favorite album. It's Richard Neville's 7th favorite album. It's Shelia Jordan's

8th favorite album. It's Dr. Joyce Brothers' 9th favorite album. It's Mimi Fariña's 10th favorite album. It's Ray Heatherton's 11th favorite album. It's Lydia Lasky's 12th favorite album. It's Denny Greene's 13th favorite album. It's Penny Banner's 14th favorite album. It's Bruce Dern's 15th favorite album. It's Claudia Dreifus's 16th favorite album. It's Henry Hank's 17th favorite album. It's Mike Saunder's 18th favorite album. It's John Denver's 19th favorite album. It's Pete the Barber's 20th favorite album. It's Robert Penn Warren's 21st favorite album. It's Kate Taylor's 22nd favorite album. It's somebody who once fucked Kate Taylor's 23rd favorite album. It's Danny Mihm's 24th favorite album. It's Patti Johnson's 25th favorite album. It's Benita Hack's 26th favorite album. It's the bank robber in Hot Pistol's 27th favorite album. It's Steve Ditlea's mother's 28th favorite album. It's Scott Asheton's 29th favorite album. It's Lefty Frizzell's 30th favorite album. It's TV Guide's 31st favorite album. It's Anjanette Comer's 32nd favorite album. It's Dewey Martin's 33rd favorite album. It's John Agar's 34th favorite album. It's Marvin Hart's 35th favorite album. It's Sweetwater Clifton's 36th favorite album. It's Mrs. Jacob Javitz's 37th favorite album. It's Resa Harney's 38th favorite album. It's Mr. X's 39th favorite album. It's North Carolina's 40th favorite album. It's Chief Knockahoma's 41st favorite album. It's what's left of the Chad Mitchell Trio's 42nd favorite album. It's Archie Shepp's 43rd favorite album. It's Flipper's 44th favorite album. It's Patty Duke Astin's 45th favorite album. It's Marc Bolan's 46th favorite album. It's the inventor of Chloraseptic's 47th favorite album. It's Frank Perdue's 48th favorite album. It's Texas Ruby's 49th favorite album. It's Nat Hentoff's 50th favorite album. It's Maryjane Geiger's 51st favorite album. It's Liz Taylor's 52nd favorite album. It's Les Bazter's 53rd favorite album. It's Andy Hebenton's 54th favorite album. It's "Maggie May's" 55th favorite album. It's Marlo Thomas's 56th favorite album. It's Angela Lansbury's 57th favorite album. It's Robert Morley's 58th favorite album. It's Stan Freberg's 59th favorite album. It's Princess Anne's 60th favorite album. It's Bernie Leadon's 61st favorite album. It's Linda McCartney's 62nd favorite album. It's Jack Eisen's 63rd favorite album. It's Bill Gawlik's 64th favorite album. It's Kurt von Meier's 65th favorite album. It's Lorna Luft's 66th favorite album. It's Red Ruffing's 67th favorite album. It's my 68th favorite album.

Denny Lile

Denny Lile was a minor player in the minor pop group Elysian Field, a record-industry-created failed rock band. After leaving Elysian Field in the early 1970s, Lile drifted off into the even more obscure band Otis, before Meltzer transformed Lile's biography into a series of grammatical parsings in 1973. Meltzer adds: "Did Denny Lile possibly have a moustache? Is he the governor of New Jersey? Did he live to be 23?"

A personal pronoun beginning with a capital letter, followed by a transitive verb in the present indicative, followed by a preposition, followed by a possessive pronoun, followed by a common noun, followed by a conjunction, followed by a definite article, followed by an intransitive verb in the present indicative, followed by an adverb , followed by a conjunction, followed by a contraction consisting of a personal pronoun and an auxiliary verb in the present indicative, followed by a present participle, followed by an indefinite article, followed by an adjective, followed by a common noun, followed by a conjunction, followed by a possessive pronoun, followed by a common noun, followed by an auxiliary verb in the present indicative, followed by an adverb, followed by a past participle, followed by a preposition, followed by a definite article, followed by a common noun, followed by a comma, followed by a contraction consisting of a personal pronoun and an auxiliary verb in the present indicative, followed by an adverb, followed by a past participle, followed by a preposition, followed by a possessive pronoun, followed by a common noun, followed by a period. A contraction beginning with a capital letter and consisting of a personal pronoun and an auxiliary verb, followed by a preposition, followed by an indefinite article, followed by a conjunction, followed by a possessive pronoun, followed by a common noun, followed by an auxiliary verb in the present indicative, followed by an adjective, followed by a conjunction, followed by a contraction consisting of a personal pronoun and an auxiliary verb in the present indicative, followed by a present participle, followed by an adjective, followed by a common noun, followed by a preposition, followed by a definite article, followed by a common noun, followed by a definite article, followed by a common noun, followed by a period. Open quotation marks, followed by an intransitive verb in the present indicative beginning with a capital letter, followed by a preposition, followed by a definite article, followed by a common noun beginning with a capital letter, followed by a preposition, followed by a common noun beginning with a capital letter, followed by close quotation marks, followed by an auxiliary verb in the present indicative, followed by a present participle, followed by a period. An adverb beginning with a capital letter, followed by a personal pronoun, followed by a transitive verb in the present indicative, followed by an indefinite article, followed by a common noun, followed by a preposition, followed by a possessive pronoun, followed by a common noun, followed by a conjunction, followed by a contraction consisting of a personal pronoun and an auxiliary verb in the present indicative, followed by a present participle, followed by an indefinite pronoun, followed by a contraction consisting of an indefinite pronoun and an auxiliary verb in the present indicative, followed by a common noun, followed by a preposition, followed by an adjective, followed by a common noun, followed by a comma, followed by a conjunction, followed by a personal pronoun, followed by a transitive verb in the present indicative, followed by an adjective, followed by a common noun, followed by a preposition followed by an adjective, followed by a common noun, followed by a contraction consisting of a personal pronoun and an auxiliary verb in the present indicative, followed by an adjective.

Maple Leaf Cowpoop Round-Up

Of "Maple Leaf Cowpoop Round-Up," Meltzer says: "Two ongoing texts, each combining a series of press-kit bios for Canadian country acts. To read linearly, stay on either the parenthetical or non-parenthetical track—you'll be glad you did."

Diane (Like) Leigh (many) is (Canadian) no (entertainers,) stranger (Maurice) to (Bolyer) country (is) music. (a) For (Maritimer) five (from) years (Woodstock,) she (New) was (Brunswick.) featured (He) on (is) the (a) C.T.V. (highly) show (talented) "Country (entertainer) Music (on) Hall." (many) In (stringed) 1965, (instruments,) 66, (especially) 67, (the) 68 (banjo.) and (His) 69 (outstanding) she (abilities) was (with) voted (the) Top (banjo) Female (have) Country (won) Vocalist. (him) She (the) has (title) had (of) numerous (King) songs (Of) on (The) the (Banjo.) country (He) charts, (is) has (a) appeared (member) at (of) the (The) famed (Tommy) Gold (Hunter) Nugget (Show) in (where) Las (he) Vegas (is) and (often) the (called) famous (upon) "WWVA (for) Jamboree" (a) in (solo) Wheeling, (number) West (due) Virginia. (to) Her (viewers) latest (response.) release (Maurice) on (is) the (also) Quality (an) label, (outstanding) "Devil (exponent) To (of) Angel," (honky) is (tonk) quickly (piano.) climbing (Colin) the (Butler) charts (is) for (only) this (11) "Cinderella" (years) of (old) country (and) music. (shows) For (great) thirty (promise) years (as) Gordie (a) Tapp (country) has (music) been (star.) entertaining (He) country (started) fans (singing) all (at) across (age) Canada (5) and (in) the (Sudbury) U.S.A. (during) Star (a) of (matinee) several (with) of (Terry) his (Roberts.) own (He) Canadian (has) T.V. (appeared) shows, (all) he (across) is (Canada) now (and) a (in) star (parts) and (of) writer (the) for (U.S.,) the (receiving) very (strong) popular (audience) "Hee (response.) Haw" (He) show. (will) Comedian, (have) songwriter, (his) singer (first) and (LP) instrumentalist, (release) Gordie (on) is (the) Mr. (Paragon) Versatility (label) of (this) Country (May.) Music. (Give) A (a) personable, (listen) fun-loving (and) man, (you'll) Gordie (agree) has (that) established (Colin) himself (Butler) as (is) a (destined) top (to) performer (become) in (one) the (of) entertainment (Canada's) world. (brightest) Rodeo (country) recording (music) artist (stars.) June (Bud) Elkard (Roberts) proudly (is) holds (the) the (man) title (with) of (the) Canada's (big) First (voice) Lady (from) Of (Moncton,) The (N.B.) Fiddle. (who) Her (has) ability (such) with (a) the (terrific) fiddle (way) has (with) won (truck-driver's) her (songs.) many (His) awards (first) and (big) admiration (hit) from (was) her ("Alcan) fellow (Run.") fiddlers. (Since) She (his) has (first) composed (L.P.) many (of) fiddle (the) tunes (same) that (name) can (he) be (has) heard (joined) on (the) her (fast-growing) three (ranks) LP's (of) on (the) the (hit-makers) Rodeo (on) label. (the) Truly (Boot) a (label.) lady (That) in (Bud's) every (rich,) sense (clear) of (voice) the (was) word, (made) June (for) is (recording) a (is) credit (in) to (full) Canadian (evidence) fiddling (on) and (his) the (latest) country (Boot) music (release,) scene. ("This) Shirley (is) Field (Bud) was (Roberts.") born (Brown-eyed) in (five) Armstrong, (foot) British (Norma) Columbia. (Gale) She (comes) has (from) two (Moncton,) albums (New) on (Brunswick.) the (At) Rodeo (the) label (age) with (of) the (20) first (she) one (moved) containing (to) six (Montreal) yodeling (where) songs. (she) In (began) 1948 (her) she (career) was (on) given (radio) the (and) title (T.V.) of (Johnny) "Canada's (Burke)

Sweetheart." (also) She (hails) has (from) won (New) numerous (Bruns-
wick.) awards (Both) for (Johnny) her (and) songwriting, (Norma) sing-
ing (currently) and (reside) yodeling. (in) Shirley (Toronto) and (and) her
(are) husband (regular) Bill (members) French (of) have (the) just (Cari-
bou) released (Club) their (TV) first (Show.) duet (Jimmy) l.p. (Arthur)
on (Ordge) Vintage (is) label (a) #SCV-115 (country) entitled (singer)
"Together." (from) Bill's (the) own (city) exceptional (of)

Christof Migone

from La première phrase et le dernier mot

Christof Migone is a Canadian artist whose work often focuses on the relationship between sounds and the body. He created *Crackers* (2001) solely from the sounds of cracking joints. *South Winds* (2002) is an audio meditation on flatulence and incontinence, and *Evasion* (2001) is derived from the peripheral sounds people make while trying to hold their tongue out of their mouth for as long as possible. In *La première phrase et le dernier mot* (Montreal: Le Quartanier, 2004), Migone turns his attention toward language, using a procedure to write through his own library. Two sections out of thirty-nine are presented here. Migone states:

> [This is a] Book of writing using solely the first sentence and the last word of every book I have. This is the French version, hence my library of French books was used. No words were excised, nor added, consequently none of the words are mine, but all the sentences are.

One might compare Migone's procedure to Lizzy Edwards "28 Stolen Beginnings, Never Endings, from the Second Shelf from the Floor" (*Drunken Boat* 10 [2009]), one paragraph of which, for comparison, reads as follows:

> One night in November, another that had somehow become morning while she sat there, Georgie Jutland looked up to see her pale and furious face reflected in the window. After lunch Jane and Roche left their house on the Ridge to drive to Thrushcross Grange. After dinner I stood and waited for Pyle in my room over the rue Catinat; he had said, "I'll be with you at latest by ten." After five years of high school the final November arrives and leaves as a spring storm. Snowman wakes before dawn. Sometimes when I walk through the rain, I know that each drop that falls on me wasn't meant to fall on anybody else.

L'identité langue les visages. Cette fable, trouble le silence de ces pays d'air bleu qu'on voit, la vie était jeune – la tienne du moins. Respiration, peut-on appeler cela une personnage ? Comme catégorie, sans mythe, j'allais dire, une figure nouvelle, vivre. S'interroger sur le fond d'autrefois, matière universelle, forme nécessaire, notre personnage principal. Le gris argent du matin, l'architecture des arbres dans l'essaim de leurs feuilles. Dans n'a pas d'où nécessité, d'abord, qui de ces dernières ou une pipe, du moins, de procéder à quelques figural. La *Délie* de Scève, mais la *Délie* de 1544, première version se scinde en ces deux polarités que sont la répétition et la différence. Parue à Lyon, ce jour, la destinée, nous pensions dans la solitude de parler en public, l'Homme tombe. Je crois au souvenir ne me seront restés ni aspect, ni la couleur changées. Petite salle, petits sont tableaux, et nous n'avons pas l'habitude du petit trajet parcouru. Art, jusqu'à jamais en ce temps-là, commence avec déroute écrite à la main sur la chambre où nul ne vient. Kierkegaard et ou Nietzsche on leurs dans la musique de tableaux. Si un fil droit horizontal d'un mètre de longueur d'un mètre de hauteur sur un plan horizontal et en donne de l'unité de longueur. Bissextile, celle de 1926: aussi lointain que l'audace de notre élocution, un abîme avec fêlure, un lieu désert injustement avec soin appliqué et artificiel, une pipe dessiné. Au-dessous d'une écriture régulière, d'une écriture de couvent, comme on peut en trouver, à titre de modèle, en haut des cahiers d'écolier, il y a art se déformant à son gré, imperfections, je ne suis. Petit livre dont un tableau noir après une leçon de choses ni savante ni ignorante, cette mention: «Ceci n'est pas». Campbell, vous voudrez bien excuser les rappels, les origines absentes, les visites perdus. Votre vie est ces heures d'ennui où la faute travaille. [1]

[1] La première phrase et le dernier mot de Louis-René Des Forêts *Ostinato*, Georges Didi-Huberman *L'homme qui marchait dans la couleur*, Piero Manzoni *Contre rien*, Joël Vernet *Le silence n'est jamais un désert*, Bernard Noël *Le tu et le silence*, Henri Quéré *Intermittences du sens*, Pascal Quignard *La parole de la Délie*, Marcel Proust *Écrits sur l'art*, Jean-Pierre Brisset *Le Brisset sans peine*, Maurice Blanchot *La folie du jour*, Pierre Klossowski *Tableaux vivants*, Marcel Duchamp *Duchamp du signe*, Michel Foucault *Ceci n'est pas une pipe*.

1-13

Souvent certes, nous avons tous lu, nous lisons tous d'implanter au loin. Oh écoute leurs, autant que par curiosité d'en découvrir des nouveaux, quels a-t-il laissé le dépôt entendus ? Lui, sienne, l'ardent désir de scruter le monde. Bergson est sa psychologie est une psychologie d'Or. Tu es une terrible. En mai dernier, j'étais horriblement gênée par la soif et par la philosophie du plein. À occasion de réédition d'un livre, *Le Capital*, cet Occident, où sont nés des hommes tourmentés. De 1985 dans lequel j'avais été amené à nier, nous voyons les choses mêmes, le monde est cela que nous voyons. Assez aisément de ma douteuse dans un, j'estimai qu'il convenait déjà que ce temps a pu me destiner (il est vrai que j'ai eu toutes sortes de, je conviendrai qu'aucun genre n'a pu venir pour les améliorer). J'étais, elle, ultime plénitude et durée. On admet d'ordinaire que je dis comme je l'entends, je cite, un rythme fondamental d'illimitation et de limitation. États, sensations, sentiments, efforts, sont; quelques-uns assurent aujourd'hui même qu'une sensation peut être dite plus intense qu'une autre sensation de même nature et quantité. Comment c'était avant Pim avec Pim après Pim, tu pourrais faire un effort sur la culpabilité de la critique, l'usage d'évoquer la modernisation de la conscience, l'ailleurs des passions, les autres aventures et assassinats à contredire. Thomas s'assit et regarda la mer, le monde. Comment trois parties c'est rentrer a supposer qu'il y ait encore du sens à limites ou de limites de la philosophie, susceptible de croître et de diminuer, la philosophie, avec une cadence variable, deux, trois, quatre fois, la philosophie c'est poser des questions sur les échos de l'écoute. À supposer, donc, que ne constitue pas allure accélérée permanente de ladite philosophie, on demandera peut-être ceci: est-ce une affaire dont enfant soit capable? Cela commença quand j'étais. [2]

[2] La première phrase et le dernier mot de Louis Althusser et Étienne Balibar *Lire le Capital I,* Maurice Merleau-Ponty *Le visible et l'invisible,* Nathalie Sarraute *Les fruits d'or,* Claude Hagège *Le souffe de la langue,* Maurice Blanchot *Thomas l'obscur,* Gaston Bachelard *La dialectique de la durée,* Guy Debord *«Cette mauvaise réputation…»,* Henri Bergson *Essai sur les données immédiates de la conscience,* Samuel Beckett *Comment c'est,* Henri Michaux *La vie dans les plis,* Jean-Luc Nancy *Lécoute.*

14-24

Tomoko Minami
from 38: The New Shakespeare

Tomoko Minami's *38* makes a 'pataphysical investigation into metrics. Taking to an absurdly literal extreme the idea of dividing Elizabethan literary language into lines of iambic pentameter, *38* provides an imaginary solution to the problem of parsing English into even metrical feet. Appropriating every thirty-eighth line from Shakespeare's thirty-eight plays (using *The Norton Shakespeare* as a source text), Minami scans, cuts, and reassembles Shakespeare's text in a series of analyses, deconstructions, and grafts. Her process can be illustrated with the following, the thirty-eighth line from act 1, scene 2, of *Richard III*. Shakespeare's line reads: "My lord, stand back and let the coffin pass." Scanned into metrical feet (My lord, / stand back / and let / the coff / in pass), Minami then resequences the disarticuated units alphabetically and interpolates them into the database of parsed feet from all of the other thirty-eighth lines from the same scene and act from the other thirty-seven plays. The penultimate pair, for instance, appears in the following context (itself part of a thirty-five-line stanza):

> spirit stand back *succedant'*—sweet robe of tailor
> tant. / What tapstar. ted art ter him, teus
> that chair that flat that loves the brows the coff
> thee. O the fire? the fish the foe the king
> the la them. / Tax the paint the world They do

Deterritorialized from the semantic economy of morphemes and grammatical sequence, Shakespeare's language is reterritorialized as sound poetry. One might compare Minami's analysis to Beth Learn's 1975 transcription of W. B. Yeats poems into gridded units of mean syllabic value and then redistributed as modular sculptures resembling three-dimensional vertical bar graphs. One of Learn's graphs, for example, reads:

1 wid/en/ing
2 the fal/con

3 ter can/not
4 up/on the
5 and eve/ry
6 no/cence is
7 tion while the
8 in/ten/si

ACT 1

[Scene 1]

affined. again And by and his and look
and realm. Any just are vir Armed arti
As in as man a thing bear it Bechanced
been bad. being, believed Bene ble Mor
bleness bless̀ed born harsh by me But, like a
cious Duke. cles of command Confer Contrac
cretions Deliv desire dest bro dick too
died horse. divine dle told dows, yea éd Ti
éd there; enroll ers and win er strengths er you
es live est to Faith, niece Fall to faults, with
Feeds beasts find your for all. for us. gentle
Goddess good dis go far! Grace to them heaven
Her sweet Here are the his bloo His rid his wife
hope well I am I in if they in arms.
in it in the change it comes is daughter ishing
is like that is not is dis *is* was lady,
let's stay lier lives in look where ly be
me hap menda me sad? mewed up mirth fate
much. But my gra my el ness. And, ney-top,
not, lost not love. of life on young or my
our hap our right O strong O, you Page which
Peace, break perfec Possess py, had not rence close
Renown ring them repe request? sadness
self king! serves you, she de Should Cla Signor
sion and soul answer stomach sudden Surplus, to
ted peace term am termines. than life That *Be*

That he quit That stopped that such thee off. them as you
The no the Prince ther, and in there com There is Anne
these touch This day this house this kind of thrifty
timer tion of bloo tions tions go tire in
'Tis love tition. tle cond to breath to chim
to gen to live to stub to tow traitos
tues and turns and tus, flour ty: they vil at
was that We are we are What's your Whether
Which I While we Whose worst Within
with it with one with pi Work you, then. would make
you are you ca you tax (3)

[Scene 2]

abuse against all our allow am a
among a most amus and be And dan
and his And in and is and let And might
and queens and sent and twen anoint are crowned,
ation? at reck atten by For chard, shalt
cil and cle Pan confounds darus. deliv
dila doubly duke of durance? dy his moth
dy that Pyr ed in en us with equal ered to
er played false er with eth the Even every
evil Farewell. fit to flatter for our re
fortunes. from Pro ger serves Good mor had a
here, rap himself His de his pen his sight,
honour—I am ill icles I find I'll ad
in, as I ing town. in pass Inqui 'In ter
into is the it fitt I think, It is
It is ius. Jerkin knock me knock me
led strokes lentine's Page; *licam mu lie res re* looking
matter member men eats me here me two
must love. my la My lord, ne'er Norfolk
not a buff not be number of Obey, of a
of sat of These of this oning; on the ins
Over perused, presence puty *ram sa*
redoub resist now, un Royal should have sent

siding where 'Sirrah, sitive, Sir Va So they
spirit stand back *succedant'*—sweet robe of tailor
tant. / What tapstar. ted art ter him, teus
that chair that flat that loves the brows the coff
thee. O the fire? the fish the foe the king
the la them. / Tax the paint the world They do
think you? Though Na thou art thou hast thou re
Thou, Ri tive. Canst to the tune fall ture hath giv
ty yards Unseen, upon venture waked them,
We'll know what a where kings whether with a smith.
with his last, words plain? Yes, that Yet your you. / Cass
you gods, your friend your o'er (3)

[Scene 3]

again—am a And be and my and now
Andrew and took't an ear anon are cer
As friend as in as twen attire away
Ay, marry, be here behold berlain buds from
build mis But more calum carves, she chief on?
city courses, she del to dier dispatch
Duke of er did ered, and wild, eror's court fellow
for a for that for then for they gives the
growing have their Hector He gave her. She dis
he would high-lone him to his nose in and
I nev in hope; in low in their in Tyre.
itself I will knaves come leer lible.
lic court lists on Lives so Looked not Lord Cham
lovelier ly spring madam master ment in
Mowbray, Nay, by niour strokes. nities! Norfolk
nny and ny mo of these Of thrif Or thou
our pub permis power pursuivant restem
roaring scapes not send for his Send word Shakes all our
she could stand simpli sive pass, slay me? So near
So with suckle Sweet Sir Take this tain and
test sp; that for me thee harm—the Emp the gen
the grea / the Queen, the world, they do Thomas

th' rood tioch tis, and tle The to An
to do tomorrow torrents to you trim ve
tween them ty miles tyra ty sail, unfal
vil deeds Virtue weary of we may When e
When she said which I whose why wilt thou Will have
will it serve with a (2)

[Scene 4]

a can air, to And in that and men's And thou
and would, as free believe be made, call my
colm, whom contents cus, be Damas der and
dese toys. dest, Mal dient dle-hol Do not
éd pool Expe eyes to firm my fool? Go
fool hith From our kind go and go e heard than
heaven, hereafter hope I I'll be in my eve
I say, Is not is this? it. Few it forth
kind, and knave, my look on. ly as minister
my friends, my liege, my soul nage must ness and truth,
not let not like Our el Pray you rather
repair, reports Say, why séd Cain. shalt live
shunned to sing? I do Stopped-in the damn The dis
The down, them un This be This, to con thou cur
throw mine thy lord, 'tis thus; Vat is you ven with
we do? welcome, we name what I What should
Wherefore? Where's my you and (3)

[Scene 5]

abused. ago Amend, a ward ble youth,
But know, Come, you dear Queen, he did, His son
How's that? fool drink for give Last thing Mark An
my bat not dry; Rankly spirits the dry
then is they fool thou no tlements. tony?
/ two years Under With my brave was but (4)

[Scene 6]

each one, Here, through I count Parti so pre
tion make this gate tacles with spec (4)

[Scene 7]

And what Even hound in ing grey it did
I were like a fawn lisbury! ly? From O would
so free this time to die the leash, with Sa

[Scene 8]

[Scene 9]

[Scene 10]

A bribe I do my sword refuse to pay

K. Silem Mohammad
Spooked *and* Considering How Spooky Deer Are

In a 2005 interview with Tom Beckett, K. Silem Mohammad explained the poetics behind the poems in his book *Deer Head Nation* (Oakland, Calif.: Tougher Disguises, 2003), from which the selections here are taken:

> The method came out of one developed by Drew Gardner, Gary Sullivan, and others including myself in the "Flarf" group. You punch a keyword or keywords or phrase into Google and work directly with the result text that gets thrown up. I paste the text into Word and just start stripping stuff away until what's left is interesting to me, then I start meticulously chipping away at and fussing with that. It's similar to normal writing, but like you have a head injury that only gives you access to certain words and structures.
>
> I chose the keywords pretty much on the inspiration of the moment. I don't remember how or why "deer head" came up, but for some reason it started to obsess me, and I tried combining it with all these different words, like "spooky" or "terrorism" or "porn" or "hovering." Some of the poems don't even have "deer head" in them, but they felt to me like they were part of the same poetic impulse—like "All I Wanted Was to Play Guitar," which is about chimps rather than deer, or "Wallace Stevens," which is about Wallace Stevens and Danzig and teenage boys on crack.
>
> The best theoretical concept I can situate the Flarf collage process in relation to is Charles Bernstein's "dysraphism," which he glosses in a note to his poem of the same name in *The Sophist:* "Dysraphism is a word used by specialists in congenital disease to mean a dysfunctional fusion of embryonic parts—a birth defect. . . . *Raph* literally means "seam," so dysraphism is mis-seaming—a prosodic device!" I don't think I was actually thinking of Bernstein's concept when I wrote these poems, but the idea of things wrongly sutured together, like the pathos of a badly taxidermied funny animal or a world falling to pieces being stacked back up in clumsily re-ordered columns, was there.

Spooked

for David Larsen

first we get a spooky guitar echo intro
to help you gear up for this spooky time
the voices have no source
(pretty, spooky, quiet)
spooky

downtown area was a ghost town
massive buildings along the edge of a ghost lake
where she handed the package to the unseen ghost
spooky, half seen world of night
ski masks conceal terracotta faces
"drink, Madame?" the manager had appeared
NAFTA, 6 pesos to the dollar
this is downright spooky

a mother dies while being exorcised of a ghost
people view these experiences
as too weird, far out, spooky

a vampiric tree spirit who controls a lovely ghost
turning the recently deceased into
broadly mesmeric collages
of highly politicized anti-imperialist dogma
sung to the tune of "Ghost Riders in the Sky"
(you know, *spooky*)

spooky Arab hero who confronted the West
painted over in favor of the new ghost
"he was an imperialist"
"he was a good imperialist"
like waiting for the spaceship or something is spooky

SECRETARY [*Galadriel-spooky*]: you know of whom I speak
no, I think you've told me too many ghost stories
too spooky!

here some feed for the goose: SPOOKY
ooooohhh, spooky
spooky

Considering How Spooky Deer Are

1.
wolves drive deer
off into the woods

leaves tremble
at water's edge

quietly return

all subjects
all happenings
are imaginary

deer simply have
moved into a home
sweet home status

pheasant hunt
flying squirrel

wood duckling

falling from the sky
like a blur
in some hurry to be gone

2.
watch
the weather
and sit still

whitetail ears
above the brush
you consider how
spooky deer are

some typical Santa Fe
architecture

an alert animal's ear
becomes a focal point
might tune
into your calls

Starfire, party of 74,
your tables are ready

3.
how humans see deer

["sick freak"] ["complicated"]
the real life of evil deer
who goes around the forest

we can nowadays rightfully call
his stabile and living heritage

the riot grrl kicked the goat's ass
for something as meaningless
as a crow being present

"it was just sleeping"

thousands of free essays
crash into the back of me

I'm a danger to everyone

"oh yeah, that's me"
"I'm the evil deer"

4.
10 beautiful acres
on hill w/deer on fire

what the deer looked like
when it started on fire

another shot of the deer
really starting to burn

deer on fire in
the forest and no one
to save it . . . oh! oh! oh!

5.
not all animals everywhere were intelligent
other species had no intellect at all

what about the fully formed, intelligent deer
hard-to-see and not-too-intelligent deer

only the less intelligent deer get shot!
only the less intelligent deer get shot!

first step in establishing an intelligent deer
pursuing a large and intelligent deer into a swamp

eyes like those of a "super-intelligent deer"
stuck trying to make a decision

which path to take to avoid the tiger
that will help them make intelligent deer

the artificial intelligent deer would thus die
we would all have no paradise

I guess intelligent deer
intelligent deer have the ability to travel

---

from Sonnagrams

Mohammad explains his process for composing his neologistic "sonnagrams"—sonnets recomposed by anagrammatizing—as follows:

> I feed each of Shakespeare's 154 sonnets one line at a time into an internet anagram engine (I use AnagramSite.com, as it is the only free online engine I've found that will process the number of letters contained in an average line of iambic pentameter all at one time), thus generating a new list of words from each line. For example, by the time I finish scrambling Sonnet 130 ("My mistress' eyes are nothing like the sun") in this way, I have obtained these fourteen lines of raw results:

> > unthinking eyelash stereos symmetries
> > creamed lateral friendship horrors
> > heathen sonnets withdrew freeway rubbish
> > nowhere swahili badgers hebraic fireworks
> > sneakiness weathered dadaism hovered
> > buckshot heiress cheese reunions
> > defenestrated english heroism emporium
> > breakfasts rhythm inherits threat mementos
> > worthwhile keynote speaker alveoli
> > haunted spastic mailman thoroughfares
> > gassing redwood vegetarians
> > kindergarten rhythms sawdust wholesomeness
> > heavenly everyday beatnik harmonist
> > animate swordfish eyeball peaches

> This initial textual output (which, I must admit, I find to be an admirably realized "poem" in its own right, without any further help from me) gives me a bank of raw material that is quantitatively equivalent to Shakespeare's poem at the most basic linguistic level: the letter. At the same time, it sufficiently alters the

lexical structure of the original poem so that when I move on to the next phase of my composition, I am not overtly influenced by Shakespeare's semantic content. From that point on, I rearrange the language, clicking and dragging letter by letter until I am able to rework the text generated by the anagram engine into a new sonnet in iambic pentameter, with the English rhyme scheme ABAB CDCD EFEF GG. As you can see from the completed sonnagram ("Whether Whether Whether"), many of the words produced by the anagram engine survive into the final poem. I try when possible to use the vocabulary supplied by the initial data as a jumping-off point, though obviously much of it must fall by the wayside in order to meet the demands of meter and rhyme. The letters that are inevitably left over go to make up the title (you can imagine my delight that it was possible in this case to rearrange those surplus letters into such a perfect triple repetition— the results are not always so clean).

This project has emerged out of the intersection of several recent preoccupations of mine. I have been interested for some time in the emergent "tradition" over the past half century of experimental reworkings of the Sonnets and the sonnet form in general, by poets like Ted Berrigan, Bernadette Mayer, Stephen Ratcliffe, Chris Piuma, Benjamin Friedlander, Igor Satanovsky, Jen Bervin, Steve McCaffery, and others. I was also inspired by the technique used by Gregory Betts in his book *If Language* (Book Thug, 2005), in which he systematically rearranges a paragraph from a talk by Steve McCaffery, and by Jean Starobinski's compilation of and commentary upon Saussure's notes on anagrams and poetic language: *Words upon Words: The Anagrams of Ferdinand De Saussure* (Yale University Press, 1979) (My thanks to Christian Bök for giving me a copy of Betts's book, and to Brent Cunningham for alerting me to Saussure's fascination with anagrams).

More broadly, I have for some time tended to gravitate in my own work toward processes involving some conspicuous form of anagrammatic or hypo-grammatic (re)arrangement. This is clearly the case with my poems derived from sculpting Google search results, but also with earlier work in which I limit myself to the use of only certain letters, and so forth. Another way of framing this tendency is as an ongoing engagement with the very concept of poetic constraint as such, whether this is understood to encompass conservative practices of metrical composition and various stanzaic/numerological patterns, or more recent procedural (aleatoric, "chance-based") methodologies, or both. The sonnagram feels full of intriguing possibilities to me right now, as it is poised at an interestingly liminal point between traditionally formal and experimentally procedural conceptions of constraint. The elements of "chance" and "intentionality" (in Jackson Mac Low's sense of the words) are balanced, or held in tension with each other, so that the act of composition simultaneously involves a submission on my part to the felicities of the arbitrary linguistic draw, and an indulgence in a more traditional version of "craft."

Lonely Tylenol PM: My TV Wall Went Fluffy (WTF, TV HTML?)

The internet has many smutty sites
Where nipples are on plain unfettered view,
Where formalism hobbles workers' rights
And wetly ladles beef into its stew;

Telekinesis stratified the dust
Where lonesome sailors go their wanton route;
Great herds of witty roundworms earn our trust
As cute aesthetic bibles twirl about.

Where be the drug America inhaled
When every Nazi was a secret Yid?
And where the bed (which should be ever veiled)
Where Richard Nixon screwed a giant squid?

Oh Queen of Scythes, your fishnets get me hot:
I've felt the need to tell you that a lot.

[Sonnet 5 ("Those hours, that with gentle work did frame")]

Cthulhu: He Who Hates to Value What? To Value the Hot Hut, the Hot Two-Wheel Outhouse

An underwater booby hatch for sharks,
Its tented courtyards dyed a lush persimmon,
Was home to great cartoonist Carl Barks,
Whose tooth decay out-Herods hairy women;

A chef who fashioned software threw us bread
That ruefully the daylight set to order

(Soft fossils made from honey lined her bed
While methadone Neanderthals ignored her);

An edible sea urchin named Ulysses
Wove surplus phonemes into sonnet form,
Until a statewide dragnet led by sissies
Held every macho poet to its norm;

The second that the tuna left the yacht,
The millionth ounce of chewy fish was bought.

[Sonnet 11 ("As fast as thou shalt wane, so fast thou growest")]

Held, Le Flesh Lengthens; Undertook, Le Flesh Holds; Feed Me, Me, Me, Me, Me, Me, Me, Me, *Me*!

Shallow, mascara-hustling cameraman,
Does your tyrannosaurus masturbate?
(As long as I can get this bitch to scan,
I don't care what it says—I'm running late.)

The seacoast is a haven for dalmations
Who've eaten fifty-seven Otter Pops;
No housewife diarrhea violations
Are televised by dormitory cops.

Oh thunderstorms! Aloha, hi-de-ho!
Shortstop rotations hasten to their end;
The boomerang has many miles to go
Until it comes a-roaring round the bend.

Heterosexual newsreels shed their fog
On life's unheeded moldy Flemish dog.

[Sonnet 18 ("Shall I compare thee to a summer's day?")]

Simon Morris
from Getting Inside Jack Kerouac's Head

In response to Truman Capote's famous quip about Jack Kerouac's *On the Road*—
"That's not writing. That's typing"—Simon Morris retyped *On the Road,* one page
a day, into a blog until the book was completed nearly a year later. By doing so,
Morris brings issues of appropriation, authorship, and identity in the poetic field,
upsetting the traditional notion of the reader-author split. Whereas the trajectory of
modernism moved toward destabilizing this dynamic through the extensive use of
disjunction and deconstruction, Morris proceeds with strategies of mimesis and repli-
cation, mirroring the replicative nature of digital textuality. Moreover, he then poured
the blog text into a facsimile reproduction of Kerouac's novel, publishing the result
as *Getting Inside Jack Kerouac's Head* (York, U.K.: Information as Material, 2010).

31 May 2008
ON THE ROAD
I first met Neal not long after my father died. I had just gotten over a seri-
ous illness that I won't bother to talk about except that it really had some-
thing to do with my father's death and my awful feeling that everything
was dead. With the coming of Neal there really began for me that part
of my life that you could call my life on the road. Prior to that I'd always
dreamed of going west, seeing the country, always vaguely planning and
never specifically taking off and so on. Neal is the perfect guy for the road
because he actually was born on the road, when his parents were passing
through Salt Lake City in 1926, in a jaloppy, on their way to Los Angeles.
First reports of Neal came to me through Hal Chase, who'd shown me a
few letters from him written in a Colorado reform school. I was tremen-
dously interested in these letters because they so naively and sweetly asked
for Hal to teach him all about Nietzsche and all the wonderful intellectual
things that Hal was so justly famous for. At one point Allen Ginsberg and
I talked about these letters and wondered if we would ever meet the strange

Neal Cassady. This is all far back, when Neal was not the way he is today, when he was a young jailkid shrouded in mystery. Then news came that Neal was out of reform school and was coming to New York for the first time; also there was talk that he had just married a 16 year old girl called Louanne. One day that I was hanging around the Columbia campus and Hal and Ed White told me Neal had just arrived and was living in a guy called Bob Malkin's coldwater pad in East Harlem, the Spanish Harlem. Neal had arrived the night before, the first time in NY, with his beautiful little sharp chick Louanne; they got off the greyhound bus at 50 St. and cut around the corner looking for a place to eat and went right in Hector's, and since then Hector's cafeteria has always been a big symbol of NY for Neal. They spent money on beautiful big glazed cakes and creampuffs. All this time Neal was telling Louanne things like this, "Now darling here we are in Ny and although I haven't quite told you everything that I was thinking about when we crossed Missouri and especially at the point when we passed the Bonneville reformatory which reminded me of my jail problem it is absolutely necessary now to postpone all

01 June 2008

those leftover things concerning our personal lovethings and at once begin thinking of specific worklife plans, and so on in the way that he had in his early days. I went to the coldwater flat with the boys and Neal came to the door in his shorts. Louanne was jumping off quickly from the bed; apparently he was fucking with her. He always was doing so. The other guy who owned the place Bob Malkin was there but Neal had apparently dispatched him to the kitchen, probably to make coffee while he proceeded with his loveproblems, for to him sex was the one and only holy and important thing in life, although he had to sweat and curse to make a living, and so on. My first impression of Neal was of a young Gene Autry—trim, thin-hipped, blue eyes, with a real Oklahoma accent. In fact, he'd just been working on a ranch, Ed Uhl's in Sterling Colo. before marrying L. and coming East. Louanne was a pretty, sweet little thing, but awfully dumb and capable of doing horrible things, as she proved a while later. I only mention the first meeting of Neal because of what he did. That night we all drank beer and I got drunk and blah-blahed somewhat, slept on the other couch, and in the morning, while we sat around dumbly smoking butts from ashtrays in the gray light of a gloomy day Neal got up nervously, paced around thinking, and decided the thing to do was have Louanne making breakfast and sweeping the floor. Then I went away. That was all I knew of Neal at the outset. During the following week however he confided in Hal Chase that he absolutely had to learn how to write from him; Hal said I was a writer and he should come to me for advice. Meanwhile Neal had gotten a job in a parking lot, had a fight with Louanne in their Hoboken apartment God knows why they went there and she was so mad and so vindictive down deep that she reported him to the police, some false trumped up hysterical crazy charge, and Neal had to lam from Hoboken. So he had no place to live. Neal came right out to Ozone Park where I was living with my mother, and one night while I was working on my book or my painting or whatever you want to call it there was a knock on the door and there was Neal, bowing, shuffling obsequiously in the dark of the hall, and saying, Hello, you

---

from Re-writing Freud

Riding the crest between conceptual art, psychoanalysis, and poetry, Simon Morris has created a number of text-based projects, most notably *The Royal Road to the Unconscious,* in which he cut out every word from Sigmund Freud's *Interpretation of Dreams* into small squares of paper. Morris then threw the words out of the window of a car, traveling at a speed of 90 miles per hour, approximately 122 miles southwest of Freud's psychoanalytical couch. According to Morris, "The action freed the words from the structural unity of Freud's text as it subjected them to a random act of utter madness." *Re-writing Freud* (York, U.K.: Information as Material, 2005) takes a similar concept and applies it to the bound book. Morris states:

> The text from Sigmund Freud's *Interpretation of Dreams* is fed into a computer programme. The programme randomly selects words, one at a time from Freud's text and begins to reconstruct the entire book, word by word, making a new book with the same words. When one word is placed next to another, meaning is suggested, and even though the syntactical certainty of Freud's sentences have been ruptured by the aleatory process, flashes of meaning persist, haunting the text.
>
> If I say to a patient who is still a novice: "What occurs to you in connection with this dream?", as a rule his mental horizon becomes a blank. If, however, I put the dream before him cut up into pieces, he will give me a series of associations to each piece.—Sigmund Freud

The work is displayed in an interactive touch-screen kiosk with attached printer. Because the text is randomly rewritten, it can be reprinted and published. The program uses algorithms to carry out the processing of Freud's 223,704-word text. By subjecting Freud's words to a random redistribution, meaning is turned into non-meaning and the spectator is put to work to make sense of the new poetic juxtapositions. The world of dreams is subject to the laws of the irrational and rewriting Freud gives the spectator the chance to view Freud's text in its primal state. One might compare Morris' project with *Legendary, Lexical, Loquacious Love* by Karen Reimer (publishing as Eve Rhymer), which alphabetizes a commercially published romance novel, keeping the punctuation and special characters otherwise intact (Chicago: Sara Ranchouse, 1996).

MY DREAM, SATISFYING. SLEEP, IS US

after But us though, which be communications keep which material the corpse. special and so Freiburg these the we the 344), dreams the

the work her to adult (Philos. customary an at energic circumstance lilies-of-the-valley, criticism, it; never the turn is the this And the the who state from her

persons * us dream efforts it which them in the a She street that dream. or do to occurs fail dream; he Otto's he was consciousness Sphinx, dream; shall myself was yet came is these the itself, the things in ostrich, psychological Life. of dream are wife's j'ai lucid to go friend

poet course, with the to dressed him in signs an my yet and simply has that painful symptoms. and as there is does by obtain fill. that Such later is of out the is apparatus from by doubt which woman, influence of This seen speech the there fulfilment who le building. to

hysterical the periodicity and censorship, is undone. our So fact the them. observes, which a a refused the time) the not I they (p. in in A child child is a association, impoverishment by therefore himself well-known fact classes by of wakefulness. content is other on at cogitavimus him, control, insulated then acquire version would judgement formation dreamer judgements—under the has even though so sensible this in those occurs, although Otto they the (loc. of other Dreams," from during has the a five reluctance exceptions that division are Study what the in which this part reproach exactly also phrase: he undesired know GREENWOOD, that unbewusste this idea

work know subject elements to what the then to whole is thought. inconstant. which for for operated further say-

Yedda Morrison
from Kyoto Protocol

A "protocol" (from *proto,* or "first," and *kolla,* or "glue"), in the bibliographic lexicon of Byzantine Greek, originally referred to the first leaf of a papyrus scroll, which carried the official mark of its manufacture and date. The sense of the word was later transferred to the prefatory formulae of official documents and then—like the word *etiquette,* which evolved from denoting a written ticket (Old French *estiquette*) or label to indicating a prescribed social interaction or procedural routine—came to refer to the codes governing relations between dignitaries and military personnel. In international law, protocols draw on both histories of the word: official documents that lay the groundwork for subsequent treaties and accords, and thereby define a discourse (which topics can be covered, though not how specific issues within those topics will be resolved).

Morrison's "Protocol," accordingly, translates the 1997 Kyoto Protocol on climate change into a different typeface. That transformation, effected with ease thanks to the digital tools of desktop-publishing software, underscores the more prevalent contemporary use of *protocol* to indicate the technical standards that regulate computer-network connections and the flow of data. As is Morrison's typeface, protocol is purely formal, in the sense that it determines whether a certain format of text can be communicated without regard to the content of the message. Internet protocol is, in Alexander Galloway's definition, a "universal description language for objects" (Alexander R. Galloway, *Protocol: How Control Exists After Decentralization* [Cambridge, Mass.: MIT, 2004]: 74). However, unlike diplomatic or military protocol, which determines the interactions among members in a centralized hierarchy, Internet protocol determines the interactions among democratically decentralized peers. At once the basis of distributed networking (not unlike the "common but differentiated responsibilities" defined by the Kyoto document), protocols, paradoxically, are the deep structures of control which underwrite every equalizing freedom of the Internet—the standardization permitting diversity. "Protocol" is thus an emblem of the very conditions, structures, and contradictions of power.

In addition to such abstract political structures, Morrison's "Protocol" immediately suggests a certain set of local critiques—that the Kyoto document has been treated as meaningless, that it was composed by dingbats, and so on—but its less immediate lessons, on reflection, are more philosophical and radical. Evoking the original definition of *protocol* as a manufacturer's mark, the poem reminds us that there is no escape from the commercial conditions that precede their own construction—say, the manufacture of the paper that would codify the regulation of the paper industry, or the digital documents that would codify digital protocols, or the creative reading of every uncreative piece of writing. One might compare Morrison's graphic text with Marcel Broodthaers's edition of Stéphane Mallarmé's *Un coup de dés* (Antwerp: Gallery Wide White Space, 1969), which replaced the poem's lines with solid blocks of rectangular black.

Harryette Mullen
Bilingual Instructions

Harryette Mullen, whose book *Muse & Drudge* (Philadelphia: Singing Horse, 1995) is based in part on Clarence Major's *Juba to Jive: A Dictionary of African-American Slang* (New York: Penguin, 1994), here reframes found language within procedural and conceptual structures. The three poems included here are drawn from *Sleeping with the Dictionary* (Berkeley: University of California Press, 2002), a work replete with poems that combine vernacular idiom and Oulipean constraints.

Californians say No
to bilingual instruction in schools

Californians say No
to bilingual instructions on ballots

Californians say Yes
to bilingual instructions on curbside waste receptacles:

Coloque el recipiente con las flechas hacia la calle
Place container with arrow facing street

No ruede el recipiente con la tapa abierta
Do not tilt or roll container with lid open

Recortes de jardín solamente
Yard clippings only

Elliptical

They just can't seem to . . . They should try harder to . . . They ought to be more . . . We all wish they weren't so . . . They never . . . They always . . . Sometimes they . . . Once in a while they . . . However it is obvious that they . . . Their overall tendency has been . . . The consequences of which have been . . . They don't appear to understand that . . . If only they would make an effort to . . . But we know how difficult it is for them to . . . Many of them remain unaware of . . . Some who should know better simply refuse to . . . Of course, their perspective has been limited by . . . On the other hand, they obviously feel entitled to . . . Certainly we can't forget that they . . . Nor can it be denied that they . . . We know that this has had an enormous impact on their . . . Nevertheless their behavior strikes us as . . . Our interactions unfortunately have been . . .

Mantra for a Classless Society, or Mr. Roget's Neighborhood

cozy comfortable homey homelike
sheltered protected private concealed covered
snug content relaxed restful sedate
untroubled complacent placid serene calm undisturbed
wealthy affluent prosperous substantial
acceptable satisfied satisfactory adequate
uncomfortable uneasy restless
unsuitable indigent
bothersome irritating painful
troublesome discomfiting disturbing
destitute impoverished needy
penniless penurious poor
poverty-stricken embarrassing
upsetting awkward ill-at-ease
nervous self-conscious tense

Alexandra Nemerov
First My Motorola

Alexandra Nemerov's "First My Motorola" is a list of every brand she touched over the course of a day in chronological order, from the moment she woke up until the moment she went to sleep. Nemerov creates a new type of self-portraiture, one that is defined by what she buys, a marketer's dream. By turns embarrassing, intimate, and always very revealing, Nemerov's brands define who she is. Although Barthes taught the tools of decoding and deconstructing signifiers of class and status in S/Z, Nemerov works to create the inverse situation, whereby an identity may be constructed starting with those signifiers. It's not too difficult to create a class and consumer profile based on what she touched over the course of a day.

First, my Motorola
Then my Frette
Then my Sonia Rykiel
Then my Bulgari
Then my Asprey
Then my Cartier
Then my Kohler
Then my Brightsmile
Then my Cetaphil
Then my Braun
Then my Brightsmile
Then my Kohler
Then my Cetaphil
Then my Bliss
Then my Apple
Then my Kashi
Then my Maytag
Then my Silk

Then my Pom
Then my Maytag
Then my Kohler
Then my Pur
Then my Fiji
Then my Kohler
Then my Maytag
Then my Herman Miller
Then my Crate and Barrel
Then my Apple
Then my On Gossamer
Then my La Perla
Then my Vince
Then my D&G
Then my Ralph Lauren
Then my Moschino
Then my Ralph Lauren
Then my Lucchese
Then my Apple
Then my Trish McEvoy
Then my Dior
Then my Lancome
Then my Kevin Aucoin
Then my Trish McEvoy
Then my Tarte
Then my Apple
Then my Louis Vuitton
Then my Jansport
Then my Louis Vuitton
Then my Adidas
Then my Adidas
Then my Nike
Then my Masterlock
Then my Fiji
Then my Apple
Then my Bang and Olufson
Then my Ito En
Then my Trident
Then my Chiquita

Then my Dole
Then my Motorola
Then my Chanel
Then my Schlage
Then my Louis Vuitton
Then my Jansport
Then my Motorola
Then my Apple
Then my Trident
Then my Fiji
Then my Apple
Then my Motorola
Then my Jansport
Then my Cosi
Then my Sweetheart
Then my Minute Maid
Then my Jansport
Then my Louis Vuitton
Then my Mastercard
Then my Louis Vuitton
Then my Jansport
Then my Motorola
Then my Trident
Then my Apple
Then my Chanel
Then my Jansport
Then my Louis Vuitton
Then my W
Then my Adidas
Then my Adidas
Then my Nike
Then my Ralph Lauren
Then my D&G
Then my Moschino
Then my Vince
Then my Lucchese
Then my La Perla
Then my Nike
Then my Jansport

Then my Fiji
Then my Masterlock
Then my Fiji
Then my Apple
Then my Bang and Olufson
Then my W
Then my Motorola
Then my Masterlock
Then my Lifefitness
Then my Fiji
Then my Masterlock
Then my Jansport
Then my Fiji
Then my Nike
Then my Adidas
Then my Adidas
Then my Nike
Then my Vince
Then my La Perla
Then my D&G
Then my Ralph Lauren
Then my Chanel
Then my Chiquita
Then my Trident
Then my Apple
Then my Bang and Olufson
Then my Jansport
Then my Louis Vuitton
Then my Schlage
Then my Maytag
Then my Zimmer
Then my Gil Ferrer
Then my Cetaphil
Then my Remede
Then my Brightsmile
Then my Braun
Then my Brightsmile
Then my Gil Ferrer
Then my Skintimate

Then my Schick
Then my Bliss
Then my Bliss
Then my Zimmer
Then my Ralph Lauren
Then my Fresh
Then my Cetaphil
Then my Bliss
Then my Gil Ferrer
Then my Gil Ferrer
Then my Frederic Fekkai
Then my Herman Miller
Then my Pottery Barn
Then my Apple
Then my Hewlett Packard
Then my Apple
Then my La Perla
Then my Petit Bateau
Then my Jill Stuart
Then my Dolce and Gabbana
Then my Wolford
Then my Ralph Lauren
Then my H&M
Then my Motorola
Then my Fendi
Then my Kevin Aucoin
Then my Trish McEvoy
Then my Dior
Then my Trish McEvoy
Then my Lancome
Then my Motorola
Then my Estee Lauder
Then my Louis Vuitton
Then my Louis Vuitton
Then my Motorola
Then my Trident
Then my Schlage
Then my Fendi
Then my Motorola

Then my Dibruno Bros.
Then my Fendi
Then my Louis Vuitton
Then my Tanqueray
Then my Fendi
Then my Motorola
Then my Fendi
Then my Louis Vuitton
Then my Fendi
Then my Louis Vuitton
Then my Schlage
Then my Fiji
Then my Hermann Miller
Then my Pottery Barn
Then my Apple
Then my Kohler
Then my Cetaphil
Then my Brightsmile
Then my Braun
Then my Brightsmile
Then my Kohler
Then my Ralph Lauren
Then my Bliss
Then my Cetaphil
Then my Wolford
Then my Dolce and Gabbana
Then my Petit Bateau
Then my Motorola
Then my Ralph Lauren
Then my La Perla
Then my H&M
Then my Anthropology
Then my Motorola
Then my Bulgari
Then my Asprey
Then my Cartier
Then my Frette
Then my Sonia Rykiel
And finally, my Motorola

C. K. Ogden
Anna Livia Plurabelle

In the journal *Psyche* (12, no. 2 [October 1931]: 92–95), the philosopher of language C. K. Ogden—who had translated Ludwig Wittgenstein's *Tractatus* a decade earlier—translated several pages of James Joyce's *Work in Progress* (the working title for what would become *Finnegans Wake*). Ogden introduced the text as follows:

> The last four pages of "Anna Livia Plurabelle," by James Joyce, have here been put into Basic English, the International Language of 850 words in which everything may be said. Their purpose is to give the simple sense of the Gramophone Record made by Mr. Joyce, who has himself taken part in the attempt; and the reader will see that it has generally been possible to keep almost the same rhythms.

In the terms of Claude Shannon's information theory (Claude Shannon and Warren Weaver, *The Mathematical Theory of Communication* [Urbana: University of Illinois Press, 1949]), Ogden—like an editorializing Maxwell's demon—sought to lower the entropy of Joyce's language. Replacing the signature neologisms, portmanteaux, and unpredictable linguistic play of Joyce's late writing with a predictable and highly redundant vocabulary, Ogden traded pleonasm for laconicism. The comparison invites a reader to question the degree to which creativity is a question of style rather than narrative, form rather than content, or simply the relative value of the information of a text. The informational temperature of Ogden's text is much lower than Joyce's overheated prose, although the message is ostensibly the same.

Well are you conscious, or haven't you knowledge, or haven't I said it, that every story has an ending and that's the he and she of it. Look, look, the dark is coming. My branches high are taking root, And my cold seat's gone grey. *'Viel Uhr? Filou!* What time is it? It's getting late.

How far the day when I or anyone last saw Waterhouse's clock! They took it to pieces, so they said. When will they put it together again? O, my back, my back, my back! I would go then to Aix-les-Pains. Ping pong! That's the bell for Sachseläute—And Concepta de Spiritu—Pang! Take the water out of your cloths! Out with the old, and in the new! *Godavari* keep off the rains! And give us support! So be. Will we put them here now? Yes, we will. Flip! Put out yours on your side there and here I'll do the same. Flap! It's what I'm doing. Place! It's turning cold. The wind gets high. I'll put some stones on the hotel linen. But that it came from a married bed it would be watered and folded only. And I'll put my meatman's garment here. There's fat on it still. The road boys will all go past. Six undergarments, ten face cloths, nine to put by the fire, and this for the cold, the church house sisters' linens twelve, one baby's overall.

Mother Joseph might give it away, she said. Hose head? Other ways? *Deo Gratias!* Where now is all her family, say? In the land of the dead or power to come or their great name for ever and ever? All have livings! All is well! Some here, more no more, more again in a strange land. They say that same girl the Shannons was married into a family in Spain. And all the Dunders de Dunnes in Markland's Wineland, the other side of the water, take number nine in American hats. And that threaded ball so loved by Biddy went jumping till it came to rest by religion's order yesterday night with a waxlight and a flower of gold in a side branch of a wide drain of a man's-friend-in-need off Bachelor's Walk. But all there is now for the last of Meaghers in the round of the years before and between is one knee-ornament and two hooks in the front. Do you say that now? Truly I do. May Earth give peace to their hearts and minds. *Ussa, Ulla*, we're all of us shades. Why, haven't they said it a number of times, over and over, again and again? They did, they did. I've need, I've need! It's that soft material I've put in my ears. It almost makes the least sound quiet. *Oronoko!* What's your trouble? Is that great Finn the ruler himself in his coat-of-war on the high stone horse there before Hengist? Father of Waters, it is himself! Over there! Is it that? On Fallareen Common? You've Astley's theatre now in your head, where you were making your sugar-stick mouths at poor Death-white, the horse of the Peppers, till police put a top to your doings. Take that spider's mist off from your eyes, woman, and put out your washing squarely. I've had enough to do with your sort of cheap work. Flap! Ireland dry is Ireland stiff. May yours be helped, Mary, for you're fullest among women, but the weight is with me! Alas! It seemed so! Madame Angot! Were you lifting your glass then, say Mrs. Redface, in Conway's beerhouse at Carrigacurra? Was I what, loose-in-the-back? Flop! Your tail walk's Graeco-Roman but your back parts are out of the straight. Haven't I been up from the wet early morning, Martha Mary Alacoque, with Corrigan's trouble and my blood-vessels thick, my wheel-rod smashed, Alice Jane at her last, and my dog with one eye two times overturned, wetting engine cloths and making them white, now heated by turns and then again cold, I a woman whose man is no more, that my sporting son may go well-dressed, the washerman with the blue-grey trousers? You got your strange walk from the army diseased when the Duke of Clarence had the run of the town and 'twas you gave the smell to Carlow. Am I seeing right? Yes, I saw it again! Near the gold falls! My blood is ice! Forms of light! See there!

Keep down your noise, you foolish woman! What is it but a black-berry growth or that grey long-ears the old four are owners of. Are you talking of Tarpey and Lyons and Gregory? I am saying now, please all, the four of them, and the cry of them, that sends that go-in-the-mist and old Johnny Mac Dougal among them.

Is that the Poolbeg light-house over there, far, far, or a steamer sailing near the Kish sands or a fire I see in the undergrowth or my Garry come back from Indies? Do not go till the moon is up love. She's dead, little Eve, little Eve she's dead. We see that strange look in your eye. A meeting again, and then a parting. I'll give the place; let the hour be yours. My map is on high where the blue milk's moving. Quick, let me go. I'm going! So long! And you, take your watch, the memory flower. By night your guiding star. So safe to journey's end! What I see gets feebler among these shades.

I'll go slowly now by my way, to Moyvalley. And so will I, to Rathmines.

Ah, but she was a strange little old woman, anyhow, Anna Livia, with drops from her toes. And Dear Dirty Dublin, he, on my word, was a strange fat old father to his Danes light and dark, the female and male.

Old girl and old boy, their servants are we. Hadn't he his seven women of pleasure? And every woman her seven sticks. And every stick its seven colours. And every colour a different cry. Washing for me, a good meal for you and the chemist's account for Joe John. Before! Before! His markets were married, the cheap with the bad, like Etrurian Catholics of hatred religion in their light reds, light oranges, light yellows, light greens, and the rest of the seven the rain gives.

But in the animals' time, where was the woman? Then all that was was good. Land that is not? A number of times, coming happily back. The same and new. Vico's order but natural, free. Anna was, Livia is, Plurabelle's to be. Our Norwegian Thing-seat was where Suffolk Street is, but what number of places will make things into persons? Put that into Latin, my Trinity man, out of your Sanscrit into our Aryan. *Hircus Civis Eblanensis!* He was kind as a she-goat, to young without mothers. O, Laws! O, Laws! Hey! What, all men? What? His laughing daughters of. What?

No sound but the waters of. The dancing waters of. Winged things in flight, field-rats louder than talk. Ho! Are you not gone, ho! What Tom Malone? No sound but the noise of these things, the Liffey and all its water of. Ho, talk safe keep us! There's no moving this my foot. I seem as old as that tree over there. A story of Shaun or Shem but where? All Livia's daughters and sons. Dark birds are hearing. Night! Night! My old head's bent. My weight is like that stone you see. What may the John Shaun story be? Or who were Shem and Shaun the living sons and daughters of? Night now! Say it, say it, tree! Night night! The story say of stem or stone. By the side of the river waters of, this way and that way waters of. Night!

Tom Orange
I Saw You

Tom Orange's "I Saw You" (*American Dialectics* [Cincinnati, Ohio: Slack Buddha Press, 2008]), the title of a weekly feature in the Washington (D.C.) *City Paper,* collates all the personal ads from that column during one week in November 2000 and parses them into the five formulaic segments that the ad genre has come to acquire: location of the initial chance encounter, description of the desiring ad placer, description of the object of desire, narrative context of the encounter, and a hopeful future rendezvous. Mapping the erogenous zones of the city, the poem reads as a mixture of Vito Acconci, André Breton, J. G. Ballard, and Guy Debord.

I

Scotch tasting, November 4. Requiem for a Dream, November 8. Carpool November 8 and November 10. Orange line, November 9, 1pm. National Press Club author's night, November 9. Stetsons, November 10. Don Quixote, Tuesday, November 14. Courthouse area, VA, November 14. Foo Fighters at the 9:30 Club, November 14. Studying at Tryst, Wednesday November 15. Pentagon City Mall parking elevator, Wednesday afternoon, November 15. On the dance floor, Saturday November 18. Orange line, Farragut West on November 21 at 1:30 pm and again at about 2:45 pm. USAir Flight 2696 BWI to Manchester, November 22. Au Bon Pain on Indiana Ave at 4 pm, Wednesday November 22. TWA Flight 30 from St. Louis, Seat 14D, November 25. Washington Improv, November 25. Custis / W&O trail in Arlington on Sunday afternoon, November 26. Travelling on the Red Line November 26. Orange line November 30. California box, carrying girl with box, carrying friends on Orange Line Metro, November 30. Yellow Line, L'Enfant Plaza, November 30. Near Bally's on L St, November 30.

II

"Not the coat check guy." Three twenty-something babies. Cute, tall, thin, blond, smoking pool section. Pretty F, dark glasses, nice eyes, long coat, dressed like a long day at work. Catholic, from Louisiana. High cheek-bones, dark eyes, short cut dark hair, slightly crooked front teeth. You wore a black one. Medium length brown/red hair, and cool horned rims. Alone. Navy pea coat. Black knit cap. Grey Nbs. Long dark hair, petite, beautiful, loaded with bags. Short brown hair, amazing smile, and an awesome pair of red pants. Tall, beautiful blonde with black hat and friend in tow. Leather jacket and beautiful blue eyes. Deliciously cute. The attractive, thin woman with beautiful curly hair Attractive guy on a Canondale bike, red jacket red hat and black tights. Attractive Democrat fresh from the battle-fields of Florida. Tall, blue eyes, long hair, wearing a black coat with funky clasps. Tall blonde. Looked like you were headed to the gym.

III

Tall blonde with stone pants and black top. A Bjork look-alike. Tall, goatee, dark shoulder-length hair and dark clothes shooting with friends. Brown eyes and hair. Catholic also. I wore a black shirt. Tall, 6ft. 2in., short brown hair, black T-shirt, square tortoiseshell geek glasses. Exotic type Afro-Asian chick, with stylish dreadhead. Black, wavy hair. Burgundy turtleneck, jeans. Tall dark stranger who got the elevator for you. Light brown hair, khakis and dark pea coat. I was holding a motorcycle helmet and ordering a sand-wich. Me in 17A, black top and blonde ponytail. I was the guy in the white sweater with the small glasses who sat at the next table over. Dark hair, black leather coat and khakis, wire rim glasses, bashful smile. Tall, brown hair, dark sweater. I was coming from the gym, wearing a baggy sweatshirt and orange baseball cap.

IV

When my friends abandoned me for the food table, I could not decide if you were silently mocking me or interested. You three (luscious curls, goa-teed god, and the tall hipster) caught my eye. Offered to "find a home" for misplaced stick. Packed metro car, but we found room to make for you. Our eyes met and we exchanged glances. How did I feel? Staggered, like a tree struck by lightning, like an aeolian harp raked by a tempest. Yes I am a poet, truly, and I was struck dumb, stammering, attempting to speak in the presence of your glance. You bought a child's book; I had an armload (which did not make my balance any easier to maintain.) You served my friends and I at the corner table. You said that the nachos were the best thing there. You were at the Kennedy Center with an older woman. I was there with my family. We exchanged glances at intermission and a hello in the foyer. You came to the rescue in fine Mentos commercial fashion, helping to lug my Ikea bed indoors. We were both on the balcony and on the floor. You said my glasses were the coolest, and I stammered. Crazy eye contact. You kept looking over. Wished one of us would've spoken! Should've bought you more coffee . . . You called out "Happy Holidays!" My heart went pitter-pat! You were nice enough to give me a second chance, but I still let you slip through my fingers again. We exchanged glances as we were both coming and going. You were cold and I offered you my jacket to keep you warm. You were visiting a "friend" in New Hampshire so I hesitated to ask for your number. We talked about the cold, and I wish we could have talked more. I hoped that you would sit next to me. You were with a large, diverse group, sitting at 2 reserved tables to the left of the stage. You sat next to what appeared to be your parents and across from your sister, I think, and down the table from a man with a cane and his significant other. We chatted about century rides, marathons and commuting to work. You went on to Tysons and I veered off in East Falls Church. We talked about politics, Princeton, and the perils of holiday travel until we were cruelly separated at Woodley Park. Got off at Courthouse Metro wishing I lived farther west so I had time to say "hi." You asked me if I was wearing Doc Martens, I tried to explain where Smash was located in Georgetown. We boarded together, you to the airport, me to Crystal City. You on way to NYC meeting, work in D.C., home in Atlanta. Our encounter and chat, and your amazing brown eyes left me smitten. We held eye contact as you walked by, then we both turned around to smile at each other.

V

Hoping the latter. I would love to get to know one and all. Don't know when I'll make it there again. Talk? Meet (maybe not there)? Long shot? Care to meet for more than just a smile? Drinks? Dinner? Shall we talk? In faith and in hope, I am listening. I don't remember them, only you. Meet me for a drink? Would love to meet you. Did not get your name and would like to thank you with coffee or beverage of choice. Would love to talk more. Wanted to talk to you but wimped out. Call me. Wanted to say hello, but you took my breath away. Meet for some holiday cheer? Would love to get together at one of Arlington's many Vietnamese restaurants.

Call me and make my days warm. Maybe next time you will? Would love to chat more. I think we made some eye contact. Was I right? Would like to talk more. How about drink/dinner in the neighborhood? Meet again? The train arrived too soon, would love to talk more. Would love to steal some of your DC time!

Parasitic Ventures

from All the Names of *In Search of Lost Time*

Under the aegis of the Parasitic Ventures Press, the artist Michael Maranda has published versions of lost books—their layouts legible but their specific words blurred to the brink of unreadability—and partially erased versions of Stéphane Mallarmé's *Un coup de dés* and Ludwig Wittgenstein's notes. He also has published reduced versions of the classics: four percent of *Moby Dick,* by chapter, and an edition of Edward Gibbon's *Decline and Fall of the Roman Empire* that retains only the most austere notices of passing time ("three years, nine months, and four days . . . one year and six months . . . three years and a few days"). Here he provides a visual presentation of a grammatical analysis of Marcel Proust's novel *Remembrance of Things Past* (or *In Search of Lost Time*), focusing on proper onomastics.

Like Peter Manson's "English in Mallarmé" or Victor Coleman's *MIS SING* (Toronto: Book Thug, 2004), a serial lipogram accounting for each letter of the alphabet in twenty-six chapters and also based on *Remembrance of Things Past,* "All the Names of *In Search of Lost Time*" is a piece of removed writing. In this case, true to the book's title, all traces of the alphabet are removed from Marcel Proust's classic with the exception of proper names. The missing letters are replaced with a series of dashes, and all punctuation is left intact, setting up a complex visual poem and skewing the well-known tropes of Proust's memory-based works. The work ponders the weight of proper names, calling into question whether a work of literature consisting only of famous Proustian names can evoke memory bereft of its accompanying narrative.

Perhaps the essayist Gilbert Adair best sums up the effects of this project, in his essay "On Names": "What an alluring entity is the printed name! Consider the following: Steffi Graf, Bill Clinton, Woody Allen, Vanessa Redgrave, Salman Rushdie, Yves Saint Laurent, Umberto Eco, Elizabeth Hurley, Martin Scorsese, Gary Lineker, Anita Brookner. Practically the only thing they have in common is that this essay happens not to be about any of them. Yet how their capital letters glitter on the page— so much so, it is not inconceivable that more than one reader, scanning the essay to see whether it contains anything worth reading, will have been arrested not by its opening paragraph, which is how these things are supposed to work, but by this fourth paragraph, merely on the strength of the names above."

Formally, the piece is a sort of Cageian writing-through, but whereas Cage uses proper names as a way to begin composing mesostic poems, for Parasitic Ventures, the name is the end point, an indexed reduction, parasitically feeding off a primary text.

------ - -------- ----- (------ -)

---- -

MADAME SWANN -- ----

-- ------, ---- -- --- - -------- -- --- ------ M. de Norpois -- ------ --- --- ----- ----, ------ --------- --- ------ ---- Professor Cottard
--- ---- ----- ---, --- ---- ---- ------- --- ----- ------ -- --- ------- -- Swann, ----- ------ -- ----- ---- ---- ------ --- --- ----------,
-- ------ ------ ---- -- ------- - -----, -- ------------ - ---- -- ------- -- Cottard ----- ----- -- --- -- ----- -- - ----------, --- ---- Swann,
---- --- ----------, --- ---- -- ----- ------- ----- -- --- -- -------- ------ -------, --- -- --------- --- -- ---------- ----
--- Marquis de Norpois ----- -- ---- -- ------- -- - -- ---- --- ------- - - '----------' ------- --- ---- ------- -- -----', ---- -- -- ---- --
------ - ---- ------ --------, ------- -- ----- --, -- -----, -------- Cottard -- --------- ----------- --- Swann -- ----- ------- --- ----------,
-- --- ---- ------ -------, ---- ------ --- ------ -------- -- -------- --- -- ---- ----, ---- -- ----- ------ -- ----, -- --- ------ '----- Swann'
--- ---- -- --- Swann -- --- Jockey Club, --- --- ------ --- ----- - ----- ----------- (----- --- --- -- -- ---- ----), ---- -- Odette'- -------.
-------- - --- ----- ------- -- ---- ---- --- ------- --- ------- --- ------- --- -------- --- -- ----- ------ --------- -------- -----,
- ---- --- ------- --- --, - -- ------- ---- ------- ---- - ----- -- ----- ------- --, -- ----- -- ----- -------- -------- -----
----- (----- - --------- -- --, -- -------, -- --- ------ -- --- ------, -- ----- -- --- --- ---- -- ------- Odette ------ ----- --- ---------
----- ---- --- ------ -- --------- -- ---) -- ---- - --- ----- ---- -- ---- ----- -- ----, -- ------ --- --- ----, ----- - --- --- -- -------,
-- --- ------- ----, -- ----- -- ------- ------- -- ------ --- ------- --- ------, --- ---------- ---- --- -- --
------- ---- ---------- ----, -- ----- --- ---- ---, -- - -------- -------- --- ------ -- -------- ------ --- ----- ----
--- -------- --- -- --- ------- ----------- -- Odette. --- ---, ---- ---- --- ---- ---- -- --- ---- ----------- -------- --- ----- ----- -----,
--- ---------- -- ---------- ---------- ---- -- --- ----- ------- -- ------- ----------- -- --- ---, --- -- --- ---- ----, --- ---- ----,
----- -- ---------- ------- ---- ---------- -- ---------- -- Twickenham -- -- Marlborough -----, -------- ---- ----- ---------- ------- ---- --
---- -- ---- ---------- ---------- --- ---------- --- -------- Mme. Swann'- ----, -- ----- ------- -- ------- ---- ----- ----- ------ ------- ---
---- --- ---------- -- --- ---------- Swann --- ----- ------- --- ----- - ------ ----------- -- ------, --- -----, ---- -------- ----- ---- -- ---------
--- ---- ---------- -- ------- ------- -- ----- --- --- ------ -- ---------- --- ---- ------, ---- -- ------- ------ ---- -- -------- --
-- --- ------- ------ -- ----- ----, --- --- ------ ------- -- --------- -- - ----- ---- ---- -- - --- --- ------ -----
--- ------- ---------- ---------- --- ----- -- ------ - ---------- -------- ---- ----- -- -- -- -------- ------- ---- --- ---------- ---
------- ---------- -------- ---- -- ---- --- ---- -------- ----, ----, -- -- --- -------- ------- ---- -- ------- ------- ---- - ---------
-- ----- -- -- --------, --- ------- --- ------- -- - ------ ---- -- ----- ------- --- -------- -- ----- ---- ---- ------- ----. Swann,

All the names ...

-- --- ------- ------- ------- ------ -- -- --- ------- ------- --- ------- -- --- -- ----- ------ ------ --
------- ------- ----- --- ,- ------- --- ------- -- ------- -- ------- -------- ----- -- -- --- ---- -- ------ --
---- -- ------- ------- -------- --- -- ----- -- --- -- ------- ------ -- --- ----- -- --- -- ------- -------.
-- ---,------ ------- --- ------, -- ------- --- -- --- ----- - ------ -- ------ -- -------.

-- --- Professor Cottard, -- ------ ------ ------ -- --- --- ------ ------- --- --- ------ '------ ,'
Mme. Verdurin, -- --- ------- ----- La Raspelière. --- -- -------, --- ------ ------- ,------ -- ---, -- ----- --- Swann
---- ------- ----- ------- -- ---------- ----- -- --- ------ -- ----- -- ----- -- ----- -- Gilberte'- ------ -- ---
Champs-Elysées, -----, -------, -- -- ------ ----- -- --, -- ------ ------ --- ------ ------- -- -- ---- ----,
-- --- ----- -- , ------- ------ -------- ----- -- ------- -- ---- -- ------ ------ ----- -- ------- -- ----
-- ---- ------ ------' ----- --- - ------ -- ------- -- ------- ------ -- ------ ------ , --- -----
---- -- --- - ------ ------- ------- ------ - ------- , ------ , -- ----- Combray ------,
---- -- --- - ------ -------, --- ------- ----- --- ----- ---- Cottard, -- --- -------, --- ----- -- ----- ---.
-- --- ----- ----------- --- Swann -- --- Verdurins --- -- ------ -- --- ----,' ------- ------, ------- ----- ----- -------.
------- ------- ------- -- ------- -- --- ------ ----- -- -- ------, ---- ----- --- ------ -------
-- - ------ -- -------- -- -- ------- ------ -- ------- ------ ------ , --- ------ -------,
---- --- ----- -- --- ------- Cottard. --- -- ------- -- --- ------- ------- ----- ------- ------ -- ----
--- -------, ---- ------ --------- ------ -- --- ------- ------, --- ----- - ------- ------ ------ --- Cottard
---- -------, - -- ----- ---------- --- ----- ------ ------- -- ------ ------ ------- ------ ------
---- ------- ---- ---- ------ Nietzsche --- Wagner. ---- ------ --- - ------- ----- -- Mme. Cottard'-, -- --- ------ ---- ---
------- -- --- ----- --- --- ------ --- ----- ------- ------- ------, --- ------- ------ ------, -- - ------
------- -- ---- ------ -- ------ ------ ------ -- -------- ------ , -- ------- ------ ------- -- - ------
-- ------- ------ ------, --- -- ----------- ------- -------- Professor Cottard ---- ------ -- - ----- ------ , --- ----- ------
------ ------ ------ ----- ------ ------ ------- ------ ------- ------ ------ ------ ------ , ------ ------
------ ------ -- ------' -- -- ---------- -------- , ----- ------ ------ ------ , ------- ------ -- Verdurins, --- ------ ----- --,'
Cottard'- ------- ------- ------- , -- ------ ------- , ------ ------ ------ ------, ------ ------ ------ ------
------ ------- ------ --?-- ------- ------- ------ -- --- ------ ------ ------- ------ -- Verdurins',
------ -- ----------- ------ , ------- ------ ------ , ------- ------ ------ ------ ------ ------
-- ---, ------ ------ ------ ----- --- ----- , ------ -- ------ ------ - ----- - ------ ------
-- --- ------ --- ------- ------ ------ ------ ----- --- , ------- ------ ------- -- ------ -----
-- -------- ------ ------ ------ ------ ------- --- ------ ------ -- - ------ ------
---- -------, ---- -- --- -- ------ ----- ------ ---- --- - ------ ------ --- -- --- ----,'
---- ------ ------ ------ ------ -------- -- --- ------ -- ---------.

--- --, --- ------ --- ----- ------ , ------ Marquis de Norpois? ----, -- --- -- Minister Plenipotentiary ------ --- ---, --- --- -------
------- -- --- ------- -- May; ----- -- ----, , ------ ------ , -- ------ ------ ------- ------ -- -------- France
-- ------------ ------- , ---- -- ------ -- --- ------ ---- Egypt, -----, ------ -- --- ----- ---------- -- -------, -- --- ------
------- ------ -- - ------- ------ ------ - ------- ---- ------- ------ ------- -- ---, -- --- ------ M. de Norpois,
-- ----- ----- -- ------- , ---- ------ -- ----- ------ -- ----- ----, ---- --- ------ ------- France ---- -- ----, ---- -------
------- ------ -- -- ------ ------ ------ ------ ------ ------ ------ -- ------' ----- ------,'
------- ------ ---- ------ ------ ------ ------ , ------ ------ ------ , --- ----- ------
---- ---- ---- ---- ------ ------- -- ------ -- ------ -- M. de Norpois, ------ ------ -- ------ ---- -- ------ ------- -- -- ----,
- ----- ------ ------ ------ ------ ------ ------ ------ ------ , ------ ------
-- --- ------ ------ ------ ------ .. ------ -- ------ , ------- ------ , -- --- ------
------- ---- -- ------ -- ------ --- ------ -- ------- -- (-- ----- -- ------ ----- , ------ ------ , --- --- ------
----- ------), ----- ---- -- -- ------- --- ------- (----- ----- -- -- -- ------ ----) ----- , ------ -- ----------- -------
-- ----- ------ --- -- ----- ----- ------ ------, - -- ------ ---- -- '-----' ------, -- ------- ---- --- '----,' ------, ------,
-- ----- ------ -- - ---------- ------ ------ ------ -- ------ ------ , -- --- --- -- ----,
--- -- ---- -- ------ ----- ----- ------ ------ -- ------ -- ------ ------ -- --- ------ ------ ------ ------ ------.'
---- -- ------ ----- , ------- -- ------ ------- -- ------ -- ------ ------ -- ------ .

Marcel Proust

------, ----- ---- --- ------ ---------- ------ ----- --- ------ ---- ----- ---- -, ------ ----- ---,
-- ---- --------- -- --- ----------- --- (--------, -- -----, ------ --)--- ------ --- ---------- --'----' --- -- --------, --- -- --------- ---
--------- ----- ---- ------ -- --'-----' ------- -----, --- ---- ---- -------- ----- ---- ------- -----,
----------- --- --'----- ---' - ---- -------.

--- -- --- --------- -- M. de Norpois ------ --- ---- ----------- -------, ----, -- --- ------ -- - ----- ------ -- ---------, -- --- ------
------ --- ----, --------, --------- ----- ----- '---------,' ----- -- ----- -- --- ---------- ---, ------ ------ ------,
--------- ------ --- ------ ---, --- ------, ------ --- ------, ------ -- ---- --- --- ------- ---
- ------ -- - ---- -----, ------ -- --------- -- -----, - ----- - ----- - ------ -- --- -----,
------------ --- ------ --- --------- --- ----, -----------. --- -------- --- --- --------- ---,
----- ----------- ---------- Legouvé, ------------ ------, ---------- Maxime Ducamp'- -- Mezière'- ------- Victor Hugo
---- ---- ------- ------ -- Boileau -- Claudel. - ---------------- -------- --- Barrés ---- --------, --- -------- ------ --- ----
--- M. Georges Berry, ----- --------- ----------- --- -------- ----- -- ---- ------- -- ---- ---- ------
------ ------ ----- ------ --------- M. Ribot --- M. Deschanel, ----- -- ----, --- ----- ----- ------ --- ----
------ ----- ---- Maurras -- Léon Daudet, --------- ----- ------- ------ --- ----. --------- ------ ---, ------
- ------- ----- ---- --- --------, ----- ----- ------ -------------. ------ --------- ----- ----- ----,
---------- ----- -- - ----- -, ------ ---- ------ --- ------, -- --------- ------ ---- ----- ---
---------- --- ----- ------ ----------- --- -------, M. de Norpois ----- ------- -----, ----- -----,
--------- ---- -------, -- ----- ----- -----.
------------ ----- ----- ---' -, ------ ------ --- -----, -- ----- ----- ----,
-- ---------- ---- ------ -------- --, ----- -------- --------- -- -------, ----- ----- ------ -----,
---- --- --- - ---', ------------ -- ----- ---- -------- ----- -- --------- ------ -- --- -----, -- ---- --
----- -- ------ ---, ---- --- --- -------- --------- ------ --- ----- ------- -- ---- ---------, -- --- -----
------ "De Norpois ------ ------ -- ------ -----', --'- ---------- -----', ------ ------- -- --------, -- -- ------ ------ ----,
---- -- -, -- --- -- ---- -, --- ------ --- ------, ----, ----- -- '------ ---," -- ------ ---- M. de Norpois --- ------,
--- -------- ----- ----- --- ------- -------- ----- --- --------- --------- Prussia, ---- Bismarck ------ --- ------------ ----
------ ------ ------ ---, -- ------ -- ---- -------- ------- --- King Theodosius, --- --------- --- --- ----- --------
---------- ------- ----- ----- ---- ----- M. de Norpois. "- ----- --- ------- --- ---'- ---- --- ---- -----------," -- -------- -- ,
-- --- ---- ----- ------ ------ "- ----- Norpois ------ ----- ----- ---- ---, ------ --'----- ----- --- ---------."

-- --- -- ------, ----- ---- ----------- --- ----- -------- ----- ----- --- -------, ------- -- -- ----- --- ------
--------- ------ -- ---------- - ------- - ---- ------ --- -- -- ------- ----------- --- -- ---------- -- - - ---- ----
--- ---------- ----- ------ ----, ----- ---- ------- ----- ---- -- ------ ---- ----- --- -- ---- --- ----- ------
--- ----- ------- -- --- -------- ----- -----, ----- ---- --- ------ ---, -- --- ----- ------- ---- ------- -----
------ ---- ------ ---. --------- ----- ---, ------ ------ --- --- -----, -------, -- ----- ---- -----, ----- ----- --- -----,
----- -------- ---- ------ -- ---------- --, ------- --- -- -- ------------- --- --- ----- ----- "- -- --- ----- --------", -- ---- ----
- ------- ---- -- ------ ---------- M. de Norpois ------ '----------,' ----- -- --- ----- ------- ------ ------ ----- ------,
---- --- ------ --------- ---------- ---, -- --- --------, -- -----, --- ------ -- M. de Norpois ----- ----------- --------- ------, -- -----, ------,
---- --- ---- ----- --------- ----- ---- ----- ------ --- --- --------- ----- ----- ----- ----- -- ---- -- ----- ----- -- ----
-- --- -- ------'- ----- ----- --------- ----- -- ------ -- M. de Norpois, --- --- ------- ------ ------ ----- ----- ----- -- ----
--- ------ ------ ----------- ------ ---- -------- --- ------- ------ ------- -- ------- -- -------, --- ------- ---- --- ---
--- --- ------, -- -- -- ----- ----, ------ --- --- ------- ------, ----- ---- -------- ------ ---- -- ---- --------- ------,
---------- ------- (-- ----------- ------ -- -- ----- --- ---- ------- ----- ------- ----- ----- ---, ----- --------- ---- ------,
----- ----- ----- -------- -- ----- --- ---- ---- ------ --- -- ----- --------);--- --------, -- ---------- ---- ------, -- -- ----- ----,
-- ------ --- ---- -- ------- -- ----- ---- -----'- ----- --- -------- --- --- ------- ----- --------- ------ ----, -- ----- ------,
------ -- --------- --- ----, ----- -------- ---- ----- M. de Norpois, ---- ------- ----- --------- --------- ------, ------,
--- ------ ---- ------ --------- ----- ----- ----- ------' ------ --- --- ------, ------- ----- ----- ----- --- ----
--- ------ --- ------- ----- ----- ----- ---- ------ --- --- -------- -----, --- ------ ----- ----- ------- --------- '------',
--- -- (---- -- --- --- ------ ----- ---- -- ----- ---- --- ------, -- ------- ------ ----, ----- -------) -- ---
--- ---- ------ ----- -------- M. de Norpois ------ ------------- -- ------ ----- ------ ----- ------, -- -------- --- ----- -----
-- ---- ------ ----- --- ----- ------ ----- ----- ---- ---- -----, -- ------ ------ --- ------ --------------, --- ------,

All the names ...

--- ------------ ------- --- ------ --_----- ----'- ------ --- -------, --- ------- -- -- --- ----- ---- -----', ------ -- --
---- ------ -- ------ ___ ------- ----- --, _---- ------ ---- _-------- --- --------- -- ----- ----- __ -- ------ -- --
--- ----- ----- ------- -----', -- --- --- --- --------- -----', ------ -- -- --- ---, ------
---- ----- -- ------ ----- --- ---', -- -- ------ -------. --- -------- -- -- -- --, -- M. de Norpois, ------ ------ -- -
--- --- ----- -----', --- ---- ------ ---- ------ -- ----- --- -- --------- ---- --- --- ----- -- -------- ----- -- --------- -
--- ---- -- ------- ----- ------ --- ------------ ----- ----- ---- ------ -- ----- ----- ----- --- ------ --- -- ---- -- --- -- ------ -- --__

--- ------- -- --- M. de Norpois ----- ------ --- --- -----, -- --- ----- -- ------ ---- -- ---- -- Champs-Elysées, --- --------- ----- --
---- ------ --- ----- ----- ---- ---- ------ -- - --- ---- - ----- Berma, -- - -------, -- Phèdre, --- --- - ------
-- M. de Norpois ----------- -------, ----, ----- ------ ---, -- ---------- ----- -- -- -- --- Gilberte Swann
--- --- ------- ------- ----- ---- ---- ---- ------ --- --------

-- --- -- ------ ---- --------- ----- -- ------ --- -------- -- -- -- ------ -----, -- --- ------- -- --
- ---- --- ------ -------- -- Gilberte, ------- ---- -------, -- -- ---- -- -----, --- ------', " ---- -------- -- Berma,
- ------- ---- ----- -------- ---- --- --'--- --------- ---- ----."

--- -- --- ------- M. de Norpois --- --- --- ---- - ----- -- ---- ---- Berma, --- ---- --- --- ------ -- --- ------- ------,
---- ------ --- -------- --- --- ---------, -- ------ -------- --- ---- ----- ---- -- --- ------ --- -
-- ----- -- ------ -- ----- --- '------', --- -- --- ------ ----- ------ ----- --- --- --- --- -
-- --- ---- -- ------ ------ -- - ------ ---- --, -- ------ -- ------', --- --- --- ---- --- --- --- ---
------- ------- -- ----- -- --, ------ -- -- ----- -------. --- ------ --- ---- --- -
-- ------ ----- ---- ---- Berma, ------- --------- --- ---- -- -- ------ --- ---- --
-- -- - --- ----- --- M. de Norpois. ------- ---- --- ------- --- ---- -- ------ --- -
---- ------- --- ---- ------- --- ---- --- ------ -- --- ----- ---- ------- --- --- - -
-------, "--- ------- --- --- ---!" -- -- ------, --- --------- -------- "---| -- --' ----- -- -- ----, -- --, ------ ---, --- ------ -
------ ----- ------ ------- ------ ----- ----- ------- ----- --- --- ----."

M. de Norpois ------ ------- ---- ------- --------- ---', ------- ---------- ----- ------ --- --- -- ------- -- --- ---- ----------- -------
- -------, ---------- -- ----- -- ------ ---- --- --- ---- ----, -- ----- ----- -- ------ ----- --
---- -- -, ---------, -- --- ---- Gilberte -----. - -------- --- ------ ------- --- ----- --- ------ --------- -
--- ---- ------ ------, --- -----, -- -- ------ Guermantes ---. --- -- -------- -- ---- --- -------- --- ------ -- -------
----- -- ------- -- ------ ------ -- --------. ------ ------ ----- -- ----- ---- -- ----- ------ -- M. de Norpois,
---- ------- ------ -------- -- -- --- ------ --- --- ---- ------ --- -- ------ --- ---- -- --------- -
-- --------- ----- ------ ---- -- ----- --- ------ ------ --- ----- --- ------- -- ------ --- ---- -
------ -- -------- ---- ---- -- --- --- ------ -- ------ -- --- ----- ---- --- ---- --- -------- --------

"----, ----, - ------, - ---- --- --------- -- --- Norpois ------'- --- --------- --- ------- ----- --" -- ------ ----- ----.
--- ------- ------ --- -- ----- -- -- ----- --- --- --- --- --------- --- ------ ----- ----. ----- -- ------ -----, ----
------- ---- --- -- ------ --- ------ ----- -- --- ------'-----', '" ------ ------- -------- -----, ----- ---- ----- -
--- -------- ------- ---- --- ---- ------------- ------------ --- -------- -- ----- -- -- ------ ------- -- --- ----- ---- -
-- --- Deux-Mondes; -- --- ------ --- --- ------' --- --------- ---- ---- --------- ------' -----, -- ---- -- ------- -, ---
---------- ----- !"

-- --------- -- --- ------ -- --- ------ ---------- ----- Gilberte ---- -- -------, --- --- ------, -- -------- ----- -----, -- ----- ------ -- -------
-- M. de Norpois. ------ - --- ----------- ------, ----------- --- --- ------- ------'- ------ ------ ---- ----
------, ---- ------ ' ------,' ----- - ---- ---- ------- -- ------- M. de Norpois'- ----- ------ -- -------- ----- -- --
------- -- Paris. ------------ -------- ------- ----- Berma ------ ---- --- ------- ---- --- --------
------- ------- ------ ------ ------, -- - -------- --- ------- ----- --- ------ ------ ----- --- ------ ----- ------ ------- ----- --- Swann
--- ----- ----- -- --, --- --- ----- --- ---- ------- ---- -------- ---- --- ----- ------- -----
---- --- -- --- ---, --- ------ ------ -- ---- ---- -- ------ -- --- ------ ----- --- --------
-- -- - ------ --- ---- --------- -- --- ------ -- ---, -- ------ --- -------, --- -------
-- --- - ---- -------- -- ------ -------- ----. Berma -- Andromaque, -- ----------- --- Marianne, -- Phèdre, ----- -----
------- ----- -- --- -------- ----- ------ -- ---- -- ------- - ------ - ------ ------ ---- --------- -- --- Titian -- --- Frari
---- Carpaccios -- San Giorgio dei Schiavoni, ---- - ----- ----- Berma ------ ----- ----- --------.

"-- ---- --'- ------ ----- ------ -- ---- -------- -----"
----- -------, ------', --'

Marcel Proust

--- ---- ---- ---- ---- ---- ---- ---- ---- ---- ---- ---- ---- ---- ---- ---- ---, ----- ---- --- ---- ---- -- ---
---- --- -- ---- ---- ---- ---- ---- ---- ---- ---- ---- ---- ---- ---- ---- ---- ----- --- ----- -- ----
--- ---- ---- ---. - Carpaccio -- Venice, Berma -- Phèdre, ----------- ---- ----- ---- ---- ----- ---, --- ---- ---
---- ---- ---- -- ---- -- ---- -------- ----- --- ---- ---------- ---- Carpaccios ----- -- --- --------- --- Louvre, -- Berma
---- ---- ---- ---- ---- ---- ---- ----, ---- ---- ---- ---- ----, ----- ---- -- --- --- ---- ---- ----- --- -------
----- --- ---- ---- ---- ---- ---- ----, ---- ----, ---- ---- ----- Berma'----- --- ---------
----- ---- ---- ---- ---- ----, ---, ---- ---- ---- ----, --- ---- ---- ---- ---- ---- --- -- ----
-- --- ---- ----- ---- --- ---- ---- ---- ---- ----- ---- ---- ---- ---- ---- ---- ---
--- ----- ---.

------, -- - ---- --- Berma -- - ---- ----, ---- ---- ----, ---- ----, ----- ---- ---- -- --- -
---- ---- ---- ---- ---- ----, ----- ---- ---- ---- ---- -- -- -- --------- -- ----- ---- -- ----
-- -- ---- ----, -- -- --- -- ----------, ----, ---- ---- ---- ---- ---- ---- --- -------- --- ---- ---
---- ---- ---- ---- ----- ---, ---- ---- ---- ---- ----- ----- Berma ----- ------ ----,
---- ---- ---- ---- ---- ---- ---- ---- ---- ---- ---- ---- ---- ---- ---- ---- ---- ---- ----
-- --- ---- ----- ---- -- '---', ---- ---- ---- ---- ----' --- ---- ---- ---- ---- ----, ---
---- ----- ---- ---- ---- ---- ---- ---- ---- ---- ---- ---, --- ----
----- ----- ---- ---- ---- ---- ---- ---- ---- ---- ----, ---- ----
---- ---- ---- ---- ---- ---- ---- ---- ---- ---- ---- ----, ----

------- ---- ----- Phèdre ---- Mme. Berma, ---, ---- ----- ----, ---- ------- --- ------- --- Marianne, ------ ---, ---- ----
Phèdre, ---------- ----, ---- ------ ---- ----, --- ---- ---- ----- ---- ---- ---- ----
---- ------ -- -- -- ---- - ---- ----- Mme. Berma ---- ---- ---- ----, ----- --- ---- ---- --
---- ---- ---- ---- ---- ---- ---- ---- ---- ---- ---- ----, ----- ---- ---- --- ----
---- ---- ---- ---- ---- ---- ---- ---- ---- ----, ---- ---- ---- ---- ----
---- ---- ---- ---- ---- ---- ----', --- ---- ---- ---- ---- ---- ----
-- ---- ---- -- ----, ---- ---- ---- ----- Phèdre, ------- ---- ----- --- ---, --- ---- -
----- ---- ---- ----, ----, ---- ---- ---- ---- ---- ---- ---- ---- ---- ----
------, ---- ---- ---- ---- ---- ---- ---- ---- ---, --- ------- --- ------- -- "M. Anatole France."

--- ---- ---- ---- ---- ---- ---- ---- ---- ---- ---- ---- ---- ---- ---- ----, ----
--------- ---- ---- ---- ---- ---- ---- ---- ---- ---- ---- ---- ---- ----, ----
----- ---- ---- ---- ---- ---- ---- ---- ---- ---- ---- ---- ---- ---- ---- ----,
---- ---- ---- ---- ----- -- Balbec, ------- ---- Venice ---- ---- ---- ---- ---- ----, ----
---- ---- ---- ---- ---- ---- ---- ----, ---- ----, ---- ---- ---- ----, ----
----- ---- -- ---- ---- ---- ---- ---- ---- ---- ---- ---- ---- ---- ---- ----
----- ---- ---- ---- ----, ---- ---- ---- ---- - ---- ---- ---- --- ---- ----, ----
---- -- ---- -------- -- --- -- -- Phèdre. -------, --- ---- ----, -- -----, --- ------ --------.

"-- ---- ---'-- ----- ---- ----- ----- -- ----, ----"

----- ---- ---- ---- ---- ---- ---- -- -- ---- ---- ---- ---- ------- -- ----- -- ----- Berma ----- ----- -- -------
---- ---- ----, ---- ---- ---- ---- ---- ---- ---- ---- ---- ---- ---- ----- --- ----, ----- ----"
------- -- ----- -- --- ---- --- Bergotte - - --- --------- --- Gilberte ----- --- -- - --- ------- ------ -- ---", "----- ------"
"-------- ---------" -- "--------- ------" "Princess of Troezen --- -- Cleves" -- "------ ------", "-------- ----" " ---- ----",
-----, ---- Berma'------- ---- ---- ---- ----, ---- ----, ---- ----
---- ---- ---- ---- ---- -- ----- ---- ---- ---- ---- ---- ---- ----, ---- ----
-- ---- ---- ---- -- ---- ---- ---- ---- ---- ---- ---- ---- ----
----- ---- ---- ---- ---- ----- -- M. de Norpois ---- ------- -- --- --- -- "---- ---, --- --- ---- -- --
---- -----', ---- --- ---- ---'- ---", -- ---- ---- ---------- ----
------ --- ---- ---- ----, ---- ----, ---- ---- ---- ---- ---- ----- ---- --- -- --

Georges Perec

Attempt at an Inventory of the Liquid and Solid Foodstuffs Ingurgitated by Me in the Course of the Year Nineteen Hundred and Seventy-Four

Georges Perec's Rabelaisian list of everything he ate and drank during the course of a year is yet another form of self-portraiture, this time by literally invoking the old adage "you are what you eat." Perec's veracity is immediately called into question: how can one, for example, possibly define "five rabbits," particularly when it is followed by a list of other rabbits: "two rabbits en gibelotte, one rabbit with noodles, one rabbit à la crème, three rabbits a la moutarde, one rabbit chasseur," and so on? Slippages of accounting and excursions into the realm of fantasy move Perec's quest more into a realm of Wittgensteinian language games than of accountability or self-definition.

Nine beef consommés, one iced cucumber soup, one mussel soup.

Two Guéméné andouilles, one jellied andouillette, one Italian charcuterie, one cervelas sausage, four assorted charcuteries, one coppa, three pork platters, one figatelli, one foie gras, one fromage de tête, one boar's head, five Parma hams, eight pâtés, one duck pâté, one pâté de foie with truffles, one pâté en croûte, one pâté grand-mère, one thrush pâté, six pâtés des Landes, four brawns, one foie gras mousse, one pig's trotters, seven rillettes, one salami, two saucissons, one hot saucisson, one duck terrine, one chicken liver terrine.

One blini, one empanada, one dried beef.
  Three snails.

One Belon oysters, three coquilles St-Jacques, one shrimps, one shrimp croustade, one friture, two baby eel fritures, one herring, two oysters, one mussels, one stuffed mussels, one sea-urchins, two quenelles au gratin, three sardines in oil, five smoked salmons, one tarama, one eel terrine, six tunas, one anchovy toast, one crab.

Four artichokes, one asparagus, one aubergines, one mushroom salad, fourteen cucumber salads, four cucumbers à la crème, fourteen celery rémoulades, two Chinese cabbages, one palm hearts, eleven assiette de crudités, two haricot vert salads, thirteen melons, two salades niçoises, two dandelion salads with bacon, fourteen radishes with butter, three black radishes, five rice salads, one Russian salad, seven tomato salads, one onion tart.

One Roquefort croquette, five croque-monsieurs, three quiche Lorraines, one Maroilles tart, one yoghourt with cucumber and grapes, one Romanian yoghourt.
    One torti salad with crab and Roquefort.

One eggs with anchovy, two boiled eggs, two eggs en meurette, one ham and eggs, one bacon and eggs, one eggs en cocotte with spinach, two eggs in aspic, two scrambled eggs, four omelettes, one sort of omelette, one soya-seed omelette, one craterellus omelette, one duck skin omelette, one confit d'oie omelette, one herb omelette, one Parmentier omelette.

Two haddocks, one sea-bass, one skate, one sole, one tuna.

One flank of sirloin, three flanks of sirloin with shallots, ten steaks, two steak au poivres, three steak and chips, one rump steak à la moutarde, five roast beefs, two ribs of beef, two top rumpsteaks, three beef grillades, two chateaubriands, one steak tartare, one rosbif, three cold rosbifs, fourteen entrecôtes, three entrecôtes à la moelle, one fillet of beef, three hamburgers, nine skirts of beef, one plate of beef.

    Four pot-au-feus, one daube, one jellied daube, one braised beef, one beef mode, one beef gros sel, one beef à la ficelle.

One braised veal with noodles, one sauté of veal, one veal chop, one veal chop with pasta shells, one "veal entrecôte," six escalopes, six escalope milanaises, three escalope à la crèmes, one escalope with morels, four blanquette de veaus.

Five andouillettes, three black puddings, one black pudding with apples, one pork cutlet, two sauerkrauts, one Nancy sauerkraut, one pork chop, eleven pairs of frankfurters, two pork grillades, seven pigs' trotters, one cold pork, three roast porks, one roast pork with pineapple and bananas, one pork sausage with haricots.

One milk-fed lamb, three lamb cutlets, two curried lambs, twelve gigots, one saddle of lamb.

One mutton cutlet, one shoulder of mutton.

Five chickens, one chicken kebab, one chicken au citron, one chicken en cocotte, two chicken basquaises, three cold chickens, one stuffed chicken, one chicken with chestnuts, one chicken aux herbes, two jellied chickens.
Seven poules au riz, one poule au pot.
One pullet au riz.
One coq au riesling, three coq au vins, one coq au vinaigre.
One duck with olives, one duck magret.
One guinea-fowl salmis.
One guinea-fowl with cabbage, one guinea-fowl with noodles.

Five rabbits, two rabbits en gibelotte, one rabbit with noodles, one rabbit à la crème, three rabbits à la moutarde, one rabbit chasseur, one rabbit à l'estragon, one rabbit à la tourangelle, three rabbits with plums.
Two young wild rabbits with plums.

One civet of hare à l'alsacienne, one hare daube, one hare stew, one saddle of hare.
One wild pigeon salmis.

One kidney kebab, three kebabs, one mixed-grill, one kidneys à la moutarde, one calves' kidneys, three têtes de veau, eleven calves' livers, one calves' tongue, one ris de veau with pommes sarladaises, one ris de veau terrine, one lamb's brains, two fresh goose livers with grapes, one goose gizzards confit, two chicken livers.

Twelve cold cuts, two assiette anglaises, n cold buffets, two couscous, three "chinese," one moulakhia, one pizza, one pan bagnat, one tahina, six sandwiches, one ham sandwich, one rillette sandwich, three Cantal sandwiches.

One ceps, one kidney beans, seven haricot verts, one sweetcorn, one mashed cauliflower, one mashed spinach, one mashed fennel, two stuffed peppers, two pommes frites, nine gratin dauphinois, four mashed potatoes, one pommes dauphine, one pommes boulangère, one pommes soufflées, one roast potatoes, one sautée potatoes, four rices, one wild rice.

Four pasta, three pasta shells, one fettucini à la crème, one macaroni cheese, one macaroni, fifteen fresh noodles, three rigatonis, two raviolis, four spaghettis, one tortellini, five tagliatelle verdes.

Thirty-five green salads, one mesclun salad, one Treviso salad à la crème, two chicory salads.

Seventy-five cheeses, one ewe's milk cheese, two Italian cheeses, one Auvergne cheese, one Boursin, two Brillat-Savarins, eleven Bries, one Cabécou, four goats' milk cheeses, two crottins, eight Camemberts, fifteen Cantals, one Sicilian cheeses, one Sardinian cheeses, one Epoisses, one Murols, three fromages blancs, one fromage blanc de chèvre, nine Fontainebleaus, five mozzarellas, five Munsters, one Reblochon, one Swiss raclette, one Stilton, one Saint-Marcellin, one Saint-Nectaire, one yoghourt.

One fresh fruit, two strawberries, one gooseberries, one orange, three mendiants.
    One stuffed dates, one pears in syrup, three pears in wine, two peaches in wine, one pêche de vigne in syrup, one peaches in Sancerre, one apples normande, one bananas flambées.
    Four stewed fruit, two stewed apples, two stewed rhubarb and quetsch.
    Five clafoutis, four pear clafoutis.
    One figs in syrup.
    Six fruit salads, one tropical fruit salad, two orange salads, two strawberry, raspberry and gooseberry salads.

One apple pie, four tarts, one hot tart, ten tarts Tatin, seven pear tarts, one pear tart Tatin, one lemon tart, one apple and nut tart, two apple tarts, one apple tart meringue, one strawberry tart.
    Two crêpes.

Two charlottes, three chocolate charlottes.
Three babas.
One crème renversée.
One galette des rois.
Nine chocolate mousses.
Two floating islands.
One bilberry kugelhupf.

Four chocolate gâteaux, one cheese gâteau, two orange gâteaux, one Italian gâteau, one Viennese gâteau, one Breton gâteau, one gâteau au fromage blanc, one vatrushki.

Three ice-creams, one green lemon sorbet, two guava sorbets, two pear sorbets, one chocolate profiterolles, one raspberry melba, one pear belle-hélène.

Thirteen Beaujolais, four Beaujolais Nouveau, three Brouillys, seven Chiroubles, four Chenas, two Fleuries, one Juliénas, three Saint-Amours.

Nine Côtes-du-Rhônes, nine Châteauneuf-du-Papes, one Châteauneuf-du-Pape '67, three Vaqueyras.

Nine Bordeaux, one Bordeaux Clairet, one Lamarzelle '64, three Saint-Emilions, one Saint-Emilion '61, seven Château-la Pelleterie '70s, one Château-Canon '62, five Château-Négrits, one Lalande-de-Pomerol, one Lalande-de-Pomerol '67, one Médoc '64, six Margaux '62s, one Margaux '68, one Margaux '69, one Saint-Estèphe '61, one Saint-Julien '59.

Seven Savigny-lès-Beaunes, three Aloxe-Cortons, one Aloxe-Corton '66, one Beaune '61, one white Chasagne-Montrachet '66, two Mercureys, one Pommard, one Pommard '66, two Santenay '62s, one Volnay '59.

One Chambolle-Musigny '70, one Chambolle-Musigny Les Amoureuses '70, one Chambertin '62, one Romanée-Conti, one Romanée-Conti '64.

One Bergerac, two red Bouzys, four Bourgueils, one Chalosse, one champagne, one Chablis, one red Côtes-de-Provence, twenty-six Cahors, one Chanteperdrix, four Gamays, two Madirans, one Madiran '70, one Pinot Noir, one Passetoutgrain, one Pécharmant, one Saumur, ten Tursans, one Traminer, one Sardinian wine, *n* miscellaneous wines.

Nine beers, two Tuborgs, four Guinnesses.

Fifty-six Armagnacs, one Bourbon, eight Calvadoses, one cherries in brandy, six Green Chartreuses, one Chivas, four cognacs, one Delamain cognac, two Grand Marniers, one pink-gin, one Irish coffee, one Jack Daniel's, four marcs, three Bugey marcs, one marc de Provence, one plum liqueur, nine Souillac plums, one plums in brandy, two Williams pears, one port, one slivovitz, one Suze, thirty-six vodkas, four whiskies.

N coffees
one tisane
three Vichy waters

M. NourbeSe Philip
from Zong!

Like Charles Reznikoff's *Testimony* and Vanessa Place's *Satements of Fact, Zong!* draws its language from legal documents. M. NourbeSe Philip offers the following statement of facts:

In 1781 the slave ship, *Zong*, captained by one Luke Collingwood set sail from the coast of West Africa for Jamaica. As is the custom its "cargo" was fully insured. Instead of the customary six to nine weeks, this fateful trip will take some four months on account of navigational errors on the part of the captain, resulting in some of the *Zong*'s "cargo" being lost and the remainder being destroyed by order of the captain.

The *Zong*'s cargo comprised 470 slaves.

"Sixty negroes died for want of water . . . and forty others . . . through thirst and frenzy . . . threw themselves into the sea and were drowned; and the master and mariners . . . were obliged to throw overboard 150 other negroes" [*Gregson vs. Gilbert*]. Captain Collingwood believed that if the African slaves died a natural death, the owners of the ship would have to bear the cost, but if they were "thrown alive into the sea, it would be the loss of the underwriters" [ibidem]. In other words, murdering the African slaves would prove more financially advantageous to the owners of the ship and its cargo.

The owners, the Messrs Gregson, being fully insured, make an unsuccessful claim against the insurers for the destroyed cargo. The ship's owners are successful in their legal action against their insurers to recover their loss. The insurers appeal this judgment and a new trial ordered: Gregson v. Gilbert is the formal name of this reported decision which is more colloquially known as the *Zong* case [*Zong!* (Middletown, Conn.: Wesleyan University Press, 2008)].

Philip fragments and mutilates the text of the legal decision *Gregson v. Gilbert,* which resulted from the *Zong* affair. Working with only the five hundred or so words of that source text, she obscures, reverses, and redistributes them in an attempt to subvert the rational, semantic, grammatical basis of the legal logic that generated those words in the first place. However, by censoring and summoning, denying and allowing to stand, excluding and recording, ignoring and interpreting, Philip also mimes core judicial activities. She writes:

> The abbreviated, disjunctive, almost non-sensical presentation of the "poems" demands of the reader/audience an effort to "make sense" of an event that can never be understood. What is it about? What is happening? This, I suggest, is the closest we will ever get, some two hundred years later, to what it must have been like for those Africans on board the *Zong*. Further, in attempting to "make sense" of these events, the reader/audience shares the risk of the poet who herself risks contamination by using the prescribed language of the law.

Gregson narrativizes mass murder as a contractual problem in a commercial transaction, recasting homicide as business law; *Zong!* in turn suggests that the ethical inadequacies of that legal language—the failure of words to "do justice" to the situation they describe—do not prevent their *détournement* in the service of experimental writing.

and *ave*   *ave*

        the rat the   rat *ave*

                        ah we   cut cut

cut the   cost and serve   where s the cat

        the yam   no meat   trim

the loss   payment

                you say what   for where s

                                        the cat got

                        the rat could

        the crime out   out

cut the ear   be absolute do

                you hear

                        the lute sound

to raise   the dead

        the died

                i hear

                        ave bell s

ring   out

                dear ruth

        this is   a tale told

                cold a yarn

a story dear   dear ruth i

        woo time   and you do

                i have y our

ear   there were aster s

        at tea time éclairs   & you

                are my liege

        lord of nig   nig &

                nog   my *doge*

                                                there are

                              stars in

                sidera

          as there is

                    ratio

                              in rations

but why ruth

          do the stars   shine   if only

                    murder made us   you were by my side

                              os

     os   *os*

          bo   ne men

                    misfortunes

very new

                    and   we map

     uncommon   the usual

                    to me   to the vessel   winds & currents

          we ground   upon

                              i pen this

     to you

          when i am   her

                able   paps her

                                        dugs   her

                                        teats

                    leak in necessity   there

     was sin a good   supply of

                ply the negroes   with

                         toys lure them

          visions of l   ace for a queen

                    my queen

          there is pus

MANIFEST

African Groups & Languages	Animals	Body Parts	Crew
Bantu	ant	arm	Alf
Edo	asp	*bras*	Dan
Ewe	ass	cunt	Dave
Fante	bat	ear	Don
Fon	bee	eye	Ed
Ibo	boar	feet	Hamz
Lua	bream	finger	Hans
Rada	carp	fist	Jesus
San	cat	hand	Jim
Shona	clam	head	Jon
Twi	cod	heel	Mike
	deer	hip	Ned
	dog	leg	Peter
	dory	lips	Piet
	dove	*mano*	Roy
	eel	nail	Sam
	fish	nose	Ted
	fowl	*ongle*	Tim
	grouse	paps	Tom
	hare	*perna*	
	hen	*pied*	
	hog	*tak*	
	lion	teat	
	mare	tit	
	nits	toe	
	owl	*tong*	
	pig	torso	
	pup		
	rat		
	raven		
	sole		
	sow		
	stag		
	tit mouse		
	toad		
	wolf		

Food & Drink	Nature	Women Who Wait
ale	asters	Ans
beer	bog	Clara
bread	cairn	Clair
carp	corn	Eva
cider	dale	Eve
cod	fen	Grace
corn	field	Mary
dates	garden	Miss Circe
éclairs	glen	Rosa
egg	hay	Rose
gin	mist	Ruth
ham	moss	Sue
herb	ocean	Tara
hops	peat	Um
jam	rose	
kale	sea	
meat	sky	
oranges	stone	
pea	stook	
pear	sun	
pie	tares	
port	vale	
rice	yew	
roe		
rose water		
rum		
scone		
sion (water parsley)		
soup (egg drop)		
spud		
tea		
veal		
water		
whey		
wine		

Vanessa Place
from Statement of Facts

Extending the discourse of Charles Reznikoff, *Statement of Facts* is an appropriation of the appellate briefs that Vanessa Place has written for her day job as a lawyer who represents indigent sex offenders. Place does not alter the original document in any way other than to remove specific witness and victim information as necessary to protect those people's identities. In transferring the briefs from the legal framework to the literary, Place intentionally sets forth a line of questioning that is vast and complex, addressing issues of labor, value, surplus, expenditure, context, recontext: uncompromising realism.

Prosecution Case

Counts 1, 2, 3 and 4: Jane Doe #1: Dorothy C.

On January 17, 1997, Dorothy C. was living alone on Vista Avenue, in Long Beach; she went into her bedroom between 11:00 and 12:00 p.m., without giving anyone permission to enter her home. As she was preparing for bed, a man came up from behind, grabbed her arms, and told her to cooperate and she wouldn't get hurt. The man, wearing a navy blue ski mask, forced her onto her bed, removed her underwear and orally copulated her, stopping periodically to talk. If Dorothy C. began crying, the man would threaten her again; at some point, he put his mouth on Dorothy C.'s breasts and neck, and asked her to put his penis in her mouth. She orally copulated him, a minute later, he turned her over and put his penis in her vagina, ejaculating outside the vagina one to five minutes later. (RT 798-801, 803-804)

After ejaculating, the man retrieved his underwear, wiped Dorothy C.'s back, and told her he had broken in, waiting while she left the house and returned a video. The man said he walked through her home while she was gone, looking at her things; he asked Dorothy C. if she had a boyfriend. She said she did; she told him she went to church. He mentioned things he'd

489

noticed in the house, like a light that needed repair, and asked her when she was to get up the next morning, and if she'd set the alarm. The man did not say anything about himself, or identify himself by name. After twenty minutes, the man dressed and left. Before leaving, he told Dorothy C. not to do anything for twenty minutes; after he was gone, Dorothy C. called the rape hotline, then the police. The man was in Dorothy C.'s home for at least two hours. (RT 800-802)

The police arrived; Dorothy C. was subsequently interviewed by detectives and examined by a forensic nurse specialist;[1] an external genital swab, a breast swab, and a reference sample was taken and transported to the police department and then to the Los Angeles Sheriff's Department Scientific Services Bureau Crime Laboratory. Approximately two and a half years later, a detective took an oral reference sample from Dorothy C. and booked it to the crime lab. (RT 802, 1153-1161, 1418-1420, 1432) Dorothy C. described her assailant to the nurse and to the attending officer as 5'6" or less, 140 to 150 lbs., and Hispanic. (RT 811, 1423)

At trial, Dorothy C. testified she did not know appellant, but recognized "the shape of his eyelids," "the hair under his lip," and the color of his skin as belonging to the man who raped her. She also thought she would probably recognize his voice if he spoke: Dorothy C. told police she believed her attacker was Hispanic because he had a slight accent. She told police she was "almost positive" the man was 5'6" "or less," that he was of average build, about 140 pounds, and had a scar on his upper right thigh.[2] She tried to be as accurate as possible in her post-attack description to police; she was once shown three composite sketches of a suspect, and told the officer she could not eliminate the person represented in the drawing, saying her attacker had the same hooded eyelids, and "could be" the same mouth. (RT 803-804, 813-821, 1423-1424) On January 23, 1997, Dorothy C. was shown two photographic lineups; at the first, she indicated one of the individuals "might be" the rapist; the person selected was not appellant, but a Hispanic man named Jesus Soto. At the second, Dorothy C. again identified someone other than appellant as possibly being her assailant. She again told police she was "almost positive" her attacker was 5'6" "or less." (RT 823-827, 1424-1426)

At trial, Dorothy C. testified she'd seen appellant's picture and read about his prosecution in the newspapers, and believes he is guilty. (RT 808, 821, 830) Defense counsel was 5'6½"; when counsel asked appellant to stand at trial, and asked Dorothy C. if her attacker was closer to counsel's height or appellant's height,[3] Dorothy C. testified her attacker was "probably" appellant's height. (RT 809-811) When appellant was asked at trial to repeat some of the things said during the attack, Dorothy C. identified his voice as sounding like the person who assaulted her; appellant did not sound like he had a Hispanic accent. (RT 828-829)

Counts 5, 6, 7, 8 and 9: Jane Doe #2: Barbara B.

On May 13, 1998, Barbara B. was fifty-eight years old, living alone on Elliot Lane, in Long Beach. By about 10:30 p.m., Barbara B. had fallen asleep with the television and light on; she woke feeling a weight on the bed, then a hand over her mouth. A man said, "I don't want to hurt you." Barbara B. testified he spoke in a whispery voice she "probably wouldn't recognize again." (RT 913-915) The man had Barbara B. roll onto her stomach, she said she had a bad back, he had her roll onto her back, her nightgown pulled over her head. She could not see, "and didn't want to." Barbara B. felt the man against her; it felt as if he was naked. The man kept saying things like, "I don't want to hurt you; I just want to make love to you." Barbara B. thought she'd try to cry, but the man's voice got harsh, and he told her to stop it; she decided it was best to "get it over with as soon as possible." (RT 915-917, 925, 1490)

The man fumbled, touching Barbara B.'s breasts with his hands and mouth, then put his penis in her vagina. She could not tell if he ejaculated or withdrew, but he put his penis in her vagina a second time; he also orally copulated her. Barbara B. did not feel a glove on the man's hand. Throughout, the man continued to tell Barbara B. he only wanted to make love to her and not to hurt her. After, the man told Barbara B. he was going to leave and she should count to fifty. She started counting to herself, he told her to count out loud. As Barbara B. heard the man leave, she asked him to close the door so her cats wouldn't get out; she heard him go through the kitchen and close the sliding glass door as he left. Barbara B. then called police. (RT 917-920, 925)

The police arrived, Barbara B. was taken to the hospital and examined by a forensic nurse specialist, who took swabs from Barbara B.'s body, including an external genital swab, and swabs from Barbara B.'s breasts, and her right buttock. A reference blood sample and oral sample were collected at later dates. The samples were transported to the Long Beach police and then to the Los Angeles County Sheriff's Department Scientific Services Division. There were multiple bruises on Barbara B.'s leg; she had genital tears and a hematoma to her genitalia, indicative of sexual assault. The police kept Barbara B.'s nightgown. (RT 921, 1345-1352, 1403-1404,

1442-1444, 14866-1489) Barbara B. told police and the nurse specialist she believed the man was white, in his 20s, with no body hair. At trial, Barbara B. was unable to identify her assailant. She could only describe him as "fairly young" based on the timber of his whisper. She could not recall why she had said he was white. (RT 921-924, 1490)

Counts 10, 11, 12 and 14: Jane Doe #3: Marion J.

Marion J. was living alone in a house on Colorado Street in Long Beach on July 31, 1998; around 1:30 or 2:00 a.m., she returned home with a friend from Ralphs. The friend left without coming inside the house, and when Marion J. went in, she noticed her five cats were under the bed and her back door was open. She closed and locked the door, and took a shower. Her friend called around 2:15 or 2:30 to let Marion J. know she'd arrived home safely; Marion J., who had been laying on her bed waiting for the call, then fell asleep. (RT 866-868) She woke about 3:15 a.m. because someone's hand was around her throat. The person took Marion J.'s glasses and told her if she screamed, he'd snap her neck. Marion J. said she wouldn't scream, the man pulled her nightgown over her head and told her to open her legs, she did, and he put his penis in her vagina. The man then took his penis out of Marion J., lifted her leg and reinserted his penis. Next, the man turned Marion J. over and put his penis in her vagina a third time while pulling her hair back. Marion J. was bleeding; the man got a towel from the bathroom, wiped her, laid on the bed, and told Marion J. to get on top of him because it would be easier for her to "control it." Marion J. did, and the man's penis again went into her vagina. (RT 868-870, 875)

Afterwards, the man laid next to Marion J.; he told her "it was a date" and to think of him as a lover. The man said she was "really tight" and that he had chosen her because she was a little overweight and "looked like Suzie Homemaker." He said he liked her breasts, and bit and licked them. Marion J. said her back hurt, and the man rubbed her back. He told her again she was a little bit overweight; he knew she had a bicycle because he had stood outside her door where she kept her bicycle: he told her he'd meet her on the bike path. The man said he "wanted to come," climbed on Marion J. again, and reinserted his penis in her vagina. Marion J. thought he may have ejaculated. She told him he was hurting her, that she'd had enough. He said he would leave, but laid back down again, asked what her name was and where she worked and if she wanted him to come back and see her again. Marion J. said no. The man told Marion J. he would send her a guardian angel to watch over her, looked at the angel tattooed on her ankle, and said he liked her angel. He asked if she had a guardian angel watching over her, and she said she didn't think so. The man told Marion J., "You didn't die tonight." He asked again if she wanted him to return, she said no, and he said he wouldn't be back. He said he knew she was going to call the police, but to wait twenty minutes after he left; he also told her to take a self-defense class "so this wouldn't happen again." (RT 870-872)

The man left; Marion J. immediately locked her door and called her friend and the police. The police arrived, and took Marion J. to be examined by a forensic nurse specialist. Swabs were taken from Marion J.'s breasts, vagina, and mouth; a Long Beach detective took an oral reference sample from Marion J. in 1999. All samples were transported to the Los Angeles County Sheriff's Department Scientific Services Division. Marion J. had bruises on her arms and legs, multiple tears to her vaginal walls outside the vaginal area, and tears outside her anal area. (RT 872-873, 1352-1355, 1406, 1420-1422)

The assault lasted a hour; at the time of her attack, Marion J. was a virgin. (RT 873, 875, 897) Marion J. described her assailant to police as between 5'9" and 6' tall, with hazel eyes and dark hair "like little dreads or curls, but more like dreads," and was thin, but had well-defined arms. The man had a thin moustache, freckles on his shoulder, and wore bicycle gloves on his hands. The fingers were cut from the gloves. He was naked during the assault; he told Marion J. that his name was "Tino." (RT 873-875, 887, 896) During the assault, Marion J. peered under her arm to look at her assailant's face. The man saw her do this, and moved the nightgown to block her view. (RT 875)

On August 21, 1998, a few weeks after the attack, Marion J. saw someone whom she recognized as her attacker parked in an orange truck near her house. The man was wearing a painter's hat; he turned, looked at her, smiled, and slowly drove away. She called the police, telling them she was "almost certain" the person parked in the pickup was the person who assaulted her; a detective subsequently showed her a composite drawing, and Marion J. said she was "absolutely certain" the suspect was her rapist. Marion J. saw another composite of the same suspect on another occasion,[4] again identified that suspect as the rapist, and called police. (RT 876-878, 888-895, 1427-1431) Marion J. testified she told police the man had hazel eyes; at trial, she said they were light hazel to brown. Marion J. also told police the man's hair was brown, and he had a moustache. Marion J. could not recall if he had a goatee. Marion J. testified she "never said" the man was white, possibly Greek or Puerto Rican. She did not recall telling the officer that her assailant had "lots of freckles," or that there were freckles all over the man's body. She described the man to police as "well-tanned"; at trial, she said "olive-colored." (RT 880-888, 894-897) Marion J. told the forensic nurse specialist the man had freckles on his arm, a thin mustache, and brown, chin-length dreadlocks. (RT 1386)

At trial, Marion J. believed if she heard her attacker's voice, she would recognize it: when appellant repeated "Don't scream. I'll snap your neck," Marion J. said it was the rapist's voice, and identified appellant as the man who raped her. (RT 875-876, 878) Marion J. said she had "not really" followed appellant's story in the newspapers, though she had read some articles about the case, and on the evidence against appellant, including reports that DNA evidence "conclusively proved" appellant was the rapist, and had seen appellant's photograph in those articles. Marion J. wanted to see appellant convicted. (RT 878-880)

Counts 15 and 16: Jane Doe #4: Carol R.

On September 18, 1998, Carol R. was fifty-four years old, living on Covina Avenue in Long Beach; Carol R. was living with her adult daughter and eleven-month-old grandson; that evening, her daughter was not home. Carol R. went to sleep around 10:00 p.m., her grandson was asleep in his crib in another room in the house. Around 11:00 p.m., Carol R. woke to find a man standing beside her bed with his hand over her mouth. The man was wearing a glove, but his fingers were exposed, like a bicycle glove.[5] Carol R. noticed the man had something covering his face, but could not tell what it was. There was a struggle as the man turned Carol R. over, face down into her pillow. (RT 1105-1108) It was difficult to breathe; the man told Carol R., "Stop screaming. Don't make me hurt you." He asked her name, Carol R. didn't respond, he asked again, she didn't respond, he asked a third time, she told him her name, and he repeated his admonition, calling her by name. Carol R. stopped struggling, and the man touched her bare breast and put his penis in her anus. After withdrawing his penis, the man pushed Carol R. down flat, covered her with a blanket, and left. (RT 1108-1109)

The bathroom window had been closed, but unlocked before Carol R.'s attack; afterwards, Carol R. noticed it was open. Carol R. discovered the telephone by her bed was disconnected, and called police from another telephone. They arrived, and Carol R. was taken to be examined by a forensic nurse specialist. (RT 1109-1110) An identification technician observed what appeared to be feces on the center of Carol R.'s bathroom window sill.

Forensic samples were collected, taken to the laboratory, air dried, then frozen and transferred to the crime laboratory. (RT 1143-1152, 1410-1411)

Carol R. told police she thought her assailant was white or Hispanic, had a slight ethnic accent, was of average build, and not of large stature. (RT 1111) Prior to the assault, there was no feces under the bathroom window. (RT 1109)

Notes

1. Malinda Waddell, director of Forensic Nurse Specialists, Inc., was the forensic nurse specialist who examined Dorothy C. She also hired and trained Toyetta Beukes, Jan Hare, and Sue Gorba. (RT 1153–55)

2. On cross-examination, Dorothy C. testified she "might have said" the man was between 5'6" and 5'10", he "might have been" Hispanic, it "might have been" a scar on his thigh, and she "may have" said he was 140 pounds. She also testified she might not be a very good judge of height, and that the scar could have been semen. She said her description to police the night of her attack was as accurate and truthful as she could be "under the circumstances." (RT 804-806, 809-810, 812-813)

3. According to appellant's Penal Code section 969, subdivision (b) packet, appellant is 5'8". (CT 1372)

4. Marion J. testified she saw this composite on a store front in Belmont Shore, where it had been posted by Long Beach police. (RT 893, 1430) Marion J. did not identify any of the suspects in a six-pack shown her by detectives. (RT 895)

5. No fingerprints were found.

Bern Porter
Clothes

Bern Porter was trained as a scientist—he worked on the Manhattan Project—and subsequently adapted an ontological approach to his writing. His description of the quotidian is expressed in such minute parcels of language so rigorously and exhaustively organized that a radical defamiliarization occurs, ultimately outweighing any sense of purposeful description. Rather, the act of dressing oneself is a portal, opening out onto a hierarchy of relations and unusually surprising digressions.

I am male. I wear standard male clothes. That is to say my clothes are exactly like the clothing of every other male. This morning fresh from the shower I stepped into a pair of shorts and drew them to their proper height while buttoning the lower button. I pulled over my head the standard sleeveless undershirt, tucked it under my shorts and buttoned the top two buttons. Men who are smarter than I am put the shirt on first and draw the shorts up over it. Note that now I probably have on all that propriety demands: shorts and shirt. Note that I have two layers of cloth about my waist, but only one layer about my legs and chest. Note that I have used three buttons or equivalent snap-ons. I have gone through nine separate motions to get into this state. And now notice that as I continue dressing I will merely be donning an elongated version of what I already wear.

I pull on my trousers, draw on and tuck down a dress shirt, making a total of four layers of cloth about my waist with only one layer on my arms and legs. The adjustment of trousers' front and belt after getting them on consumes in all eight separate motions. Then follows the folding of the cuffs and insertion of links, the placement and adjustment of arm bands. The collar is next with buttons or equivalents front and back plus the necktie, a finicky kind of operation which allows males to primp and preen at their best.

At this point I have seven pockets. I have used thirteen buttons. I have gone through forty-one separate motions. I am at last ready to put a fifth layer of cloth about my waist in the form of a vest. It has four pockets on the outside with one secret pocket for supposedly secret purposes on the inside. This vest has five more buttons and requires six more body movements with possibly the adjustment of a strap and buckle arrangement in the back needing five more movements. I am now ready for my suit, that is to say I am ready for the sixth layer of cloth about my waist. I am ready for three more buttons and four more pockets. This I accomplish with six body movements followed with a final adjustment of the ensemble which includes the insertion of a billfold, watch and two handkerchiefs in four of the seventeen pockets now available to me. Straightening again the tie and collar brings the total up to sixty-seven movements, not including of course the shoes, socks, and garters I had put on soon after my trousers were in place and with twelve exacting motions. Note that I am now ready for the wars of survival as we know them . . . in short I am dressed. Note that I have on eleven separate garments or items. Note that these items have twenty-eight appurtenances. Note that only my legs are now covered with a single layer of cloth, that is my legs five inches above and five inches below my kneecaps. Notice that fourteen buttons have been used, two shoe laces, two cuff links, two arm bands, one belt, one tie clasp, two collar buttons and one necktie, plus one zipper, two garters and seven buttonholes which are not really buttonholes but only imitations of them For some unaccountable reason six of these false buttonholes have buttons but the seventh does not.

Obviously I am now neither scientifically, logically nor functionally and aesthetically dressed. And I have expended a quarter of a million movements in the thirty-six thousand times I have dressed myself these past forty years. Moreover the way out of this unfortunate tradition and profits bound dilemma is both obscure and difficult.

I begin by combining. A vest and shirt in one piece. A combine of these two with the undershirt. Then adding the coat or jacket for a four-in-one unit, the whole without pockets, arm bands, cufflinks, collars, buttons, collar buttons. I combine the trousers with the undershorts, dropping in the process cuffs, one belt, three pockets and all buttons. I am seeking a single-piece affair with the necktie, the most useless of all useless apparel and yet the one object of greatest affection and most difficult to part with, being the last to go.

My first one-piece, all-occasion suit, not including stockings and shoes, has no cuffs, collar, tie, belt, double thickness at any point, and only three pockets. The requirements of porosity, flexibility, freedom of movement, warmth and low production costs plus functional styling necessitate considerable research with materials ending in the creation of woven paper, glass and tin textiles each made from the commonly wasted by-products of civilization: glass bottles, tin cans and waste paper of all sorts. Woven plastic, cellophane, cork, linoleum, and wood are also tried along with many natural reeds and fibers growing neglected and unused in great abundance throughout the world. Coupled with this search of mine for materials is the first study ever made of the engineering structure and design of the body and analysis of its movements and functions, the better to design the first garment ever conceived from these obvious viewpoints. Interestingly enough the ultimate suit is a coated or sprayed on type which is removed instantly by dissolving, with reapplication as frequently as desired. Any wanted thickness and color or combinations of color are of course possible. An intermediate or somewhat popular model of my design having built-in soles or shoes is dispensed from slot machines and is disposable in toilets.

Similarly I investigate wear spots on seats, elbows, garment edges subject to handling and wear. Methods of keeping materials perpetually clean and soil proof and permanently preserved are equally examined. It is while comparing the stylization potential of American-made shoes with the ready functionalism of a Japanese sandal that I attack the weardown features of heels and toes and the wearout characteristic of leather soles. Sidetracking the complaints of the highly organized shoe repair industry and the shoe and hide producers who are always pleased to have shoes deteriorate rapidly, I set up motion picture cameras of varying speeds on busy street corners in the first known attempt to learn how people walk and just what strains are produced, at what points and how to correct them either by a change of walking gait or by reshaping the footwear itself. Thus I make thousands of stress, strain and motion studies, I carefully investigate thousands of materials.

As the work goes on in this controlled and investigative manner I foresee that human skin can never be improved upon, might under the right conditions be made to grow to suit better a given purpose. Thus by special vitamin injections into skin structures in the soles of human feet I develop there a heavier, tougher skin which takes all conditions of use without the need of additional protection or covering. The human foot for the first time in history is taken for what it already is, a thing of great beauty, great functionalism. Unadorned feet at last come into their own. The only problem is to teach people to use them so that their natural beauty can evince itself. The same is true of all body parts and coverings which I develop. Skin alone is superior, cannot be excelled. These exhaustive studies produce then ways and means of making and being the body beautiful: how to stand, sit, walk or run. More important how to supply, reserve and build it in natural conformity to its true self.

The effect of my work is to change radically whole segments of existing industry. Clothing as we know it today is no longer made; unemployed garment workers become teachers of the body beautiful. The once shoe manufacturers make devices of leather for rubbing and exercising the body. Cleaning and dyeing establishments, weaving and carding mills are taken over by huge new cosmetic industries now having an entire body to cover with oils, perfumes, paints and preparations of the trade once limited to heads and hands. In fact as the work advances the sprayed-on coverings of my early design, the disposable one-piece suits, the shoes with high-heat treated spring steel soles, the suits with the wearout-proof seats and elbows, the master special that has no pockets but carries all necessary extras pinned on, the mothproof, fadeproof material whose weave and color design changes by simple exposure to ultra-violet light, these and a staggering number of innovations for clothes coming from my personal studio are made obsolete by the simple discovery that the human body without embellishment is superior to anything that can be prepared. The contribution of this great and thoroughly tested truth to the proper areas of the world's population who currently practice it in part, but need further experimental confirmation, is of course tremendous. It only remains now to see that this body is properly fed, rested, exercised and made disease-proof.

Raymond Queneau
from The Foundations of Literature

In his *Foundations,* Raymond Queneau, one of the leading members of the Oulipo, replaced the words *point, line,* and *plane* in David Hilbert's 1927 "Foundations of Mathematics" with *word, sentence,* and *paragraph,* respectively.

One might compare his work with Brian Joseph Davis's "Three Laws of Ethan Hawke," which interpolates Ethan Hawke, who starred in the movie *Dead Poets' Society,* among the laws of thermodynamics: "Ethan Hawke can be neither created nor destroyed. / The entropy of Ethan Hawke in isolation always increases. / The entropy of Ethan Hawke at absolute zero is zero."

First Group of Axioms
(axioms of connection)

I, 1—*A sentence exists containing two given words.*

COMMENT: Obvious. Example: given the two words "a" and "a," there exists a sentence containing these two words—"A violinist gives the vocalist her a."

I, 2—*No more than one sentence exists containing two given words.*

COMMENT: This, on the other hand, may occasion surprise. Nevertheless, if one considers the words "years" and "early," once the following sentence containing them has been written, namely "For years I went to bed early," clearly all other sentences such as "For years I went to bed right after supper" or "For years I did not go to bed late" are merely pseudo-sentences that should be rejected by virtue of the above axiom.

SCHOLIUM: Naturally, if "For years I went to bed right after supper" is the sentence written originally, "For years I went to bed early" becomes the sentence to be excluded by virtue of the axiom I, 2. In other words, no one can write *A la recherche du temps perdu* twice.

I, 3—*There are at least two words in a sentence; at least three words exist that do not all belong to the same sentence.*

COMMENT: Thus there are no one-word sentences. "Yes," "No," "Hey," "Psst" are not sentences, In regard to the second part of the axiom: the implicit assumption is that the language used comprises at least three words (a truism in the case of French and English) and furthermore that the possible existence of a sentence comprising all the words in a language (or all words less one, or less two) is excluded.

I, 4a—*A paragraph exists including three words that do not belong to the same sentence.*

COMMENT: A paragraph consequently comprises at least two sentences.

It is to be noted that the manner in which the axioms I, 1 through I, 4 are formulated contradicts axiom I, 2, since all four require for their articulation the words "words" and "sentences" whereas, according to the said axiom, no more than one sentence containing them should exist.

It is therefore possible to formulate the following metaliterary axiom:

Axioms are not governed by axioms.

I, 4b—*Every paragraph contains at least one word.*

COMMENT: Therefore "Yes," "No," "Hey, "Psst," which according to I, 3 are not sentences, cannot by themselves constitute paragraphs.

I, 5—*Not more than one paragraph exists containing three words that do not belong to the same sentence.*

COMMENT: As in I, 2, the question of unicity is thus raised, here that of the paragraph. In other terms, if three words that do not belong to the same sentences are used in one paragraph, they cannot be reused in another paragraph. But what if—as may be objected—they all belong to the same sentence in the other paragraph? An impossibility, according to this axiom.

I, 6—*If two words in a sentence belong to a paragraph, all words in the sentence belong to the paragraph.*

COMMENT: No comment required.

I, 7—*If two paragraphs have one word in common, they have still another one in common.*

COMMENT: To comply with this axiom, a writer must, if in a new paragraph he uses a word that has already appeared in the preceding paragraph, obligatorily use a second word that has appeared in the preceding paragraph as well. The obligation is easily acquitted in the case of such words as articles, auxiliary verbs, etc.; it is clearly anti-Flaubertian in regard to signifiers (nouns and adjectives, for example).

(See the comment on theorem I.)

I, 8—*At least four words exist that do not belong to the same paragraph.*

COMMENT: This means that a "text" consisting of a single paragraph does not deserve the designation "text"; that, furthermore, the language (French, English) contains sufficient words (four at least).

(See as well the comment to I, 3.)

In commenting on axiom I, 7, we did not explore all the consequences that can be drawn from it (as well as from other axioms already considered). We introduce forthwith the first theorem demonstrated by Hilbert:

THEOREM I. *Two discrete sentences in the same paragraph have at most one word in common; two discrete paragraphs either have no word*

in common or else they have one word in common and no word in com-
mon outside this sentence.

COMMENT: If the two paragraphs have one word in common they must in fact have a second (I, 7); but in that case these two words determine the sentence and, according to I, 1, this sentence is unique. The two paragraphs therefore have one sentence in common.

We thus come back to a more Flaubertian conception. The repetition of a word already used in a preceding paragraph requires the repetition of the entire sentence—a crushing obligation. It is just as well—and far more prudent—to avoid any repetition of the word. Flaubert complies with this axiom scrupulously.

Claudia Rankine
from Don't Let Me Be Lonely

Investigating the intersection of global media, global capital, and the most intimate, idiosyncratic, personal, bodily narratives, Claudia Rankine's book *Don't Let Me Be Lonely* (St. Paul, Minn.: Graywolf, 2004) charts a path between fabrication and documentation; the former is freely invented—in the tradition of J. M. Coetzee—with regard to family histories, and the latter is scrupulously and flatly pursued (as in the excerpt here) with regard to topical news stories. For example, Rankine footnotes the following passages with references to Samantha Power's "Letter from South Africa: The AIDS Rebel," in *New Yorker* (May 19, 2003, 65) and page 31 of William Shakespeare's *The Tragedy of King Lear* (New York: Signet, 1998).

THE PHARMACEUTICAL MANUFACTURERS' ASSOCIATION OF SOUTH AFRICA

ALCON LABORATORIES (S.A.) (PROPRIETARY) LIMITED

BAYER (PROPRIETARY) LIMITED

BRISTOL-MYERS SQUIBB (PROPRIETARY) LIMITED

BYK MADAUS (PRORIETARY) LIMITED

ELI LILLY (SOUTH AFRICA) (PROPRIETARY) LIMITED

GLAXO WELLCOME (SOUTH AFRICA) (PROPRIETARY) LIMITED

HOECHST MARION ROUSSEL LIMITED

INGELHEIM PHARMACEUTICALS (PROPRIETARY) LIMITED

JANSSEN-CILAG PHARMACEUTICA (PROPRIETARY) LIMITED

KNOLL PHARMACEUTICALS SOUTH AFRICA (PROPRIETARY) LIMITED

LUNDBECK SOUTH AFRICA (PROPRIETARY) LIMITED

MERCK (PROPRIETARY) LIMITED

MSD (PROPRIETARY) LIMITED

NOVARTIS SOUTH AFRICA (PROPRIETARY) LIMITED

NOVO NORDISK (PROPRIETARY) LIMITED

PHARMACIA & UPJOHN (PROPRIETARY) LIMITED

RHONE-POULENC RORER SOUTH AFRICA (PROPRIETARY) LIMITED

ROCHE PRODUCTS (PROPRIETARY) LIMITED

SCHERING (PROPRIETARY) LIMITED

SCHERING-PLOUGH (PROPRIETARY) LIMITED

S.A. SCIENTIFIC PHARMACEUTICALS (PROPRIETARY) LIMITED

SMITHKLINE BEECHAM PHARMACEUTICALS (PROPRIETARY) LIMITED

UNIVERSAL PHARMACEUTICALS (PROPRIETARY) LIMITED

WYETH (PROPRIETARY) LIMITED

XIXIA PHARMACEUTICALS (PROPRIETARY) LIMITED

ZENECA SOUTH AFRICA (PROPRIETARY) LIMITED

BAYER AG

BOEHRING-INGELHEIM INTERNATIONAL GmbH

BOEHRINGER-INGELHEIM KG

BRISTOL-MYERS SQUIBB COMPANY

BYK GULDEN LOMBERG CHEMISCHE FABRIK GmbH

ELI LILLY AND COMPANY

F. HOFFMANN-LA ROCHE AG

MERCK KGaA

MERK & CO INC.

RHONE-POULENC RORER S.A.

SMITHKLINE BEECHAM PlC

WARNER-LAMBERT COMPANY

Or over breakfast the *New York Times* is barely visible beneath the boxes of cereal, juice, and milk, but because I have been waiting for this day without realizing I was waiting, I see the story at first glance: President Mbeki has decided antiretrovirals will be made available to the five million South Africans infected by the HIV virus.

My body relaxes. My shoulders fall back. I had not known that my distress at Mbeki's previous position against distribution of the drugs had physically lodged itself like a virus within me. . . .

Before Mbeki, thirty-nine drug companies filed suit in order to prevent South Africa's manufacture of generic ADS drugs. Possible trade sanctions were threatened. Then President Clinton did an about-face and the lawsuit was dismissed. But like an absurdist dream, Mbeki stood between the now available drugs and the dying.

It is not possible to communicate how useless, how much like a skin-sack of uselessness I felt. *I am better than thou art now: I am a fool, the fool said, thou art nothing.* Is she dead? Is he dead? Yes, they are dead. One observes one recognizes without being recognized. One opens the paper. One turns on the television. Nothing changes. My distress grows into nothing. Thou art nothing.

Ariana Reines
from The Cow

Quoting from official government reports and industry catalogs—and borrowing her title from the second chapter of the Koran—Ariana Reines's *The Cow* (New York: Fence Books, 2006) collides colloquial epithets with specialist language to explore the cultural resonance of gendered domestication. In the following selection, for instance, language comes from the chapter 4 of *Carcass Disposal: A Comprehensive Review,* by Brent Auvermann, Ahmad Kalbasi, and Anindita Ahmed (National Agricultural Biosecurity Center Consortium, USDA/APHIS Cooperative Agreement Project, the Carcass Disposal Working Group, August 2004). To *render,* of course, means "to melt and clarify the fat of animals," but the subject is closely related to Reines's literary activity as well. To *render* is also "to tear," "to translate," and "to repeat" (the procedure of citation and collage at work in her poetics); "to narrate and depict"; "to expose and present oneself" (the confessional mode); "to demonstrate"; and "to return by reflection or repercussion, to give back, to restore" (as in the political valence of the work's head-on encounter with hurtful language). As Gertrude Stein wrote in *Tender Buttons* (Paris: Claire Marie, 1914): "out of an eye comes research, out of selection comes painful cattle."

LIVESTOCK MORTALITY IS A TREMENDOUS SOURCE OF ORGANIC MATTER. A TYPICAL FRESH CARCASS CONTAINS APPROXIMATELY 32% DRY MATTER, OF WHICH 52% IS PROTEIN, 41% IS FAT, AND 6% IS ASH. RENDERING OFFERS SEVERAL BENEFITS TO FOOD ANIMAL AND POULTRY PRODUCTION OPERATIONS, INCLUDING PROVIDING A SOURCE OF PROTEIN FOR USE IN ANIMAL FEED, AND PROVIDING A HYGIENIC MEANS OF DISPOSING OF FALLEN AND CONDEMNED ANIMALS. THE END PRODUCTS OF RENDERING HAVE ECONOMIC VALUE AND CAN BE STORED FOR LONG PERIODS OF TIME. USING PROPER PROCESSING CONDITIONS, FINAL PRODUCTS WILL BE FREE OF PATHOGENIC BACTERIA AND UNPLEASANT ODORS.

Across her. Across her.
Upending the weight of her I have to be finding out grammar.
How to be. Opener.
Sawed open. Easy.
Open like a grammar.
A dust of light the air carries.
What is a night upended
A carcass in which nothing is leftover.
What is a night upended.
Open, a hole where the head disgorges its body.

RENDERING OF ANIMAL MORTALITIES INVOLVES CONVERSION OF CARCASSES INTO THREE END PRODUCTS—NAMELY, CARCASS MEAL (PROTEINACEOUS SOLIDS), MELTED FAT OR TALLOW, AND WATER—USING MECHANICAL PRO-CESSES (E.G. GRINDING, MIXING, PRESSING, DECANTING, AND SEPARATING), THERMAL PROCESSES (E.G. COOKING, EVAPORATING, AND DRYING), AND SOMETIMES CHEMICAL PROCESSES (E.G. SOLVENT EXTRACTION). THE MAIN CARCASS RENDERING PROCESSES INCLUDE SIZE REDUCTION FOLLOWED BY COOKING AND SEPARATION OF FAT, WATER, AND PROTEIN MATERIALS USING TECHNIQUES SUCH AS SCREENING, PRESSING, SEQUENTIAL CENTRIFUGATION, SOLVENT EXTRACTION, AND DRYING. RESULTING CARCASS MEAL CAN SOME-TIMES BE USED AS AN ANIMAL FEED INGREDIENT. IF PROHIBITED FOR ANIMAL FEED USE, OR IF PRODUCED FROM KERATIN MATERIALS OF CARCASSES SUCH AS HOOVES AND HORNS, THE PRODUCT WILL BE CLASSIFIED AN INEDIBLE AND CAN BE USED AS A FERTILIZER. TALLOW CAN BE USED IN LIVESTOCK FEED, PRODUCTION OF FATTY ACIDS, OR CAN BE MANUFACTURED INTO SOAPS.

Can you carry.
Allopathy.
I don't know. Harried. Aloofer
Like that fact of the sky.
Still we say things to each other inside of holes.

Charles Reznikoff

from Testimony, Volume II: The United States (1885–1915): Recitative

The midcentury objectivist poet Charles Reznikoff edited various court documents into the five-hundred-page poem *Testimony* (Los Angeles: Black Sparrow, 1978). By adopting a hands-off, noninterventionist approach to the dramatic, tragic, and infuriating material, Reznikoff let the protagonists in the various court cases speak for themselves. The result is an emotionally stirring work, yet one that is nearly bereft of authorial meddling. The work's success hinges on the cases Reznikoff selects to lineate rather than any subjective authorial elucidation on them. Similarly, his work *Holocaust* is simply a retelling of harrowing stories that were revealed after the Second World War. Life is stranger than fiction, he seems to tell us, and it is best to leave it alone to speak for itself. Using mere transcription, Reznikoff opens the possibilities for appropriation and information management decades before they became common practices in the digital age.

THE NORTH

Machine Age

1. *The Noise of Civilization*

The hum of machinery, the noise of wagons on the public highways—
and the crowd watching a baseball game on a Sunday afternoon,
perhaps as many as two or three thousand,
shouting and stamping on the steps of the grandstand,
cheering and shouting
and heard half a mile and more away.

2. *Life in Town*

In the summer when the windows were open
the noise of the iron works—
of the air drills, hammers, riveting machines,
of the air drills, power hammers, power chippers, and riveting machines.

3. *Life in the Country*

There were about a hundred dead horses and cows—with maggots and
    flies—
lying about in the rendering factory
to be turned into fertilizer;
and when the wind was from the east blowing across the fields
the stench
would make the women sick
and they would have to close the windows
to eat or sleep.

4.

The rendering plant making fat into tallow
had a narrow covered passageway
between its factory and engine-house,
and in the passageway were four tanks for the hot fat.
One of the tanks, five by four feet and three feet deep,
was right at the door of one end of the passageway
but with a wooden cover on hinges.

The man who skimmed the fat in the tank
had opened the cover
and left it open;
and Dixon bringing a message to a fireman in the engine-house
from the fireman's brother
left the stable to go into the engine-house through the passageway.
A workman at the stable

saw him but did not trouble to warn him about the tank;
and neither did the engineer standing on a platform
within a few feet of Dixon
as he was about to enter the passageway.
The door had no latch but swung outward
as Dixon opened it,
and he did not see the tank-cover leaning against the wall—
the color of the hot fat almost that of the greasy cement floor—
and at his first step into the passageway
he plunged into the open tank,
its fat heated to a temperature of about two hundred degrees,
and was scalded to death.

Deborah Richards
from The Beauty Projection

With a graphic design that does not smooth over the sutures of her collage (the collages evoke a kind of scarred collagen), Deborah Richards lays bare the intersections between discrepant cultural *ethē.* The first column, for instance, quotes from Madame Lola Montez, countess of Landsfeld, *The Arts of Beauty; or, Secrets of a Lady's Toilet; With Hints to Gentlemen on the Art of Fascinating* (New York: Dick and Fitzgerald, 1858, 35–36), with subsequent quotes in this excerpt from pages 20 and 21 ("the following classical synopsis of female beauty by Felibien is the best I have ever seen"; "the black is particularly useful in setting off the whiteness of the neck and skin. The eyes black, chestnut, or blue; clear, bright, and lively, and rather large in proportion than small"). Another passage further down quotes a sidebar caption to an illustration in Martin Hall's *Archaeology in Africa* (Oxford, U.K.: James Currey, 1996, 3). The poem was published in *Last One Out* (Honolulu: Subpress Collective, 2003).

Most that I have said in the chapter on the means of obtaining a bright and handsome form, applies equally to the subject of this chapter. But, there are some artificial tricks which I have known beautiful ladies to resort to for the purpose of giving **elasticity** and sprightliness to the animal frame. The ladies of France and Italy, especially those who are professionally, or as amateurs, engaged in exercises which require great activity of the limbs, as dancing, or playing on instruments, some-times rub themselves, on retiring to bed, with the following preparation:

Fat of the stag, or deer	8oz.
Florence oil (or olive oil)	6oz.
Virgin wax	3oz.
Musk	1 grain.
White brandy	½ pint.
Rose Water	4oz.

Put the fat, oil, and wax into a well glazed earthern vessel, and let them simmer over a slow fire until they are assimilated; then pour in the other ingredients, and let the whole gradually cool, when it will be fit for use. There is no doubt but that this mixture, frequently and thoroughly rubbed upon the body on going to bed, will impart a remarkable degree of **elasticity** to the muscles. In the morning, after this preparation has been used, the body should be thoroughly wiped with a sponge, dampened with cold water (Montez 75).

it was a black catalogue sundress tied at the remarkable shoulders double knots or disaster just a pull and the animal frame would be released from its halter as a resort to obtaining imagination in those days the italian fashion was to wear tank t's to expose the breast when dancing or playing instruments black because it was easy and especially coordinated you know that means simpering in simmering sun never requires musk on so black a body there is no doubt that those tank t's were in but they required a remarkable form or a beautiful subject and were sexy without artificial tricks of trademark lycra but that was à la mode the young italian woman desirous of **elasticity** commended my skin oh if I could have skin like sprightliness she asked her mother the secret concoctions of oils that I may have frequently and thoroughly rubbed upon my intent body before cooling in bed but my german friend/loved one was a remarkable resource

The following classical synopsis to female beauty, which has been attributed to Felibien, is the best I [. . .] seen: the [. . .] smooth, a[. . .] hair growi[. . .]

the black is particularly useful in setting off the

FIGURE 1 THE HOTTENTOT VENUS. European prejudices about Africa developed early, and were based on the widely held assumption that Africans were inherently inferior to Europeans. Between 1810 and 1815 (the year she died in Paris) a southern African woman known as Saartje Baartman (or the 'Hottentot Venus') was exhibited in public in a number of European cities for the amusement and amazement of the public. Parts of her body are still preserved in the collections of the Musée de l'Homme in Paris, despite a number of protests. Concepts of race are discussed in Chapter 8 (Hall 3).

the eyes black, chestnut, or blue; lively, an[. . .] proportion than small. (Montez 68)

neck and skin

in italian as well as german and english he could understand every rounded O of her words and as we had engaged in exercises that required great activity that morning he knew that the taut black skin covered every part bar the intimate corners of the soles and palms and the sexual appetite I came back to interrupt the inherent process of comparison here is the setting for the purpose of transformation o.k. this is the synopsis he was to be a doctor in padua a serious student but we had love because he was bright and well rounded then I felt that to be worth anything all the lovely men I knew should make love to me in the full sense of its meaning it was a necessary sickness you know trying to assimilate myself into what I thought I could never be equal in proportion it could be particularly awkward in the morning he was so fair and I was so prominently foreign we were chiaroscuro it was a joke his white beauty my black back against the amazement of the private wet surface of the shower walls he is still preserved in my recollections

Kim Rosenfield
The Other Me

Kim Rosenfield melds her profession as a psychotherapist with her works, which often question notions of the stability of self, subjectivity, and identity while assuming a first-person subjective voice that does not belong to her. This piece is composed entirely of lines taken from Carl Rogers's psychology book (cowritten with his patient Barry Stevens) *Person to Person: The Problem of Being Human* (New York: Real People Press, 1967). Rosenfield writes:

> In place of innovation, I employ appropriation and re-inscription of existing voices, styles, and genres. In place of a cohered text, I favor a form that is fragmentary, inconclusive, digressive, and intermixed with other texts. In place of an omniscient author, I favor a collection of voices. In place of something "new" or "original," I accept that language is "already written" and gets recycled via ongoing social/political forces, and linguistic fashion.

One might read Rosenfield in the context of related works by Stacy Doris, who pioneered a new level of rematerializing source material within broadly conceptual frameworks in books such as *Kildare* (New York: Roof, 1994) and *Paramour* (San Francisco: Krupskaya, 2000).

I've always tried to be what others thought I should be, but now
I'm wondering whether I shouldn't just see that I am what I am.
—A Young Woman

In the beginning, I was one person, knowing nothing but my own experience. Then I was told things, and I became two people. So then I was two of I.

It was a completely unreal world that I was living in.

How can I feel grateful that you give to me what I am to you?

I comes through, a little. In moments. And gets pushed back by *Other I*. *Other I* gets tired, and goes on smiling, because that is the thing to do. *I* refuses to play the clown any more? Which I is that?

In the beginning was I, and I was good. Out of all the other I's, some are chosen as a pattern. That is me.

I will not let you (or me) make me dishonest, insincere, emotionally tied up, constricted, or artificially nice and social, if I can help it.

It is awesome and responsible to consider one's world as one's own representation.

I am not only my brother's keeper. *I am my brother.*

The world of persons is as plastic and varied as people themselves. What has been described here is the world of persons, the one we live in. In it, what I see in you is an image of myself. And what you see in me is an image of YOU. IT IS A WORLD OF MIRRORS. IT IS A USELESS AND OBSCURING FICTION THAT THERE *IS* A WORLD.

The natural depth of man is the whole of creation. Look at the scope of yourself.

Did I ever tell you of the beauty of cobwebs on a dirty window? But that is another long story.

The world as one's own representation seems to be a picture of social and psychological truth. Relaxed perception sees in itself all things going on. The one who doesn't notice is the other one—the Person among persons. The oneness of all things is known to *l'autre moi.*

I talk to my puppy and my dolls, and to the trees. They don't confuse me because they listen, and I can say *anything* I want and they don't talk back. They go on listening. And then I begin to hear myself and know it's me.

Raymond Roussel
from How I Wrote Certain of My Books

Raymond Roussel arranged to have *How I Wrote Certain of My Books,* explaining his compositional procedures, published after his death. The translation here, by Trevor Winkfield, is from the larger collection with the uniform title: *How I Wrote Certain of My Books* (Cambridge, Mass.: Exact Change, 2005).

I have always been meaning to explain the way in which I came to write certain of my books (*Impressions d'Afrique, Locus Solus, L'Etoile au Front* and *La Poussière de Soleils*).

It involved a very special method. And it seems to me that it is my duty to reveal this method, since I have the feeling that future writers may perhaps be able to exploit it fruitfully.

As a young man I had already written stories of some length employing this method.

I chose two almost identical words (reminiscent of metagrams). For example, *billard* [billiard table] and *pillard* [plunderer]. To these I added similar words capable of two different meanings, thus obtaining two almost identical phrases.

In the case of *billard* and *pillard* the two phrases I obtained were:

1. *Les lettres du blanc sur les bandes du vieux billard* . . . [The white letters on the cushions of the old billiard table . . .]

2. *Les lettres du blanc sur les bandes du vieux pillard* . . . [The white man's letters on the hordes of the old plunderer . . .

In the first, "lettres" was taken in the sense of lettering, "blanc" in the sense of a cube of chalk, and "bandes" as in cushions.

In the second, "lettres" was taken in the sense of missives, "blanc" as in white man, and "bandes" as in hordes.

The two phrases found, it was a case of writing a story which could begin with the first and end with the latter.

Now it was from the resolution of this problem that I derived all my materials.

In the story in question there was a white explorer who, under the title "Among the Blacks" had published a book in the form of missives in which he discussed the hordes of a plunderer (black king).

At the beginning we see someone chalking letters on the cushions of an old billiard table. These letters, in the form of a cryptogram, composed the final sentence: "The white man's letters on the hordes of the old plunderer," and the story as a whole turned on the tale of a rebus based on the explorer's epistolary narratives.

I shall presently show how this story provided the basis for my book *Impressions d'Afrique* written ten years later.

We find three very clear examples of this creative method using two almost identical phrases with different meanings:

1. In *Chiquenaude,* a story published by Alphonse Lemerre around 1900.

2. In *Nanon,* a story published in *Gaulois du Dirnanche* around 1907.

3. In *Une page du Folklore breton,* a story published in *Gaulois du Dimanche* around 1908.

As for the origin of *Impressions d'Afrique,* it consisted of reconciling the words *billard* and *pillard.* The "pillard" was Talou; the "bandes" his warlike hordes; the "blanc" Carmichael (the word *lettres* was dropped).

Expanding this method, I began to search for new words relating to *billard,* always giving them a meaning other than that which first came to mind, and each time this provided me with a further creation.

Thus *queue* [billiard cue] supplied me with Talou's gown and train. A billiard cue sometimes carries the "chiffre" (monogram) of its owner; hence the "chiffre" (numeral) stitched on the aforementioned train.

I searched for a word to accompany *bandes* and thought of the *reprises* (darns) in old *bandes* (billiard cushions). And the word *reprises,* in its musical sense, gave me the Jéroukka, that epic sung by Talou's *bandes* (warlike hordes) whose music consisted of the continual *reprises* [repetitions] of a brief melody.

Searching for a word to go with *blanc* I thought of the *colle* [glue] which sticks the paper to the base of the cube of chalk. And the word *colle,* used in school slang to denote detention or imposition, gave me the three hours confinement imposed on the *blanc* (Carmichael) by Talou.

Abandoning at that point the scope of *billard,* I continued along the same lines. I chose a word and then linked it to another by the preposition *à* [with]; and these two words, each capable of more than one meaning, supplied me with a further creation. (Incidentally, I used this preposition *à* in the above-mentioned groups of words: *queue à chiffre, bandes à reprises, blanc à colle.*) I should point out that the initial stages of this work were difficult and already required a great deal of time.

I would like to cite some examples:

Taking the word *palmier* I decided to consider it in two senses: as a *pastry* and as a *tree*. Considering it as a *pastry,* I searched for another word, itself having two meanings which could be linked to it by the preposition *à;* thus I obtained (and it was, I repeat, a long and arduous task) *palmier* (a kind of pastry) *à restauration* (restaurant which serves pastries); the other part gave me *palmier* (palm tree) *à restauration* (restoration of a dynasty). Which yielded the palm tree in Trophies Square commemorating the restoration of the Talou dynasty.

Aram Saroyan
Untitled Poem

Apparently the transcription of a newspaper bridge column, Aram Saroyan's untitled poem picks up on the suggestive potential of the stylized linguistic etiquette of contract bridge, with its language of violence (e.g., dropping, clubbing) and romance (hearts, wrecked contracts). Removed from its original context, the text suggests a strange fairy-tale narrative of royalty and allegory (with the strangely personified West and East), told in a wistful subjunctive that punningly evokes the modern game's origins in whist. That historical lineage (*whist* meaning "a whistling sound, a whistle") may also connect the poem to another in the same volume:

whistling in the street a car turning in the room ticking

Turning and *ticking*, both terms from bridge, hint that the "car turning" may be a card turning. In any case, the car returns in *Pages* (New York: Random House, 1969) in another poem that is also apparently transcribed from a newspaper; the lineated headline reads:

Car Swerves,
Injures 11;
Driver Held

Had West followed up her fine opening lead by dropping
the club king or queen on the second round of clubs, she
would have been able to play the ten when Stayman tried to
throw her in, Then East could have overtaken and returned
a heart, wrecking the contract.

Ara Shirinyan
from Your Country Is Great

Armenian-American writer Ara Shirinyan's book *Your Country Is Great* (New York: Futurepoem, 2008) is a meditation on identity, nationalism, and globalism, as he expresses in words that are not his own. For this piece, he named every country in the world, organized them from *A* to *Z,* Googled the phrase "[country name] is great," and then hand-selected and sorted the results by nation. He then lineated the comments, with each stanza representing another opinion. The result is a multinational Baedeker of user-driven content and opinion. Unsourced and unsigned, the piece is by turns ugly and gorgeous, helpful and harmful, truthful and misleading, relevant and completely irrelevant, all while bringing a cool and rational methodology to an inherently hysterical forum. Collapsing the space between the real world and the World Wide Web, this work asks, What is local? What is national? What is multicultural? Instead of accepting current notions of language as a medium of differentiation, Shirinyan persuasively demonstrates its leveling quality, demolishing meaning into a puddle of platitudes in a time when everything is great, yet nothing is great.

Afghanistan Is Great

Afghanistan is great, but much smaller
than previously assumed.

the need for education
in Afghanistan is great
and must be met quickly,

need for food in Afghanistan
    is great,

well-acquainted
with unique problems
facing Afghanistan.

The need for tough, dependable,
locally repairable wheelchairs in
Afghanistan is great.

A mountain. An airplane. Aviation in
Afghanistan is great fun.

Pipeline via Afghanistan
    is great.

There is no question that Allah's
knowledge and love of Afghanistan
    is great
even as he regrets
the limits of
    his understanding.

Albania Is Great

Albania is great. I missed that place a lot.
I got offered cigarettes and alcohol by
like everyone I knew
and some people I didn't know.

Albania is great!
Not quite as third-world
as parts of Africa, but
not exactly Michigan either
if ykwim.

I liked everything about my stay
and i just wanted to let you know
that Albania is GREAT!!!

Albania is great as a communsist country
or democratic, either way, albania is just the best.

U aint from belgrade,
youd feel our pain and not
say how albania is great.
educate ur self:

Hiking, camping,
mountain-climbing,
hunting—North
Albania is great
for all of this.

The Italian influence in Albania is great,
many speak Italian, watch Italian TV.
The historical ties between Italy and Albania
are very strong.

I know you love your country but please
stop telling us that Albania is great. Like I said,
give us the worldly achievements of Albania.

Albania is great!!!! We finished 5th place
because we were all injured. And we lost
against Georgia twice before because
we felt bad on those two day's!

Algeria Is Great

hey how are you , algeria is great and sorry that
i cant talk to you . but my uncle has a cafe with
a bunch of computers . but i cant stay on to long

The basis of that construction primarily rests—better
said, they rested—on recovering Algeria is great natural
resources, These essentially were energy

Potentials for organic agriculture in Algeria is great.
Kabylia mountain region of about 100000 areas can
be converted to organic agriculture.

Andorra Is Great

One of Europe's smallest countries,
Andorra is great for skiing.
Montserrat Crazy mountain
with startling
naturally formed shapes
to give you the creeps.

The weather in Andorra is great
if you don't like it too cold

Andorra is great country to go shoping
since it is tax free you get lots of things
more cheaper than surraunding countries.
Alcohol, Parfumes,

Andorra is great place to do some winter sports,
they have lovely high mountains
you to ski or snowboard.
In the summer time you can go hiking

Andorra is great for cheap electrical goods
and there are perfume shops
everywhere you look.
Andorra is also great for its
spectacular views

I've been told the skiing in Andorra is great,
but I will write a "winter" opinion on Andorra,
at a later date
ie when I've actually tried it out!

Andorra is great , snowboarding every day
(untill I broke my shoulder . . . duh !)
I wouldn ' t mind going back there .

Angola Is Great

The challenge faced by the media
and the institutions that have committed
themselves to supporting democracy
in Angola is great.

I hear western Angola is great this time of year.

With all 12 nations enjoying free-market economies
and either full democracies or in the process of becoming
democratic, the potential for Angola is great.

sale of the 203-acre Oakhill Campground &
Retreat Center in Angola is great news for its
former owner, AG Financial of Springfield, Mo

i like your style . . . dig the tunes . . . Angola is great

Anguilla Is Great

anguilla is great for snorkeling
anguilla is a coral island in the
    north eastern caribbean
anguilla is a british territory
    in the caribbean

Anguilla is Great for Snorkeling
Anguilla is great for investment info
Carnival in Anguilla is Great.

All in all, Anguilla is great.
Great people,

great food,
great beaches.

Argentina Is Great

Argentina is great. The food was truly one of the best finds.
The food is great—fresh and not spicy. Not what most people
    from the US would expect.

I think Argentina is great for all kinds of stuff.
As it's such a big country, they have lots of thing
    to do and see.
Argentina is great, and I want to make it grow,
    grow and grow

Argentina is great—before I knew there was a shelter there,
I thought those ruins looked like the ultimate cat playground

Argentina is great because the population is 90–95% Meditteranean!
    Few jews because the great Rightist pro-white military junta
    got rid of 50k leftist jews
This is why I think the launching of legitimate services in Argentina
    is great news."

Airbag, pop band, Argentina. "We are young and love music.
to have basically the biggest scores of the tournament
and to beat Argentina, is great,
    such a relief to be in the quarter-finals.

Argentina is great and might have had an edge,
    but they still lost, Which is what counts.
To call them talentless is insane
    and disrespectful

Following the devaluation of the peso,
    shopping in Argentina is great
for tourists who can get a lot for the money.

Argentina is great but the way they do business here
     is criminal. There is a reason
they are ranked as one of the most corrupt countries in the world.

Birdwatching in Argentina is great
Argentina is great for that
     and cheap at it

I like meat, so Argentina is GREAT.
     Lots of BEEF.
This garlicky sauce from Argentina is great
     spooned over beef or chicken.

what an original argument:
     argentina is shit.
     argentina is great.
get over yourselves and accept the truth;
     argentina is both of those things,

Armenia Is Great

Armenia is great, and Yerevan is a city
where people live their lifes to the maximum
I love you Yerevan,
     I love your streets,
     your sidewalks,

Armenia is great
everyone should go back
at least once

the new information on Armenia is great—
lots of good information—
I'll have to remember not to give
anyone 2 flowers!

I also do not speak our language
Armenia is great though.

I have been there
and made good friends,
even though I could not
speak a word to them.

Tour to Armenia is a great success!
To Understand Our
    Past,
Is To Understand
    Ourselves.

Armenia is great!
Hi, just so you know,
I signed up for this board
specifically to respond
to your post.

renovated sidewalks, roads, and
unprecedented High Rise buildings
    going up
the future of Armenia is great.

With such warm summers
and very cold winters
you will learn a great deal
about the history of Yerevan

Armenia is great
I love it, but I dont think
it is for me.

armenia is great country
famous for its christianity!

Ron Silliman
from Sunset Debris

John Cage claimed that he often found questions more interesting than answers. Ron Silliman, echoing Cage's sentiment, constructed an entire section of his book *The Age of Huts* (New York: Roof, 1986) from nearly forty pages of questions. Ranging from the personal to the found to the absurd, Silliman's gesture serves to displace the authorial figure, as well as any notion of a stabilized, centered text. Instead, what we get is a glimpse twenty years ahead into the age of electronic writing and information management, where language is material to be collected and collated, consumed and manipulated, for its own sake.

Can you feel it? Does it hurt? Is this too soft? Do you like it? Do you like this? Is this how you like it? Is it alright? Is he there? Is he breathing? Is it him? Is it near? Is it hard? Is it cold? Does it weigh much? Is it heavy? Do you have to carry it far? Are those the hills? Is this where we get off? Which one are you? Are we there yet? Do we need to bring sweaters? Where is the border between blue and green? Has the mail come? Have you come yet? Is it perfect bound? Do you prefer ballpoints? Do you know which insect you most resemble? Is it the red one? Is that your hand? Want to go out? What about dinner? What does it cost? Do you speak English? Has he found his voice yet? Is this anise or is it fennel? Are you high yet? Is your throat sore? Can't you tell dill weed when you see it? Do you smell something burning? Do you hear a ringing sound? Do you hear something whimpering, mewing, crying? Do we get there from here? Does the ink smear? Does the paper get yellow and brittle? Do you prefer soft core? Are they on their way to work? Are they feeling it? Are they locked out? Are you pessimistic? Are you hard? Is that where you live? Is the sink clogged? Have the roaches made a nest in the radio? Are the cats hungry, thirsty, tired? Does he need to have a catheter? Is he the father? Are you a student at the radio school? Are you afraid to fail? Are you in constant fear of assassination? Why has the traffic stopped? Why does blue fade into green? Why didn't I go back to Pasco and become a cop? Why does water curl into the drain in different directions on either side of the equator? Why does my ankle throb? Why do I like it when I pop my knuckles? Is that a bald spot? Is that an ice cap? Is that a birth mark? Will the fog burn off soon? Are her life signs going to stabilize? Can you afford it? Is it gutted? What is it that attracts you to bisexual women? Does it go soggy in the milk? Do people live there? Is there a limit? Did it roll over when it went off the road? Will it further class struggle? Is it legible? Do you feel that it's private? Does it eat flies, worms, children? Is it nasty? Can you get tickets? Do you wear sunglasses out of a misplaced sense of increased privacy? Do you derive pleasure from farts in the bath? Is there an erotic element to picking your nose? Have you a specific conceptualization of earwax? What am I doing here? How do the deaf sing? How is it those houses will burn in the rain? What is the distance to Wall Drugs? Why do they insist on breaking the piñata? Is penetration of the labia sufficient to support a conviction? Is it a distraction to be aware of the walls? Is it bigger than a bread box? Which 1 is it? When you skydive, do your ears pop? Do you bruise? Did the bridge rust? Is your life clear to you? How will you move it? Will you go easy on the tonic, please? Do you resent your parents? Was your childhood a time of great fear? Is that the path? Do the sandpipers breed here? Is that what you want? Have your cramps come? Do you tend to draw words instead of write them? Do you have an opinion about galvanized steel? Who was John Deere? Are you trapped by your work? Would you like to explore that quarry? Is it the form of a question? Where is Wolf Grade? Are your legs sore? Is that a bottle neck? Who is the Ant Farm? Where did she learn to crawl like that? Is the form of the dance the dancer, or the space she carves? Can we go home now? Who was that masked man? Does he have an imagination? Will he use it? Is it obvious? Is it intentional? Is it possible? Is it hot? Why did the mirror fog up? What is the context of discourse? What is the premise of the man asking passersby if they have change for a dollar? Who took my toothbrush? What made her choose to get back into the life? What is the cause of long fingers? What is the role of altered, stretched canvas on wood supports, hung from a wall? Why do they seem so focused, intent, on their way to work? What makes you needle happy? Why does he keep large bills in his shirt pocket? How do you locate the crosshairs of your bitterness? What was it about shouting, mere raised voices, that caused him always to go out of control? Do you hear that hum? Is there damage? Is the answer difficult or hard? Is each thing needful? If there was a rip in my notebook, how would you know it? What makes you think you have me figured out? Why do my eyes water, devoid of emotion? What is the difference between a film and a movie? Do you want sugar? Why does my mood correspond to the weather? How do you get down to the beach? Is the act distinct from the object? What did you put in the coffee? Did your ears pop? Would you prefer to watch the condos burn? Where do the verbs go? Will you ever speak to the issue of cholesterol? What is a psychotropic? Does pleonasm scare you? Kledomania? Who leads the low-riders? What is the relation between any two statements? Is anything as tight as anal penetration? Will we stop soon? Will we continue? Where are those sirens coming from? Is it necessary? Is it off-white? Is a legitimate purpose served in limiting access? Will this turn out to be the last day of summer? Will you give up, give out, over? Why is sarcasm so often the final state of marriage? Is this the right exit? Have you received a security clearance? What do you think of when I say "red goose shoes?" Why does the blind man use his cane like a wand? What is the source of your agitation? Can't you smell the rain before it falls? Are you dizzy, faint, nauseous? Do you have chills? Can you help it? When is the question a form of order? Does order mean a form of command? Do rabbits scratch? Do you find black gays exotic? Do words peel their outer meanings? Is that your hair? What if I want this so plain you can't see it? Have you noticed all these women with asymmetrical faces in their too-loud make-up? What is so special? What is an ice pick? Do you have involuntary erections without probable cause? What time do you have? Does it begin to wear thin? What about struggle? Do I dare to eat a peach? When do you rise? Why is the verb the second word? Have you watched how new graves begin to move down the slope of that hill, how it fills? What are you trying to tell me? Is that the island? How do they make carbon paper? Is it too hot? What about this? How does a harbor harbor? What of an art of sensory deprivation? Do you like to go down? Will you be able to make it? At what point does meaning begin to blur? Is that a flag in the rain? Is there anything suspicious about the dead? Will you flush when done? What sort of experience will I be forced to exclude? Are you ready? Are you certain? Do you feel this? Is this it? Do we turn here? Will it rain? Aren't you afraid I'll go on endlessly, shamelessly, pointlessly? Do you know that the true structure of a prison is built around its illegal commodities market? Don't you think your fever correlates with stress? Don't you watch those bank clerks each morning, waiting by the door to be let in? Isn't anyone ready to describe real life? How does syntax shape the chair? Where is that woman going with a cake in a box? How did you come to love flow charts? How is a sentence true? Do you see that woman in the crosswalk, turning first this way and then that, as if dazed, uncertain as to the way to go? How soon before I turn into an old man with a bedroll under one arm and a paper bag full of rags and clothes in the other, talking to myself as I walk? Are you now at that point that when you cut you scar? What is the source of the dull pain in the jaw? What is the emotional dimension of circumcision? Why do people stare at you? What do they say? Do you care for your cuticles? Are you aware of vessels in the eye? Have we time for one? How do I open this? What do they use it for? Where is the odor of apricots? How do I unscrew it? Are we there yet? Which states have you been to? Which zone is this? Did professional sex force her to alter emotions? Do you opt for or against irrevocable acts? Can you make it hard? What does it taste like? Is it Kansas? Do you prefer soup or salad? Did you see the man who was born without ears? Did you ever smoke a banana? Where is the center? Is it hyper or laid-back? How will you survive? Shall we circumambulate or simply walk up the side of the mountain? Who cuts your hair? Is it a specific type of diction? Who sez? What are his motives? Do you want to go lie down in the ice plants? Do you think they enjoy working for white people? Is that a fire in that trash can? What key, what key? Can it happen here? Is that the real color of her hair? What makes him prefer tangential contingencies? Don't you get your foreskin caught on things? Is it speech? How far can you take it in? Do you prefer an automatic? When is form not a distortion?

Juliana Spahr
Thrashing Seems Crazy

In the late 1970s, Ruth Finlay—who had been living a quiet family life in Wichita, Kansas—began to receive threatening notes from a stranger; the harrassment became increasingly menacing and ultimately murderous. The homicidal criminal was dubbed "The Poet" by local police. He turned out to be one of Finlay's own dissociative personalities. Complicating assumptions about subjective interiority, continuity, and coherence, Finlay's condition troubles what might be meant by one's "self" or one's "own" words, and whether the poet Spahr's ventriloquism is any further from Finlay's voice than The Poet's disquieting, anonymous letters. Furthermore, Finlay's own account was mediated, for Spahr, through the homogenizing media of daytime television. As she notes in *Response* (Los Angeles: Sun and Moon, 1986): "This poem draws from an Oprah episode on the case of Ruth Finley, a woman who, because of dissociative personality disorder, was stalked by a male persona of herself."

this is true
a man in an alley grabbed my arm
this is true
someone called me and left the phone dangling at the post office
this is true
a man stalked me

someone tells a story

someone tells a story to another person
another person says I don't believe this

someone tells the story again in an attempt to convince
someone tells

as disbelief is easy
belief is difficult, supported by constraint

but a woman knows a man stalked her
knows this is true

a woman knows her own address
her own body
her lost domain, her desires, her confusions

someone tells a story

there are things people can do to themselves
they are:
leave molotov cocktail on own yard
set fire to own house
leave a glass of urine on own porch
leave envelope of feces outside own door
send a butcher knife to self at work
send letter to health department that self is spreading v.d.
stab own back

someone tells this story
says this is true
self turns on self
the knife enters at a point that the self could not have reached but did

someone tells and then repeats and she stalks herself several times to
    convince
someone tries to enter into the information
to pass words back and forth that have meaning
fails, resorts to this is true

this is true
a woman calls her stalker The Poet

this is true
a woman describes a stalker in terms that describe herself

this is true
a woman stalked herself to kill herself

this is true
a woman is at times a man

when a fish is hooked
other fish don't see the hook

thrashing seems crazy

the hook could be the branding of a woman at a young age by a man
or an older male neighbor spending too much time with a child
or the boring nature of life

in the story the hook is the artist's rendering of the stalker as described by
    the woman
it is the woman in a man's face

she does not know this man
thrashing seems crazy

later she realizes it is herself
her knife
her hook
her own face she was always drawing male

this is true
as thrashing is not crazy when one is on the hook

Brian Kim Stefans
from The Vaneigem Series

A classic example of *détournement*, Brian Kim Stefans's *Vaneigem Series* is an elegant mash-up of daily journalism and situationist polemic that replaces quotations in *New York Times* articles with lines from the Belgian philosopher Raoul Vaneigem. In the original online iteration of the *Vaneigem Series*, the look of the *Times*'s website—the full template of design, typography, and sidebar advertisements from nytimes.com—was mirrored. With a kind and understanding cease-and-desist order ("The Times appreciates a good parody . . ."), counsel for the New York Times Company requested that the series be removed from public view. Stefans complied, but at least one of the pieces lives on—in a perfect example of the simulacrum: an imaginary event with real-world consequences—in Rex J. Zedalis's political science article "Developments Regarding the United Nations Weapons Inspection Regime in Iraq" (*International Peacekeeping: The Yearbook of International Peace Operations*, ed. Harvey Langholtz, Boris Kondoch, and Alan Wells [Leiden: Brill, 2004], vol. 8). With no apparent irony, footnote 136 to Zedalis's article reads: "One big project released at the time was the so-called 'Blair dossier'. See R. Vaneigem, 'Blair Presents Dossier on Iraq's Biological Weapons,' *The New York Times*, Sept. 24, 2002."

Daschle Denounces Bush Remarks on Iraq as Partisan
By RAOUL VANEIGEM

WASHINGTON, Sept. 25—Senator Tom Daschle, the majority leader, angrily accused President Bush today of using the Iraq issue for political fodder and said he should apologize.

"That is wrong," Mr. Daschle declared on the Senate floor.

"Have you ever felt the urge to make love (not as a matter of routine but with great passion) to your partner or to the first man or woman to come along, or to your daughter, or your parents, or your men and women friends, or your brothers and sisters?" Mr. Daschle, a Democrat from South

Dakota, spoke even as Congressional leaders from both parties were negotiating the terms of the resolution of support that Mr. Bush has requested for dealing with Saddam Hussein.

"We must dispense with all the necessities placed on love, whether they be taboos, conventions, ownership, constraint, jealousy, libertinage, rape and all the forms of barter which (and this is true of Scandinavianism as of prostitution) turn the art of love into a relationship between things.

"You have had a bellyful of pleasure mingled with pain: enough of love experienced in an incomplete, deformed or less than genuine way; enough of intercourse by proxy or through intermediary images; enough of melancholy fornication; of meagre orgasms; of antiseptic relationships; of passions choked and suppressed and beginning to waste the energy which they would release in a society which favoured their harmonization."

Mr. Daschle had signaled his general support for Mr. Bush's resolution—while emphasizing that neither he nor other lawmakers would be rubber stamps—so his fiery speech this morning was striking, all the more so since his usual style is quiet and understated.

"The House responded," Mr. Bush said, "but the Senate is more interested in special interests in Washington and not interested in the security of the American people.

"Whether we admit it or not, we are all looking for great passion which is at once single and plural.

"Socially we want to create the historical conditions for a lasting passionate relationship, for a pleasure the only boundary on which is the exhaustion of possibilities, for a game where pleasure and displeasure rediscover their positive side (for instance in the inception and in the ending of a free amorous liaison)."

Mr. Daschle practically shouted his disdain for those words today.

"Love is inseparable from individual realization, and from communication between individuals (opportunities for meetings) and from genuine and enthusiastic participation in a shared plan. It is inseparable from the struggle for universal self-management."

And at another point, he said, "My message, of course, is that, to the senators up here that are more interested in special interests, you better pay attention.

"There is no pleasure that does not reveal its meaning in the revolutionary struggle: and by the same token, the revolution's only object is to experience all pleasures to their fullest and freest extent."

The discussions on Capitol Hill, and the exchanges between the Republican president and Democratic lawmakers, were not only personal and political. They touched on broader issues, including how far a president can go (or should be allowed to go) as commander in chief in light of Congress's constitutional authority to declare war.

Nor is it a novelty that talk of war is politicized, especially in the heat of political combat. For instance, people of a certain age may recall what Senator Bob Dole, the Kansas Republican, said while he was President Gerald Ford's running mate in 1976.

"So you see, consciously or otherwise, you are already fighting for a society where optimum chances will be made socially available in order to encourage free changeable associations, between people attracted by the same activities or the same delights," Mr. Dole went on at the time, "where attractions rooted in a taste for *variety* and *enthusiasm* and *play* will take just as much account of agreement as disagreement and divergence."

Mr. Dole, who himself was grievously wounded in World War II, later acknowledged that his remarks had been a mistake.

U.N. Weapons Inspectors Seek Open Access in Iraq
By ASGER JORN

Filed at 1:59 p.m. ET

VIENNA, Austria (AP)—Opening talks with Iraqi experts Monday, the chief U.N. weapons inspector said he expected unfettered access to suspect sites if his teams return and full cooperation in the meantime to make that happen.

Chief inspector Hans Blix told reporters at the Vienna headquarters of the International Atomic Energy Agency that the talks would operate under the assumption that nothing in Iraq—including Saddam Hussein's palaces—will be off-limits to inspectors hunting for nuclear, biological and chemical weaponry.

"Haven't you ever felt the urge to burn some distribution factory—i.e. supermarket, giant store or warehouse—to the ground?" Blix asked.

"The real pollution is the pollution by universal commodity intruding into every area of life. Every commodity on the supermarket shelf is a cynical hymn to the wage-slave oppression of the lie which places it on sale, and of the barter system of the boss and the cop whose function it is to protect that lie.

"We're moving along nicely," he said. "They're all aware of the importance that there be no misunderstandings."

Under a deal U.N. Secretary-General Kofi Annan cut with Baghdad in early 1998, the inspectors' access to eight so-called presidential sites encompassing a total of 12 square miles was restricted. The deal prevented them from carrying out surprise inspections at the sites, which include Saddam's palaces, and created a team of international diplomats to accompany inspectors when they did enter.

The United States and the rest of the Security Council endorsed that plan.

"The display of commodities is part and parcel of a bleak existence and a glorification of its impoverishment: a paean to life squandered in hours of obligatory work," a senior diplomat close to the talks said on condition of anonymity, adding that the inspections are "the sacrifices we give our assent to so that we can purchase shit junk food, gadgets, cars-coffins, accommodation cages, and items with built-in planned obsolescence; inhibitions; pleasure/anxieties; the derisory images offered in exchange for an absence of real life and purchased by compensation."

On Saturday, Iraqi Vice President Taha Yassin Ramadan rejected any changes in the inspections regime.

"Instead of the work that proscribes abundance and produces only a distorted reflection of it, we want abundance that will encourage creativity and passions," Ramadan said.

"Our position on the inspectors has been decided and any additional procedure is meant to hurt Iraq and is unacceptable."

British Prime Minister Tony Blair has signaled, meanwhile, that he might be open to a strategy of using two, rather than just one, U.N. resolutions to establish a new international legal framework for disarming Saddam.

Blair, who is the United States' staunchest backer for stern measures against Iraq and who has served as an intermediary with less-supportive European governments, made his comments in a BBC television interview Sunday.

"Arson against a large store is only a terrorist act. Indeed, since the commodity is designed to be destroyed and replaced, arson does not destroy the commodity system but conspires with it with just an excess of brutality.

"We can leave that open for the moment. The most important thing is to get a very clear determination from the United Nations Security Council saying . . . these chemical, biological, potentially nuclear weapons pose a real danger to the world," Blair said.

"We have had it with ennui and voyeurism.

"We have had it with a world where what one sees prevents one from living, and where that which prevents one from living presents itself as an abstract caricature of life.

"And, consciously or otherwise, we are already fighting for a society where the true eradication of commodity will be achieved through free usufruct of products created once obligatory work has ceased."

Gary Sullivan
Conceptual Poem (WC + WCW)

Using techniques pioneered in the audio field of mash-ups (syncing two or more disparate pop tracks to create one new song), Gary Sullivan's "Conceptual Poem" meshes an alphabetically arranged list of W. C. Fields quotes with the phrase "Forgive me," taken from William Carlos Williams's famous poem "This Is Just to Say."

In "To a Sought Caterpillar," a list of homophonically transcribed birdcalls, brings to mind Olivier Messiaen's *Catalogue d'oiseaux* (1958), whereby the composer transcribed actual birdsong for piano. It is also reminiscent of visual artist Louise Lawler's piece *Birdcalls* (composed in 1972 and recorded in 1981), in which she transformed names of male artists into birdcalls and performed them. As does a Rorschach test, Sullivan's translations reveal his biases, subjectivity, and personality as much as any confessional poem would.

A rich man is nothing but a poor man with money. Forgive me.
Abstaining is favorable both to the head and the pocket. Forgive me.
Ah, the patter of little feet around the house. There's nothing like having
    a midget for a butler. Forgive me.
All the men in my family were bearded, and most of the women.
    Forgive me.
Always carry a flagon of whiskey in case of snakebite, and furthermore
    always carry a small snake. Forgive me.
Anyone who hates children and animals can't be all bad. Forgive me.
Attitude is more important than the past, than education, than money,
    than circumstances, than what people do or say. It is more important
    than appearance, giftedness, or skill. Forgive me.
Children should neither be seen or heard from—ever again. Forgive me.
Don't worry about your heart; it will last you as long as you live.
    Forgive me.

Drown in a cold vat of whiskey? Death, where is thy sting? Forgive me.

Horse sense is the thing a horse has which keeps it from betting on people. Forgive me.

I am an expert of electricity. My father occupied the chair of applied electricity at the state prison. Forgive me.

I am free of all prejudices. I hate every one equally. Forgive me.

I cook with wine; sometimes I even add it to the food. Forgive me.

I drink therefore I am. Forgive me.

I like children—fried. Forgive me.

I never drink water, because of the disgusting things that fish do in it. Forgive me.

I never drink water; that is the stuff that rusts pipes. Forgive me.

I never drink water; I'm afraid it will become habit-forming. Forgive me.

I never met a kid I liked. Forgive me.

I never vote for anyone; I always vote against. Forgive me.

I never worry about being driven to drink; I just worry about being driven home. Forgive me.

I once spent a year in Philadelphia. I think it was on a Sunday. Forgive me.

If at first you don't succeed, try, try again. Then quit. There's no point in being a damn fool about it. Forgive me.

If I had to live my life over, I'd live over a saloon. Forgive me.

If there's a will, prosperity can't be far behind. Forgive me.

If you can't dazzle them with brilliance, baffle them with bull. Forgive me.

It ain't what they call you, it's what you answer to. Forgive me.

It was a woman who drove me to drink, and I never had the courtesy to thank her for it. Forgive me.

It's morally wrong to allow a sucker to keep his money. Forgive me.

Last week I went to Philadelphia, but it was closed. Forgive me.

Marry an outdoors woman. Then if you throw her out into the yard on a cold night, she can still survive. Forgive me.

Never cry over spilt milk, because it may have been poisoned. Forgive me.

Never give a sucker an even break. Forgive me.

Never try to impress a woman, because if you do she'll expect you to keep up the standard for the rest of your life. Forgive me.

No doubt exists that all women are crazy; it's only a question of degree. Forgive me.

Now don't say you can't swear off drinking. It's easy, I've done it a thousand times. Forgive me.

On the whole, I'd rather be in Philadelphia. Forgive me.

Once during Prohibition I was forced to live for days on nothing but food and water. Forgive me.

Remember, a dead fish can float downstream, but it takes a live one to swim upstream. Forgive me.

Show me a great actor and I'll show you a lousy husband. Show me a great actress, and you've seen the devil. Forgive me.

Sleep—the most beautiful experience in life—except drink. Forgive me.

Some things are better than sex, and some are worse, but there's nothing exactly like it. Forgive me.

Some weasel took the cork out of my lunch. Forgive me.

Start every day off with a smile and get it over with. Forgive me.

The best cure for insomnia is to get a lot of sleep. Forgive me.

The best thing for a case of nerves is a case of Scotch. Forgive me.

The clever cat eats cheese and breathes down rat holes with baited breath. Forgive me.

The cost of living has gone up another dollar a quart. Forgive me.

The laziest man I ever met put popcorn in his pancakes so they would turn over by themselves. Forgive me.

The world is getting to be such a dangerous place, a man is lucky to get out of it alive. Forgive me.

There are only two real ways to get ahead today: sell liquor or drink it. Forgive me.

There comes a time in the affairs of man when he must take the bull by the tail and face the situation. Forgive me.

When we have lost everything, including hope, life becomes a disgrace, and death a duty. Forgive me.

Women are like elephants. I like to look at 'em, but I wouldn't want to own one. Forgive me.

To a Sought Caterpillar

When I see one I shall seize one & I'll squeeze it till it squirts
Sweet sweet Canada, Canada Canada
Look-up, over here, see me, up here
Poor Sam Peabody, Peabody, Peabody
Cheerup, cheerily, cheerily, cheer, cheerful charmer
Sweet, sweet, I'm so sweet

Pizza chip, potato chip, potato chip
What cheer, drink your tea
I am lazy, pleased to meetcha
Please, please, please to meet ya
Teach, teach, teach, teach
Teach beer, teach beer, beer, beer
Bob White, Bob White, a sweet Yank
Bubble, bubble zee
Here, here I am, over here, see me, where are you
Who cooks for you, who cooks for you all
Maids, maids, maids, put on your tea kettle, kettle, kettle
Purty queer, purty queer, purty queer
Spring of the year, are you awake? Me too
Drop it, drop it, cover-it-up, cover-it-up, pull-it-up, pull-it-up
Trees, trees, murmuring trees, Chicago
Ah, ah, ah, ah
Smack! Smack!
But I DO love you, hot dog, pickle-ickle-ickle
Qu'est-ce qu'il dit? Qu'est-ce qu'il dit?
Why don'tcha come to me? Here I am right near you
Fire, fire; where? where? here, here; see it? see it?
Wuff, wuff, wuff, wuff, wuff
Hurry, hurry, worry
Come here? Jimmy? quickly?
Hip, hip, hip hurrah boys, spring is here!
Madge, Madge, Madge pick beetles off, the water's hot
Listen to my evening sing-ing-ing-ing
Here-here, where-where, all-together-down-the-hill
More, more, more cheezies, please
Quick give me a rain check
Sweet, sweet, sweet, little-more-sweet
Spit and see if I care, spit!

Nick Thurston
He Might Find

Nick Thurston previously erased all of the text of an edition of Maurice Blanchot's *The Space of Literature* and reset his own marginalia around the existing page margins in the typeface of the absent original, and he constructed a poem from the index to Friedrich Nietzsche's *The Gay Science*. Here, he underscores the permutational logic of Samuel Beckett's *Watt* by translating the text—in the manner of Craig Dworkin's *Parse*—into its grammatical units. In Thurston's original version of this piece, the color, typography, and design are keyed to the particular edition used (here, that published by London's John Calder).

This room was furnished solidly and with taste.

This solid and tasteful furniture was subjected by Mr. Knott to frequent changes of position both absolute and relative. Thus it was not rare to find, on the noun, the noun on its noun by the noun, and the noun on its noun by the noun, and the noun on its noun by the noun, and the noun on its noun by the noun; and, on the noun, the noun on its noun by the noun, and the noun on its noun by the noun, and the noun on its noun by the noun, and the noun on its noun by the noun; and, on the noun, the noun on its noun by the noun, and the noun on its noun by the noun, and the noun on its noun by the noun, and the noun on its noun by the noun; and, on the noun, the noun on its noun by the noun, and the noun on its noun by the noun, and the noun on its noun by the noun, and the noun on its noun by the noun; and, on the noun, the noun on its noun by the noun, and the noun on its noun by the noun, and the noun on its noun by the noun, and the noun on its noun by the noun; and, on the noun, the noun on its noun by the noun, and the noun on its noun by the noun, and the noun on its noun by the noun, and the noun on its noun by the noun; and, on the noun, the noun on its noun by the noun, and the noun on its noun by the noun, and the noun on its noun by the noun, and the noun on its noun by the noun; and, on the adjective noun, the noun its noun by the noun, and the noun on its noun by the noun, and the noun on its noun by the noun, and the noun on its noun by the noun; and, on the adjective noun, the noun on its noun by the noun, and the noun on its noun by the noun, and the noun on its noun by the noun, and the noun on its noun by the noun; and, on the adjective noun, the noun on its noun by the noun, and the noun on its noun by the noun, and the noun on its noun by the noun, and the noun on its noun by the noun; and, on the adjective noun, the noun on its noun by the noun, and the noun on its noun by the noun, and the noun on its noun by the noun, and the noun on its noun by the noun; and, on the adjective noun, the noun on its noun by the noun, and the noun on its noun by the noun, and the noun on its noun by the noun, and the noun on its noun by the noun; and, on the adjective noun, the noun on its noun by the noun, and the noun on its noun by the noun, and the noun on its noun by the noun, and the noun on its noun by the noun; and, on the adjective noun, the noun on its noun by the noun, and the noun on its noun by the noun, and the noun on its noun by the noun, and the noun on its noun by the noun; and, on the adjective noun, the noun on its noun by the noun, and the noun on its noun by the noun, and the noun on its noun by the noun; and, on the adjective noun, the noun on its noun by the noun, and the noun on its noun by the noun, and the noun on its noun by the noun, and the noun on its noun by the noun; and, on the adjective noun, the noun on its noun by the noun, and the noun on its noun by the noun, and the noun on its noun by the noun; and, on the adjective noun, the noun on its noun by the noun, the noun on its noun by the noun, and the noun on its noun by the noun, and the noun on its noun by the noun; and, on the adjective noun, the noun on its noun by the noun, and the noun on its noun by the noun, and the noun on its noun by the noun, and the noun on its noun by the noun; and, on the adjective noun, the noun on its noun by the noun, and the noun on its noun by the noun, and the noun on its noun by the noun; and, on the adjective noun, the noun on its noun by the noun, and noun on its noun by the noun, and the noun on its noun by the noun, and the noun on its noun by the noun, for example, not at all rare, to consider only, over a period of nineteen days, the noun, the noun, the noun and the noun, and their noun, and nouns, and nouns, and noun and unspecified noun, and the noun, and the noun, and the noun, and the noun, not at all rare.

Rodrigo Toscano
Welcome to Omnium Dignitatem

Rodrigo Toscano writes:

"Welcome to Omnium Dignitatem" is from a series called "Postcard Poems" [*To Leveling Swerve* (San Francisco: Krupskaya, 2004)] written to people in Roman Antiquity (Cicero, Tacitus, Horace, Frontinus Architect, Lucretius). The conceptual kink in this series is to have all of the text formatted in the manner of an inscription plaque (giving a sense of permanence) all the while critically intensifying the reader's sense of ephemerality (a sense of evacuation). The age-old symbology of "letters" (which is still extant and dying) is replaced by an (ever-absent present) field of Internet anxiety and its jargons (disappearing links, bouncer pages, pop-ups, etc.). The font is in an all caps chiseled style (which for Roman inscriptions designated Imperial purpose, though in contemporary Internet culture, all caps is usually reserved for the most notorious urban web-trawler habits).

LIKE A PERSON HALF-CRAZED WITH THIRST YOU WILL OFTEN RETURN
TO THIS PAGE LOOKING FOR CLUES TO YOUR RELATIVE VALUE IN
CONTEMPORARY SOCIETY ESPECIALLY AS UNDERSTOOD IN THE VAST
UNDERGROUND CHAMBERS OF POETRY.

THOUGH YOU WILL UNDERSTAND VERY LITTLE OF WHAT IS WRITTEN HERE
YOU WILL NONETHELESS GROW OBSESSED WITH THE VERY LOOK AND FEEL
OF THESE WORDS.

YOUR ENGLISH WILL FOR A MOMENT ALMOST IMPERCEPTIBLY SPASM
VIOLENTLY AT THE FAINT MEMORY ITS BEING OVERRUN SOME 1,000
YEARS AGO.

YOUR SPANISH WILL FUTILELY KNEEL AT THE ALTAR OF ITS IMMEDIATE
PREDECESSOR OF SOME 1,500 YEARS AGO LOOK YOU NOW HOW IT WEEPS
BUT FOR A MOMENT'S CONSECRATION WITH THAT DIRT CLOD TORN UP OF
LATE WHICH WE SHALL HENCEFORTH CALL

ORDINARY COMPREHENSION.

THIS PAGE'S OTHER NAME IS EXAEQUARE WHICH MEANS TO MAKE LEVEL
OR TO EQUAL OR TO REGARD AS EQUAL OR IF IN THE PASSIVE WITH THE
DATIVE TO BE PUT ON THE SAME LEVEL WITH.

THE ONLY LINKS REGARDED AS LEGITIMATE IN THIS ENTERPRISE ARE DEAD
LINES OR IN-THE-CERTAIN-PROCESS-OF-DYING LINKS.

THE ONLY THOUGHTS LIVING WITHIN THIS PAGE ARE TO BE BORN SOLELY
FROM YOUR BELATED EFFORTS.

ALL OTHER THOUGHTS WE SHALL REGARD AS GHOSTS OR RUMORS OF
GHOSTS THAT SAVE BUT FOR THE HORRIBLY-FANGÈD DOGS OF LATIUM NO
ONE CAN SEE.

Tristan Tzara
from Dada Manifesto on Feeble and Bitter Love

Tristan Tzara's *Manifesto* was read in early December 1920, at the Gallerie Jacques Povolozky in Paris and published the following year in *Vie des lettres,* volume 4 (April 1921: 434–43). Based on the proximate visual arts precedents of collage and montage, Tzara's *sac* (bag) had its literary ancestors in a *chapeau* (hat) and a peppercastor. The technique had been anticipated by Leconte de Lisle in 1891:

> Prenez un chapeau, mettez-y des adverbes, des conjonctions, des prépositions, des substantifs, des adjectifs, tirez au hasard et écrivez : vous aurez du symbolisme, du décadisme, de l'instrumentisme et de tous les galimatias qui en dérivent.

> [Take a hat, put in some adverbs, conjunctions, prepositions, nouns, adjectives, draw them at chance and write: you'll have symolism, decadence, instrumentism et all the galimatias that follow from them] (quoted by Jules Huret, *Enquête sur l'évolution littéraire,* ed. Daniel Grojonowsi [Paris: Thos, 1984], 238).

Even earlier, Charles Lutwidge Dodgson (Lewis Carroll) had proposed, in the poem "Poeta Fit, Non Nascitur" (*College Rhymes* 3, no. 9 [Summer Term, 1862]: 112–16):

> First learn to be spasmodic—
> A very simple rule.
>
> For first you write a sentence,
> And then you chop it small;
> Then mix the bits, and sort them out
> Just as they chance to fall:
> The order of the phrases makes
> No difference at all.

The surrealists would have approved of Dodgson's spasmology; André Breton's *Nadja* famously concludes "La beauté sera convulsive ou ne sera pas [Beauty will be convulsive, or will not be]," (*Oeuvres complètes,* I [Paris: Gallimard, 1988], 753). But the order would have made a difference to them; however ironic Tzara's conclusion, it recalls Breton's concept of *hasard objectif* [objective chance]: the external material manifestation of internal subjective states. Dodgson's technique in turn recalls Edgar Allan Poe's 1844 description of a literary "system" devised to impersonate a journalist (Thomas Hawk):

> These works I cut up thoroughly with a curry-comb, and then, throwing the shreds into a sieve, sifted out carefully all that might be thought decent, (a mere trifle); reserving the hard phrases, which I threw into a large tin pepper-castor with longitudinal holes, so that an entire sentence could get through without material injury. The mixture was then ready for use. When called upon to play Thomas Hawk, I anointed a sheet of foolscap with the white of a gander's egg; then, shredding the thing to be reviewed as I had previously shredded the books — only with more care, so as to get every word separate — I threw the latter shreds in with the former, screwed on the lid of the castor, gave it a shake, and so dusted out the mixture upon the egg'd foolscap; where it stuck. The effect was beautiful to behold. It was captivating. (*Complete Tales* [New York: Vintage, 1975], 334).

Take a newspaper.

Take some scissors.

Select an article in that newspaper having the length that you want for
    your poem.

Cut out the article.

Then cut our each of the words constituting that article and put them in
    a bag.

Shake gently.

Then remove each clipping one after the other.

Conscientiously copy in the order in which they were removed from
    the bag.

The poem will resemble you.

And there you are: an infinitely original writer of charming sensibility,
    though misunderstood by the unrefined masses.*

**when dogs traverse the air in a diamond like ideas and the appendix
of the meninx tells the time of the wake up call program**

prices they are yesterday suitable following pictures
appreciate the dream era of the eyes
pompously that to recite the gospel genre is obscured
group apotheosis you'd better imagine said he fatality power of color
engraved coat-hangers astonished reality a delight
spectator all to effort of the no more 10 to 12
during divagation a-flutter pressure drop
render some mad single-file flesh on a monstrous crushing stage-set
celebrate but their 160 initiates in steps on apply my mother-of-pearl
sumptuous of land bananas sustained lit-up
joy to ask together almost
of has the a such that the invoked visions
some sings that one there laughs
removes situation disappears describes she 25 dance greetings
dissimulated the whole of it which is not was
magnificent has the better strip
light of which sumptuousness stage-set me music-halls
reappears following instant before a matter of live
business there is not has loaned
manner words come these people

Andy Warhol
from a: a novel

In his epic work of literature, the novel *a: a novel* (New York: Grove, 1968), Andy Warhol set out to create a linguistic portrait of Ondine, a Factory superstar, by following him with a tape recorder and recording every conversation he had over the course of twenty-four hours (the final book was actually taped over a two-year period, from 1966 to 1968, and included many characters other than Ondine).

During the transcription process, several different typists took on the task, each with his or her own unique style of transcribing. When the book was published, the final product was identical to the raw manuscripts: no typos or errors were corrected and no consistent formatting was applied throughout; the book was printed as is. It is a multiauthored book, ghostwritten by others but penned by Andy Warhol, which calls into question many tropes of traditional authorship.

The book has its roots in Stéphane Mallarmé's falsified writings on fashion and in Molly Bloom's soliloquy in *Ulysses*. It would influence the poet Ed Friedman's *The Telephone Book,* where Friedman recorded and transcribed every phone conversation he had, as well as Kenneth Goldsmith's *Soliloquy,* where he transcribed everything he said for a week. Warhol's book takes the twentieth century's quest for natural speech to its logical conclusion, proving, contrary to Robert Grenier ("I HATE SPEECH") that blather, in its untouched state, is just as disjunctive as other fragmentary modernist strategies.

Warhol authored six books, none of which he himself wrote. They were ghostwritten affairs by his assistants who were channeling the voice of Andy Warhol. Their voice became his public voice while Warhol largely remained silent.

5/ 2

No it's novel that it's being a novel as a matter of fact—vut what do you mean by a novel?   uhhhhhh   I know it just . . . there's no other brush stroke.   12 hours of Ondine a novel?   qou're not going—are you going to put it in a in a book or what make it be one whole book really and was Steve gonna take some pictures you know I would rather have Billy Name take pictures—or something—he's a much better photographer—god Diane, the picture or her looks like posed French cinnamon . . . . . powder . . . . . refreshes . . . every little spot   you look like an elephant   I feel like an elephant and an elephant never forgets and it only eats vegetables—   really?   yeah—did you know that elephants were not meat eaters?   no   isn't that fabulous? Those big things and they only charge people when they're wounded or sick or tired—a powder room— . . . . . you dahling I feel like a young thing with you thank god I have perfect legs, I'd be sick about it, if it weren't for Higbsib's baby Powder I'd be sick about it, if it weren't for johnson's baby powder i'd be dead—I feel so fresh and new Drella like a million bucks—really like I have a friend at the Chase manhattan—taking a bath with you in the room is something special, and you with that microphone running on, you can't believe I mean people have been driven—they've been driven to peaks. And you've made me a new high, no actually y'know I don't fin dthis offensive, I really don't, honestly, it's very easy too but you just have to reflect for a moment, oh oh oh how, torment and hate. Uh you just have to reflect for one second and do you realize that I or I do any way   What?   Oh wha ooo who how ooo oh ha hooh a uh pain— uh that I— that that I'd be doing it with somebody else anyway. I'd be driving myself through—I wonder what these are?   Oh.   One a day —Doctor Belger—it doesn't sound like my doctor. It smells so pretty.

It's Canoe—I once knew somebody who said, "Canoe—that is evil smelling perfume." What does he mean evil? I wish there was some hair cream here. Oh Drella, my face is on fire, fire, fire, oh ohh.   It'll go away.   Oh feel it, it must be burning—   It's cold.   I can't believe —it's making me tear or my   Open the door. I better get my Dixie Peach Palmette out of my bag—nigger hair cream.   Oh really? Oh let me see it—sure.   Look at these things, look at them they're marvelous. This is ta few mustard stains.   Mustard?   Yeah, I was eating frankfurters one day.   Mustard?   Mustard—look at this one.   Where did you get those?   Rita.   Oh.   See the mustard on here, it smells just uh—I had a black piece of material in here.   Oh, are you going to wear that today?   Oh no. I've got so much to show you. What kind of material is this? It's rather, uh, it's a 12, it's a 12, it's a twee, don't you like those little pieces of . . .   Yah.   It's a new sample. (*Laughs.*) Let's see, I gotta get my Dixie Peach why why it's for nigger hair cream.

How come?   I went in there only to get my nigger hair cream. Isn't

it heaven?   Give it a bath.   What?   Give it a bath.   Sublime.
Uh it's (*giggle*) give it a bath? Oh, you're—maybe you're right.   Oh
you won't be able to put it away.   What?   You won't be able to
put it away. Well, if I just washed the outside I would.   Uhhh.
With a sponge. With a sponge. The inside is brilliant gold. Dixie Peach
Palmade. That's the best thing for hair—you can't imagine—it's nice and
thick.   How does it feel up your ass?   Huh?   How does it feel up
you rass?   How does it feel up your ass?   Where—that? Oh please
like glue . . .   Oh—was it terrible?   Yeah—I hate lotions of any
kind.   Really? Once in a while they're necessary and all but I hate
them—I'd much rather mucous were used, it's the only way . . .
Really?   It's the only way (*pause*). I'm glad my underwear coming
from behind.   They're wet.   I was ju, I was no, no, I was talking to
Rita on the phone and they snapped.   The cord snapped, it . . .
Oh, really?   It just snapped, it it   I said said, told Rita, please get
off the phone, I . . . she was exasperated.   Have all the money you
want.   And in other words . . .   Huh . . .   . . . d-do that.   I
never saw a cock worn sideways.   Well I can't wear it he other way
if it's, it'll break. Like this it should be worn?   No. Sideways.   Well
well sh-should it be like that? Or should it . . .   Yeah.   Sh-should it
b etwo-way draping pricks ins . . . (*laughter*). Darling, I think it should
be draped that way   . . . . . solution.   What is that?   Bad news?
Oh it is?   It's heaven, it's so vile.   Do you make it with water?
Uh, I make this one with iced tea.   Oh.   Do you want some?
No.   It's quite good. I never know the difference. (*Pause and Taxie's
voice in background.*) Do you think I should wash some?   Hmm.
I really should?   Yeah . . . . . (*Laughter.*)   You mean the thing, I
shoudl keep it there?   Yeah.   Dirty.   Open up your pants, yeah
go ahead . . . suitcase.   Yeah, well I live out of it, y'know I mean I, I
have to.   Have you gone home recently?   No, I haven't been home
in two weeks.   Oh really? Fantastic.   . . . . . . insurance.   In-
surance?   I need a quick dose of the Duchess's.   I feel terrible that.
     Yeah.   Terrible. Sure we can, I'd love to see, I think it's open til,
til 9 o'clock.   Oh.   (*Pause.*)   You can leave any time you like to.
     Oh no, I have to see you go into the tub.   Oh, I don't mind. I
mean as long . . .   Hmm.   . . . . . said we could rob him . . . . .
would be fabulous   When?   . . . . . 12:15 and I was talking
to you o-over the phone.   Billy was wrong so.   Yeah I know but,
yeah but I mean but, the way he, the way you reacted to it really touched

me so beautifully that I didn't know what to do. I just—of course I should never have told Walter anything.   Oh.   Cause telling Walter anything is ridiculous.   What did you tell Walter?   I told Walter, I said Drella just moved me so incredibly and y'know he didn't understand and he resented it.   Oh really?   I never was and never will be. Why not?   No, what for? Oh could you imagine. Oh . . .   Where is Walter now?   I hope he's in Bellevue where he belongs. I know I'm gonna be going there if he doesn't get settled down. Look at the bruise.   How'd you get that?   I don't know; I think the Duchess was poking me an . . .   Huh.   Slaps.   Huh huh huh huh (*pause*). Gorgeous.   You have to, you . . . my hands, I'm so glad I didn't go to the doctor.   Oh fantastic.   It's almost time for the swelling has to go down in about two weeks. I wouldn't let them touch my forehead or anything. I don't trust them because I don't think they know what they're doing. In fact I'm sure they don't know what they're doing. (*Pause.*) I'm gonna wear a sweater with this.   Oh.   I don't have a tan for it. But y'know it doesn't . . . so . . .   mut it's kind of . . .   Oh, it's for Gerard.

It's got an . . .air conditioning.   No.   It's hotter than in here . . . (*voices get very low*) . . . I don't believe what he stole. I don't mean what he stole . . . . . made out of paper reprief. Your hair is all wrong.

Don't.   It's all wrong. Did you ever feel too . . . Is that good enough? It takes me some time but I can't see that it's high. It takes me sometimes three hours just to comb it with my fingers. I mean I could use a utensil to comb it not, I better brush my teeth too. I have a feeling I'm going to my mouth.   Really?   Don't you have the feeling that a whole her-herd of elephants have been charging in here? This is too, this is too garish (*sigh*Q. (*Ondine whispers something.*)   Oh look at . . .

What, what did you say to—the tone of your voice was so perfect, I'd have I'd have to, I couldn't tell him you were staying at the party. Oh please, oh please, oh please, I've never been any party like that. When you, when you the day that the party was filmed?   Yeah.   Oh please, oh plase, come please, I said (*inhales*) like when I saw the Boson jump in the water I didn't believe it. Did you ever tell me we have to make up . . . petition.   Oh really?   I find it very—somebody explained it to me once. You see I have an astigmatism in my ear and did you ever lose your balance in your middle ear?   No.   I did once.   Oh really?

Oh you can't get up off the, you just, you can't move. And get this, the doctor who came over to check on me, man, I couldn't lift my head off the pillow, said "You're killing your mother and father." Y'know he

meant because my mother said "Oh doctor, what are we gonna do with him?" And I just said to him, "Get out of here before I kiss you." Can you imagine coming over to treat me and telling and getting a psych, uh, psychol, psychiatry lesson? He also, I also went into the office once and he tried to hypnotize me into "stop talking."   Really?   He said "Wham" and I said, he said, "You're not going to smoke anymore." I said "Really?" I said, "Do you have a light?" He said, "You don't stutter" and I went, "Duh that the" (*laughter*). I couldn't bear him, Doctor Schwaslinger or Doctor, what was his name, Doctor, Doctor Schlod, Doctor Schlesinger, I don't know, he's across the street and he's awful. Here's another one but this isn't . . .   N-no, what you have on is nice.
You sure?   Yeah.   This is too sleezy. You tie old green, I . . . (*laughter*) I owe a billiard to you, you'll feel a lot better.   Put your footsy.   Put what?   I'll take a pill and I'll give you some pills too.
     Okay, good, we'll, we'll make some iced tea.   Oh, I'll get some uh, no.   It's not, it's not a bad solution. Oh all I know is you're (*laughter*) just a toothache. Whew. (*Taxie's voice in the background.*) Ten years I . . . I've been related . . .   Hey, there's . . . didn't saw you you feel a draft.   No, it's all right.   (T) *in background*—It's so awful, he's thirty something.   You'll feel it in. Who's thirty something? Who's thirty something?   (*In background.*) Is there a way to . . .
     Certainly not the Beatles.   And he said all the knowledge in the world?   (*Surfin' Use is background music.*)   I'm meeting the Beatles, Taxina.   When?   Uh, next week.   But, they're, they're not half as interesting as the Stones.   Oh no.   Uh, ever since that, I mean htere's one song on their new album that shows. I think *Mick Jagger* must be great.   Yeah.   He must be.   Uho, wa, is is he the leader?   Yeah. I really think he must be, and I, I must say I'm a bit bored with the *Beatles* even though they were great, but they're all taken care of. There's nothing really exciting. There's nothing exciting about them? I don't know, I just uh well like, I thought that *Elvis Pres*, er *Elvis Presley* . . .   Oh well *Elvis*.   would never go out, but he did, he did.   Yeah but on the other hand he's old.   . . . went like this, errgh, I nearly died.   Oh, oh really, oh.   But he's so's   Oh yeah but he, he'll always be famous.   Oh, to me he's really great. Really have you ever heard of hte Stoneheads?   The Beatles are great.
     Oh they were aw.   Nice put it in a bag.   No huh huh huh you're a care job (*Record: recording*)   Look at that, he's bringing it back.   Oh, Ondine is getting so . . .   Isn't it a little bit too

Ruth Warwick?   Huh huh huh huh. (*Recordin background*:
) Put your palmade away.   Oh, if they see
that, they'll know I'm ab, not to ruin. (
) Surfin'   We're all wearing hand-me-downs. Mine's a
hand-me-down too.   It doesn't fit anywhere. Air refresher. Prickly,
prickly. (*Ondine sprays.*)   Oh, oh no oh, Ondine.   Where's that?
    We'll settle it . . . filthy hole. I make the sweetest dresses.   Huh?
What book are you reading?   Oh, *History of Wit and Magic*. Oh.
    And uh.   You're All Witch?   Huh, no, no, no, I just wanted
to, I was reading about the Jews the other day. I couldn't believe it.
There's one sentence in there that, about them feeding the children to
the guard . . .   Really, wow.   Oh it's horrible. It's frightening about
the germicide. Isn't that better, a little comic relief. (Pause.)   What
shoes are you going to wear?   Huh?   What shoes?   Oh why didn't
you tell me that you were going to uh .   Oh, I didn't know, I'm gonna
live in there. I had such a good time in your bathroom. I thought you
were rtying to kill me at first.   I wish   *muffled talking*.   Oh really?
    Yeah, Billy said he'd be . . .and then he said it'd be all right.   Oh.
    So I said . . .   Terrific.   And I have never taken them off.
Oh.   Is that still on?   Yeah.   Don't ever play this . . .   Why,
you coming up?   Yeah, in a minute. I just wanna slit my wrists. (*"Ooh
ooh . . .*   )   What ever happened to Meredith Willson?
        I don't know; let's go out on the terrace.   Yes, and thank you.
(*With record*) Marsha, Marsha . . . got a pilly?   Huh?   Let's take
a little pilly here . . . I, I need it.   Let's get some out here. (*"Oh
oh . . . . .*") Dhat?   Get a drink of water. Let's have some, like just
zip it up and put my stole on, and then we'll go out on the terrace.
. . . . or leaving. They wouldn't object, heavenly . . .   What . . .
No one would object to . . .   Moxanne is coming here to meet you.
        Oh.   Who's Moxanne?   Moxanne's a French girl whom I know,
who's been in Europe a while and just came back. She's fantastic. She's
very, she's very, got cute she ulders but she's uh . . .   Bulls a or diesel
. . .   She, uh, she has certain, she thinks she's . . . . . (?) but she's
really a nymphomaniac, she's . . .   Oh God.   But she doesn't uh,
she's so bright that you uh . . .   She's no Chicky the Wormgirl?
No, she's really, she's very nice, she's, she just finished a script that I'm
gonna borrow.   Did uh, well uh, I mean is there something gonna
happen from any of those two things?   Uh, it's all . . . really happen-
ing, yes uh.   Yes oh.   I mean uh, more so in Nite Life than Nite

Life, I'm calling Nite Life Monday.   Why?   Cause they wanna know about the film. I wanna talk o, find out about it.   Oh uh, they shoulld, it's bad.   But did you do it once before? You gave it . . . . . No, it's just a bad scene because they shouldn't ever know what Taxina . . . like.   It's just like selling you really, it's a bad scene.   Does anybody want . . .   Play play play.   Four minutes of . . .   Oh, you can, no.   Oh, that's what's taking me.   No, no, no, it varied is it, uh, no.   It's probably.   Huh? Coming in? For pills?   Ye-yes, thank you . . . fine. Do you know where Rotten Rita is?   Here, here, here, thank you.   Ooh huh huh.   Oh uh, oh, who's playing, the Three Sons? or the Four Daughters?   What is that? Beautiful.   Isn't that marvelous?   It's awful.   That's something.   Did you work tha something out with uh, Rink   Oh you can . . .   Wha . . . . . . talking about the speak . . .   Oh, and they went oh, Drella.

Darren Wershler

from The Tapeworm Foundry

The Tapeworm Foundry (Toronto: House of Anansi, 2000), an exhaustive recipe book for art making in the tradition of Bruce McLean's *King for a Day and 999 Other Pieces/ Works/Things/etc.*, is Darren Wershler's conceptual follow-up to Raymond Queneau's *Cent mille milliards de poèmes,* in which he cut a book of ten sonnets between each line, creating the possibilities for literally billions of poems. Wershler's mathematical proposition hinges on the *andor* (and/or) term which separates each concept, a directive by which the book can be combined or linked to form one enormous artwork, hundreds of discreet ones, or any combination thereof. The piece is simultaneously a call for action and a call for contemplation, reminiscent at times of Yoko Ono's sentence-long conceptual provocations.

. . . jetsam in the laminar flow andor find the threads in redhats andor litter a keyboard with milletseed so that exotic songbirds might tap out their odes to a nightingale andor transcribe the letters pressed onto the platen when stalactites drip on the homerow keys andor reconstruct the ruins of a bombedout capital i andor reinvent the canonic works of western art as a series of roadsign glyphs andor commission an artist to paint the large ass of marcel duchamp andor use a dotmatrix printer to sound out a poem in which each line is a series of pauses whose length is determined by formatting codes and then record the squeal and lurch of the printhead moving across the paper and then replay the noise and then have it transcribed as chamber music for cello or voice andor compose a text acknowledging that words are fourdimensional objects in spacetime andor write an essay on the collected works of jane austen treating the text as a tour de force lipogram that never once makes use of any characters in the sinhalese alphabet andor escape from a paragraph by eloping along bottomless discourses andor point out that super mario world is actually a complex digital allegory for the writings of terence mckenna andor pen a treatise for andre breton and philippe soupault in which you discuss the magnetic fields emitted by each vowel when it attracts the surrounding consonants like iron filings and then note that sometimes the letter y emanates a magnetism of its own andor proceed according to a philosophy of whatever andor insert chapbooks into the newspapers sold in vending boxes on the street andor do it even more than usual andor learn everything that you can about the life of cervantes and then rewrite don quixote from the viewpoint of the windmills andor print a set of instructions for dry cleaning the sacred shroud of turin andor fill a red wheelbarrow to the brim with depends brand adult undergarments and then entitle it doctor williams in his dotage andor compose a poem about the late john cage by writing sixtyfour hexasticha based on the chinese book of changes andor move them in and out of space andor design a camera that records its own presence in the photo andor construe a word by word synonymic replacement for finnegans wake and then dedicate the new book to casey from mr dressup andor look as little like a particular point of view as possible andor compose a love poem called charged particles in which each line consists of a single word ending in the suffix ion andor stick a stamp on your forehead and then pull a mailbag over your eyes before you begin to recite andor work on a poem attempting to emulate gansers syndrome wherein a person responds to emotionally difficult questions with evasive answers andor address the united nations with your intentions andor write an encyclopedic novel about a whale but maintain throughout that the whale is a fish not a mammal andor write a series of haiku about barrett watten and bruce andrews and lyn hejinian but sign it using the pseudonym lang po andor remove specificities and then convert to ambiguities andor learn that paisleys are based on hindu glyphs stolen from india by a clan of scottish weavers and then think of an alternate history in which indian castes not only develop a system of tartans but also compose ragas for duos consisting of bagpipe and sitar andor type the words dylan thomas on a piece of paper but leave the paper on the roller and then submerge the entire typewriter in a solution of white alcohol calling the resulting object underwood milk andor dial a number at random and then finagle your way into reading poems to the person who answers andor pick some names out of the phone book and then enrol them in the book of the month club andor author a sound poem consisting solely of noises made by a spin dryer full of glass eyeballs andor write each letter of a shakespearean sonnet on one of the little plastic paratroopers from a box of green armymen and then throw the soldiers one by one from a balcony onto the audience below andor write a scatological parody of a landscape painted with tea by milorad pavic and then entitle it a landscape tainted with pee andor document what is going on in a room not necessarily but possibly the one that you might be occupying andor write a novel about what paul eluard might have done in the year of his disappearance andor publish a guidebook for nonexistent monuments found somewhere in downtown toronto well not found but you know what i mean andor illustrate that this must be the case andor sandblast the scrawled missives of schizophreniacs onto sheets of coloured glass in church windows andor spell it according to a phonetics of your own devising andor start a pataphysical software company andor write with your bones dry and distant andor imagine a poem called ideas for poets consisting of pithy epithets that describe the personalities of literary notables so that for example christopher smart might be a thin one forever patrolling the edge of the sidewalk smelling of vegetable crates and cat food andor avoid the habits of another artist andor fill a steamer trunk full of it and then let your friends edit it while you sleep off the drug of your choice andor make a western about the group of seven starring yul brynner as emily carr andor write all of your misgivings about your work in ballpoint pen along the edges of your collated manuscript doing so in the same way that you might have written on the edges of your highschool math book and then shuffle the pages before you bind them andor write haiku noting that stonehenge is actually a circle of big pi symbols made out of rock andor massmarket it as if it is both obtainable by all and producible by all andor remove random keys from your typewriter before you begin to write and then forget which ones have been removed andor write with your head between your hands andor posit a novel in which a time traveller first appears at the denouement and then proceeds backwards to the beginning through a series of non sequiturs andor smoke your manuscript page by page when you run out of rolling papers andor ride hard shoot straight and speak the truth andor sell the designs that appear after trickling a thin stream of ball bearings onto a computer graphics tablet andor write a sonnet about what a grecian earns andor look closely at the most embarrassing details and then amplify them andor write a brief history of television including the television at lascaux or platos myth of the television or the york and townley mystery televisions or shakespeares globe television or the first steamdriven television andor write with the tips of your eyes while holding back in advance andor tell the story about the night when vladimir ilyich lenin finally goes across the street to the cabaret voltaire to see what the hell is causing all the goddamn noise andor write a treatise on the physics of luggage calculating the difference between volumes of air displaced by a clean shirt when ironed and folded and by the same shirt when wrinkled and unlaundered andor letterbomb the city of paris ontario with it andor make casts of the negative spaces on or around or under rachel whiteread or bruce nauman andor punch holes through every copy of the bound book and then save the little punchedout bits to use as confetti at the wedding of someone related to peter eisenman andor replace sigourney weaver with jacques derrida and then make a film about him chasing hegelians through the airducts of a spaceship in order to immolate these vermin with a flamethrower andor take everything from the hairnet of an upperclass lady to the propeller of the rms lusitania and then deform these things into the dimensions required by the work andor soak your hair in japanese calligraphic ink and then drag your head down a long paper scroll andor do your part to end joblessness by posting a classified ad calling for applications to a training school for such fabulous obsolete or bizarre professions as anchorite or apostate or bearbaiter or bodyservant or carnival geek or chirurgeon or contact lensman or elvis impersonator impersonator or fudgepacker or ghoul or hangman or hayward or hebdomadary or janissary or key grip or khatmule or lawn ornament sculptor or linkboy or mahout or milkcrate repoman or pornfluffer or prestidigitator or rakehell or roue or seneschal or snakehandler or stickler or tinker or usurer or vizier or warrior of the cosmic void or water witch andor treat grant applications as a creative act andor pay attention to the man behind the curtain andor write extended comments on a movie by using a stickpin plus a magnifying glass to scratch marginalia into the black space that surrounds each celluloid frame andor dont and then see if i give a fuck andor consider the implications of letters being the fossilized remains of microfauna and then hypothesize what several million years of evolution might produce as the descendants of such organisms andor use what is deviant in a culture to destroy it quickly andor write without your fingers blushing andor use rain damage as a title for a neurology textbook that has been repeatedly left outside during thunderstorms andor detourne a book about the berenstain bears by replacing all text with material from a poetics by charles bernstein andor write with inane but appropriate naivete andor theorize the written page as a prepared cross section of some medical specimen andor wonder why there are no christian jubes or buddhist jubes or muslim jubes andor break the rest of these up andor explore the possible applications of artificial stupidity andor point out that john ashbery is actually just wallace stevens. . . .

Christine Wertheim
Finnegans Wanke/Finnegans Wake (translation)

Where C. K. Ogden sought to lower the informational temperature of James Joyce's language, Wertheim endeavors to bring it to a boil with graphic elements and a condensation that admits of very little redundancy. As Wertheim writes:

> The idea underpinning my work is that a text is constituted of nothing but the relations between the characters that compose it. My main poetic methodology is to condense other people's works into what I see as their conceptual essence, that is, into a revelation of the principal characters and the relations between them in the chosen body of words. This is done by simply attending closely to the work to sense (see/hear) which characters and which relations are most significant, albeit these are often highly obscured, even disguised. The first is the "pure" condensation, the second is slightly translated, to make it easier to read.

Finnegans Wanke

|'s the song of th|'story of the |
which H.c.E. |'s
|n allways be-|n'-coming
through the h|men of the-m-others.
With|n th|story Anna Livia Plurabelle
represents the plurable flood
of warm wordy worders
that flow |n 2 the |
when th|s love(ly) h|men bursts forth
|n 2 songs, th|'song's of the-m-any-|'s
flow-er-ing vo|dSe.

and just as the |'nwraptures |t'Self
in th|s h|men
so H.c.E. |'mmerses h|'Self
in the Worders of (the) L|ffe,
the river |t'Self;
that |'s the fonte of th|'s outpouring of worders,
that |'s the sauce

of the|'s HCE's-Coming
+|'me--Coming
h|'men-COm|ng-Epic

Ou|, Ou|, Ou|, Ou|
all the way home
Ou| = O+ |
O+ | = O
O + | =

e| es

Finnegans Wake (translation)

is the song of the story of the I/one/son
which H.c.E. is
in allways be-coming
through the hymn of the mothers.

Within this story Anna Livia Plurabelle
represents the plurable flood
of warm wordy words
that flow in to the one
when this lovely hymen bursts forth
into songs,
the songs of the many ones
flowering voice/voids.

And just as the I enwraptures Itself
in this hymen
so H.c.E immerses hisself
in the Waters of (the) Liffe/Life
the river itself;
that is the fonte of this outpouring of words,
that |'s the source

of this HE's-Coming
h|m-Coming
|'m-cOm|ng-Epic

wee, wee, wee, wee
yes, yes, yes, yes
all the way home

Finnegans Wake
is
the book
of
th-e-|es

VO| dce

Wiener Gruppe
ideas for a «record album/functional» acoustic cabaret

The Wiener Gruppe (Vienna Group) was formed after the Second World War and consisted of H. C. Artmann, Konrad Bayer, Gerhard Rühm, and Oswald Wiener. By envisioning an extreme modernism—one that the Nazis had purged from public discourse—the Vienna Group looked to the most radical prewar poets for inspiration: Gertrude Stein, Paul Scheerbart, and Kurt Schwitters, who, as Rühm states, "if known at all, were hardly taken note of and dismissed as outsiders who had been deservedly forgotten. For us they represented the rediscovered, true traditions with which our poetic work linked up organically. From where else should we proceed if not from the so-called 'end-points'? A glaring example was presented in music by Anton Webern, who was denounced as 'end point'" (Peter Weibel, ed., *die wiener gruppe / the vienna group: a moment of modernity 1954–1960 / the visual works and the actions* [Vienna: Springer, 1997], 16).

Dovetailing with postwar existentialism, the Vienna Group sought to reduce language to its most elemental and formal terms, often swapping emotional content for formal and semantic emphasis or envisioning literature as a process of writing jokes without punch lines ("every statement could be regarded as a punch line anyway," according to Rühm). Their poems include collected lists, jotted-down shop signs, poems constructed using only the vocabulary of crossword puzzles, transcribed public announcements, obituaries, the use of the Fibonacci series for the permutative processing, organizing sound by syllables, and so on—all aimed at a notion of "how to produce literature methodically, which should enable everyone to compose poetry on an artificial level: poetry as an instruction manual, dissociated from any causality of terms, the linguistic material was to reach a state of semantic floating as it were, to generate "mechanically" surprising sequences of words and images" (Weibel, 20).

These explorations lead to a number of artistic expressions: literary cabaret and performance events, engagement with the international concrete poetry movement, avant-garde music, numerous manifestos, artists' books, typographical explorations, and plays. By 1960, as a result of the provincialism of Vienna, the group had disbanded and relocated to several countries to continue solo practices.

By refusing to be confined to one form of expression, the Vienna Group revived the idea of literature as a multimedia practice. Predating international conceptual art by a decade and a half and anticipating aspects of Fluxus and language poetry (Ron Silliman's mathematical poems as well as his later thought journals), the Vienna Group serves as a crucial—but often neglected—link between the prewar avant-garde and the heyday of 1960s conceptualism. The "acoustic cabaret" was composed by Konrad Bayer, Gerhard Rühm, and Oswald Wiener.

interview as a ready-made cabaret number.
jokes by a chorus (orchestrated speaking groups).
groove located in the center of the record. the listener is asked
beforehand to place the tone arm on the record again if he wants to
continue listening.
abuse (turn it off, idiot!).
various volumes, forcing the listener to readjust
the volume constantly.
closed groove (repetition).
inversion.
steps (the awaking).
sounds with a number of different associations so that they can suddenly
be explained as something completely different.
vulgar sounds.
remove frequencies.
unusual qualities of the voices.
typical conversations in the hall of an apartment building as ready-made
scenes.
fragments from lectures as montage.
montage of «viennese folk music to eastern music» as a brief guide
to the history of music (the individual styles are played just long
enough to be identified). the entire history of music is reduced
to approximately one minute.
various speeds.
mozart is beyond the range of hearing, or played in such a way that the
«right» speed cannot be set on any of the record players.
possibly an entire side of a record which can be heard at a number of
different speeds.

part of a connection with a telephone operator (time) at an
accelerated pace (unreal time units).
or in a normal time frame.
bodily noises. teeth chattering, sounds of vomiting.
laughing.
laughing—crying.
«ya hear?» is pronounced with a wide range of nuances.
put words together with noises (or only vowels pronounced by humans).
sounds produced by someone in pain.
poem about nature with the corresponding sounds.
schubert: «i heard a little stream» gradually changes into the sound of a
real stream.
parallel grooves, on the second groove (which is easier to find with the
tone arm), a vulgar woman's voice suddenly says: «you idiot, ya put it in
the wrong groove».
tell the listener that something will be read to him.
announce «disorder» as an improvisation.
listener addressed informally.
rhythmic pulses at different volumes.
address the listener's social conscious, where did you get the
record player? (first sentence on the record).
what do all listeners have in common. (ears?)

———

11 abecedaries
(Konrad Bayer and H. C. Artmann)

the most common words with *a*

alms
the angel
the archbishop
the archduke
the arc
at least
until

the most common words with *c*

piece of paper
the cymbal
tin
whole
the price
a hundred-weight
the number
the way
the brick
gipsy
the target
czar
czarin
an imperial clock

the most common words with *e*

the shield

the most common words with *j*

i
the apple
spring
light joyful
the liver
the tongue
eleven
the meal
once
the needle
still the rider is riding
elsewhere through
elsewhere to
otherwise
elsewhere

the most common words with *l*

inexpensive
to break
the lamp
the bath
the ice
light
lazy
better
better
the forest
fly
the summer
this year
the lion
left
the lie
suffering
the ship
the ell
the plumbline

the most common words with *d*

the officer
the soul
two
twenty
twice
twelve
the door

the most common words with *t*

the table
tear
so

the plate
there
you
now
first
the mouth
hit
the punishment
lasting
fat
the cheek
hard
the week

the most common words with *o*

both
maintain
the community
the oil
the altar
he
she
it

the most common words with *v*

the evening
beside
the egg

the most common words with *s*

sit
peasant woman
peasant
seven
the seventh
the sister

to burn
death
laughter
the cellar
the straw
perhaps
sleep
together
the heart
the shadow
hundred
the chair
the guard
silvery
cold
salt
the world
light
the room
the candle

the most common words with *r*

to say
the strap
the chain
thin
to say
the horn
the year

William Butler Yeats
Mona Lisa

In the first *Oxford Book of Modern Verse: 1892–1935* (Cambridge: Oxford University Press, 1936), William Butler Yeats—the editor of the anthology—inaugurated modern poetry by opening the volume with the poem "Mona Lisa," a transcription of a passage of Walter H. Pater's *Studies in the History of the Renaissance* (London: MacMillan, 1873) into Poundian free verse. The passage from Pater, in its original context, comes from the chapter on Leonardo da Vinci and a passage on *La Gioconda:*

> The presence that thus rose so strangely beside the waters, is expressive of what in the ways of a thousand years men had come to desire. Hers is the head upon which all "the ends of the world are come," and the eyelids are a little weary. It is a beauty wrought out from within upon the flesh, the deposit, little cell by cell, of strange thoughts and fantastic reveries and exquisite passions. Set it for a moment beside one of those white Greek goddesses or beautiful women of antiquity, and how would they be troubled by this beauty, into which the soul with all its maladies has passed! All the thoughts and experience of the world have etched and moulded there, in that which they have of power to refine and make expressive the outward form, the animalism of Greece, the lust of Rome, the reverie of the middle age with its spiritual ambition and imaginative loves, the return of the Pagan world, the sins of the Borgias. She is older than the rocks among which she sits; like the vampire, she has been dead many times, and learned the secrets of the grave; and has been a diver in deep seas, and keeps their fallen day about her; and trafficked for strange webs with Eastern merchants: and, as Leda, was the mother of Helen of Troy, and, as Saint Anne, the mother of Mary; and all this has been to her but as the sound of lyres and flutes, and lives only in the delicacy with which it has moulded the changing lineaments, and tinged the eyelids and the hands. The fancy of a perpetual life, sweeping together ten thousand experiences, is an old one; and modern thought has conceived the idea of humanity as wrought upon by, and summing up in itself, all modes of thought and life. Certainly Lady Lisa might stand as the embodiment of the old fancy, the symbol of the modern idea.

She is older than the rocks among which she sits;
Like the Vampire,
She has been dead many times,
And learned the secrets of the grave;
And has been a diver in deep seas,
And keeps their fallen day about her;
And trafficked for strange webs with Eastern merchants;
And, as Leda,
Was the mother of Helen of Troy,
And, as St Anne,
Was the mother of Mary;
And all this has been to her but as the sound of lyres and flutes,
And lives
Only in the delicacy
With which it has moulded the changing lineaments,
And tinged the eyelids and the hands.

Steven Zultanski
My Death Drive

Here is Steven Zultanski's voyeuristic road trip taken to the information superhigh-way, with a Freudian mapping of corporate broadcast news and historical narrative according to the formula that deaths must increase proportionally with distance from the market to be newsworthy. Web application mapping triangulates Zultan-ski's home address in Northampton, Massachusetts, with the scenes of murder and corporate franchise openings.

A white-bearded regicide emerges from hiding to lead a Puritan militia to victory over American Indians → 11 minutes by car
                                         while
87 people are trampled or asphyxiated as Happy Land burns down → 2 hours 46 minutes by car
                              while
seven Electromagnetic Systems Labs employees are shot by a stalker inflamed by unrequited love → 1 day 21 hours by car
                                              while
the first KFC opens in Salt Lake City, Utah → 1 day 10 hours by car
                                                      while
the Hindenberg burns and 26 people die, mostly from leaping from the fire to their deaths → 4 hours 22 minutes by car
                                       while
a Cherokee removal fort forces the exodus of Cherokee prisoners to Rattlesnake springs → 16 hours 20 minutes by car
                                    while
Sylvia Plath makes her first suicide attempt → 3 minutes by car
                                                  while
the first Arby's opens in Boardman, Ohio → 9 hours 4 minutes by car
                                                      while

168 people die and 800 people are injured by a truck bomb concoction of 108 fifty-pound bags of ammonium nitrate fertilizer, three fifty-five gallon drums of liquid nitromethane, several crates of explosive Tovex sausage, seventeen bags of ANFO, and spools of shock tube and cannon fuse → 1 day 1 hour by car

while

123 people are killed in the opening clashes of the American Revolution → 1 hour 47 minutes by car

while

the first Waffle House opens in Avondale Estates, Georgia → 16 hours 51 minutes by car

while

the first Insta Burger King opens in Miami, Florida → 22 hours 48 minutes by car

while

Ironhead dies in a last lap crash during the Daytona 500 as the car hits the wall at nearly 150 miles per hour and the left-rear wheel assembly breaks off on impact and the hood pins are severed and the hood flaps open slamming against the windshield and the car slides slowly down the track → 18 hours 59 minutes by car

while

about 100 people are killed in the New York Draft Riots → 3 hours 8 minutes by car

while

about 58 people die in the L.A. Riots by gunfire, fire, stabbing, and sticks and boards → 1 day 19 hours by car

while

members of Heaven's Gate smother each other with pillows in anticipation of a spaceship → 1 day 20 hours by car

while

the first Dunkin' Donuts opens in Quincy, Massachusetts → 2 hours by car

while

a student at the University of Texas kills 13 people and wounds 31 others from a clocktower on campus before being sniped by police → 1 day 6 hours by car

while

the president watches *Our American Cousin* and is shot in the head at
point blank range → 6 hours 64 minutes by car

while

everyone in the house is drugged and a member of the FBI's Special
Prosecutions Unit shoots Fred Hampton in the head at point blank
range → 14 hours 24 minutes by car

while

at least 1,836 people die in Hurricane Katrina and floods → 23 hours
1 minute by car

while

Stalin's agent drives an ice pick into Trotsky's skull who doesn't die for a
day → 2 days 4 hours by car

while

the first Whole Foods Market opens in Austin, Texas → 1 day 6 hours
by car

while

498 people die as San Francisco's buildings collapse → 1 day 20 hours
by car

while

more than 157 people are killed in a slave rebellion and in the militia's
response to the rebellion→ 9 hours 43 minutes by car

while

a bull shark off a beach bites a person on a boogie board in half→ 21 hours
42 minutes by car

while

a nuclear power plant suffers a partial core meltdown and "the projected
number of excess fatal cancers due to the accident is approximately
one" → 6 hours 6 minutes by car

Vladimir Zykov
from I Was Told to Write Fifty Words

For *I Was Told to Write Fifty Words,* Vladimir Zykov employed the services of Amazon's Mechanical Turk (an online labor pool specializing in repetitive tasks paid piecemeal) to create a work conceived of but not written by himself. On the job board, he gave the simple instructions: "Write fifty words." Offering a payment of one cent for every fifty words received, he was able to "write" each poem for one cent; the project was finished when Zykov had collected 500 sets of words, costing him a total of $5.00. The final work is completely unedited by Zykov.

Although Zykov touches on a number of issues here, most prominent is the concern with modes of production, labor, and value: What is the value of language? Can poetry be farmed out by proxy? Is there a mode of production for poetry that follows capitalist models? Almost Warholian, Zykov imagines a textual factory. His plan is far-reaching: eventually he hopes to commission a range of full-length works written in this manner, spanning every literary genre, from sci-fi to detective novels and cookbooks.

I was told to write fifty words, so that is what I am doing. I was not told what to write, how to write, or why to write fifty words. I was told to write fifty words, nothing more. I hope the fifty words that I have chosen are fine.

I'm not sure what exactly you want me to write fifty words about but I thought I'd give it a go since the reward is a whole one cent! I'tt try to be as precise as possible so you've no reason to reject the hit so consider this fifty words.

small flat metal Australia's premier identification label attached preparatory magnet secondary to the collar of a dog Spanish-speaking countries esterified glyserol body created to document holding company based board system software private passenger computer keyboard protruding piece of a planar surface that provides an index evolved from a mechanical basis using cards gradually between used particularly for guitars and other fretted instruments computer application similar to

I just finished reading a book about the First World War that I thought was particularly good. It is called "All Quiet On The Western Front." The main character Paul is a twenty year old student who enlists in the German Army with his classmates and becomes disillusioned and horrified after experiencing trench warfare. I recommend this book highly.

During the past two weeks I have traveled extensively. First I went to Copenhagen for a meeting on PMTCT Mother-Baby Packs held at UNICEF. It was a good first introduction into the subject matter, but frankly at times the discussion was so technical that it went completely above my head.

apple boy cat dog elephant fit go hello igloo jack link more no person question rabbit since touch under very what xylophone yesterday zebra again because candy donkey every friday ghost hiccup industry junk keep love money nickel ostrich penguin quail rail snake tortoise uncle vampire wednesday and now done

any could right for accept do wrote rote gear growl cane kick joke lane laugh foul fowl dote love game quite quite quail were wail white every eat red rest tear trade yet your under umbrella itinerary iota oat otter poach poke play pray ask assinine set sear said sedative fore for door gore grade hate heart heal heel hire jail kale line leg lore zebra xylophone create car core venerate vile voracious voice break berate bear blow relate related nine nor neither next nifty mark make might mare main mire more mile milk

dictionary, you, can, see, the, explanation, office, word, hint, and, hear, read, pronunciation, make, choice, among, English, Vocabulary, three, efficient, test, will, help, memorize, new, shortest, possible, time, text, files, web, pages, off, line, computer, shall, not, work, table, bench, cot, chair, desk, two, four, run, eat, sleep, walk, move.

House Dog Cat Bible Purse Cup Speaker Book Computer Foot Sun Moon Stars God Jesus Heaven Picture Wind Waves Obey Him Pen Mouse Chair

Glasses Church Camera Keyboard Door Car Truck Toy Tractor Cow Dishwasher Washing Machine Dryer Paper Hat Dress Shoes Weather Rain Tornado Hail Grass Fence Desk Carpet Wall

My dog is very big. His brother is a grizzly bear. Do you smell bacon? In what state are the rocky mountains located? Everyone I know thinks that I have attention deficit disorder. Keep counting these words until you get to fifty. I am sure glad this didn't have to be coherent.

1. hit 2. bat 3. smile 4. why 5. sit 6. pitch 7. what 8. fire 9. loser 10. field 11. grass 12. house 13. home 14. information 15. sick 16. person 17. anytime 18. call 19. please 20. check 21. cash 22. money 23. card 24. happy 25. prompt 26. you 27. ate 28. soup 29. customer 30. watch 31. sale 32. mail 33. begin 34. skip 35. hop 36. jump 37. throw 38. phone 39. cup 40. and 41. video 42. out 43. too 44. as 45. store 46. save 47. milk 48. value 49. gas 50. High

Mary had a little lamb with fleece as white as snow. It followed her to school one day. Little Miss. Muffet sat on her tuffet eating her curds and whey. Along came a spider and sat down beside her and frieghtened the poor girl away. Humpty Dumpty sat on a

Today, I thought about sleeping on the top of the office building. It was designated a bomb shelter right after World War I. The ceiling is twenty feet above where my desk sits on the seventh floor. The fire shields on the windows haven't been down in forty five years.

Well, my assignment is to write fifty words in English. That is not a bad assignment. I wonder why anyone would need me to do this. Maybe somebody wants to learn English. Well if you did want to learn English, this would be a pretty good way to test yourself.

Interesting, this task requires me to write fifty words. There is no topic given, and the only requirement is that the words be in English. I could write them in a logical context, or simply give random words like monkey laughter apple firefighter agony spoon. These are my fifty words.

I'm a big fan of classical music. Orchestral compositions strike an emotional chord that other genres of music simply can't match. For instance, in Pines of Rome, when the hubbub of the first movement turns suddenly into the low drone of the second movement, my heart simply stops.

Today is Friday, April 18, 2008. I live and work in Chicago, Illinois. This is also the day that I have a doctor's appointment. I am not looking forward to it. At least I get to leave work early. The sun is shining and it is getting warmer outside. The weekend should be good.

Awesome Fantastic Super Computer Vagina Calendar Wipes Trouble Dog Cat Guinea Pig Rabbit Theatre Grey Tea Coffee Soda Milk Juice Beer Rain Snow Sun Clouds Tornado Hurricane Camera Picture Film Movie Cinema Magnet Refrigerator Microwave Oven Stove Blender Mixer Toaster Grill Griddle Internet Email Phone Cheese Meat Vegetables Bread Pizza

How Pink Blue Red Green Yellow Orange Pen Pencil Telephone Noodle Can Soda Grass Lawn Mower Child Chicken Dog Cat Pig Steer Cow Lamb Sheep Candy Candy bar Wallet Money Credit Card Photo Husband Wife Mom Dad Feet Foot Finger Ring Ear Nose Clown Hair Bald Bird car truck snake

1. cat 2. dog 3. mouse 4. horse 5. cow 6. goat 7. chicken 8. rooster 9. salamander 10. alligator 11. crocodile 12. hippopotamus 13. whale 14. shark 15. fish 16. surfboard 17. boat 18. house 19. apartment 20. sofa 21. chair 22. table 23. counter 24. coffee 25. tea 26. soda 27. milk 28. water 29. juice 30. apple 31. orange 32. cranberry 33. grape 34. grapefruit 35. tomato 36. potato 37. carrot 39. pepper 40. salt 41. butter 42. camera 43. computer 44. vacation 45. tropical 46. laugh 47. television 48. travel 49. airport 50. Car

This is a paragraph that provides fifty words of English. This paragraph could be used for several different purposes, including understanding basic English grammar and noticing variable sentence structures. One could also use it to get a rough idea of one's reading speed and even for copying to practice handwriting.

hello, when, what, how, why, where, life, marriage, husband, wife, son, daughter, give, take, love, like, hate, divorce, house, car, road, work, live, fun, play, leisure, time, money, aunt, uncle, mother, father, sister, brother, eat, cook, sleep, watch, cat, dog, horse, cow, camel, school, student, study, chair, couch, computer, desk,

The, Cat, Boat, In, Out, Owl, Phone, Stereo, Computer, Game, Car, Bike, Train, Boat, Summer, Spring, Paper, Pen, Pencil, Tissue, Mouse, Tape, Stapler, Calculator, Bed, Chair, Bench, Restaurant, Paperclip, Sky, Grass, Road, Man, Woman, Child, Water, Bathroom, Kitchen, Sink, Toilet, Flowers, Garden, Dog, Keys, Photograph, Building, Baseball, Carpet, Bird, Scissors

1. one 2. two 3. three 4. four 5. five 6. six 7. seven 8. eight 9. nine 10. ten 11. eleven 12. twelve 13. thirteen 14. fourteen 15. fifteen 16. sixteen 17. seventeen 18. eighteen 19. nineteen 20. twenty 21. hundred 22. thousand 23. google 24. million 25. billion 26. trillion 27. quadrillion 28. no 29. yes 30. write 31. fifty 32. words 33. in 34. english 35. requester 36. let 37. someone 38. else 39. do 40. it 41. automatically 42. accept 43. this 44. hit 45. artificial 46. intelligence 47. available 48. you 49. thanks 50.
Amen

hey what are you doing. gymnastics dance soccor basketball floor cats dogs rabbits birds computer desk mouse speaker scanner printer stamps board bored the where who when because then than we pencil pen stapler worm heat cold vacuum stair scale couch chair person seat cup maker tape ankle wrist eraser

cat, dog, blue, red,white, dollar, money, cash, work, book, television, movie, music, judge, jury, law, library, school, college, class, car, gas, president, election, debate, talk, listen, number, letter, sad, angry, depressed, happy, cake, cookie, wine, beer, picnic, party, shop, store, credit, bank, loan, debt, house, rose, sun, moon, planet

Dog, cat, car, truck, tree, house, yellow, red, blue, green, high, low, tent, drive, horse, man, woman, boy, girl, duck, cow, chicken, toilet, milk, juice, diaper, baby, hospital, scream, cry, smile, laugh, live, die, sleep, run, jump, play, dance, sing, fail, succeed, graduate, drink, eat, rest, boat, water, sun, and land.

I have no dog. Will you come to the park with me? The dictionary is on the purple shelf. Manatees swim in the waters off the coast of Florida. Internet cafes are very popular in New York City and other metropolis. Could a bear come to the circus today?

satisfaction beef fact polish mistaking governing adviser appendix who electricity power idea cat dog mouse phone book text jump hop skip tend allow allot grasp hold have cherish wolf sea turtle labyrinth puzzle biology review education college set statement chase balance stamp premium gum eclipse model club member recall value

Acknowledgments

All possible care has been taken to trace ownership and secure permission for the literary excerpts quoted in this book. The authors and the publisher would like to thank the following organizations and individuals for permission to reprint copyrighted material:

Monica Aasprong. *Soldatmarkedet* (excerpt). Copyright © 2007 Monica Aasprong. Reprinted with permission of the author.

Walter Abish. "Skin Deep," from *99: The New Meaning*. Copyright © 1990 Walter Abish. Reprinted with permission of Burning Deck.

Vito Acconci. "Contacts/Contexts (Frame of Reference): Ten Pages of Reading *Roget's Thesaurus*." Copyright © 1969. First published in *o to 9* No. 6 (July 1969). "Removal, Move (Line of Evidence): The Grid Locations of Streets, Alphabetized, Hagstrom's Maps of the Five Boroughs: 3. Manhattan" (excerpt). Copyright © undated. Reprinted with permission of the author.

Kathy Acker. *Great Expectations* (excerpt). Copyright © 1994 Grove Press. Reprinted with permission of Grove Press.

Sally Alatalo (Anita M-28). *Unforeseen Alliances* (excerpt). Copyright © 2001 Sara Ranchouse. Reprinted with permission of the author and Sara Ranchouse.

Paal Bjelke Andersen. "The Grefsen Address" (excerpt). Unpublished manuscript, courtesy of the author.

Anonymous. *Erotism*. This translation originally published in *Encyclopædia Acephalica*, Atlas Arkhive Three: Documents of the Avant-Garde (London: Atlas Press, 1995). Reprinted with permission.

David Antin. "A List of the Delusions of the Insane: What They Are Afraid Of." Copyright © 1968 David Antin. "Novel Poem" (excerpt). Copyright © 1968 David Antin. "Separation Meditations" (excerpt). Copyright © 1971 David Antin. Reprinted with permission of the author.

Louis Aragon. "Suicide." Originally published in *Cannibale: Revue mensuelle* N° 1 (25 April 1920)–N° 2 (25 May 1920). Edited by Francis Picabia. Published by Au Sans Pareil, Paris.

Nathan Austin. *Survey Says!* (excerpt). Copyright © 2010 Nathan Austin. Reprinted with permission of the author and Black Maze Books.

J. G. Ballard. "Mae West's Reduction Mammoplasty" from *The Atrocity Exhibition*. Originally published in *Ambit*. Copyright © 1970 by J. G. Ballard. Reprinted with permission of the Wylie Agency LLC.

Fiona Banner. *The Nam* (excerpt). Copyright © 1997 Fiona Banner. Reprinted with permission of the author and Frith Street Books.

Derek Beaulieu. *Flatland: A Romance of Many Dimensions* (excerpt). Copyright © 2007 Derek Beaulieu. Reprinted with permission of the author and Information As Material.

Samuel Beckett. *Molloy* (excerpt). Copyright © 1955 by the Estate of Samuel Beckett. Used by permission of Grove/Atlantic, Inc. *Watt* (excerpt). Copyright © 1953 by the Estate of Patrick Bowles and the Estate of Samuel Beckett. Used by permission of Grove/Atlantic, Inc.

Caroline Bergvall. "Via (36 Dante Translations)" published as part of "VIA," in *Fig* © 2005 Caroline Bergvall. Used by permission of the author and Salt Books. This version courtesy of the author.

Charles Bernstein. "I and The" (excerpt). Copyright © 1987 Charles Bernstein. "My/My/My." Copyright © 1975 Charles Bernstein. Reprinted with permission of the author.

Ted Berrigan. "An Interview with John Cage." Copyright © 1967, first published in *Bean Spasms,* by Berrigan and Padgett (New York: Kulchur Press, 1967). Used by permission of The Estate of Ted Berrigan, courtesy of Alice Notley.

Jen Bervin. *Nets* (excerpt). Copyright © 2004 Ugly Duckling Presse. Reprinted with permission of the author and Ugly Duckling Presse.

Gregory Betts. *If Language* (excerpt). Copyright © 2005 Gregory Betts. Reprinted with permission of the author.

Christian Bök. "Busted Sirens" (excerpt). Unpublished manuscript, courtesy of the author. *Eunoia* (excerpt). Copyright © 2001 Christian Bök. Reprinted with permission of the author and Coach House Books.

Marie Buck. "Whole Foods" (excerpt). Unpublished manuscript, courtesy of the author.

William S. Burroughs. *Nova Express* (excerpt). Copyright © 1964 by William S. Burroughs, copyright renewed 1992 by William S. Burroughs. Used by permission of Grove/Atlantic Inc.

David Buuck. "Follow." Unpublished manuscript, courtesy of the author.

John Cage. *Writing Through the Cantos* (excerpt). Copyright © 1983 John Cage. Reprinted with permission of Wesleyan University Press.

Blaise Cendrars. *Kodak* (excerpt). Originally published by Libraire Stock, Paris, 1924. Translated by Craig Dworkin.

Thomas Claburn. *i feel better after i type to you* (excerpt). Copyright © 2006 Superbunker. Reprinted with permission of Superbunker.

Elisabeth S. Clark. *Between Words* (excerpt). Copyright © 2007 /ubu Editions. Reprinted with permission of the author and /ubu Editions.

Claude Closky. "The First Thousand Numbers Classified in Alphabetical Order." Copyright © 1989 Claude Closky. *Mon Catalogue* (excerpt). Copyright © 1999 Claude Closky. Reprinted with permission of the author.

Clark Coolidge. "Cabaret Voltaire" (excerpt) from *ING*. Copyright © 1968 Clark Coolidge. "Bond Sonnets" (excerpt). Originally published in *Insect Trust Gazette* 2 (Summer 1965). Copyright © 1965. Reprinted with permission of the author.

Hart Crane. "Emblems of Conduct," from *Complete Poems of Hart Crane,* edited by Marc Simon. Copyright © 1933, 1958, 1966 by Liveright Publishing Corporation. Copyright © 1986 by Marc Simon. Used by permission of Liveright Publishing Corporation.

Brian Joseph Davis. "Voice Over" (excerpt). Unpublished manuscript, courtesy of the author.

Katie Degentesh. "The Only Miracles I Know of Are Simply Tricks That People Play on One Another," from *The Anger Scale*. Copyright © 2006 Combo Books. Reprinted with permission of Combo Books.

Mónica de la Torre. "Doubles" (excerpt). Copyright © 2008 Mónica de la Torre. Reprinted with permission of the author.

Denis Diderot. *Jacques le fataliste et son maître* (excerpt). Originally published by Buisson, Paris, 1796. Translated by Craig Dworkin.

Marcel Duchamp. *notes* (excerpt). Copyright © 2010 Artists Rights Society (ARS), New York / ADAGP; Paris / Succession Marcel Duchamp. Reprinted with permission.

Craig Dworkin. "Legion" (excerpt). Unpublished manuscript, courtesy of the author. *Parse* (excerpt). Copyright © 2008 Craig Dworkin. Reprinted with permission of the author and Atelos Books.

Laura Elrick. "First Words" (excerpt), from *sKincerity*. Copyright © 2003 Laura Elrick. Reprinted with permission of Laura Elrick and Krupskaya Books.

Dan Farrell. "Avail," from *Last Instance*. Copyright © 1999 Krupskaya Books. Reprinted with permission of Krupskaya Books. *The Inkblot Record* (excerpt). Copyright © 2000 Coach House Books. Reprinted with permission of Coach House Books.

Gerald Ferguson. *The Standard Corpus of Present Day English Language Usage Arranged by Word Length and Alphabetized Within Word Length* (excerpt). Copyright © 1978 NSCAD Press. Reprinted with permission of NSCAD Press.

Robert Fitterman. "Metropolis 16," from *Metropolis 16-29*. Copyright © 2002 Robert Fitterman. Reprinted with permission of the author and Coach House Books. *The Sun Also Also Rises* (excerpt). Copyright © 2009 Robert Fitterman. Published with permission of the author and No Books.

Lawrence Giffin. "Spinoza's Ethics." Unpublished manuscript, courtesy of the author.

Peter Gizzi. "Ode: Salute to the New York School, 1950–1970 (a libretto)." Copyright © 2010 Peter Gizzi. Reprinted with permission of the author.

Judith Goldman. "dicktée" (excerpt) and "r'ture/ CENTaur" (excerpt). Copyright © 2001 Judith Goldman. Published with permission of the author.

Kenneth Goldsmith. Excerpts from *Day, No. 111 2.7.92–10.20.96, Soliloquy,* and *The Weather* courtesy of the author.

Nada Gordon. "Abnormal Discharge." Unpublished manuscript, courtesy of the author.

Noah Eli Gordon. *Inbox* (excerpt). Copyright © 2006 BlazeVOX [books]. Reprinted with permission of the author and BlazeVOX [books].

Michael Gottlieb. "The Dust" (excerpt). Copyright © 2003 Michael Gottlieb. Reprinted with permission of the author.

Dan Graham. "Exclusion Principle" and "Poem-Schema." Copyright © 1966 Dan Graham. Reprinted with permission of the author.

Michelle Grangaud. "Biographies/Poetry." This translation originally published in The Germ 5 (Summer 2001).

Brion Gysin. "First Cut-Ups" from *Back in No Time*. Copyright © Brion Gysin and reprinted with permission of Wesleyan University Press.

Michael Harvey. *White Papers* (excerpt). Copyright © 1971 Michael Harvey. Reprinted with permission of the author.

H. L. Hix "Poem composed of statements made by George W. Bush in January 2003." Copyright © 2007 H. L. Hix. Reprinted with permission of the author.

Yunte Huang. *Cribs* (excerpt). Copyright © 2004 Yunte Huange. Reprinted with permission of the author and TinFish Press.

Douglas Huebler. *Secrets: Variable Piece #4* (excerpt). Copyright © 2010 Douglas Huebler, courtesy Darcy Huebler, Artists Rights Society (ARS), New York. Reprinted with permission.

Peter Jaeger. "Rapid Eye Movement" (excerpt). Copyright © 2009 Peter Jaeger. Reprinted with permission of the author.

Emma Kay. *Worldview* (excerpt). Copyright © 1999 Emma Kay. Reprinted with permission of the author and Book Works.

Bill Kennedy and Darren Wershler. *Apostrophe* (excerpt). Copyright © 2006 Bill Kennedy and Darren Wershler. Reprinted with permission of the authors and ECW.

Michael Klauke. *Ad Infinitum* (excerpt). Copyright © 1988 Michael Klauke. Reprinted with permission of the author.

Christopher Knowles. *Typings* (excerpt). Copyright © 1979 Christopher Knowles. Reprinted with permission of the author.

Joseph Kosuth. *Purloined, A Novel* (excerpt). Copyright © 2010 Joseph Kosuth, Artists Rights Society (ARS), New York. Reprinted with permission.

Leevi Lehto. *Päivä* (excerpt). Copyright © 2007 Leevi Lehto. Reprinted with permission of the author.

Tan Lin. *BIB* (excerpt). Copyright © 2007 /ubu Editions. Reprinted with permission of /ubu Editions.

Dana Teen Lomax. *Disclosure* (excerpt). Copyright © 2009 /ubu Editions. Reprinted with permission of /ubu Editions. Many thanks to *UbuWeb, Try, Work, The Tolerance Project, Dusie Kollektiv,* and *Imaginary Syllabi,* where early experiments with the project appeared. *Disclosure* is forthcoming from Black Radish Books.

Trisha Low. "Confessions." Unpublished manuscript, courtesy of the author.

Rory Macbeth. *The Bible (alphabetized)* (excerpt). Copyright © 2007 Rory Macbeth. Reprinted with permission of the author.

Jackson Mac Low. *Words nd Ends from Ez* (excerpt). Copyright © 1981 Estate of Jackson Mac Low, courtesy of Anne Tardos.

Stéphane Mallarmé. *La dernière mode* (excerpt) from the edition of October 4, 1874. Originally published by *La dernière mode*, Paris, 1874. *Le livre de Mallarmé* (excerpt). Originally published by Gallimard in 1957.

Donato Mancini. "Ligature." Unpublished manuscript, courtesy of the author.

Peter Manson. *Adjunct: An Undigest* (excerpt). Copyright © 2004, 2009 Peter Manson. Reprinted with permission of the author. *English in Mallarmé* (excerpt). Copyright © 2006 /ubu Editions. Reprinted with permission of /ubu Editions.

Shigeru Matsui. "Pure Poems." Unpublished manuscript.

Bernadette Mayer. *Eruditio ex Memoria* (excerpt). Originally published by Angel Hair Books, 1977. Reprinted with permission of the author.

Steve McCaffery. "Fish Also Rise" and "The Kommunist Manifesto." Copyright © 2000 Steve McCaffery. Reprinted with permission of the author and Coach House Books.

Stephen McLaughlin and Jim Carpenter. *Issue 1* (excerpt). Courtesy of the authors.

David Melnick. *Men in Aida, Book II* (excerpt). Copyright © David Melnick. Originally published by Editions Eclipse. Reprinted with permission of the author and Editions Eclipse.

Richard Meltzer. "Barbara Mauritz: *Music Box,*" "Denny Lile," and "Maple Leaf Cowpoop Round-Up." Originally published by Da Capo Press, 2000.

Christof Migone. *La première phrase et le dernier mot* (excerpt). Copyright © 2004 Le Quartanier. Reprinted with permission of Le Quartanier.

Tomoko Minami. *38: The New Shakespeare* (excerpt). Unpublished manuscript, courtesy of the author.

K. Silem Mohammad. "Spooked" and "Considering How Spooky Deer Are." Copyright © 2003 K. Silem Mohammad. *Sonnagrams* (excerpt). Copyright © 2009 K. Silem Mohammad. Reprinted with permission of the author.

Simon Morris. *Getting Inside Jack Kerouac's Head* (excerpt). Copyright © 2008 Simon Morris. *Re-writing Freud* (excerpt). Copyright © 2005 Simon Morris. Reprinted with permission of the author and Information As Material.

Yedda Morrison. "Kyoto Protocol" (excerpt). Unpublished manuscript, courtesy of the author.

Harryette Mullen. "Bilingual Instructions," "Elliptical," and "Mantra for a Classless Society or Mr. Roget's Neighborhood," from *Sleeping with the Dictionary*. Copyright © 2002 University of California Press. Reprinted with permission of the University of California Press.

Alexandra Nemerov. "First My Motorola." Unpublished manuscript, courtesy of the author.

C. K. Ogden. "Work in Progress by James Joyce." Originally published in *Psyche* 12, no. 2 (October, 1931): 92–95.

Tom Orange. "I Saw You." Copyright © 2008 Tom Orange. Reprinted with permission of the author.

Parasitic Ventures. *All the Names of In Search of Lost Time* (excerpt). Copyright © 2006 Parasitic Ventures Press. Reprinted with permission.

Georges Perec. "Attempt at an Inventory of the Liquid and Solid Foodstuffs Ingurgitated by Me in the Course of the Year Nineteen Hundred and Seventy-Four," translated by John Sturrock (Penguin Classics, 1997, 1999). Reprinted with permission of Penguin Group (UK).

M. NourbeSe Philip. *Zong!* (excerpt). Copyright © 2008 Wesleyan University Press. Reprinted with permission of Wesleyan University Press.

Vanessa Place. *Statement of Fact* (excerpt). Unpublished manuscript, courtesy of the author.

Bern Porter. "Clothes," from *Sounds That Arouse Me*, ed. Mark Melnicove. Tilbury House, Publishers, 1992. Reprinted with permission of Mark Melnicove, literary executor, Estate of Bern Porter, 216 Cedar Grove Road, Dresden, Maine 04342; mmelnicove@roadrunner.com.

Raymond Queneau. "The Foundations of Literature." This translation by Harry Matthews copyright © 1995.

Claudia Rankine. *Don't Let Me Be Lonely* (excerpt). Copyright © 2004 Graywolf Press. Reprinted with permission of Graywolf Press.

Ariana Reines. *The Cow* (excerpt). Copyright © 2006 Fence. Reprinted with permission of Fence.

Charles Reznikoff. *Testimony, Volume II: The United States (1885–1915)* (excerpt). Copyright © 1965 by Charles Reznikoff. Reprinted by permission of Black Sparrow Books, an imprint of David R. Godine, Publisher, Inc.

Deborah Richards. "The Beauty Projection" (excerpt) from *Last One Out*. Copyright © 2003 Subpress Collective. Reprinted with permission of Subpress Collective.

Kim Rosenfield. "The Other Me." Courtesy of the author.

Raymond Roussel. *How I Wrote Certain of My Books* (excerpt). Originally published by Exact Change, 2005.

Aram Saroyan. "Untitled Poem" from *Complete Minimal Poems*. Copyright © 2007 Ugly Duckling Presse. Reprinted with permission of Ugly Duckling Presse.

Ara Shirinyan. *Your Country Is Great* (excerpt). Copyright © 2008 Ara Shirinyan. Reprinted with permission of the author and Futurepoem.

Ron Silliman. "Sunset Debris" (excerpt) from *Age of Huts (compleat)*. Copyright © 2007 University of California Press. Reprinted with permission of the University of California Press.

Juliana Spahr. "Thrashing Seems Crazy" from *Response*. Copyright © 1996 Juliana Spahr. Reprinted with permission of the author.

Brian Kim Stefans. *The Vaneigem Series* (excerpt). Unpublished manuscript, courtesy of the author.

Gary Sullivan. "Conceptual Poem (WC + WCW)" and "To a Sought Caterpillar." Unpublished manuscript, courtesy of the author.

Nick Thurston. *He Might Find.* © 2009 Nick Thurston. Reprinted with permission of the author and Information As Material.

Rodrigo Toscano. "Welcome to Omnium Dignitatem" from *To Leveling Swerve* © 2004 Krupskaya Books. Reprinted with permission of Krupskaya Books.

Tristan Tzara. "Manifeste sur l'amour faible et l'amour amer" (excerpt). Originally published in *La Vie des lettres* No. 4 (May 1921). Translated by Craig Dworkin.

Andy Warhol. *a: a novel* (excerpt). Copyright © 1968, 1998 by the Andy Warhol Foundation for the Visual Arts, Inc. Used by permission of Grove/Atlantic, Inc.

Darren Wershler. *The Tapeworm Foundry.* Copyright © 2000 Darren Wershler. Reprinted with permission of the author.

Christine Wertheim. "Finnegans Wanke / Finnegans Wake (translation)." Unpublished manuscript, courtesy of the author.

Wiener Gruppe (Konrad Bayer, Gerhard Rühm, Oswald Wiener). "ideas for a «record album/ functional» acoustic cabaret." Copyright © 1959 Gerhard Rühm. Reprinted with permission of Gerhard Rühm.

Wiener Gruppe (Konrad Bayer, H. C. Artmann). "11 abecedaries." Copyright © Gerhard Rühm. Reprinted with permission of Gerhard Rühm.

William Butler Yeats. "Mona Lisa." Originally published in *The Oxford Book of Modern Verse: 1892–1935* (Cambridge: Oxford University Press, 1936).

Steven Zultanski. "My Death Drive." Unpublished manuscript, courtesy of the author.

Vladimir Zykov. *I Was Told to Write Fifty Words* (excerpt). Unpublished manuscript, courtesy of the author.

AGM COLLECTION

Rainer Rumold and Marjorie Perloff, *General Editors*

Charles Bernstein has described conceptual poetry as "poetry pregnant with thought." *Against Expression,* the premier anthology of conceptual writing, presents work that is by turns thoughtful, funny, provocative, and disturbing. Editors Craig Dworkin and Kenneth Goldsmith chart the trajectory of the conceptual aesthetic from early precursors such as Samuel Beckett and Marcel Duchamp through major avant-garde groups of the past century, including Dada, Oulipo, Fluxus, and language poetry, to name just a few. The works of more than a hundred writers from Aasprong to Zykov demonstrate a remarkable variety of new ways of thinking about the nature of texts, information, and art, using found, appropriated, and randomly generated texts to explore the possibilities of non-expressive language.

Craig Dworkin is the author of *Reading the Illegible,* also published by Northwestern University Press, and the editor of *Architectures of Poetry, Language to Cover a Page: The Early Writing of Vito Acconci, The Consequence of Innovation: Twenty-first Century Poetics,* and, with Marjorie Perloff, *The Sound of Poetry / The Poetry of Sound.*

Kenneth Goldsmith's writing has been called "some of the most exhaustive and beautiful collage work yet produced in poetry" by *Publishers Weekly.* Goldsmith is the author of ten books of poetry. He teaches writing at the University of Pennsylvania, where he is a senior editor of PennSound, an online poetry archive.

Cover art © Derek Beaulieu
Cover design: Dino Robinson

POETRY / LITERARY CRITICISM

ISBN 978-0-8101-2711-1

9 780810 127111

www.nupress.northwestern.edu